The State of Development Economics

The State of Development Economics

Economics

Progress and Perspectives

Edited by

GUSTAV RANIS & T. PAUL SCHULTZ

Basil Blackwell

First published 1988
First published in USA 1988

Basil Blackwell Ltd
108 Cowley Road, Oxford OX4 1JF, UK

Basil Blackwell Inc.
432 Park Avenue South, Suite 1503
New York, NY 10016, USA

British Library Cataloguing in Publication Data

The State of development economics: progress
and perspectives.
1. Developing countries – Economic conditions
I. Ranis, Gustav   II. Schultz, T. Paul
330.9172′4   HC59.7

ISBN 0-631-15377-2

Library of Congress Cataloging-in-Publication Data

The State of development economics: progress and perspectives
edited by Gustav Ranis and T. Paul Schultz.
    p. cm.
Papers from a conference held at Yale University, April 11–13 1986.
Bibliography: p.
Includes index.
ISBN 0-631-15377-2
1. Economic development – Congresses. 2. Developing countries –
Economic policy – Congresses. I. Ranis, Gustav. II. Schultz, T. Paul.
HD73.S7 1987
338.9 – dc19   87-29389
                                                                CIP

Typeset in 10 on 11½ Times
by Unicus Graphics Ltd, Horsham
Printed in Great Britain by T.J. Press Ltd, Padstow, Cornwall

Contents

Preface

During 1986 the Economic Growth Center at Yale University observed the 25th anniversary of its founding. Created with the help of the Ford Foundation during the early halcyon days of the renewed postwar academic concern with development, we thought it fitting to celebrate the event by means of a scholarly symposium addressed to an assessment of the accomplishments in this area of inquiry over the past quarter century, combined with an inevitable look at the agenda of the future. Consequently, we approached some of the major contributors and "wise men" in the field – sprinkled with as many of our own "alumni" as appropriate – and commissioned papers on the specific topics indicated. The Symposium, at which 16 of the 18 papers included here were presented, took place in New Haven from 11 to 13 April, 1986. We have included the comments of the invited discussants, but not the floor discussion. A list of Symposium participants is included at the back.

We would like to express our gratitude to the Ford Foundation, the Rockefeller Foundation, and the U.N. University for their support. Our thanks also go to all the participants who helped make this an intellectually rewarding experience; to Dorothy Nitshke and Louise Danishevsky who carried most of the administrative burdens; and to a number of graduate students, including Jim Stodder and especially Kolleen Rask, who provided invaluable help all along the way and thoughtfully reviewed the proofs to make corrections and identify ambiguities for authors and editors.

Gustav Ranis
T. Paul Schultz
New Haven

Dedication

This volume is dedicated to the memory of two individuals whose absence from our midst will be lamented for many years to come: Carlos Díaz-Alejandro, one of the most lively and productive members of the Economic Growth Center faculty, cherished in both the North and the South; and Simon Kuznets, the intellectual father of the Center, our perennial guide and long-term Advisory Committee member.

Introduction

GUSTAV RANIS AND T. PAUL SCHULTZ

The editors of this volume, who organized the symposium on which it is based, are aware that there usually exists some trade-off between the quality of contributors and the ability of the organizers to achieve uniform coverage of a subject. We opted for inviting recognized leaders in the field and believe we achieved what we were after – a *tour d' horizon* of development economics. If necessarily less than complete, this volume presents a survey of prominent macro- and microeconomic issues in the field. We will, of course, acknowledge that this subdiscipline of economics is both broader and more amorphous than most, and therefore especially difficult to encapsulate. Thus, we do not claim to present here the "state of the art" at every boundary of this vineyard in which so many people of such varying intellectual backgrounds and experiences labor, even using different methods of analysis. Inevitably, we have not been able to cover every facet of work in this area. But what we have been able to accomplish, we believe, is to provide some evidence that intellectual progress has indeed been continuous and that development economics continues to be alive and well. Moreover, and perhaps most importantly, it has before it a realistic and lively agenda for the future.

This volume does not engage in *Methodenstreit*; in other words, it does not champion either orthodox or heterodox approaches to a complicated set of problems. But it does carry the positive message that the consistent and ever more empirically oriented application of the tools of our trade has increasingly served to illuminate these problems, provided for the testing of analytical insights and perspectives and, one would dare to assert, even led to considerable convergence in the policy sphere.

The volume is divided into three parts. Part I is devoted to an overview of the field of development economics from an historical and macroeconomic perspective. Part II presents a survey of theoretical constructs, policy-relevant tools, and development experience in different corners of the heterogeneous development landscape. Part III focuses on a variety of specific microeconomic and sectoral issues which have in recent years received an increasing share of the attention of development economists.

No attempt will be made here to summarize the content or even the basic message of each of the contributions included. These must be allowed to speak for themselves. The editors will attempt no more than to provide something of a road map and guide to the volume.

W. Arthur Lewis's lead-off piece affirms that the past 40 years have provided us with the experience and the data to analyze many problems and resolve many issues, but by no means all. His contribution represents a necessary, i.e. healthy, reminder that all that pessimism concerning the prospects for development, vintage 1945, was seriously in error and that substantial growth has occurred – and can occur again – under widely varying initial conditions and circumstances. Among the admittedly still unresolved problems is the seemingly inevitable rise of unemployment in the course of development, the appropriate role to be accorded to "openness," and the associated ideal role of government from both the quantitative (resources) and qualitative (extent of interventionism) points of view.

Raúl Prebisch, the father of the so-called Latin American school of development, takes a backward look at the dependency concept, distinguishing between the overall hegemony of the "center" and specific elements underlying the various aspects of North–South interaction. The more recent insertion of power relations, mainly by political scientists, is seen to enrich the purely economic explanations. Contrasts are drawn between those advocating "delinking" and those advocating the intelligent or "mutual gains"-oriented use of various types of links. Unconditional submission by the "periphery" to the theories of the "center" is rejected, along with the wholesale adoption of the center's consumption or technology patterns. Prebisch also examines some specific cases of theories emanating from the periphery, contrasting with those from the center as they relate to issues of development policy. Interdependence as a positive sum game is seen as a real possibility in circumstances in which both parties decide to make optimal use of the various strands of interconnectedness. The growing importance of this North–South dimension of global economic interdependence is emphasized.

Hollis Chenery explores our perceptions of the stylized facts of transition growth, as well as the feedback of such studies of comparative structural change on development theory and policy. The paper is expressly forward-looking in suggesting revisions of the structural change research program, among them the extension of model comparisons to include labor markets and the distribution of income. It is suggested that policy analysis be integrated more fully into the program, taking advantage of expanding data availability to analyze the effects of past episodes of policy change. Chenery suggests that a broadened research program would incorporate the best features of both neoclassical and structural approaches.

Ronald Findlay's essay points us in a direction which some recent development literature has taken, i.e. the incorporation of political economy elements in the explanatory apparatus. Focusing attention on a developing country's trade policy, he shows how the historical experiences of primary product exporters reveal the importance of links between various economic groups and the nature of the state. While government policies in Latin America, for instance, are shown to cause oscillations in trade, and thus in overall economic performance, the underlying causes of these policies are explored in terms of the nature of the state and its effect on the extent of external orientation. Findlay is drawn to the not-so-happy conclusion that the so-called bureaucratic-authoritarian state may be a necessary but not sufficient condition for developmental success.

John Fei and Gustav Ranis in two separate symposium essays, combined for publication here, point in a similar direction: the incorporation of political economy elements in presenting typologies of development theory and policy. Kuznets essentially excluded policies from his descriptive canvas but recognized their powerful influence in either obstructing or accommodating the "natural" structural evolution of an economic system over time. Chenery and his associates have tried to build policy choices into the very typology they have progressively constructed. What Fei and Ranis suggest in their essay is the increasing need to explain such policy choices endogenously, that is, as a function of some combination of initial conditions, economic as well as institutional, and the evolutionary interaction between changes in economic performance and a changing institutional and policy setting. Using the "newly industrializing countries" (NICs) of East Asia in contrast to the NICs of Latin America as an example, the authors try to indicate the direction future research might take. They suggest, for instance, that the relative size and persistence of natural-resource-based rents may be a determining factor in how macroeconomic policies are deployed to shift incomes from some groups to others, in the process centrally affecting the overall performance of the system over time.

Turning to Part II, Vittorio Corbo examines the combined influence of development theories and economic conditions on the growth strategies and development performance of the Latin American countries over 70 years. Changes in trade policy – from free trade or comparative-advantage-based to "natural" import substitution, to crisis management, to forced import substitution – are selected for particular attention. His analysis then turns to more recent efforts at reform, aimed at reducing the anti-export bias of policies generally in place in the 1970s. Corbo emphasizes the importance of coordinating liberalization efforts in various markets with appropriate macroeconomic policy management, since the expected gains from the reduction of distortions emanating from the liberalization can be too easily offset by external shocks and ill-considered stabilization efforts. As a regional subfamily of developing countries, Latin America is unique in the extent of its heterogeneity. Corbo manages to convey a flavor of this, *inter alia*, by distinguishing between the particular recent policy experiences of the Southern Cone (Argentina, Chile, and Uruguay) and those of other Latin American countries, including Brazil and Mexico.

Turning our attention to the African "type," Uma Lele's paper focuses on the generally acknowledged central issue of that region's agricultural performance and its interaction with the overall pattern of development. Five special features of African agriculture are related to past performance and future policy. Lele calls for technology-based increases in labor productivity in food crops and enhanced public investment in research and infrastructure, that is, a higher level and improved balance between private and social capital formation. She also deals with the important dimensions of domestic price stabilization and the conditions affecting exchange in domestic intersectoral markets. Throughout the paper, an effort is made to relate the recent lively academic debates on the causes of the lagging performance of most African countries to aid-donor advice and to the internal policies actually pursued in much of the continent.

Part II concludes with three papers on Asian development, all focusing heavily on the role of the rural sector within the overall developing country experience. K. N. Raj reminds us that poverty can only be alleviated by mobilizing the rural economy as part of a total development effort. Three essential links for forging a reliable rural mobilization chain are emphasized, based on the overall Asian experience. The first is related to the mobilization of idle labor within peasant households for the purpose of rural capital formation; the second considers technological advances within agriculture assisted by modern nonagricultural inputs; the third emphasizes the transfer of resources over time from agriculture to nonagriculture, mainly through the mechanism of various intersectoral markets. Shigeru Ishikawa's contribution focuses exclusively on this latter issue – the net direction and magnitude of intersectoral resource flows. He emphasizes the substantial diversity of the Asian experience, including the (net) investment needs of agriculture at an early stage of development, and presents relevant statistical findings. Direct government intervention affecting the size and direction of these intersectoral capital flows is seen to be of greater importance at low levels of income, especially with respect to the development of adequate systems for financial intermediation. The relationships among Asian countries' differing initial conditions, saving mobilization capacities, intersectoral transfer mechanisms, and the overall relevance of competitive development theories are discussed and analyzed from both positive and normative points of view.

Finally, Dong Fureng's paper deals with one of Asia's giants – the Chinese economy – from the point of view of a socialist developing economy. Although public ownership is seen as a continuing requirement in a socialist economy, certain forms of public ownership are acknowledged to hinder productivity growth. Reforms allowing a limited role for private enterprise are seen as conducive to economic development, but may in turn also create new problems – widening income gaps, or causing inflation and unemployment. Early socialist development theory and strategy are contrasted with China's post-Cultural Revolution reforms which stress economic incentives and consumer needs. The content and economic consequences of China's well-known recent strategy shifts, first in agriculture, then in rural non-agriculture, and most recently in urban industry, are described and analyzed.

Turning to the individual contributions of Part III, Theodore W. Schultz considers the possibility that an increasing division of labor may, for a time, generate increasing returns. This notion carries with it the implication of disequilibria and opportunities for economic growth in excess of factor accumulation. Modern growth theory is criticized by Schultz because it omits disequilibria and neglects the contribution of entrepreneurs to deal with these disequilibria. To support his contention, he notes the diminishing economic importance of land and natural resources. In contrast, the economic importance of the health, vigor, and acquired abilities of people increases as we approach the contemporary era of modern economic growth. The complementary returns to human capital and the available pool of productive knowledge provide a viable explanation for the increasing returns of our era, but no assurance that this fund of knowledge will continue to yield such unprecedented returns or encourage continued increases in the level of investment in human capital. Schultz illustrates increasing returns with reference to modernizing agriculture and the transformation of the traditional autarkic family. One way to explain increasing returns to specialized human capital is to posit social externalities that have no counterpart in the accumulation of physical capital.

Anne Krueger's paper bridges the literature on trade and comparative advantage with what has been written on labor markets. Both areas have played an important role in the evolution of thinking about development; yet, she points out, the question of the relationship between trade and employment has been neglected by researchers. Trade economists have proceeded some way in translating their Heckscher–Ohlin–Samuelson models into empirical predictions. Effective protection has been used to explain the factor proportions governing output and the composition of exportables, import substitutes, and non-tradeables. This research measures the magnitude of inefficient structural responses to protection and provides a framework for explaining why the outward-looking developing countries have achieved relatively rapid growth, compared with those countries that encouraged import substitution and neglected their comparative advantage. Labor markets have also played a central role in distinguishing how developing countries differ from the more industrialized high-income countries. Distortions and the segmentation of labor markets are a keystone to many models of development, but in this case, there has been much less effort to extract from these theories predictions that can be tested empirically. There is virtually no evidence on the efficiency consequences of Harris–Todaro type distortions in the labor markets of developing countries. Krueger argues that these two areas have much to learn from each other; trade restrictions may have an important impact on wage levels and structure that, in turn, influence employment composition and growth. Effective labor market restrictions in the form of minimum wages and national social insurance schemes can add to differences in labor costs between covered and uncovered sectors, thus modifying a country's comparative advantage and its ability to choose the outward-looking development course.

Ronald McKinnon's paper reevaluates and amends his influential thesis advanced more than a decade ago that financial repression and regulatory distortions in the banking system can slow the rate of economic growth. First, he notes the widespread positive correlation between the rate of growth of financial assets relative to GNP, the growth in the money supply relative to GNP, and real economic growth in those countries with higher levels of real interest rates. But on closer scrutiny, it is also shown that many of the most rapidly growing countries, such as Japan and Taiwan, did not start with financial liberalization. Rather, they maintained considerable control of the financial system, while working to stabilize the price level and channel domestic savings to investors. The sequence of policies in the Southern Cone of Latin America is noted; here financial liberalization was used to halt rapid inflation and, without regulations or governmental monitoring, banks made risky loans and assumed governments would protect them from massive bankruptcy. To explain how seemingly desirable moves toward financial liberalization could precipitate collapse, McKinnon refers to adverse risk selection models, in which rising real interest rates drive out sound borrowers, while government insurance of banks creates a problem of moral hazard. Thus, macroeconomic instability can result from financial liberalization, if the proper sequence of policies is not followed. Testing these conjectures and bringing them into consonance with McKinnon's own earlier work remains a challenge for the field.

T. Paul Schultz's survey of economic demography and development begins with Malthus's influential blend of macroeconomic diminishing returns to labor and microeconomic constraints on mortality and fertility. Evidence from both preindustrial and modern periods confirms fertility's responsiveness to economic circumstances, but does not always support Malthus's other working assumptions. The theory of household demand and production has been used more recently to account for the variation in fertility and to interrelate fertility with family labor supply and investments in the productivity of adults and children. Progress in the modeling of household demographic and economic behavior suggests that population growth should not be viewed as an exogenous shock. Consequently, the effects of population growth on economic development are very difficult to infer from historical experience. Increasingly, population growth is seen as a complex reflection of the economic opportunities facing individuals and families. The recognition that fertility and even mortality (i.e. health) are constrained household choices has led to the development of entirely new analytical approaches for evaluating health, family planning, education, and extension programs that seek to improve family production and consumption opportunities. These policy evaluation tools promise to be particularly relevant to low-income countries, according to Schultz.

Gary Fields reviews the evolution of knowledge concerning the relationship between income inequality and economic development. Kuznets first drew our attention to the inverted-U pattern in cross-country comparisons of family income inequality and per capita income levels. He speculated in the 1950s that developing countries might follow a path of first increasing inequality and then decreasing inequality only at a later stage of development, as has been the case in the twentieth century for high-income countries. But the diversity of subsequent experience within developing countries does not confirm that this tendency was of paramount importance. Nor is it clear, as some speculated from a few examples, that rapid growth would necessarily tend to be associated with increased inequality. Macroeconomic models of growth and inequality in personal incomes have not yet been satisfactorily integrated. However, microeconomic explanations for individual earnings have made headway, and more limited progress is noted in the study of family formation behavior. Thus, the distribution of family income soon may be approached within a coherent microeconomic theoretical framework. Understanding how policy options can alter the resulting distribution of family income is still a major challenge. Once a suitable theory of family income formation is at hand, there will be no shortage of alternative ways to measure inequality and even decompose the sources of that inequality, Fields notes. We already have a number of high-quality, labor-force household surveys and samples of population censuses from low-income countries. In combination with local area administrative records, these data may illuminate the actual impact of public programs and policies on the level and distribution of personal incomes.

Robert Evenson's paper presents an intellectual history of our methodological search for the sources of factor productivity growth which account for most of modern economic growth. It is also a summary of our current knowledge of the pattern of expenditures on research and development (R&D) and on technology transfer, on who is investing in these activities, the returns to these investments, and the distributional consequences and interactive effects of the new technologies. The paper includes a review of Evenson's recent findings on the payoff to the international agricultural research centers, a most influential institutional development of the postwar period with respect to the dynamism observed in Third World agriculture. Evenson begins by estimating the level of research expenditures relative to GNP in agriculture, forestry, and industrial activities. His data show that the developing countries have a research intensity that is between one-half and one-fifth that which is sustained by the industrialized countries in agriculture and forestry, respectively. The distribution and ownership of patents and expenditures on technology transfer (licensing arrangements) add further dimensions to his international overview of R&D activity. The hard question is: What is the optimal mix of institutions (e.g. patent laws) and policies to encourage efficient long-run production in and transfer of technology to the developing countries? Part of the answer to this question turns on the realized rates of return to these two interrelated aspects of a country's science and technology policy. Studies of industrial R&D and invention are more limited than those focused on agriculture; but Evenson summarizes what is known and what patterns have thus far been replicated across countries.

T. N. Srinivasan thoughtfully surveys the long-standing economic policy debate of how international trade in goods and the movement of factors contributes to economic development. This issue has been at the forefront of a reappraisal of development strategies in the last decade. Srinivasan describes both the additions to our analytical tool kits that clarify the critical parameters which determine trade's contribution to growth and the accumulating evidence on the magnitude of these crucial parameters and assumptions – what Balassa in his comments calls elasticity pessimism or optimism. Srinivasan concludes from general equilibrium models of the form developed by Whalley that global static gains from trade liberalization are modest, whereas the more difficult to pin down, dynamic consequences of outward-looking economic regimes can be a major source of economic gains over time. He then examines the literature on the macroeconomic responses of countries to shocks, such as the oil price increases of 1973 and 1979 and the increase in real interest rates in the early 1980s. At issue is whether the degree of reliance on trade affected the ability of an economy to adapt quickly its relative prices, and if necessary, its trade balance. Balassa's and Mitra's conclusions are contrasted and evaluated. Rent-seeking activities are then analyzed and their implications for welfare considered in the presence of economic distortions. In a situation where disequilibrium foreign exchange regimes encourage rent-seeking behavior, the elimination of the underlying cause of the distortion along with the ensuing rent-seeking may have a more substantial benefit than merely restricting the rent-seeking. Srinivasan then illustrates other models whose distinctive conclusions depend on distortions, rigidities, or peculiar elasticity assumptions, and discusses a variety of models emerging from an exchange of approaches between the industrial organization and trade literature. Seemingly desirable flows of factors can also yield welfare losses, if the economy is initially distorted; the "second best" may not be approached by achieving stepwise fewer restrictions to factor mobility. Although the richness of theoretical models can illustrate cases where movement toward outward-oriented trade strategies need not improve welfare, a growing number of empirical studies confirm that the countries following such strategies have done better in the postwar era and weathered better the recent series of shocks to the world economy.

Kenneth Kletzer presents a closely reasoned survey of the recent theoretical literature on external borrowing by nations and on the peculiar features and consequences of incentive-compatible debt contracts for sovereign borrowers. The waves of debt crises have not abated yet, but in the last decade economists have developed many convincing insights into the special features of this process. As Kletzer notes, the rigorous insights of general equilibrium theoretical models make the existing empirical analyses easy to criticize. Most of the empirical models are specified within a partial equilibrium setting and explain, without full justification, one attribute of the debt crisis or borrowing behavior with other jointly endogenous market outcomes or indicators. Relatively little thought has gone yet into the difficult task of developing a more appropriate estimation strategy to identify the structural parameters derived from convincing general equilibrium models, according to Kletzer.

The repayment of loans between sovereign parties cannot be enforced by third parties but must somehow be made self-enforcing. Special institutions are thereby spawned, but residual uncertainties continue to attach to international credit markets, and this unresolved uncertainty may be a critical impediment to international capital flows and efficient development. Kletzer reviews the first generation of optimizing models of borrowing which ignored the possibility of repudiation and imposed a solvency budget constraint. Added to these models was a sanction for default to deal with the enforcement problem. Asymmetries in information then were added to raise the level of realism; such models are seen to be helpful in explaining the behavior of syndicated bank loans, their changing length of maturity, rescheduling exercises, etc. in the current period. Finally, the implications of insurance policies for the behavior of banks and the effect of credit rationing and inadequate regulation of financial intermediaries on market outcomes and on macroeconomic instability are examined. These topics also surfaced in the papers of Corbo and McKinnon.

PART I
Overall Perspectives

1

Reflections on Development

W. ARTHUR LEWIS

These reflections deal with matters that have emerged throughout 40 years of events and of argumentation. What have we learned in that time, and what major concerns are still at issue? This is a brief review.

THE GROWTH RATE

We have established that less developed countries (LDCs) can grow very fast, a phenomenon that was widely denied in the 1950s and 1960s. I have calculated from the World Bank's *World Development Report* (1984, table 5) growth rates of gross domestic product (GDP) for all LDCs whose population exceeds five million. There are 50 such countries. Some of these countries show GDP growth between 1960 and 1982 at 3 percent or more per man per year; 3 percent attained by one-third of the countries is a formidable statistic. If you take 2 percent a year per head, the proportion making it is 50 percent. Growth is not confined to the "gang of four" – South Korea, Taiwan, Hong Kong and Singapore. Of these only Korea makes our list.

The statistics are not firmly founded. For example, services are a large element in the GDP, but the size and growth of that item year by year is highly speculative. Again, the volume of agricultural exports is known (except from countries that encourage smuggling) but the volume of domestic food production, which is usually much larger, is only an informed guess. The choice of sectoral weights is fundamental. The same sectoral growth rates, coupled with different sectoral weights, give differences in the overall growth rate of GDP to the extent of one percentage point. In other words, there is a statistical bias against the poorer countries. This makes the wealthier LDCs seem to be rising faster than they are, in comparison with the less rich ones. Our domestic prices for LDCs are not much good, and one may sometimes overthrow a model simply by moving from one index number to another. I believe we accept the GDP figures despite known weaknesses, partly because anyone visiting these countries can see firsthand the great improvements in their infrastructure – the doubling of ships in port, the piped water supplies, the children in school, and so on – and partly because we can do no better.

Leaving aside the accuracy of the data, the resulting indices of growth are attacked on two fronts: that of distribution and that of failure to assess development capacity.

On distribution, the fruit of growth is concentrated in a fe·
Here, emphasis is usually put on the capitalists, landlord
paid professionals. The elasticity of supply of unskilled lab
(whether in the dual or the classical models) that it dampen·
The workers benefit more than is realized because the soci
are expanded – health, piped water, free schooling – and the
are where the workers get some share of the industrial revo
Besides, the Gini coefficient ought to rise in the early stages of de
ment, this because a new middle class comes into existence. One s
also add on the positive side the pleasure that the poor derive from
seeing their children go ahead in the world: a daughter has become a
teacher or a nurse; a son has become a mechanic. We cannot measure
such pleasures, but should count them all the same (both positively and
negatively).

Coming back to growth, what do the figures suggest as to the causes of growth? In the mid-fifties we generalized from sparse historical data on growth in the countries already industrialized. Now we can look at data of our own times and see what it suggests.

Using data from the World Development Report (WDR), we can look at LDCs with populations of 5 million or more. These LDCs can be divided into three groups, the countries in each group listed in increasing order of GDP per head (averages over a period, e.g. 1960–80, are calculated by the method of least squares):

Group I: GDP growth more than 3 percent
Indonesia, Egypt, Thailand, Nigeria, Dominican Republic, Ecuador, Turkey, Tunisia, Colombia, Syria, Malaysia, South Korea, Brazil, Mexico, Azuna, Yugoslavia   (16)

Group II: GDP growth between 1 and 3 percent
Ethiopia, Mali, Burma, Malawi, Upper Volta, India, Rwanda, Tanzania, Guinea, Sri Lanka, Pakistan, Kenya, Bolivia, Philippines, Zimbabwe, Morocco, Cameroon, Ivory Coast, Guatemala   (19)

Group III: GDP growth 1 percent or less
Bangladesh, Nepal, Zaire, Uganda, Haiti, Niger, Madagascar, Ghana, Sierra Leone, Sudan, Zambia, El Salvador, Honduras, Peru, Chile   (15)

Group III contains the countries where GDP grew at 1 percent or less per year per head over two decades. A glance shows what they have in common. Either, like the Sudan, they have not enough natural resources to yield a sizeable surplus (as Steuart called it) that could be the base of further industrialization, or else their economies have been disrupted by internal war. There are degrees of disruption, and countries vary in their ability to continue economically, even in the face of maximum disturbance (e.g. Nigeria). Still, the outstanding teaching of the Group III countries is that domestic peace is one of the conditions of growth; without it professionals, capital and entrepreneurs flee the country (as also do hundreds of thousands of farmers).

Africa is the continent most prone to industrial disturbance, because nearly every African country is engaged in the painful process of trying to create a nation from people of different tribal allegiances; it is at the same time seeking political systems that will permit peaceful transfer of authority from one mixed group to another. Much of Africa also suffers from inadequate rain, inadequate in total or unreliable. So the economic problem is as formidable as the political problem. Perhaps we should think of the disincentives and deficient agricultural programs as endogenous, rather than prime causes.

What do the Group I countries, the fastest growing, have in common? Regression analysis across countries does not help because the data are particularly unreliable at this level. Of course, one can begin here with the mirror image of the lessons of Group III. The fundamental requirements of growth are water and internal peace; together, these raise output and create surplus. So new industry is attracted, and taxes can be raised for social infrastructure. Capital comes out of its hiding places, and human capital again accumulates.

Continuing, note that a high growth rate of income associates with high per capita income – all the Group I countries have per capita income in excess of $500. They invest more and save more than the Group II countries, but which is cause and effect we need not ask. The mean investment ratio of Group I rose from 18.3 to 26.5 between 1960 and 1982; the mean domestic saving ratio from 15.7 to 22.7. Group II countries were less self-reliant, their investment ratio rising by 7 points, while their saving rose only by 2 points (9.6 to 11.6).

The incremental capital–output ratios (ICORs) are on the high side, about 5.5 for Group I, and about 8.0 for Group II. This is subject to a variety of possible explanations. Thus, the world-wide inflation had raised the prices of capital goods more than those of primary commodities, especially in 1982, which was a slump year. Again to take real factors, production capacity may be a positive function of output per head; output may depend more on the stock of capital than on its annual inflow. Productivity may rise as the economy and its institutions learn by doing. Or the growth rate may be asymptotic, since growth can be too fast for proper use, a familiar sight in oil-rich countries, which indeed may even reduce their growth rates by investing more. For a country to be in Group I shows that it can grow faster, but not necessarily that it should do so.

It is possible that each country has its own optimal rate of growth, depending on its resources and institutions, and that this rate itself changes as the country develops.

Still, looking at all these groups together, one is puzzled by some of the results. All things considered, some countries turn out to have done better than one expected (e.g. Thailand, Kenya, Malaysia); while others have done worse (e.g. India, Tanzania, Sri Lanka). These a priori expectations took into account how well endowed the country was with skilled and professional people. Superimposed on this resource is the further quality of mutual respect that enables persons of different ethnicity (races, tribes, religions) to work together. Economists normally state their objective function in terms of output of GNP, but in many Third World countries the principal product is politics, and this takes precedence over raising the GNP. However, the relationship is not simple. Sometimes economic development is the cause of political strife; the tribes were at peace with each other until money began to flow. In other cases, it is development that offers a prospect of peace, since the flow of money makes possible such remedies as affirmative action, subsidies to rural works and other emollients.

UNEMPLOYMENT

We first must distinguish the cyclical from other macroeconomic causes of unemployment. In the United States, there is a Kuznets great depression every 20 years or so (1873, 1893, 1907, 1929, 1956, 1973) which raises unemployment from a minimum of 3 to 4 percent to perhaps 20 percent. The pattern of the cycle in the 1970s and 1980s is dissimilar from that of Kuznets great depressions in the century from 1873 to 1973, mainly because the economy was thought to be overheating in the late 1970s. Deliberate steps were taken in 1979 and the next two or three years to bring it down, when precedent would have required policies to push it up. So much has changed, especially in monetary policy and the reactions thereto, that we shall spend a quarter of a century before we have models with which we are completely comfortable.

The opinion that the short-term movement of the world economy should be controlled internationally (commodity prices, terms of trade, short-term exchange rates) is gaining by experience. Ultimately the case for freedom of prices has been based on a diversity of demand and supply in world markets, but this is not how markets work. For example, in the economists' theories of foreign exchange, surplus or deficient situations are brought into line by real goods and real services; but in the real world, the amount of money available for speculation in the foreign exchanges is several times that required for trade, and for foreign exchange, rates are determined by speculation that has little to do with the trade in real goods and services.

During the coming decades, the international community will be forced to make alternative and more civilized means of dampening the phenomena that create Kuznets depressions, and those of the leading countries of Europe. In the early part of the twentieth century, the general public still believed that depressions came from God. Once the public fully understands that depressions can be turned on and off (as in 1979) by ordinary men, they will no longer tolerate them and will force the financial and governmental communities to create and adopt less volatile institutions. It takes a long time for communities to learn new lessons, especially lessons involving ceding power to nationals of other countries, but ways of governing the economy must be found and brought into effect that are less costly than making 20 percent of the population unemployed.

Now turn to the domestic macroeconomy. Unemployment is an almost inevitable product of economic development. Development raises the rate of natural increase of population in an LDC. If the land–labour ratio is favorable, the group simply brings more land under cultivation. If the ratio is unfavorable, the land absorbs more labour – by subdivision of family farms or otherwise. At some point, diminishing returns drive young men off the farms into other occupations, especially into the towns, if that is where the development is occurring. The rates of change have been astonishing. At the end of the nineteenth century, urban population was growing at 2.5 percent per annum from farming, at 3.5 in the United States and 3.5 percent in Australia. But the 1960s and 1970s saw many urban populations in LDCs growing at 6 percent per annum; LDCs averaged about 4.5 percent. It is not possible for infrastructure to keep up with such rates of growth. Everything falls behind – schools, municipal transport, piped water, electric power, and so on. The only thing to be said in favor of excessive urbanization is that it tends to reduce the birthrate.

An obvious remedy for a high urbanization rate would seem to be to restrict the growth of the towns, for example, by requiring residence permits of all who live in cities of a certain size. This presupposes that it is cheaper to have development occur in the countryside than in the town. This is probably so, not because it is cheaper to build in the countryside, but because less infrastructure is supplied. Rural areas get schools for 25 percent of their children (in contrast with 75 percent in the urban areas) fewer hospital beds per thousand, no street lighting, no piped water, and so on. This policy has some potential: entrepreneurs do open up in rural areas, especially where rural entrepreneurs are indeed encouraged, and particularly if the population is used to rural towns with already some level of business sophistication. But the results are limited. The alternative policy – to license living in towns – is not popular in democracies and also is not very successful, except perhaps in China.

The economists' remedy for excessive urbanization, as for many other situations, is to let market prices roll. If all prices are flexible, they will adjust to each other in such a way that every person who wants to work will find work; those who have no work will not be "unemployed." One condition for this is that the wage level be consistent with international prices of those commodities which the country could expect to export. This was so, in the days before LDC trade unionism and minimum wages. It is still so in many LDCs, where wages are determined endogenously, but it is not true in other LDCs where wages are determined other than by supply and demand.

It is especially not the case where some highly profitable natural resource can be exported at high wages, while also earning a lot of foreign currency. Wages in the rest of the economy are attracted upwards, beyond the level that they can afford, so there is unemployment. And the abundance of foreign exchange has the effect that there is also no pressure to devalue the currency. This is now known as the Dutch disease.

Productivity is playing an increasing role in wage negotiations, as are fringe benefits, training and job security, suggesting that the obsession with money wages that has reduced such negotiations' contribution to price and incomes policy is diminishing. The use of medium-term (five years) settlements in real terms might also help cool industrial disputes, just as the three-year contract did when first introduced. Just because there is a three- or four-year macroeconomic cycle is no reason to expect real wages to rise and fall every four years. Salaries ride the cycle; why should not wages? In Japan, "rigidities" in industrial relations teach the rest of us that we do not need the range of fluctuations that we have supposed.

We had hoped to get some relief from the development of a new "intermediate technology," but while there have been some good results, the new techniques have not spread rapidly. Their relevance is limited, especially in the choice of manufacturing plant. For some jobs you must have the latest technology, or a precise cut, or access to a storeroom of expensive parts. Construction is easier to adapt; man has been building huge works for the last 5,000 years, much of it with slave labor valued erroneously at zero, so we still have before us access to all the various tricks of labor-intensive construction.

The problem here is not the absence of techniques but the absence of the human will. The benefit-cost analyst may show for a particular project that it would cost more in domestic currency if done by hand than if done by machine, but the real cost by hand is lower (say when shadow pricing for foreign exchange, to be noncontroversial). The project should go ahead in the labor-intensive version. But this will not happen unless it is subsidized. Therefore, the government has the opportunity of demonstrating the benefits of shadow pricing. Ministers of finance, however, will look with distaste on proposals that they spend more where they could spend less. And if one cannot get the subsidy through for public projects, getting it through for private projects is all the more difficult.

I have pointed out before that what economists maximize and what ministers maximize are not the same – and now I make the point again in relation to employment. The economists claim to be maximizing real output, whereas ministers have to watch out for what is happening to employment. They will even employ people to dig holes and fill them up again – a list of such schemes has been published by the International Labor Organization (ILO).

EXTERNAL TRADE

The rate of growth of world trade is determined by two principal factors: the demand of industrial countries for primary commodities, and the ratio of net imports of manufactures into industrial countries from other industrial countries (Lewis, 1981). The extraordinary acceleration of world trade in manufactures after World War II can be traced almost entirely to these two factors. Fast growth of industry induced fast growth of demand for primary commodities, which in turn, stimulated the demand of commodity producers for manufactures. The ratio of commodities to industrial production remained constant from 1873 to 1929, and again after World War II until 1973.

The ratio of net imports of manufactures to consumption of manufactures is the other principal determinant of the share of manufactures in international trade. The changes were striking. Organization for Economic Cooperation and Development (OECD) countries barred their markets to each other, but besides their trade with one another, had only a restricted effect on trade in manufactures outside the OECD. Table 1.1 shows that ratio of imports of manufactures to absorption of manufactures.

The results could have been modified by the terms of trade or the volume of capital export, but these seem not to have changed significantly in the 1950s or 1960s. The only major ratios that changed were the growth rate of industrial production and the share of domestic production in net consumption of manufactures. Only one of these seems open to speculation in the near future, not the growth rate of industrial production, nor the ratio of commodities to manufactures in world trade. But one may hazard a guess that the rush to import manufactures which distinguished both Britain and the United States in the fifties and sixties will not be repeated.

Now to the individual country in world trade. The slogan that LDCs should specialize in agriculture has surfaced again, but does not need to

TABLE 1.1   *Ratio of imports of manufactures to absorption of manufactures*

	1959/60	1973/74 (ratio)	Change
Japan	6.0	7.1	+ 1.1
EEC net	7.6	10.1	+ 2.5
USA	3.3	8.0	+ 4.7
EEC intra	6.6	15.6	+ 9.0
UK[1]	17.1	29.0	+ 11.9

[1] UK includes imports from EEC.
Source: UNCTAD, *Handbook of International Trade and Development Statistics* Supplement 1977, p. 236.

be refuted once more for this audience, for whom a country should specialize in the opportunities where it has a comparative advantage. In most LDCs these opportunities have centered on natural resources (commercial crops and minerals) to the exclusion of producing food for export – although this generalization is not wholly true, since rice has been a major export. The snag is that superficially it looks as though the countries with the poorest agricultural resources (due usually to inadequate or unreliable rains) have a comparative advantage not in food production, but in export crops or in light manufacturing.

These matters lend themselves to benefit–cost analysis, and we shall not find ourselves disputing measurable quantities. LDCs range all the way in the nature and value of their natural resources; they should not be treated as if they are all alike. That surely is one of the first lessons of the last 30 years. Another lesson is the importance of technological change. We have had the wheat and the wet rice revolutions, and are spending liberally to bring about the maize and other tropical cereals, and the livestock revolutions. Creating all the institutions needed to support an agricultural revolution takes time. Continent-wide drought has plagued mankind for as long as we know. It will not be ended by altering the price of rice – although better agricultural programs were unquestionably essential, along with water, canals, transport and all the rest.

The recent and continuing assault of LDCs on the markets for manufactures in "more developed countries" (MDCs) is due partly to the exhaustion of import substitution, and partly to the collapse of the myth that tropical peoples do not have what manufacturing takes. Import substitution offers a limited market, since the ratio of substitutable imports to national income is itself small. Once the backlog has disappeared, imports grow at more or less the same rates as national income and contain the 7 to 10 percent potential rates that fast-moving LDCs require. The myth collapsed as LDC after LDC joined the ranks of successful exporters of manufactures.

The episode has many lessons, of which we shall pick only one, namely the importance of marketing. Production depends mainly on internal discipline and MDCs have no comparative advantage in discipline. But in marketing the seller must radiate energy and skill.

Organized markets exist for most agricultural and mineral products, but manufactures are sold face to face. Buyers and sellers establish contacts on which they rely for continuing trade. LDC manufacturers, therefore, soon discovered that they depended on their foreign contacts to the point in many cases that subsidiary companies, branches, and long-term contracts were fundamental to selling. In the early 1960s, theorists argued hotly over the role of private foreign entrepreneurship and investment. This argument has cooled. Instead, in the mid-eighties we can see the procession of government leaders of all per-suasions – from free traders to self-styled neo-Marxists – visiting New York to talk about joint enterprises and all the concessions now offered to private business.

At one stage of the argument, customs unions between adjacent countries were seen as a possible substitute, reducing the need for foreign enterprise by opening up a new category of integration industries. It has not worked out this way. In the first place, opening up the local markets to competition from adjacent markets massacred a lot of small firms as average market size increased, but it did relatively little to productivity or employment. This created a small gain and a large anti-unionist body, but these were not the main purposes of the union. The main purpose was to increase the economies of scale, by bringing in new industries or by bringing down costs of existing ones. The chief lesson, presumably, is that one should not begin a customs union with internal free trade.

A second point is that the countries in a customs union are not equally attractive to manufacturing. A union intensifies this, since a dis-proportionally large part of new industries sets up in the more favored places. This is a source of tension and instability.

The third lesson is that customs unions may flourish in depressions rather than in booms. The 1960s and 1970s were boom decades. It was then easier for an LDC to export to the United States or France than to infiltrate a market in Brazil. Recession since 1973 has hit the customs union hard, though it is too early to assess the ultimate effect.

To watch manufacturers from the most industrialized nations running away from competition with newcomers and resorting to illegal discriminations is both bizarre and tragic. They claimed that compe-tition between peoples of different levels of wages was "free" but not fair. The classical economists disposed of this a century and a half ago, by demonstrating that the difference in wages is the equilibrating element.

The argument was supported by the events of the 1960s and 1970s in all the industrial states except the United States. The rest ran short of labor and had to import labor; they could not argue that the import of low-wage goods was causing unemployment. In the United States, on the other hand, the theory did not work. People without jobs in textiles or shoes were theoretically to move into high-wage industries – automobiles, agricultural machinery, steel, and electronic equipment – but these were in equal disarray.

Critics divided into those who thought this simply a matter of domestic and foreign prices being out of line, and those who said fundamental disequilibria exist in institutions or in outlook. If merely a matter of prices, this would be corrected by devaluation of the dollar; if more fundamental, it could even be beyond solution. The United States was not alone in maintaining an overvalued currency through most of the 1960s. To devalue was a sign of weakness in most countries. We have abandoned long-term stability of the currency without new rules to take its place. This is one place where we have yet to learn the lessons of the fifties and sixties, whatever these lessons may be.

The principal lesson we have all learned, LDC and MDC alike, is that inflation is a terrible scourge. But how to avoid it in face of all the pressures is yet to be seen – pressures for higher real wages, for more public services, for more housing, and so on. Such pressures did not exist a century ago. In the twentieth century, governments have undertaken to provide a rising standard of living, at say 5 percent a year, whereas in fact they do not know how to reach 2 percent. By their own efforts, the political novels and parliamentary speeches of a century ago carried no such undertaking. Until this incompatibility of purpose and ability is removed, inflation will always challenge the market economies and the stability of their currencies.

FISCAL

Lastly, a few words on the financial situation. As I pointed out earlier, Group I countries have distinguished themselves, by raising their domestic savings ratio from 16 to 23 percent over two decades. Whereas in the mid-seventies, we were still urging LDCs to save more, and especially to tax themselves more, today talk is widespread that the share of the national income passing through the government's tills is too large. The arguments are the same as are made for MDCs in the same context and can, therefore, be tackled at several levels of meaning.

First, one may argue that in physical terms the amount of some public service is too large (whether publicly or privately provided), in the sense that part of the resources that it uses up would be better used for something else. This is the basic statement.

In one version of this statement, the government's problem is not how to raise the funds in domestic currency, but how to translate domestic into foreign funds. This was the concept that eighteenth-century economists were seeking when they insisted on distinguishing between productive and unproductive goods. In our day, this turns up as tradeable goods and as the basis of the two-gap model. We see this typically when a country borrows money to build, for example, schools and hospitals, financing the original costs from loans or grants, but thereby putting a strain on foreign exchange reserves to meet current expenses and debt charges that cannot be reached simply by raising more domestic finance. This is all part of the general lessons on the management of the economy, which turn out to be the central priority.

Pursuing the concept of the burdensome government, one may agree that the burden is not unacceptable in the real terms measured above, but be hostile to the size of the portion that is administered by the government. Here the argument is usually about managerial efficiency. It derives from the proposition that government management tends to be more inefficient than private management. One of the lessons over the last 30 years is that Third World governments differ widely in this respect. Some countries are more ready for, and more able to cope with management, and programs should take this into account. Finally the government's share may appear more burdensome in some countries than in others because of differences in the way the programs are financed.

If the tax paid is concealed in the price of the taxed commodity, it will not be felt as much of a burden, since it will not be noticeable. This is the difference between "strident" taxes and taxes that do not draw attention to themselves. An important element, for tax purposes, is the extent to which the rich users of a program are subsidizing it. The Beveridge principle requires that all members of the public get the same service and pay the same fee. Since the upper-middle classes insist on receiving higher levels of service than the poor would accept, a Beveridge-type plan bears heavily on the government's budget. Finally, the acceptability of government expenditure depends partly on whether it is enacted or "comes about." By comes about, I mean that the elasticity of revenues as a whole with respect to tax national income is significantly greater than unity. A number of LDCs may have reached this situation.

The record of three decades is not bad. If economic growth continued at this pace for another 30 years, the standard of living of the Third World would be unrecognizable.

REFERENCES

Lewis, W. Arthur 1981: "The Rate of Growth of World Trade." In Sven Grassman and Erik Lundberg (eds), *The World Economic Order, Past and Prospects*, London: Macmillan.
World Bank 1984: *World Development Report*.

Comments on
"Reflections on Development"

JEFFREY G. WILLIAMSON

Professor W. Arthur Lewis poses the question: What have we learned about development over the past 30 years? In searching for the answers, Sir Arthur ranges far and wide over recent Third World history. My remarks will dwell on 12 of his lessons from history.

Lesson 1

Lewis LDCs can grow very fast, a statement that was denied in the 1950s and 1960s, and is still often unappreciated in the popular press in the 1980s. That is, one-third of the 50 developing nations exceeding 5 million in population had per capita growth rates of 3 percent per annum or more from 1960 to 1982. Half had growth rates 2 percent per annum or more (based on *WDR* tables).

Williamson We can, in fact, say far more. First, this growth experience was spectacular, compared with previous industrial revolutions in Europe. Based on McGreevey's (1985) summary, European per capita income growth rates were much slower:

1800–1850	0.74
1850–1900	1.27
1900–1950	1.35

Second, Third World growth tended to accelerate up to the first Organization of Petroleum Exporting Countries (OPEC) crunch. Trend acceleration is a common attribute of all developing countries, past and present. Third, the growth slowdown in the 1970s was far less dramatic in the Third World than in the industrialized countries. While conditions at the center clearly mattered to performance in the periphery (as Sir Arthur's Nobel Laureate lecture on the "Slowing Down of the Engine of Growth" reminded us in 1980), it is still striking how well the non-African Third World has done in an otherwise difficult economic environment.

Lesson 2

Lewis Three conditions seem essential to growth from an agrarian base, conditions which are not satisfied by 15 of the 50 countries in the World Bank sample. These three conditions are: (1) internal peace, (2) a large enough natural resource endowment to yield a sizeable agricultural surplus, and (3) sufficient water to yield a sizeable agricultural surplus.

Williamson The importance of peace would, of course, be appreciated by any economic historian. Two important examples come immediately to mind (Williamson, 1985a chap. 11). From 1760 to 1820, Britain was at war more than half the time. Crowding-out associated with war finance, price twists associated with trade deflection, and uncertain investment expectations associated with wartime stop–go, all served to generate low rates of accumulation and resource allocative distortions, even during the "heroic" First Industrial Revolution. There was no capital-deepening, real wages were stable, and growth was slow. During Pax Britannica after about 1820, growth rates doubled, real wages surged and, led by Korean exports, a mini-take off occurred. The acceleration in Japanese industralization after 1905 can be explained by much the same factors.

While a favorable natural resource endowment rarely appears as an important explanatory variable in most economic histories, rapid productivity advance in agriculture does. Indeed, some would argue that an agricultural revolution is an essential condition for modern economic growth. The interesting issue, of course, is exactly what role institutional reform and pricing policy play in creating an environment favorable to rapid rates of agricultural productivity growth and a growing agricultural surplus.

Lesson 3

Lewis The fruits of growth are concentrated in a few hands. This fact should occasion no surprise since the Gini coefficient ought to rise in the early stages of development. This follows largely because the elasticity of unskilled labor supply is so high that it dampens real wage growth.

Williamson The upswing of the Kuznets curve is *not* an unambiguous stylized fact of history, past or present. Indeed, the variance around any estimated Kuznets curve is greatest from low to middle levels of development. This serves to dramatize a point worth recalling whenever the Kuznets curve is debated: inequality is unlikely to rise systematically across a pooled cross-section of early industrial revolutions; such correlations are bound to be poor, since history and geography have given less developed countries very different starting points (Lindert and Williamson, 1985). Furthermore, at least in the case of Brazil, the behavior of the income share at the bottom may be the result of population growth, rather than of relatively low rates of growth of income of the poor (Morley, 1981). But most important, there is no evidence which supports the view that it is elastic unskilled labor supplies that account for rising inequality where in fact it can be found. I know of no comprehensive evidence from the Third World which establishes that point. Certainly the evidence from Britain's industrial revolution fails to support the labor surplus view, and that, after all, was the economy which the classical economists were writing about (Williamson, 1985a). It appears that labor demand conditions underlying growth strategies may play the more important role in accounting for rising inequality when it occurs.

Lesson 4

Lewis   Unemployment is an almost inevitable product of economic development, and it is manifested mainly in the cities. Industrialization triggers the demographic transition; although we are not entirely clear how, rising rates of population growth put pressure on the land, and outmigration to the cities results. The rates have been astonishing, averaging about 4.5 percent per annum in the Third World as a whole.

Williamson   It is simply not true that rapid rates of urbanization in the Third World since 1960 can be explained by Malthusian forces and pressure on the land. Demographers have advocated this view, and it has always seemed plausible, but when submitted to test within a full general equilibrium model, the thesis fails (Kelley and Williamson, 1984). Rather, it has always been pull conditions in the city that have played the key role.

Lesson 5

Lewis   The Third World has overurbanized.

Williamson   The term overurbanization is overworked. I am not sure just how Professor Lewis is using it here.

One of the central arguments used to support the overurbanization thesis is that Third World populations are supported by an unusually small industrial labor force. The evidence on this point was first marshalled by Hoselitz, who found that Third World ratios of industrial employment to urban populations were small in contemporary developing nations compared with currently developed countries in the late nineteenth and early twentieth centuries. Not too long ago, Bairoch replicated Hoselitz's finding, and using World Bank data from the 1960s, Berry and Sabot have made the same point. Hoselitz's thesis has encouraged the view that Third World city growth is being driven by somewhat different forces than has been true historically. According to this view, sometime after 1930, "urbanization without industrialization" began to appear in the Third World, and the problem took on alarmist dimensions in the 1960s, when urban unemployment and underemployment captured our attention.

Since so much seemed to ride on the issue, fresh new tests of the overurbanization thesis gained high research priority with the appearance of more employment data as the last two decades of Third World city growth experience unfolded. Based on an exhaustive assessment of industrial employment trends between 1950 and 1970, Preston has been unable to find any evidence of deterioration in industry–urban ratios for the Third World as a whole (Preston, 1979). A more recent study by Gregory (1980) has offered an even sounder rejection of the Hoselitz thesis. Furthermore, there is no evidence to support the view that informal sector urban employment has grown at an exceptionally rapid rate.

If Hoselitz and Lewis were right, then urban service sectors – the informal service sector, in particular – should exhibit relatively low wages, high unemployment, and they should be dominated by migrants. Yap, Mazumdar, Kannappan and a whole host of scholars have shown that this simply is not so. The evidence is simply not consistent with the overurbanization thesis.

Lesson 6

ewis   One remedy for overurbanization is to legislate restrictions on city growth. Another is to get the prices right.

Villiamson   Of course, Third World cities may be growing too fast, because incentives promote that growth and the incentives may be due to policy distortions. Legislative restrictions would be a bad idea under such circumstances, while eliminating the distortions would, presumably, be a good idea.

Lipton and Keyfitz have both reminded us that an urban bias favors city growth. There is no shortage of policies which serve to have that effect: the domestic terms of trade are twisted against agriculture, thus encouraging more rapid rural emigration to the city than would be true in the absence of such policies; tariffs and overvalued exchange rates also serve to protect urban industry at agriculture's expense; financial markets are manipulated by policy to create cheap capital for favored urban industries; and social overhead is allocated disproportionately to the cities, all offered at less than user costs, and all financed from general tax revenues rather than from urban land taxes. The components of the urban bias are, therefore, well known: what we *don't* know, however, is their empirical relevance or how they interact in a world of multiple distortions.

Lesson 7

ewis   One of the reasons for the disappointing employment growth in Third World industry has been the persistence of a capital-intensity bias. Benefit–cost analysis, if implemented by shadow pricing rules, will reveal the bias. But the labor intensive project will not be selected, of course, unless the project is subsidized. Government financial constraints make subsidized projects unpopular for public investment projects, and even more so for private projects.

Villiamson   I agree. Perhaps this explains, in part, why development strategies in the nineteenth century were far more labor-intensive.

Lesson 8

Lewis   Exports from the Third World have been driven in large part by two forces in the industrialized nations: fast growth of industry stimulated buoyant demand for primary products; and the ratio of net imports of manufactures to consumption of manufactures rose. The export engine of growth in the Third World has slowed down, and it is unlikely ever to repeat the experience of the 1950s and 1960s.

Williamson   I agree. Indeed, we all appreciate that one of the reasons for the unusual growth in world trade in the 1950s and 1960s was because the world economy was attempting to return to normalcy after the disastrous economic events of the interwar period. These included the spectacular slowdown in industrialization associated with the Great Depression and competitive commercial policy responses, which suppressed world trade. To argue that impressive Third World growth in the quarter century after 1950 was driven by favorable growth conditions in the industrialized nations, is to argue that dramatic Third World growth was postponed by interwar failure. It is not clear whether the Third World has achieved greater economic independence in the 1980s than it had in the 1930s, and a comparative assessment is long overdue.

Lesson 9

Lewis   Getting the prices right hardly guarantees that an agricultural revolution will ensue. Creating all the institutions needed to support an agricultural revolution takes time and resources.

Williamson   I agree. Indeed, it is easy to be misled, as many governments past and present have been, that agricultural productivity advance requires little investment. This has rarely been the case during any country's successful industrial revolution, and certainly not during the First Industrial Revolution, where more than a third of Britain's investment was allocated to agriculture. Furthermore, "getting the prices right" in agriculture often requires institutional reform and changes in property rights of profound proportions. We now know, for example, that the English enclosures in the late eighteenth and early nineteenth centuries were in large measure a response to under-renting in an environment of sticky rents and massive double-digit inflation.

Lesson 10

Lewis   Import substitution offers a limited market, since the ratio of substitutable imports to national income is itself small. The myth that tropical LDCs cannot exploit manufacturing exports collapsed as LDC after LDC joined the ranks of successful exporters of manufactures.

Williamson   I agree, although it has been hard to communicate that lesson to the Latin nations who suffered a collapse in world markets during the 1930s and then enjoyed industrialization in the 1940s, due to special wartime conditions elsewhere. In the nineteenth century, it is almost impossible to find examples of industrial revolutions without rapid export growth.

Lesson 11

Lewis   Fast growing LDCs have been extraordinarily successful in raising their domestic saving ratios over the past two or three decades, helping achieve high rates of accumulation and capital deepening. Yet, large governments may have become "too large." First, public services often crowd out other more valuable activities. Second, government management often tends to be less efficient than private management. Third, the (rural) poor may be subsidizing public projects which are consumed primarily by the (urban) rich.

Williamson   I agree. We often fail to appreciate just how spectacular the rate of accumulation has been in the Third World compared to past historical standards. It took America more than six decades to do what the Third World has done in two or three: that is, the investment ratios in the successful developing countries today are what they were in America in 1900 after 60 years or more of industrialization. In the absence of government intervention, the rate of accumulation in England during the First Industrial Revolution was about a third of that in contemporary LDCs, and the saving rate was less than half.

   On the other hand, nineteenth-century developing countries selected a less capital-intensive development strategy, manifested primarily by lower social overhead investment in the cities. While this more labor-intensive development strategy freed up resources for greater rates of job creation than would have been true otherwise, it was purchased at great cost – namely, at the price of far more unpleasant urban environments and far higher urban mortality rates.

   One of the most favored explanations of the rise in the saving rate across industrial revolutions has been rising inequality. Indeed, ever since Adam Smith, development economists and economic historians have stressed the growth-inequality trade-off, and it is central to the classical labor surplus model tailored for Third World experience by Lewis. The evidence, however, has not been kind to the trade-off thesis. Rising inequality accounted for little of America's nineteenth-century accumulation experience, it accounted for none of Britain's accumulation experience during the First Industrial Revolution, and it appears to have accounted for little of contemporary Third World experience as well (Williamson and Lindert, 1980, chap. 12; Williamson, 1985b; Lindert and Williamson, 1985). Instead, investment demand seems to have been the driving force behind private saving and accumulation, past and present.

Lesson 12

Lewis   The record of the past three decades in the Third World is not bad. If the pace continued for another three decades, the standard of living in the Third World would be unrecognizable.

Williamson   We can say more. The record of the past three decades in the Third World has been spectacular by the standards of practically all industrial revolutions since Britain initiated the first experiment 200 years ago. However, it is very unlikely that it will be replicated over the next three decades. In any case, we would understand this experience far better if more development economists would engage in serious comparative economic history, much like Sir Arthur has done throughout his illustrious career.

REFERENCES

Gregory, P. 1980: "An Assessment of Changes in Employment Conditions in Less Developed Countries." *Economic Development and Cultural Change*, 28 (July), 673–700.

Kelley, A. C. and Williamson, J. G. 1984: *What Drives Third World City Growth?* Princeton, N.J.: Princeton University Press.

Lewis, W. Arthur 1980: "The Slowing Down of the Engine of Growth." *American Economic Review*, 70 (Sept.), 555–64.

Lindert, P. H. and Williamson, J. G. 1985: "Growth, Equality and History." *Explorations in Economic History*, 22 (Oct.), 341–77.

McGreevey, W. P. 1985: "Economic Aspects of Historical Demographic Change." *World Bank Staff Working Papers No. 685*, Washington, D.C.: The World Bank.

Morley, S. A. 1981: "The Effect of Changes in the Population on Several Measures of Income Distribution." *American Economic Review*, 71 (June), 285–94.

Preston, S. H. 1979: "Urban Growth in Developing Countries: A demographic Reappraisal." *Population and Development Review*, 5 (June), 195–215.

Williamson, J. G. and Lindert, P. H. 1980: *American Inequality: A Macroeconomic History.* New York: Academic Press.

Williamson, J. G. 1985a: *Did British Capitalism Breed Inequality?* London: Allen and Unwin.

Williamson, J. G. 1985b: "The Historical Content of the Classical Labor Surplus Model." *Population and Development Review*, 11 (June), 171–91.

2

Dependence, Development, and Interdependence

RAÚL PREBISCH

In the 1960s, a ferment of controversy and concern seethed around theories on dependence and the long-standing problems it posed. On looking backwards from the mid-eighties, when ideas have settled, two major approaches are discernible. One of them, representative of more traditional thinking, identified the problem of dependence with the familiar hegemony of the stronger countries over the weaker. It was a one-sided and invariably negative relationship to which all the ills of the periphery were attributed. The other stream of thought took for granted the fact and the significant implications of hegemony and attempted to go further by clarifying elements on which that hegemony was based and elucidating the complex manifestations of it that appeared in the center-periphery concept. Thus, for example, the nature of the trend towards deterioration of the terms of trade was highlighted as a clear expression of the disadvantageous positon of the periphery. Later, the center-periphery concept was enriched with valuable contributions by sociologists, political scientists and economists, who took pains to point out internal phenomena inherent in the periphery which strengthened dependence relations. Special mention should be made of a work by Fernando Cardoso and Enzo Faletto, prepared under the aegis of ECLAC.[1]

How does ECLAC's thinking on the subject stand today, with all this wealth of theory to draw upon? Something may usefully be said of its significance, now that so much time has elapsed, in discussing the sweeping changes that have taken place in real conditions.

The first step will be to review the role of the periphery in capitalist development in preindustrialization days. The very dynamics of the centers had left the periphery on the sidelines of industrial develop-ment, in its appendicular role as producer and exporter of primary products. The increase in productivity, which technical progress in the centers brought in its train, did not spread throughout the world via a fall in the price of manufactures, but was reflected in the centers them-selves in income growth and the consequent expanded demand for goods and services, and in the capital accumulation required to meet it. Demand for primary products from the periphery also increased in this process, generally very briskly, and the resultant additional income was transferred to the centers in exchange for manufactured goods.

This model began to crack up during World War I. But the decisive impulse to industrialization was given mainly by the Great Depression of the 1930s. It was a move dictated not by doctrinaire considerations, but by adverse circumstances which likewise made import substitution essential. No one could have dreamed of exporting manufactures to the centers either then or afterwards, during World War II and the difficult postwar days. Later on came times that were favorable to the export of manufactures; some countries turned these opportunities to good account, while others, like my own (Argentina), failed to use them in an intensive and unswerving pursuit of objectives.

I said before, that since the periphery had no share in industrialization, broad masses of the population had been excluded from development. This was a consequence of the dynamics of the centers and of change and diversification in demand. Demand for manufactures is apt to increase rapidly, whether in the periphery or in the centers, in contrast with the relatively slow growth of primary exports. There is an immense disparity in the income-elasticity of demand. That is why it is so important to export manufactures. It so happens, however, that the manufactures which the periphery is in a position to export are just those in whose case demand in the centers tends to shift towards diversified goods. Hence the unwillingness of the centers to do away with their protectionism, which if anything is tightening up. The great trade liberalization of the Kennedy and Tokyo rounds scarcely reached the periphery, since the goods concerned were those for which demand was boosted by the technological innovations of the centers. The inference would seem to be that here again the dynamics of the centers does not benefit the periphery as it does the centers themselves. We shall revert to this point later.

It was said at the outset that in the controversy on dependence, the center-periphery thesis had been enriched. Perhaps the most important contribution was the insertion of power relations in this concept. In the appendicular development of the periphery, links had been forged between the dominant groups in the centers and those in the periphery. These social groups had certain interests in common, albeit the peripheral groups were clearly in a subordinate position. The hegemony of the centers, and especially of the main dynamic center, was based on their own economic, financial and technological superiority, on the fragmentation of the periphery, on the trend towards an imbalance in trade, and on this subordination or dependence, whichever name is preferred.

That superiority of the centers continued to make itself felt – and to assume new modalities – during the industrial development of the periphery. To the siphoning off of income from the enterprises producing and exporting primary goods and importing manufactures in the pre-industrialization phase, as well as from public utility companies, was added the absorption of income by the transnational corporations through their increasing participation in industrial development, frequently under the shelter of overprotection. Nor, of course, must the banking and financing companies be omitted. Thus a change took place in the composition of the dominant groups linked to the centers and a web of relations was woven which favored the economic, political, and strategic interests of the groups in question.

This was a way – blatant or subtle – in which the hegemonic weight of the centers made itself felt. And when the periphery reacted against this dependence and jeopardized those interests, the whole constellation of dominant elements in the centers lost no time in mobilizing themselves to apply penalizing measures.

It is desirable to draw a distinction, not always clear-cut, between these dependence phenomena and the nature of the center-periphery relations to which we have referred before, and which are bred of the time lag in the integrated development of the periphery, of its economic, financial, and technological inferiority and of its economic fragmentation.

We shall now go on to discuss the other stream of ideas on dependence. Among its most significant expressions was the allegation that the high level of living in the centers was basically due to systematic exploitation of the periphery, with various forms of transfer of income to the centers and a deterioration of the terms of trade for the periphery's primary products. Undoubtedly, history can show elements of exploitation which ECLAC has repeatedly exposed. But then to leap to such a conclusion on the peripheral origin of the centers' welfare is to overlook the influence of their enormous technological progress.

It is not surprising, then, that some have gone so far as to recommend delinking from the centers, a more or less sharp severance of center-periphery relations, in order to enable the periphery to take full advantage of its own potential and thus give a decisive impulse to its development.

It is true that the centers, in particular the main dynamic center of capitalism, have concerned themselves with the development of the periphery only in so far as it served their own interests, and generally with little foresight or breadth of outlook. They have been indifferent to the development of the periphery in social depth, nor have they cared to look for ways in which interests could converge.

An enormous and enlightened effort, a tenacious and long drawn-out effort of its own, will be necessary before a peripheral country can cease to be peripheral. That was what took place in the United States, until the country came to be the main dynamic center. And in the same way, we have witnessed the transformation of Japan into an exceptionally thriving center, notwithstanding its lack of natural resources – such as were available in the other case – other than the power of its mind and will. They did not take pains to cut off their relations with the centers, but sought to make intelligent use of them to further their own development.

Generally speaking, in the stream of thought under consideration, little emphasis was placed on the internal flaws of peripheral development. For instance, just as there is a persistent trend towards external disequilibrium, to which we have referred, so too in the periphery there is a propensity towards a dynamic internal imbalance between the rate of expenditure and that of the reproductive capital accumulation, which is indispensable if employment, productivity and the global income of the economy are to multiply. In this respect, there is in the periphery – and I am alluding first and foremost to the Latin American region – a fundamental flaw.

With an average productivity lower than that of the centers, we make haste to imitate their life styles, to step up demand for diversified goods and services. A privileged consumer society has thus evolved in the social strata that are favorably placed, as regards the appropriation of the fruits of technical progress, to the obvious detriment of reproductive capital investment. And in the course of the structural changes in society, as the distributive power of the labor force has developed, its private and social consumption has also gradually increased, and the state (i.e. government) has considerably raised its own civil and military expenditure. All these outlays are not made at the expense of spending by the favored strata, which is incessantly stimulated by technological innovations, but are superimposed on their privileged consumption. In this way, sooner or later, the rate of reproductive accumulation has suffered deleteriously to the rate of development and to distributive equity. And this dynamic imbalance inevitably ends in a new type of inflation which cannot be efficaciously combated with a restrictive mo____ry policy that is counterproductive because of its economic, so____ ____ ____ ences.

The fact that all these forms of private and social, civil and military ex____ ____ ____ imitation of the centers might induce the th____ ____ ____ to likewise attribute to dependence the sl____ ____ ulation as well as its inflationary consequences which would mean carrying delinking to an extreme almost inconceivable in development practice.

I shall now refer to another conspicuous manifestation of dependence: unconditional submission, in certain circles in the periphery, to theories formulated in the centers. I am not going to deny the value of these theories, but I maintain that they are not generally in keeping with the real conditions in the periphery, of which I have tried to give a very succinct description in earlier pages. It is not surprising, therefore, that the concept of periphery should be regarded as a mere change of nomenclature, or that it should be attributed to the intention of working out a theory of the periphery's own, distinct from the thinking of the centers. Nothing of the sort: the phenomena of peripheral capitalism must be inserted in a global theory of capitalist development. I consider it very important to clear up this point in order to dispel misunderstandings.

When the force of international circumstances began to drive the periphery into industrialization, the very idea of this deliberate industrial development, based on protection and import substitution, was attacked in the centers. It is worthwhile recalling this, for despite the time that has gone by, substitution is still being assailed as a monstrosity spawned by ECLAC.

I remember that in the early 1950s, the eminent Professor Jacob Viner took up the cudgels against us in the University of Rio de Janeiro, attributing to us the fantastic idea that agriculture was a symbol of poverty. I had an opportunity of replying to him shortly afterwards. How could I uphold such a view, if it was (thanks to its agriculture) that my own country, Argentina, had attained an extremely high level of per capita income at the beginning of the twentieth century? Instead of becoming industrialized, said Professor Viner, the thing to do was to introduce technical progress into farming, in order to increase productivity and expand exports. Agreed, I responded in my turn, but technical progress in agriculture would leave redundant manpower. And upon industry, as well as upon other activities that develop along with it, developed the role (among others) of absorbing that redundant population at rising levels of productivity. Otherwise, there would be a risk of increasing exports beyond what was required by the expansion of demand, with the consequent deterioration of the terms of trade. Protection of industry would help to deploy capital and labor from agriculture to industry, counteracting the tendency to deterioration. That protection has been exaggerated and abusive does not invalidate this thesis. It has indeed been so, and in some cases (once again I am alluding to Argentina) it has had an adverse impact upon agriculture and exports.

The theoretical defense of adequate protection was very simple. Given the extremely low income-elasticity of international demand for agricultural products – and also for primary products in general – expansion of such exports tended to bring down relative prices. Protection was a good thing, if the increase in costs for a country proved less than the losses caused by the fall in agricultural prices.

But the argument did not end there. Import-substitution industry had to be built up and, at the same time, the export of manufactures had to be initiated and furnished with incentives similar to those received by import substitution for the domestic market. I believe that in ECLAC we were among the first to defend this thesis in a study presented to the governments (Prebisch, 1961), in which it was noted:

> ...the need for import substitution and for consequent protection of substitution activities has been unavoidable. But there has been a failure to boost exports to the same extent. There has been discrimination in favour of industrial substitution and against exports, mainly industrial exports. The ideal policy would have been to promote exports in order to place them on an equal footing again with substitution activities, which does not necessarily mean equal incentives.

> This aspect is sufficiently important to merit examination; in a nutshell, it is the following. Limitation of external demand for primary exports makes it necessary to devote part of the *increase* in the factors of production to substitution activities. As their productivity is lower than in the industrial centers, they need to be given a certain subsidy in the form of tariff protection. Yet there would be possibilities of using a smaller subsidy to develop new industrial export activities, whereby a greater quantity of industrial goods could be obtained through trade than those that could be manufactured by substitution production.

> By subsidizing substitution production rather than production intended for *new* exports (industrial or primary), export opportunities have been lost which, had they been properly used, would have reduced the scope of substitution policy or made more rapid economic growth possible.[2]

Industrialization had been asymmetrical: besides being based on a generally excessive degree of protection, it had not given the appropriate encouragement to exports of manufactures. And yet we have been accused of shutting our eyes to the necessity of combining import substitution with exports of manufactures.

Now that I have mentioned Professor Viner, I shall also refer to Professor Bela Balassa, who has always reproached us for having overlooked the need to make that combination. And, what is more serious, in a recent report he attributes all the ills of Latin American development to this onesidedness on ECLAC's part.

Obviously, he has had only a fragmentary acquaintance with our studies, culled from quotations at second or third hand, generally mutilated or incomplete. Thus, he mentions a paragraph of my 1961 study in which I denounced exorbitant protection, but makes no reference to my recommendation that import substitution be combined with exports to broader markets than those of individual countries. At all events, I am glad that Balassa has come to express agreement with me at long last; and I hope he may introduce an emendation in the study on Latin American development which he is preparing.

If I allude to this case it is not only because of the influence wielded by Balassa as adviser to the World Bank, but also because he is representative of certain attitudes which would seem to frown upon ECLAC's endeavor to apply a criterion of its own in interpreting the region's development phenomena. Generally speaking, no serious effort is made to understand ideas before attacking them. No recognition has been accorded to our determination to free ourselves from a persistent intellectual dependence which has serious implications for the praxis of development.

Since ECLAC's earliest days – to cite an important example – objective consideration has never been given to the theoretical grounds on which we maintained that, owing to technical progress, a trend towards deterioration of the terms of trade existed. I said this before: If increasing productivity raised production beyond the requirements of demand, the terms of trade would show a tendency to deteriorate. Why did this not occur in the case of manufactured goods? Simply because when deterioration supervened, the flexibility of industry allowed a redeployment of capital and labor in response to the diversified demand that technological innovations ceaselessly bring in their train. But this did not happen with agricultural products, save to a very limited extent. It was argued, then, that deterioration was a mere illusion, since the price of diversified goods was higher because of the improvement in their quality and efficiency. If a farmer has to pay a higher price for a tractor, that is why. Yet when for similar reasons the price of a machine used by manufacturers rises, there is no deterioration. And the reason there is none is that diversification (plus other factors) prevents industrial prices as a whole from falling correlatively with the increase in productivity. Hence the fundamental difference between agricultural and industrial prices, which is of such great importance in peripheral development.

As regards the other primary products, there are cases in which, besides the above-mentioned trend, demand is also weakened by technological innovations which substitute new manufactures for natural products. Technical progress thus works unfavorably at both ends. Unfavorably for the periphery, but not for the centers.

The peripheral countries have not the same possibilities of counteracting the tendency to deterioration that exist in the United States, where production of grain is restricted, or in the European Economic Community, whose surplus output due to the fixing of high prices is launched on the world market, with seriously prejudicial effects on other producer countries, especially those of the periphery. And, nevertheless, it is still being urged that the deterioration theory is fallacious.

This double standard of judgment is by no means uncommon. It can be seen in the field of protection. Criticism has been leveled at the periphery for the protection it accords to its manufacturing output. Undeniably, of course, its costs (at least initially) are higher than in the centers because of the economic and technological superiority of the latter. Why not devaluate, then, it is queried, instead of resorting to measures that represent arbitrary interference with market laws? But to devaluate means lowering the prices of primary products that were already internationally competitive; and this, while beneficial to the centers, has adverse effects on peripheral development.

As I have remarked, the centers have unremittingly advised us to export manufactures instead of resorting to import substitution. We have followed the advice, we have acquired the necessary technology and we are exporting goods which, thanks to that and to lower wages, are competing favorably with goods from the centers, which are having recourse to protection. Why is devaluation not counseled for them as the way to tackle the problem? I believe that common sense prevails: the consideration, *inter alia*, that such a course would bring down the prices of their competitive exports, making them lose part of the profits of their technical progress.

The effects of the intellectual dependence to which I have referred have in general been serious, owing to the academic authority which is customarily attributed to those who advocate certain ways of thinking. The damage done by the Chicago theories, as they are called, in several Latin American countries, especially mine, is still fresh. Matters are even worse when such theories become operative, as in the conspicuous case of the International Monetary Fund (IMF). This institution took several years to recognize that external disquilibria came not only from insufficient internal monetary expansion, but from international factors, as we long had been maintaining in ECLAC. And to cope with these disequilibria, contraction of economic activity and reduction of imports were recommended, since respect for market laws made the pursuit of a selective import policy inadvisable. The economic, social and political consequences of the compression of the economy seem not to have come into the picture – to say nothing of substitution policy, which the IMF has resolutely impugned.

Another very serious step has been recourse to monetary contraction to combat inflation, an efficacious formula in the days of the bygone form of capitalism, when the labor force submitted to market laws and the State adopted a *laissez-faire* attitude to income distribution. To prevent, or at least to attenuate, this monetarist extreme, it would have been necessary to adopt an income policy in which capital accumulation was given the great importance that it deserves. The IMF did once mention this idea, but unfortunately it would seem to have gone on clinging to its inveterate orthodoxy.

A reduction of imports is also currently advocated as a means of facing up to interest payments on the external debt, to the very serious detriment of internal activity and employment. It must be recognized that the IMF is not responsible for the debt. It was simply set aside when the large banks, guided by the profit incentive, took advantage of the abundant resources of the Eurodollar market to issue loans to countries which accepted those resources without even a glimmering of foresight. There was a convergence of irresponsibilities on both sides, except in so far as an attempt was made to cope with the rise in petroleum prices. The private banks proclaimed the virtues of their own wisdom and market laws in resource allocation, extolling their superiority over international institutions formed by states.

It is playing with fire to sidestep a political solution of the problem, which has been aggravated by the deterioration of the terms of trade and the increasing difficulties of expanding exports in present circumstances. The Baker Plan implies recognition of the problem's political character. But this is nothing more than a beginning, while astronomical interest rates continue to prevail. The debt has accentuated our countries' dependence. The financial factor has always been extremely important, and it is now even more so than in the past. Countries whose capital accumulation has fallen inordinately low, principally owing to the inflation crisis and to debt servicing, are going to need foreign capital. Hence the necessity of a political arrangement which, besides resolving the immediate problem, will pave the way for a selective investment policy.

The foregoing considerations bring us to conditionality. International credit operations require conditionality. But what conditionality? This is a question that must be raised now that the World Bank is talking of conditionality too. The private banks do not, of course, observe it. However, conditionality cannot be allowed to consolidate our dependence upon the thinking of the centers. The matter would have to be discussed objectively with economists independent of the periphery until a reasonable body of ideas was compounded that might serve as guiding principles for the action of the institutions aforesaid, as well as for that of the Inter-American Development Bank.

Nevertheless, conditionality could have a constructive meaning only in the context of a definite policy of economic expansion. And to that end, highly significant changes are essential. International financial cooperation, however broad and enlightened it were, would not have really lasting positive effects on the peripheral countries, unless the latter were to take efficacious measures to correct the tendency for the rate of expenditure to exceed that of reproductive investment. Nor would such effects be fully achieved unless measures were likewise adopted to correct the trend towards external disequilibrium. Herein lies the key role of the centers, especially the main dynamic center.

We have talked of dependence, but we have said nothing of interdependence. We are all interdependent, but some are less interdependent than others. Like Orwell's equality in which some are less equal than others.

There is positive interdependence and negative interdependence. And therein the dynamic center's role is of primordial importance. That center's vigorous and continuing expansion would shed its favorable effects throughout the rest of the world, especially in the periphery, if it were to make up its mind to respond to the stimulus thus provided. In contrast, weak and fluctuating growth of that center represents a disquieting case of negative interdependence.

I am not saying that a peripheral country would have no means of attenuating, if not counteracting, the adverse consequences. In so far as, despite its intentions, it was unable to increase its exports fast enough, it would be forced to carry its substitution policy farther than would otherwise have been necessary.

Would this substitution policy do any harm to the centers? It would merely change the composition, not the quantity of imports from them, whose growth would have to keep pace with development.[3] This is an interesting case of asymmetry, which, as a rule, is not clearly grasped. The imbalance, as we have explained above, is basically due to the disparity between the relatively slow growth of exports and a relatively rapid increase in imports of diversified goods. If a peripheral country substitutes its own production for certain imports it does so in order to increase others. In contrast, when above all the main center does the same thing, and restricts its imports, it deprives the peripheral countries of the means to continue importing at a rate as high as or higher than before, with a consequent slackening of the rate of development.

Accordingly, it is easy to understand the adverse implications of the diminished rate of development of the centers at the present time, aggravated as it is by the recrudescence of inveterate protectionism. Multilateral formulae will have to be found enabling the peripheral countries to participate without hindrances in the centers' increase in consumption as long as persistent unemployment precludes measures of more far-reaching scope. In any event, could it be argued that this will provide an in-depth solution for the problem of disequilibrium?

Those of us who are unconvinced that it will, must continue to urge the need for combining exports with import substitution. It is to be hoped that understanding on the part of the centers and the emancipation of the periphery from its intellectual dependence will facilitate the application of this policy.

Substitution will impel our countries to enter upon new lines of production that would necessitate the technological cooperation of the advanced centers. This would open up a promising field for exploitation of a technology which has already been developed and which in the centers is being ousted by new technological advances.

Obviously, for the success of such a policy, it would be indispensable for these new lines of production, these changes in the structure of production, to have access to broader markets than the individual countries can provide. We have hammered at the centers' doors to induce them to favor our exports. But we have not found a way to do so ourselves. Here, too, more efficacious formulas must be sought than those designed in the 1960s.

For the first time in the history of capitalist development the periphery, passive hitherto, might exert a dynamic influence on the centers, provided new forms of cooperation were devised. An increase in exports of goods requiring less advanced technology than that of the centers and their exchange for more highly developed goods would mean that both parties could obtain well-recognized advantages with the consequent increase in productivity. While exploitation in the periphery of a technology that is incessantly being updated in the centers would also afford undeniable reciprocal benefits.

I have said elsewhere that the centers had shown interest in peripheral development only in so far as it suited their own interests. Nobody could blame them. We should have to blame ourselves for not having been able to shake off an intellectual dependence that has blurred out perception of our own interests. We have reached a stage in our relations with the centers, however, in which great possibilities of convergent interests arise.

These converging interests, however, are not only economic but political and of enormous importance. Our Latin American countries – to continue confining myself to them – are passing through an acute structural crisis whose consequences are evident. To the problem of the broad masses of human beings that are left at the bottom of the social structure with very precarious incomes, must now be added that of unemployment and an increasing distributive struggle, which inevitably leads to inflation and in some cases to hyperinflation. The life horizon of the new generations is narrowing and their dynamic elements find themselves seriously frustrated – very potent seeds of resentment and rebellion. The problem is not so much one of ideologies from outside as of a breeding ground for any ideology of violence. Its tendency is important, of course. But much more so is its capacity to overset social coexistence and the advance of the democratization process.

The hegemonic power of the United States is an unalterable fact. It may be exercised in different ways. Events in Latin America may be allowed to drift, and the consequent upheavals may be met with penalizing measures or the use of force; or a far-sighted and enlightening practice of interdependence may be adopted. There is no other choice.

NOTES

[1] See Fernando Cardoso and Enzo Faletto, "*Dependencia y desarrollo en América Latina. Ensayo de interpretación sociológica*," Mexico, D.F., Siglo XXI Editores, 1974, 166 pp.

[2] See Raúl Prebisch, "Economic development on monetary stability: the false dilemma," in *Economic Bulletin for Latin America*, Santiago, Chile, ECLA, 6(1), March 1961, pp. 1–25.

[3] Aníbal Pinto, the eminent Latin American economist who has contributed so much to the evolution of ECLAC's ideas, stated in a 1980 study on external openness in Latin America ("La apertura exterior en la América Latina", *El Trimestre Económico*, 187, Mexico, D.F., July–Sept. 1980) that for Latin America to be able to continue up to the year 2000 with a growth rate of 6.4 percent, such as had been recorded between the years 1965 and 1974, it would have to double its imports in each decade. The question, therefore, is not one of keeping them up, but of changing their composition in accordance with the requirements of development.

Comments on
"Dependence, Development, and Interdependence"

JAGDISH N. BHAGWATI

This is the third time in recent years that I have been asked to comment on Professor Prebisch concerning the theme of dependence and interdependence. I have no doubt that he feels, as much as I do, that we too are destined, like his center and the periphery, to be locked into a relationship of interdependence on each other! Indeed, our gracious host, Professor Ranis, whom I confronted with this curious fact, could find no one, not even among the exchange-oriented and mutual-gain-seeking neoclassical economists present here, to trade places with me. So, you should find it credible that, as Prebisch fears, the periphery's efforts to break the fetters of dependence face often-insuperable difficulties.

In many ways, Prebisch's views tend to be unique. As many of you must know, he entertains his friends by dividing the world into developed countries, the developing countries, Japan, and Argentina. Development economists similarly divide into the mainstream neoclassicals, the radicals, and then Prebisch. His present paper, characterized by his customary blend of thought-provoking and provocative arguments, underlines this only too well.

He puts himself squarely in the middle of the "dependence" school of thought, which he identifies as having been enriched by Latin American intellectuals, such as Cardoso, and by economists such as himself and Aníbal Pinto, the amiable CEPAL economist of portly dimensions who is Keynesian not merely in macro but also in micro, having married one of Chile's most gifted ballerinas.

It is not quite clear, from the capsuled version that Prebisch provides in this paper, which of the many versions of the *dependencia* thesis he would embrace without reservation. Consider a statement (p. 31) such as: "The very dynamics of the centers had left the periphery on the sidelines of industrial development." This suggests the *mildest* version of the center-periphery relationship: i.e. simply that there is none, whether detrimental or beneficial. Then again, for later phases of this interaction, Prebisch reiterates this theme differently (p. 32): "The influence would seem to be that here again the dynamics of the centers does not benefit the periphery as it does the centers themselves." In this view, the periphery has what Prebisch calls an "appendicular" role, although I doubt whether his English translator has gotten the better of his Spanish here, since if the anatomical appendix is what Prebisch has in mind, presumably the weak periphery must eventually cause acute distress to the powerful center; whereas if the reference is to the impressively incomprehensible material which we remove from the text and consign to a separate existence at the end of our papers, the periphery must possess more prestige than the center! Prebisch surely means, rather, that the periphery is a "sideshow."

But this would be an anemic version of the *dependencia* thought indeed. And Prebisch does not disappoint us. For he turns the screw again and says (pp. 32–33): "To the siphoning off of income from the enterprises producing and exporting primary goods and importing manufactures in the preindustrialization phase, as well as from public utility companies, was added the absorption of income by the transnational corporations... Nor, of course, must the banking and financing companies be omitted." In short, Prebisch transcends then to what I call the "malign neglect" view of the center-periphery relationship, in contrast to the "benign neglect" framework of mainstream economists.

There is evidence of a shift into a *yet higher* gear, into what I call the "malign intent" view when, having mentioned how the elites of the periphery have changed and evolved relationships with the elites in the center, Prebisch declares (p. 33): "This was a way – blatant or subtle – in which the hegemonic weight of the centers made itself felt. And when the periphery reacted against this dependence and jeopardized those interests, the whole constellation of dominant elements in the centers lost no time in mobilizing themselves to apply penalizing measures." Does Prebisch have in mind International Telephone & Telegraph and Henry Kissinger arrayed against Salvador Allende, or perhaps the Hickenlooper Amendment? – which, incidentally, was never effective because of calculated accommodation, rather than the "penalizing" mobilization that Prebisch writes of (you should read the brilliant work *Standing Guard*, by Charles Lipson, on the evolving conduct towards multinationals since the nineteenth century). The sentence is too cryptic; but its import is loud and clear.

But then Prebisch shifts focus and turns his wrath on the elites of the periphery more directly. He observes that other countries in the past, including the United States and Japan, have emerged with "an enormous and enlightened effort, a tenacious and long drawn-out effort of [their] own" from their peripheral status. They apparently "did not take pains to cut off their relations with the centers, but sought to make intelligent use of them to further their own development" (p. 34).

By contrast, the peripheral countries, especially of Latin America, have elite behavioral patterns that constitute a "fatal flaw." In particular, these elites hasten to imitate the life styles of the centers, thus making impossible demands on available resources and thereby contributing to low investment and high inflation. Permit me to quote again from page 34, lest you think that *I*, rather than Prebisch, have these damaging views of Latin America's elites:

...as the distributive power of the labor force has developed, its private and social consumption has also gradually increased, and the state has considerably raised its own civil and military expenditure. All these outlays are not made at the expense of spending by the favored strata, which is incessantly stimulated by technological innovations, but are superimposed on their *privileged consumption* (my italics). In this way, sooner or later, the rate of reproductive accumulation has suffered, deleteriously to the rate of development and to distributive equity. And this dynamic imbalance inevitably ends in a new type of inflation ... all these forms of private and social, civil and military expenditure constitute overt imitation of the centers...

In this description of the center-obsessed and imitative elite of Latin America, I recognize the witticism that an Argentinian is an Italian who speaks Spanish, thinks he is English, and aspires to be French.

But Prebisch does not connect up his critique of the Latin Americans with his views on IMF conditionality and its alleged adverse impact on Latin America in the postwar period. If indeed inflation of occasionally three digits was caused by the profligate excesses of Latin American elites, reinforced rather than curbed by government expenditure, presumably you have here the classic model where there is excess spending through the budget, financed by money printed as necessary, spilling over into balance of payments deficits that necessitate visits to the International Monetary Fund for support. Put yourself then in the position of Jacques Polak: What would you do except tell these governments to cut their spending, ease up on their printing presses, and also to devalue to bring their exchange rates in line with the inflated nominal prices? And, when you retired to the quiet of your desk, you would develop the simple "monetarist" model to think about payments deficits. This, of course, is what appears to have happened throughout the 1950s and early 1960s.

The much-maligned IMF model, if you buy this stylized history inspired by my reflection over Prebisch's remarks, is then a gift of *Latin America* to the world. The Latin American periphery, not the IMF in the center's de facto capital, cast the mold. The tragedy was that this model of adjustment then came to be applied by the IMF to other countries and situations which were characterized by "structural" sources of payments difficulties, rather than simply to the excess-expenditure, massive-inflation-characterized clients from Latin America. The IMF model, thoroughly apt for the latter class of situations, had no applicability to the countries of, say, the Indian subcontinent where even a double-digit inflation can cause riots and macroeconomic tranquility prevails. I sometimes think that macroeconomics reflects literature: The profligacy and wild inflations of Latin America, if you know your Prebisch and Hirschman, appear to have been facilitated by extravagance that reminds you of the surreal and exuberant characters in Gabriel García Márquez, whereas India's macroeconomics reminds you of R. K. Narayan's peaceful and harmonious village of Malgudi!

What we have been witnessing recently, therefore, is the realization that *other* models of adjustment are necessary to keep in the IMF tool kit, though it is evident that there is not yet available a neat taxonomy of what models are appropriate to what types of structural problems and what kinds of economies (e.g. classified by their openness on trade, portfolio capital flows and direct foreign investment, by their debt overhang or its absence, and so on). As always, it is easier to define what should not be done, rather than what should be.

Let me return now to Prebisch's grand theme of the center-periphery relationship. If you reflect on what I have quoted from him earlier, Prebisch seems to be evenly balanced between the views that: (1) the center-dependent periphery is locked into an embrace where the center's influence, through the periphery-elite's value formation and through the center's muscle-flexing, is inhibiting development in the periphery, and (2) the periphery, as in the early Japan and the United States, may still reach out for development, somehow using the opportunities provided by the center in an intelligent and creative way. The former is evidently more the "deterministic," radical-variety view of historical processes; the latter, on the other hand, fits more nicely into the conventional economists' viewpoint, where elites and governments can and will pursue the social interest in a benign fashion. I frankly do not see how Prebisch really reconciles these two contrasting philosophical underpinnings of his recent writings; all I can do is to confront him with the unease with which they seem to me to coexist in his vision.

This tension reflects itself fully in his discussion of the two major areas that seem to preoccupy him and dominate the bulk of the paper in consequence – one from the past and the other from the present. The former is, unsurprisingly, the contribution of Prebisch and Latin American economists to the strategy of import substitution; the latter is naturally the enormity of the debt crisis. Let me consider each in turn.

1   As we age, even if we do this as gracefully as Prebisch, our thoughts turn back to the old battles. Prebisch's mind is focused on the IS (import-substitution) strategy, on whose merits he faced the indomitable Jacob Viner, then, and confronts the indefatigable Bela Balassa now. Viner ruled the center's minds; Balassa rules the center's institutions, chiefly the World Bank. Prebisch darkly hints that even the intellectuals in the periphery broke ranks, in a "conspicuous manifestation of dependence" by "unconditional submission ... to theories formulated in the centers" (p. 34). I wonder whom he has in mind. But you have here the dual theme: elites in the periphery locked into slavish imitation of the center's world view, and the center's militancy in confronting the periphery's attempt at autonomous development.

But I am afraid that, while I recognize that Prebisch was there in the thick of the battle while I was still in my unshaven early teens, I find Prebisch's interesting observations less than compelling.

For one thing, it is difficult to see how the question of IS versus EP (export-promoting) strategy, although absolutely central to debates about developmental policy and the thinking of nearly all the creative developmental economists in the postwar years, can be elevated into a center versus periphery issue. The question has always been in the *mainstream* of economic science, with arguments about the relative merits of protection and free trade attending the birth of our discipline and debated ever since by Mill, List, and countless other economists who could not be remotely described as peripheral or from the periphery.

The novelty in Prebisch's conception seems, rather, to have been that he based his case for protection on the assumption that the terms of trade would decline secularly against Latin America's primary-product exports, developing in turn an analytical rationale (based on asymmetric wage and price responses to technical change in manufactures and in primary production) to buttress a presumed historical tendency for such a secular decline. This is not the occasion to re-examine the Prebisch thesis in depth; the informed reader needs no such assistance. I simply wish to stress that this Prebisch scenario, a specific version of export (or elasticity) pessimism, does not necessarily imply a case for protection. For, as the terms of trade improve for manufactures, resources will shift through market incentives alone to producing more manufactures. To produce an argument in support of protection for manufactures, you would have to throw in something more to demonstrate that the market signals and incentives would not translate into the appropriate degree of pattern of industrialization. I have no doubt Prebisch and ECLA did; but I frankly have never seen what exactly that extra element was.[1]

Prebisch, as it happens, appears a trifle beleaguered by the critics of IS, to which group I consider myself to belong. Many of these foes in fact happen to be present today: Krueger, Little, Balassa among them. Indeed, the weight of numerous empirical studies, and of theoretical argumentation by international economists, has been severely anti-IS and pro-EP. Prebisch therefore resorts to the strategy of saying: I was for EP too! But his solitary quote to that effect is like the quotes from Mahalanobis (whose model was autarkic) stressing exports – what counts, surely, is the central thrust of your argumentation and advice. Besides, on EP versus IS, you simply cannot have it both ways, unless the Hispanics share with the Hindus the acceptance of the rules of discourse where the answer to a question can be simultaneously "yes," "no," and even "maybe."

I would be delighted, of course, to have Prebisch walk over to our side of the street. But I think I would rather defend him, more sensibly and also more realistically, by saying that the documented excesses of the IS strategy in Latin America cannot be blamed on Prebisch any more than the follies of the first Reagan Administration can be blamed on the more sober supply-siders who simply felt that incentives matter but cannot usher in the golden age.

I believe this caveat may be particularly true for the IS strategy in Latin America and Prebisch's role in it. I have long argued that the IS strategy was often a consequence of reluctant exchange rate adjustments in the teeth of substantial inflation. The resulting overvaluation of the exchange rate implied a de facto IS strategy, of course. The chaotic pattern of import substitution, as also the excessive level of it, were attendant consequences. I would suspect that the Prebisch–ECLA arguments for an IS strategy were occasionally cited to legitimate this situation, rather than were the cause of it. Certainly, it is doubtful whether Prebisch's prescriptions for the *type* of IS strategy that he desired were in consonance with the *actual* outcomes that we have long criticized.

2 Let me turn now to the debt crisis. Here, I find Prebisch again vascillating a little between the two views: of a dominant, thoughtless and self-absorbed center and a self-indulgent periphery elite. The blame is divided between both for the enormous borrowings of the 1970s. But the center and the Bretton Woods institutions get the major blame for the crisis-management failures, while Prebisch does not confront the periphery elites for their role in this at all.

It is true that the banks were eager to invest and blandished money. But they did that with other countries, too. India could have borrowed, for example, but did not. Cross-sectional reflection suggests that the fault, if any, may lie mainly with the borrowers, reminding us again of Prebisch's earlier castigation of Latin American elites.

Arguably, no one could have foreseen the difficulties ahead in the heyday of recycling of petrodollars. But looking to the present, I wonder if the criticisms of the center by Prebisch over the conditionalities attached to the IMF's (and now to the World Bank's) assistance of the debt-crisis countries should not be equally directed to these countries in some measure. Is it not their desire to resume the net inflows, to which they got addicted during the 1970s, which makes them go along with these conditionalities, even as they complain? An alternative is to coalesce behind some plan, such as Felix Rohatyn's or President García's, to address the debt-overhang issue directly and then to reconcile oneself to the prospect that new net inflows may resume only as memories fade, as they historically have (after defaults). This delinking of the stock and the flow aspects of the problem does require that the elites and policymakers in these high-income developing countries be willing to live within their means for the foreseeable future. It is doubtful, on current evidence and from Prebisch's characterization of Latin American elites, whether they will want to.

NOTE

[1] I might add that, in contrast, Nurkse's use of export pessimism to justify the IS strategy (which he called the balanced-growth strategy) implied a less than perfectly elastic foreign offer curve facing the country and hence did justify the use of an optimum tariff. If Bela Balassa is correct in asserting at this conference that Nurkse did not want protection or governmental intervention to promote such balanced growth, I might ask: How was this recommended balanced-growth outcome to be ensured? Moreover, Nurkse wrote to me when he read my 1958 *Review of Economic Studies* piece on Immiserizing Growth, shortly before his death, and said that my analysis captured more fully what he had in mind in his Wicksell Lectures. And it is pretty evident that immiserizing growth cannot arise if an optimal tariff is being used.

3

Structural Transformation: A Program of Research

HOLLIS CHENERY

To assess the state of development economics, we need some agreement on what it is trying to accomplish. In his presidential address to the American Economic Association (1984), W. Arthur Lewis identifies its subject matter as "the structure and behavior of economies where output per head is less than 1980 US $2,000." This agenda is divided into two parts: "matters relating to the allocation of resources in the short run, and matters relating to long-term growth." The long-run issues are further categorized as "the search for the engine of growth and the patterns of growth."

My assignment concerns the last category: the patterns of growth. In Lewis's assessment – with which I agree – "we know more about the patterns imposed by growth than we know for certain about the causes of growth." In the view of Kuznets (1971), who did the pioneer studies of most of these patterns, this state of affairs is almost inevitable in a well-ordered research program, since description of empirical phenomena should precede the elaboration of theories. For sympathetic critics such as Díaz-Alejandro (1976) and Perkins (1981), however, the search for uniform patterns of structural transformation has already reached sharply diminishing returns and needs to be more closely related to historical studies of individual countries.

It is futile to try to evaluate one aspect of a research agenda without considering its relationship to other parts of the program. This is not to say that the empirical validation of individual patterns, such as Engel's law or the factor proportions implied by the Heckscher–Ohlin theory, is not worthwhile in itself. The more interesting question, however, is the one raised by Lewis: Does the study of patterns of structural change help to identify sources of growth, and perhaps more important, to do something about them?

Since many of the questions raised here are discussed in subsequent chapters, I will take as my principal topic the usefulness, past and future, of empirical research focused on the structural transformation of developing countries. To simplify the discussion, I will imagine that the historical, statistical, and theoretical work on this topic can be treated as a single research program in which individual scholars collaborate implicitly, if not explicitly. While individual participants tend to stress the differences in their approach and findings, all involve some inter-action between generalizations from comparative studies, on the one hand, and the elaboration of theory, on the other. Where the individual research programs tend to diverge is in the subsequent step from empirical results to policy implications.

In looking back at the 30 years since Kuznets began his series of articles on the *Quantitative Aspects of the Economic Growth of Nations* (1956–64), one can identify shifts in objectives, working hypotheses, statistical methodology, and theoretical interpretation – in short, all the attributes of an active research program.[1] Here I am mainly concerned with how they all fit together. I will, therefore, concentrate on three sets of questions:

1   What have been the main changes in our perceptions of the "stylized facts" or uniform features of the transformation?
2   How has the evolution of development theory been affected by studies of structural change?
3   What policy implications emerge from comparative studies of structural transformation?

Since these are broad questions, I will illustrate my analysis by two or three examples under each heading.

THE STYLIZED FACTS

Although the term is widely used, the concept of "structural transforma-tion" is hard to define with any precision. In general, it connotes the set of changes in economic and institutional structures necessary to con-tinued growth of GNP. These terms have taken on more precise mean-ings in the course of several decades of comparative studies of the relations between structure and growth.

A minimal definition of the required structural transformation would include the accumulation of physical and human capital and shifts in the composition of demand, production, trade, and employment. These comprise the economic core of the transformation and have received the principal attention of researchers. Closely related are socio-economic processes such as urbanization, demographic transition, and changes in income distribution, which extend beyond the central processes and will be identified as peripheral.

Before 1955, these structural changes were studied as separate phenomena subject to different sets of influences. An outstanding example is Engel's law of demand, which was amply verified in cross-section and time-series analyses over the preceding century

(Houthakker, 1957). Similarly, Colin Clark (1940) demonstrated the uniform shift of labor from agriculture to manufacturing and services as income levels rise. Like Engel's law, this dimension of the structural transformation has been confirmed in both time-series and cross-country data.

The Kuznets synthesis

Simon Kuznets (1966, 1971) achieved a great advance in the study of long-term growth by dealing with the structural transformation as a whole, rather than as a set of separate phenomena. The statistical foundation for this approach had been established by the postwar spread of national accounting to developing countries. This made possible both cross-country analysis and comparison of the results to historical time series for the developed countries. The structural transformation could now be defined by a consistent set of changes in the composition of demand, production, trade, and employment, each reflecting different aspects of the shifts in resource allocation that take place as income levels rise. Furthermore, Kuznets used a consistent disaggregation of the economy into three (or more) sectors – agriculture, industry, and services – that later provided a basis for more formal modeling efforts.

Although this procedure requires a minimum of deductive theory, it has led to the establishment of some quite robust estimates of the central features of the transformation. While Kuznets himself preferred to speculate about their significance, rather than to test formal hypotheses, his speculations have been very fruitful for other researchers. For example, by applying the three-sector breakdown across countries and comparing the shift in the composition of value added to the corresponding shift in employment, Kuznets derived a U-shaped curve describing the relative decline and subsequent rise in relative agricultural productivity as per capita income rises. By extension, he speculated that income distribution typically exhibits a similar U-shaped curve of growing inequality followed by a reversal toward greater equality. Both of these hypotheses have stood up well in subsequent econometric tests and have stimulated the search for more complete explanations.

Although most of Kuznets's studies are concerned with historical patterns of structural change in advanced countries, his general synthesis (1966, chap. 8) provides a summary of cross-country patterns for all income levels in 1958. These concentrate on the central features of demand, production, trade, and factor use. They are measured by changes in the average structure of five or six groups of countries classified by income levels. Although the accuracy of these estimates has been improved by subsequent increases in data and the adoption of econometric methods, the later results have generally served to reinforce Kuznets's main findings. This is particularly true of his description of the structural transformation in terms of the shift of production from agriculture to other activities, and the lagging movement of labor in the same directions. Kuznets gives less attention to trade and capital flows, which play a larger role in subsequent accounts of the sources of structural change.

The fruitfulness of Kuznets's approach is reflected in the list of intriguing questions that he left for his successors. Perhaps the most important is the interpretation to be given to the observed similarities – and differences – between cross-country and time-series estimates of development patterns. Closely related are the problems of translating speculations as to causal sequences into more formal models and testable hypotheses. Which of the changes observed in the past will prove to be necessary to further development?

Alternative patterns

Since Kuznets's main concern was to identify the common features of "modern economic growth," he focused on the universal aspects of the structural transformation. His successors have been more interested in theoretical explanations of these uniformities and in their policy implications. This shift in focus led to a search for the sources of systematic variations in development patterns, caused either by differences in resource endowments and institutions or in policies.

Coincidental with Kuznets's studies of the late 1950s, development theorists were arguing the advantages of specialization versus balanced growth. Nurkse reflected the current debate in his 1959 Wicksell Lectures, in which he identified three alternative patterns of specialization (Nurkse, 1961, p. 323):

1 growth through exports of primary products;
2 growth through exports of manufactured consumer goods;
3 expansion of output for domestic markets.

He argued that external conditions were then favorable to a shift away from pattern 1 to pattern 3, which was subsequently described as import-substitution industrialization.

The studies of development patterns by Chenery (1960), Maizels (1963), and Chenery and Taylor (1968), tried to identify the principal alternative patterns of trade and production inductively, starting from econometric estimates of some of the relations already established by Kuznets. In addition to per capita income, two exogenous variables were shown to have a substantial effect on the composition of production: population size (interpreted as a measure of market size), and the extent of specialization in exports of primary products or manufactures. These findings led to a proposed division of country development patterns into three categories very much like Nurkse's (although the similarity was not recognized at the time). Since there is a strong inverse correlation between country size and the extent of international trade, the effects of specialization are most pronounced in small countries. Nurkse's first two categories thus became small, primary-oriented (SP) and small, manufacturing-oriented (SM) in Chenery–Taylor. Since import-substitution policies were characteristic of almost all large countries in the period studied (1950–64), effects of this policy were incorporated in the typical large-country (L) pattern.

These three country groups were used to make a number of statistical tests of the differences in development patterns, notably of the uniformity of changes in the composition of manufacturing and the relation between time-series and cross-section estimates. (See Chenery and Taylor, 1968; Chenery and Syrquin, 1975; Syrquin, 1985; Wood, 1986.) Of the three patterns tested, the large-country group proved to be the most homogeneous. The difference in specialization among small countries was also identified as a major source of the variation in the timing of the structural transformation. Explanations of the differences in these typical patterns of structural transformation became the main objective of several of the modeling attempts discussed in the section beginning on page 60.

Extensions

For Kuznets, the main purpose of comparative statistical studies was to identify the universal elements of 'Modern Economic Growth' (MEG), and the relation between growth and structural change. His basic method was the comparison of historical time series although cross-country comparisons were added to extend his study to less developed countries. Kuznets's numerous followers have broadened the scope of the processes studied, added to the postwar time series, and used a variety of statistical techniques.

One of the most ambitious extensions of Kuznets's agenda was undertaken by Adelman and Morris (1967, 1973, 1984). Their main objective was to establish quantitative relations among economic, social, and political aspects of development. By adopting ordinal measures for variables such as the modernization of agricultural techniques, for which no cardinal measure is available, they are able to apply factor analysis and other less conventional forms of multivariate analysis to explore a broad range of statistical associations. Although the significance of the results is hard to evaluate, at a minimum they suggest that socioeconomic and political factors have as much to contribute to the explanation of the uniform features of the structural transformation as do more narrowly defined economic relations.

An example of both the attraction and limitations of the Adelman–Morris approach is their analysis of income distribution in relation to different socioeconomic structures (1973). Their statistical technique is a form of the analysis of variance that seeks to subdivide the total sample of countries in such a way as to explain the variance of selected measures of income distribution. The variables that are shown to have the greatest significance for the results include the extent of dualism, the improvement in human resources, and the availability of natural resources. Although these results are suggestive for policy-makers, they do not get us much closer than other techniques to establishing the nature of causation.

Other analysts have tried to validate and extend Kuznets's results by using conventional econometric methods of combining cross-section and time-series analysis to test alternative formulations. Since these are frequently associated with attempts to model the structural transformation, they are taken up in the next section.

MODELING THE TRANSFORMATION

Success in identifying the uniform features of the structural transformation must ultimately be judged by its contribution to explaining the way development takes place. If there were no common features, the methodology of comparative analysis that has been built up would have little to contribute, since each country's experience would be dominated by its unique characteristics. In fact, however, the stylized facts just discussed account for more than half of the intercountry variance in the economic structure. It is, therefore, timely to ask what this accumulation of statistical knowledge can contribute to our basic understanding of development.

One attractive approach to this problem is to compare this "structural" research program to other research programs in economics. While this would be too ambitious for present purposes, the methodological surveys of Blaug (1980a, 1980b), Cross (1982) and others will at least serve to frame the questions.

Scientific research programs

Although the philosophy of science is noted more for its controversies than for its areas of agreement, Kuhn's "paradigms" and Lakatos' "scientific research programs" both suggest that we should focus our attention on common premises and styles of analysis rather than on particular theories.[2] The Lakatos approach to evaluating a research program involves three steps:

1   Identification of the "hard core" of the program, defined as "that set of purely metaphysical beliefs whose abandonment is tanta-mount to abandoning the program itself" (Blaug, 1980b, p. 225).

2   Examination of theories that flow from the hard-core premises plus the additional assumptions needed to produce testable implications.
3   Is the research program "progressing" or "degenerating"? This test implies a comparison to competing theories and a judgment as to whether the modifications required in step 2 increase or decrease the program's empirical content.

The hard core of the structural (or MEG) research program was succinctly outlined by Kuznets (1959, p. 170):

> If there were no substantial transnational factors, there would be no common features of significance in the economic growth of nations – and comparative study would hardly be warranted, for it would amount to no more than a compilation of historical detail, and there would be no hope of finding intellectual order in it. Indeed a general model of a nation's economic growth, following a more modern growth pattern, is possible only because the industrial system has certain elements of identity throughout the world, because human nature responds in similar ways to rising real income per capita, and so on.

The central "metaphysical" aspect of this position is its reliance on a range of social and technological characteristics to produce common patterns of behavior, going beyond the corollaries of neoclassical welfare maximization.

The research program that stems from the hard-core assumptions has followed two main lines. First, the identification and measurement of the essential features of the "modern growth pattern" for different sets of countries and periods of time. This is the heart of Kuznets's program, whose results have been illustrated above.

The second line of analysis is to model the typical relations among the central variables identified with the structural transformation – demand, production, trade, and employment. The importance of such modeling, even with quite limited data, was stressed by Tinbergen (1959) at an early stage. He recommended starting from reduced-form equations that could be estimated from available data and then proceeding to more explicit specifications – a recommendation that has been followed in several recent studies.

The "structural" research program of the past 20 years developed from the interaction of these two approaches. The principal stylized facts – surplus labor, industrialization, Engel effects, differential productivity growth, the results of international specialization – have been periodically reformulated and tested for different countries, periods, and typologies. In this process a characteristic form of theorizing has evolved, which I will call the method of prototype modeling, that seeks to clarify the implications of the different hypotheses that have emerged. The following sections illustrate the uses that have been made of prototype models both in historical analyses and in comparisons of alternative hypotheses.

Prototype models

Prototype models emerge early in the process of trying to formalize a set of complex interactions. In order to focus on a manageable set of relations, the analyst deliberately omits others. In a classic example, Samuelson (1939a, 1939b) studied the interaction of the multiplier and the accelerator in a numerical simulation of the effects of alternative values of two structural parameters. Such numerical simulations are popular in modeling the structural transformation for similar reasons.

The term "prototype" applies to two aspects of this analytical technique. Although the general specification of the economic structure is derived from comparative studies, the model itself does not apply to a particular country but to a country "type." Secondly, the structural relations are often specified in general terms that can be refined in country-specific applications. Thus the Harris–Todaro model (1970) of LDC labor markets and rural-urban migration started from the general hypothesis that workers migrate in response to expected earnings; this proposition was subsequently restated in alternative forms on the basis of empirical testing.

The dual economy   One of the first and most influential prototype models of the structural transformation was Lewis's dual-economy model (1954), which was elaborated in geometric form by Fei and Ranis (1964). It applies to countries and time periods in which the supply of labor from the traditional to the modern sector is relatively elastic. This assumption leads to a separate phase or regime in the structural transformation in which there is a rising share of investment and accelerated growth, as long as surplus labor persists. Although it has proved difficult to test the basic assumptions of the Lewis model in its original two-sector form, it has had an impact on virtually all attempts to model the transformation.[3]

Understanding the principal features of the transition to modern economic growth as perceived by Kuznets requires an analysis of shifts in demand, trade, and production at the commodity level as well as of the reallocation of factors of production. While these relations were debated in general terms by Nurkse (1961) and others in the fifties, development of the required multisectoral models only became feasible after the widespread application of input-output analysis to developing countries in the sixties.[4]

Industrialization   Multisectoral prototype models were first used to explain industrialization as a system-wide phenomenon involving the central features of demand, production, and trade. While it is commonly assumed that Engel's law is the driving force underlying the rise of industry, the necessity of industrialization in an open economy has often been challenged. To explore the effects of factors other than demand, a prototype model of industrialization was designed that included intermediate and final demand as well as trade and technological change. This type of model was first tested in a historical study of the transformation of the Japanese economy (Chenery, Shishido and Watanabe, 1962); it was subsequently revised and reestimated from cross-country data (Chenery and Watanabe, 1964; Chenery and Syrquin, 1980).

Developing a prototype from country experience has both advantages and disadvantages. On the plus side it forces the analyst to use a form of disaggregation that corresponds to the availability of data and is likely to be replicable in other countries. In the present instance it became possible by the mid-seventies to apply a similar model to the historical experience of eight additional countries and to use a common accounting framework to refine the stylized facts. The results of this study are given in Chenery, Robinson, and Syrquin (1986). However, it is only quite recently that the development of applied general equilibrium models has led to the introduction of prices in multisectoral models and the incorporation of labor market behavior as in the Lewis model.[5]

The cross-country version of the industrialization model incorporates the stylized facts that result from reestimating Kuznets's basic relations together with several additions that have emerged from the use of input-output accounts. (See Chenery, 1979, chap. 3; Chenery and Syrquin, 1980, 1986.) Among the latter the most notable is the trend toward greater intermediate use of manufactured goods in virtually all the countries studied. This is partly due to the shift in the composition of demand and partly to technological changes reflected in changing input-output coefficients.

This prototype model attributes the growth of output in each sector to four factors:

growth of domestic demand
growth of exports
effects of import substitution
growth of intermediate demand (including technological change).

The structural transformation can be analyzed in numerical terms by solving the corresponding Leontief model at different levels of per capita GNP. This procedure is illustrated in table 3.1, which compares the structure of demand and production at an income level near the end of the transformation to the structure at a level near the beginning. Each

TABLE 3.1   Simulation of structural change over the transformation.[a]

Sector	Domestic demand (D)			Net trade (T)			Intermediate demand (W)			Total output[b] (X)			Value added (V)		
	Initial	Final	Increment	Initial	Final	Increment	Initial	Final	Increment	Initial	Final	Increment	Initial	Final	Increment
Tradeables															
I Primary	19	4	−15	13	−2	−15	14	14	0	46	16	−30	38	9	−29
II Mfg.	27	34	+7	−14	−1	+13	23	51	+28	36	85	+49	15	36	+21
Nontradeables															
III Social overhead	15	20	+5	0	1	1	5	7	+2	20	28	+8	11	16	+5
IV Services	41	42	+1	0	2	+1	9	10	+1	50	54	+4	36	39	+3
Totals[c]	102	100	−2	−1	−1	0	51	82	+31	151	182	+31	100	100	0

[a] The initial period is defined by a GDP level of 140 ($1970) per capita; the final period by a level of $2070. Each element is expressed as a percentage of GDP.
[b] $X = D + T + W$.
[c] Totals may not add because of rounding.
Source: Chenery and Syrquin (1986a)

element is shown as a percent of GDP so that total domestic demand (minus net trade) is equal to 100, as is total value added. These results simulate a typical transformation based on structural parameters that are representative of postwar experience: the 23 sectors in the basic model are aggregated here to four.

The main effect of this presentation is to view the structural transformation as a whole. In the essentially non-tradeable sectors, which account for about half of total value added, changes in domestic demand (Engel effects) are closely reflected in domestic value added. This is far from the case with tradeable commodities, for which changes in net trade (exports minus imports) are at least as important as Engel effects in explaining the changing composition of output.

The transformation of the productive structure is characterized in the last column as a shift of 29 percent of total GDP from primary production to manufacturing (21 percent) and to social overhead (5 percent) over the course of a 10-fold increase in per capita GNP.[6] The direct effects of changing domestic demand are concentrated in the primary sectors, while rising intermediate demand is concentrated almost entirely in manufacturing. Both sectors are affected by changing patterns of trade.

We can move a step closer to the causal factors involved by using the Leontief model to attribute intermediate use to the elements of final demand – domestic demand, imports and exports. This is done in Chenery and Syrquin (1980), which decomposes the causes of the rising share of industry for several subsectors and time periods. This more detailed analysis does not change the principal finding of table 3.1, however: typical shifts in the pattern of exports and imports with increasing income levels contribute more to the rise of manufacturing than do changes in domestic demand. Secondly, a significant proportion of industrialization – perhaps 10 or 20 percent – stems from rising coefficients of intermediate use.

This analysis also provides a basis for answering the question: Is industrialization necessary? To avoid this result, the trade surplus of the primary sectors would have to increase sufficiently to offset the substantial growth in both intermediate and final demand for manufactures that is shown in table 3.1. While such increases in primary exports have been observed for limited periods, very few developing countries have grown for as long as two decades without some increase in the share of manufacturing to maintain the balance in tradeable commodities.

Several analysts have created more general prototype models to study the effects of alternative policies on related aspects of the transformation. One of the most useful is the "Representative Developing Country," designed by Kelley and Williamson (1984) to study the urban transition in a general equilibrium framework. This model is used in the section which begins on page 62 to illustrate the relation between industrialization and the peripheral aspects of the transformation.

Typologies

The search for uniform features of development almost inevitably leads to a division of countries into more homogeneous groups. Such country types may be based on similarities in their initial conditions (size, resources) or on their policies in a given period – or perhaps on both. The most widely accepted division is between the developed countries (those that have completed the transformation) and the less developed. Beyond this basic division, categories tend to stress alternative development strategies.

There are two objectives to these typologies. One is to group together countries thought to be following similar policies, however these policies may be identified. This is characterized by Ranis (1984) as the comparative historical approach. It is illustrated by comparisons between a resource-rich but inward-looking "Latin American type" and a labor-surplus but outward-looking "East Asian type." The analysis is designed to establish similarity of subphases of the transition within each group, leading to a comparison of development strategies among two or more development groups.

A second objective of typologies is more narrowly statistical: to establish more homogeneous subgroups for which average shares and regression equations will have greater significance. If there are only one or two rich but underdeveloped mineral exporters, for example, the tendency is just to omit them from the study. When they become more numerous, they can be included as a separate category. From an econometric standpoint, establishing a few homogeneous groups makes it possible to specify different statistical relations for each type within the same general prototype model.[7]

In the present context typologies may be regarded as a useful adjunct to the development of prototype models. If the analysis starts with the identification of a characteristic that is thought to distinguish among development patterns or regimens such as surplus labor or outward orientation – the identification of countries exhibiting this feature should go hand in hand with the development of a prototype model to explore its implications. A recent example is the study of deindustrialization in mineral exporters (Dutch disease), which has been redefined and extended several times as it has become better understood in different countries (see Corden and Neary, 1982).

The attempt to move on from stylized facts to prototype models of development has led to a form of analysis that can be described as model-based comparisons. The general procedure adopted in several recent studies is to establish a common analytical framework that can be applied to all the countries to be studied and to base the analysis in large part on what can be learned from comparison among both country models and cross-country prototypes. A byproduct of this approach is the application of a given country typology to a large group of developing countries as a basis for selecting the sample.[8] This helps to interpret the conclusions reached from the countries that are studied in detail.

STRUCTURE AND POLICY

The structural transformation links together many of the policy problems of developing countries. This is apparent in the relations among demand, production, trade, and employment that have already been discussed. Recognition of this interdependence is spreading to more peripheral phenomena such as urbanization, education, health, and population growth, which have traditionally been treated as separate areas of policy. This has led to a reconsideration of the choice of direct versus indirect policy instruments, as well as substantial reorientation of policy objectives.

The movement toward a general-equilibrium view of development policy has also acquired empirical support from the formulation and tabulation of social accounting matrices (SAMs). These extend the production-based, input-output accounts to include the generation and distribution of income as well as the identification of different categories of institutions and income recipients. Such a statistical framework is a first step in defining the economic structure and identifying the indirect consequences of proposed changes in resource allocation. Even without the next step of using the SAM as a basis for a general equilibrium model, the structural equations underlying it can delimit some of the indirect effects of policy choices. This approach was demonstrated in the World Bank's recent report on China's future development (World Bank, 1985), which linked projections of the labor force with other major aspects of the structural transformation (Wood, 1986).

Population policy

Most of these trends can be illustrated in the field of population policy. Ten or 15 years ago it centered on the effectiveness of various means of contraception and their provision at lower cost. More modern approaches start from the household's demand for children and the changing effects of other aspects of the transformation – urbanization, education, health – on fertility choices. Current policy recommendations rely more heavily on the indirect effects of these changes in the socioeconomic environment and less on direct measures to increase the acceptance of family planning. An exposition of this general view and supporting references are given in the World Bank's 1984 *World Development Report*.

A similar progression from broadening the analytical framework to reconsidering policy instruments and putting greater reliance on indirect measures can be seen in other policy areas. The inefficiency of relying on direct measures alone to stimulate agricultural or industrial growth has long been recognized. A comparable reorientation is under way in policies toward urbanization, where direct efforts to limit or redirect urban growth have been generally unsuccessful. This example is developed further below.

Recognition that the principal dimensions of the structural transformation are highly interrelated does not in itself provide an argument for greater government intervention or overall planning. It is only where market forces may not lead to optimal results – as in population growth, urbanization or income distribution – that there is an a priori case for selective intervention. The nature of this problem has been highlighted in a recent study of urbanization by Kelley and Williamson (1984), which is one of the most comprehensive attempts to study long-term policy choices in the context of the structural transformation.

Urbanization

The argument for considering various aspects of the transformation together is nowhere stronger than in the area of urban policy. It is hard to find a government that does not intervene in a substantial way in urban development or a country in which the various interventions are mutually consistent. Kelley and Williamson argue that both governments and scholars misjudge the causes of rapid urban growth and often try unnecessarily to slow it down. My main interest is the contribution that their study makes to the structural research program and the extent to which it may serve as a guide to policy analysis in related fields.

The Kelley–Williamson study of *What Drives Third World City Growth?* (1984) is designed to explain the relative importance of the principal factors that affect the urban transformation. Their approach is very much in the spirit of the structural research program outlined here. The stylized facts of the structural transformation are either incorporated directly in their simulation model or at least consistent with its results. The model itself follows the neoclassical computable general equilibrium format pioneered by Johansen (1960) and Adelman and Robinson (1978). The results take the form of alternative simulations over several decades designed to bring out the changes in the principal parameters.

This approach has notable advantages in studying related aspects of the transformation. It incorporates adjustment mechanisms that depend on relative prices, such as the Harris–Todaro migration functions, or the demand for exports as a function of world prices. In contrast to earlier studies of urbanization, which tend to exaggerate the effects of a few factors such as population growth or "urban bias," the general equilibrium prototype gives greater weight to indirect effects such as differential productivity growth. Although *What Drives Third World City Growth?* has numerous speculations that remain to be verified in country studies, it demonstrates the possibilities of combining theoretical analysis and stylized facts in a fruitful interaction.

The areas of policy for which this approach is likely to be useful include those for which the initial economic structure is important to the outcome and cannot be changed rapidly. Although the limits to structural change have been studied primarily in the field of trade, they are equally important in human capital formation, income distribution, and demographic processes.

REVISING THE PROGRAM

Any active research program is periodically revised in the light of empirical and theoretical findings. Revision takes the form of modifying hypotheses and designing empirical tests to discriminate among alternative formulations. In the structural research program described here, new information has usually been successfully absorbed by elaborating the existing assumptions, but occasionally there is a challenge that has deeper ramifications.

A notable example of such a challenge was Jorgenson's "Testing Alternative Theories of the Development of a Dual Economy" (1966), which compared particular forms of the classical (surplus labor) and neoclassical models to Japanese experience and found the latter to be superior. While the controversy over his findings did not cause the abandonment of either model, it did lead to a reexamination of their basic assumptions and the data supporting them. A similar confrontation between neoclassical and structural analyses of the trade constraint on the transformation took place at about the same time, with similarly inconclusive results (see Fei and Ranis, 1968; Bruton, 1969; Chenery, 1969).

In the Lakatos–Blaug assessment of Scientific Research Programs, a program is "progressing" if the theoretical extensions required to meet such challenges add to the empirical content of the results, rather than limiting them to more special cases. In a new field such as postwar development, another source of progress has been the rapid accumulation of experience and data. If one were to compare the results of the past 25 years of research to the objectives outlined at the NBER conference of 1959, it would not be hard to reach a favorable assessment on both counts. However, I would agree with Díaz-Alejandro (1976) and Perkins (1981) that the mere repetition of existing studies over longer periods is likely to meet diminishing returns.

Apart from reacting to neoclassical critiques, the structural research program has progressed by examining the interaction among different aspects of the transformation, as illustrated in the previous section. This approach becomes more promising as the data base for comparative analysis expands from 10- to 30-year time series. Comparisons based on this data have produced a broader understanding of the postwar relations between trade and industrialization. A logical next step would expand these model-based comparisons to include labor markets and income distribution.

The main limitation to the structural research program, as it was conceived by Kuznets, is the absence of policy analysis. One remedy is to take advantage of the expanding time series to analyze the common effects of changes in policies – such as the shift from inward to outward orientation – on groups of similar countries. This would complement the proposals of Ranis (1984, 1986) for a more detailed form of typological analysis of policies.

Although it is customary to regard the neoclassical and structural approaches as competitors (for example, see Little, 1982), I would argue for trying to combine the best features of both. The hard core of the neoclassical program – its reliance on economic rationality as the source of theory – is both its strength and its limitation. Although this approach has had some notable successes in applying household economics and human capital theory to developing countries, they are mainly at the micro end of the spectrum.

The structural research program has opposite strengths and weaknesses. Its hard core is the presumption that there are various common elements of social, political, and technological behavior that lead to uniformities in the structural transformation. The search for these development patterns has been most successful at the economy-wide level. Models based on this approach combine some of the assumptions of the neoclassical system with constraints that are inferred from structural analysis. This approach has been most successful in establishing links among aspects of the structural transformation that extend over several decades.

These summaries suggest that the two research programs should be more complementary than competitive. Both could be encompassed in a broader Walrasian system in which the stylized facts of transformation would appear as constraints on the form of various functions or on the speed of adjustment of different markets. Positing such a system should stimulate the type of research on individual markets that in the past followed the setting out of the Lewis and Harris–Todaro models of labor markets or Nurkse's and Prebisch's hypotheses as to the limited flexibility of LDC exports. In charting progress, it is probably more important to note when such questions are raised, rather than whether the first answer suggested turned out to be correct.

NOTES

[1] The common elements in this research program in the late 1950s are discussed in the report of a National Bureau of Economic Research (NBER) conference on *The Comparative Study of Economic Growth and Structure* (1959). Views of Kuznets, Tinbergen, and other contributors are cited later in this chapter.

[2] Blaug (1980a) concludes that "This notion that theories come to us, not one at a time but linked together in a more or less integrated network of ideas, is however better conveyed by Lakatos' 'methodology of scientific research programmes.'" Evidence for this statement is given in Blaug (1980b), which applies the Lakatos approach to nine branches of economics that are off-shoots of the general neoclassical research program.

[3] The essential features of the several versions of the Lewis model have been recently reviewed by Findlay (1982) and Bhagwati (1982).

[4] While the 1959 Conference on Economic Growth and Structure recognized the potential value of the input-output system for this purpose (NBER, 1959, pp. 71–4), it doubted its practicality, at least in the following decade.

[5] The pioneering country application of this technique is the study of Korean development and income distribution by Adelman and Robinson (1978). A prototype model derived from this approach is given in Chenery, de Melo, Lewis, and Robinson (1986). An alternative general equilibrium approach is used by Kelley and Williamson (1984).

[6] The underlying model was estimated by converting per capita incomes by means of exchange rates. A shift to purchasing power conversion would reduce the income range from 15 times to perhaps ten, based on the findings of Kravis, Heston, and Summers (1978). If we also correct the results for the rising relative price of services, there is probably no real increase in the service share.

[7] Apart from their use in modeling, typologies have another attraction in facilitating experimentation with groups defined by socioeconomic indices, such as those used by Adelman and Morris (1973).

[8] For example, 38 semi-industrial countries are classified by Chenery and Syrquin (1986b) into four types on the basis of their initial structures and trade policies; comparisons are made among countries over time within a given type as well as across types.

REFERENCES

Adelman, I. and Morris, C. T. 1967: *Society, Politics and Economic Development: A Quantitative Approach*. Baltimore: Johns Hopkins.

Adelman, I. and Morris, C. T. 1973: *Economic Growth and Social Equity in Developing Countries*. Stanford: Stanford University Press.

Adelman, I. and Morris, C. T. 1984: "Patterns of Economic Growth, 1850–1914, or Chenery–Syrquin in Perspective." In M. Syrquin, L. Taylor and L. E. Westphal (eds), *Economic Structure and Performance*, New York: Academic Press.

Adelman, I. and Robinson, S. 1978: *Income Distribution Policy in Developing Countries: A Case Study of Korea*. Stanford: Stanford University Press; Oxford: Oxford University Press.

Bhagwati, J. N. 1982: "W. Arthur Lewis: An Appreciation." In M. Gersovitz, C. F. Díaz-Alejandro, G. Ranis, and M. R. Rosenzweig (eds), *The Theory and Experience of Economic Development*, London: Allen and Unwin.

Blaug, M. 1980a: "Kuhn versus Lakatos, or Paradigms versus Research Programs in the History of Economics." In G. Gutting (ed.), *Paradigms and Revolutions*, Notre Dame: University of Notre Dame Press.

Blaug, M. 1980b: *The Methodology of Economics*. Cambridge: Cambridge University Press.

Bruton, H. J. 1969: "The Two-Gap Approach to Aid and Development: Comment." *American Economic Review*, 59 (June), 439–46.

Chenery, H. B. 1960: "Patterns of Industrial Growth." *American Economic Review*, 50 (Sept.), 624–54.

Chenery, H. B. 1969: "The Two-Gap Approach to Aid and Development: A Reply to Bruton." *American Economic Review*, 59 (June), 446–9.

Chenery, H. B., de Melo, J., Lewis, J. and Robinson, S. 1986: "Alternative Routes to Development." In H. Chenery, S. Robinson and M. Syrquin, *Industrialization and Growth*, New York: Oxford University Press.

Chenery, H. B., Shishido, S. and Watanabe, T. 1962: "The Pattern of Japanese Growth, 1914–54." *Econometrica*, 30 (Jan.), 98–139.

Chenery, H. B. and Syrquin, M. 1975: *Patterns of Development, 1950–70*. London: Oxford University Press.

Chenery, H. B. and Syrquin, M. 1980: "A Comparative Analysis of Industrial Growth." In R. C. O. Mathews (ed.), *Measurement, History and Factors of Economic Growth*, New York: Macmillan.

Chenery, H. B. and Syrquin, M. 1986a: "Typical Patterns of Transformation." In H. Chenery, S. Robinson and M. Syrquin, *Industrialization and Growth*, New York: Oxford University Press.

Chenery, H. B. and Syrquin, M. 1986b: "The Semi-Industrial Countries." In H. Chenery, S. Robinson and M. Syrquin, *Industrialization and Growth*, New York: Oxford University Press.

Chenery, H. B. and Taylor, L. J. 1968: "Development Patterns among Countries and Over Time." *Review of Economics and Statistics*, 50 (Nov.), 391–416.

Chenery, H. B. and Watanabe, T. 1965: "The Process of Industrialization." Paper read at the World Congress of the Econometric Society, Sept. 9–14, Rome, Italy.

Clark, C. 1940: *The Conditions of Economic Progress*. London: Macmillan.

Corden, W. M. and Neary, J. P. 1982: "Booming Sector and De-Industrialization in a Small Open Economy." *Economic Journal*, 92, 825–48.

Cross, R. 1982: "The Duhem-Quine Thesis, Lakatos and the Appraisal of Theories in Macroeconomics." *Economic Journal*, 92 (June), 320–40.

Díaz-Alejandro, C. F. 1976: Review of H. B. Chenery and M. Syrquin, *Patterns of Development, 1950–70*. In *Economic Journal*, 86 (June), 401–3.

Fei, J. C. H. and Ranis, G. 1964: *Development of the Labor Surplus Economy*. Homewood, Ill.: Irwin.

Fei, J. C. and Ranis, G. 1968: "Foreign Assistance and Economic Development Revisited." *American Economic Review*, 58 (Sept.).

Findlay, R. 1982: "On W. Arthur Lewis's Contributions to Economics." In M. Gersovitz, C. F. Díaz-Alejandro, G. Ranis, and M. R. Rosenzweig (eds), *The Theory and Experience of Economic Development*, London: Allen and Unwin.

Harris, J. R. and Todaro, M. 1970: "Migration, Unemployment, and Development: A Two-Sector Analysis." *American Economic Review*, 60 (March), 126–42.

Houthakker, H. S., 1957: "An International Comparison of Household Expenditure Patterns: Commemorating the Centenary of Engel's Law." *Econometrica*, 25 (Oct.), 532–51.

Johansen, L. 1960: *A Multisectoral Model of Economic Growth*. Amsterdam: North Holland.

Jorgenson, D. W. 1966: "Testing Alternative Theories of the Development of a Dual Economy" (with comment by S. A. Marglin). In I. Adelman and E. Thorbecke (eds), *The Theory and Design of Economic Development*, Baltimore: Johns Hopkins Press.

Kelley, A. C. and Williamson, J. G. 1984: *What Drives Third World City Growth? A Dynamic General Equilibrium Approach*. Princeton, NJ: Princeton University Press.

Kravis, I. B., Heston, A. W. and Summers, R. 1978: "Real GDP Per Capita for More Than One Hundred Countries." *Economic Journal*, 88 (June), 215–42.

Kuznets, S. 1959: "On Comparative Study of Economic Structure and Growth of Nations." In National Bureau of Economic Research, *The Comparative Study of Economic Growth and Structure*, New York: NBER.

Kuznets, S. 1956–64: "Quantitative Aspects of the Economic Growth of Nations." *Economic Development and Cultural Change* (a series of ten articles).

Kuznets, S. 1966: *Modern Economic Growth*. New Haven: Yale University Press.

Kuznets, S. 1971: *Economic Growth of Nations: Total Output and Production Structure*. Cambridge, Mass.: Harvard University Press.

Lewis, W. A. 1954: "Economic Development with Unlimited Supplies of Labor." *Manchester School of Economic and Social Studies*, 22 (May), 139–91.

Little, I. M. D. 1982: *Economic Development: Theory, Policy and International Relations*. New York: Basic Books.

Maizels, A. 1963: *Industrial Growth and World Trade. An Empirical Study of Trends in Production, Consumption and Trade in Manufactures from 1899–1959, with a Discussion of Probable Future Trends*. Cambridge: Cambridge University Press.

National Bureau of Economic Research, 1959. *The Comparative Study of Economic Growth and Structure*. New York: NBER.

Nurkse, R. 1962: "Balanced and Unbalanced Growth." In G. Haberler and R. M. Stern (eds), *Equilibrium and Growth in the World Economy*, Cambridge, Mass.: Harvard University Press.

Perkins, D. 1981: *Three Decades of International Quantitative Comparisons*. Cambridge, Mass.: Harvard Institute for International Development.

Ranis, G. 1984: "Typology in Development Theory: Retrospective and Prospects." In M. Syrquin, L. Taylor and L. Westphal (eds), *Economic Structure and Performance*, New York: Academic Press.

Ranis, G. 1986: *Development Economics: What Next?* New Haven: Yale Growth Center.

Samuelson, P. A. 1939a: "Interactions between the Multiplier Analysis and the Principle of Acceleration." *Review of Economics and Statistics*, 21 (May), 75–8.

Samuelson, P. A. 1939b: "A Synthesis of the Principle of Acceleration and the Multiplier." *Journal of Political Economy*, 47 (Dec.) 786–97.

Syrquin, M. 1985: "Patterns of Development since 1960: A Comparison for China." Cambridge, Mass.: Harvard Institute for International Development.

Temin, P. 1967: "A Time-Series Test of Patterns of Industrial Growth." *Economic Development and Cultural Change*, 15 (Jan.), 174–82.

Tinbergen, J. 1959: "Comparative Studies of Economic Growth." In National Bureau of Economic Research, *The Comparative Study of Economic Growth and Structure*, New York: NBER.

Wood, A. 1986: "Growth and Structural Change in Large Low-Income Countries." World Bank Staff Working Paper 763.

World Bank, 1984: *World Development Report.* New York: Oxford University Press.

World Bank, 1985: *China: Long-Term Development Issues and Options*, New York: Johns Hopkins Press.

Comments on
"Structural Transformation: A Program of Research"

IRMA ADELMAN

The paper by Hollis Chenery provides a very thoughtful summary of the history of the empirical research program into the economic structure of developing countries during the transition process. It delineates the evolution of the research, its major findings, and its relationship to development theory and policy. It also evaluates the structural research program within the more general context of the ideal methodology of scientific research.

The summary provided by Chenery constitutes a mature assessment of the 30-year history of research into the structural transformations of developing countries. If the assessment can be faulted at all, it is on the grounds of excessive modesty. The number of citations to his own work is somewhat smaller than any other development economist surveying this area of research would tend to make, and the paper is quite generous to both antecedents and successors.

My comments will concern three areas: (1): how the major findings of the research relate to the historical experience of currently developed nations during the second half of the nineteenth century and early twentieth; (2) how the methodology of the structural research program fits into the general methodology of economics; and (3) where the research program should go in the future.

The structural research program and methodology

The history of doctrine in economics is marked by sharply diverging views concerning the methodology which is appropriate to the development of economics viewed as a science.

The English classical economists, though referring to particular historical episodes, on the whole espoused deductive methods. Their primary contributions were to provide conceptualizations which organized large bodies of nonsystematic observations into consistent systems. Starting from premises based on particular views of human nature, they deduced generalizations concerning patterns of individual behavior. Embedding these into assumptions concerning specific institutional arrangements, they then inferred the dynamics of national income, accumulation, income per capita, and income distribution among classes.

The role of observation in their work was limited to introspection concerning human motives (Smith's Scotchman, Bentham's hedonist, and Malthus's sex fiend) and to verification by specific experience – comparing the results of reasoning with the results of particular historical episodes relating to analogous problems. Ricardo and Mill favored the method of "thought experiment" of comparative statics. Mill (1874, pp. 144–6) specifically rejected empirical methods as inefficient ways of arriving at a body of valuable truths, but he thought they could be usefully applied to problems of verification. Efforts to make economics into a "science" were limited to evolving a consistent method of quantification, such as provided by the utilitarian calculus of Bentham and Jevons.

The English views of scientific method of economics were, by and large, adopted by continental economists such as Pareto, Walras and Cassel. But they were sharply challenged by the German historical school. Under the influence of Hegel, who believed in historical relativism, Schmoller and his followers espoused the inductive approach to economic science. They believed that the task of the economist who really wished to contribute to the development of the subject was to be devoted to the accumulation of empirical evidence. Only when a sufficient body of empirical evidence has been accumulated could the building of theory profitability begin.

The structural research program originated by Kuznets and Chenery owes much of its methodology to the German historical school. But it differs from it in three important respects: it uses systematic statistical techniques to summarize the historical process; it develops typologies applying to groups of countries, rather than historical descriptions applying to individual countries; and in the hands of Chenery et al., concentrates primarily on the quantification of the structural changes in the major components of the national income and product accounts, rather than on the wider process of development encompassing institutional and technological change. It also uses more theory to guide the specification of the functional relationships it estimates.

The *Methodenstreit* which raged in Germany during the 1870s and 1880s between inductive and deductive economics continues to be rife a century later between the devotees of theoretical and mathematical economics, on the one hand, and applied economists, policy analysts, and economic historians, on the other. Both branches of economics have developed greatly in technical sophistication, applying more powerful mathematical methods and more powerful statistical techniques to their preferred approaches. Also, the development of large data bases and powerful computers has helped increase the scope of analysis of empirical regularities. Nevertheless, the cleavage among empirical and theoretical economists continues, despite writings on the methodology of science which espouse iterative interaction between a priori and a posteriori methods as ideal models of scientific research.

It is now generally accepted in the philosophy of science that the classical idea – that the basic data from which the scientist forms hypotheses are provided by an unmediated faculty of observation – is wrong. Rather, the logical positivists stress the need for a scientific approach to the generation of factual propositions by means of controlled experiments or statistical analysis of data.

On the other hand, the logical positivists also introduced the notion of science as a system of pure logic and the distinction between factual truth and analytic truth. The main influence of positivism in economics has manifested itself in model-building activities that search for analytic truth, as evidenced by internal consistency and clarity, rather than for factual truth, as evidenced by explanatory or predictive power.

Philosophers of science now generally agree that the aim of science is explanation, i.e. factual truth (see, for example, the article on the philosophy of science in the *Encyclopedia of Social Sciences*, 1968). Explanation, in turn, requires deducing events or regularities from a set of premises containing one or more "laws" (i.e. scientifically established, stylized facts) and one or more conditioning statements (Morgenbesser, 1968). Explanation thus requires a combination of stylized facts with analytic models.

The growth of scientific knowledge, therefore, involves using scientific methods – statistical or experimental – to generate stylized facts and incorporate the stylized facts into a system of deductive explanations. These deductive explanations consist of analytic models that are used to derive consequences similar to the new stylized facts by applying mathematical-logical principles to premises that combine previously confirmed stylized facts with other propositions and use conceptual-semantic categories that are generally accepted in the discipline.

As Kuhn (1970) and Lakatos (1970) point out, ideally empirical research should interact with theory. Empirical research should generate some of the premises upon which analytic models are built; it should be used to verify the deductions of analytic models; and it should be used to reformulate the premises upon which the theories are built. In turn, the conceptual categories used in analytic models, the deductions from the models, and the regularities asserted in the premises upon which the models are built should define the research agenda of empirical research.

The structural research program surveyed in the paper by Chenery has followed the ideal methodology. It has quantified the stylized facts of development and has incorporated them into a system of deductive explanations, based mostly on the systematics of change in the structure of demand and supply during the transition process to industrial economies. The stylized facts of economic development as initially postulated by Colin Clark (1940) and Kuznets (1966) have been found to be quite robust.

Additional stylized facts, relating mostly to the role of international trade, and to alternative paths in economies with different initial resource endowments and of different sizes, have been documented. The research has become more sophisticated over time as it progressed from single equation analysis, to reduced form systems, to interdependent structural models. Basic theoretical ideas – comparative advantage, production functions, demand systems – have been used to generate the models estimated and to explain the stylized facts uncovered by the research. Other stylized facts – Engel's law, the inverse correlation of the share of trade with the economy's size – have been invoked in structuring the search for further stylized facts and in explaining empirical findings.

Thus, much has been learned from this research program concerning the stylized facts of economic development. Furthermore, the feedback from this research into development policy has been substantial. The research has been used to identify changes in the barriers to growth, and hence to argue for differing roles and forms of foreign assistance in countries at different stages in the transition process. It has been used as a diagnostic tool to see whether an economy is doing well or poorly, both in general and in more specific structural features (patterns of accumulation and resource use). It has also been used to decompose growth into its sources and to try to identify superior development strategies.

But the feedback from empirical research into development theory has not been as strong as the feedback from theory to empirical research. In part, this has been due to the fact that many of the important new stylized facts of economic development concern multi-sector patterns of growth and only two, or at most three, sectors can be accommodated in analytic models. In part, this has been due to the fact that the feedback from empirical research to theory is weak throughout all branches of economics. With a few notable exceptions (e.g. Keynes), there is still a large preference in theoretical economics for viewing economics as a search for analytic rather than factual truth, and for relegating the search for factual truth to applied fields.

The stylized facts of development

The structural research program summarized in the Chenery paper has described the transformations occurring in less developed countries during the transition from very underdeveloped to semi-industrial countries. The aspects of the transition it has focused on are the accumulation of physical and human capital and the shifts in the composition of demand, production, trade and employment. Since the findings of the research program have been well summarized by Chenery, I shall not dwell on them.

Rather, I shall concentrate on the contrasts between the historical and the contemporary process. I will base my comments on the extension of the empirical methodology of the Kuznets–Chenery research program to the historical process of 23 countries from 1850 to 1914 undertaken by Adelman and Morris (see Adelman and Morris, 1986; Morris and Adelman, forthcoming).

As compared with the historical record of currently developed countries during the Industrial Revolution, there are both similarities and differences. Then, as now, development changed the structure of production and exports from mostly primary towards manufacturing. But technological and productivity change played a more important role in the historical than in the contemporary process. Indeed, technological change has generally been identified as the prime mover of the Industrial Revolution. Then, as now, most countries started with an import-substitution phase and only later proceded to an export phase. But the share of trade did not bear as strong a negative correlation to country size historically, because both some small and some large countries had colonies and used trade extensively to supplement their resource base and sell their manufactures.

The distinctions in development strategies between small manufacturing, small primary, and large countries were important historically as well. But the distinctions by country size were not as significant historically, since some small countries had colonies and used them to diversify and supplement their natural resources and enlarge their markets. In addition, the distinction between early industrializers and late industrializers was important historically since the latter used government-sponsored mercantilist policies to attempt to catch up with the first comers to the Industrial Revolution.

Historically, the accumulation of physical capital played an important role in fueling industrialization. But the accumulation of human capital was considerably less significant in the production process than it had been in less developed countries. And historically, capital transfers from commerce played a more important role as a source of finance for industrialization, while transfers of resources from agriculture played a less significant role.

Finally, the most important contrasts between the historical and the contemporary records are in the behavior of agriculture and of population. In all the industrializing countries, the industrialization process either started from a productive agriculture as a base or else was accompanied by agricultural modernization. Agricultural productivity improvements through biological or institutional change either preceded or coincided with the Industrial Revolution. In current LDCs improvements in agricultural productivity (as Kuznets and Chenery have taught us) lag improvements in industrial productivity significantly.

Unlike the contemporary experience with population growth, historically the population explosion preceded the Industrial Revolution, and its residual effects were mitigated by very significant outmigration. Birthrates had dropped before the Industrial Revolution and mortality rates rose during the early phases as a result of population flows into cities whose environmental sanitation was worse than in the country-side. By contrast, LDCs have had to contend with a population explosion at the samé time as they try to shift public resources into the construction of infrastructure.

Also, while per capita income comparisons across centuries are very risky indeed, as far as one can tell from the data, currently developed countries started their industrial push from levels of per capita income which were significantly higher than those of LDCs in the 1950s. And they grew considerably more slowly than have LDCs in the last 30 years.

Thus, comparing the historical with the contemporary development experience, one can conclude that LDCs started from more adverse initial conditions and have performed considerably better than did developed countries in the nineteenth century.

The research agenda

The research agenda posed by Kuznets called for "a clearer perception of past trends and of the conditions under which they occurred, as well as knowledge of the conditions that characterize underdeveloped countries today" (Kuznets, 1955, p. 26). For the recent period, covered by the last 30 years, much of this agenda has been carried out in the systematic research of Chenery and his co-authors. The results they obtain delineate both the nature of the transformations in factor use which have taken place in developing countries and serve to indicate the limited contribution to growth in per capita GNP which these trans-formations alone can make. Thus, as with a good growing science, they serve to pose questions which need to be answered by future research.

One of the major findings of the general structural quantitative research program has been to point out that resource reallocation pro-cesses by themselves, whether occurring under the impetus of trade policy or under the impetus of fiscal policy, lead to at the most, one to two percentage point changes in growth rates. But intercountry dif-ferences in long-term growth rates range from negative to about. 11 percent. This means that the bulk of the variance in growth rates among developing countries must be attributed to forces other than the ones covered so well by neoclassical analysis.

Instead, we must look to the factors stressed by the classical econo-mists (accumulation of factors and technical change), to the forces emphasized by the mercantilists (trade policy and the catalytic role of governments), and to the processes stressed by the early development economists (external economies and linkages) for the bulk of the explanation of intercountry differences in growth rates. Of these, differences in factor accumulation and use and differences in trade policy have been the major focus of the past research program. The study of the other forces should constitute the bulk of the research agenda of the structural research program for the future.

In my comments on future research, I shall discuss only those agenda items which can, I think, be analyzed with the general methodology of the structural research program.

A major feature of the transformation process is the transformation of agriculture from a low-productivity, extensive sector, whose increase in output is due primarily to increased factor use, into a high-productivity sector, whose growth is due primarily to technological change and in which resources are used in an intensive fashion. The "patterns" work has not focused at all on how this transformation is achieved. It has looked into the manufacturing sector and decomposed shifts in its output and sources of growth, but has treated agriculture as an undifferentiated blob. The qualitative transformation of agriculture is at least as important to the change in structure of developing countries in their development process as is the quantitative transformation in structure involved in the industrial sectors. Understanding this transformation could profitably become an important direction in which the "patterns" work might move. An educated guess would ascribe the sources of this transformation to institutional change, terms of trade policy, technical change, and indirect domestic demand effects arising from the nonagricultural urban sector.

Another under-researched area identified by the patterns work as important is productivity growth, both in manufacturing and overall. It accounts for about 40 percent of total growth in the typical developing country. The study of the sources of productivity growth – external economies, winds of competition, technology transfer, investment in research, price policy, institutional change (into, for example, conglomerates) – has important growth policy implications.

Are there typical sequences in the mastery of new technologies, going from imitation to adaptation, to innovation? How are these related to other aspects of the transformation process, particularly trade policy and foreign investment policy? This again would seem like an important, somewhat neglected area for future research in using both micro-analysis, as done by Westphal and Pack, and the patterns framework.

Institutional change, a common factor to agricultural transformation, technological absorption, income distribution, and the quality and impact of government policy, also requires more study. The extension of the Chenery et al. research methodology to the historical realm (Morris and Adelman, forthcoming) has identified it as the single most important differentiator of development performance among groups of countries. While the insights into institutional change that can be gained by macro-quantitative, cross-country analysis are limited and must be enriched by micro-level analysis, there is still scope for establishing the stylized facts of institutional and political structure and their interaction with the overall economy.

Finally, the time would appear ripe to return to the study of forces affecting the size distribution of income and the extent of poverty. In the patterns work, the typical changes in the size distribution of income which occur in the development process are treated as a byproduct of other transformations, particularly the shift out of agriculture.

While these shifts are important explanatory variables affecting the long run course of poverty, other aspects are also important. The patterns work has not really focused on the other structural sources. Historical analysis and case histories of particular episodes, such as famines, indicate that institutions in commodity and factor markets are very important in explaining how development affects the poor. Institutions tend to vary in systematic ways during the development process; they also differ in systematic ways among countries in which policy is responsive to the interests of different types of elite or nonelite groups and in countries that are pursuing different development strategies.

The study of the systematics of how the distribution of income and poverty change with development, the construction of analytic and policy models aimed at the design of anti-poverty policy have been the focus of structural, modeling and typology work for only above five years. The Arabs pushed these concerns out of the mainstream research agenda. A byproduct of the falling oil prices and interest rates might be to bring these concerns back. After all, the problems of poverty have hardly been solved. And this is what economic development is all about.

REFERENCES

Adelman, I. and Morris, C. T. 1984: "Patterns of Economic Growth, 1850–1914, or Chenery–Syrquin in Historical Perspective." In M. Syrquin, L. Taylor, and L. E. Westphal (eds), *Economic Structure and Performance*, New York: Academic Press.

Chenery, H. B. and Syrquin, M. 1975: *Patterns of Development, 1950–1970.* London: Oxford University Press.

Clark, C. 1940: *The Conditions of Economic Progress.* London: Macmillan.

International Encylopedia of Social Sciences 1968: D. L. Sills (ed.), London: Macmillan and The Free Press.

Kuhn, T. 1970: *The Structure of Scientific Revolutions* (2nd edn). Chicago: University of Chicago Press.

Kuznets, S. 1956–64: "Quantitative Aspects of Economic Growth of Nations." *Economic Development and Cultural Change* (a new series of ten articles).

Kuznets, S. 1966: *Modern Economic Growth.* New Haven: Yale University Press.

Lakatos, I. and Musgrave, A. (ed.) 1970: *Criticism and the Growth of Knowledge.* Cambridge: Cambridge University Press.

Mill, J. S. 1844: *Essays on Some Unsettled Questions of Political Economy.* London: London School of Economics.

Morgenbesser, S. 1968: "Scientific Explanation." In D. L. Sills (ed.), *International Encyclopedia of Social Sciences,* London: Macmillan and The Free Press.

Morris, C. T. and Adelman, I. Forthcoming: *Where Angels Fear to Tread: Quantitative Analysis of Economic History.* Baltimore: Johns Hopkins Press.

4

Trade, Development, and the State

RONALD FINDLAY

The role of international trade and factor movements in the process of economic development has always been a major cause of contention in the literature. It is fair to say that the pioneers of development theory in the fifties – Nurkse, Prebisch, and Lewis – were all pessimistic or at least skeptical about the power of trade to continue to serve as an "engine of growth" in the less developed regions of the world as it had done up to 1914, before the disruptions of the interwar period. Hence the emphasis on "balanced growth" and the possibility of tapping the alleged hidden potential of rural underemployment. The Soviet example of the 1930s, based on the so-called "law of the superiority of heavy to light industry," inspired Mahalanobis and others in India to extol a pattern of building up domestic capital goods industries, neglecting the possibility of obtaining such goods more cheaply by exporting primary products or manufactured consumer goods, for which adequate markets were not felt to exist internationally.

The sixties and early seventies, however, saw tremendous expansion of world trade, driven by historically unprecedented growth rates in Japan, Western Europe, and the United States. A wealth of evidence has been assembled, showing that those LDCs which were willing to take advantage of this expansion of external markets did exceptionally well, while those which cut themselves off by overvalued exchange rates, high tariffs, and export controls of one sort or another performed much more poorly by the yardstick of GNP or other associated measures. While it is possible to dispute the shades and nuances of this bold

I would like to thank Ian Little both for the generosity and the acuteness of his written comments. Several important questions were raised in the discussion at the Yale Symposium, and Raquel Fernandez and Andres Velasco also had much to criticize in private conversations. I am grateful to all these people and to the editor of this volume for forcing me to think more deeply about the difficult issues with which this paper has attempted to grapple. I hope to be able to respond to at least some of the points raised in future work.

assertion I shall simply take it for granted in what follows, since I believe that the basic contention is incontrovertible.

This experience has pushed the most urgent analytical task one step further back. The issue is no longer one of whether "outward looking" or "restrictive" trade policies are most conducive to development, but what factors determine whether a given state, i.e. nation-state, in the Third World has followed one type of policy or the other; more correctly, what determines the particular point on a continuum between complete free trade and autarky that each country chooses. The problem thus transcends the familiar technical bounds of our discipline and becomes one of "political economy."

The broader issue raised by this question is the nature of the links between international trade and the state, under conditions corresponding to those of the Third World in the present day. Under colonialism the question simply does not arise, since the state is then simply that of the metropolitan power, which can be assumed to conduct economic policy in the colony in its own self-interest, of whatever degree of "enlightenment" that may be.

What follows will be an "essay in trespassing," an attempt to explore the subtle and recalcitrant issues involved in the mutual interactions of trade, development and the state from the perspective of an economist, but drawing on historical experience and the insights of writers from a variety of disciplines in the social sciences. Not surprisingly, I have found myself following some of the tracks of the Great Trespasser himself – I allude, of course to Hirschman (1981, chap. 4, 5, and 8; 1971, chap. 3).

The first section will look at the problem in the context of primary exports of the traditional type. The second examines the sociopolitical framework of industrialization based on import substitution. The third considers the role of the state in the so-called "newly industrializing countries" (NICs), in which development is spearheaded by manufactured exports.

PRIMARY TRADITIONAL EXPORTS

The familiar "nineteenth-century pattern" of international trade was one in which Britain, followed by other Western European countries, exported manufactures to the rest of the world, while the colonies and the "regions of recent settlement," in the Eurocentric terminology of the League of Nations, exported raw materials and food in return, with capital exports from Europe financing the creation of the necessary physical infrastructure in the primary exporting regions. This process in the real world found its expression in the world of ideas in Ricardo's famous theory of comparative advantage, which demonstrated for all time how specialization and trade benefit both sides of the exchange.

The symmetry of mutual gain, however, should not be allowed to obscure the *opposite* implications for income distribution and growth in each region that were derived by Ricardo in the very same analysis in his *Essay on Profits*. He showed that cheaper food reduced rents and raised profits in the exporter of manufactures, i.e. England. Since landlords, in his view, essentially spent their income on luxury consumption while the frugal capitalists accumulated more capital out of theirs, this shift in the distribution of income would raise the rate of growth. This, and not the increase in the real income of consumers as stressed by later economists, was his reason for being in favor of the repeal of the Corn Laws. By the very same reasoning, however, the effect on the exporter of corn would be to raise rents and reduce the rate of profit, and with it the growth rate of capital and output. (For a description of the formal model, see Findlay, 1974.)

Thus in England, the course of free trade was associated with all the positive features of the Victorian concept of "progress" – abolition of "rotten boroughs" and the extension of suffrage, religious toleration, civil liberties, and so on. In the regions exporting primary products, however, the social and political thrust of the free trade interest was in the opposite direction. To take the most dramatic and obvious example, consider the case of cotton and the antebellum South in the United States. Free trade in England was spearheaded by the cotton textile industry of Manchester, which was inconceivable without the supply of raw cotton from the American South, which in turn was inextricably linked to slavery before the Civil War. Free trade, thus, was socially and politically progressive in the "centre" of the world economy but reactionary in such key areas of the "periphery" as the United States.

This Janus-like aspect of free trade has been noted for an earlier era by M. M. Postan (1973). In the late Middle Ages and early modern times, Europe east of the Elbe had developed an economy specializing, to a large extent, on the export of corn to the industrially more developed areas of Western Europe, such as Holland. The social consequences of this specialization in Eastern Europe were the decay of towns and urban mercantile interests, and a great extension in the power of feudal landed magnates, who used the political and military means at their disposal to coerce their recalcitrant peasantries to provide labor on their estates for the production of marketable surpluses, handled by merchants of the Hanseatic League and others. Postan contrasts the growing power of urban mercantile interests in alliance with the state in the West, accompanied by a decline in the power of the aristocracy, with the *resurgence* of feudalism east of the Elbe that the corn trade generated. This development had fateful consequences for the whole future *divergent* historical development of Europe on the two sides of the Elbe. (See Anderson, 1974, for an extended investigation of this theme.) As Wallerstein (1979, chap. 2) has not been slow to note, in this era, Poland fits very well into the pattern of "dependency" more familiar in our own times. (Significantly, however, he does not mention Prussia, which had a similar economic pattern, but one in which the evolution of the state was in the opposite direction to the dissolution of central power in Poland.)

The United States from the War of Independence to the Civil War, the era between the "First and Second American Revolutions" as Charles Beard put it, provides us with a fascinating case history in the political economy of trade and development. The pattern of interdependence that developed between Britain and its former colony was the classic one of raw material exports, namely cotton, in exchange for manufactures (Keohane, 1983).

In 1860, about 80 percent of Britain's imports of raw cotton came from the United States. Much of the economy of the U.S. North was also based on providing financial, marketing, and transport services for cotton exports from the South. The trade policy of the new nation involved a compromise between the free trade interests of the Southern plantation oligarchy and the protectionism of Northern industrialists. The Constitution itself prohibited export taxes, a clear indication of how importantly regional conflicts over trade policy were regarded.

As is widely known, the antebellum South should not be viewed in romantic terms as a feudal chivalry persisting with noneconomic plantations to preserve a culture or way of life. The slave-based cotton plantation was a profitable "capitalist" enterprise. While the South was capitalist, however, it was not bourgeois, meaning by that term the complex of values, practices, and sentiments that are commonly associated with the dominant middle class of Western Europe and England, which was also emerging in the Northeast of the United States. Capitalism based on slavery could not *politically* and *culturally* unite with the classical capitalism of at least ostensibly free contract within the *same* state, though it could of course inhabit the same "world-system," as Barrington Moore (1966) has pointed out. A coalition of Northern capitalists and Southern planters, swapping high tariffs on imports of manufactures in exchange for acceptance of the legitimacy of slavery (a "marriage of steel and cotton" preceding the famous German one between "iron and rye") was thus socially and politically impossible. Instead, according to Moore, the North found its coalition partner in the free farming interests of the West. Opening up the public domain in the West appealed both to Western farming interests and Northern labor, and in return for their support, Northern capitalists could get higher tariffs on manufactures. "Vote yourself a farm – vote yourself a tariff," was the Republican slogan in 1860. Once slavery was overthrown, the North could offer the dismantling of "reconstruction" for acquiescence to further tariff increases, which rose sharply in the decades following the Civil War.

In appraising the counterfactual question, "What if the South had won," Moore (p. 153) offers the following scenario: "…the United States would have been in the position of some modernizing countries of today, with a *latifundia* economy, a dominant antidemocratic aristocracy, and a weak and dependent commercial and industrial class, unable and unwilling to push forward toward political democracy."

The experience of Latin America from independence to the onset of the Great Depression in 1930 provides a rich source of case histories on the relationship between the state and economies based on primary exports as the leading sector. The general experience was for the state to provide the institutional framework for the systematic exploitation of natural-resource-based comparative advantage by the establishment of property rights, physical infrastructure such as railroads and ports, and the provision of an elastic supply of labor either internally or through immigration. A wide range of primary products was involved – from the wheat, beef, and wool of the temperate plains of Argentina and Uruguay; the tropical products such as coffee and sugar from Brazil, Colombia, and Cuba; and minerals, such as nitrates and copper, from Chile; and oil from Mexico. The forms of government were varied, but the essentials were the same – a very limited range of participation, less than 5 percent of the male population are estimated to have voted in any election, and strong executive rule dominated by an "oligarchy" of landowners in the case of countries such as Argentina and Brazil, or *caudillos* such as Porfirio Diaz in Mexico, who provided a hospitable framework for foreign investment in extractive industries.

Looked at in terms of export growth rates and even of GNP, the experience of this era (that Carlos Díaz-Alejandro (1984) has called the "*Belle Epoque*" for Argentina), was quite impressive (see Reynolds (1985) for a summary and some useful statistics). What is disappointing from a liberal perspective is the failure of this undeniable economic progress to be reflected in a corresponding "democratization" of the political systems. How is this to be explained? Marxists and associated radicals of course have an easy answer: that it was not in the interest of the "imperialists," informal or otherwise, to permit the emergence of any such tendencies that could threaten the security of their profits. Another line of thought would bring in the political culture and the former metropolitan countries, with Spain and Portugal hardly being stirring examples of political "modernization" themselves.

Yet neither of these factors was able to prevent the Mexican Revolution of 1910, which in spite of the fact that it has even now failed to produce a genuine liberal democracy, nevertheless did lead to progress in land reform and national control over the exploitation of natural resources. If poor backward Mexico, "so close to the United States," could defy Iberian traditions and Yankee imperialism in this way, why not the affluent Argentines, for example, particularly since they did not have any African or American Indian populations to worry about?

Argentina and Australia offer an interesting comparison. Manufacturing and labor interests in Australia were able to prevent domination of the political system by livestock-rearing rural capitalist interests. Tariff protection for manufactures and restrictive immigration laws prevented the vast natural resources of Australia from being exploited with the same neoclassical efficiency as was the case with the similar natural resources of Argentina, where dependence on manufactured imports was much greater and where the urge to "people the wilderness" of successive governments by Spanish and Italian immigration led to a much better allocation of the world's resources, not to mention higher rents for the landed elites that dominated the governments. As Smith (1978) has shown, the rise of the middle-class "Radical" party that governed Argentina from 1916 to 1930 only succeeded in annoying the Conservatives and the Army without effectively incorporating the interests of workers, leaving them outside the system until they fell prey to the demagoguery of Juan Perón.

Thus large-scale, land-intensive agriculture, whether in the ranches of the Argentine *pampas* or the coffee plantations of Brazil, seems to produce social and political structures that are inherently resistant to change in a democratic direction. Comparative advantage and democracy are at odds, instead of mutually complementing each other, as in the Victorian England of John Stuart Mill and the other heirs of David Ricardo.

Commercial agriculture in Latin America has been of the large-scale type that we have been discussing. What, however, of peasant agriculture for the market, such as we find in most of Africa and Southeast Asia? Surely here the conflict that we have noted in the Latin American context between efficiency and equity, between the dictates of comparative advantage and a representative polity, would disappear since the benefits of higher world prices would spread to the mass of the population or at least major segments of it. Ironically, colonial regimes, particularly the British, have generally provided the framework within which this type of commercial agriculture could flourish. Thus, with the coming of independence, one would have hoped that the traditional pattern could have been continued, with more state support in the form of extension services, transport, credit and so on.

Regrettably, however, the record has been one in which the new regimes, whether civilian or military, have treated this sector simply as a source of revenue to be squeezed by the monopolistic pricing policy of marketing boards that were ostensibly established for the purpose of "stabilizing" the incomes of the peasant producers. Instead of giving them the average world price of their products, these organizations have typically drained substantial fractions away. The rationalization has been that "development" requires sacrifice and saving and that the "propensity to save and invest" by the government is higher than by the peasant producers themselves. Thus, the redistribution, while admittedly reducing output below the optimal level, nevertheless increases the "investible surplus" of the society and hence the rate of growth, ultimately to benefit society as a whole in the form of a higher level of per capita consumption. The argument in essence is that of the "primitive socialist accumulation" of the Soviet economist Preobrazhenski, which has been elaborated upon by myself and others. (See Erlich, 1960, for a fascinating discussion of the Soviet debates of the 1920s. Findlay, 1973, chap. 4, develops the formal analysis and makes the extension to the open economy.)

In practice, however, the outcome has been very different. For one thing, the price squeeze has often gone beyond any rational "optimal monopsony" level. The relative price of the export product in terms of importables is diminished not only by the lower-than-world nominal purchase prices set by the marketing boards but also by the higher-than-world nominal prices for importables, resulting from quotas, tariffs, and other trade restrictions. Thus not only output, but even government revenue, is probably lower than it would be under a more rational policy. The expenditure, on the other hand, has frequently simply gone into the private consumption of the urban beneficiaries or into armaments and other "public" goods of dubious social value.

Bates argues (1981) that this phenomenon in West Africa is simply a redistribution from a productive segment of the population that is vulnerable because it is geographically dispersed and unorganized in the rural areas, favoring small and concentrated urban elites such as army officers, civil servants, and perhaps factory workers. The irrationality from the standpoint of Paretian welfare economics of these policies is perfectly explicable in terms of interest-group behaviour as in the "new"' political economy.

Thus the experience of peasant agriculture and the state in Africa and parts of Southeast Asia such as Burma and the Philippines is, if anything, even more dismal than with the *estancias* and plantations of Latin America during the *Belle Epoque*. Only the case of Thailand offers encouragement, with a healthy expansion of peasant exports that is taxed in the interests of urban manufacturing and service sectors, but in a manner that still permits the "goose" to go on laying its "golden eggs" – a sharp contrast to the irrational government policies and rural misery of adjacent Burma.

IMPORT-SUBSTITUTION POLICIES

Few terms have been used more widely in the literature of development economics than "import substitution." A vital distinction has not always been made between the domestic production of previously imported goods arising from the natural forces of capital accumulation and technological change, on the one hand, and such replacement occurring as the outcome of a series of protective measures such as tariffs, quotas, and overvalued exchange rates. This has resulted in much needless confusion and controversy, since the welfare consequences of the two distinct processes are obviously quite different, at least from a "mainstream" neoclassical perspective.

Our concern here is with the "political economy" of import substitution, and hence we will use this term in the latter of the above two senses. Thus, we will try to consider what constellation of social and political forces induces the state to establish a trade and payments regime that is oriented towards import substitution. Since it is manufactured goods that are usually the target for such strategies, the issue becomes one of the promotion of industrialization behind a wall of implicit or explicit protection.

Once again it is convenient to begin with the experience of Latin America, where the process has been going on far longer than in the much more newly independent Asian and African countries, and where a sophisticated literature on the political economy aspects has grown up.

Despite several earlier attempts, particularly in Mexico and Brazil, it was not until the Great Depression of the thirties that industrialization in Latin America got substantially under way. The massive adverse shift in the terms of trade against primary products gave a market incentive to reallocate existing resources towards the domestic production of imported manufactures, particularly in the more labor-intensive and less technically sophisticated lines. The countries with larger domestic markets, such as Brazil and Mexico, naturally went furthest in this direction. This tendency was reinforced during World War II, when trade channels were disrupted for a considerable time. When the world economy started to function normally again, the terms of trade for primary products had vastly improved and much of the earlier industrialization might have now become uneconomic. Not surprisingly, however, the gains made were consolidated by protective measures, and additional more ambitious attempts at further industrialization were also undertaken.

These economic trends produced a shift in the rural–urban balance of the population, creating a mass of urban workers who had not hitherto been part of the political process. In Western Europe the political expression of this class was through mass-based political parties that entered the legislative arena and successfully struggled for the adoption of a welfare state and full employment policies. In Latin America the process took the form of "co-operation from above" rather than "pressure from below." Charismatic politicians, such as Getulio Vargas in Brazil and Juan Perón in Argentina, adopted policies that catered to the interests of these new groups while retaining political power in their own hands. This was in conformity with the Latin tradition of a dominant executive, even when coming to power in popular elections, as was the case with both Perón and Vargas. The term "populism" has been coined to denote this political phase in Latin

American history, somewhat reminiscent of the policy of Bismarck, which emasculated the radicalism of popular movements by paternalistic provision of social welfare services. (See Cardoso and Faletto, 1979, and Wynia, 1984, for interesting accounts and analyses of this process.)

The success of such regimes would naturally be judged on the basis of the extent to which they were able to "deliver the goods." The only two sources available were redistribution from the old elite, the "agro-export oligarchy" of cattle ranchers and coffee planters, and development, which in practice meant industrialization based on import substitution. Perón's policy of low internal purchase prices for beef and wheat provided the masses with cheap "bread," his wife Evita, of course, helped with the "circuses." The consequences were that the supply of exportables from the productive rural sector shrank drastically, while internal relative prices shifted in favor of the establishment of domestic industry. The intense nationalist fervor associated with the regime resulted in the use of substantial foreign exchange reserves for the nationalization with compensation of extensive public utilities, which also meant a reduced ability to deal with the inevitable balance of payments pressures of the "populist" program. This crisis finally led to the fall and exile of Perón in 1955.

In Brazil, Vargas, and after him Kubitschek, were much more pragmatic and less confrontational in their political style. Rather than sharply pitting one group against another, as Perón did with the urban masses and the agro-exporting interests, they attempted to forge cooperative alliances between all of the organized segments of the population. Economic performance, particularly in exports, thus was much better in Brazil than in Argentina. The supply of coffee and other agricultural exports was not sharply cut, since there was some attempt to maintain price incentives. The state also generally seems to have put more into the industrialization drive with massive investments in social overhead, steel, and other "heavy industry" sectors. The presence of an elastic labor supply from the large subsistence or traditional sector also helped. As several commentators have noted, Brazil fits well into the Veblen–Gerschenkron model of a "great spurt," with the state playing an active promotional role in the development process, albeit in conjunction with local entrepreneurs and multinationals (Veblen, 1915; Gerschenkron, 1962).

Latin American development has tended to be marked by "cycles," in which a boom in investment and employment is started, with rising real wages and consumption, and industrialization stimulated by a regime that discriminates against exports. The inevitable balance-of-payments crisis then requires a period of austerity, with the International Monetary Fund (IMF) supervising the swallowing of the bitter medicine. The populist leader goes off into exile, waits in the wings, or is sometimes even killed, as in the tragic case of Salvador Allende in 1973.

A period of "liberalization" in economics, necessary to restore some semblance of sanity to the structure of relative prices, unfortunately is usually accompanied in the political field by its exact opposite – "repression," under the auspices of a military junta. "Close the polity in order to open the economy" seems to be the motto during this phase. The generals get the job done, go back reluctantly to the barracks, the populists return and the whole cycle starts again. In Brazil, the cycles seem to have been around a sharply rising trend in GNP per capita, exports and other relevant variables; whereas in Argentina, the end result simply seems to have been stagnation. Brazil's per capita GNP was one-third of Argentina's in 1945. It is approximately equal to it today. The performance of the other major Latin American economies lies between the limits of Brazil at one end and Argentina at the other (see Stepan (ed.), 1973, for several excellent essays on the political economy of Brazil).

How is the "import-substitution syndrome" to be accounted for? One approach in line with Keynes's famous quote, is to stress the influence of ideas of some particular "defunct economist," from whose thoughts a "madman in authority...distills his frenzy." Vittorio Corbo's very interesting paper at this conference follows such an approach, associating the ideas of Raúl Prebisch and ECLA with various phases of import substitution, and of Olivera Campos and others with orthodox approaches to economic policy. My own view is that ideas *per se* are not the exogenous force that Keynes makes them out to be. I prefer to proceed from "interests," with particular groups or leaders selecting those ideas that serve them best from the "menu" currently available. Thus, I do not believe that any amount of lectures on neoclassical economics will induce protectionists to see the errors of their ways and to reform.

But how do we go from particular interests to protection, which must of necessity be a national policy? One possible model is to conceive of the state as an inert "black box" that can, however, be prodded into doing something for a particular interest – for example, setting a tariff, if enough resources are devoted to influencing it in that direction by the concerned parties. Other groups may, of course, wish to block this, which they can if they in turn are prepared to spend enough on lobbying activities. This process can be modeled *à la* Cournot, with each group making the optimal political input for itself (given what the other is doing) with equilibrium established at the tariff level corresponding to political inputs by each faction, given by the intersection of their respective "reaction functions." This is the approach taken in Findlay and Wellisz (1982). The model presupposes a "democratic pluralist" parliamentary regime of the Anglo-Saxon type, in which state action is simply the resultant of the pushes and pulls of the particular interest groups.

By contrast, the tradition not only in Latin America but throughout the developing world is for a strong executive – heir to the all-powerful colonial governors and viceroys of the past – with control augmented by the communications technology of the twentieth century. Thus, instead of a Madisonian struggle between factions within well-defined rules of the game involving checks and balances, we have a case of the "autonomy of the state," a situation in which the "ruler" is to a large extent able to implement his own "agenda" of action, constrained only by the availability of domestic and external resources.

The "autonomy of the state" need not be a mere piece of Hegelian mysticism. After all, Hegel himself had the perfectly concrete nineteenth-century Prussian state in mind, in which the king could exercise almost absolute power, with the bureaucracy as a "universal class" suspended above the petty concerns of "civil society." (See Avineri, 1972, for a very informative discussion. The famous analysis of the "Eighteenth Brumaire of Louis Napoleon" by Marx seems to have owed much to Hegel.)

It is not surprising that several Latin American social scientists have put forward a model of the "bureaucratic-authoritarian" state reminiscent of this Hegelian one, with a faceless junta instead of an individual "strong man" at the apex of the pyramid, exercising power through, and in the interest of, the military and civilian bureaucracy itself. (See Collier, 1979, for several very interesting papers on this topic, inspired by the writings of the Argentine political scientist Guillem O'Donnell.) The self-imposed tasks of the regime are "national security," with its concomitant of "internal order," and "development," which serves both as an end in itself and, if successful, as a means to further expansion of the role of the state, and therefore, of the bureaucracy itself. The Parkinson–Niskanen model of departmental or corporate bureaucracy can be applied to the state as a whole to produce the concept of a particular type of "Leviathan," a Frankenstein monster in which the entities such as army and civil service, ostensibly created to serve the "people's will," instead arrogate to themselves the task of defining the goals of the state, which they make to coincide with their own. (See Brennan and Buchanan, 1980, and Findlay and Wilson, 1984, for models of the Leviathan. Lal, 1984, is a broader analysis in a similar vein.)

The only constraint on the Leviathan's appetite for the pursuit of what it sees as its "tasks" is revenue. Given the well-known difficulties attendant upon collection of corporate and personal income and other direct taxes in developing countries, particularly in Latin America, one is left largely with taxes of one sort or another on foreign trade, and of course, the inflation tax. The stubborn persistence of inflationary cycles in the Latin American context is proof that the process is driven by something more deep-seated than governmental ignorance of the quantity theory of money. Indeed, it may be that a "rational" government will systematically use the inflationary tax to fleece its own populace. Once powerful inflationary forces have been generated it is almost impossible to prevent them from distorting the structure of relative prices. If adjustment of the exchange rate tends to lag, as it generally does, a bias is introduced against tradeable goods. Quantitative import restrictions imposed to stem the loss of foreign exchange reserves tilt relative prices against exportables within the tradeable sector itelf. Combined with high maximum revenue tariffs and export taxes, also imposed to satisfy the Leviathan's appetite for revenue, the outcome can be very heavy discrimination against exports, in short the "import-substitution syndrome," which thus appears in this analysis as a byproduct of the revenue- or expenditure-maximizing activities of the Leviathan. This approach is spelled out more fully in Wellisz and Findlay (1984).

Urban manufacturing interests would of course be delighted with this outcome, since it provides the market incentive for investment and profits on their part. Since the resultant structure of industrialization is likely to be haphazard, leaving all sorts of gaps, there are likely to be calls for "coordination," "rationalization," "deepening," etc. The end result of all this is, of course, that there are more "tasks" for the bureaucracy to perform – and so on, and so on, and so on. Democratic reformers, who complain that various sections of the masses are being impoverished, may also have their criticisms answered by yet more distortionary schemes, ostensibly designed to protect the living standards of the poor and deprived, but in reality further reducing real national income.

The military is always a key component of the bureaucracy and, for a number of obvious reasons, its influence will be to encourage the more extravagant aspects of the import-substitution syndrome. For one thing, there is the "national defense" argument for self-sufficiency in armaments, which leads to the demand for domestic production of the necessary metallurgical and chemical inputs. Military intellectuals and staff officers also tend to be fascinated with technology for its own sake, regardless of the humdrum economic criterion of cost-effectiveness.

Foreign multinationals are usually the only source of the technology and capital that such an ambitious agenda requires. Consequently the "triple alliance" between the state and local and foreign capital, which writers such as Evans (1979) have noted, is readily explicable in these terms. Ironically, radical writers such as Cardoso and Faletto (1979) tend to be more approving of direct foreign investment when it is directed toward production for the domestic market than the earlier pattern of orientation towards the export enclaves. The neoclassical analysis of Brecher and Díaz-Alejandro (1977) and Brecher and Findlay (1983), shows that the latter enhances national welfare while the former *reduces* it – if induced by protection, as it almost always is.

THE NEWLY INDUSTRIALIZING COUNTRIES

One of the most remarkable aspects of the stormy decade of the 1970s was the rise to prominence of the so-called "newly industrializing countries," NICs. This label has been attached to the celebrated East Asian "gang of four" – South Korea, Taiwan, Hong Kong, and Singapore – as well as Brazil, Mexico, and some other countries in Latin America, Southern Europe, and Asia. The elite members of the club, on the basis of levels and growth rates of *manufactured* exports, are clearly the Asian Four and Brazil. The experience of these countries has aroused very extensive debate, not only on the reasons for their obvious success, but on the implications for broader questions related to the relative role of the state and markets in the process of development and of "inward" versus "outward" orientation in development strategy.

Both sides of these debates seem to have shared a false premise – that the roles of "state" and "markets" (particularly the world market for tradeable goods and factor services), are necessarily inversely related. Except for Hong Kong, however, the experience of all the NICs has been marked not only by strong reliance on world market forces, but also by very far reaching and pervasive intervention and control by the state in almost all segments of the economy. Gunnar Myrdal's famous characterization of India as a "soft" state would certainly not apply to South Korea, Taiwan, Singapore, or Brazil.

Korea, Taiwan, and Brazil all initially followed the import-substitution path that we have discussed in the last section. In the case of Korea and Taiwan, the change in the orientation of development strategy occurred in the early sixties. In neither case was there any alteration in the nature of the political regime, the military being firmly in power already. In Korea, however, there does seem to have been a tightening of the severity of military control over the society under General Park, who took power in 1963 and presided over the most spectacular phase of export-oriented development until his assassination in 1979.

In Brazil the turning point was 1964, when the populist regime of Goulart was overthrown by the military. The period 1964 to 1967 was devoted to reducing inflation and getting the balance of payments under control, a task that was accomplished by the orthodox economist Roberto Campos. Controlling the rate at which nominal wages were adjusted brought inflation down while redistributing income from wages to profits and government revenue. Needless to say, the power of the state was an essential element in the ability to accomplish this. From 1968 to 1973 there was a big spurt in exports and GNP, with a policy of automatic mini-devaluations and other measures providing the market incentive. A big influx of foreign capital also took place. The oil shocks did cause setbacks in the seventies, but growth of GNP per capita was at the impressive rate of 5 percent per annum from 1965 to 1983, with exports growing at about the same rate. Another economist, Delfim-Netto, presided over most of this era.

Despite the apparent shift from populism to sternly authoritarian military rule, students of Brazilian politics point to the essential institutional continuity of the Brazilian state from the 1930s under Vargas to the present. (See chapters by T. Skidmore and P. Schmitters in Stephan (ed.), 1973.) The polity is organized "from above" along the lines of the bureaucratic Leviathan that we have outlined, with social classes and interest groups co-opted into the system on "corporatist" lines rather than competing freely in the political arena. In spite of the large differences in location, history, culture, and size, all three of these countries thus conformed broadly to the same bureaucratic-authoritarian or Leviathan pattern.

In each of these cases the shift from import substitution to export promotion took place as a policy shift within an essentially unchanged political regime. There was no shift in power from classes or factions with a stake in import substitution to those with a stake in export promotion as, for example, in the case of landowners and capitalists in nineteenth-century Britain.

How can we then account for such a drastic reorientation of trade and development strategy from "inward" to "outward" orientation in political economy terms? It seems that the answer lies in the perception of the Leviathan that its organic interest in *autonomy* is better served by the latter policy. Attempting rapid growth with import substitution is a policy that is bound to founder on the eventual shortage of foreign exchange, a condition that this particular development strategy is ostensibly designed to alleviate. As is well known, requirements for intermediate imports and capital goods tend to rise faster than any replacement of final goods imports by domestic production. The squeeze that the strategy places on exports means a country must resort to foreign aid or borrowing. This in turn eventually causes further outflows due to interest payments, with dim prospects of repayment because of the poor export performance. Eventually the IMF has to come in with all the attendant humiliations for the regime. Why not, instead, try to ride the world trade boom of the sixties and early seventies, with rapid growth in the open markets of the United States, Japan, and Western Europe? Even after the oil shock, the prosperous OPEC countries provided another lucrative market.

Everything could remain as before in terms of control over the economy and polity. The role of the bureaucracy is preserved – perhaps even enhanced – with success in world markets, instead of domestic markets being the criteria for the technocrats and the domestic business sector to follow. True the requirements for capital goods and imported intermediates might still outpace even the rapid growth of exports. But borrowing could now be resorted to with an assurance of better terms and more elastic supply, as a result of favorable ratios of debt services to exports. The top echelons of the state have even more patronage and influence to disburse, in terms of which domestic sectors or firms are to obtain government guaranteed international loans and which foreign firms are to get what contracts and concessions. Rents from some of the existing trade distortions, such as import licenses for restricted items, could be used as incentives for exporters. The same pool of entrepreneurs and skilled workers could be switched into activities where they could earn more foreign exchange, doing better for themselves while enhancing the ability of the economy to accelerate growth on an autonomous footing, due to the easing of the external resource constraint. Diversification of export markets and supply sources ensures that increased participation in the world economy, measured by higher trade ratios, implies less dependency and more autonomy, contrary to *dependista* dogma. (See discussion on Korea by Haggard and Moon in Ruggie (ed.), 1983.)

This is not to say, however, that the success of these NICs is evidence that they must be following classical liberal principles of *laissez-faire*. The government intervenes massively on both sides of the savings–investment nexus and even the trade and payments regime is not free from extensive intervention, particularly in the larger countries such as Brazil and Korea. Emphasis on exports as such, which is what these systems tend to stress, is after all, a *mercantilist* and not a liberal objective. Selling TV sets domestically at several times the world price in order to swell the volume of exports, for example, is not something that one would find recommended in the writings of James Meade or Harry Johnson. It is sometimes said that the pro-export bias simply cancels out the previous biases in the opposite direction, so that the net effect is close to free trade. One should be suspicious of such confident assertions of Pareto-optimality by inadvertence. Why not then dismantle everything and make life easier for everybody? To simply ask the question is to realize that there must be powerful vested interests involved for which the outcome will not be neutral.

The relationship between import-substitution and export-oriented development on the basis of comparative advantage also is not as mutually exclusive as it appears in simple static models. Today's bad investments can become tomorrow's "sunk costs," leading to the possibility that projects or sectors whose existence could not have been justified *ex ante* might become so *ex post*.

Brazil today exports over $3 billion worth of cars and trucks, and low wages and an extensive network of parts and component suppliers give it very strong potential comparative advantage in this field for decades to come, if it is not dissipated by policy errors. Yet this base would not exist in its present form were it not for the legacy of some very costly episodes of import substitution in this area. Korea's difficulties with strategic heavy industries in the late 1970s similarly may have laid the basis for upgrading her export pattern into product lines where economies of scale and quality are of paramount concern, as in automobiles. The experience of Japan also points in a similar direction, of a period of learning behind some form of at least implicit protection. The evidence is ample that protection is not *sufficient* for successful industrialization in more technologically complex and capital-intensive lines, but the argument that it is not *necessary* seems to be largely an a priori one, in view of the fact that most historical examples from Germany and the United States to Japan have involved protection.

Perhaps the most difficult and contentious issue associated with the NICs is the relationship between their economic success and their authoritarian domestic politics. Once again it is obvious that authoritarianism is not sufficient to explain their success, since there are so many cases of dictatorships that are economic disasters. The real question is not sufficiency but necessity. The internal autonomy of these "bureaucratic authoritarian" Leviathans has meant that they have been able to overcome internal resistance to "rational" economic policies, for example, such cases as the Brazilian stabilization of the mid-sixties, the withdrawal of price supports for coffee producers, lowering of the minimum scale of direct foreign investment against the opposition of small business in Korea, and many other instances. Most important of all is some assurance to domestic and foreign firms that the outward orientation is a lasting commitment of the government that will not be eroded by domestic pressures in the other direction, such as is now occurring in Brazil under its first democratic presidency in more than 20 years. It is very difficult, if not impossible, to imagine a genuinely democratic regime that can insulate itself from domestic pressure groups to the extent necessary, even if the outward-looking strategy is to everyone's best interest in the long run.

REFERENCES

Anderson, P. 1974: *Lineages of the Absolutist State*. London: New Left Books.

Avineri, S. 1972: *Hegel's Theory of the Modern State*. Cambridge and New York: Cambridge University Press.

Bates, R. 1972: *Markets and the State In Tropical Africa*. Berkeley, California: University of California Press.

Brecher, R. and Díaz-Alejandro, C. F. 1977: "Tariffs, Foreign Capital and Immiserizing Growth." *Journal of International Economics*, 7, 317–22.

Brecher, R. and Findlay, R. 1983: "Tariffs, Foreign Capital and National Welfare." *Journal of International Economics*, 14, 277–88.

Brennan, G. and Buchanan, J. 1980: *The Power to Tax*. Cambridge and New York: Cambridge University Press.

Cardoso, F. H. and Faletto, E. 1979: *Dependency and Development in Latin America*. Berkeley, California: University of California Press.

Collier, D. (ed.) 1979: *The New Authoritarianism in Latin America*. Princeton, New Jersey: Princeton University Press.

Díaz-Alejandro, C. F. 1984: "No Less Than One Hundred Years of Argentine Economic History Plus Some Comparisons." In G. Ranis et al. (eds), *Comparative Development Perspectives*, Boulder, Colorado: Westview.

Erlich, A. 1960: *The Soviet Industrialization Debate*. Cambridge, Mass.: Harvard University Press.

Evans, P. 1979: *Dependent Development*. Princeton, New Jersey: Princeton University Press.

Findlay, R. 1973: *International Trade and Development Theory*. New York: Columbia University Press.

Findlay, R. 1974: "Relative Prices, Growth and Trade in a Simple Ricardian System." *Economica*, Feb. 1974.

Findlay, R. and Wellisz, S. 1982: "Endogenous Tariffs, the Political Economy of Trade Restrictions and Welfare." In J. N. Bhagwati (ed.), *Import Competition and Response*. Chicago: University of Chicago Press.

Findlay, R. and Wilson, J. D. 1984: "The Political Economy of Leviathan." Mimeo.

Gerschenkron, A. 1962: *Economic Backwardness in Historical Perspective*. Cambridge, Mass.: Harvard University Press.

Haggard, S. and Moon, C. 1983: "The South Korean State in the International Economy: Liberal, Dependent, or Mercantile?" In J. Ruggie (ed.), *The Antinomies of Interdependence*. New York: Columbia University Press.

Hirschman, A. O. 1971: *A Bias for Hope*. New Haven: Yale University Press.

Hirschman, A. O. 1981: *Essays in Trespassing*. Cambridge and New York: Cambridge University Press.

Keohane, R. O. 1983: "Associative American Development, 1776–1860: Economic Growth and Political Disintegration." In J. G. Ruggie (ed.), *Antinomies of Interdependence*. New York: Columbia University Press.

Lal, D. 1984: "The Political Economy of the Predatory State." Mimeo.

Moore, B. 1966: *Social Origins of Dictatorship and Democracy*. Boston, Mass.: Beacon Press.

Postan, M. M. 1973: "Economic Relations Between Eastern and Western Europe." In *Medieval Trade and Finance*. Cambridge and New York: Cambridge University Press.

Reynolds, L. G. 1985: *Economic Growth in the Third World, 1850–1980*. New Haven and London: Yale University Press.

Ruggie, J. G. (ed.) 1983: *Antinomies of Interdependence*. New York: Columbia University Press.

Schmitter, P. 1973: "The 'Portugalization' of Brazil." In A. Stepan (ed.), *Authoritarian Brazil*. New Haven and London: Yale University Press.

Skidmore, T. 1973: "Politics and Economic Policy Making in Authoritarian Brazil, 1937–71." In A. Stepan (ed.), *Authoritarian Brazil*. New Haven and London: Yale University Press.

Smith, P. H. 1978: "The Breakdown of Democracy in Argentina 1916–1930." In J. Linz and A. Stepan (eds.), *The Breakdown of Democratic Regimens: Latin America*. Baltimore, Maryland: Johns Hopkins University Press.

Stepan, A. (ed.) 1973: *Authoritarian Brazil*. New Haven and London: Yale University Press.

Veblen, T. 1915: *Imperial Germany and the Industrial Revolution*. London: Macmillan.

Wallerstein, I. 1979: "Three Paths of National Development in 16th Century Europe." In *The Capitalist World-Economy.* Cambridge and New York: Cambridge University Press.

Wellisz, S. and Findlay, R. 1984: "Protection and Rent-Seeking in Developing Countries." In D. C. Colander (ed.), *Neoclassical Political Economy,* Ballinger.

Wynia, G. W. 1984: *The Politics of Latin American Development.* Cambridge University Press.

Comments on
"Trade, Development, and the State"

I. M. D. LITTLE

I welcome Ronald Findlay's exploration of some of "the subtle and recalcitrant issues involved in the mutual interactions of trade, development and the state...." (p. 79).

He first explores the long-run influence on both economic and political development of trading in accordance with apparent comparative advantage. I have no quarrel with his finding that when comparative advantage lies with the export of primary products, and title to these products or the land that produces them is highly concentrated, then political development towards democracy may be inhibited – as it evidently was in Latin America and Eastern Europe (and probably would have been in the United States if the South had won). In contrast, England became "progressive" after the repeal of the Corn Laws and the resultant stimulus to further industrialization. It is, perhaps, less clear that growth is inhibited by concentrating on primary exports, despite Ricardo's view that industrial capitalists were frugal and landlords spendthrift.

Of course, it is not agriculture or mining as such that is antidemocratic. The argument depends on a prior inequality of asset ownership. Where, as in parts of Africa and much of Southeast and East Asia, land ownership is relatively equal and farming is more the province of peasants than an aristocratic oligarchy, there is no ground for associating primary product exports with a lack of political participation; and Findlay rightly laments the fact that most governments in these areas have gone far towards killing the golden goose by exploiting agriculture in favor of urban beneficiaries and in the pursuit of statist aims. One must also remark that rapid industrialization is no royal road to democracy, as South Korea and Taiwan have made clear, and as also emerges from Findlay's second exploration, that of the socio-political framework of industrialization based on import substitution.

Industrialization via import substitution has created a large urban industrial labor force in most Latin American countries. But the resultant political development has differed greatly from that of the older industrialized countries. An economic restructuring supposedly favorable to the development of democratic institutions instead resulted in the "populism" that has been typical of Latin America, permitting the retention of economic power in the hands of charismatic leaders, until their excesses result in economic breakdown and the arrival of the generals who, according to Findlay, "restore some...sanity to relative prices" (p. 87) before reluctantly retiring to barracks. Findlay does not discuss why they retire. Perhaps they find that the costs of buying the support that even they need is so great that there is little surplus left to satisfy their own objectives, and governing ceases to be fun.

Findlay also asks what accounted for the import-substitution syndrome. He discounts the role of the Economic Commission for Latin America (ECLA), declaring his belief, *pace* Keynes, in the dominant role of interests rather than ideas (Vittorio Corbo's paper at this symposium leans the other way). But how to go from particular interests to a national policy of industrial protection? In the OECD countries, this has tended to result from the cumulative appeasement of sectoral interests. Not so in Latin America. Here Findlay introduces the "Bureaucratic-authoritarian" state, an appealing Latin American concept. As I understand it, "authoritarian" implies that the state has its own objectives independent of the welfare of the citizens,[1] while "bureaucratic" implies that the bureaucracy is to a large extent both ruler and beneficiary, and not purely an instrument. There is no longer a clear distinction between the sovereign and the laws and institutions, including the military, that constitute the state.[2] We have, as Findlay says, "a Frankenstein monster in which the entities such as army and civil service, ostensibly created to serve the 'people's will,' instead arrogate to themselves the task of defining the goals of the state, which they make to coincide with their own" (p. 88). Their self-imposed tasks expand, and the urge to spend explains import substitution, via inflation, balance-of-payments crises, and quantitative trade restrictions; and via trade, taxes to raise revenue. The "need" of the military for domestic production of guns and gunpowder is an additional cause. The resultant economic disarray further increases the tasks of the bureaucracy.

While this is a persuasive story, I do not think that ideas can be dismissed altogether. It must be a comfort for the Leviathan to find professional economists forcibly arguing that policies adopted in pursuit of its own interests are also in the best interests of the mass of the people. We do not need to see ideas either as the driving force or as superficial floss. In alliance with interests they are supportive; and since there are usually competing interests, they may surely influence the outcome.

Findlay's third exploration discusses the role of the state in the NICs, or more precisely in the "gang of four" and Brazil. Apart from Hong Kong, all conform to the authoritarian-bureaucratic mold featuring fairly massive intervention, and all switched to more outward-looking policies between the late 1950s and mid-1960s. These switches, he says, did not come about as a result of any shift in the power or influence of particular interest groups. The political setup was essentially unchanged. So he explains it in terms of the Leviathan coming to see that import substitution soon inevitably lost its driving force for growth, and not only failed to reduce extensive dependence, but even increased it.

I have more doubts about this exploration than the others. First, it is awkward to explain both the onset of import-substitution policies, and then the (partial) revulsion from them in terms merely of the Leviathan's changing perceptions of its interests. Why in particular did so many other authoritarian countries fail to perceive that import substitution was failing and take action, and why was Brazil's conversion so much less thorough than that of South Korea, Taiwan, or Singapore? Perhaps one needs to appeal to ideas. After all, the Leviathan must change its view about how the economy would work when more open to the outside world. There is evidence that ideas working through a few key personalities were important in Taiwan, which was the first to see the disadvantages of import-substitution policies and to change.[3]

Secondly, although there was, as Findlay says, no great shift in the power or influence of particular interest groups, nevertheless interests were less unfavorable to increased export orientation than is now the case in many other countries. The older import-substitution industries which could not compete in world markets mostly belonged to Leviathan himself, while the newer ones started in the 1950s were of the light "primary import-substitution" type which might more easily turn to exports (rather similarly in Korea, the older heavy industries were in the North).

Thirdly, I would question the extent to which the bureaucratic-authoritarian model, which Findlay associates with a massive role for the state in industrialization, applies without much qualification to South Korea, Taiwan, and Singapore. It certainly applies less in Taiwan than the others. My own interpretation of Taiwan's success is different from Findlay's (see Little in Galinson, *op. cit.*). And in Korea it can be argued that success occurred despite the state's direct intervention in the pattern of industrialization. It was not the "cars" of steel, shipbuilding, petrochemicals, or the "pony" car that drove the economy; such intervention occurs much less in Taiwan which, I believe, has the edge over South Korea in terms of performance when growth equity and stability are taken into account. Nor should one forget Hong Kong's performance, where there has been no intervention.

In conclusion, I think Findlay has written a bold and most interesting essay in "trespassing." But it is, I am sure he would agree, an early effort in a growing area of interest in comparative political economy on the part of economists of all persuasions. I hope his concluding sentence, to the effect that true democracy and an open economy are irreconcilable in the developing world, may yet prove to be pessimistic.

NOTES

[1] In another paper, "The Political Economy of Leviathan," Ronald Findlay and John D. Wilson point out that the citizens may be better off in a predatory state than in the state of nature, and explore the welfare consequences in a model where the state both provides law and order while also maximizing its own objective function.

[2] In a recent book (*The State*: Basil Blackwell, 1985), A. E. de Jesay explores in depth the consequences of assuming that the state has a will of its own.

[3] See Maurice Scott (chapter 5) and Ian M. D. Little (chapter 7) in Walter Galinson (ed.), *Economic Growth and Structural Change in Taiwan*, Cornell University Press, 1979.

5

Development Economics: What Next?

GUSTAV RANIS and JOHN C. H. FEI

INTRODUCTION

In recent years the profession seems to have yielded an extraordinary outpouring of agonizing reappraisals and laments about the state of development economics, remarkable for even this difficult branch of our dismal science. The funereal orations range from Deepak Lal's diatribe,[1] which disputes the very legitimacy of the field, to Ian Little,[2] who sees it as a legitimate branch of pure applied microeconomics, to Albert Hirschman,[3] who thinks we have self-destructed en route to monotheism. In between – as usual – some more modest voices, such as Henry Bruton's[4] and Paul Streeten's[5] can be heard who, while not in unison, urge us to hang on to both the baby and most of the bath water.

It is not entirely clear whether this period of self-flagellation has its cause in some specific, identifiable illness – e.g. that we have not experienced any major analytical breakthrough in recent years, or that we have simply been infected by the depressed state of economics in general, or that of all manner of North–South relations. Admittedly the bloom is off the rose and both our theoretical and applied hurdles in the 1980s and 1990s are likely to tower above those of the 1950s and 1960s. Nevertheless, I believe a case can be made, without risk of polyannaism, for the claim that substantial, if not spectacular, advances have indeed been made over the past decade. And, perhaps as meaningful for the vitality of the subdiscipline, a promising research and policy agenda for the future has been established.

After all, we have learned a great deal about the ingredients of success in development. We are now universally convinced, and have convinced policy-makers, about the responsiveness of peasants at the micro level and about the importance of the role of the agricultural sector at the macro level; about the importance of technology choices and alternative directions of technology change; about the importance of initial typological differences among developing countries in affecting the chances of a successful transition to modern growth; and about the overall importance of policies emphasizing workable competitiveness in domestic markets and openness in foreign markets, as opposed to resource-oriented planning models.

We vigorously concur, therefore, with those who believe that reports of the death of development economics have been greatly exaggerated. That does not mean that we should not recognize or be concerned that we may be in the diminishing-returns range of the major advances of the early postwar era. And each of us undoubtedly has his or her own idea of how the intellectual production function in development economics will once again be shifted. In this paper, we present one candidate for such a possible shift.

THE POLITICAL ECONOMY OF POLICY CHANGE

Beyond comparative statics

Kuznets's seminal contribution on modern economic growth[6] focused on the speed of per capita income change and on the importance of technology, structural change, and the diffusion of growth across regions and borders once a system has reached the "promised land." Kuznets also described the pre-modern growth era of agrarianism, in which most of the world found itself before the middle of the eighteenth century. But, while providing many insights and hints, he essentially stopped short of examining the nature of the transition from one epoch to the next and the reasons for success or failure in different contexts.

For the contemporary LDCs, the postwar era (1950–85) represents a unique period of attempted transition from colonial agrarianism towards what Professor Kuznets refers to as the epoch of modern economic growth, emulating the long-run historical experience of the now developed countries. The relatively short-run nature of this transition effort raises issues in economic theory, organization, and policy quite different from those embedded within the long-run analysis emphasized by Kuznets. To the LDCs, this transition represents an extremely growth-conscious period[7] during which macroeconomic policy instruments (the money supply, the interest rate, the foreign exchange rate, domestic taxes, import and export duties) were used to promote growth. As a result, their imperfect markets, which had been focused on colonial objectives, were penetrated by the political forces of nationalism, reflecting a "political will" dedicated to growth promotion and contrasting rather sharply with the early postwar policy aim of the developed countries.[8]

Considerable work has, of course, been done by Kuznets himself, as well as by Chenery, Bhagwati, Krueger, Fei and Ranis, Balassa,[9] and others, in describing the way an LDC typically changes it structure as it moves into modern growth. Of necessity, much of this work was initially cross-sectional in nature but has in recent years increasingly utilized the rich, newly available, laboratory of postwar time-series data on individual (or groups of) developing countries. In this effort Chenery and his associates, for instance, have moved toward the pooling of time-series and cross-sectional data for subfamilies of LDCs; Bhagwati, Krueger, and Balassa et al. have conducted extensive country comparisons in the Little, Scitovsky and Scott tradition;[10] and Fei and Ranis have turned to comparing the historical experience of members of one subfamily (e.g. South Korea and Taiwan) with each other, as well as with members of other subfamilies (e.g. Colombia and Brazil). The objective of most of these efforts has been, on the one hand, to describe a variety of sectoral and aggregative dimensions of performance and to link these more or less casually to initial conditions; and, on the other, to relate policy to bottom-line success or failure in reaching underlying development objectives.

Policy choice

The role played by organizational or policy choices in this analytical context has varied considerably. Kuznets preferred to think of policies as either obstructing or accommodating the natural evolution of a system over time, but he essentially excluded policy formulation from his descriptive canvas. Chenery and associates, however, built policy choices into the very typology they constructed (e.g. see their division into "outer-oriented" and "inner-oriented" systems). Fei and Ranis focused on subphases of transition and described the differential evolution of policy choices along the way as crucial to differential performance. And World Bank economists like Corbo and Edwards, following Anne Krueger's lead, have examined the sequential policy experience of Southern Cone countries in recent years.[11] The common denominator of most of these efforts – and we have by no means enumerated more than a subset – resides in the recognition, implicit if not explicit, that organizational and policy choices are basic to the explanation of developmental success and failure. For example, it is now more widely accepted, though by no means universally, that increased openness and reduced government intervention are generally associated with improved development performance. The role of the pursuit of rents has opened up an important related area of inquiry.[12] But what still has eluded observers and constitutes an important field for investigation is just how to endogenize policy change over time. Different LDC societies have clearly made substantially different policy choices in the course of their effort to achieve modern growth. Such choices have either been simply described as fortunate or (less fortunate) *deus ex machina* events attributed loosely to superior or inferior states of cultural preparedness of the population, or, usually in the land of political scientists, linked to theories of the state and the role of interest groups. More and more frequently, both in academic studies of the development process and in efforts to undertake economic reforms and/or negotiate related conditions for assistance from the outside (currently under the label of overcoming the debt crisis), we have come up against our incapacity to understand just how different systems make their oganizational and policy choices in a decidedly non-random fashion. While all this is admittedly likely to prove a somewhat inexact science at best, it is increasingly becoming a consensus priority area for research at the macro level of development economics.

In this connection, it is good explicitly to recall two implicitly well-recognized facts. First, most LDCs start out as mixed economies marked by a substantial volume of government intrusion and control, partly as a reaction to prior colonial objective functions, market deployment, and resource allocation patterns, and partly to help create a unified national entity capable of starting on an import-substitution industrialization pattern in the first place. Second, the pattern followed by the developed countries in the epoch of modern growth is characterized, not only by the aforementioned statistically observable production, speed, and diffusion features *à la* Kuznets, but also by institutional and organizational features. That is to say, "mixed" developed countries, while they of course differ from each other, cover a spectrum exhibiting a much greater exposure to market forces than the equally substantial spectrum covered by post-independence LDCs. We may thus hypothesize the need to include policy convergence, i.e. the study of how societies organize themselves as they move into modern growth, in our analysis. Our understanding of how a society gets from here to there must include organizational and policy changes as just as integral a part of the story as statistically observed changes in economic structure and performance.

All the statistical evidence which can (and has been) brought to bear, clearly indicates that, of all the postwar LDCs, the newly industrializing countries of East Asia (i.e. the so-called "gang of four" – Taiwan, South Korea, Singapore, and Hong Kong) have registered by far the best development performance over the past 35 years. There exists, moreover, the general assessment, not only among academicians but also among practitioners such as the World Bank, the IMF, etc., that this success mainly was due to these systems' more pronounced external orientation and their greater overall willingness to subject themselves to the competitive discipline of the market. This in turn suggests that a trend towards the liberalization of various markets has helped to fundamentally transform the systems of this small group of countries and made them relatively more "successful," i.e. has instilled in them a flexibility, a sensitivity to technology change, and an ability to adjust to shocks, which is the hallmark of the industrially advanced market economy. Successful LDCs, in other words, seem to converge toward the pattern of organizational choice as well as production characteristics of the "mixed" developed economy type.

In other more typical parts of the developing world, including Latin America, Africa, and other parts of Asia, we have been witness to a somewhat different, less clear-cut, and more oscillatory pattern of organizational choice, with market-oriented episodes replaced by a return to import-substitution policies in a more or less continuous fashion and accompanied by generally less successful outcomes in terms of the statistical record of economic performance.

It is a challenge for development economics to try to understand the fundamental causes of this divergent pattern. In that sense, it is necessary to proceed beyond a description of divergent growth performances and towards the generation of a comparative, typologically sensitive, development perspective which includes the evolution of organizational and policy changes as part of the explanatory framework. In other words, it is time to proceed beyond the effort to quantify "average" LDC economic structure over time and explain deviations from that average in a rather *ad hoc* fashion. Instead, we must endeavor to answer the question of why, in a minority of cases (e.g. East Asia), a conformable evolution of policy resulted, by and large, in the linearity of policy change, while in the majority of cases (e.g. Latin America), we have been witness to inconsistency and oscillation in spite of the profusion of advice offered by the profession and the international donor community. To explain this divergence in the choice and sequencing of organizational and policy changes largely on the basis of intrinsic cultural differences or other "special case" dimensions challenges the power of positive economics as applied to development; moreover, it is undoubtedly factually incorrect.

Instead, it is more likely that the bulk of the explanation for the observed divergence of performance must be found in a combination of the initial, marked, typological differences among developing countries, when the curtain rises, and in various political and economic forces which shape the adoption or rejection of different institutional changes and policy mixes over time. It is fair to start with the assumption that all LDCs initiate their transition growth efforts with strong political forces penetrating their mixed economies. The subsequent deviation between monotonicity and oscillation, en route to the convergence of both economic and policy structures in the mature economy, can be explained by a combination of initial typological differences and alternative ways in which the political economy of policy change plays itself out over time. Since policy change is clearly achieved through a political process, such research must go beyond the normal confines of economic analysis, including an investigation of the political economy of policy change. It should be recalled that such considerations represented an essential component of classical economics and were artificially excised from consideration only by the neoclassical school after the last quarter of the nineteenth century.

Given the record of almost four decades of postwar development efforts behind us, we are now in a position to examine LDC policy evolution in a fashion which is complementary rather than antithetical to the empirically focused, policy-neutral analysis which we are accustomed to. While the search for any sort of economic determinism relating policy sequences and economic events would be highly inappropriate, such an effort clearly involves reasoning about both economic and political phenomena in order to understand the logical necessity of differential orderings of policy events, i.e. the timely adoption and/or abandonment of particular policy measures within the total matrix of the essential components of the liberalization trend. We are by no means in a position to present a deterministic model of such a complex set of relations and interrelations, but can only hope to demonstrate a methodology to be followed with the help of particular country cases.

Traditionally, policy analysis stresses the economic impact of various policy options, on, for example, employment, labor reallocation, the pattern of trade, growth and the distribution of income, without much reference to political arguments – including the processes of adoption and/or abandonment of policies within a particular political milieu. It stresses comparative statics, that is, the situation before and after some individual reform or package of reforms. But it has little to offer on the dynamics of getting from here to there and in what preferable sequence.

The research which we believe will have a substantial payoff must start out with a comparative typological perspective, in terms of important differences in the initial setting, and must base itself on at least three components to trace the evolution of a society over time: (1) development theory sensitive to different initial conditions: (2) evolutionary tracing of events, both in the economic performance sense and in terms of a focus on policy events over time; and (3) quantification of both of the above in the context of an effort to trace causal relations among them. Our fundamental hypothesis here is that major development policy instruments – e.g. the interest rate, the foreign exchange rate, the rate of protection, and the tax rate – must be interpreted as political instruments to promote growth through the transfer of income among social groups, that is, to manufacture profits for one class at the expense of others. In other words, once political force has penetrated the post-independence developing country, it is necessary to differentiate between the conventional "on the table" or overt revenue and expenditure-related policies of government, which focus on taxation and the provision of overheads, public goods and welfare, and the much more pervasive use of "under the table," i.e. indirect or implicit, income transfers among groups. In the context of a political process, such indirect transfers are usually sanctioned by the powerful need of governments (especially the newly independent) to try to solve current problems while putting aside the possibility of a social conflict arising later, i.e., with a time lag. One leading example of this is, of course, a policy of monetary expansion which seems to solve an unemployment problem today, but leads to inflation after a time lag, culminating in conflict among various constituent groups of the body politic. When the familiar macro-policy tools, including the foreign exchange rate and the interest rate, are interpreted as growth promoting political instruments to effect income transfers, the concrete meaning of liberalization becomes the gradual withdrawal of such political forces from the economic arena over time. Differentiating between the covert and overt types of policy then permits us to render the analysis more politically sensitive, as well as realistic. Shifting from the former to the latter clearly does not necessarily mean, it should be noted, a diminished role for government but merely a different role; its direct functions may actually increase with the continued process of liberalization, even as its implicit or indirect functions diminish.

Policy evolution

During the transition effort in the so-called "open dualistic" developing economies, the evolution of policy passed through well-recognized subphases, namely, an early import-substitution subphase (IS) and a later external-orientation subphase (EO), both of which can be defined in terms of certain observable statistical time series data.[13] Moreover, superimposed on the long-run trends of the speed of growth and structural change in the statistical tradition of Kuznets – with speed measured in per capita income terms and structural change in the sectoral allocation of the labor force – we note disturbances traced to externally originating fluctuations in the prices of primary products in world markets.[14] In the early IS subphase the LDCs, almost without exception, adopted an internally oriented policy as an essential component of their growth promotion strategy in which macro-policies were deployed to provide protection from these exogenous disturbances. During this period, policies (especially monetary policies) were used extensively to accommodate "deficit finance" and to assist private entrepreneurs by "manufacturing" profits on their behalf. A corrupted version of the "Keynesian" monetary approach lurks beneath the surface here, as policy practice seems to be based on the conviction that: (1) interest rates can be artificially repressed in order to generate profits for the private entrepreneurial class; and (2) government can acquire all the goods and services it needs from the market by "covert taxation without consent." Price inflation lightens the repayment burden of the entrepreneurs and "forces" the public to save.

To refer to this monetary approach of the LDCs as "Keynesian" is actually somewhat misleading since, for Keynes, an expansion of the money supply meant to create a "liquid asset" in the Cambridge tradition in order to meet the demand for liquidity. No such roundabout way of thinking is required in the typical LDCs where monetary expansion is a convenient way to create purchasing power, allowing the beneficiary (i.e. the government and/or the favored private entrepreneur) to "costlessly" acquire goods and services from the market. As long as money must be accepted involuntarily as a medium of exchange, this convenient method of finance can be practiced extensively, with an effectiveness quite similar to that of "counterfeiting." All such growth promotion tasks can be undertaken without difficulty as the government of a sovereign state has the power to monopolize the printing of money. All it takes is the political will to use this power persistently, giving the LDCs – and especially those of Latin America – a virtually perpetual inflationary bias.

The core thesis of this paper rests on two ideas. First, with the arrival of the EO phase, a "liberalization" process is likely to set in as the market mechanism which regulates the exchange behavior among economic actors is gradually depoliticized and perfected. This amounts to the gradual atrophying of the political will in the sense that Keynesian monetary activism is gradually abandoned.[15] The monetary policy which replaces it is based on the recognition that money (M) should serve principally as an internal medium of exchange, while the foreign exchange reserve stock (R) should serve as an external medium of exchange. The manipulation of these quantities as "purchasing power," amounting to the exercise of the monopoly powers of government to promote growth, is thus gradually eroded. The postwar policy experience seems to suggest that LDCs cannot afford the convenience of monetary management to promote growth with impunity any more than the DCs can indulge in the same for "aggregate demand management" to promote stability.

The gradual movement towards liberalization in some LDCs entails a change in thinking with respect to both fiscal and monetary matters. It represents a movement toward rationalism and a more mature nationalism and away from the notion that an all-powerful, newly independent government can "take care of everything." The movement also suggests that, to narrow budgetary gaps, the government should not shy away from the onerous task of seeking social compromises through "taxation with consent," and that private entrepreneurs should learn, as soon as possible, to earn their profits through competitive productive performances in internal and world markets, rather than via rent-seeking activities on the political stage. This movement, while still most pronounced in East Asia, seems to be gaining ascendancy elsewhere. In long-run historical perspective, it constitutes a natural organizational evolution, companion to the transition toward the epoch of modern economic growth. As the economy becomes increasingly complex, sooner or later the idea seems to surface that command by political forces is cumbersome and that economic decisions must be decentralized in order to achieve economic efficiency.[16]

The second component of this paper's basic thesis is that the above liberalization process may not be smooth and linear. In particular, in the natural-resources-abundant Latin American countries, the birth of liberal reform tends to be a slow, painful process, as the very existence and abundance of economic rent (in the production of the exported primary products) invites "rent-seeking" policies to enter the political stage.[17] The slow liberalization process is disturbed, moreover, by exogenous shocks – such as the fluctuations in the prices of primary products in world markets and the business cycle in the industrially advanced countries. The superimposition of cyclical fluctuations on the long-run liberalization trend clearly yields what appear to be periodic revivals of the earlier IS phase, with all its well-known observable symptoms.

One area in which liberalization has proved difficult to maintain is in the realm of international reserves and the exchange rate. In the LDCs, the monopoly of management of the foreign exchange reserves by political power is usually accompanied by the prohibition of private international financial transactions. The isolation of domestic interest rates from the international rate is a cornerstone of the government's pursuit of an independent, low-interest rate policy when combined with the printing of money.[18] Moreover, as discussed above, the periodic revival of IS policies is more likely to occur in the natural-resources-abundant Latin American countries than in the natural-resources-poor countries of East Asia. Under the condition of a centralized reserve system (i.e. with government monopoly on capital movements) and given the prospect that price inflation will continue for some time to come, the art of management of the foreign exchange rate and the stock of foreign exchange reserves becomes a critical issue. Clean and/or dirty floats in LDCs represent another aspect of the political economy, in view of the fact that when the LDC government is obsessed with its growth promotion responsibilities, the "affluence" of a large foreign exchange reserve stock tends to inflate the government's desire to spend. Business cycles and fluctuations of the reserve stock then trigger additional government economic policy changes in the same direction, exacerbating the initial movement.

Moreover, the usually politicized application of macro-policies in the LDCs differs from that of the DCs in that, especially during the IS phase, the government's political will penetrates the market system to determine, not only the over-all volume of aggregate demand, but even individual investment decisions governing resource allocation.[19] One manifestation of policy evolution during the EO phase is the atrophying of such "directional controls" as the economy becomes more complex, calling increasingly for a market solution to replace civil service discretion in determining resource allocations. The frequently encountered residue of directional controls (e.g. a government-sponsored joint venture with foreigners to produce cars) is likely to constitute "selective window dressing" that can do far less damage than the pervasive macro-policies that become more and more directionally neutral as a sheer evolutionary necessity.[20] In our view, in the years ahead LDC governments should redirect their attention to the macro-policies (money, interest and exchange rates) as a primary focus of LDC policy redesign.

To maintain the momentum for liberalization, a vexing issue is not *why*, in order to close the budget gap, a social consensus should be generated to support "taxation with consent," but *how*. For the natural-resource-abundant LDCs, the politics of tax reform involves the vested interests of at least three social groups: urban consumers, urban entrepreneurs, and spatially dispersed (small) family farmers, i.e. the non-elite in any policy matrix. All realistic tax reform proposals would have to proceed by stages. While consumers may have to bear the burden of tariff protection to subsidize entrepreneurs for a while, the latter must gradually learn to compete successfully, first with foreigners in foreign markets and subsequently in domestic markets. The urban classes as a whole must begin to learn to suffer pain so that more income and purchasing power can be made available to spatially dispersed farmers – so they also can participate fully in the transition process.

Unionism, conspicuous by its presence in Latin America and its relative absence in East Asia, represents another relevant political economy phenomenon. First of all, union unrest and strikes may be seen as a thermometer of social unrest traceable to the unevenness, for different social groups, of the impact of over-the-cycle price inflation. In most instances, social upheavals with union involvement are induced by monetary malpractice.[21] However, the political phenomenon of a differentiated wage structure in the natural-resources-abundant LDCs (i.e. a much higher union wage for a small minority of the labor elite) can be damaging to the cause of export diversification; the export of labor-intensive manufactured goods is effectively blocked, contributing to the persistence of unemployment. A tight monetary policy (at least a more modest pace of inflation) represents the most effective and equitable way of restraining labor unions at the present time.

While the initial politicization may be quite inevitable, both its extent and the speed and sequencing of subsequent liberalization may vary substantially across countries. In fact, it is our basic hypothesis that policy linearity occurs when the role of government does not atrophy but is changed from implicit to explicit actions; policy oscillation occurs when covert policies which are adopted for short-term political convenience sooner or later self-destruct because of the insufficiently anticipated, delayed, and adverse impact on some groups whose income is being transferred in the absence of a clear political consensus.

In other words, to explain the differential behavior of developing economies, we may focus on two particular issues which represent underlying hypotheses for future work – both relating to dimensions of the initial conditions of a particular developing society. The first concerns the extent of political intervention during the essentially inevitable, early import-substitution subphase, i.e., how severe and how prolonged the array of normal interventions is likely to be, based on the maturity of the initial nationalism the newly independent government can count on. It is no accident, for example, that relatively "soft states," those lacking at the outset a relatively homogeneous population focused on national development objectives, are likely to be much more concerned with artificially creating a unifying atmosphere, not only by promising much more as to what the government can accomplish through a series of interventions in various markets, but also by being much more vehement in their undervaluation of the benefits of participating in the international economy. In this setting of a "synthetic" nationalism, there seems to be a clearer need to claim that the all-powerful, newly independent government can "take care of everything" in situations where, in fact, it is able to take care of very little effectively.

Our second hypothesis deals with the evolution of policy in a linear versus an oscillating fashion at the end of the inevitable early import-substitution subphase, i.e. as the country enters its export-orientation subphase. We are quite convinced that the absence or presence of substantial natural resources becomes a critical element at that point in time in determining the political economy of policy change and, thus, of the evolution of the economy's development prospects over time. In other words, we believe that the periodic revival of import substitution in the Latin American type of developing country is much more likely to occur in a natural-resources-abundant setting than in the natural-resources-poor East Asian type. The ability to manage a gradual shift from covert to overt policies of resource transfer seems to be related inversely to the relative abundance of natural resources. In a later section, we hope to demonstrate how the evolution of policies in one East Asian system fits the case of relative policy linearity, based on the initial twin conditions of an organic nationalism and relative natural resources scarcity.

Liberalization trends and oscillations

Seen in long-term perspective, the evolution of the LDCs in the direction of modern economic growth tends to repeat the historical experience of the DCs in terms of indicators of structural change. This is equally true in the organizational sense, that is, we witness a general evolutionary trend from heavy direct market interference by LDC governments towards a gradual abandonment of that interference and a greater reliance on the market. Not untypically, an internally oriented IS (import-substitution) phase is followed by an EO (external-orientation) phase.[22]

Most postwar LDCs, given their high aspirations in the wake of political independence, were concerned with growth promotion directly via the use of macro-policies, as was typical in the IS phase. Accordingly, all the major policy instruments (e.g. the interest rate, the money supply, the foreign exchange rate, the rate of protection, the rate of government taxation) must be viewed as tools for such direct growth-oriented activism by government. A basic principle that underlies growth promotion is the implementation of an income-transfer strategy, so that purchasing power generated in the production process can be transferred, covertly, either as purchasing power by the government (i.e. taxation without consent) or as politically manufactured windfall profits for favored private entrepreneurs.

During the EO phase, liberalization experiments usually begin hesitantly, because its *laissez-faire* connotations run counter to the lingering political ideology which holds that growth is a public concern that must be managed directly, via the exercise of political power. Thus, when the EO phase is reached, the growth process has to contend with the legacy of the prior primary IS phase, which constitutes a substantial control-oriented institutional and organizational package. Consequently, liberalization is likely to proceed in an oscillating manner as the idea of "growth through controls" atrophies only slowly.

In the primary product-exporting economy, policy oscillations are induced by exogenous shocks manifested as the superimposition of a sequence of (externally originated) "cycles" C_1, C_2 – on top of the EO growth phase. A typical cycle contains recovery, prosperity, and recession subphases corresponding to the forces of the demand for the export product in international markets.[23] This long-run trend of "liberalization" is, therefore, not a smooth process, as it encounters short-run policy oscillations; liberalization packages are adopted and experimented with for a time, only to be abandoned under the impact of the external shocks. The periodic revival of IS usually occurs during difficult periods of recession and thus may be viewed as a temporary "retreat" to that "heritage." It was after all, the fear of the unfavorable impact of externally originated fluctuations, e.g., the decline in primary product prices, that provided the underlying rationale for the inward strategy of easy IS in the first place.

All the statistical evidence that can be brought to bear indicates that the East Asian countries (i.e. the so-called "gang of four," bordering mainland China) have registered by far the best growth (and equity) performance over the past 35 years. It is also well recognized that this performance is related to their more pronounced external orientation, as they moved, organizationally as well as structurally, towards convergence with the market-oriented economy of the DCs. In our language, they have followed a more or less linear liberalization policy trend once they emerged from the IS phase, in contrast to the marked oscillation along a more gradual liberalization trend in the majority of LDCs. The behavioral differences in the evolutionary pattern as between the East Asian and the more typical Latin American LDC type can be explained largely in terms of the differentiated factor endowment, namely the "rent-seeking" Latin American countries are more favorably endowed with natural resources and hence more sensitive to the fluctuations of raw material prices in world markets.

BEHAVIOR IN THE "TYPICAL" LATIN AMERICAN CASE

Growth promotion via macro-policies

In the "typical" open LDC, macro (including money-related) growth promotion policies involve the exercise of a set of major policy instruments, such as government revenue (T), foreign exchange reserves (R), money (M) and its creation (dM/dt), price (p), the interest rate (i), the foreign exchange rate (r), as well as a host of ancillary policies (e.g. import restrictions, foreign exchange allocations and export bonuses) woven around that "major set."[24] As motivated by political considerations, the deployment of the "major set" usually goes through a somewhat predictable time pattern of variation within a typical cycle (C_i). This pattern will be analyzed in this section by emphasizing the political motivation of the government to act; the creation of purchasing power and price inflation; the manufacture of profits plus the covert transfer of income; and external monetary management. The ultimate purpose of this section is to show how the periodic revival of the import-substitution policies during the EO subphase results from the interplay of political and economic forces. It concludes by suggesting the possibility of a change in macro management in the "typical" Latin American LDC.

The government's power to spend

The typical LDC interventionist government springs into action (or alternately, relative inaction) during the recovery (recession) period of the cycle, not only because of its sense of a growth promotion mission but also, and just as importantly, due to the waxing and waning of the feeling that it has the power to spend. Exogenous fluctuations automatically induce the government to be active (passive) during the recovery (recession) period by way of two channels: its foreign exchange reserves, R (i.e. its accumulated external purchasing power) and its tax revenue, T (i.e. its internal spending power), both with an over-the-cycle characteristic that can be statistically verified.

Foreign exchange reserves (R) as a source of government power In a politicized economic system, R represents something considerably more than international reserve assets to help defend against short-run fluctuations in the balance of payments. The memory of the experience of previous cycles often leaves the LDC government with little doubt that mercantilist affluence $(dR/dt > 0)$ is necessarily good, while the opposite $(dR/dt < 0)$ is surely a sign of government weakness that causes national anxiety of crisis proportions.

Thus, an externally sensitive LDC government never fails to try to stockpile R as much as it can at the beginning of each cycle C_i for later use. Moreover, a sovereign government can always "promote exports" by buying foreign exchange, thus permitting its own exchange rate to decline in value. Towards the end of each C_i, on the other hand, the reluctance to release the rapidly diminishing foreign exchange (FE) reserves implies that the import surplus is politically curtailed as the government's political power to rule is threatened by the depletion of the FE reserves. Thus the cyclical pattern of the FE reserve management system amounts to a distortion of the trade deficit within each C_i by encouraging it to promote exports or cut imports to allow more imported resources to flow in during the "middle" portions of C_i.

Tax revenue and the power of government spending Exogenous events also give the government an enhanced sense of the domestic power to spend as total government revenues T increase during the recovery period. The boom and bust nature of the political power to spend is mainly traceable to the appropriation of windfall economic rents from primary producers which become more abundant in the recovery period. Thus the relative tax burden index T_a/T rises during the recovery period.[25] Such an involuntary expansion of the political power to spend then emboldens the government to promote growth through the voluntary act of spending even more, i.e. via expansionary fiscal policies. Total expenditures of government, G, are accordingly likely to zoom up and, with a time lag, to produce a budget deficit $(B < 0)$. As compared with the typical DC, we note here the trendal characteristic of B towards a budget deficit, such that the deficit years (more frequent and longer than the surplus years) can occur right in the middle of prosperity.[26]

Internal purchasing power creation and price inflation

Soon after the recovery the activist government is emboldened to assist domestic entrepreneurs by manufacturing profits through the "printing of additional money" (dM/dt) by the banks to accommodate the demand for money for private investment finance.[27] In LDCs, money creation is more appropriately interpreted as the creation of "market power" granted to private entrepreneurs, the government, and state enterprises by the political act of the sovereign government's monopoly power to manufacture money. By way of a footnote to the history of monetary thought, such an idea of a "demand for finance," that is, a demand for monetary purchasing power to command goods and services in the market, was rendered all but obsolete by the "liquidity preference" theory of Keynes, according to which an increase in the quantity of money has mainly psychological effects.

Accordingly, money is printed to solve three types of growth-related problems. First, as a complement to the "centralized" foreign exchange system, it allows the government to acquire FE reserves at zero cost, as the FE earnings of exporters can be forcibly acquired via money creation. Second, it allows control over domestic resources without the inconvenience of taxation. Third, it allows the government to manufacture profits for private entrepreneurs by accommodating their demand for finance with impunity. Money creation (dM/dt) can thus become an all-problem-solving device for the typical LDC government.[28]

Monetary expansion thus constitutes the most important policy instrument in "typical" LDCs. Its citizens have no choice but to accept money, involuntarily, as the medium of exchange – even when the monetary system functions very badly (e.g. at times of hyper-inflation). In the absence of the tradition of some central bank autonomy, the convenient power of money printing is thus monopolized by the government – with the Central Bank performing merely as an arm of the executive branch of the "growth-minded" government. It is primarily for these reasons that a change in monetary philosophy is essential if the liberalization trend is to become "linear."

When the government persistently indulges in the convenience of money printing this will, sooner or later, produce price inflation – with a time lag. The duration of that time lag, which blinds almost everyone into believing in a "cost-push" theory of inflation, depends on both the memory of the inflation experience of the past and the strength of "expectations" of future price inflation in the present. Price inflation will be brought under control only when, in the absence of price controls,[29] moderate increases in the quantity of money (not too much in excess of the GNP growth rate), are held for transactions purposes at the increased price level, taking into consideration changes in velocity. Some such monetary mechanism is at work toward the end of each cycle C_i to bring price inflation under control.

Covert transfers and the manufacture of profits

We know that when the government and/or private entrepreneurs borrow from the banks the repayment burden that falls due at a later date can be lightened or even rendered negative by price inflation.[30] An expansionary monetary policy is always popular, as the borrowers can benefit from negative real interest rates – i.e. as the delayed price inflation lightens the repayment burden. This manufacture of purchasing power plus inflation represents a key growth promotion mechanism in the LDCs. It has been likened to an "act of burglary" by classical monetary theorists.

Rational expectations and indexing The arguments of the "rational expectations" school make it abundantly clear that, in any rational society, such "thefts" can only be occasional – only as long as the expectations of savers are not yet fully "rational" (when the real interest depressing effects of inflation are only "perceived" and defended against *ex post*, rather than "anticipated" *ex ante*). In the long run, as savers gradually learn from experience, the indexing of bank deposits can become a permanent feature of monetary institutions and thus weaken the government's capacity to act in this fashion. Profit manufacture by political force is always based on the cardinal principle of the exploitation of a victimized class – the savers in the present case. With indexing, the market rate of interest is close to its natural level and the entrepreneurial class must rely on its own entrepreneurial capacity to make a real profit, not augmented by political patronage.[31]

However, "equity through total indexing" is really a contradiction in terms, because an "agreement" on "total indexing" (at best an unstable pseudo-agreement) is only reached when citizens cannot reach a consensus on equity under the customary methods of a constitutional democracy.[32] The very fact that governments continue to print money (for deficit finance), in spite of total indexing, is concrete proof of this contradiction. For if the body politic has the capacity to agree on something equitable (e.g. total indexing) the same capacity should have led the citizens to agree on taxation with consent in the first place.

In an evolutionary perspective, however, the practice of indexing the interest rate is contributory to the cause of liberalization because it leads to the emergence and firming up of the idea that the government, in spite of all its good intentions and power, cannot persistently use an expansionary monetary policy to suppress the interest rate to an artificially low level, i.e. much below the natural rate, according to the loanable funds theory.[33] Monetary maturity paves the way to political maturity when the citizens demand an explicit accounting of the "costs of growth" expressed in terms of the dollars-and-cents tax burdens on various groups, instead of the "under the table" covert transfers of resources to the government by money printing, while relying on price inflation as the mollifier, with or without indexing.

External monetary management

The external monetary management of a country refers to the management of the FE rate (foreign exchange rate) and of R (its foreign exchange reserves). In LDCs, both the internal and external dimensions of monetary management are inseparable from "growth promotion policies" and bear little resemblance to the use of R as a first line of defense of the FE rate (under the pressure of balance-of-payments imbalance), as in the DCs. In each cycle C_i, we may picture a three-stage political life of external monetary management complementary to that of the domestic growth promotion policy.

If we start with R in a state of near depletion we first witness a drive to accumulate R via the adoption of a more realistic FE rate through devaluation. However, in the absence of a clear cut "precautionary motive," there is no assurance that the same reserve stock will not be used up quickly.[34] In the second stage, expansionary domestic monetary and fiscal policies create a tight resources situation and build up pressures for an import surplus. The decline of R is accommodated by an overvaluation of the domestic currency. This well-known "import-substitution" type policy serves to transfer incomes from the producers of the export primary product to benefit the importing urban entrepreneurial class. Such a political act of "profit manufacture" is facilitated by a de facto overvaluation when, with creeping price inflation, the FE rate is "pegged" (i.e. not promptly devalued).[35]

In the final stage, that is, during the recession, the overvaluation of the domestic currency becomes more pronounced. Some now claim that the FE rate is overvalued due to an accelerated inflation rate. Believers in the "import cost-pushed theory of inflation" then assert that devaluation at such a time would "cause" more inflation. In the midst of such confusion only one thing is clear, namely that the artificially overvalued domestic currency is expected to act as an "inflation fighter" as devaluation is postponed.[36] The rapid dissipation of the FE reserves can only mean that their inflation fighting power is rapidly diminishing. All the symptoms of an IS strategy are revived, as improvised quantitative import restrictions and foreign exchange allocations are installed to protect the quickly depleting R. And yet, given the customary national anxiety about devaluation, such action is postponed as long as possible, usually until the FE rate has to be devalued abruptly. Finally, when it comes, the devaluation has a "big bang" effect. In the wake of this crisis atmosphere, the economy then makes a resolute effort to try liberalization once again, thus starting a new cycle with a vision that the FE rate will be cleanly floated this time.

Policy oscillation and the temporary revival of import-substitution policies thus come about *ex post*, with nobody planning it that way. The basic reason is that there was insufficient realization of the seriousness of the political commitment that had been made (i.e. one that separates FE management and domestic monetary management from growth promotion) when the "floating rate" was first announced. The FE managers, in other words, did not promptly devalue the currency in order to nip the expansionary policies in the bud. Growth promotion through artificial purchasing power expansion is clearly not without its social costs and should be reflected promptly in terms of the endearment of imported resources. A dirty float and an oscillating pattern of externally oriented growth basically result from an incomplete commitment to the "rationalism" of a liberalization trend.

Possible change in internal and external monetary management

The design of growth promotion policies in the postwar years has suffered from the absence of a sound monetary theoretic foundation. Whether or not Keynesian theory is sound for the industrially advanced country is a debatable issue, but we believe it is irrelevant to the problems and the political reality of the LDCs. Here dM/dt represents the creation of purchasing power to be spent rather than "held," that is, giving the holder a sense of "security with liquidity." In the years ahead the rehabilitation of a monetary philosophy based on an older, classical wisdom might be useful.

To ensure that the equilibrium rate of interest and the equilibrium FE rate prevail during the EO phase, the motto to be considered is "watch and limit quantity." Since the government cannot control both price and quantity without rationing, "watching quantity" implies keeping an eye on quantity and largely forgetting about the price that is determined in the market place.

In the case of domestic monetary policy, the principle of watching quantity is Friedman-like advice, namely that even the world's most experienced central bankers should watch the quantity of money (M) and forget about controlling the rate of interest, which is to be determined in the loanable funds market. This suggests that the smoothly expanding money growth rate should be limited to approximately the growth rate of GNP. In the case of foreign exchange management, the same principle implies a clean float system where the quantity of reserves (R) is watched and the level of the FE rate, no longer viewed as "sensitive" for political and/or economic reasons, is left to be determined in the FE market. This motto further implies that the quantity of FE reserves held should be limited to a relatively small, constant amount; an LDC cannot afford the luxury of a large R.

The simultaneous application of a quantity restriction for both internal and external monetary management is not accidental. In both cases, money would then be interpreted strictly as a medium of exchange for transactions purposes, i.e., M as a domestic medium of exchange required for the internal division of labor, and R as a medium of exchange for international transactions purposes to accommodate the international division of labor. In both cases, this motto implies an emphasis on efficiency through decentralized choices by market participants.

Gradual liberalization implies the substitution of the market for government direct controls. As the interest rate is liberalized there will be less need for credit rationing by political force, and, as the FE rate is liberalized, there is less need for FE rationing. While not all government controls (e.g. import duties) are eliminated, the most serious ones are. No government, DC or LDC, makes daily adjustments in its tariff structure, but they do make daily discretionary decisions with respect to the supply of money and the foreign exchange rate. Distortions by tariffs represent less of a case of oscillating inefficiency and can be reduced at a later stage.

The sovereign state's exercise of monopoly power via the printing of money and the compulsory purchase and dissipation of FE is thus seen as far more damaging than the retention of import duties, at least for some time. We might say that the liberalization movement is very much co-extensive with the acceptance of a new monetary philosophgy, i.e. to regard M and R as mediums of exchange suggests relative monetary inactivism. In other words, they are not to be viewed as purchasing power that can be artificially created and/or manipulated by political will to achieve socially desirable purposes. This view clearly represents something of a rebellion against the postwar mainstream position in the industrially advanced countries which regards the creation of money as the augmentation of a socially desirable liquid asset that is being "held" mainly for psychological reasons rather than spent aggressively.

But it also represents a rebellion against the postwar mainstream view in the LDCs which regards the government as being responsible for growth via expansionary monetary policies. For, in spite of all the slogans of "growth with equity," this policy implies the manufacture of profits by a strategy of income transfer that victimizes the politically less powerful social groups, i.e. consumers, unorganized workers and, especially, spatially dispersed rural entrepreneurs and farmers. With a limited government capacity to borrow, a commitment to monetary conservatism also implies fiscal responsibility; that is, covert income transfers by and to the government can and should be replaced by taxation with consent, with the costs of growth explicitly calculated and apportioned to various social groups. The achievement of modern economic growth also requires the gradual switch to a modern organizational and institutional framework. LDC governments have the perfect right to think they can and should promote growth by means of all kinds of intervention. It is the responsibility of prefessional economics to remind them of the limitations.

THE EAST ASIAN CASE IN COMPARATIVE PERSPECTIVE

The data

The contemporary East Asian NICs, of which Taiwan is a prominent member, may be seen as belonging to a group of open dualistic economies characterized by the initial co-existence of a relatively large agricultural and a small non-agricultural sector internally and, given their relatively small size, the importance of international trade externally. Taiwan, moreover, exemplified the natural-resources-poor country case, Not only were there no large deposits of exportable minerals or reproducible raw materials on hand, but even the amount of good arable land was very limited, i.e. only 22 percent of the total land area, with a population density of about two persons per hectare. A type of "organic nationalism," acquired from an awareness of one's own history and the belief that one continues to exist as a member of a cohesive social group, was very much in evidence. Even though there existed differences between the indigenous Taiwan population and the migrants from mainland China after 1948–49, there is clearly in evidence a common heritage which could be melded, partly in response to the threat from the mainland, into institutions of orderly reform which could express calculated sympathy with all members of the community without endangering the underlying principles of a self-interested and acquisitive reward system. The fact that a mature nationalism already existed and did not have to be invented meant that it was easier for the population to realize that government patronage was not likely to be a permanent feature over time. It does not stretch the imagination to see the significance of such pragmatism in terms of less rigid or severe import-substitution policies, as well as the better chances for gradual depoliticization in a linear fashion once the system entered its export-orientation phase in the early 1960s.

In Taiwan, emerging from a more or less colonial situation after World War II, four subphases of transition can be identified approximately as follows:[37]

1 a primary import-substitution subphase – from 1953 to approximately 1961;
2 an export-orientation subphase of the primary export-substitution type, i.e. emphasizing labor-intensive industrial exports – from 1961 to approximately 1970;
3 an export-orientation subphase of the secondary import- and export-substitution type, i.e. emphasizing production and export of consumer durables, capital goods, and the processing of raw materials – from approximately 1970 to 1980;
4 a technology-intensive subphase of secondary import- and export-substitution – beginning around 1980 and continuing.

Primary import substitution represents a natural metamorphosis out of colonial triangularism in three senses. First, the essential fuel governing the system's import capacity still resides in natural-resource-intensive, agriculturally-based exports. Second, these exports pay for the producers' goods, which are now allocated to support the new industrial sector's displacement of imported non-durables. Third, the pre-existence of a domestic market for these non-durables makes it easy for new, relatively inexperienced, domestic entrepreneurs to take it over with the help of protection.

Table 5.1 provides a basis for a comparison of the performance of a "typical" East Asian case, represented by Taiwan, and of a "typical" Latin American case, represented by Colombia. It demonstrates that even during the import-substitution subphase of the 1950s Taiwan's performance, while not as good as later, was quite favorable by international standards, e.g. compared with Colombia. This is very much related to the relative mildness of this phase and its relatively short duration.

Turning to the export-orientation subphases of the 1960s, the Taiwan economy began its more or less monotonic shift in the liberalization direction early in the decade. As table 5.1A shows, the performance in terms of both growth rates and income distribution improved dramatically, fueled by spectacular increases in labor-intensive exports. By the end of the 1960s, as we may note from the more pronounced rise in unskilled real wages around that time, the unlimited supply of labor condition came to an end, inducing a shift towards a second subphase of export orientation characterized by more capital and skill-intensive production and output mixes during the 1970s. Thus, the continuation of the policy liberalization trend accommodated the march of a changing comparative advantage as the system moved up the skill ladder. The final evolution of this process in the 1980s was to one of science and

TABLE 5.1   *Performance indicators*

A. Taiwan

	1950s	1960s	1970s	1980–84
	(averages of annual data, unless otherwise indicated)			
Growth of real GDP (%)	('53–'59) 8.2	9.2	10.1	6.8
Gini coefficient	(1953) 0.56	(1964) 0.36	(1970) 0.32	(1980) 0.31
Exports/GDP (%)	('52–'59) 9.11	18.79	44.02	53.53
Industrial exports/ total exports (%)	('52–'59) 10.8	50.21	85.1	('80–'83) 92.05
Taxes/GDP (%)	('52–'58) 12.71	11.20	14.40	15.84
Change in unskilled real wage (%)	('52–'59) 5.09	('60–'68) 4.89	('74–'79) 7.63	

B. Colombia

	1950s	1960s	1970s	1980–84
	(averages of annual data, unless otherwise indicated)			
Growth of real GDP (%)	('52–'59) 4.86	1.62	2.10	('80–'82) 2.00
Gini coefficient		(1960) 0.53	(1970) 0.56	(1979) 0.51
Exports/GDP (%)	19.6	15.4	13.0	(1980) 14.1
Industrial exports/ total exports (%)	('57–'59) 3.0	8.0	21.3	('80–'82) 24.5
Taxes/GDP (%)	(1950) 2.85	(1960) 4.21	('72–'79) 9.0	('80–'81) 10.0
Change in unskilled real wage (%)	('56–'59) 6.26	('61–'69) 3.09	1.74	(1980) 2.4

Sources: UN Statistical Yearbook; IMF Yearbook; World Bank World Table; Statistical Yearbook of the Republic of China; The Trade of China; UNCTAD Yearbook of Trade and Development Statistics.

technology-intensive output and export patterns, with an emphasis on the domestic generation of indigenous science and technology as the next logical step in the international product-cycle context, as Kuznets describes it for the modern epoch. In brief, once export orientation began, it was maintained more or less linearly; the economy grew rapidly, was able to absorb its labor surplus by the end of the sixties, and moved on to perform exceedingly well, even under the deteriorating international circumstances of the seventies and early eighties.

The policies

Our purpose here, however, is not to retell the Taiwan success story once more in substantial detail but to advance our understanding of the underlying reasons *why* appropriate policies were adopted during three decades of postwar growth, in contrast to the less successful and more oscillatory nature of other LDC experience (see table 5.1B). To assist in this effort, we present the "Economic Policy Matrix of Taiwan," describing the major policy events in that economy over the past 35 years. It contains the main elements of a policy evolution that accommodated the previously described metamorphosis of the system's economic structure as it moved towards the epoch of modern growth. Significant landmarks separating import substitution from export orientation (ca. 1961) and the termination of the (unskilled) labor surplus condition (ca. 1968) are indicated by the vertical lines in the policy evolution chart.

Such a policy evolution chart represents a manifestation of a change in organization in various markets of the Taiwan economy, with policies consequently classified into macro and sectoral components. The major policies indicated on page one of that matrix – i.e. the fiscal policies related to domestic taxes (I), trade related taxes and regulations (II), policies impinging on the interest rate (III), the foreign exchange rate (IV) and international capital movements (V) – all represent macroeconomic policies focused on the government's overall management of purchasing power. The sector-specific policies indicated in subsequent sections of the chart – the role of public enterprises and of infractructural investments (VI), agricultural policies (VII), manpower (education and population) policies (VIII), science and technology related policies, (IX) and development planning (X) – although all important in their own right, require a somewhat different framework of reasoning, since they are not directly related to the central issue of the direct or indirect management of purchasing power by the government. It is mainly in the area of macroeconomic policies that the evolving rationality of the policy mix of a country over time can be assessed, since such policies are not only more "pervasive" in their impact but also intertwine in a particular way with the political forces that underpin them.

Taiwan's primary import-substitution subphase (1952–61) already bears evidence of policy events which differ from those of the more typical developing country in terms of the milder-than-usual version of that particular policy package, planting the seeds of the linear liberalization trend which was to follow. It is relatively easy to identify the typical array of IS policies, such as the imposition of tariffs and import controls, a multiple exchange rate system, relatively large government budget deficits coupled with rapid inflation, a substantial emphasis on public enterprises, and a pronounced dedication to the idea of "economic planning." All these are familiar symptoms of an internally oriented import-substitution strategy. Nevertheless, on the other side of the ledger, we may also note, in Taiwan unusually early concerns with inflation, the early implementation of land reform, and an early shift to welcoming the contribution of both domestic and foreign private actors.

More specifically, given the fresh memory of the nightmarish hyper-inflation on the mainland (1940–48) the new government of Taiwan attacked inflation early, earnestly, and on all fronts, i.e. in relation to its fiscal, monetary and capital market policies. With respect to the latter, for instance, the substantial inflow of foreign aid into Taiwan in the 1950s was primarily used as a prominent "inflation fighter" which helped meet a budget gap that was unusually large, given the customary initial substantial requirements for LDC overhead construction plus Taiwan's special security requirements. Decision-makers, however, never subscribed to the notion that foreign aid should be viewed as a necessary, persistent injection of resources on a long-term basis. In fact, Taiwan was the first LDC that agreed (V), to terminate her status as an aid recipient by 1965.

A balanced government budget was viewed early and persistently to have high private and public "value." In the early postwar years, when the government's direct tax capacity was still severely limited, it resorted to a rice–fertilizer barter program (VI; 1949), terminated in 1974 in favour of direct taxation. Through the introduction of a con-solidated income tax reform (I; 1955), budget deficits were gradually brought under control by 1961 (I), and, as early as 1964, we witness the emergence of budgetary surpluses. In 1979, we have another major overhaul of the income tax system and, in 1983, the consideration of further tax reform, this time a value-added tax. The system has con-sequently enjoyed considerable price stability, i.e. both during the early EO subphase (1961–70) and the later EO subphase (1970–80), in spite of oil shocks and other elements of a deteriorating international economy. The emergence of the slightest government budget deficit in the 1979–85 period consistently evoked a search for new taxes. The Taiwan government has thus stubbornly resisted, right from the beginning, the temptation to finance government expenditures by "under the table" covert taxation and never shied away from imple-menting new rounds of tax reform to generate adequate government revenues "on the table."

Taiwan's monetary and interest rate policies fully supported such fiscal restraint. Whenever inflation occurred, the government did not try to suppress the interest rate by further monetary expansion but, instead, moved the interest rate up towards its "natural" level. A high interest rate policy to help combat inflation was, in fact, adopted remarkably

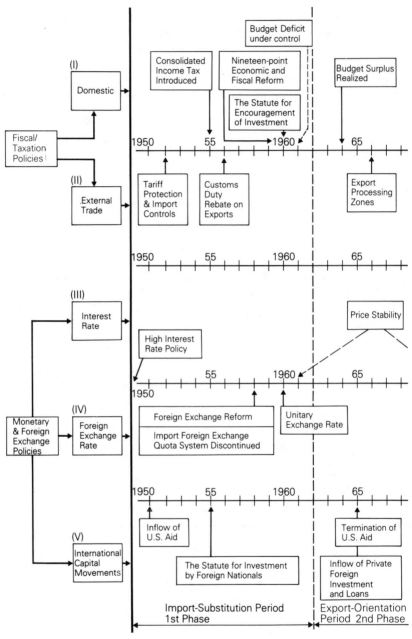

Fig. 5.1a

POLICY MATRIX OF TAIWAN

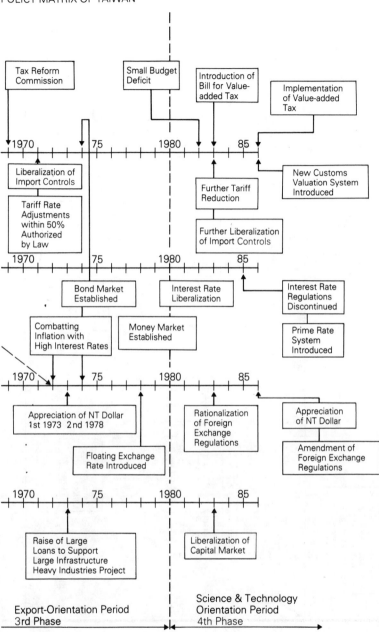

Fig. 5.1a   *cont.*

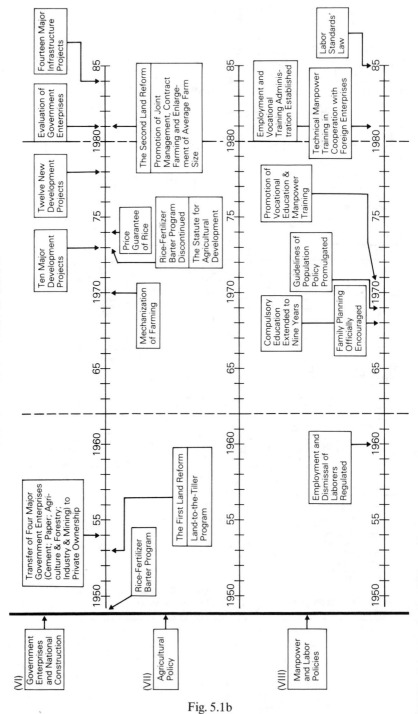

ECONOMY POLICY MATRIX OF TAIWAN

Fig. 5.1b

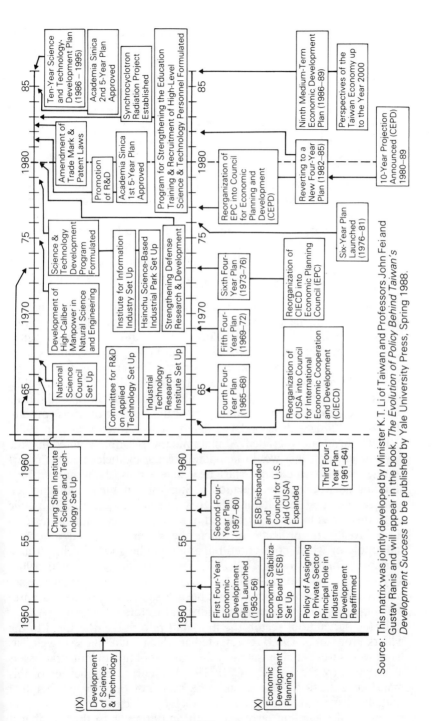

Source: This matrix was jointly developed by Minister K. T. Li of Taiwan and Professors John Fei and Gustav Ranis and will appear in the book, *The Evolution of Policy Behind Taiwan's Development Success* to be published by Yale University Press, Spring 1988.

Fig. 51b   *cont.*

early, i.e. during the primary import-substitution period (III; 1955). The same high interest rate policy was reaffirmed (III; 1972) when the rest of the world was just about to enter into a period of unprecedented inflation.

Taiwan did, of course, resort to "money printing" to some extent in order to transfer incomes to the industrial entrepreneurial class in both the sixties and the seventies. However, the practice was always moderate, i.e. it became tradition to link the level of the interest rate to price inflation. In other words, whenever price inflation was a problem, the government thought it necessary to index the interest rate, more or less in acordance with the loanable funds theory. The evolution of these ideas logically culminated in another credit market liberalization in 1980, when a national slogan emerged emphasizing the social value of the "natural rate of interest," relatively unfettered by political controls. As part of this cumulative linear movement, the idea has gradually taken hold that money creation is not to be consistently used for the manufacture of profits on behalf of private entrepreneurs or state enterprises.

Thus, the seeds of a linear trend towards liberalization were indeed planted early in the IS phase, when a policy of assigning the private sector the principal role in development was also, at least implicitly, agreed upon. This reflected the sense that in a natural-resources-poor and human-resources-abundant country, the creative talents and energies of individuals have to be fully mobilized. The role of public enterprise, substantial in the early IS phase, gradually atrophied during the 1960s, briefly re-appeared as part of the "ten big projects" push in the 1970s (along with secondary IS), but finally, 30 years later, in 1980, (VI), was firmly downgraded. At that time it was formally stated that the government not only would liquidate existing inefficient public enterprises, but also would not start new ones – thus abandoning a long standing doctrinaire interpretation of Sun Yat Sen, the founding father. This accelerating search for efficiency meant that the role of public investment was increasingly limited to social and economic infrastructural investment projects in which the government had a natural monopoly or which constituted bona fide public goods, such as transportation, communication (VI; 1973, 1978) and education (VIII; 1968, 1970, 1981). The primary role for the growth of directly productive activities has, therefore, increasingly been assigned to private entrepreneurs in both the agricultural and industrial sectors.

In the agricultural sector, the first land reform (i.e. the Land to the Tillers Program of 1953) represented anything but a "class struggle," as landowners were compensated by the transfer of title to industrial assets abandoned by the Japanese (VII; 1953). The true significance of this major organizational change may be seen not only in the fact that spatially dispersed farmers were no longer neglected (or exploited) on the political stage, but also, and more importantly, in the fact that it paved the way for the deployment of individual initiative in decentralized nonagriculture. Under the conditions of relative price stability and a unitary exchange rate established in 1960 (IV), the Taiwan farmer could hold his own and, with respect to the export of nontraditional mushrooms and asparagus, behave quite like the Hong Kong exporter of labor-intensive products, i.e. produce wave after wave of new items directed at the world market and thus spearhead the external-orientation drive in the early years of the EO phase. The fact that there was a decade-long time lag between land reform and the beginnings of a spectacular nontraditional agricultural export drive (1963), plus the fact that a nondiscriminatory foreign exchange rate with a stable price level can eventually promote growth by stimulating farmers, offers a sober lesson to Latin American LDCs, where liberalization is sometimes unrealistically expected to bring quick results over a three- or four-year period. As a result of disappointment and exogenous terms of trade shocks, what often happens instead in such situations, as we have noted above, is retrenchment to import-substitution type policies, oscillation and relative non-success.

With respect to the manufacturing sector, the well-known dramatic success of Taiwan's external-orientation drive was built on the seemingly "paradoxical" policy foundation of only a partial liberalization over the course of the last 30 years, i.e. only in the 1980s is Taiwan approaching what might be called full liberalization in various relevant markets. The foreign exchange institutions were depoliticized, linearly and cumulatively, starting with the abandonment of the import licensing and quota system in 1958 (IV), and of the multiple exchange rate system in 1960 (IV), both during the IS phase. This was followed by the discretionary appreciation of the currency in 1973 and 1978 (IV), finally leading to a more automatic foreign exchange rate adjustment under the managed floating peg system in 1978 (IV). The foreign exchange regime, in other words, moved linearly towards a more liberal system, recognizing the cardinal principle that the determination of a foreign exchange rate should be influenced increasingly by market, rather than political, forces. By 1983 (IV), this trend was taken even further via the decentralization of the control of foreign exchange reserves in the hands of commercial banks. Today the full integration of Taiwan's domestic capital market with that of the rest of the world, allowing for less control over even short-run capital movements, seems not far off. Such persistent liberalization of the foreign exchange regime represents an excellent example of an evolutionary process conducive to the gradual perfection of one of the most important markets and is essential if private initiatives are to be mobilized for successful competition in the world's industrial markets.

Of course the liberalization drive, even in Taiwan, has been incomplete in the sense that there always remain political forces at work, manufacturing profits and transferring incomes towards the urban entrepreneurial class, both overtly and covertly. In the quasi-covert category we may include the policy of exempting certain "new and strategic" industries (I) from corporate income tax obligations under the 1960 "Statute for the Encouragement of Investment." Although such tax exemption schemes appear as a form of discretionary control (and hence work against liberalization trends) the basic result is one of growth activism, in the sense that in this way the tax burden is shifted away from reinvestible profit incomes and towards the incomes of other unidentified classes.

The most important covert income transfers from agricultural to industrial interests were, however, as is typical, effected via protection (II; 1952), but the customs duty rebate system (II) installed in the IS phase (1956), in combination with the export-processing zones (II; 1966) established during the EO phase, combined to ameliorate their impact. This package of policies reflected an awareness that, while the competitiveness of domestic producers in foreign markets is crucial for growth in the labor surplus economy, domestic consumers can, and perhaps should, be exploited as long as it is politically feasible. The sequential order of Taiwan's liberalization package implies that, while a sovereign state cannot exploit foreign consumers, it can, in the name of growth, exploit its domestic consumers for some time, i.e., as long as the latter are ignorant of the price they are paying.

The more recent replacement of this partial liberalization by a full dosage seems to have resulted from three related events. First, domestic entrepreneurs, having demonstrated their competitive fitness in foreign markets, now have less to fear from going head-to-head with foreigners in the domestic market. Second, as the number of items of imported goods multiplies, it becomes increasingly impossible for civil servants to make discretionary decisions on selective import controls, preferential target industries, etc. And finally, in an increasingly open world economy, domestic consumers will ultimately become aware of the exploitation they have been exposed to and generate their own political pressure for tariff reductions. Thus, in the later stages of the EO phase, in 1971 and again in 1983 (II), import controls were further liberalized and tariff rates reduced, persistently and cumulatively. This movement is still gathering momentum at the present time, partially under pressure from the United States, with which Taiwan has a substantial bilateral trade surplus.

These quasi-covert income transfers used in Taiwan differ significantly from those developed in Latin America and described earlier. While the Latin American LDCs relied extensively on overvalued exchange rates to transfer the income of primary product exporters to the urban industrial class, this instrument of foreign exchange market intervention was not used extensively in Taiwan, primarily because it is not a natural-resources-abundant system, i.e. there was never as much "rent" to be sought after by the urban entrepreneurial class. While

Taiwan also made use of the tariff to protect infant industries, the victimized group was mainly its consumers rather than its producers. Therefore, the impact of the income transfer strategy was much less detrimental to growth because the incentive to produce was not dampened as much. When the problem is only a matter of "fairness," it tends to become less of an issue, because what is perceived as "fair" is only relative to one's awareness. To the extent consumers are less aware of the fact that they are being "exploited" by high import duties, the government faces less of a constraint in continuing the same policy mix.

When we, finally, take a longer time perspective by examining the latter half of the EO phase (since about 1970) in comparison with the years before, we see an evolutionary principle at work; the pragmatic orientation of the government becomes more and more clearly established, with the more romantic and nationalistic notions as to which direct government actions can be counted on as beneficial to growth gradually receding.

This increased maturity of nationalism over time has led to a role of government increasingly pointed in the direction of institution construction and organizational reforms – including the areas of education, science and technology, agricultural finance, long-run capital movements, etc. – which are both sensitive to the new problems brought about by development at a higher stage and conducive to a fully liberalized market economy. For example, once the labor surplus condition had terminated (shortly before 1970), the economy entered a situation in which the need for further development of its human resources pointed to greater emphasis on the quality dimensions of growth. From rows VIII (manpower and education) and IX (science and technology) of our policy matrix, we can see that government activism gradually shifted towards these areas in the second EO subphase. In the realm of science and technology, for example, the setting up of new and the revamping of old science and technology institutions (1965, 1967, 1973, 1975), culminating in the formation of a national "Science and Technology Development Program" (1979), is but a case in point. The promotion of R&D, as well as the strengthening of trade mark and patent laws (IX) under way in 1985, suggests that the country has effectively entered the mature growth phase of Kuznets, in which indigenous science and technology can be expected to play a major routinized role. With respect to the former, most government policy change centered on education and training (VIII), with the competitive examination system followed by vocational education and engineering-oriented programs in 1968, 1970 and 1981. The government also instituted (1968) and strengthened (1969) its program of family planning (VII), which initially was supported only by the private sector.

In the realm of agricultural policies, the advent of the labor shortage condition led, by the end of the 1960s, to a farm mechanization movement in response to the resulting higher wages. This, in turn, stimulated new thinking on the appropriate role of that sector and on how this could be accommodated by policy action. What resulted was the "Statute of Agricultural Development" (1974) which contained the seeds for what was later (1981) termed the second land reform, including the promotion of joint farm management, contract farming and the enlargement of farm size, i.e., land consolidation schemes induced by the unskilled labor shortage. As early as 1974, Taiwan even began to adopt measures to subsidize the agricultural sector (VII), which is symptomatic of the industrially advanced countries once the agricultural sector has fulfilled its historical mission in support of growth and has become a politically sensitive, but economically less significant, appendage to the rest of the economy.

At a higher stage of economic development, another important dimension of institutional reform resides in the area of "investment finance" where, given an increasingly differentiated "financial intermediation" network, "informal" financial institutions outside the government-controlled banking system are increasingly drawn into the formal sector. In the later EO subphase, the Taiwan government moved into the area of organizational reforms to establish, in quick succession, a bond market in 1974 (III) and an organized money market in 1976 (III). The financial system has thus become more flexible with the help of institutional construction and innovation, with commercial banking becoming more competitive and widening its scope of operations, independent of the government-controlled commercial banking system. The establishment of these additional financial institutions is a prerequisite for the gradual movement toward something approaching an equilibrium or natural rate of interest which, in turn, provides guidelines for the interest rate to be used in official commercial bank lending (III; 1980). Borrowers have become more carefully stratified according to size and credit-worthiness as the notion of a prime rate began to emerge in the 1980s.

With respect to the international capital market, Taiwan realized quite early in the IS phase (V; 1955) that foreign investment had a positive role to play and should be encouraged by statute. Substantial flows began in earnest only after the termination of U.S. aid in 1965. In addition to the institutionalization of direct investment in this early effort, the liberalization of long-run private capital inflows continued in the eighties via a further reduction of government restrictions on foreign firm operations, e.g. with respect to export prohibitions, as well as via the positive government encouragement of joint ventures. A further opening up of the domestic financial market by allowing for a wider scope of operations by foreign banks in the domestic capital market has already taken place (1985).

In addition to all these activities to institutionalize private foreign lending, the government has increasingly borrowed directly in foreign markets (1973) to finance infrastructure and heavy industry (V) or, even more recently (1983), to promote joint ventures with foreign corporations. However, judging from the slow pace of progress in negotiating a Taiwan–Japan joint venture in large-scale automobile assembly, it is very doubtful that "government sponsored" joint ventures will play a significant role in the future, compared with private joint ventures in the past.

It is equally unlikely that Taiwan, which escaped the "debt problem" thus far, will suffer from it in the foreseeable future. Having shifted from natural-resource- to human-resource-intensive production and export mixes in the 1960s, Taiwan, in sharp contrast to other LDCs, proceeded rather cautiously in borrowing from foreign commercial banks in the 1970s. Moreover, it was able to adjust successfully to the deterioration of the international environment of the 1980s by a further relative expansion of its exports.

Two additional remarks complete this synopsis of the policy evolution in Taiwan. Although the reorganized Council of International Economic Cooperation and Development (X; 1963), succeeded by the Economic Planning Council in 1973, had continued to compile economic development plans (X; 1965, 1973, 1976), these plans were increasingly viewed as "think pieces" or general guidelines to convey a sense of national purpose, and not, in any sense, as mandatory or regulatory. In fact, when the planning machinery was once again reorganized in 1977, this time into the Council for Economic Planning and Development, it became concerned even less with formal resource-oriented planning and more with policy debate and formulation comparable to the functions of the Council of Economic Advisers in the United States.

Finally, with respect to the labor market, the union movement has been conspicuous by its relative absence as compared with other LDCs, including especially the Latin American countries. The only policy event of any real significance in this area was a 1960 law on the employment and dismissal of labor (VIII). Labor legislation, e.g. dealing with employment, labor relations, working conditions, and retirement benefits, has generally not been of major importance in raising the real costs of labor on Taiwan. Nor has minimum wage legislation. In many LDCs, including the Latin American type, such legislation is more the result of domestic political preferences or of international demonstration pressures on governments, rather than a consequence of the voluntary association of the workers themselves.

CONCLUSIONS AND PERSPECTIVES

During the decade of the seventies, the field of inquiry labeled development economics has substantially changed its character. In consonance with changes elsewhere in economics, there has been a marked shift towards microeconomic research, moving out from Beckerian household utility maximization models, on the one hand, and contemporary industrial organization models, applied to agricultural as well as non-agricultural production units, on the other. But all too often, again in consonance with what is happening in "domestic" macroeconomics, the links between this microeconomic research and the improved macro-economic analysis towards which it claims to be directed are both weak, and worse, receiving inadequate attention.

The overwhelming emphasis on the production of finely tuned deter-ministic models and, less frequently, their econometric implementation as an end-product has turned our profession increasingly away from its less respectable and murky border areas, e.g. with sociology, with political science, even with history. As admittedly overambitious and ill-conceived postwar programs of interdisciplinary or multidisciplinary research fell of their own weight, our subdiscipline has tended to retreat into "fortress purity," rather than fashioning a better set of disciplinary tools to tackle partly interdisciplinary problems.

We have pointed to but one area in which macroeconomic analysis is increasingly running up against disciplinary boundary constraints which seriously impede the further progress of our applied branch of economic science. While economists have managed to achieve an improved understanding of what makes for better performance across different developing countries, we have substantially lagged behind in our effort to explore why some societies manage to move from here to there, and why most do not.

This paper is intended to do little more than indicate one future direction for our subdiscipline, if we are to approach an answer to this question. Our quick review of macro-policy oscillation in Latin America in contrast to more linear economic and organizational changes in Taiwan over the past 35 years has taken a first inductive stab at exposing the vital interactions between two neighboring and usually relatively isolated fields of inquiry. The political process through which policy either accommodates or obstructs the evolution of an economic system towards modern growth lies at the heart of the issue – as do the roles of natural resources and foreign capital. We believe further pro-gress will come by way of such typologically sensitive analysis, e.g. focusing on the contrasting historical experiences of the East Asian linear with the Latin American oscillatory case.

The linear Taiwan case to which we have given most of the detailed attention in this paper is intended to illustrate this inductive process. In the early import-substitution subphase, we noted the virtual necessity of governments to undertake massive infrastructural expenditures, on the one hand, and massive direct interventions in the market, on the other. This resulted in the government's viewing money creation as a necessary instrument for acquiring the purchasing power for itself and the where-withal to shift resources to others. Implicit is the fact that the larger the supply of rents emanating from natural-resource-based production and exports, the greater the temptation for governments to transfer them, under the table, to the public sector and to favored private parties – and the greater the temptation for various private sector participants to engage in DUP (directly unproductive profit-seeking) activities in fighting over the spoils. If natural resources are limited, by the same token, there is a much better chance for import-substitution policies to be less severe and less prolonged and for a linear liberalization trend to accompany the beginnings of export orientation.

We, of course, need a better understanding, not just of the nature of organizational changes in each sector or market, but also of the ideal – and less ideal – sequencing of such changes. Specifically, future efforts must focus on: (1) the evolution of policy and performance over time, by sector; (2) the ideal (and less ideal) sequential ordering of policy change in each sector, based on historical experience; (3) the causal relatedness among the sectoral sequences, i.e. packages of policy change, especially the more "ideal" ones; and (4) the identification of constraints on such sequences and how these can be reduced.

As we have seen in Taiwan, the decision was made early not to squeeze agriculture unduly – and to do most of that squeezing explicitly. Land reform was instituted in the early 1950s and the usual IS policies were less discriminatory of agriculture than usual. Even during the fifties, credit policy began to shift away from the customary low-interest rate, money printing *cum* inflationary pattern of shifting resources and towards the more pronounced use of on-the-table direct taxation. A second major step was to shift towards a unitary and more realistic exchange rate by the end of the 1950s giving first nontraditional agricultural and then nonagricultural exports a competitive chance in international markets. While QRs were reduced or abolished by the early 1960s, virtually equivalent tariffs were instituted in their place. Liberalization of the current account thus initially took the form of an important qualitative change. Next in the sequence were tariff rebates and export-processing zones in the mid-sixties as transition measures, with full import liberalization postponed until much later. This sequencing clearly indicates that, in East Asia, domestic consumers could continue to be squeezed substantially longer, even as competitive export substitution proceeded apace with respect to the rest of the world – moving from land- to labor-intensive and hence to skill- and capital-intensive products.

The contrast with Latin America is both marked and instructive. For one thing, the import-substitution subphase there lasted longer and was more severe. Moreover, the nontraditional, export-oriented phase which followed was more limited and based on the long-term subsidization of a whole variety of export products, from consumer durables to capital goods and processed raw materials. We may also note that Latin America's much greater availability of natural resources, and thus its much greater continued dependence on land-based rents, provided an obstacle to the shift to a human-resource- and ingenuity-based pattern of production and exports. This pattern, moreover, continued to expose the economy to the vagaries of terms of trade fluctuations which we believe to be instrumental in causing oscillations in policy, i.e. periods of liberalization followed by a return to import-substitution policies.

With respect to what we have called sectoral policies, the Taiwan liberalization experience indicates that the role of public enterprise, while never publicly deprecated, has continued to gradually decline. On the other hand, the role of government increased elsewhere as the system moved into its skilled labor-dependent subphase in the 1970s and its science and technology-dependent subphase in the 1980s. Government never moved off stage but concentrated its scarce energies on providing physical and organizational infrastructure, on responding to the advent of labor shortage by implementing the so-called second agricultural revolution (i.e. land consolidation and the development of the cultivating firm), and by responding via capital market reforms to the needs for larger-scale private investment projects.

In the areas of planning and the labor market, it is fair to say that government policies were marked by self-negation. Comprehensive centralized planning was, of course, never attempted here but, contrary to many other LDCs, planning exercises turned quite early into indicative rather than directive activities. Labor markets, beyond minimal ILO-type conditions governing work, were not substantially interfered with – either via strong minimum wage legislation or the encouragement of union activities. As a consequence, employment was favored and wage incomes rose rapidly, even as wage rates remained low, until the labor surplus had been eliminated.

In other words, in the absence of an ample endowment of natural resources and, after the 1950s, large-scale foreign capital inflows, policy packages in Taiwan were directed to accommodate production and trade adjustments in keeping with the system's changing human resource capabilities, rather than responding to the natural desire of various interest groups, i.e. industrialists, elite workers, and civil servants, anxious to maintain their unearned rents. The challenge before us is to examine the evolution of policy and of performance, sector by sector, in various types of developing economies over time, and to explain the contrast in terms of differences in initial resource endowments, differences in the extent and nature of external shocks and, most importantly, differences in the capacity to overcome the inevitable political economy constraints to policy change.

NOTES

[1] Deepak Lal, 1984: *The Poverty of Development Economics*, London: Hobart Paperbacks, no. 16.

[2] Ian M. D. Little, 1982: *Economic Development; Theory, Policy and International Relations*, New York: Basic Books.

[3] Albert O. Hirschman, 1982: "The Rise and Decline of Development Economics," in Gersovitz, Díaz-Alejandro, Ranis and Rosenzweig, eds, *The Theory and Experience of Economic Development*, London: George Allen, Unwin, 1982.

[4] Henry Bruton, "The Search for a Development Economics," *World Development*, 13(10/11), Oct./Nov.

[5] Paul Streeten, 1981: *Development Perspectives*, London: Macmillan.

[6] Simon Kuznets, 1966: *Modern Economic Growth*, New Haven: Yale University Press.

[7] The period is comparable to the Meiji period in Japan, or the period of the Industrial Revolution in England during which a growth consciousness found its academic consonant in the emergence of classical growth theory. Growth theory revived after World War II for the same reason.

[8] In the aftermath of the Great Depression, this political will (as reflected, for example, in the Full Employment Act of 1946 in the United States) was focused on the battle against unemployment. While concerns were with the deficiency of effective demand, the urgent social problem was instability and not the rapidity of growth.

[9] Hollis B. Chenery, 1979: *Structural Change and Development Policy*. London and New York: Oxford University Press; Jagdish Bhagwati and Anne Krueger, 1973: "Exchange Control, Liberalization and Economic Development," *American Economic Review*, May; John C. H. Fei and Gustav Ranis, 1975: "A Model of Growth and Employment in the Open Dualistic Economy – The Cases of Korea and Taiwan," *Journal of Development Studies*, Jan.; Bela A. Balassa et al., 1982: *Development Strategies in Industrial Economies*, World Bank, Baltimore: Johns Hopkins University Press.

[10] Ian M. D. Little, Tibor Scitovsky, and Maurice Scott, 1970: *Industry and Trade in Some Developing Countries; A Comparative Study*. Development Center, OECD, New York: Oxford University Press.

[11] Vittorio Corbo, 1985: "Reforms and Macro-Economic Adjustments in Chile During 1974–84," *World Development*, 13(8), Aug. And Sebastian Edwards, 1985: "Economic Policy and the Record of Economic Growth in Chile: 1973–82," in G. Walton (ed.), *National Economic Policies in Chile*, Greenwich, CT.: J.A.I. Press.

[12] See Anne Krueger's path-breaking article "Political Economy of a Rent-Seeking Society," *American Economic Review*, June, 1974.

[13] One key statistical indicator in this connection is the trade ratio (i.e. total value of exports as a fraction of GNP). The economy takes on an internal (external) orientation when the trade ratio declines (increases).

[14] A point that deserves comment is that this "externally originated" cause of instability in LDCs is basically different from the "internally originated" cause in DCs. Thus, while aggregate demand management in the DCs is directed at "internally originated instability", demand management in LDCs is directed at growth in the context of externally originated instability.

[15] The resulting relative monetary passivity apparent in Taiwan and, to a lesser degree, Korea, but not in Latin America, is a part of the East Asian liberalization movement from the very beginning of the EO phase in these countries.

[16] Even contemporary socialist LDCs, e.g. the Chinese Communist authorities,

have rationalized their own brand of liberal reform (post-1979) by tracing it, with considerable justification, to what they now call the "fundamental teachings of Marx," according to which "forces of production" will always be liberated from artificial and outdated institutional constraints while the Party only expedites the process at the present time in an "experimental" way. In this regard, the Communist authorities were quick to learn from their inflationary experiences of 1984–85 that the convenience of purchasing power creation is not something to be used lightly.

[17] In the East Asian countries (Taiwan, South Korea, Hong Kong and Singapore), in which natural resources are conspicuous by their absence, the laborers and entrepreneurs must earn an income competitively in the world market – rather than through rent-seeking political patronage. Exogenous shocks are less of a problem because of their more diversified export capacity.

[18] This is not to suggest that full integration with world financial markets is foreseeable anywhere in the near future. Given completely free international capital movements, the basic sovereign economic power of the LDC government would collapse. Given rapid inflation, the inverse of Graham's Law implies that a stable foreign currency (e.g. the U.S. dollar) would drive out the domestic currency as a standard of value and even as a medium of exchange when not protected by the political force of "legal tender." Even in contemporary Taiwan, the full integration of the domestic financial market with the rest of the world is still stubbornly resisted.

[19] The multiple exchange rates, the import licensing system, the differential interest rate structure and/or availability of bank credit to "favored" public or private sector industries are typical examples. In the industrially advanced countries aggregate demand management is, generally speaking, more likely to be directionally neutral as, aside from public goods, the private sector is left alone to determine the direction of resource allocation. Under the U.S. Federal Reserve System, for example, the monetary authorities only control the overall levels of new bank lending, leaving the market to determine the precise direction of individual allocations.

[20] The U.S. action in "bailing out" Chrysler may be considered "selective window dressing" for the DC case.

[21] In the inflationary epoch of the 1970s an institutional (or cost-push) theory of price inflation (analytically, the Phillips curve literature) emerged in the industrially advanced countries. Recently cost-push theory has receded as inflation was finally brought under control by tight monetary policies. As long as the growth rate of money does not exceed the GNP growth rate too much, most people will now agree, unions are powerless to "cost-push" prices to higher levels by their "money" and "power" illusion. Thus, a tight monetary policy can effectively discipline labor unions by leaving them a choice of either a high-wage gap (favoring their own members only) or higher employment with stable price levels, leading to higher incomes for all working families.

[22] The demarcations of the subphases are matters related to the use of statistical time series to implement growth theoretical reasoning that supplies the turning points of the phases.

[23] These external demand forces represent combinations of the world prices of

primary products and the business cycle in the industrially advanced countries.

[24] The interrelatedness among the policy variables is a matter of macro-economic theorizing. In the case of LDCs, policy exercises in postwar years have been conducted in a theoretic vacuum in view of the irrelevance of stabilization policies to growth-related issues.

[25] Total tax revenue T is the sum of T_a (taxes on income of agriculture) and T_q (taxes on income of nonagriculture).

[26] This noncompensatory characteristic is very different from the usually compensatory nature of fiscal policies in the United States, where budget deficits decrease during relatively full employment years.

[27] The various Keynesian motives for holding on to money (i.e. not spending) are contradictory to the perceived political economy reality of the typical LDC, where the government's willingness to spend is the primary reason for monetary expansion – with little or no regard for "liquidity preference."

[28] The existence of these three components can be statistically verified by the so-called "money base" approach to the decomposition of dM/dt as traced to its internal and/or external origins. A general rule is that, within C_i, money creation shifts towards money of "internal origin."

[29] When price inflation is brought under control by the political force of price control, inflationary pressures are only suppressed. As long as the quantity of money is more than adequate to meet transaction demands, price inflation can be expected to be rekindled once the controls are lifted.

[30] It is a historical misfortune that the elementary fact that bank loans must be repaid becomes almost an irrelevant minor detail in the liquidity preference theory of interest. To put the emphasis on the total money stock (M) rather than the flow of its creation (dM/dt) renders the Keynesian theory almost entirely irrelevant to the political economy of LDCs. Far more relevant are the Swedish and the forced saving schools of thought based on the loanable funds theory, in which the obligation of the repayment of a bank loan is implicitly recognized.

[31] In an industrially advanced country (e.g. the U.S.), given its highly developed financial institutions (e.g. stock and money markets) which compete effect-ively with the commercial banks, rational expectations which tend to restore the natural rate of interest can be effective at times of anticipated price infla-tion. Under competitive pressure from the money market, commercial banks have to "index" the interest rate for savers, de facto, i.e. without a government decree – as is the case for government-controlled commercial banks in LDCs.

[32] Taxation with consent can be more readily realized through fiscal reforms in the East Asian countries because their higher capacity to agree is ensured by a deep-rooted cultural trait that emphasizes "obligation" (to oneself and to the society) rather than "human rights," a Western cultural trait. This Chinese cultural trait has often been crudely seen through "Western" eyes as "oriental despotism" or the readier acceptance of an "authoritarian" government.

[33] We really cannot blame the LDCs for their slow acceptance of such a non-Keynesian idea which was popularized only in the 1970s in the U.S. through the preachings of both the monetarists and the rational expectations group, as well as the practitioners of the Federal Reserve system. In historical perspec-

tive, we see that it was the de facto indexing in the money market that destroyed the crude liquidity preference theory of Keynes. For with indexing the market rate of interest moves upward, rather than downward (as the Keynesian theory would predict), at the news of an increase in the quantity of money.   .

[34] This is, in fact, almost certain to happen when there is a political election cycle to contend with since it is foolish to leave the external purchasing power to be spent by the next administration when it can be used to enhance the popularity of this administration.

[35] It is at this juncture that the government also begins to think about "export promotion" (e.g. by means of an export bonus scheme) to partially compensate for the overvaluation of the currency. Such selective export promotion schemes are bound to fail because of the basic contradiction between the government's desire to discriminate against existing exports and its desire to promote (i.e. to diversify into) new (potentially profitable) exports.

[36] The fact that an overvalued domestic currency (conducive to an import surplus) can act as an "inflation fighter" was a popular idea at the time (1984) in the United States. The same idea is routinely in vogue in the recession phase in most LDCs.

[37] There is no need to elaborate the content of these four subphases at great length here. The interested reader is, however, referred to Kazushi Ohkawa, Gustav Ranis and John Fei, 1985: "Economic Development in Historical Perspective: Japan, Korea, and Taiwan," in *Japan and the Developing Countries: A Comparative Analysis of Development Experience*, K. Ohkawa and G. Ranis (eds), Oxford: Basil Blackwell.

Comments on
"Development Economics:
What Next?"

PRANAB BARDHAN

I wholeheartedly endorse the suggestion of Gustav Ranis that one of the major directions in which development economics can fruitfully move is toward a political economy of organizational and policy change. In trying to understand developmental success and failure, we have often come up against our basic incapacity to explain "how different systems make their organizational and policy choices" and "why some societies manage to move from here to there, and most do not."

In this connection he points to the differential performance of the newly industrializing countries of East Asia *vis-à-vis* other parts of the developing world, say Latin America, where the last two or three decades have been marked by an oscillatory pattern of policy choice and less successful policy outcomes. In the context of his compact but incisive account of the evolution of development policy in Taiwan over the last 35 years, he attempts to explain the differential performance by pointing to two types of initial conditions. The first has to do with "the extent of political intervention during the essentially inevitable early import-substitution subphase, ... based on the maturity of the initial nationalism the newly independent government can count on." The weaker states, often "lacking at the outset a relatively homogeneous population focused on national development objectives," tend to promise too much on what government intervention can accomplish and to undervalue the benefits of participation in the international economy. The second initial condition has to do with the absence or presence of natural resources. In natural-resource-scarce economies, there is less rent to be squeezed out of the natural-resource-intensive sectors in the initial phase and outward orientation tends to come quicker.

While there is no doubt that Ranis puts his finger on two important initial conditions, my judgment is that his explanation of differential development performance based on them is a trifle too easy. The key issue, I think, is not maturity of nationalism (except in a tautological sense), or pragmatism of leadership, or scarcity of natural resources; it is the ability of the state to insulate economic management from the pressures of short-run rent-seeking by powerful interest groups. The Taiwanese military regime, like its South Korean counterpart under Park and Chun, centralized decision-making power in the executive branch of the government, granted considerable operational space to economic technocrats, and carried out a corporatist restructuring of relations with labor, business, and the rural sector to an extent unmatched by the Latin American states – even in the peak of their "bureaucratic-authoritarian" phase.

The early land reforms carried out by an invading army clipped the wings of any potentially anti-industrial landlord class. The state control over a weak labor movement made the switch to export orientation, since the middle sixties, politically much easier than in other countries. Taiwan never witnessed the kind of populist labor mobilization we associate with the postwar import-substitution phase in Latin America. Profits and exports were helped substantially by the control over rise in real wages: on a rough estimate, between 1960 and 1978 value-added labor productivity in the industrial sector went up more than five times, whereas the industrial real wage went up about three times in the same period.

Unlike in South Korea, the state in Taiwan generally has not allowed large conglomerates in domestic business (partly out of fear of concentrated economic power in the hands of any indigenous Taiwanese group) and as such, carries even more clout than in Korea in its dealings with this class. Through its control over finance, industrial licenses, foreign loan and technology agreements, and use of selective incentives and threats, the state has redirected private business into targeted sectors (the latter knew very well that the government could put the deviant out of business in a matter of months).

It is this "relative autonomy" of the state and its dominance over domestic social classes, which provides the crucial contrast between Taiwan (and Korea) and most countries in Latin America or South Asia. A pragmatic growth-oriented leadership and the relative abundance of human capital (compared to land or natural resources) have certainly been important. But negotiating the short-run political hurdles of large policy switches as the economy graduates from one phase to another and getting away with upsetting entrenched interests at each stage would have been a much more formidable task in a system where the channels of interest articulation were less tightly under the control of the state. The relative social homogeneity of the population in Taiwan or South Korea, in contrast to, say, South Asia, also helped – by keeping the social conflicts and the attendant problems of conflict management in periods of transition somewhat more manageable. Compared to Latin America, the entrenched foreign interests in the import-substitution phase in Taiwan have also been fewer. Foreign firms and foreign banks were allowed to operate in any significant way only after the export boom of the late sixties was well under way.

Comments on
John Fei's "Evolution of Development Policy"

HELEN HUGHES

John Fei draws a sharp distinction between developing and developed countries' policies and experience since World War II: he argues that the developed countries, in reaction against the depression of the 1930s, opted for stability and full employment, while developing countries concentrated on the transformation of their poor and backward economies through rapid growth to achieve rising standards of living. This involved turning limited and imperfect markets into fully articulated and competitive ones. The transformation of developing countries occurred in two phases. An import-substitution phase, characterized by inflation as a means of taxation, has generally been followed by an external-orientation phase, with appropriate fiscal policies ending inflation. Paths of transformation, however, differed. The East Asian "gang of four" achieved a linear and rapid movement from import substitution to export orientation with tax probity, whereas other developing countries, notably the resource-rich Latin American countries, took a longer, more complex, indirect, and "oscillating" route to export orientation.

Keeping with the spirit of the mid-1980s in discussing the evolution of developing policies associated with these two principal transformation paths, John Fei emphasizes financial, exchange, and fiscal macroeconomic policies, with trade policies playing a more limited role than they did in John Fei's writing a decade ago. Policies act on the money supply and rate of interest, the level of reserves and rate of foreign exchange, the relative prices of tradeables and non-tradeables, and the relative level of national inflation. Also in keeping with the spirit of the times "rational expectations" explain the limits to the use of inflation as an instrument of taxation.

Two exogenous conditions – commodity price fluctuations and business cycles in developed countries – affect the transformation process in Fei's model. The pessimistic scenario introduced by Arthur Lewis and Jeff Williamson in the first chapter of this book concludes John Fei's argument. Exogenous influences are the principal sources of growth for developing countries. In contrast to the rapid growth of markets for developing country exports in the "golden age" of the 1950s and 1960s, future global economic conditions are expected to be much less favorable than those of the past. Despite the poor record of economic forecasts during the past 40 years, a belief in the ability to foretell future economic trends remains a constant in economic thought. Export pessimism is again attracting a large following. In the stringent environment that John Fei foresees, conventional macro-economic instruments will remain the key to economic performance.

While unrealistic economic constructs have at times contributed sharp insights to economic analysis, more generally the fit of a model's stylized facts to reality is critical to its explanatory power. Binary approaches rarely succeed in clarifying economic analysis for this reason. The real world does not consist of "developing" and "developed" countries, or of "inward"- and "outward"-oriented ones, but of overlapping spectrums of countries varying only slightly in terms of per capita income, total income size, population size, natural-resource endowment, administrative capacity and the appropriateness of policies. In each analytically relevant area, analysts are generally more ready to disagree than to agree on all but the extremes of the spectrums. The economy of Chad is clearly different from Singapore, but there are great similarities between Mauritania and Chad, and Hong Kong and Singapore. The precise characteristics of policies and their impact on economic growth and development are particularly difficult to describe and analyze. Thus, a Martian economist well might conclude that the Republic of Korea and India had similar trade regimes, but the effects of these regimes quite generally are recognized to be at opposite ends of the inward/outward-oriented spectrum.

The usefulness of a model also depends on its internal logic. John Fei's paper provides only the bare bones of "development policy," but it is clear that "development" policy is differentiated from "economic" policy just as "development economics" is often thought to be different from the economics used to analyze industrial or "developed" countries. The analytical insights accumulated since World War II suggest that this dichotomy neither describes reality accurately nor contributes to the effective management of developing countries. On the contrary, the economic management of many developing countries has been weakened by the special pleading of "development economics." The claims that the economic, institutional, and political conditions of "underdevelopment" mean that policy solutions based on standard economic analysis will not be effective are extremely dubious.

In economies at the very beginning of the modern development process, low savings, the lack of entrepreneurial and other skills, and the prevalence of subsistence activities with a concomitant absence of clearly defined markets certainly make special demands on policy formulation. However, the majority of people in developing countries do not live in such circumstances but in countries in which entrepreneurs abound and market conditions prevail in most of the economy. For example, a tendency of markets to break through the attempts to regulate them away has been one of the most consistent aspects of

Chinese development. And recourse to markets quickly led to the burgeoning of entrepreneurship and to rising productivity. The market economy is thus more prevalent than is sometimes supposed or admitted.

The role of government has, nevertheless, been central to lifting global growth trends to unprecedented and unexpected heights during the past 40 years. The balance between the role of markets and governments has thus emerged as a critical determinant of growth and development. Governments clearly have an important role to play in the establishment of law and order (without which a country cannot flourish), in creating an overall intellectual climate that favors growth and development, and in regulating sectors characterized by natural monopolies and high externalities. Markets should be left to determine prices and hence supply and demand decisions where the numbers of economic actors are large and information flows are serviceable. The area between these two extremes remains a no man's land, where decisions about the appropriateness of government intervention and its form must be made for each country and each period of time.

Macro- and microeconomic policies, similarly fairly clearly defined at their extremes, run into each other to affect many types of economic activity simultaneously. Thus, monetary policies not only affect levels of inflation and exchange rates but day to day investment decisions about capital–labor ratios in production. Migration policy not only has microeconomic effects, but has been an effective instrument of anti-inflationary policy in countries such as Singapore and Hong Kong.

Indirect policies that act on economic behavior through price incentives are generally preferable to direct regulation and other forms of government intervention, such as investment in public enterprises. Indirect intervention is usually thought of as having fewer unintended byproduct effects than direct intervention, being administratively simpler and hence less costly, and leading to less rent-seeking. However, in developing as in industrial countries where external benefits from an activity are large or competition is not effective so that private ownership has to be controlled by public regulation to protect consumers, there is often little sense to privatization. At times a bold stroke of direct intervention can be highly effective. The debate between balanced and unbalanced growth continues in ever new guises about the nature of intervention. Was the successful post World War II land reform in the Republic of Korea and Taiwan an "unbalancing" act that cleared the way to rapid agricultural development or the first step toward balanced agricultural and industrial growth?

Despite their distributional importance, intertemporal trade-offs, notably in investment versus consumption, have rarely been explicitly recognized in the decade in which distributional issues have often held center stage despite dubious logic and even more dubious data. As high savings and investment ratios came to be associated with rapid growth in the late 1960s, the emphasis came to be increasingly on the maximum that could be saved and invested. Borrowing for investment (and sometimes for consumption) was encouraged, almost without regard to effectiveness of the investment. Despite a revival of concern with timing and sequencing issues, particularly after acute liberalization problems in Latin America led to rapid income declines, inter-temporal issues have remained "too hard" for most economic analysts.

Tracing the way in which political action by farming, business and other vested interests affects economic policies has joined more traditional quantitative aspects of economic analysis in recent years. The factors influencing the supply and demand for protection are as real as those that determine supply and demand for apples. Moreover, not only do vested interests affect the content and form of policy, the form of policies can affect the attitudes of political interest groups and the vigor with which they pursue their interests. The new political economy of policy formulation has thus far largely been applied to industrial country policy analysis, but the resistance to moving from John Fei's import substitution to export orientation through "structural adjustment" is so considerable in many developing countries, that greater attention to formal political economy issues in policy formulation in developing countries is likely to have a high pay-off.

Economic analysts no doubt will continue to disagree on questions of form and substance as they sift through past development experience for clues to the improvement of development policy. Tedious and repetitive though such debate often seems, it has contributed to a rapid evolution of development policy. With the improvement of economic performance in South Asia and more recently in China, many more people were affected by rapid growth in the 1970s than in the 1960s, despite the relatively slower growth of the world markets in the later period. Many aspects of policy effectiveness remain unsolved, but enough is known to accelerate growth in slowly growing countries. There is now no excuse for the governments of developing countries that do not approach the high, long-run GNP growth of the East Asian countries.

PART II
Typological Experience
and Prospects

6

Problems, Development Theory, and Strategies of Latin America

VITTORIO CORBO

ABSTRACT

In this paper, I examine the influence of both economic problems and development theories on the growth strategies followed by Latin American countries in the last 70 years. Up to the Great Depression, most countries in the region were fairly open to trade, and comparative advantage was the basis for the leading development theory. From the Great Depression to World War II, most countries practiced crisis management as a reaction to the sharp external shocks coming from the Depression. Toward the end of the 1940s, the first attack on free trade orthodoxy was launched by the structuralist school, headed by Raúl Prebisch. It championed import-substitution industrialization. By the early sixties, however, disappointed with the perspective for growth, Brazil and Colombia and to a lower degree Chile, started reforms aimed at reducing the anti-export bias of their import-substitution policies. In Brazil and Colombia, the supply response of exports to the new economic incentives was dramatic: they grew even faster than did world exports in the golden decade of world trade. Later on, a second frontal attack on structuralism was launched, this time by the Southern Cone countries, which recently instituted liberalization attempts. Had it not been for ill-fated stabilization programs and the external shocks of the seventies and early eighties, the reform measures would have lifted the Southern Cone countries out of their economic stagnation. However, from these recent experiences, we have also learned that the coordination of macroeconomic policies with the liberalization policies is fundamental to achieve the expected gain from a less distorted economy.

I thank Edgardo Barandiarán, Albert Berry, Arnold C. Harberger, Jaime de Melo, Guy Pfefferman, Julio Nogués, Gustav Ranis, and Luis Riveros, for their helpful comments on a previous draft of this paper and Peter Bocock for editorial assistance. I am also indebted to participants at a seminar at Harvard University and at the 25th Anniversary Symposium of the Economic Growth Center of Yale University for their perceptive comments.

INTRODUCTION

The purpose of this paper is to study the role that economic theories have played in shaping economic policies in Latin America in the last 70 years. The paper is organized as follows.

The first section reviews events in the period from World War I to the Great Depression, a time when many Latin American countries began to move toward import substitution, some more extensively than others. Overall, however, most were still guided by the classical theory of international trade.

That pattern was disrupted by the Great Depression. The second section looks at the economic evolution in Latin America during this crisis up to World War II, a period during which Latin America responded to the economic upheaval by pursuing discriminatory switching and aggregate demand policies. Growth was now to be led by import-substitution industrialization.

By the end of World War II, most countries in Latin America had accumulated substantial foreign reserves, while it seemed certain that there would be a resurgence in world trade. The logical next step was to reduce the anti-export bias resulting from the trade policies implemented in the previous 15 years. Instead, as described in the next section, Latin America pursued and even intensified the import-substitution strategy, influenced in large part by the recommendations of Raúl Prebisch and the Economic Commission for Latin America (ECLA). This strategy of import-substitution industrialization is called here Structuralism I. When the increasing cost of this approach, especially for the medium-sized and small countries of the region, could no longer be ignored, and the times seemed to call for a lessening of import substitution, most countries simply switched to another version of the same strategy – regional integration – ideally to be complemented by foreign aid. This second phase of import-substitution industrialization, called here Structuralism II, is reviewed in the section beginning on page 162. The first attempts at reducing the anti-export bias of economic policies in the 1960s is revised in the following section.

The discussion then focuses on the eventual response of the Southern Cone countries to the continued economic difficulties that dogged their import-substitution strategies. Their positive experience with some of their liberalization reforms was unfortunately overcome by an ill-fated stabilization program and, in Chile and Uruguay, by the severe external shocks of the 1970s. Nevertheless, the progress they made until that point suggests the wisdom of adopting more open policies and promoting exports. These and other conclusions can be found in the final section.

FROM WORLD WAR I TO THE GREAT DEPRESSION

From World War I to the Great Depression, economic policies in most countries in Latin America were very much shaped by classical trade theory, and those countries were still very open to international trade. Although some countries raised their average tariff levels in the 1920s, they did so mainly for fiscal reasons. Further, most of them returned to the gold standard after World War I, and their macro adjustment was thus closely related to balance-of-payments adjustments (Furtado, 1976).

Critics of the prevailing free trade orthodoxy did, however, point to signs of growing protectionism in the most advanced countries (the United States, European nations, and Japan), although there was no clear trend. In Latin America, Argentina continued with export-led growth based on extensive agriculture that in part involved bringing new land into production (Díaz-Alejandro, 1970; O'Connell, 1986). At the same time in Argentina, discussions on alternative development strategies had already gotten under way in the second half of the 1920s, as access to export markets became more restricted. For example, in January 1927, the U.S. Department of Agriculture prohibited the import of fresh and refrigerated meats from countries with foot-and-mouth disease, the case in Argentina. Although almost all Argentina's meat exports were going to Great Britain, this policy promised restricted future access to the growing U.S. market and also created doubts about the security of the British market.

The idea of import restrictions was not new to Argentina – in the early 1920s the government had already toyed with establishing a protective tariff structure. President Marcelo Alvear, at the behest of his finance minister, Herrera Vargas, had even appointed a commission to look into the matter. Headed by Alejandro Bunge, the father of protectionism in Argentina, it proposed a very protectionist tariff structure that contained four categories of imports, with nominal tariff rates ranging from 0 to 80 percent, the lowest to be applied to raw materials and machinery, the highest to luxuries. This tariff structure was never implemented, however, and the commission was dissolved when Herrera Vargas resigned the Ministry of Finance (O'Connell, 1986).

As to Chile, it had benefited during the war from very favorable external markets, whereas its import channels had been interrupted. While its export levels remained constant, imports fell to almost half. As a result of this temporary natural protection, there had been a substantial expansion in manufacturing output (Muñoz, 1968; Palma, 1984). Although at the end of the decade of the teens, nitrates, Chile's main export product at the time, collapsed, they did recover in the second half of the 1920s. The final collapse of the nitrates industry was a result of the Great Depression and the development of cheaper synthetic fertilizers.

Nevertheless, during this period, Chile raised its tariffs first in 1916 and then again in 1928. The 1928 revision further gave the president the right to increase tariffs on individual products up to 35 percent, a power that would be used extensively during the late 1930s (Ellsworth, 1945). Another important fact of Chilean economic life was that it borrowed heavily in the second half of the 1920s to finance some ambitious public investment projects. As a consequence, it had to contend with important real appreciation of the currency in the 1926–29 period, with negative effects on the profitability of tradeable activities.

Brazil's economic evolution was still tied to the coffee cycle. Nevertheless, some import-substitution measures had been taken during the previous 50 years, and they were intensified during World War I. By 1920, import substitution was of importance in the consumer goods sector, especially with respect to textiles. However, in the middle of the twenties, when the real exchange rate appreciated as a result of good coffee prices and conservative monetary policies, the import-competing sectors lost some of their dynamism (Furtado, 1963).

Mexico was a special case, in that it was in the process of restructuring following 10 years of revolution that had started in 1911. Its most dynamic sectors were mining and agriculture. Given that the United States was its main market, the Mexican economy followed the economic cycles of its neighbor very closely. Mexico also differed from the rest of Latin America in that the country generally discouraged direct foreign investment, except where it involved new manufacturing technology. Only a little industrialization took place in this period, and it was more the result of high income growth in agriculture and mining and of internal integration than of increased protection (Díaz-Alejandro, 1982; Cárdenas, 1984).

Colombia came later to export-led growth. After a long period of stagnation following the civil war at the end of the nineteenth century, the country experienced an important expansion of exports in the first quarter of this century. This export boom was associated with the introduction of coffee into the economy and good performance of minerals and banana exports. From 1925 to 1928, important public works – financed by heavy external borrowing and good export performance – resulted in substantial growth. During this period, protection was moderate and imposed with some selectivity; tariffs were mainly used for fiscal purposes. Manufacturing output had already expanded at the beginning of this century, partly as a result of the natural protection provided by the interruption of import channels during World War I (Ocampo, 1984).

The picture that one gets from the above review is that the economic policies of most Latin American countries in the 1914–29 period were very much guided by the classical theory of international trade. At this time, economic ideas were to be found in political writings or general essays on Latin America (Hirschman, 1961). However, some import substitution did develop – both naturally, as part of the normal development process following income growth, and more artificially, when the flow of imports was interrupted during World War I. Nevertheless, in general, exports were the main engine of growth. Aggregate demand was highly diversified, with that for industrial products (mainly food, textiles, machinery, and equipment) taking an increasing share, while agriculture and mining constituted the main components of the production sector. Sectoral equilibrium between supply and demand was provided through international trade, which faced few restrictions, mainly in the form of low tariffs and export taxes on primary products. Also at that time, tax revenues came primarily from the foreign trade sector and government expenditures were oriented toward the development of physical infrastructure. Macro-policies were mostly governed by the rules of the gold standard, and there was relative price stability. Capital inflows became important in the second half of the twenties but fell substantially in 1929. Until that time, balance-of-payments crises were the exception.

Although primary data on growth in manufacturing output and overall GDP are relatively poor for the pre-1930 period, some information exists for the largest countries in the region. At the country level, we observed that manufacturing growth in Argentina was closely related to export expansion and the growth of the domestic market. Import substitution was not important before the Great Depression: the import–GDP ratio, which was 26 percent in the 1900–4 period, fell only marginally – to 25 percent in 1925–29 (Reynolds, 1985, p. 88) Industrialization had occurred with a manufacturing sector that grew at an average rate of 11.5 percent per year between 1900–4 and 1910–14, and by 5.4 percent per year between 1900–4 and 1925–29 (Díaz-Alejandro, 1970).

In Chile, manufacturing output grew at an average annual rate of 5 percent between 1914 and 1925–9 (Palma, 1984). Fragmentary information also indicates that manufacturing grew more rapidly than GDP in the pre-1914 period. Export-oriented sectors were again the main sources of growth in manufacturing and income (Muñoz, 1968).

In Brazil, manufacturing activity closely followed the income effect of the coffee cycle. Manufacturing grew at about 4.6 percent per year from 1911 to 1920, and by 3 percent per year from 1920 to 1924 (Reynolds, 1985).

In Colombia, export quantum grew at the respectable rate of 7 percent per year between 1905–9 and 1925–9. GDP figures are available only for the latter part of the period and show 8.6 percent average annual growth rate for the 1925 to 1928 period (Ocampo, 1984).

FROM THE GREAT DEPRESSION TO WORLD WAR II

The Great Depression sent many unfavorable shocks through Latin America's economies. First, as the international commodity markets collapsed, export prices fell more than import prices, and the terms of trade in individual countries dropped between 21 percent and 45 percent (CEPAL, 1976). Second, the capital inflows that had become important up to 1928 had almost disappeared by 1929. Third, the collapse in export prices increased substantially the real burden of external debt.

A fourth factor was rising protectionism in the key industrialized countries, which made the prospects for world trade very discouraging. Protectionist pressures in this period resulted in the Smoot–Hawley tariff of 1930 in the United States, the British Abnormal Importation Act of 1931, and the Ottawa Commonwealth Preferences of 1932.

In light of these large external shocks and given the dark prospects for world trade, the Latin American economies were forced to adjust. (For the policies followed by the most important Latin American countries in the 1930s, see also Maddison, 1985.) In modern terminology, there were, in principle, three adjustment policies or policy combinations available to them. The first, a gold standard policy, involved engineering a monetary contraction and, via domestic deflation, reducing the level of imports and increasing exports. The second was to alter the exchange rate so as to combine a cut in absorption with demand and supply switching. Third was to encourage selective switching through import restrictions, combined with exchange controls and expansionary demand policies.

The first course was judged politically infeasible for countries with a high proportion of their population in the urban sector. Since most of the urban labor force owned no agricultural land, they had nothing to fall back on if their employment in the industrial sector was terminated as a consequence of contractionary measures.

Given the pessimistic view of future world trade, the second option was also disregarded. During and following the Depression, most industrialized countries were closing their doors to international trade, a situation that reduced the market for Latin American exports significantly. Furthermore, because most imports of developing nations did not have close domestic substitutes, their short-term import price elasticities were very low. Within this framework, a real devaluation was not favored as the main instrument for restoring an external balance.

Thus, most Latin American countries ended up following the third option – a mix of discriminatory switching and aggregate demand policies. To implement it, they abandoned the gold standard, imposed exchange controls and discriminatory trade restrictions (such as quotas tariffs, and multiple exchange rate systems) on imports of consumer goods, and adopted countercyclical fiscal and monetary policies. This set of policies has been called the model of domestically oriented growth. Import-competing manufacturing activities were given an advantage not only through protective trade policies, but also through tax and credit incentives. Specifically, the dynamic growth element, instead of being the export sector as it was up to the eve of the Great Depression, was private and public investment in import-substitution industries and public investment in infrastructure geared to these industries' needs.

A last point is that by the end of 1933, all Latin American countries except Argentina stopped full service of their external debt. Argentina continued meeting its obligation only because most of its debt was held by Great Britain, which also happened to be its largest export market. But an emerging confrontation was developing with the increasingly restricted access of Argentinian exports to Great Britain.

It should be noted that, although most Latin American countries ended up pursuing the third option, they did so not as a conscious policy choice, but as the end result of their implementation of *ad hoc* policy measures designed to accelerate adjustment to the severe external shocks they were facing. Indeed, those countries that broke away from the gold standard while they followed active public expenditure policies (in particular Argentina, Brazil, Chile, Colombia, and Mexico) still pursued a fiscal policy aimed at achieving a balanced budget. This approach did not keep them, however, from running small deficits. Even in Brazil, whose coffee price support system that dated from 1906 resulted in a large increase in expenditures, the fiscal implications of these measures were only moderately expansionary (Furtado, 1963; Fishlow, 1972; Silber, 1977; Cardoso, 1979). In Argentina, Prebisch, then the director of research at the Central Bank, was recommending fiscal discipline to avoid an outburst of inflation. With respect to the appropriateness of the use of orthodox fiscal policies, Prebisch (1986, p. 134) notes:

> I do not think it was mistaken, given the need to stop inflation and check the fiscal deficit before they become uncontrollable. What did this orthodox economic policy, for which I was totally responsible, consist of? In the first place, it took the form of a considerable fall in public expenditure, including a 10 percent cut in public sector wages; these were brutal measures that allowed for a drastic reduction. In the second place, it meant an increase in taxation; in this area we decided to seek new paths by introducing an income tax.

In Colombia, the Lopez Government introduced a major stabilization program in 1934, and a fiscal surplus was achieved in 1935.

Thus, in most Latin American countries in the pre-World War II period, fiscal policy was still relatively conservative. Except in

Argentina, however, monetary policy was more active. As shown in table 6.1, growth in the real money supply in Brazil, Chile, and Colombia was higher than in the United States, in spite of a sharp drop in international reserves. Thus, those countries more than compensated for the drop in reserves with expansion in domestic credit.

On the relative price side, three main factors were at work: (1) the world Depression, with the resultant collapse in the prices of primary commodities; (2) widespread exchange controls and devaluations following the devaluation of the pound in September 1931; and (3) the multiple exchange rate system and an increase in the levels and variations of nominal tariffs, with effective rates of protection many times the nominal rates and increasingly a function of the stage of fabrication. Grouping output into three categories – importables, exportables, and non-tradeables – the relative prices of importables and non-tradeables in terms of exportables increased. Within importables, the sharpest increases were for consumer durables.

Real exchange rates, exclusive of the tariff and non-tariff effects for importables in terms of non-tradeables, are presented in table 6.2. The table shows that large real devaluations took place in most of the large countries during the 1930s. If the effects of the tariffs and other constraints on trade (such as multiple exchange rates and import quotas) are added to these rates, the increased incentives to import substitution

TABLE 6.1   *Real money supplies*

Year	Argentina	Brazil	Colombia	Chile	U.S.
		(1931 = 100)			
1928	99.6	76.4	111.9	n.a.	105.9
1929	97.4	78.5	91.2	n.a.	104.4
1930	96.5	85.6	91.3	n.a.	104.4
1931	100.0	100.0	100.0	100.0	100.0
1932	110.5	106.1	143.2	126.2	100.6
1933	96.6	104.1	172.6	120.9	93.6
1934	109.8	113.3	147.7	139.0	99.7
1935	103.2	118.6	145.3	154.4	116.5
1936	104.5	128.2	164.9	164.2	124.9
1937	108.1	122.5	166.9	154.7	120.7
1938	106.7	147.3	164.1	159.7	127.7
1939	108.3	151.2	162.2	172.8	142.2

Sources: The data for nominal money supplies and price indexes, except for Chile, are taken from tables 1.9 and 1.6, respectively, in Díaz-Alejandro (1983). The Chilean price level data comes from table V (which refers to the cost of living index in Santiago) in Ellsworth (1945, p. 165). The data for nominal money stock in Chile refer to the end of the year stock figures obtained from table 11 of Deaver (1970, p. 60), found in Meiselman (1970).

are seen to be even sharper. Indeed, the evidence shows that protection became redundant in Chile (Ellsworth, 1945), Argentina (Díaz-Alejandro, 1970) and Brazil (Reynolds, 1985). The non-tradeable sector expanded not only as a response to improvement in its relative price, but also because government services and public investment in infrastructure (an important non-tradeable) grew. Not surprisingly, there was substantial government intervention in this decade, not only in economic management but also in important infrastructural projects.

With respect to overall economic performance, Latin America did quite well in the 1931–40 period in comparison with the most advanced countries. As six tables (6.3 through 6.8) show for Latin America as a whole and for Argentina, Brazil, Colombia, Chile and Mexico individually, the average annual rate of GDP growth for the decade was 4.8 percent in Chile, 4.2 percent in Colombia, 3.6 percent in Brazil, 2.5 percent in Argentina, and 2.4 percent in Mexico, with the countries that followed the more expansionary monetary and fiscal policies growing at the highest rates. For the same period, the average annual rate of growth was 2.7 percent in the United States, −1.2 percent in France, 3.4 percent in Great Britain, and 4.1 percent in Japan (Maddison, 1982). In all Latin American countries for which we have comparable informa-

TABLE 6.2   *Real exchange rates*

Year	Argentina	Brazil (1929 = 1.00)	Colombia	Chile
1929	1.00	1.00	1.00	1.00
1930	1.09	1.19	1.22	0.97
1931	1.41	1.84	1.34	0.89
1932	1.61	1.61	1.46	3.00
1933	1.15	1.45	1.65	2.35
1934	1.50	1.68	1.68	1.84
1935	1.41	1.87	1.71	1.74
1936	1.32	1.89	1.64	1.79
1937	1.23	1.63	1.65	1.59
1938	1.30	1.73	1.48	1.49
1939	1.43	1.83	1.37	1.45

Sources and methods: The real exchange rates are calculated in 1931 constant prices and converted into indexes with 1929 = 1.00 as follows:

$$\text{Real exchange rate} = \frac{\text{Nominal exchange rate} \times \text{U.S. price index.}}{\text{Price index of each country}}$$

The data for the nominal exchange rates and price level indexes, except for Chile, are taken from tables 1.5 and 1.6, respectively, in Díaz-Alejandro (1983). The Chilean price level data come from table V (which refers to the cost of living index in Santiago) in Ellsworth (1945, p. 165). The data for the nominal exchange rates are obtained from de la Cuadra and Cortés (1984).

TABLE 6.3   *Trade and output growth in Latin America as a region, 1931–80*

	1931–40	1941–50	1951–60	1961–70	1971–80
			(percentages)		
Exports: current dollars	− 4.0	13.1	1.2	5.4	20.1
1963 dollars	− 1.2	1.5	3.7	4.1	6.0[a]
Imports: current dollars	− 2.5	13.7	0.9	5.8	17.0
1963 dollars	1.5	5.7	1.0	4.5	7.0[a]
GDP[b]	n.a.	4.0	4.5	5.0	5.3
GDP primary[b]	n.a.	2.0	3.6	3.2	3.2
GDP manufacturing[b]	n.a.	5.3	5.9	6.0	5.4
GDP construction and services[b]	n.a.	1.7	4.3	5.2	5.8
Terms of trade[c]	89.0	109.8	122.5	100.8	123.2

[a] 1982 dollars for this decade.
[b] Figures in 1970 constant dollars.
[c] This is an index with average 1963 = 100.
Sources: The trade data up to the last decade are from CEPAL (1976); the last decade is from IDB (1985). The GDP data are from CEPAL (1978 and 1984a). The terms of trade data are from CEPAL (1976 and 1984b).

TABLE 6.4   *Trade and output growth in Argentina, 1931–80*

	1931–40	1941–50	1951–60	1961–70	1971–80
			(percentages)		
Exports: current dollars	− 5.1	9.7	− 0.8	6.3	16.5
1963 dollars	− 3.5	− 0.6	3.5	5.3	5.9[a]
Imports: current dollars	− 5.9	13.5	− 1.7	1.4	17.4
1963 dollars	− 1.0	4.1	0.3	− 0.4	6.8[a]
GDP[b]	2.5	2.9	2.6	3.6	2.0
GDP primary[b]	2.5	− 0.8	1.9	2.9	2.6
GDP manufacturing[b]	4.2	3.5	3.8	4.6	0.7
GDP construction and services[b]	1.9	4.1	2.3	3.3	2.8
Terms of trade[c]	90.0	113.4	91.7	93.8	88.7

[a] 1982 dollars for this decade.
[b] Figures in 1970 pesos.
[c] This is an index with average 1963 = 100.
Sources: The trade data up to the last decade are from CEPAL (1976); the last decade is from IDB (1985). The GDP data are from CEPAL (1978 and 1984a). The terms of trade data are from CEPAL (1976 and 1984b).

TABLE 6.5   *Trade and output growth in Brazil, 1931–80*

	1931–40	1941–50	1951–60	1961–70	1971–80
			(percentages)		
Exports: current dollars	−4.1	14.2	−3.2	6.9	21.4
1963 dollars	1.3	−0.6	0.9	5.8	8.9[a]
Imports: current dollars	0.6	14.7	−3.1	6.9	20.0
1963 dollars	4.1	7.7	−2.3	6.1	6.5[a]
GDP[b]	3.6	3.9	6.2	5.0	7.3
GDP primary[b]	2.8	1.4	4.4	2.8	4.9
GDP manufacturing[b]	5.6	6.8	8.5	5.8	7.5
GDP construction and services[b]	3.4	3.8	5.7	5.2	9.1
Terms of trade[c]	82.1	101.0	140.6	105.3	104.9

[a] 1982 dollars for this decade.
[b] Figures in 1970 cruzeiros.
[c] This is an index with average 1963 = 100.
Sources: The trade data up to the last decade are from CEPAL (1976); the last decade is from IDB (1985). The GDP data are from CEPAL (1978 and 1984a). The terms of trade data are from CEPAL (1976 and 1984b).

TABLE 6.6   *Trade and output growth in Colombia, 1931–80*

	1931–40	1941–50	1951–60	1961–70	1971–80
			(percentages)		
Exports: current dollars	−6.0	17.9	0.0	5.3	19.8
1963 dollars	3.6	2.8	2.2	3.8	6.1[a]
Imports: current dollars	1.1	14.2	2.2	4.2	18.3
1963 dollars	4.9	5.7	2.8	3.4	7.5[a]
GDP[b]	4.2	3.5	4.3	4.7	4.9
GDP primary[b]	3.1	1.8	3.1	3.3	3.7
GDP manufacturing[b]	8.8	6.9	6.2	5.4	5.1
GDP construction and services[b]	4.9	4.3	4.6	5.3	5.4
Terms of trade[c]	93.1	97.6	135.0	105.5	127.7

[a] 1982 dollars for this decade.
[b] Figures in 1970 prices up to 1970 and in 1975 prices for the last decade.
[c] This is an index with average 1963 = 100.
Sources: The trade data up to the last decade are from CEPAL (1976); the last decade is from IDB (1985). The GDP data are from CEPAL (1978 and 1984a). The terms of trade data are from CEPAL (1976 and 1984b).

TABLE 6.7   *Trade and output growth in Chile, 1931–80*

	1931–40	*1941–50*	*1951–60*	*1961–70*	*1971–80*
			(percentages)		
Exports: current dollars	2.1	5.9	2.8	9.5	17.2
1963 dollars	3.9	− 1.1	2.1	2.6	10.6[a]
Imports: current dollars	− 5.2	9.0	4.3	4.7	18.2
1963 dollars	− 1.3	1.1	4.0	2.8	4.3[a]
GDP[b]	4.8	3.4	3.4	3.8	1.8
GDP primary[b]	3.5	0.7	2.2	3.3	2.4
GDP manufacturing[b]	7.0	4.3	4.5	4.6	0.0
GDP construction and services[b]	16.0	4.5	3.4	3.7	2.4
Terms of trade[c]	115.0	91.6	105.5	128.7	110.0

[a] 1982 dollars for this decade.
[b] Figures in 1970 prices up to 1970 and in 1977 prices for the last decade.
[c] This is an index with average 1963 = 100.
Sources: The trade data up to the last decade are from CEPAL (1976); the last decade is from IDB (1985). The GDP data for the first decade are from Palma (1984) and from then on from CEPAL (1978 and 1984a).

TABLE 6.8   *Trade and output growth in Mexico, 1931–80*

	1931–40	*1941–50*	*1951–60*	*1961–70*	*1971–80*
			(percentages)		
Exports: current dollars	− 5.0	14.3	1.9	5.5	27.3
1963 dollars	− 6.8	1.9	4.0	3.1	7.8[a]
Imports: current dollars	1.9	11.5	3.7	8.0	22.6
1963 dollars	2.4	3.8	1.4	6.3	11.4[a]
GDP[b]	2.4	5.4	5.1	6.5	6.2
GDP primary[b]	1.2	4.3	4.7	4.1	4.4
GDP manufacturing[b]	5.4	6.5	5.6	8.5	6.9
GDP construction and services[b]	2.3	5.6	5.1	6.5	6.4
Terms of trade[c]	82.0	132.6	128.5	98.9	127.3

[a] 1982 dollars for this decade.
[b] Figures in 1970 pesos.
[c] This is an index with average 1963 = 100.
Sources: The trade data up to the last decade are from CEPAL (1976); the last decade is from IDB (1985). The GDP data are from CEPAL (1978 and 1984a). The terms of trade data are from CEPAL (1976 and 1984b).

tion, manufacturing was the leading sector, followed by construction and services and finally by the primary sector. Initially, the discrimination against exportable activities did not create efficiency-loss costs during the decade, as the expanding area of activity was labor-intensive light manufacturing where the cost disadvantage *vis-à-vis* imported goods was not significant. Besides, most of the export markets were highly protected and/or in major recession.

The creation of a domestic industry geared to the production of previously imported non-durable consumer goods and some raw material inputs obviously decreased imports of these goods. However, at the same time, imports of other raw materials and capital goods required for those same industries increased. To relieve the pressure on the external accounts, "nonessential" imports were restricted, a move that accelerated the process of import substitution and its costs. Finally, World War II created both a boom in the prices of mineral exports and a natural suspension in the flow of imports from industrial countries. These conditions also stimulated demand in the import-competing sector.

LATIN AMERICA IN 1945–60: STRUCTURALISM I

It is evident that the protectionism of the thirties and the first half of the forties resulted mostly from crisis management. Eventually, the effects of the crises – that is, the Great Depression and World War II – came to an end.

As the postwar period opened, most Latin American nations found themselves with substantial foreign reserves in their central banks (although, there were convertibility problems with the pound sterling). Despite conflicting signals about the future evolution of world trade, the Marshall Plan and the creation of international institutions geared to avoid the trade wars of the previous 20 years provided positive indications of an expansion in world trade. It seemed that the stage was set for a reduction in the discrimination against exportables that had evolved over the last 15 years.

However, an important initial condition had been built up during the previous decade. The expansionary policies of the thirties and the boom in commodity markets during war years had indeed resulted in a large expansion in the demand for manufactured products. At the same time, the suspension of normal trade during World War II – a product of interrupted worldwide flows of manufacturing goods, combined with lack of international transport facilities – created a situation in which almost all manufacturing was sheltered from foreign trade. Not surprisingly, a large expansion of manufacturing resulted. New industrialist and labor groups in the emerging manufacturing sectors strongly lobbied for the enactment of tariff protection to replace temporary natural protection; differentiated tariffs and multiple exchange rates were important elements in the arsenal of import-substitution policies deployed in the 1945–60 period. Manufacturing output achieved substantial growth immediately after the war, but started to decline when the "easy" import-substitution phase was completed. One common result of these policies was slow growth in total exports and in manufacturing exports in particular: exports practically stagnated between the early postwar years and the beginning of the 1960s. This was especially the case for the Southern Cone countries (Argentina, Chile, and Uruguay) and to a lesser degree for Brazil and Colombia.

Some exceptions to these policies were performed during this period. Thus, by the early 1950s, Mexico and Peru realigned their exchange rates and lifted import-repressing policies so as to increase incentives to foreign trade (Díaz-Alejandro, 1983). The most important exception was Peru, who, after World War II, dismantled trade barriers and continued an export-led growth process until 1960, when ECLA's ideas begun to be influential (Nogués, 1985).

At this time, however, a debate emerged over what long-term development strategy Latin America should follow. Initially, the debate was at the country level. On the one side were the producers of exportables (agriculture and mining) and the traders of imported goods, who argued for reducing the bias of the trade regime against them. They were supported at the time by the mainstream economists of the region, who also favored a more balanced trade regime. On the other side were the leaders of the manufacturing associations, the new industrialists and labor in the new manufacturing industries, all of whom advocated keeping and even intensifying the protectionism. Clear manifestations of this debate appeared in Argentina, Brazil, Chile, and Colombia.

In 1948, ECLA, the special Economic Commission for Latin America (then still temporary) was set up in the United Nations. It soon entered the debate. Consisting of a group of economists under the leadership of Prebisch, ECLA proposed a development strategy for Latin America that differed from the earlier recommendations of most economists that trade be liberalized. ECLA's was the first school of thought about regional economic development to emerge in Latin America (Hirschman, 1961). An article by Prebisch (1950) that summarized the thinking of this group proved very influential with a large number of Latin American economists, including Furtado in Brazil, Noyola in Mexico, and Ahumada and Sunkel in Chile (all of whom bcame part of the staff of ECLA when it became permanent in early 1951). Prebisch (1950) presented what is called today the structuralist critique of the export-led growth model of the pre-1930 period. A central argument in Prebisch's thesis was that the main determinant of the rate of growth of per capita GDP was technical progress, a thesis few economists questioned.

Prebisch also asserted that the international terms of trade of primary exports from peripheral countries had a secular tendency to deteriorate *vis-à-vis* their imported manufactured goods. He therefore concluded that countries needed to industrialize if they were to keep the fruits of technical progress. A second component of Prebisch's thesis was that import-substitution manufacturing produced dynamic externalities.

With respect to the secular deterioration in the terms of trade, Lipsey (1963), Kravis and Lipsey (1981) and Michaely (1985) have since concluded that there is no evidence of this trend. As to the dynamic externalities of import-competing manufacturing, again the evidence shows that export-oriented manufacturing and agriculture can create as many dynamic externalities as can import-competing manufacturing (Little, Scitovsky and Scott, 1970; Krueger, 1978).

Prebisch recommended that the state should promote industrialization through protection and investment in the infrastructure to support import-competing manufacturing. Prebisch's ideas had the most impact in Chile, the country that had called for the creation of ECLA and became its home. Furthermore, ECLA economists taught at the then prestigious Universidad de Chile and gave lectures all across Latin America. They were also very influential in Brazil, where Prebisch was invited to lecture by local manufacturing interest groups in the late 1940s. In Argentina, in contrast, the Perón government was quite hostile to Prebisch from the beginning (Prebisch, 1986; Díaz-Alejandro, 1983; Furtado, 1985), and thus ECLA's ideas were not easily disseminated. At the same time, it should be noted that under Perón's first administration from 1945 to 1954, import-substitution discrimination against agriculture was pushed further than anywhere else as a result of price controls and export taxes imposed to help urban workers, Perón's main source of political support. However, Prebisch was called by the Libertarian Revolution of 1955 to advise on economic policies. He recommended stabilization of the economy and development of the basic metal industry, which he believed should serve as the engine of growth. Here we see his dynamic "externality" argument for industrialization in action.

Receptivity to policies of import-subtitution industrialization was intimately linked to political developments in the region. Popular movements and populist governments came to power in Chile, Brazil, and Argentina in the late 1930s and the 1940s. Political developments in these countries had a common theme of removing power from conservative agrarian oligarchies and vesting it increasingly in mass movements of urban workers. These latter groups made important alliances with the new industrialists against export-oriented landowners. As a part of this scenario, programs of import-substitution industrialization built up strong institutional and political support.

By the early forties, Keynesian demand management policies were becoming fashionable in Latin American academic circles and in ECLA and soon started to influence government policies (Prebisch, 1947; Pinto, 1960). Demand management provided analytical respectability for the expansionary demand policies starting in the late forties.

The expansionary demand policies and rapid use of the foreign reserves accumulated during World War II combined with increasingly restrictive trade regimes to produce accelerated inflation, balance-of-payments difficulties and slow export growth in the early 1950s. By that time, ECLA was developing another argument for import-substitution industrialization. It was based on a foreign trade gap that could be reduced only by decreasing import requirements through further import substitution. This argument was derived from a comparison of the relations over time in individual Latin American countries between import and output growth, on the one hand, and export and output growth on the other. The rationale for the first type of calculation, after accounting for relative prices, is clear. However, the relationship between exports and domestic output growth could hold only in countries where exports were a residual after satisfying the domestic market. This case hardly applied to most Latin American countries. Prebisch (1959a) postulated that the relation between the rate of growth of imports and the rate of growth of output (a total income elasticity concept) was substantially higher than the ratio of the rate of growth of exports to the rate of growth of output. Therefore, without further access to external financing, the only way to increase output growth without a balance-of-payments crisis was to reduce the income elasticity of imports through further import-substitution industrialization. He did not consider that, given the industrialization of the previous 30 years, manufacturing exports, not to mention primary exports, could respond to price incentives.[1]

In summary, most Latin American countries from the end of World War II to the late 1950s encouraged industrialization by strongly promoting industries that produced for the local market. This import substitution was implemented by means of a set of policies designed to shift the domestic terms of trade between agriculture and industry in favor of the latter. The major tool was the trade regime. Moreover, in these years of increasing state intervention, the state itself often became directly involved in import-substitution industrialization by setting up public enterprises in highly protected sectors, such as steel, petroleum, and chemicals.

The result of this policy was discrimination against exports. Through a combination of an overvalued currency, tariffs and quotas, the trade regime produced a structure of effective rates of protection that, besides being biased against existing exports (especially agricultural and mining products), was characterized by considerable dispersion of the rate of protection among industrial products.

As has by now been widely documented (Little, Scitovsky, and Scott, 1970; Balassa and associates, 1971; Bhagwati, 1978; and Krueger,

1978), these policies not only failed to halt the steady growth of imports; they also led to the stagnation of exports and a series of other undesirable effects. First, an inefficient, ever-growing bureaucracy emerged to enforce the often contradictory regulations enacted to support an overvalued currency.

Second, although the creation of a domestic industrial sector geared to the production of previously imported consumption goods led to a decline in imports of these goods, it simultaneously raised imports of the raw materials and capital goods required to produce consumption goods domestically. One consequence of this shift in the composition of imports was a greater dependence on importing. The availability of raw materials and capital goods became fundamental to the smooth functioning of the economy: if the supplies of foreign inputs were interrupted, not only would consumption levels fall as before, but unemployment and underutilization of the industrial capacity would result as well.

Third, there was a lack of competition within the industrial sector: the small size of the market either precluded the existence of many efficient firms, or very few firms were present, and they did not compete among themselves. This was a more acute problem in the smaller countries of the region (Chile and Uruguay).

Fourth, resources were socially misallocated, as indicated by the substantial dispersion in the computed domestic resource cost of the different import-competing industries (Taylor and Bacha, 1973, Berlinsky and Schydlowsky, 1982; Bergsman, 1970). This outcome was attributable mainly to the protectionist policies that closed the door on external competition and to the whole range of government intervention built up to promote industrialization.

Finally, in many cases, subsidized imports of capital goods (stemming mainly from the fact that they attracted the lowest rate in a multiple exchange rate system) led to factor price distortions that penalized employment. (For another evaluation of the structuralist-ECLA type of policies, see Fishlow, 1985.)

The proponents of the import-substitution model probably did not clearly envisage the protective regimes that finally emerged. Indeed, their recommendations were designed to achieve a degree of industrialization as a precondition for future growth based on manufacturing exports. Over time, however, as the typically small and scattered industrial sector became obsolete, protection usually increased (rather than decreasing, as had initially been envisaged by the proponents of this strategy). In this connection, it is illuminating to make a comparison with the South Korean model where the government also intervened to promote industrialization. In Korea, however, while import restrictions (tariffs and non-tariff barriers) were used as major protective devices, the government simultaneously also provided important export incentives to compensate for the bias of the import regime. Indeed, one of the most careful studies of the system of incentives in Korea has concluded that it was equally attractive for a Korean producer to produce for sheltered local markets and for world ones (Westphal, 1978). This was hardly the case in Latin America. Even in Brazil, despite the export promotion strategy of the 1960s, there was still an anti-export bias in the trade regime (Carvalho and Haddad, 1981).

THE CRISIS OF IMPORT-SUBSTITUTION INDUSTRIALIZATION: STRUCTURALISM II

The main problems facing an important group of Latin American countries (Argentina, Chile, Colombia, Uruguay, Bolivia, and Brazil) in the late fifties and early sixties were recurrent balance-of-payments crises and periodic outbursts of inflation. As a consequence, some of these countries entered into International Monetary Fund (IMF) agreements to stabilize their economies. Most of the time, the IMF-type recommendations were in direct conflict with the policies being recommended by ECLA.

Not surprisingly, a structuralist view of inflation was developed in response to the stabilization prescriptions of the IMF (Baer, 1967; Noyola, 1965; Pinto, 1960; Seers, 1962; and Sunkel, 1958). (For an evaluation of the monetarist and structuralist views of inflation, see Corbo, 1974, Chapter 5.) This new view proved very influential in delaying the implementation of the policies required to reduce inflation. The structuralist focus on supply response diverted attention from important ways of cutting inflation, such as making the adjustment of the real value of contracts more flexible and implementing credible policies for eliminating the monetization of government deficits (Harberger, 1964). Furthermore, when inflation expectations are taken into account, the trade-off between inflation and output level (or unemployment) disappears. Interestingly enough, the recent stabilization attempts in Argentina and Brazil (and also in Israel), which have been more radical than those implemented by the Southern Cone countries in the 1970s, show that the breaking by indexation schemes and nominal contracts of the monetization of the fiscal deficits is centred together with the halting components of a stabilization program. These types of policies are at odds with structuralism.

The main constraint on growth, however, was seen by the structuralists to be the scarcity of foreign exchange. Their view was that to deal with the foreign exchange constraint, Latin American countries needed to plan their economic development and to increase the size of their markets through economic integration. As planning was new to most Latin American governments, ECLA provided both training and direct collaboration in the preparation of plans. Indeed, a new United Nations Institute, ILPES (Instituto Latino-Americano de Planificación

Económica y Social) was created in the early sixties to assist Latin American countries in the preparation of their development plans. The first director of ILPES was Raúl Prebisch – indicating the importance attached to planning in the early sixties.

The programming exercises taken with the help of ILPES in many countries of Latin America followed quite closely the guidelines already laid down in CEPAL (1955). They consisted of simple multisectoral models of the static input–output type. Through its assistance with economic planning, ECLA extended its area of influence well beyond Chile and Brazil. As the policies to achieve the targets considered in the plans were never clearly articulated, the entire effort did not have much influence on economic development in the region, although it tied up some of the best professionals. In fact, the strongest incentive for planning came about with the establishment of the Alliance for Progress in 1961; it required that countries prepare a plan as a precondition for aid.

Along with the planning effort, ECLA also recommended that Latin American countries needed to move on to a second stage of import substitution (Hirschman, 1961, pp. 18–19). They were quite aware by now that growth through import substitution at the country level was becoming increasingly costly. For this reason, Prebisch (1959a and 1959b) concluded that further import substitution would have to take place at a regional level.

Thus, in the sixties, ECLA became the champion of regional economic integration. In 1959 Prebisch had written:

> Trade between Latin American countries forms only 10 percent of their total foreign trade, and industrial exports are relatively very small by contrast with countries such as Italy, Japan, and others with similar income levels. All this has resulted in the splitting of the industrialization process into as many watertight compartments as there are countries, without the advantages of specialization and the economies of scale. (1959a, pp. 267–8)

This result was only to be expected, given a strategy that encouraged import-substituting industrialization and discriminated against actual and *potential* export activities, many of the latter in labor-intensive manufacturing. However, instead of concluding that the system of protection should be rationalized to reduce its anti-export bias, Prebisch recommended that:

> The response to this should be the enlargement of national markets through the gradual establishment of a common market...Without the common market, there will be a continued tendency by each country to try to produce everything – say, from automobiles to machinery – under the sheltering wing of very high protection. (1959a, p. 268)

With the intellectual leadership of ECLA and the support of the U.S., a Latin American Free Trade Association (LAFTA) was created in 1961. However, reduction of the trade barriers within the region was to be negotiated commodity by commodity, and the industrialists in the highly protected manufacturing sectors were to play a central role as members of the country negotiating teams. Not surprisingly, it proved very difficult to reach agreement on tariff reductions, except in the case of a small number of commodities whose production within the region was minimal.

Parallel with this development, Professor Hollis Chenery and his associates in the United States were formalizing the ECLA-type foreign exchange constraint on growth first in a Harrod–Domar framework (Chenery and Bruno, 1962; Chenery and Strout, 1966) and later in a more neoclassical framework that allowed for substitution in production (Chenery and Raduchel, 1971). In Chenery's type of framework, growth is limited *ex ante* by the larger of two gaps, one being the difference between investment and savings, and the second being the trade gap – the difference between imports of goods and services (including financial services) and total exports. These models were mostly used to articulate the potential contribution of foreign aid to growth in a foreign exchange constraint (trade-gap-binding) economy.

That latter solution was given a boost by the Alliance for Progress and the creation of the Inter-American Development Bank. However, it soon became apparent that the foreign aid being provided would not be sufficient to finance a resumption of growth. As such, regional economic integration became the central strategy.

Findlay (1971) pointed out that the binding gap (usually the foreign exchange one) must be the result of imperfections in the relevant markets or the nature of the assumptions built into the model. In particular, he questioned the assumption that trade flows do not respond to relative prices between tradeable and non-tradeable goods. More importantly, the shadow prices of foreign resources implied by two-gap models are absurdly high.

In 1969, with the LAFTA initiative going nowhere, a subset of middle-sized LAFTA members formally approved an Andean Common Market Pact, an initiative that had actually first been launched in August 1966. In designing its rules of operations, members of the Andean Pact took into account many of the lessons learned from the LAFTA initiative. Tariffs and non-tariff barriers were to be fully eliminated among member countries by the end of 1980; Chile and Colombia had advocated an even faster decline (Díaz-Alejandro, 1973). Instead of proceeding commodity by commodity, tariffs were to be reduced each year by 10 percent of the minimum *ad valorem* tariff then existing in Colombia, Chile, and Peru, which in no case was to exceed 100 percent. Thus, reduction of the tariffs was going to be automatic.

The less developed members (Ecuador and Bolivia) were, however, given more favorable terms.

Parallel with the general rule of automatic reductions, the Andean Pact called for the allocation of new manufacturing activities to individual countries to avoid duplication and to reap benefits from economies of scale. The result would be import substitution at a regional level. The countries were also to negotiate a common external tariff.

If the alternative to regional cooperation were continued import substitution at a country level, the Andean market was a definite improvement, in that it allowed countries to carry out intra-industry specialization and to create trade. However, for the whole process to be sustainable in the long run, a mildly protective common external tariff had to be implemented. This goal was never achieved, a failure that undermined the allocation of specific branches of manufacturing. That process involved a very tricky calculation of the costs and benefits for individual countries, and without agreement on a future common external tariff, it was very difficult (if not impossible) to allocate activities among member countries rationally. As to the main thrust of the sectoral agreements, it was continued import substitution, but at a regional level. This shift by itself could have reduced the economic cost of import substitution, in comparison with the alternative option of developing these industries at a country level. Here again, however, unless the common external tariff were moderated, the welfare cost of this further import substitution could have been substantial.

The politics of import substitution at a regional level proved much more difficult than that within a country, and the Andean Pact lost its dynamism in the second half of the 1970s. The final blow came when Chile, which had played a central role in the creation of the Pact, withdrew from it after failing to obtain agreement on its proposals for sharply reducing the common external tariff and for lifting the Pact's restrictions on direct foreign investment.

In the meantime, new developments were taking place on the analytic front, especially in the area of applied commercial policy. The concept of effective protection, which had been in the process of development since at least the early 1950s, became widely known to professional economists through the seminal paper of Corden (1966). His work was particularly important in terms of producing a framework for evaluating the effects of the tariff structures on value added, as well as the economic effects of different types of distortions.[2] In addition, the difference between promotion and protection was made explicit. These developments in applied commercial policy were used to evaluate the trade regimes of developing countries.

The studies (an important set of them is summarized in Little, Scitovsky and Scott, 1970; Balassa and associates, 1971; Bhagwati,

1978; and Krueger, 1978) highlighted the large economic costs associated with the import-substitution strategy and the strong anti-export bias that arose out of these policies. The costs were inversely related to the size of the economy and directly related to the intensity of import substitution. To make matters worse, according to recent work by Krueger et al. (1981) and Krueger (1983), in general the strategy of import substitution also hindered the growth of employment.

As such, it is ironic that as early as 1950, Viner (1953), in a series of lectures delivered in Rio de Janeiro, had rejected most of the arguments for protecting import-competing industry and recommended eliminating the discrimination against exports and improving the operations of the price system. (See Furtado, 1985, for an evaluation of ECLA's reception of Viner's talk.) Nor was Viner's the only challenge in the region to ECLA's ideas. They were questioned both by some academics and by other economists in the public and private sectors.

One of the early critics was Roberto Campos (1961), who questioned the emphasis in favor of industry and against agriculture, the confidence shown in the theory that by substituting public initiative for private initiative, new resources would be created, and the assumption that inflation could be used to increase capital formation in a sustainable way. In particular, Campos stated that economic incentives are one of the main factors accounting for the economic performance of Latin America. Nevertheless, it was ECLA's thoughts on the role of the state in providing protectionism that reigned supreme up to the early 1960s. With inflation a major problem in the region, rationalization of the protection system did not seem as pressing as stabilization.

Still, in the context of the stabilization programs, overvalued exchange rates were adjusted and the multiple exchange rate system eliminated or improved as ways to reduce part of the anti-export bias. However, usually the overvalued exchange rate returned fairly quickly, and the anti-export bias remained.

There were, however, a few more substantial departures from excessive import-substitution policy, stimulated in part by the exposure of a new generation of economists to alternative schools of economic thought. In the late 1950s, and especially in the 1960s, there was a substantial increase in the number of Latin Americans pursuing graduate studies in economics abroad, both in the United States and Europe. On returning to their countries, most of these newly trained economists contributed to a marked improvement in the level of economic debate. In particular they called into question stabilization policies, trade policies, and the selection of public investment projects (Diz, 1966; Universidad de Chile, 1963; Ffrench-Davis, 1971).

For example, Chile decided in 1964 to establish a stable real exchange rate through the introduction of a crawling-peg system, followed by some rationalization of the trade regime. Chile still retained a substantial bias against exports, however, and the first major break with ECLA-type policies was actually initiated by Brazil that same year, and some 15 years after Viner questioned ECLA's views. This and subsequent policy initiatives in the direction of greater liberalization are discussed in the next section.

LIBERALIZATION ATTEMPTS OF THE 1960s

As just noted, while the rest of Latin America was still struggling to deepen import substitution, Brazil undertook a set of reforms designed to improve the functioning of its markets and the profitability of export activities. The measures included: (1) a more realistic real exchange rate and elimination of most export taxes; (2) introduction of subsidized credit and tax incentives for export activities; (3) reduction of the public sector deficit and control of inflation; (4) development of a capital market; and (5) downward adjustment of real wages. Some of these new ideas were later incorporated into economic policies implemented elsewhere in the region; this was partly true during the lifetime of the Ongania Government (1966–71) in Argentina, and the Frei Government in Chile (1964–70).

After three years of adjustment without growth, Brazil's economic performance in this period was remarkable. GDP at constant prices grew at an average yearly rate of 11 percent between 1968 and 1973, and by 7.7 percent between 1973 and 1977. The value of exports rose by 23.1 percent a year on average between 1968 and 1977. By way of comparison, during the latter period, the value of world exports grew at an average annual rate of 19.1 percent.

Chile attempted to introduce some liberalization and stabilization measures during the Frei Government (1964–70). The Chicago-trained economists who were running the Central Bank at the time announced that inflation (then running at an annual rate of close to 40 percent) could not be reduced abruptly without substantial unemployment, and devised a system to adjust the value of the nominal exchange rate in accordance with the evolution of domestic inflation, international inflation and the terms of trade. The main contribution of this policy, which was subsequently adopted by many other countries, was to avoid periodic stop–go macroeconomic crises and to reduce the uncertainty facing potential exporters. On the trade side, the anti-export bias of the tariff structure was reduced with the introduction of a drawback system and later on with a reduction in tariffs, when the copper boom had produced an accumulation of foreign reserves that was having unwanted monetary consequences. Attempts to make a more substantial cut in tariffs had, however, faced strong opposition from an alliance of workers and entrepreneurs in the highly protected sectors.

Chile was soon followed by Colombia, which in 1967 also moved to reduce the bias against exports and to establish a more predictable and realistic real exchange policy. Export incentives were introduced to compensate for the anti-export bias of tariffs, and the average tariff level was reduced. The exchange rate was adjusted through the use of a crawling-peg formula. The value of Colombia's exports grew at an annual rate of 2.7 percent between 1961 and 1967, and at an annual rate of 19.1 percent between 1968 and 1977.

The favorable export performance of the late sixties and seventies allowed Colombia to avoid the periodical balance-of-payment crises of the previous 15 years. Indeed, it has been argued that the macroeconomic gains from liberalization were more important than the static resource allocation ones (Díaz-Alejandro, 1976).

Somewhat later, beginning in the mid-1970s, Argentina, Chile, and Uruguay also initiated a comprehensive set of reforms aimed at increasing the role of the markets in resource allocation and at reducing the bias against exports. Their experience is discussed in detail in the next section.

Thus a number of economic experiments were carried out in Latin America in the late sixties (and early seventies). Meanwhile, however, countries in the subcontinent had not performed as well during the 1960s as other countries at a similar level of development. Average annual growth during the decade was 5.0 percent in Latin America (table 6.3), while the upper-middle-income countries (a group that included most of the large nations in Latin America) grew at 6.4 percent. In the area of inflation, Latin America did even worse.

The early seventies witnessed an acceleration of inflation in most of the region as well as chronic balance-of-payments problems. At that time, a very strong reaction against the extreme distortions that had been accumulating during the previous 40 years emerged in the Southern Cone of Latin America. Some have called this liberalization effort a monetarist experiment, while others have called it neoliberalism. As with all reform programs, it had a little of everything.

LIBERALIZATION ATTEMPTS OF THE 1970s

Disenchantment with import-substitution policies and government intervention was deeper in those countries that were suffering from extreme macroeconomic problems and widespread microeconomic distortion. The countries where these sentiments were more pronounced were in the Southern Cone of Latin America. When military governments took over there in the 1970s, they implemented, to different degrees, important economic reforms that were opposite to the standard ECLA-type recommendations. Along with the earlier policy recommendations of the ECLA school, they have had the strongest effect on the design of economic policies in Latin America. A group of Chicago-trained economists played a key role in the Chilean reforms and a somewhat smaller one in the other two countries.[3]

The reforms started around 1974 in Uruguay and Chile, and in 1976 in Argentina. At that time, all three countries were in severe macroeconomic disequilibrium, with acute foreign exchange shortages and severe fiscal deficit-induced inflation. Hence, the reform packages entailed short-term rescue operations and stabilization policies, as well as long-term policies aimed at progressively removing government intervention in the product and factor markets.

On the micro side, the three countries suffered from severe distortions. Relative prices were distorted as a result of a combination of price controls, protective tariffs, quotas, subsidies and export taxes. Inefficient public enterprises were an important cause of high public sector deficits. Effective rates of protection of over 100 percent were more the norm than the exception. It was no wonder that only a few natural-resource-based primary commodities were the main export products.

The first task facing the new economic teams in each country was to control galloping inflation. The teams also diagnosed excessive government intervention as a fundamental cause of inefficient resource allocation and low growth. In their view, they had to deregulate the commodity and factor markets, including reducing the barriers to free trade and capital flows. Such measures would benefit resource allocation, eliminate recurrent bottlenecks, and lead to higher growth.

Chile went the furthest in its economic liberalization. Uruguay was in the middle, and Argentina moved the least.

Reform Measures

The economic teams in each country immediately had to contend with two forms of macro imbalance: extremely high inflation rates, and major balance-of-payments crises. Programs to redress these imbalances were implemented in two identifiable phases.

In the first phase, the countries based their anti-inflationary policies on major reductions in fiscal deficits and monetary growth. (The fiscal deficits were substantial long before the collapse of the civilian governments; see table 6.9.) The substantial chronic fiscal deficit of Chile was eliminated by drastic across-the-board expenditure cuts (15 percent in 1975), together with a later tax reform. In Uruguay, the fiscal deficit was reduced with the introduction of a value-added tax (VAT). However, the total deficit after reaching a balanced budget in the period 1979–81 (table 6.8), increased to 10 percent of output in 1982. In Argentina, the fiscal deficit was never really controlled (Cavallo and Peña, 1984).

TABLE 6.9 *Macroeconomic performance in the Southern Cone*

	Import substitution period	Pre-reform crisis	Reforms			Post-reform recession
			Pre-Tablita		Tablita	
	1965–70	1971–73	1974–76	1977–78	1979–81	1982–83
CHILE						
Average annual growth rate (percent)						
Gross domestic product	4.3	0.5	3.1	9.0	7.3	−7.8
Expenditure	5.1	1.3	−8.2	11.9	10.2	−14.4
Gross fixed investment	5.3	−9.8	−7.8	16.7	17.8	−26.6
Consumer price index	23.3	149.7	358.0	79.0	30.2	11.7
Average (percent)						
Fiscal deficit/GDP	2.1	16.1	5.1	1.3	−2.1	3.1
Unemployment rate	6.0	4.6	14.2	13.6	12.2	22.2
Real wage (1969 = 100)	98.0	98.0	69.0	82.0	100.0	82.0

URUGUAY

	1965–70	1971–73	1974–76	1977–78	1979–81	1982–83
Average annual growth rate (percent)						
Gross domestic product	1.9	−0.4	4.3	3.2	4.7	−7.2
Expenditure	2.9	−0.2	1.9	3.6	5.6	−11.2
Gross fixed investment	7.3	−10.8	25.0	10.5	6.9	−24.8
Consumer price index	49.8	62.7	69.2	51.3	54.0	33.3
Average (percent)						
Fiscal deficit/GDP	1.9	3.2	3.8	1.9	0.0	6.4
Unemployment rate	8.2	8.1	9.7	12.4	8.4	13.7
Real wage (1968 = 100)[a]	104.0	102.0	86.0	70.0	64.0	54.0

ARGENTINA

	1965–73	1973–75	1976–78	1978–80	1981–83
Average annual growth rate (percent)					
Gross domestic product	4.2	2.9	0.8	3.7	−3.0
Expenditure	4.2	3.3	−1.6	8.6	−6.1
Gross fixed investment	6.6	0.1	4.9	4.0	−15.1
Consumer price index	23.5	77.6	245.6	128.3	188.5
Average (percent)					
Fiscal deficit/GDP	3.0	12.0	7.7	7.9	17.8
Unemployment rate	5.7	2.4	3.4	2.2	4.7
Real wage (1976 = 100)	125.0	154.0	100.0	118.0	111.0

[a] Until October 1980, the index reflects only legislated increases in wages.

Sources: Corbo, de Melo, and Tybout (1986, table 1).

These "orthodox" measures were recognized to be contractionary, but it was thought that the potential benefits would easily outweigh the temporary costs of recession. Reducing absorption was much more important in Chile than in Argentina and Uruguay; hence, not surprisingly, the Chilean recession was the most extreme (table 6.9). This problem was compounded by a severe terms-of-trade loss in 1975.

Anti-inflationary policy measures were, in themselves, viewed as insufficient to eliminate the balance-of-payments crises. Hence, stabilization policies in each country also included major attempts to switch expenditures. Switching policies were implemented concurrently with policies designed to change relative prices among importables and between importables and exportables. In Chile, this switching of policies, accompanied by within-tradeables price adjustment, was achieved through a large real devaluation and a reduction of the barriers to imports. In Argentina, this same process was accomplished with a combination of real devaluation, reduction of taxes on exports, and some reduction of import barriers. In Uruguay, the switching included a combination of real devaluation, reduction of barriers to imports, and subsidies for nontraditional exports. To avoid a repetition of the external crises, these initial adjustments in each country were complemented by a passive, crawling-peg, exchange-rate regime aimed at maintaining purchasing power parity adjusted by changes in the terms of trade.

These initial policies successfully eliminated the balance-of-payments crises. However, although the rate of inflation came down considerably in each country, it remained disturbingly high several years after the contractionary policies had been implemented (table 6.9). The persistence of inflation motivated a major shift in stabilization tactics toward the use of the exchange rate as the main stabilization device. Expectations about inflation and devaluation were recognized as important in determining the dynamics of stabilization, and it was assumed that exchange rate targets – pre-announced up to six months in advance and with forward devaluations at a decreasing rate – would break inflationary expectations. In practice, the rate of devaluation, set according to a pre-announced schedule known as the *tablita*, was less than the existing difference between domestic and world inflation. This policy corresponded to an "active" crawling peg.

Important reforms took place on the microeconomic front. With different timing and intensity, all three countries removed price controls, liberalized interest rates, decentralized government intermediation, and partly deregulated the labor markets. All three countries also relaxed the restrictions on international trade and liberalized capital inflows. However, with the exception of domestic financial market deregulation, which proceeded rapidly in all cases, the sequencing of the reforms differed in each country. Uruguay removed all controls on capital flows and many commodity price controls early on, but progressed more slowly on the liberalization of foreign trade. Chile, to the contrary, went the furthest in eliminating domestic price controls and the endemic fiscal budget deficit and in reducing trade barriers, but it kept the controls on short-term capital flows for a long time and maintained important labor market regulations. On the other hand, Argentina also elminated price controls and removed most restrictions on short-term capital flows and quantitative import restrictions (with some important exceptions) before it implemented some *ad hoc* tariff reductions.

Rapid deregulation of the domestic financial markets, a common feature of the reforms in the three countries, was important because of the many years of non-price allocation of credit and highly negative real interest rates. All three countries substantially deregulated the domestic capital markets in two ways. First, they progressively eliminated the ceilings in interest rates. Second, they reduced the restrictions on financial intermediaries. Argentina went from 100 percent reserve requirements and directed credit programs to a decentralized fractional reserve system. The Chilean government first loosened its control of the financial system by allowing nonbank intermediaries to operate without interest rate controls. Then, in the next several years, it removed the interest ceilings on commecial banks and returned publicly held commercial banks to the private sector. In Uruguay, dollar deposits were legalized early on, and direct credit programs were dismantled. Later, in 1977, the controls on entry to the banking system were lifted.

Each country also tried to open its economy to international capital flows, but the speed and extent of this action varied. Uruguay legalized movements of private capital as early as 1974 and reached full convertibility by early 1977. Argentina eliminated most controls on capital movements in 1979. Chile progressively deregulated medium-term capital flows, eliminating the global limits on borrowing in 1979 and the restrictions on monthly inflows in April 1980. Restrictions on short-term capital inflows were not dismantled until late 1981, however.

In all three countries, there was relatively minor liberalization of the labor markets. These markets continued to be controlled through penalties or prohibitions on labor dismissals, legislated wages and/or wage indexation. However, the weakening of trade union power amounted to de facto deregulation in the early stages of the reforms.

The Results

In the early stage of the reforms, when the markets were being liberalized and inflation was being reduced through an exchange rate policy that was trying to keep an "appropriate" real exchange rate, the three countries did quite well (table 6.9). Most of their problems started when major macro imbalances developed in the post-1978 period, as they were implementing a second stabilization attempt. In Argentina, the pre-announced decreasing rate of devaluation was incompatible with the financial reforms (Calvo, 1986) and the irreducible fiscal deficit. As a consequence, significant capital inflows followed to finance the government deficit. In turn, the capital inflows fueled a large peso appreciation that became unsustainable. When real domestic interest rates sharply increased in anticipation of a major devaluation, the stage was set for a deep recession and the collapse of the heavily leveraged financial sector. In Chile, 100-percent-plus backward wage indexation was incompatible with a pre-announced decreasing rate of devaluation and resulted in a peso appreciation that the country was unable to reverse without a crisis.[4] Furthermore, the availability of easy external financing at a time when it was very profitable to borrow abroad sustained the real appreciation of the peso for a long period, a situation that hurt the exportable activities, which had started to make inroads in the external markets, and the import-competing sectors, which had just completed a quite successful adjustment to the commercial policy reforms (Corbo and Sanchez, 1985). In addition, the abrupt reduction in inflation, together with some contractionary monetary policies, resulted in 1981 in a large increase in real interest rates that created substantial hardship, especially for firms in tradeable activities (Tybout, 1986; Sjaastad, 1983). Uruguay was somewhat in the middle. By historical standards it did quite well up to 1979, when it suffered from the external shocks originating in Argentina, and then in early 1981, when a fiscal deficit emerged that was incompatible with the exchange rate policy. The ensuing real appreciation discouraged the new export activities and, to a lesser extent, the still highly protected import-competing activities.

Another problem common to all three countries was the expansion of risk-taking by the financial system. The lack of appropriate supervision and evaluation of portfolio quality on the one hand, and the de facto deposit insurance on the other, resulted in extremely risky loan portfolios and very high real interest rates. Lately, McKinnon (1986), one of the strongest advocates of financial liberalization, proposed that, to avoid adverse selection, a cap should be put on real interest rates, with financial intermediaries spending more to evaluate the quality of their loans.

CONCLUSIONS

At the risk of oversimplification, it could be said that, up to World War I, economic policies in Latin America were derived from general economic principles based on comparative advantage. During that period, growth was led by exports. While industrialization in light manufacturing was progressing, it was the result of income growth rather than of government intervention.

In the interwar period, however, and especially during the worldwide Great Depression, most Latin American countries developed substantial balance-of-payments difficulties, and they resorted initially to tariff restrictions and/or devaluations to deal with them. By the early 1920s, most had also returned to the gold standard and had put in place trade regimes that discriminated slightly against exports as a result of taxes on exports and mild tariffs on imports. When the Great Depression hit and the export and international capital markets collapsed, these countries intensified their import controls by increasing tariffs and instituting non-tariff barriers to trade. Although some reduction in import restrictions took place in the second part of the 1930s and early 1940s, the trade regime in existence at the outbreak of World War II was substantially biased in favor of import-competing manufacturing and against export activities.

As world trade resumed in the post-World War II period, Latin American exports grew, but at a slower rate than that for the world as a whole because of the anti-export bias. The average annual rate of increase for Latin America between 1951 and 1960 was 1.4 percent, as against a worldwide rate of 4.0 percent. (Latin America did experience unusually high average annual rates of growth immediately after the war – from 1945 to 1950 it was 15.5 percent – as a result of the reconstruction in Europe and the resultant high level of demand for raw materials.) In addition, industrialization was already under way, spurred by import substitution stemming from the biases in the trade regimes and by the concomitant growth in income.

Although world trade was picking up at this time, many countries in Latin America were pessimistic about the possibility of returning to export-led growth. This pessimism led to what I call "import-substitution industrialization – Structuralism I." This strategy was articulated by Prebisch at the Economic Commission for Latin America (ECLA), where he recommended import-substitution industrialization as a long-term approach.

There ensued a period of further import substitution. After two or three decades of this strategy, however, most countries found themselves facing a slowdown in their growth and increasingly severe balance-of-payments problems. Their response in the late 1950s added a new twist to the structuralist theory, one that I call "Structuralism II."

According to this version, further growth was being limited by the unavailability of foreign exchange. Given that import substitution had already been pushed too far, a new form of this strategy – regional integration – had to be pursued, preferably in combination with increased foreign aid. Economic planning would provide the coordinating framework for evaluating the policy options.

The first element in this policy prescription found expression in a movement toward regional economic integration, as ECLA had recommended in the late 1950s. The second element, based on the two-gap model of limits to growth, gave rise to the gap theory of foreign aid, given the virtual absence at the time of international capital markets for medium- and long-term capital flows and the pessimistic outlook on export growth. As to economic planning, although ECLA had been pushing planning techniques, especially projections for the trade sector since the mid-1950s, the Alliance for Progress, established in 1961, provided the strongest incentive: it made an overall economic plan a precondition for aid.

It should be noted that despite Prebisch's prescription of government intervention to pursue import substitution, he expressed early concern about the anti-export bias of existing import-substitution policies. Indeed, after his period as director of ILPES Prebisch's move into the United Nations Conference on Trade and Development (UNCTAD) showed his clear interest in improving the trade prospects of developing countries. Clearly, import substitution was carried to extremes in the late 1950s and early 1960s, and the cost of the resulting distortions became all too explicit. Moreover, in those countries that had gone the farthest with this approach, macro stabilization became a major problem in the face of recurrent balance-of-payments crises and accelerating inflation.

Some countries did recognize the dangers and instituted reforms. The first was Brazil in the mid-sixties, followed soon thereafter by Chile in 1965 and Colombia in 1967. Somewhat later, in the mid-1970s, three Southern Cone countries – Argentina, Chile and Uruguay – initiated a set of reforms oriented toward liberalizing their economies and controlling inflation. For a time their efforts proved quite successful, and they might well have worked had it not been for the substantial appreciation that resulted from ill-fated stabilization efforts and ill-advised capital inflows during the late 1970s. External shocks, particularly the oil price increases, the rise in international interest rates and the subsequent worldwide recession, coming on top of the macro errors helped the collapse of the three economies.

From the previous review of the development theories followed in Latin America, we find that up to World War II, economic policies were shaped by classical trade theory and *ad hoc* emergency strategies designed to cope with the Great Depression. Most writing on economic matters at the time was done by historians and political scientists. Only with the creation of ECLA did a Latin American view on economic development start to emerge. The main policy prescription it called for was import-substitution industrialization. In the initial stages of this strategy, when the anti-export bias was small, Latin American countries performed quite well. However, by the time the easy import substitution was completed, the increasingly distorted trade regimes that resulted created a strong anti-export bias that constrained overall growth. Many other forms of state intervention arose to complement the restrictive trade policies. They included direct public investment in some key sectors, price controls, credit allocation, and so forth. As the costs of further import substitution at a country level became too high, there was a movement toward regional integration. However, it was really just another form of import substitution, and the integration process was unsuccessful. An exception was the Central American Common Market, which functioned for a number of years.

Some movement toward reducing the anti-export bias and introducing a more realistic real exchange rate was attempted by Chile in 1965, Brazil in 1965, and Colombia in 1967, and the growth of nontraditional exports in all these countries were impressive. The most radical attack on import-substitution industrialization policies, however, had to wait until the military governments took power in the Southern Cone in the 1970s. To different degrees, they implemented policies oriented toward diminished state intervention, a reduced anti-export bias in trade policies, a reduced variance of effective protection rates, and liberalized markets. In Chile and Uruguay, where the reforms went the furthest, important gains in efficiency resulted in a resumption of growth. In Uruguay, it followed 25 years of stagnation; in Chile the sharp 1975 recession. Argentina was never able to keep a coordinated set of policies in place, and there was thus no clear trend in its performance.

A common policy implemented in the three countries in the late 1970s was a stabilization program that used the exchange rate as the main tool. Because of the inconsistency between the exchange rate policy and other macro-policies, the stabilization attempts ended up creating a high rate of real appreciation, a sharp recession, and a bankrupt financial sector.

The lesson from these experiences is not that liberalization does not work, but rather that inappropriate macro-policies are bound to result in crisis, especially in a deregulated economy. Indeed, after correcting the macro inconsistencies and some vacillations, the Chilean economy has recaptured some economic growth, despite the burden of its large foreign debt and a crippled financial sector.

NOTES

[1] It is difficult to understand the assumption that the relation between the rate of growth of exports of a country and its *own* rate of output growth is given. In fact, no such causality exists. Also, the value of this ratio depends crucially on

the bias of the trade regime. With the anti-export bias of the trade regime in Latin America of this period, it is not surprising that this ratio was very small.

[2] Interestingly enough, Macarios (1964), then the director of research at ECLA, had already used effective protection concepts to evaluate industrialization in Latin America critically.

[3] A large body of literature has been written in the last three years on this topic. This section draws mostly on Corbo (1985), Corbo, de Melo, and Tybout (1986), and Corbo and de Melo (1985). Other references are Calvo (1986), Edwards (1985), Harberger (1982), Rodriguez (1982), and Sjaastad (1983).

[4] With backward 100-percent-plus wage indexation, the dynamic of inflation in Chile was bound to result in a long period of temporary peso appreciation (Corbo, 1985).

REFERENCES

Baer, W. 1967: "The Inflation Controversy in Latin America: A Survey." *Latin America Research Review,* 2 (2).

Balassa, B. and associates 1971: *The Structure of Protection in Developing Countries.* Baltimore: Johns Hopkins University Press.

Bergman, J. 1970: *Brazil: Industrialization and Trade Policies.* London: Oxford University Press.

Berlinski, J. and Schydlowski, D. M. 1982: "Incentive Policies and Economic Development: Argentina." In B. Balassa and associates, *Development Strategies in Semi-industrial Economies,* Baltimore: Johns Hopkins University Press.

Bhagwati, J. 1978: *Anatomy and Consequences of Trade Controls Regimes.* New York: National Bureau of Economic Research.

Calvo, G. 1986: "Fractured Liberalism: Argentina under Martinez de Hoz." *Economic Development and Cultural Change,* July.

Campos, R. 1961: "Two Views on Inflation in Latin America." In A. O. Hirschman (ed.), *Latin American Issues,* New York: Twentieth Century Fund.

Cardenas, E. 1984: "The Great Depression and Industrialization: The Case of Mexico." In R. Thorp (ed.), *Latin America in the 1930s,* New York: St. Martin's Press.

Cardoso, E. A. 1979: "Inflation, Growth and the Real Exchange Rate: Essays on Economic History in Brazil." Ph.D. dissertation, Massachusetts Institute of Technology, Cambridge, Mass.

Carvalho, J. L. and Haddad, C. 1981: "Foreign Trade Strategies and Employment in Brazil." In A. O. Krueger et al. (eds), *Trade and Employment in Developing Countries,* vol. 1, Individual Studies, Chicago: Chicago University Press.

Cavallo, D. and Peña, A. 1984: *Deficit Fiscal, Endeudamiento del Gobierno y Tasa de Inflación en Argentina: 1940–82* [Fiscal Deficit, Public Debt and the Rate of Inflation in Argentina: 1940–82]. *Estudios IEERAL.*

CEPAL 1955: *Introducción a la Técnica de la Programación* [Introduction to Programming Techniques]. Mexico City: United Nations.

CEPAL 1976: *América Latina: Relación de Precios del Intercambio* [Latin America: Terms of Trade]. Santiago, Chile: ECLA.

CEPAL 1978: *Series Históricas del Crecimiento de América Latina* [Historical Series of Latin America's Economic Growth]. Santiago, Chile: ECLA.

CEPAL 1984a: *Statistical Yearbook for Latin America, 1983.* Santiago, Chile: ECLA.

CEPAL 1984b: *Estudio Económico de América Latina 1982* [Economic Study of Latin America: 1982]. Santiago, Chile: ECLA.

Chenery, H. and Bruno, M. 1962: "Development Alternatives in an Open Economy: The Case of Israel." *Economic Journal*, March.

Chenery, H. and Raduchel, W. 1971: "Substitution in Planning Models." In Chenery (ed.), *Studies in Development Planning,* Cambridge, Mass: Harvard University Press.

Chenery, H. and Strout, A. 1966: "Foreign Assistance and Economic Development." *American Economic Reviews,* Sept.

Corbo, V. 1974: *Inflation in Developing Countries. An Econometric Study of Chilean Inflation.* Amsterdam: North-Holland Publishing Co.

Corbo, V. 1985: "Reforms and Macroeconomic Adjustments in Chile during 1974–84." *World Development,* Aug.

Corbo, V. and de Melo, J. 1985: "Liberalization with Stabilization in the Southern Cone: Overview and Summary." *World Development,* Aug.

Corbo, V., de Malo, J., and Tybout, J. 1986: "What Went Wrong with the Recent Reforms in the Southern Cone." *Economic Development and Cultural Change,* July.

Corbo, V. and Sanchez, J. M. 1985: "Adjustment by Industrial Firms in Chile during 1974–82." In V. Corbo and J. de Melo (eds), "Scrambling for Survival. How Firms Adjusted to the Recent Reforms in Argentina, Chile and Uruguay," Staff Working Paper No. 764, World Bank. Washington, D.C.

Corden, M. W. 1966: "The Structure of a Tariff System and the Effective Protective Rate." *Journal of Political Economy,* Aug.

Deaver, J. 1970: "The Chilean Inflation and the Demand for Money." In D. Meiselman (ed.), *Varieties of Monetary Experiences,* Chicago: University of Chicago Press.

de la Cuadra, S. and Cortés, H. 1984: *Recesiones Económicas, Crisis Cambiarias y Ciclos Inflacionarios: Chile 1936–1982* [Economic Recessions, Exchange Rate Crisis and Inflation Cycles]. Santiago, Chile: Instituto de Economie, Pontificie Universidad Católica.

Díaz-Alejandro, C. F. 1970: *Essays on the Economic History of the Argentine Republic.* New Haven: Yale University Press.

Díaz-Alejandro, C. F. 1973: "The Andean Common Market: Gestation and Outlook." In R. S. Eckaus and P. N. Rosenstin Rodan (eds), *Analysis of Development Problems: Studies of the Chilean Economy.* Amsterdam: North-Holland Publishing Co.

Díaz-Alejandro, C. F. 1976: *Foreign Trade Regimes and Economic Development.* New York, N.Y.: Columbia University Press.

Díaz-Alejandro, C. F. 1982. "Latin America in Depression, 1929–39." In M. Gersovitz, C. F. Díaz-Alejandro, G. Ranis, and m. F. Rosenzweig (eds), *The Theory and Experience of Economic Development.* London: George Allen and Unwin.

Díaz-Alejandro, C. F. 1983. "Stories of the 1930s for the 1980s." In P. Aspe-Armella, R. Dornburch, and M. Obstfeld (eds), *Financial Policies and the*

World Capital Market: The Problem of Latin American Countries. Chicago: University of Chicago Press for NBER.

Diz, A. C. 1966: "Money and Prices in Argentina, 1935–62." Ph.D. dissertation, Chicago: University of Chicago.

Dornbusch, R. and Fischer, S. 1985: "Stopping Hyperinflations Past and Present." Massachusetts Institute of Technology, Mimeo, Dec.

Edwards, S. 1985: "Economic Policy and the Record of Economic Growth in Chile: 1973–1982." In G. Walton (ed.), *National Economic Policies in Chile,* Westpoint, Conn.: JAI Press.

Ellsworth, P. T. 1945: *Chile: An Economy in Transition.* New York: Macmillan.

Fernandez, R. B. 1985: "The Expectations Management Approach to Stabilization in Argentina during 1976–82." *World Development,* Aug.

Ffrench-Davis, R. 1971: "Economic Policies and Stabilization Programs, Chile 1952–69." Ph.D. dissertation, University of Chicago.

Findlay, R. 1971: "The Foreign Exchange Gap and Growth in Development Economies." In J. Bhagwati, et al. (eds), *Trade, Balance of Payments and Growth,* Amsterdam: North-Holland Publishing Co.

Fishlow, A. 1972: "Origins and Consequences of Import Substitution in Brazil." In L. de Marco (ed.), *International Economics and Development,* New York: Academic Press.

Fishlow, A. 1985: "The State of Latin American Economics." In Inter-American Development Bank, *1985 Report,* Washington, D.C.

Furtado, C. 1963: *The Economic Growth of Brazil.* Berkeley, Calif.: University of California Press.

Furtado, C. 1976. *Economic Development of Latin America,* Cambridge: Cambridge University Press.

Furtado, C. 1985: *A Fantasia Organizada* [An Organized Fantasy]. Rio de Janeiro, Brazil: Editore Paz et Terra S/A.

Harberger, A. 1964: "Some Notes on Inflation." In W. Baer and I. Kerstenetzky (eds), *Inflation and Growth in Latin America.* New Haven: Yale University Press.

Harberger, A. 1982: "The Chilean Economy in the 1970s: Crises, Stabilization, Liberalization, Reform." *Carnegie-Rochester Conference Series of Public Policy,* vol. 17. Amsterdam: North-Holland Publishing Co.

Hirschman, A. O. 1961: "Ideologies of Economic Development in Latin America." In A. O. Hirschman (ed.), *Latin American Issues: Essays and Comments.* New York: Twentieth Century Fund, Inc.

IDB 1985: *Economic and Social Progress in Latin America. 1985 Report.* Washington: Inter-American Development Bank.

Kravis, I. B. and Lipsey, R. E. 1981: "Prices and Terms of Trade for Developed-Country Exports of Manufactured Goods." NBER, Working Paper No. 744. Cambridge, Mass.: NBER.

Krueger, A. O. 1978: *Foreign Trade Regimes and Economic Development: Liberalization Attempts and Consequences.* Cambridge, Mass.: Ballinger Press for NBER.

Krueger, A. O. 1983: *Trade and Employment in Developing Countries,* vol. 3, *Synthesis and Conclusions.* Chicago: Chicago University Press for NBER.

Krueger, A. O. et al. 1981: *Trade and Employment in Developing Countries,* vol. 1, *Individual Studies.* Chicago: Chicago University Press for NBER.

Lipsey, R. E. 1963: *Price and Quantity Trends in the Foreign Trade of the United States*. Princeton, N.J.: Princeton University Press.

Little, I., Scitovsky, T., and Scott, M. 1970: *Industry and Trade in Some Developing Countries: A Comparative Study*. New York: Oxford University Press.

Macarios, S. 1964: "Protectionism and industrialization in Latin America." *Economic Bulletin for Latin America*, vol. 9 (March).

Maddison, A. 1982: *Phases of Capitalist Development*. Oxford: Oxford University Press.

Maddison, A. 1985: *Growth, Crisis and Interdependence 1929–38 and 1973–83*. Paris: OECD.

McKinnon, R. 1986: "Interest Rate and Foreign Exchange Management During Monetary Stabilization: Further Lessons from Chile and Korea." Mimeo, Stanford University.

Meiselman, David 1970: *Varieties of Monetary Experience*. Chicago: University of Chicago Press.

Michaely, M. 1985: *Trade, Income Levels, and Dependence*. Amsterdam: North-Holland Publishing Co.

Muñoz, O. 1968: *Crecimiento Industrial de Chile, 1914–1965* [Industrial Growth in Chile, 1914–1965]. Santiago: Universidad de Chile, Instituto de Economía y Planificación.

Nogués, J. 1985: "A Historical Perspective of Peru's Trade Liberalization Policies of the 80s." Mimeo.

Noyola, J. 1965: "El Desarrollo Económico y la Inflación en Mexico y Otros Paises Latinoamericanos" [Economic Development and Inflation in Mexico and Other Latin American Countries]. *Investigaciones Económicas*, 16 (4), Mexico.

Ocampo, J. A. 1984: "The Colombian Economy in the 1930s." In R. Thorp (ed.), *Latin America in the 1930s*, New York: St. Martin's Press.

O'Connell, A. 1986: "Free Trade in One (Primary Producing) Country: The Case of Argentina in the 1920s." In G. di Tella and D. C. Platt (eds), *The Political Economy of Argentina, 1880–1946*, New York: St. Martin's Press.

Palma, G. 1984: "From an Export-Led to an Import-Substituting Economy: Chile 1914–39." In R. Thorp (ed.), *Latin America in the 1930s*, New York: St. Martin's Press.

Pinto, A. 1960: *Ni Estabilidad ni Desarrollo: La Política del Fondo Monetario Internacional* [Neither Stability nor Development: the Policy of the IMF]. Santiago: Editorial Universitaria.

Prebisch, R. 1947: *Introducción a Keynes* [Introduction to Keynes]. Buenos Aires: Fondo de Cultura Económica.

Prebisch, R. 1950: "The Economic Development of Latin America and Its Principal Problems." New York: United Nations.

Prebisch, R. 1959a: "Commercial Policy in the Underdeveloped Countries." *American Economic Review*, May.

Prebisch, R. 1959b: *El Mercado Común Latinoamericano* [The Latin-American Common Market]. New York: United Nations.

Prebisch, R. 1986: "Argentine Economic Policies since the 1930s: Recollections." In G. di Tella and D. C. Platt (eds), *The Political Economy of Argentina 1880–1946*. New York: St. Martin's Press.

Reynolds, L. G. 1985: *Economic Growth in the Third World, 1850–1980*. New Haven, Conn.: Yale University Press.

Rodriguez, C. A. 1982: "The Argentine Stabilization Plan of December 20th." *World Development*, 10.

Seers, D. 1962: "A Theory of Inflation and Growth Based on Latin American Experience." *Oxford Economic Papers*, June.

Silber, S. 1977: "Analise da Política Económica e do Compartmento de Economia Brasileira Durante o Periodo 1929–1939 [Analysis of the Economic Policies and the Performance of the Brazilian Economy During 1929–1939]. In F. R. Versiani and J. R. M. de Barros (eds), Sao Paulo: Savarca S. A.

Sjaastad, L. 1983: "Failure of Economic Liberalism in the Cone of Latin America." *The World Economy*, vol. 6 (March).

Sunkel, O. 1958. "La Inflación Chilena: Un enfoque heterodoxo" [The Chilean Inflation: An Heterodox Approach]. *El Trimestre Económico*, (Oct.–Dec.).

Taylor, L. and Bacha, E. 1973: "Growth and Trade Distortions in Chile." In R. S. Eckaus and P. N. Rosenstein-Rodan (eds), *Analysis of Development Problems*, Amsterdam: North-Holland Publishing Co.

Tybout, J. 1986: "A Firm-Level Chronicle of Financial Crises in the Southern Cone." *Journal of Development Economics*, vol. 24, no. 2.

Universidad de Chile 1963: *La Económia Chilena en el Período 1950–1963*. Santiago: Instituto de Economía.

Viner, J. 1953: *International Trade and Economic Development*. Oxford: Clarendon Press.

Westphal, L. 1978: "The Republic of Korea Experience with Export-Led Industrial Development." *World Development*, vol. 6.

Comments on
"Problems, Development Theory, and Strategies of Latin America"

ALBERT BERRY

Professor Corbo's paper reflects nicely the gist of much of the thought and writing about twentieth-century economic development in Latin America, when it focuses on the countries' trading relations with the rest of the world (i.e. the industrialized countries), and on the related question of the extent of government intervention in that trade and in the economy more generally. This preoccupation with the region's "international economics" reflects the widespread view that the initial growth impulse came from trade (and sometimes from foreign investment), and that the later debates on trading relations needed to be reoriented in the light of the crisis of the 1930s and the economic slowdowns of the 1960s.

Whether the orientation is neoclassical, *dependista*, or Marxist, it is true that most commentators have given much weight to this sector. Without belittling its obvious importance, one may still wonder whether the emphasis has been too one-sided and whether savings, the agricultural sector, education, population growth, and other aspects of the process of economic change have been somewhat undersold as long-run determinants of Latin America's economic advance. The foreign sector is a natural focus of attention; because its crises often demand an immediate response, because it is an area where policy can obviously have an impact, and perhaps because of the intellectual glamour of a well-developed area of economic theory and the political glamour of dealing with foreign powers and potentates. If there has been a tendency to attribute to it more importance than its due, it is probably because trade-related variables (whether exogenous or policy-related) fluctuate more brusquely than many others, making it easy to identify correlations with the rate and pattern of overall growth. Many determinants of savings (income distribution, extent of financial intermediation) change more gradually, if not glacially. The same goes for educational coverage and quality, population growth rates, and many other possibly significant phenomena. May it be true, then, that trade phenomena have accounted for much of the fluctuations of Latin American growth around its long-run trends, but that the longer-run average growth rate (in relation, for example, to that in other parts of the world) would owe more of its explanation to other factors? No doubt in a longer treatise, Corbo would have given more attention to other problems and other elements of economic policy, which are far from absent in the literature, but whose place often is secondary to the international aspects.

Professor Corbo's broad "story" of the evolution of theory and policy in Latin America is, I believe, a good summary statement. Most of my comments will reflect a nagging feeling that the interpretation running through the essay – that liberalism, letting markets have more or less free rein in the allocation of resources, is and has systematically been the optimal strategy for Latin America – is too simple. In a micro-economic course, one never claims that free markets are the best way to organize resource allocation under all circumstances. What one has to say, rather, is that it all depends. While the theoretical qualifications are easy to forget in the face of massive and obvious distortions, it still behoves us to bear them in mind *and* to look at the historical record with appropriate caution. The following points, then, are in a spirit, not of disagreement with Professor Corbo's interpretation, but of somewhat less conviction and somewhat more uncertainty.

1   While it is true that it appeared that following the European recon-struction, world trade would expand, and that this would create a setting in which Latin countries might reduce their discrimination against exportables, this shift would not have been totally obvious, even in the absence of Prebisch's views on the secular trend in the terms of trade. Countries which had just come through the external shocks of the depression and World War II could surely be forgiven if they did not confidently predict that world trade was about to enter upon the longest period of continuous growth in the century.

Difficult as they may have been to quantify, the risks of hitching one's wagon to an industrial world that had just suffered the greatest economic cataclysm of the modern era, and had shown its "beggar my neighbor" fangs in trying to deal with it, cannot be overlooked. With the growth of world trade once again less smooth and more uncertain at the present time, countries must look at the potential dangers of an overly "world market-oriented" strategy.

2   Related and complementary to the above point, it should be remembered that static trade theory, powerful as are its conceptualiza-tions and results, does not have any simple and completely general implications for policy. Only in the last 10 to 15 years has the empirical evidence provided a strong case that Prebisch's surmises were wrong – that there was no worsening of LDC terms of trade, and that when one studies the cross-section, outward orientation was positively correlated with growth. But these results refer only to the unusual period of fast growth of world trade in the 1950s, 1960s, and 1970s. It would have been a shrewd surmise to predict all this in 1945–50, but it certainly would have been guesswork.

3   Given the inherent plausibility of the infant industry argument, based on the phenomenon of learning by doing (we do know that such learning can be fairly rapid), the theoretically optimal tariffs/subsidies on import substitution and exporting activities may vary a good deal from product to product. Thus, a "substantial dispersion in the computed domestic resource cost of the different import-competing industries" (p. 161) does not by itself prove that "resources were socially misallocated." Probably a substantial dispersion is exactly what one would like to see if one had any confidence in the policy process to cough up the "right" dispersion. In this sense it has always seemed to me that the argument against tariff dispersion is not an economic one, but a political-administrative one.

In any case, the important point that "export-oriented manufacturing and agriculture can create as many dynamic externalities as can import-competing manufacturing" (p. 159) is again, something which can be and has been demonstrated only by the unfolding of events. And perhaps one should stress the word "can;" I would not have bet that the exportables ranking next to cocoa in Ghana or coffee in Colombia would involve as much cost-lowering learning by doing and/or externalities as some import-substitution industries (ISI). Perhaps they have, and if so, it has often been due to an accelerated process of technological improvements in tropical agricultural products, a process which was barely beginning at the end of World War II.

4   Professor Corbo's basic point, I believe, is the qualitative one that Latin America would have done best if the ISI route had never been taken. It would be valuable, though certainly difficult, to (a) deal with the argument that ISI paved the way for successful growth of non-traditional exports, and (b) try to provide a feel for the extent of the loss resulting from the choice of the ISI strategy, assuming the first argument could indeed be dispatched. It depends on how one interprets the statistics, whether one concludes that the ISI interlude really made much difference or not.

From the data presented in the tables, one cannot see a dramatic impact of the growth of constant dollar exports on GDP growth. The gradual acceleration of Latin American growth, decade by decade through 1980, might be interpreted as reflecting the increasing shift away from ISI, but such single-factor interpretations correctly enough are frowned on by the econometricians. The basis for Corbo's assessment that the accumulated costs of 30 years of protectionism exceeded by far the short-run costs that would have been incurred had the anti-export bias been reduced in the post World War II period is not apparent, even if one tends to agree with his conclusion.

5   The macroeconomic problems plaguing a number of Latin American countries during the 1970s, and especially the 1980s, are an

important and new chapter in the unfolding drama. And they do interact in important ways with resource allocation questions. The discussion of the section "Return of Economic Liberalism" would benefit from a look at the political economy of the development of these fiscal and related difficulties. In particular, one wonders whether this return was a rather accidental result of (a) macro crises, calling clearly for a change of course and, hence, of advisors, and (b) the new advisors having strong views on resource allocation issues, as well as on macro issues.

6   My last main point will reflect my view of why we need to understand the Latin American experience better than we do and, accordingly, of where we need to be going in thinking about trade policies and their interaction with other policies. The rough reading we have of the Latin American experience, like that for LDCs as a whole, certainly highlights the potential benefits from outward orientation and comparative advantage. But our understanding is, I believe, not refined enough to permit fairly safe predictions of the difference trade policy is likely to make under rather different world market conditions, and it is on that next level of analysis that we must now focus.

Finally, the Southern Cone tangle of macroeconomic policies and "liberalization policies" reflects the same need for greater subtlety. The problems are captured in Professor Corbo's point that, "Had it not been for ill-fated stabilization programs and the external shocks of the seventies and early eighties, the reform measures would have lifted the Southern Cone countries out of their economic stagnation" (abstract). This is probably true but, in making a double counter-factual point, it is not all that reassuring.

A couple of minor points can be added. In the discussion of inflation (p. 162), the sentence "when inflation expectations are taken into account, the trade-off between inflation and output level (or unemployment) disappears" gave me a jolt. It was unclear whether it was referring to the results of a theoretical exercise (and we know that any result can be teased out, if the right assumptions are fed in), or was supposed to be an empirical statement. I presume the former.

Also on a detail, it seems to me that the Chenery et al. formulation of the foreign exchange constraint provided a valid general framework for thinking about either short- or long-run phenomena. ECLA clearly was thinking "long-run" with its structuralist arguments. Findlay was essentially arguing that the foreign sector was unlikely to be a binding gap in the long run if price responsiveness was allowed to do its work. But the Chenery et al. model was clearly relevant in analyzing the short-run situation of a country which, possibly through its own past misdeeds (which, of course, we economists think of as bygones), had an economic structure in which the payoff to the marginal import was extremely high.

7

Comparative Advantage and Structural Transformation: A Review of Africa's Economic Development Experience

UMA LELE

INTRODUCTION

Africa's poor economic performance in the 1970s has been attributed mainly to African governments' policy mistakes affecting agriculture. An important World Bank report saw the sector's resuscitation as the primary means of Africa's economic salvation (World Bank, 1981). This paper, therefore, focuses on the central issues of agricultural growth and its interaction with overall economic development.

Although agriculture's crucial role in the development of countries has long been of interest to economists concerned with structural transformation (Clark, 1951; Dovring, 1959; Kuznets, 1959a; Rostow, 1960; Johnston and Kilby, 1975; Mellor, 1967 and 1976; Okhawa and Takamatsu, 1973; Ishikawa, 1967), the implications of this role for the content of contemporary economic policy have rarely been adequately explored. This is particularly true for Africa. In his discussions of general economic policy in South Asia, I. M. D. Little (1982) attributed an earlier neglect of agriculture to the lack of familiarity of general economists with the intricacies of agriculture. Literature on agricultural development has since grown substantially – even for Africa, where empirical research has been weak. Nevertheless, the precise form and

I am grateful to Yaw Ansu, Surjit Bhalla, Dayanatha Jha, Bruce Johnston, Stephen O'Brien, Peter Oram, Ademola Oyejide, Chandra Ranade, Vernon Ruttan, T. N. Srinivasan, and T. Paul Schultz for helpful suggestions on an earlier draft of this paper and to Kim Tran for typing drafts. Henry Russell did the bibliographical work and Lien Tran some background statistical work. The views expressed in this paper are my own and do not necessarily represent those of either the World Bank or the commentators.

content of the contributions needed from the rest of the economy to agriculture, and their likely effects on the extent and speed of agriculture's response, are poorly understood in economic literature, as are the size, nature, and timing of the contributions that agriculture can make to overall development. Economists disagree about the relative effects of food and export crop growth on foreign exchange earnings and savings (Alison and Green, 1983); about the extent of underemployed resources and their likely effect on agricultural supply responses in the short and the long run; and about the relative roles of price and non-price factors, of domestic and external factors, and of the public and private sectors in the mobilization and efficient use of resources. These issues have important implications for the content of overall economic policies.

Modern economic history provides relatively few parallels to this state of affairs. In the 1940s, even the most market-oriented agricultural economists in the United States stressed the special nature of the agricultural sector at early stages of development (Schultz, 1945; Johnson, 1947). Due to the nature of risks in agriculture, and the failure of labor markets to adjust to technical change, Schultz and Johnson ascribed an important role to the U.S. government in price stabilization and in social welfare programs for low-income producers and regions. They also stressed government's role in research, extension, education, and training on grounds of externalities. Among the justifications they cited were: the small units and the dispersed nature of agricultural production, the weather-induced risks in agricultural production, in contrast to other sectors of the economy, and consequently, the greater variability of agricultural relative to other prices. In their view, the long gestation lags in realizing the benefits from investments in agricultural research and infrastructure, the free-rider nature of these benefits, and the difficulties of direct cost recovery also pointed to a valid role for government in agriculture.

In Africa, while all these arguments apply, agricultural economists who understand the internal dynamics of farm resource allocation have tended not to concern themselves with macroeconomic policy debates. General economists, on the other hand, do not sufficiently understand the factors influencing resource allocation within agriculture. Their disenchantment with the performance of governments has led them to call for market solutions without adequately exploring the optimum mix of private incentives and public goods needed to develop agriculture at the early stages of development.

Similar calls occurred in India in the mid-1960s. However, several special features of African agriculture make the focus on privatization a more serious problem in Africa. First, economic transformation is at a much earlier stage in Africa than it was in Asia in the mid-1960s. The lower technological sophistication of the agricultural production process means that labor is a major portion of agricultural value added, and labor allocation and labor productivity are important determinants of agricultural and overall economic growth. Second, markets for commodities, factors of production, knowledge, information, and risk are less well developed in Africa. This means substantial investment is necessary in public goods in the form of transportation, information, communication, education, etc. for the development of markets. In addition, governments also need to foster secure land rights and create a stable institutional environment for encouraging private investment and development of technology.

It follows, then, that taxation and allocative efficiency of public revenues are hardly trivial issues in Africa. A clear comparative advantage in export crops means that producers frequently earn a "rent" in the use of scarce factors of production, compared to the next best alternative. Rents exist due to the nonhomogeneity of land, barriers to entry, and the failure of the labor and capital markets to increase factor supply at a time needed by the requirements of the production process. Given agriculture's importance in the economy at the early stages of development, there is no reason why some of this rent should not be mobilized for the provision of public goods. The optimum level of taxation in specific cases would, of course, depend on the size of the rent, the extent of fixity of resources, and the nature of the international demand for exports. These are empirical questions which need investigation in specific contexts. Instead of being concerned with the specifics of these issues, economists concerned with African policy have focused rather exclusively on the level of price incentives to individual producers, on the assumption that, irrespective of the availability of public goods, producer response will automatically be strong enough to increase government revenues (World Bank, 1981).

The experience of agriculturally successful Japan and Taiwan with regard to agricultural taxation and public spending indicates, however, that substantial surpluses were extracted by governments from the agricultural sectors through direct and hidden taxes on land and on rice production throughout the periods of agricultural transformation (Ishikawa, 1967; Lee, 1971; Okhawa and Takamatsu, 1973). It was the level, the variety, and the quality of public expenditures that boosted the rate of productivity growth and enabled continued extraction of surpluses by governments. In the only systematic accounting of intersectoral resource flows done over a 65-year period, Lee (1971) points out that in Taiwan the tax base increased through productivity growth, despite the high levels of surplus extraction from agriculture, because of public investment in agricultural technology, irrigation, transportation, primary education, etc.

Establishing causality between investment in physical and social infrastructure and agricultural development for countries at the early stages of development is important; without a causative role, decisions about public investments are greatly weakened. Also, beneficial externalities, such as the lowering of input and marketing costs to the individual producers through the presence of physical (transportation network) and institutional (market information, standardization of grades, weights and measures) infrastructure, are often overlooked.[1]

The third salient feature of Africa involves its unusually difficult conditions of agricultural production. These discourage private capital formation and the adoption of new technology, and stress the overwhelming importance of public goods in fostering private capital formation in agriculture. An inadequate appreciation of these difficult production conditions – and the government's long-term role in alleviating them – has led governments and donors alike to underinvest in the specific types of human and institutional capital needed in the public sector to address these production conditions. Instead, general expansion of the public sector has resulted. The role of donors in promoting misallocation of public capital must not be overlooked, given their overwhelming importance in financing public expenditures in Africa (Lele, 1984a; Lele, in press) and in bringing about knowledge transfers through policy advice[2] (Krueger, 1986).

The fourth salient African feature is the large share of trade in the GNPs of African economies.[3] Two interrelated aspects of openness are relevant: the relative roles of food and export crops in growth, and the level and stability of GNP as it affects the stability of public goods supply. As regards the former, Myint (1977) had observed that, in their concern about the role of agriculture in economic transformation, agricultural economists such as Johnston and Mellor (1961) did not give much attention to export orientation. According to Myint, their primary concern with closed economies led them to stress the importance of productivity growth in the food crop sector. A more explicit consideration of openness in Myint's view would lead to a greater appreciation of the role of export crop production in structural transformation. The reasons underlying these differences in the relative stress on food and export crops by agricultural and general economists are fundamental to the discussion of African economic policy (Johnston and Kilby, 1974) and are taken up below, after spelling out their relationship to general economic instability.

Openness makes the international terms of trade a significant variable. It determines the level and stability of gross national income and the size and structure of domestic production, and it influences the ability of countries to pursue stable policies needed to achieve a dynamic agriculture. Increased instability of primary commodity markets (and foreign exchange) since the 1970s makes this as important an issue in Africa in the mid-eighties as it was in the mid-forties in the development of American agriculture, with which Schultz and Johnson were concerned.

The relationship of government revenues and export earnings is significant in this regard in the provision of public goods. Agriculture is the most important export earner and determinant of imports, except in a few mineral-producing countries. Export crop production is dominated by smallholders, with a few exceptions of enclave plantation sectors. The "cash" income of smallholders is determined by export earnings minus government taxes and transportation and processing costs. Government expenditures on the consumption or investment needs of the agricultural sector – such as rural consumer goods, research, production inputs, education, health, rural water supply, and transportation – improve production incentives. When allocated to unproductive industrialization or to other "conspicuous" urban consumption, they reduce agricultural incentives.

When a government forgoes the role of "middleman," international price fluctuations are passed on directly to the producers, thus reducing the possibility of provision of public goods. Shifts in the international terms of trade would lead to increased (or decreased) private rural consumption and investment, as well as an agricultural production response. Depending on whether annual or perennial crops are involved, short- and medium-run agricultural supply responses may or may not be significant.

All else being equal, a deterioration in the international terms of trade means a rise in the relative price of imported consumer goods and agricultural inputs and a fall in per capita income from agricultural exports. Export agriculture then becomes relatively less profitable, reducing its ability to attract labor. The reverse is true when international terms of trade move in favor of export agriculture. In the face of international price instability, an important macro-policy issue is whether stabilization mechanisms can improve the investment climate in the agricultural sector. Without macroeconomic policies and public expenditures which provide a stable supply of public goods for an expanding agricultural sector, a "traditional" production function prevails with a low ceiling on crop yields and agricultural income.

The fifth and final feature of African agriculture is the risk aversion of producers in influencing farm-level resource allocation under conditions of rainfed agriculture. Instability in yields and production, combined with the presence of fragmented rural food markets, leads smallholders to place a high value on ensuring domestic food security. Such risk-induced labor constraints on export crop production must be distinguished from the controversies about the presence or absence of surplus labor in agriculture based on productivity levels (e.g. Arthur Lewis, 1954; Ranis and Fei, 1964; Schultz, 1965). Further, rural food insecurity is typically greater than in the urban sector where public policy ensures a more reliable and low-cost food supply. The Harris–Todaro type rural-urban migration based on expected earning differentials is reinforced by rural food insecurity. When the rural food market becomes more reliable, or when technological change in food crop production reduces the labor requirements of domestic food needs, labor shifts freely to the export crop sector.[4] Recent reviews of agricultural household models have not shown awareness of even the existence of literature on risks and on the effects of insecure food markets on the behavior of agricultural households, nor of the effects of technical change on household labor supply.[5]

In the absence of technical change in the food crop sector, extension of production to marginal land leads to diminishing marginal returns. Population growth under classical Malthusian conditions means that the labor requirements of subsistence food production rise more rapidly than the growth rate of population. Supply response to rising export crop prices would then be constrained by declining labor productivity in the food crop sector. Urban migration in contrast, raises the average product of the labor remaining in food crop production, while reducing the overall supply of food, since the marginal product of labor is typically well above zero in Africa. Migration also adds to the cost of food transfers to the urban sector. In the absence of technical change and given population growth, relative prices between food and export crops then move in favor of food crops. Increased net retention of government revenues from export crops or declining prices of exports reinforce the movement of relative prices in favor of food crops (see Lele, 1985).

These, then, are some of the characteristics of the agriculturally dominated African economies, from which several policy implications follow. First, technological change which increases labor productivity in food crop production is fundamental to releasing labor for export crop production. Where rural food insecurity is heightened by population pressure, by the suppression of food markets, and by the lack of an active rural market development policy by governments, the need for technological improvements in the food crop sector is all the greater. Second, government investment in agricultural research, extension, education, transport, and so on, can help raise returns to factors of production, especially that of labor. Third, given the importance of public goods in agriculture, not only the role of fiscal policies is important, but also that of government expenditures in arriving at an optimum balance of private and social capital in agriculture.

Price incentives to agricultural producers should, ideally, complement the provision of public goods. The ability of governments to provide both, however, is frequently constrained by the existing misallocation of capital, both within and outside agriculture.[6] Higher agricultural producer prices, therefore, frequently come directly at the expense of crucial public goods in agriculture. Finally, some degree of domestic agricultural price stabilization is essential for the long-term efficient allocation of private resources in a risk-prone agriculture. The details of price stabilization will, however, differ among countries. For instance, given the small-country phenomenon, instability of export crop prices in many countries is externally induced; instability in food crop prices, on the other hand, reflects changes in domestic supply as well as the international market conditions, including the unpredictable nature of food imports. Similarly, due to differences in the nature of supply response between annuals and perennials, stabilization policies may also be different among types of crops. These policies could affect the ability of governments to maintain a steady supply of public goods and private incentives. More empirically based analysis is needed of these issues to develop situation specific policies.

In this paper, these propositions are first explained by a review of African agricultural production and exchange conditions, and responses of producers. The consequences of African policies and donor advice are then examined and finally an explanation is attempted of some of the inconsistencies which exist in conditions of agricultural production and exchange and the policy responses of governments and donors. In the course of this discussion, academic debates on several policy issues of particular concern to African agricultural policy are necessarily examined.

AGRICULTURAL PRODUCTION AND EXCHANGE RELATIONS IN AFRICA

Physical conditions

Patterns of land use, human settlement, human and animal disease, and labor availability reflect the frequently difficult physical production environment in Africa. These patterns are not well understood and their significance is rarely discussed explicitly in discussions of economic policy. By exploring these patterns, this section sets the context for later policy discussions. The generally poor nutrient content of African soils and their diversity has been well documented in the African agricultural literature. In his classical study of agricultural development in Africa commissioned by the World Bank in the early 1960s, de Wilde (1967) observed:

> There is a widespread popular fallacy that natural conditions in tropical Africa are very favorable to agriculture. The exuberant growth of natural vegetation and the rapid regeneration of bush or forest following clearing tend to conceal the fact that soils are for the most part poor. Over large parts of Africa, rainfall is either so marginal or erratic as to make farming and even herding hazardous, or so intense as to produce leaching and deterioration of soil structure, with consequent loss of nutrients and increase in erosion (p. 15).

The interactions between rainfall and human and animal health have resulted in population densities being the greatest in drier areas where health hazards are limited, but so are production possibilities. In contrast, in millions of acres of well-watered land, hazards to human and animal health keep population densities low. Tick-borne East Coast fever affects livestock in large areas of Africa. *Simulum damnosum*, or the black fly, carries river blindness and deters settlement in fertile river valleys, while the various species of the tsetse fly cause trypanosomiasis, which affects the health of both humans and ruminant livestock. Snails in water catchments cause bilharzia. Malarial diseases (Blackwater fever, encephalitis) are probably greater in Africa than in other regions. Mosquitoes carry yellow fever, a disease not found in Asia. The Quelea-Quelea bird reduces grain crop yields.

In drier semi-arid areas greater concentration of excessive population has already begun to threaten fragile ecologies. Furthermore, even in the drier areas indigenous cattle (which are resistant to the tsetse fly) are too small to be effective draft animals. Consequently farmers are forced to use hoe culture (or switch to mechanization). Low and unreliable rainfall, with short annual peaks in distribution, limits the growing season to 75–149 days and, due to yield instability, increases the risk of famine and malnutrition. Low-value cereals cover 60 to 80 percent of the cultivated land in these areas. Higher value non-food crops in semi-arid areas include only such limited possibilities as cotton, groundnuts, and some oilseeds, e.g. sesame.

Annual food crops also predominate in the semi-humid tropics, where the growing season is longer, ranging from 150 to 269 days. Taken together, semi-arid and semi-humid areas characterize about 35 to 40 percent of the area in the African continent.

Another 15 to 20 percent of the area consists of humid lowlands (with a growing season of 270 to 329 days) and equatorial tropics (330 to 365 days). The area under annual crops in the humid lowlands falls below 70 percent of the total, and the share of cereals falls sharply to 30–50 percent. Rice assumes importance in production, along with roots, tubers, and vegetables. Cocoa and oil palm dominate among the higher-value cash crops.

In the six East African countries tropical climate is modified by altitude. Here annuals account for 60 to 90 percent of the crop area, and tea and coffee are the major perennials.[7]

The development of crops, livestock, manufacturing, and the service sectors are interrelated in the process of structural transformation. This highlights the fundamental importance of local adaptive research and local entrepreneurial capability.[8]

Technological possibilities

As elsewhere most technical change in food crop production in Africa is aimed at developing faster-maturing, higher-yielding varieties and mineral fertilizers; together these are expected to produce higher and more reliable yields. However, maize is the only staple in which significant breakthroughs have been achieved and even these have been confined to the relatively higher elevation and better watered areas of East and Southern Africa. Breakthroughs in lower rainfall areas, whether for maize or for other cereals and rootcrops, have been insignificant. Fast-maturing, high-yielding, and stable production systems need to be accompanied by improvements in mechanical technologies to ensure productivity growth. In Africa, however, settled agriculture has a relatively short history, and both biological and mechanical change is being compressed in a relatively short period. In the now more developed parts of Western Europe and North America, the introduction of mechanical innovations preceded biological innovations by several decades. (See D. G. Johnson, 1986).

Increases in yields through biological improvements need to be sufficiently large to compensate for the increased cost of purchasing new inputs needed in their production. The short rainfall peaks referred to previously increase the importance of timeliness of operations, especially when adoption of new inputs is involved. This in turn necessitates the use of implements and traction power to alleviate severe labor bottlenecks faced in the seasonal peaks. The higher costs of new technologies are frequently not commensurate with the benefits, although once again there are exceptions.[9] In addition, the increased use of implements often presupposes the existence of appropriate mechanical technologies suited to the particularly diverse local soil and rainfall conditions. The increased use of animal traction depends on succcessfully integrating livestock with cropping, and this in turn requires the existence of a local manufacturing and a service sector. Thus, the growth of agricultural productivity is both constrained by and constrains the development of the nonagricultural sector.

The low level of commercialization and poor communications frequently inhibit technical change due to market limitations. The lack of a secure land tenure system and land consolidation similarly pose a problem.

Technological change is perhaps even more complex in the semi-humid regions. A system of allowing land to lie fallow at regular intervals is still practiced in many of these areas to preserve soil fertility. Here a change in the farming system has to occur before new innovations can be applied effectively. The technological questions are usually whether to turn from the fallow system to using high inputs of mineral fertilizers, planting green manure crops, or growing fodder crops for livestock under a mixed farming system.

Most past growth in African agricultural productivity has come from introduction of high-value export crops and by bringing new areas under cultivation, rather than through increased yields per acre of traditional food crops. Export crop production among smallholders stimulated capital formation in the form of land clearing and land improvements, curing barns, storage facilities, and so on (Anthony et al., 1979). Bringing previously uncultivable land under cultivation with the perennial export crops also stabilized yields in comparison with the annual (mostly) food crop alternatives. Many perennial export crops arrested soil erosion and helped reduce the sharply peaked demand for labor in the production of annual food crops. Since the labor requirements of many export crops are greater by between 50 and 400 percent, and since it is not easy to mechanize the production of perennial crops, the latter also helped increase employment – especially as demand for labor in perennial crops is more evenly distributed than for food crops.

Allocative responses of factors of production to physical conditions

The ability of African producers to adapt to their difficult natural environment and to new opportunities has been well recognized. The economic rationality of African producers also has been well established (W. Jones, 1960; de Wilde, 1967; Stolper, 1969; Hill, 1970; Helleiner, 1975). Agricultural technicians have credited them with having developed a detailed system of soil classification. Intercropping (growing several crops together on the same piece of land) is practiced in nearly 80 percent of the semi-arid parts of West Africa. It was previously considered to be primitive, but is increasingly recognized to be the most effective response of African producers to achieving maximum stable output under the constraints of prevailing rainfall regimes and labor supply.

Adaptation, however, should not be confused with building up or, indeed, even preserving soil fertility. Fertility growth is prevented by communal land rights and household labor constraints under which soil mining is frequently the best economic response of individual producers. Unless modern science and technology improve the productivity of resources, and unless more individualistic land rights are combined with concerted public efforts to encourage capital accumulation, production and resource management will continue to operate at a relatively low level.

The process of "spontaneous" intensification through increased population density has been observed by Boserup (1981) and Ruthenberg (1971). Recently it has begun to attract renewed attention among researchers (Binswanger and Rosenzweig, 1982 and 1983). Perennial cropping areas such as the former White Highlands of Kenya have experienced the greatest land intensification. Perennial cropping involves settled agriculture and usually results in individualized land rights, leading to the development of land and capital markets. However, even in these cases, technical change is a necessary condition for successful long-run intensification. Where land potential is not as great as in the Kenyan highlands, and where annual export crops are involved population pressure is typically followed by the reduction of fallow and subsequent deforestation and soil degradation.[10]

At times, low population density itself signifies the low average product of labor in agriculture under traditional technologies and the relatively low degree of associated commercialization, implying low off-farm employment opportunities in the vicinity. Thus labor may not be available for withdrawal from other activities at seasonal peaks of agricultural production at low transaction costs. And yet, research indicates that due to the sharp demarcation between wet and dry seasons, seasonal peaks in labor demand are far more acute in the semi-arid and semi-humid regions of Africa than in South Asian agriculture.[11] Often African agriculture is unable to cope with the increased workload at peak periods of agricultural activity. This climatically induced peak labor demand must also be distinguished from the academic controversies about the presence or absence of "surplus labor."

There has been relatively little empirical investigation of the nature of agricultural labor markets, although the high rates of male migration to urban areas *à la* the Harris–Todaro model is known to pose acute labor constraints in parts of Africa during the land preparation period. Hypotheses also abound about the role of cultural, sociopolitical and natural factors in the functioning of rural labor markets. There is, however, little systematic research on these issues to test these hypotheses.[12] Preference for leisure, especially of males, has often been stated to inhibit labor response to economic opportunities.[13] However this hypothesis is contradicted by the frequently observed long hours and the arduous nature of the agricultural work, dictated by short seasonal peaks and the lack of substitutability of labor between seasons. The nutritional consequences of seasonal hunger on labor supply and productivity are also observed to pose a problem. The gender-based division of labor offers yet another explanation, since often women have the responsibility for food crop production and males for cash cropping and livestock. The neoclassical assumption of maximization of a joint household utility function determining household labor allocation is contradicted by such gender-based division of labor, especially where polygamous situations prevail (C. Jones, 1983; Lele, 1986).

Tribal practices of shared, rather than hired, labor are another constraint (Shapiro, 1973). Occasionally, ethnic barriers obstruct even seasonal migration. Permanent migration and settlement are, of course, more constrained by ethnic problems (Migot-Adholla, 1977).

No obvious policies can alleviate barriers to labor mobility caused by many of these sociocultural and political attitudes in the short run, although investment in education is essential to break down social barriers and to increase factor mobility in the long run. However, to the extent that labor mobility is influenced by economic factors, even in the short run changes in policies can increase labor flow into agriculture. Urban male migration can be averted by altering minimum wage laws and government guarantees of public sector employment. Reducing urban food subsidies, raising producer prices, and removing government controls over agricultural markets can all increase relative returns to and labor flow into agriculture.

The urgent need for understanding the functioning of labor markets is stressed by the fact that African households are noted to respond to changing economic incentives with remarkable speed. When circumstances permit, individuals as well as entire households shift between farming, trade, and urban occupations (Sabot, 1983). Recent evidence from Nigeria and Senegal suggests that urban households also return to agriculture when urban opportunities decline. Both the literature and the statistical evidence on urbanization in Africa suggest more rapid occupational shifts between agriculture and other activities than were assumed earlier by agricultural economists in the case of U.S. agriculture (Johnson, 1947; Schultz, 1945; Wilcox and Cochrane, 1951). This is perhaps explained by lower transaction costs and different skill levels required for occupational shifts in low-capital economies. Since labor typically constitutes between 70 and 90 percent of the value added in African agricultural production, labor shifts *may* constitute the most important source of agricultural supply response, an issue to which we will return later.

Land access closely interacts with labor use and labor productivity. Population pressure has increased the demand for land. The breakdown of traditional communal land rights following modernization, however, has increased inequality in access to cultivation and grazing rights. Large holdings are typically underutilized, creating increased pressure on land for food crop production and grazing, especially where surplus land has been exhausted. Skewed land distribution has been followed by the breakup of large parcels and the development of a land market in some countries such as Kenya (Heyer et al., 1976). However, equalizing land access is not always possible through the market, given the unequal access to political power, institutional credit, and the *ad hoc* public policy toward land registration in many African countries. Through its effect on the patterns of consumption and investment, the process by which land access evolves has major implications for efficiency and equity in the short run and the long run (Johnston and Kilby, 1975; Mellor and Lele, 1972).[14] African governments have generally overlooked the importance of developing a long-term land policy, as have their donor supporters.

The absence of capital markets is similarly a major constraint to the growth of production. Covariance of risk over large geographical regions with uncertain rainfall increases the risks of default and reduces the scope for development of private financial markets in many parts of semi-arid regions, especially as low average labor productivity keeps surplus accumulation at a low level. A shortage of cash at critical periods of production has frequently been observed to be a constraint in purchasing fertilizers and hiring additional labor for crop production. Unlike in Asia, where the informal rural financial markets provide up to 60–70 percent of rural finance, interseasonal capital transfers among households are less developed in Africa. Also in contrast to Asia, agricultural hiring contracts are not yet sophisticated enough to alleviate the risk of financial market failure. The issue of the need for seasonal credit, imposed by the inadequate evolution of rural capital markets, is often confused with the relatively high saving rates noted among African households cultivating perennial crops or among nomads in the form of cattle accumulation. Investments in perennials or cotton are selectively more risk-free, compared to annual cropping. Capital formation of this type, and the emergence of informal saving groups, have led economists to stress the need for the development of rural financial markets (Adams, 1978; von Pischke, 1980). The erosion of formal credit institutions through subsidized interest rates and an increasing number of defaults have reinforced their call for the promotion of informal financial markets. However, the speed with which, and the conditions under which, rural financial markets naturally emerge are frequently not appreciated. There is also a tendency in the literature to equate the promotion of rural financial markets with rural capital formation, when in fact, the latter depends on relative returns to rural investments. Because agriculture pricing policies and public investments often reduce relative return to rural investments, informal sector savings frequently flow out of the agricultural sector.

Risks associated with commodity markets

The risks African farmers face in commodity markets may be classified into those related to yield, price, and supply. These risks tend to be the result of erratic rainfall, variability in market forces, and the unpredictable nature of public policy and its implementation. Risks are, however, not always independent. When they are correlated, risks cause producers to attach high priority in their resource allocation to meeting domestic food requirements, in opting for stable but lower yields through mixed cropping, varying planting dates to reduce crop failures, and stressing the production of drought-resistant crops (de Wilde, 1967; Ruthenberg, 1971; Collinson, 1972; Lele, 1975; Balcet and Candler, 1982).[15]

The inaccessibility of markets, poor and costly communications, and fluctuating yields and prices are the most important factors reinforcing producers' disinclination to be dependent on the market for food supplies. De Wilde observed in 1967:

> Subsistence entails the comparatively inefficient use of land for production when such land could much better be devoted to cash crops... The African farmers are caught in a vicious circle, for the inadequacies of the

market prevent them from raising their output through specialization, while their own desire for food security inhibits the growth of the market (p. 22).

The reliability of the domestic, especially rural, food supply depends not simply on this year's rainfall but on last year's production and carryover stocks.

Weather-induced risks are typically correlated with policy-induced risks. For instance, a domestic food crop failure leads to increased commercial food imports by governments. Where parastatal monopolies prevail in food distribution, as in much of East and Southern Africa, transportation of imported grain to rural areas increases the costs of public food distribution. Welfare considerations lead to less than full cost recovery of food imports and distribution. Consequently, the financial losses of the marketing parastatals are closely related to the size of the domestic production.[16] Cash flow problems, in turn, reduce the parastatals' ability to make timely delivery of production inputs or to pay for the purchases of output in the following year. Levels and timing of food imports themselves depend on the availability of foreign exchange or aid.

Private food trade is more prevalent in West Africa. There is no evidence to suggest, however, that interseasonal and inter-year price or supply stability is greater in West Africa than in East African countries. Consequently, allocation of household labor to meet domestic food needs is no less an overriding concern in West than in East Africa.

Unintegrated food markets and their inability to ensure adequate interseasonal and inter-year storage to deal with weather induced risks should not be interpreted to mean that spatial and intertemporal market integration could not be achieved if promotion of private markets were combined with government stocking policies. However, results will take time. Many African governments have tended to actively curtail the functioning of commodity markets. Due to the concerns of food security, many governments have instituted public sector monopolies of food marketing and have imposed restrictions on movements of even small food surpluses across administrative boundaries.[17] Inordinately long hours are spent by farm families in attempting to dispose of any significant food surpluses they have, not to mention the risks faced in "illegal" trading across administrative boundaries.

Other policy-induced risks faced by producers include unpredictable input supply caused by changes in the level and composition of imports, which are often a result of unpredictable aid allocations by donors, and shifts in trade policies by governments in response to fluctuations in availability of foreign exchange. While too little systematic empirical evidence exists at a disaggregate level to discern the relative importance of each of these risks, their collective adverse effect on farm resource allocation needs no belaboring.

Marketing and processing of export crops pose an altogether different set of problems. Export crops require lumpy public investments in transport and communication to ensure the timely supply of inputs and collection of output. The financing and management skills associated with developing export crop processing are often substantial. The presence of scale economies in agro-processing necessitates vertical integration with marketing, if not also with production. A combination of the need for these relatively more sophisticated entrepreneurial skills and the policies of colonial governments limited the participation of indigenous Africans in export crop marketing and processing, although indigenous entrepreneurs were more active in West than in East Africa because of the former's stronger trading tradition. Marketing boards, individual European companies, and Levantine and Asian traders with access to finance handled international and domestic wholesale trade and crop processing. After independence, governments did not expect African entrepreneurship to emerge rapidly enough to meet the requirements of the export industry. In any case, scale economies in processing implied possibilities of oligopolistic control by a few private entrepreneurs, creating the likelihood of economic domination by a few ethnic groups. Consequently, public monopsonies and government-imposed cooperative marketing and processing societies replaced companies run by alien European, Levantine, and Asian minorities. Government investments have, however, often exceeded any natural scale economies and donors have helped finance many large, inappropriate, capital-intensive processing facilities. These public investments have not only fostered monopolies where they need not exist, but the increased processing costs have reduced returns to producers. (See Lele, in press; Jemneh and Ranade, 1986.) Government subventions to public sector processing have become an important element of their budgets.

Expansion of employment in agricultural parastatals has also tended to be rapid. Incentives in public enterprises have been diluted to a point where it has been difficult to maintain high management standards.[18] While real wages of public employees have declined sharply since the late 1970s in many countries, reducing employment levels has been far more difficult. A decline in the quality of services, including both delays in supplying critical production inputs and payment delays to producers, has driven producers to plant food crops which can be more easily traded on the domestic market. Barter trading across national boundaries is extensive in countries where overvalued exchange rates and poor domestic producer prices are combined with shortages of consumer goods (Lele, 1984a; Ansu, 1984). The more elitist the countries, the more acute are the import-substitution strategies favoring basic industry, and the more distorted the trade and exchange rate policies, leading to a greater shortage of consumer goods and causing a reversion to food production.

A decline in the quality of export produce is also a serious problem in many countries. Grading discounts larger than those received earlier have been reported for several crops exported by African countries (Lele, 1984a). This is a result of poor planting material, an unreliable supply of production inputs, ineffective extension, poor handling of the produce in storage and processing, and inadequate price incentives for quality.

The weaknesses of public and cooperative monopsonies are easy to recount. However, relatively little is known about the structure and performance of the private agricultural markets that could replace them. Most private markets are currently confined to food crops because governments have acquired control of the distribution and processing of export crops. Even where the private sector is allowed to operate freely in marketing and agro-processing as, for instance, in Nigeria, trade by licensed buying agents for cotton and rubber is often alleged to be far less than competitive. Also, private investments have not been forthcoming in agro-processing of even those crops for which the demand for the processed products has been growing, perhaps due to the year-to-year fluctuations in the supply of raw materials. On the other hand, the inadequate level of investments in processing itself constrains the growth of the supply of agricultural raw materials. The reasons for inadequate private investments in agro-processing are not fully understood but may relate to a lack of credit facilities and poor rural infrastructure, which increase the risks associated with such investments.

Despite gaps in our knowledge about the response of market forces, however, several observations can be made. First, where domestic agricultural trade is allowed to function and where entry seems to be free in principle, in practice, certain African ethnic groups in each country have tended to dominate trading. Free entry also does not mean the absence of concentration.[19] The relative absence of domestic financial markets among Africans has also meant that aliens with access to the modern banking system have tended to exercise oligopolistic influence on domestic trade by financing local African traders involved in primary collection (Bauer, 1963; Miracle, 1968). The conglomerate nature of the commercial activities of European and Asian minorities lends support to their oligopolistic control. For instance, the Asian community has owned and operated much of the trucking in East Africa. Only recently have Africans begun to emerge in private transport. This means that the cost of transport is frequently higher for small African traders. Even Bauer has acknowledged that the scope for exercising oligopolistic control is enhanced when physical infrastructure and communications are poor, when turnover is low so that large amounts of working capital are needed, and when the instability of production and prices place a premium on access to timely market information.[20]

The most difficult policy question for African governments is, therefore, one of how to allow the development of an indigenous entrepreneurial class in an environment of intense competition from European and Asian entrepreneurs. So far they have tended to view private modern entrepreneurship as an infant industry to be developed and nurtured largely through the establishment of public enterprises. The intensity of the food issue in domestic politics combined with the absence of effective competition has tended to curtail the enthusiasm of African policymakers for liberalization of food markets in countries where aliens have been feared to control trade in the event of liberalization. It is noteworthy, for instance, that the policies of "market-oriented" Malawi exclude Asians from residing in rural areas in order to curtail their role in rural trade, in much the same way as the policies of Tanzania and Kenya curtail Asian petty trade.

This discussion is not to suggest that private monopolies will necessarily be inferior to current public monopolies, but rather to stress the likelihood of the emergence of some monopolies in the short and medium run. Overt or covert small-scale African trade is growing in importance, and due to the control of alien competition ensured by public policy, is already earning large rents (Waterbury, forthcoming; Bienen, forthcoming, Jammeh and Ranade, 1986). Bauer (1981) has argued that by guaranteeing African entrepreneurs large profits, restrictive practices of African governments have tended to undermine the importance of risk-bearing, thereby arresting the rate of their development. Efficiency losses under the current arrangements are unquestionably greater than they would be in the competitive and integrated markets that could prevail. In many countries, the rents currently accruing to African enterprises, however, seem to have been as much at the cost of alien trading monopolies as of African producers and consumers of agricultural commodities. This crucial point is frequently overlooked by donors in their preoccupation with liberalization.

Public policy in post-independence Africa has thus been directed mainly to the development of an indigenous middle class. This is consistent with Harry Johnson's description of the growth of nationalism in the developing world (1965). An active development of indigenous markets has not yet received much attention. This may be because Africa did not inherit from its colonizers the tradition of public action directed toward improving the competitiveness of domestic markets, as did India, where "Regulated Market Acts" helped improve standardization of weights, measures, grades, and marketing charges, and also established the method of collection and dissemination of price information, and broadened access by the trading class to institutional credit (Lele, 1971). The absence of such a regulatory tradition in Africa may well be explained by the absence of an indigenous class of moneylenders and traders, a sign of Africa's earlier stage in the development of rural capital and commodity markets. Yet, in their quest for liberalization, donors have paid little attention to investigating systematically the prevailing market conditions, or to identifying how governments could assist in the process of their establishment. Governments, in turn, have been happy to use the bogey of alien control to perpetuate the current rent-seeking policies.

What are the effects of controls on markets and prices on farm-level resource allocation? This depends on the extent of comparative advantage. If it is strong, the marginal return to labor – typically the scarcest factor of production – frequently tends to be much higher in the production of export crops than in competing food crops, even in the presence of an export tax.[21] Where comparative advantage is less pronounced, however, and where unreliable markets for export crops are combined with increased bartering opportunities in food crops, a shift away from export to food crops is facilitated by government controls on markets and prices, as in cotton production in Tanzania (Lele, 1985). Allocation of labor within agriculture and between competing (including non-agricultural) activities, however, depends on relative returns. The taxation of agriculture is by no means the only villain in influencing relative returns. Government expenditure patterns and subsidization of urban activities have been as responsible for diverting labor out of agriculture. It is also noteworthy that export crops are frequently grown, *despite* their less than attractive return to labor in production compared to competing food crops, as a means of security against the effects of drought on annual food crops. This explains why the shift from cotton to maize in Tanzania has been less pronounced than the relative returns would suggest.

To summarize, the incentives for export crop production involve a complex set of issues typically overlooked in general economic discussions, which have tended to focus almost exclusively on the producer price levels. The preceding discussion has stressed that reliance on markets may not necessarily ensure competitive processing or marketing of crops where monopolies exist, or where historical factors explain oligopolistic tendencies. African reluctance to relinquish public control of such activities is perhaps explained more by concerns of ethnic rivalries and consequent political instability than by ideological considerations. This suggests that donor emphasis on precipitating market liberalization in the short run may well set back the cause of market development. The development of competitive markets would, however, need to receive continued attention from a long-run point of view. Also, institutional competition between the public, cooperative, and private sectors would need to be encouraged wherever possible.

POLICY DEBATES RELEVANT TO AFRICAN AGRICULTURAL DEVELOPMENT

Through a review of both relevant economic literature and policy experience elsewhere, the discussion in this section considers the policies pursued by African governments with regard to: (1) agricultural research and productivity, (2) the terms of trade, and (3) taxation and capital formation. Donors, through their policy advice and financial investments, play an important role in the pursuit of these policies. The intention here is not to distinguish the policies attributable to governments from those attributable to donors, but rather to stress the interaction and combined influence of governments and donors.

Agricultural research and productivity

A strong consensus had already emerged by the mid-1960s in economic literature about the central importance of technical change in explaining the growth of nations (Kuznets, 1959b; Lee, 1971; Okhawa and Takamatsu, 1973). Considerable evidence had also evolved at the micro level of the high rates of return to investment in agricultural technology (Griliches, 1958; Nelson, 1964; Evenson and Kislev, 1975).[22] However, the fundamental importance of technological change in productivity growth continues to be grossly underrated in African economic policy.

Also by the 1960s, recognition had existed among economists working on Asia that the scope for a simple international transplant of agricultural technology was limited, and that the capacity of poor nations to borrow appropriate elements of specific agricultural technologies from elsewhere depended on their own scientific capability, as reflected in high levels of trained manpower and research organization effectiveness (Evenson, 1981). The urgency of developing national capacity for agricultural technology has been reinforced for small African countries because of several factors. Scale economies exist in addressing individual research problems resulting from the number of scientific disciplines required to improve technology. African micro climates tend to be highly diverse and, consequently, many research areas need attention. Finally, there is little backlog of basic research on tropical environmental problems which impede agricultural production. Opportunities for regional cooperation in scientific research among African countries have also been limited by political difficulties.

Assumptions, however, have persisted in donor-funded projects in Africa that a shelf of improved technological packages exists for large areas. Ineffective agricultural extension and inadequate savings by rural households were seen as the main constraints to its adoption. Individual area rural development projects attempted to alleviate these constraints by adaptive trials, extension, and credit (Lele, 1975). The need for developing *national* capacity to carry out adaptive agricultural research was overlooked by donors in Africa in the 1970s in their massive investments in the agricultural and rural sectors. While similar assumptions led to the establishment of the community development program in India in the 1950s, efforts to develop national capacity for technology had also been well under way. The elite in the Indian government grasped the principles involved in institutional adaptation of scientific research capability relatively early, and the trained manpower and organizational implications of its establishment were adopted vigorously by Indians from their U.S. technical advisors. In its establishment of indigenous capacity, India benefited from the supply and continuity, spanning well over a decade, of U.S. personnel experienced in the management of a highly productive U.S. agricultural research system (Lele and Goldsmith, forthcoming).

By contrast, in Africa the research, organizational, and management issues have not received the serious attention they deserve, either by African governments or their donor supporters. The donors' time horizon has been short, despite the rhetoric calling for a long-term effort. For instance the British withdrawal from some of the best established colonial research efforts was much too quick after independence, and whereas the French presence has been longer lasting, neither colonial power has assisted in the development of indigenous trained manpower nor management capability on the scale needed.[23] Some early U.S. efforts in Ethiopia, Nigeria, and Uganda became ineffective due to prolonged civil wars in all three countries.

Financial allocations to food crop research were increased substantially by some African governments following the 1973–4 drought, and international awareness of the importance of national agricultural research in Africa followed suit in recent years.[24] On the surface, the increased allocation of resources for research on food crops supports Ruttan's hypothesis of induced innovation in response to relative scarcities (Ruttan and Hayami, 1984; Ruttan, 1982). However, the Ruttan model does not explain the low productivity of research expenditures present in post-independence Africa, due to poor research policies.[25] These stem from the inadequate recognition at the senior policy-making levels in African governments of the fundamental importance of science and technology suited to particular factor endowments in African agriculture, of the lack of adequate emphasis on training and experience of African scientific staff in research and management, and of the inadequate incentives for nationals engaged in science and technology. These problems are combined with too rapid an Africanization of research in Anglophone Africa and excessive reliance on expatriate staff (exceeding 50 percent of the national scientific establishment) in many Francophone countries. Such changes in the organization of research systems that have occurred have been driven mostly by domestic and regional bureaucratic rivalries, rather than by the requirements of the research systems.

Conflicting advice from a fragmented donor community is also a serious problem. Donors embody quite different approaches to research. Typically 15 to 20 donors support well over 50 to 100 individual research initiatives in individual countries. Little relationship, therefore, currently exists among the organization, the management, and the substance of most African national research. Much of this international research effort is exclusively geared to food crops and overlooks export agriculture.

Technical assistance is provided by donors to alleviate the shortage of trained African manpower. However, the technical assistance staff tend to be short term, leading to a substantial loss of learning by doing. Also, unlike the case of the Rockefeller Foundation's assistance to India, donor-provided research manpower in Africa is typically oriented toward carrying out their own research, rather than toward training young Africans in the management or the conduct of research.

By far the greatest weakness of donor efforts in the development of national research systems is the large emphasis placed on the expansion of physical capital relative to the improvement of human or institutional capacity. Without urgent attention to the issues of priorities in the management of agricultural research by the donor community, the large resources now being devoted to research and extension are unlikely to have a significantly positive impact in the foreseeable future.

Terms of trade and agricultural pricing policy

Pessimism about primary commodity export prospects led many African countries to vigorously pursue industrialization in the 1960s and 1970s, although there were the exceptions of Malawi, Kenya, and the Ivory Coast, where import substitution was pursued less actively. The absence of a domestic entrepreneurial class and suspicion of foreign investors led to the pursuit of this objective through an active role for the public sector. Not only did many donor advisors to African countries share in this export pessimism, but donors went along with the taxation of agriculture in pursuit of economic diversification (Lele et al., forthcoming). The issue of domestic terms of trade began to receive attention in policy dialogue by donors only by the late 1970s. The reorientation of African economic policies must, thus, be viewed in the context of expenditure patterns aided by donors and developed for nearly two decades. Besides, in the absence of any systematic empirical analysis, differences have existed among economists about the magnitude of short- and long-run responsiveness of agriculture to prices relative to other non-price factors, as well as the relative importance of price levels versus price stabilization. These issues, in turn, are related to questions about the relative merits of price incentives to individual producers, as opposed to the government's retention of revenues to develop the social capital needed to develop a technologically dynamic agriculture.

Primary commodity prices were generally depressed in the 1970s, relative to the prices of imports (with the exception of the brief beverage boom in 1975–7). For several major export crops, e.g. coffee (mild arabica), groundnut meal, groundnut oil, and tea, coefficients of variation in prices increased dramatically relative to the 1950s, and especially the 1960s. (See "Discussant's Comments" by U. Lele in Davis, 1986, pp. 382–6.)

Through overvaluation of the exchange rate, discriminatory tariffs, taxes, and quotas, African governments turned the domestic terms of trade (producer prices relative to CPIs) against export crop producers at a rate even more rapid than the decline in their international terms of trade. Effective rates of taxation of export agriculture reached levels of 50 to 60 percent in several countries in the 1970s. The protection of industry, combined with excessive urban public consumption, caused a decline in the African share of world exports in all major agricultural food and export commodities, with the exception of coffee and tea. New entrants took over Africa's potential markets in some products (cocoa, palm oil); in others (pyrethrum and sisal), accelerated development of substitutes limited market prospects.

In the case of food crops, a decline in real world food prices helped offset the declining domestic per capita production and year-to-year shortages induced by weather. African food imports grew at 8 to 10 percent annually since the mid-1970s, and the rate accelerated in the 1980s, with over two-thirds of such imports being on a commercial basis. The ability of African governments to finance these food imports, however, declined with a drop in the real value of their primary commodity exports. Constrained food imports, combined with the shortages of foreign exchange, have led African governments to raise domestic official food (both producer and consumer) prices since the late 1970s. In some cases, they have raised official food prices sharply relative to prices of primary commodity exports, even though international prices of major food crops in U.S. dollars have been stable or declining. In relation to export crops, unofficial (or market) food prices in African countries show even sharper rises than official food prices.

With regard to ensuring the future performance of African agriculture, the debate has focused largely on the inadequate level of price incentives. The importance of a "positive" price policy in agricultural development, stressed earlier by economists of the Chicago school

(Johnson and Schultz), has recently been reinforced in the World Bank's World Development Reports and annual reports on Africa.

It is evident that many African countries have been operating well below their production possibility frontier, as reflected in both diversification of economic activity out of agriculture, and within agriculture from export to food crops. An important part of this phenomenon appears to be a result of labor shifts, and some of the labor shifts appear to be explained by relative price levels. I have argued, however, that food insecurity and public expenditure policies that encourage urban migration and employment all play an important part in economic diversification. The correction of domestic terms of trade in favor of agriculture should thus be expected to lead to *some* aggregate supply response in the short and the medium run, and a move towards the production possibility frontier by labor reallocation. The precise magnitudes would vary among countries, depending on the extent of past distortions and of corrections currently undertaken.

Meticulous studies of aggregate supply response are rare in Africa, due to lack of good data (Askari and Cummings, 1976). Recent attempts at calculating responses have mostly turned up statistically insignificant results (Bond, 1983). One, therefore, tends to seek refuge in non-African literature which tends to be highly divided. By using a meta production function, Peterson (1979) estimated aggregated supply elasticities in the neighborhood of 1.3.[26] Mellor and Johnston have pointed out the limitations of the underlying assumptions leading to this high estimation and have argued in favor of much lower aggregate supply elasticities (1984). A recent study by Binswanger et al. (1985) estimates short-run aggregate output supply to be remarkably price inelastic, with own elasticities never exceeding 0.06. The higher long-run supply responses in the study are attributed mainly to public investments in physical infrastructure and research.

Even with a strong supply response to prices, however, upward price adjustments cannot be expected to continue once the initial price distortions have been corrected, especially in view of the limited international market prospects for many of Africa's traditional export and food crops. Once the price distortions are corrected, important issues regarding long-term agricultural growth relate more to the stability of the pricing environment and the necessary social and physical capital needed to achieve productivity growth. There is, however, as much lack of consensus in the literature about the extent of price stability needed as there is related to aggregate supply response. Johnson's advocacy of price stability in the United States in the 1940s was based on capital rationing associated with unstable prices and the associated risks, both through the supply of and the demand for investable resources. Through the announcement of "forward" prices reflecting *expected* future changes rather than historical levels, government was to become the buyer and seller of last resort. The importance of stable prices was also stressed in Asia in the 1960s to ensure rapid adoption of the new technology made available by the Green Revolution (Schultz, 1965; Falcon, 1967).

In a recent exchange, Johnson has expressed greater scepticism about the need for price stability because of the distortionary consequences of such interventions (see Davis, 1986, session 5). Others argue that price instability may result in higher (rather than lower) private investments following the Permanent Income Hypothesis. Also, in industries where technological change is rapid, unstable prices may be less of a deterrent to growth than was argued by Johnson (for instance, see Robinson, 1973). The preceding discussion has, however, stressed that risks in African agriculture may be greater and technological change far slower than was experienced in U.S. agriculture.

In contrast to the American and Asian literature, the pro-market "African" literature has, by and large, strongly lacked any sympathy for a stable price environment. In an interlinked argument about export prices, export taxes, commodity price stabilization, and buffer funds, Bauer and Yamey (1957) rejected the concern for stability. Stephen Lewis (1967) summarized the controversy on Africa in the 1950s:

> The major arguments of the proponents of export taxation are that it can (1) absorb windfall gains that accrue to the exporters during periods of rising prices, dampening fluctuations and reducing the primary and secondary effects of the increased export earnings on the economy, (2) be adminstered with ease, (3) be made flexible by providing sliding scale rates to vary with international prices, (4) generate revenue from a low saving sector that can be transferred by government expenditure to the high saving sector and be used to diversify the economy and avoid future fluctuations, and (5) for a country in a monopoly position, serve to restrict supply and increase short run exchange earnings. The opponents of such policies, led by Bauer and his associates, argue that these devices are not likely to be satisfactory because: (1) they are likely to move domestic prices well out of line with world prices, thus reducing the country's real income by preventing it from producing at its greatest comparative advantage; (2) they discriminate against one sector of the economy, and, therefore, should be opposed on equity grounds; (3) they discriminate against crops produced for and sold in foreign markets and in favor of those sold domestically; (4) they may reduce private saving more than they increase public saving (and public investment is not as desirable as private investment anyway); and (5) even if exchange earnings are increased in the short run, new entrants on the supply side and the accelerated development of substitutes will reduce exchange earnings in the long run (p. 469).

It is noteworthy that Bauer's opposition to price stabilization incorporates both the behavioral observation about a higher marginal propensity of governments to consume relative to that of individuals, and the normative view that private spending is more desirable than government spending, irrespective of the nature of externalities. In addition, Bauer's argument seems implicitly addressed to the situation of rising, rather than declining, international terms of trade. Price increases cannot be passed on to producers without also passing on price reductions, with a consequent fall in export volumes through the supply response. Finally, Bauer does not recognize the differences we stressed earlier in relative returns to scarce factors of production of some activities implicit in the existence of comparative advantage. Yet some of Bauer's reasons for rejecting price stabilization have proved prophetic in the 1970s.

It could be argued that if more pro-agricultural attitudes had prevailed, African governments might have allocated revenues generated through price stabilization programs in the 1950s and 1960s to support agriculture. Such investments would have raised agricultural productivity and enabled countries to absorb the adverse price shocks of the 1970s more effectively. For instance, in the Ivory Coast, contrary to the general impression, smallholders producing export crops have been taxed relatively heavily at rates ranging from 50 to 70 percent.[27] It is the allocation of such government revenues to the agricultural and the rural sector which facilitated increased cocoa production in the Ivory Coast.[28] Also, the Ivory Coast's priority to agriculture has by itself been insufficient to avert the effects of the external shocks of the 1970s, without resorting to foreign borrowings.

The attribution of export crop failure to the "food self-sufficiency" policies pursued by African governments similarly needs closer analytical scrutiny. The high and rising food imports of African countries referred to earlier suggest greater openness than is generally recognized. It is doubtful that an even more trade-oriented food policy would have induced producers to allocate less labor to meet their domestic food needs in the absence of efficient and reliable domestic food markets. Moreover, the foreign exchange intensity of the trade-based approach may well exceed the resources that could be devoted to increase domestic food productivity where internal distances are long and transportation costs are high.

In view of Africa's poor infrastructure and lack of well-functioning markets, techno-organizational failures are large and require a broader concern with allocation of capital and the development of institutions, rather than simply attention to price incentives. Krishna (1967) arrived at this same judgment on the Punjab earlier:

> The marginal contribution of the price variable to the variance of growing output is much less than the contribution of other nonprice factors...such as water availability, indices of varietal improvement or progress of extension... In measuring the contribution of price movements to agricultural growth we must not lose sight of the fundamental

truth that the transformation of traditional agriculture is primarily a techno-organizational episode. The transformation cannot be brought about only or mainly by price movements (pp. 516–17).

CONCLUSION

This paper has emphasized the crucial role of agriculture in economic transformation and, in turn, the important role of government in promoting infrastructure, markets, land tenure, and technological capacity in support of agriculture. Of central concern has been the extent to which markets in factors, products, risk, and information are absent or operate inefficiently. The adverse effects of absent or fragmented markets on the efficiency of production at the farm level has been stressed. Public policy can significantly influence both the emergence of domestic markets through the development of infrastructure, tenurial arrangements, information and so on, and reduce the risks inherent in unstable markets. Finally, the pace of productivity growth in agriculture can be accelerated by governments undertaking investments in human and institutional capacity of a scientific nature. Effective government policy, however, cannot be formulated or implemented without a sophisticated understanding of the intricacies of tropical agriculture. The present debate on agriculture's role in Africa's economic development sadly lacks the extent of understanding needed for the formulation and implementation of an effective long-run policy.

NOTES

[1] Wharton (1967) argued that residual productivity growth attributed to education and research (Griliches, 1958 and 1964; Nelson, 1959 and 1964; Tang, 1963) may well have been due to the presence of much broader social capital made possible by investment in infrastructure as a whole.

[2] With the exception of Nigeria, which does not receive much official development assistance (ODA), per capita ODA ranged between $US 6.1 to $US 110.00 in the early 1980s and constituted 17.4 percent of public expenditures by all Sub-Saharan countries.

[3] Trade ranged between 30 and 50 percent of GNP in many African countries in the early 1980s.

[4] Based on Collinson's study (1972) of farming systems in Sukumaland in Tanzania, Lele (1975) documented how an increase in food crop productivity, made possible by a shift from sorghum to hybrid maize, released labor for the production of cotton. Lele later documented the shift away from cotton into maize in the same areas of Sukumaland in the 1970s, due to reduced profitability of cotton *vis-à-vis* maize and increased *un*reliability of the food market (1984a). Lele and Mellor (1981) documented in a two-sector model

the effect of technological change in the food crop sector on employment in the non-food grain sector, through the interacting food and labor markets.

[5] For example, I. Singh, L. Squire and J. Strauss (1986). The nutritional implications of inadequate food supply on agricultural labor use can also be significant. A study by IFPRI currently under way in Zambia shows the effect of inadequate caloric consumption on labor flow and labor productivity.

[6] Expansion of urban industrially-oriented expenditures in the 1970s has been followed by a near halving of per capita urban real incomes in some countries in the 1980s. Nevertheless, the urban industrial bias continues, and is itself a result of the export crop pessimism of the 1960s, which led African governments to diversify out of export agriculture. Donors supported such diversification (Lele 1984b, Lele et al., forthcoming). The recurring food crisis of the 1970s led the donor community to support either directly or indirectly, through fungibility, Africa's concern for increasing domestic food self-sufficiency through irrigation and other development schemes with relatively low rates of return. Protectionism in donor countries has also played a part in determining which of Africa's many export crops are supported (Lele, in press).

[7] P. Oram (1985), personal communication. Data from International Food Policy Research Institute. Percentages of area under each climatic zone were derived following M. K. Bennett (1962).

[8] Spencer (1985) observed that, "as is the case with biological technology, we need mechanical technology that is within the farmer's reach. Cooperative ownership and management of agricultural machinery has not worked in SSA. Neither have government tractor hire schemes. The only open avenue is research on the improvement of farmers' existing tools and equipment. A hand weeder that allows a farmer to weed twice as fast as existing weeders would have a big impact on labor productivity. The animal yoke newly designed by the International Livestock Center for Africa (ILCA), which allows the traditional Ethiopian plow to be pulled by one instead of two oxen, is likely to have more impact on agricultural productivity in the Ethiopian highlands than all the mechanization research over the last 30 years. These efforts concentrated on replacing traditional cultivation methods with mechanized methods, rather than on improving the existing methods."

[9] For instance, the number of producers using oxen in some parts of Western Kenya increased from 25 percent to 49 percent in the relatively short period of 1977 to 1981 (Oluoch-Kosura, 1983). Animal traction is also used extensively in parts of Francophone Africa. Use of traction, however, brings added costs and special problems (Delgado, 1977), and the process of learning by doing takes four to five years (Jaeger, 1984).

[10] The forced villagization attempted by the government of Tanzania in the 1970s starkly demonstrated the serious adverse consequences of shortening fallow through increased population pressure in the absence of technological change.

[11] A recent paper by Delgado and Ranade (in press) demonstrates the far greater seasonality of labor use in Africa than in India for the same crops. Labor inputs peak in Africa and Asia over a period of four months. In Africa these months account for 50 to 70 percent of total crop work, in Asia for 40 to 50 percent. In slack months the proportion of total cropping labor input is much lower in Africa than in Asia (p. 220; see also tables 3 and 4, p. 236).

[12] De Wilde observed in 1967: "While the vital role of labor supply in African agriculture is gradually receiving more attention, inadequate recognition of its importance has been a prominent cause of failure of many past efforts to increase output. Efforts to get farmers to plant early have repeatedly failed because there was not enough labor available at the recommended time, and no provision had been made to introduce implements to relieve the labor bottleneck. New settlement of irrigation projects have often proved disappointing because their labor requirements were ignored, or the demographic pressures which were supposed to furnish labor were overestimated. Again and again, attempts have been made to intensify output – i.e. to increase yields per unit of area by additional "inputs", including more labor – under conditions where farmers, not troubled by a shortage of land, obviously thought that "extensive" production was a more effective way to increase their total income" (p. 71).

[13] De Wilde (1967) notes that "the [African farmer's] ability to engage in 'social activities' is still valued rather highly by comparison with the acquisition of material goods" (p. 88).

[14] For example, in addition to causing underutilization of resources and its inefficient use, a skewed land distribution tends to lead to greater external multipliers by increasing the demand for imported rather than locally manufactured goods. This, in turn, adversely affects the pace and pattern of overall agricultural development.

[15] A survey carried out for this paper of 530 Ph.D. dissertations on African agriculture completed in U.S. universities since 1960 stresses the singular importance of food security in constraining allocative efficiency of labor in agriculture. Also see Ruthenberg (1971), Collinson (1972), and Shapiro (1973).

[16] Surplus years lead to yet another source of parastatal losses, as they result in large purchases of carryover stocks, shortages of working capital and substantial storage losses (Lele and Candler, 1984).

[17] In Kenya, no more than two bags of maize of 90 kilos each are allowed to be traded on private account across district boundaries without a permit. In Tanzania, the law has recently been changed to allow five bags.

[18] KTDA in Kenya is often cited as one of the few exceptions to this rule (Lele 1975; Lamb and Muller, 1982).

[19] Miracle (1968) described oligopolistic tendencies among Lebanese and Syrian traders, as well as the trading cartels of African "queens" in West Africa. While much less systematic research exists on East Africa, oligopolistic tendencies on the part of Europeans and Asians are known to be significant, even currently in crops in which free trade is allowed to operate as local African trading is still primarily confined to the collection of produce at the primary level. Factors underlying the concentration of European and Asian communities in certain trading and processing activities are themselves interesting, as is the genesis of the organized African protests in support of an increased share in economic activities prior to political independence (see Huttenback, 1971). Europeans had tended systematically to exclude Asian traders, through regulation, from those activities in which Asians were seen to be directly competitive. This led to the concentration of Asians in petty trade which involved direct contact with Africans. The African struggle for independence led to demands for the restriction of trading activities of

Asians in much the same way that Europeans had restricted them earlier in the more organized sector. The British government obliged Africans with such demands immediately preceding and following World War II, leading to the emergence of quite a viable and thriving African cooperative movement that captured some agricultural export trade and processing from Asians.

[20] A recent study of private grain marketing in Senegal, for example, indicated that transportation costs incurred by large wholesalers are considerably higher than the official government transport rates. See Newman, NDoye, and Alassane (1986).

[21] For instance, in Malawi the return to labor in the production of smallholder tobacco is high compared with maize – despite the fact that smallholders producing dark fired tobacco receive only 13 to 30 percent of the f.o.b. price compared to 70 to 80 percent of the f.o.b. price that is paid to estate growers for higher quality burley tobacco. See Ranade (1986).

[22] V. Ruttan (1982) provides a comprehensive survey of rates of return to investment in research.

[23] See K. Anthony (forthcoming) for review of the experience of the British support for agricultural research to Kenya, Tanzania, and Malawi.

[24] For 35 African countries (excluding North Africa), funds spent on agriculture research have risen in real terms (1980 constant dollars) from approximately $103 million in 1970 to $180 million in 1975, $276 million in 1980, and $380 million in 1984. It is not easy to determine how much of this striking increase was allocated to food crops, but the doubling of expenditures since 1975 suggests a positive reaction by governments and donors to the 1973/74 food crisis. In addition, for 35 African countries donor assistance to international and national research systems increased from $124 million in 1976, to $250 million in 1980, and to more than $300 million in 1983. (P. Oram, 1985, personal communication. Data from International Food Policy Research Institute.)

[25] This may not be surprising, given both the difficulty of African physical conditions and the long lags referred to earlier. Schultz (1965) observed a similar phenomenon in the case of the United States: "The early corn yield tests, which were based on searching for superior seed corn on Iowa farms for 12 years from 1904 to 1915...indicate how slow and difficult it was to improve corn yield by this approach – even with exceptionally competent and inspired workers and leadership...we have been blind to the fact that for decades prior to the (1920s)...(the agricultural research establishment) produced a trickle" (p. 61). Herdt (1970) made the same observation in the case of Korea. Unlike the United States in the 1920s, however, Africa cannot be said to have the best trained and most motivated scientific research establishment; nor has it identified either a clear technical solution or an organizational approach to research that would lead to finding a solution.

[26] Peterson's estimates exceed long-run supply elasticities for the United States, which were estimated to be of the order of 0.8 in the 1950s (Wilcox and Cochrane, 1951). In a personal communication, Ruttan has argued that improved statistical estimation procedures may explain the upward shift, although the latest Binswanger et al. (1985) study raises questions about this hypothesis. Even Ruttan argues, however, that supply responses may not be as high as Peterson's estimates suggest.

[27] Rates of implicit taxation for cocoa in the Ivory Coast have been estimated at 71

percent (1970–82) and 51 percent (1960–80); Gbetibouo and Delgado (1984).

[28] In this regard, the explanation of Malawian agricultural "success" typically attributed to its market-oriented policies (e.g. World Bank, 1981) is somewhat misleading – focusing exclusively on the absence of exchange rate overvaluation, rather than on the extent of explicit taxation of smallholders. It also misses the point that growth has been highly inequitable.

REFERENCES

Adams, D. W. 1978: "Mobilizing Household Savings Through Rural Financial Markets." *Economic Development and Cultural Change*, 26(3), 547–60.

Alison, C. and Green, R. (eds) 1983: "Accelerated Development in Sub-Saharan Africa: What Agendas for Action?" *Institute for Development Studies Bulletin*, 14(1), Brighton, Sussex: Sussex University.

Ansu, Y. 1984: "Monetary and Exchange Rate Policies for an Economy with Parallel Markets: The Case of Ghana." Ph.D. Dissertation, Stanford, California: Stanford University.

Anthony, K. Forthcoming. "U.K. Agricultural Research Aid to Kenya, Tanzania and Malawi" In U. Lele and E. Hanak (eds), *Experiences with Foreign Aid to African Agriculture*.

Anthony, K., Johnston, B. F., Jones, W. O. and Uchendu, V. C. 1979: *Agricultural Change in Tropical Africa*. Ithaca NY: Cornell University Press.

Askari, H. and Cummings, J. 1976: *Agricultural Supply Response: A Survey of the Econometric Evidence*. New York: Praeger.

Balcet, J. C. and Candler, W. 1982: *Farm Technology Adoption in Northern Nigeria*, vol. 1 and 2. Washington, DC: World Bank.

Bauer, P. T. 1963: *West African Trade, A Study of Competition, Oligopoly and Monopoly in a Changing Economy*, rev. ed. London: Routledge and Kegan Paul.

Bauer, P. T. 1981: *Equality, The Third World, and Economic Delusion*. Cambridge, Mass.: Harvard University Press.

Bauer, P. T. and Yamey, B. S. 1957: *The Economics of Underdeveloped Countries*. Chicago: University of Chicago Press.

Bennett, M. K. 1962: "An Agro-Climatic Mapping of Africa." *Food Research Institute Studies*, 3(2), 195–216.

Bienen, H. Forthcoming. "Politics and Agricultural Policy in Nigeria," In U. Lele and E. Hanak (eds), *Public Choice and Private Wants: The Political Economy of Agricultural Policy in Africa*.

Binswanger, H. P. et al. 1985: "Estimation of Aggregate Supply Response From Time Series of Cross-Country Data." Report No. ARU48, Washington, DC: World Bank.

Binswanger, H. P. and Rosenzweig, M. R. 1982: "Productive Relations in Agriculture," Research Program in Development Studies, Discussion Paper No. 105, Princeton, NJ: Princeton University, Woodrow Wilson School.

Binswanger, H. P. and Rosenzweig, M. R. 1983: "Behavioral and Material Determinants of Production Relations in Agriculture." Report No. ARU5 Washington, DC: World Bank.

Bond, M. 1983: "Agricultural Responses to Prices in Sub-Saharan African Countries." *IMF Staff Papers*, 30(4), Washington, DC: IMF.

Boserup, E. 1981: *Woman's Role in Economic Development*. New York: St Martin's Press.

Clark, C. 1951: *The Conditions of Economic Progress*. London: Macmillan.

Collinson, M. 1972: *Farm Management in Peasant Agriculture*. Boulder, Colorado: Westview Press, Reprint 1983.

Davis, T. J. (ed.) 1986: *Development of Rainfed Agriculture under Arid and Semiarid Conditions*. Proceedings of the Sixth Agricultural Symposium, Jan. 6-10, 1986, Washington, DC: World Bank.

Delgado, C. L. 1977: "Economic Interactions Between Peasants and Herders in the West African Savannah: A Case Study from Tenkodogo, Upper Volta." Ann Arbor: University of Michigan, Center for Research on Economic Development.

Delgado, C. L. and Ranade, C. G. 1987: "Technical change and Agricultural Labor Use." In J. W. Mellor, C. L. Delgado, and M. Blackie (eds), *Accelerating Food Production Growth in Sub-Saharan Africa*. Baltimore: Johns Hopkins University Press.

de Wilde, J. C. 1967: *Experiences with Agricultural Development in Tropical Africa*, 2 vols. Baltimore: Johns Hopkins University Press.

Dovring, F. 1959: "The Share of Agriculture in a Growing Population," *Monthly Bulletin of Agricultural Economics and Statistics*, 8, 1-11.

Evenson, R. E. 1981: "Benefits and Obstacles in Developing Appropriate Agricultural Technology." *Annals of The American Academy of Political and Social Science*, 458, 54-67.

Evenson, R. E. and Kislev, Y. 1975: *Agricultural Research Productivity*. New Haven: Yale University Press.

Falcon, W. P. 1967. Comment on R. Krishna, "Agricultural Price Policy and Economic Development," In H. M. Southworth and B. F. Johnston (eds), *Agricultural Development and Economic Growth*, Ithaca, NY: Cornell University Press.

Gbetibouo, M. and Delgado, C. 1984: "Lessons and Constraints of Export Crop-Led Growth: Cocoa in Ivory Coast." In I. W. Zartman and C. Delgado (eds), *The Political Economy of the Ivory Coast*, New York: Praeger.

Griliches, Z. 1957: "Hybrid Corn: An Exploration in the Econometrics of Technical Change." *Econometrica*, 25, 501-22.

Griliches, Z. 1958: "Research Costs and Social Returns: Hybrid Corn and Related Innovations." *Journal of Political Economy*, 66, 419-31.

Griliches, Z. 1964: "Research Expenditure, Education, and the Aggregate Production Function." *American Economic Review*, 54, 961-74.

Hayami, J. and Ruttan, V. W. 1985: *Agricultural Development: An International Perspective*. Baltimore: Johns Hopkins University Press.

Helleiner, G. K. 1975: "Smallholder Decision Making: Tropical African Evidence." In L. G. Reynolds (ed.), *Agriculture in Development Theory*, New Haven: Yale University Press.

Herdt, R. W. 1970: "A Disaggregate Approach to Aggregate Supply," *American Journal of Agricultural Economics*, 52, 512-20.

Heyer, J., Maitha, J. K., and Senga, W. M. (eds) 1976: *Agricultural Development in Kenya: An Economic Assessment*. Nairobi: Oxford University Press.

Hill, P. 1970: *Studies in Dual Capitalism in West Africa.* Cambridge: Cambridge University Press.

Huttenback, R. A. 1971: *Gandhi in South Africa.* Ithaca, NY: Cornell University Press.

Ishikawa, S. 1967: *Economic Development in Asian Perspective.* Tokyo: Kinokuniya.

Jaeger, W. 1984: "Agricultural Mechanization: The Economics of Animal Traction in Upper Volta," Ph.D. dissertation, Stanford University.

Jammeh, S. and Ranade, C. G. 1986: "Agricultural Pricing and Marketing in Senegal," Unpublished paper prepared for Managing Agricultural Development in Africa Study, World Bank.

Johnson, D. G. 1947: *Forward Prices for Agriculture.* Chicago: University of Chicago Press.

Johnson, D. G. 1954: *Agricultural Price Policy and International Trade.* Princeton, NJ: Princeton University Press.

Johnson, D. G. 1986: "Policy Issues in Rainfed Agriculture," In T. J. Davis (ed.), *Development of Rainfed Agriculture Under Arid and Semiarid Conditions,* Proceedings of the Sixth Agricultural Sector Symposium, Washington, DC: World Bank.

Johnson, H. G. 1965: "A Theoretical Model of Economic Nationalism in New and Developing States," *Political Science Quarterly,* 80(2), 169–85.

Johnston, B. F. and Kilby, P. 1975: *Agriculture and Structural Transformation: Economic Strategies in Late Developing Countries.* New York: Oxford University Press.

Johnston, B. F. and Mellor, J. W. 1961: "The Role of Agriculture in Economic Development." *American Economic Review,* 51, 566–93.

Jones, C. 1983: "The Mobilization of Women's Labor for Cash Crop Production: A Game Theoretic Approach," Ph.D. dissertation, Cambridge, Mass.: Harvard University.

Jones, W. O. 1960: "Economic Man in Africa." *Food Research Institute Studies,* 1, 107–34.

Jones, W. O. 1974: "Regional Analysis and Agricultural Marketing Research in Tropical Africa: Concepts and Experience," *Food Research Institute Studies,* 13, 3–28.

Krishna, R. 1963: "Farm Supply Response in India – Pakistan: A Case Study of the Punjab Region," *Economic Journal,* 73, 477–87.

Krishna, R. 1967: "Agricultural Price Policy and Economic Development," In H. M. Southworth and B. F. Johnston (eds), *Agricultural Development and Economic Growth,* Ithaca, NY: Cornell University Press.

Krueger, A. O. 1986: "Aid in the Development Process." *World Bank Research Observer,* 1(1), 57–78.

Kuznets, S. 1959a: *Six Lectures on Economic Growth.* Glencoe, Illinois: Free Press of Glencoe.

Kuznets, S. 1959b: "Quantitative Aspects of the Economic Growth of Nations: Part IV, Distribution of National Incomes by Factor Shares." *Economic Development and Cultural Change,* 7(3), part 2.

Lamb, G. and Muller, L. 1982: "Control, Accountability and Incentives in a Successful Development Institution: The Kenya Tea Development Authority." World Bank Staff Working Paper No. 550, Washington DC: World Bank.

Lee, T. 1971: *Intersectoral Capital Flows in the Economic Development of Taiwan, 1895-1960.* Ithaca, NY: Cornell University Press.

Lele, U. 1971: *Food Grain Marketing in India: Private Performance and Public Policy.* Ithaca, NY: Cornell University Press.

Lele, U. 1975: *The Design of Rural Development: Lessons from Africa.* Baltimore: Johns Hopkins University Press.

Lele, U. 1977: "Considerations Related to Optimum Pricing and Marketing Strategies in Rural Development." In T. Dams and K. E. Hunt (eds), *Decision Making and Agriculture,* Lincoln: University of Nebraska Press.

Lele, U. 1984a: "Tanzania: Phoenix or Icarus?" In A. Harberger (ed.), *World Economic Growth,* San Francisco: Institute for Contemporary Studies.

Lele, U. 1984b: "The Role of Risk in an Agriculturally Led Strategy in Sub-Saharan Africa." *American Journal of Agricultural Economics,* 66(5), 677-83.

Lele, U. 1985: "Terms of Trade, Agricultural Growth and Rural Poverty in Africa." In J. W. Mellor and G. M. Desai (eds), *Agricultural Change and Rural Poverty: Variations on a Theme by Dharm Narain,* Baltimore: Johns Hopkins University Press.

Lele, U. 1986: "Women and Structural Transformation." *Economic Development and Cultural Change,* 34(2), 195-221.

Lele, U. 1987: "Growth of Foreign Assistance and its Impact on Agriculture." In J. W. Mellor, C. L. Delgado, and M. Blackie (eds), *Accelerating Food Production in Sub-Saharan Africa.* Baltimore: Johns Hopkins University Press.

Lele, U. 1988: "Agricultural Growth, Domestic Policies, and External Assistance to Africa: Lessons of a Quarter-Century." Eighth Agricultural Sector Symposium on Trade, Aid, and Policy Reform for Agriculture. Sponsored by the Agricultural and Rural Development Department of the World Bank, 6-8 January.

Lele, U. and Candler, W. 1984: "Food Security in Developing Countries: National Issues." In C. K. Eicher and J. M. Staatz (eds), *Agricultural Development in the Third World,* Baltimore: John Hopkins University Press.

Lele, U. and Goldsmith, A. Forthcoming: "Development of Agricultural Research Capacity: India's Experience with the Rockefeller Foundation and its Significance for Africa." *Economic Development and Cultural Change.*

Lele, U. and Hanak, E. (eds) Forthcoming: *Experiences with Foreign Aid to African Agriculture.*

Lele, U. and Hanak, E. (eds) Forthcoming: *Public Choice and Private Wants: The Political Economy of Agricultural Policy in Africa.*

Lele, U. and Mellor, J. W. 1981: "Technological Change, Distribution Bias and Labor Transfer in a Two-Sector Economy." World Bank Reprint Series No. 205, *Oxford Economic Papers,* 33(3), 426-41.

Lele, U. and Meyers, Richard L. 1987: "Growth and Structural Change in East Africa: Domestic Policies, Agricultural Performance, and World Bank Assistance, 1963-1986." Parts I and II. World Bank DRD Discussion Papers Nos. 273, 274.

Lewis, S. R. Jr. 1967: "Agricultural Taxation in a Developing Economy." In H. M. Southworth and B. F. Johnston (eds), *Agricultural Development and Economic Growth,* Ithaca, NY: Cornell University Press.

Lewis, W. A. 1954: "Economic Development with Unlimited Supplies of Labor." *The Manchester School,* 22, 139-91.

Linnehan, A. 1984: "Senegal: The Legacy of Extensive Agricultural Growth." Draft of internal World Bank paper.

Little, I. M. D. 1982: *Economic Development: Theory, Policy and International Relations*. New York: Basic Books.

Mellor, J. W. 1976: "Toward a Theory of Agricultural Development." In H. M. Southworth and B. F. Johnston (eds), *Agricultural Development and Economic Growth*, Ithaca, NY: Cornell University Press.

Mellor, J. W. 1976: *The New Economics of Growth: A Strategy for India and the Developing World*. Ithaca, NY: Cornell University Press.

Mellor, J. W. and Lele, U. 1972: "Jobs, Poverty and the Green Revolution." *International Affairs*, 48(1), 20–32.

Mellor, J. W. and Johnston, B. F. 1984: "The World Food Equation: Inter-relations among Development, Employment, and Consumption." *Journal of Economic Literature*, 22, 531–74.

Migot-Adholla, S. E. 1977: "Migration and Rural Differentiation in Kenya." Ph.D. dissertation, Los Angeles: University of California.

Miracle, M. P. 1968: "Market Structure in Commodity Trade and Capital Accumulation in West Africa." In R. Moyer, S. Holladder, and B. Harris (eds), *Markets and Marketing in Developing Countries*, Homewood, Ill.: Irwin.

Myint, H. 1977: "Agriculture and Economic Development in an Open Economy." In L. G. Reynolds (ed.), *Agriculture in Development Theory*, New Haven: Yale University Press.

Nelson, R. P. 1959: "The Simple Economics of Basic Scientific Research." *Journal of Political Economy*, 67, 297–306.

Nelson, R. P. 1964: "Aggregate Production Functions and Medium Range Growth Projections." *American Economic Review*, 54, 575–606.

Newman, D. N., NDoye, O., and Alassane, P. 1986: "Private Sector Grain Marketing in Senegal's Peanut Basin." Paper submitted for presentation at 1986 Annual Meeting, American Agricultural Economics Association, Reno, Nev., July 27–30.

Okhawa, K. and Takamatsu, N. 1973: "Capital Formation, Productivity and Employment: Japan's Historical Experience and its Possible Relevance to LDCs." International Development Center of Japan.

Oluoch-Kosura, W. A. 1983: "An Economic Analysis of Small Farm Mechani-zation in Western Province, Kenya." Ph.D. dissertation, Ithaca, NY: Cornell University.

Oram, P. 1985: Personal communications. International Food Policy Research Institute, Washington, DC.

Peterson, W. L. 1979: "International Farm Prices and the Social Cost of Cheap Food Policies." *American Journal of Agricultural Economics*, 61, 12–21.

Ranade, C. G. 1986: "Agricultural Marketing and Pricing in Malawi." Un-published paper prepared for Managing Agricultural Development in Africa Study, World Bank.

Ranis, G. and Fei, J. C. H. 1964: *Development of a Labor Surplus Economy: Theory and Policy*. Homewood, Ill.: Irwin.

Robinson, K. L. 1975: "Unstable Farm Prices: Economic Consequences and Policy Options." *American Journal of Agricultural Economics*, 57(5), 769–77.

Rostow, W. W. 1960: *The Stages of Economic Growth: A Non-Communist Manifesto*. London: Cambridge University Press.

Ruthenberg, H. 1971: *Farming Systems in the Tropics.* Oxford: Clarendon Press.

Ruttan, V. 1982: *Agricultural Research Policy.* Minneapolis: University of Minnesota Press.

Ruttan, V. W. and Hayami, Y. 1984: "Induced Innovation Model of Agricultural Development." In C. K. Eicher and J. M. Staatz (eds), *Agricultural Development in the Third World*, Baltimore: Johns Hopkins University Press.

Sabot, R. 1983: "Urban Employees in Kenya and Tanzania: Educational Attainment and its Relation to Jobs, Pay, Mobility, and Rural Links." Mimeo, Washington, DC: World Bank.

Schultz, T. W. 1945: *Agriculture in an Unstable Economy.* New York: McGraw Hill.

Schultz, T. W. 1964: *Transforming Traditional Agriculture.* New Haven: Yale University Press.

Schultz, T. W. 1965: *Economic Crisis in World Agriculture.* Ann Arbor: University of Michigan Press.

Shapiro, K. H. 1973: "Efficiency and Modernization in African Agriculture: A Case Study in Geita District, Tanzania." Ph.D. dissertation, Stanford University.

Singh, I., Squire, L., and Strauss, J. 1986: "A Survey of Agricultural Household Models: Recent Findings and Policy Implications," *The World Bank Economic Review*, 1(1), 149–79.

Southworth, H. M. and Johnston, B. F. (eds) 1967: *Agricultural Development and Economic Growth.* Ithaca, NY: Cornell University Press.

Spencer, D. S. C. 1985: "A Research Strategy to Develop Appropriate Agricultural Technologies for Small Farm Development in Sub-Saharan Africa." In H. W. Ohm and J. G. Nagy (eds), *Appropriate Technologies for Farmers in Semi-Arid West Africa*, West Lafayette, Ind.: Purdue University.

Stolper, W. F. 1969: *Planning Without Facts: Lessons in Resource Allocation from Nigeria's Development.* London: Cambridge University Press.

Tang, A. M. 1963: "Research and Education in Japanese Agricultural Development 1880–1938." *Economic Studies Quarterly* (Tokyo), 13, 27–42 and 91–9.

von Pischke, J. D. 1980: "The Political Economy of Specialized Farm Credit Institutions." World Bank Working Paper No. 446, Washington, DC: World Bank.

Waterbury, J. Forthcoming: "Agricultural Policy Making and Stagnation in Senegal: What is There to Explain?" In U. Lele and E. Hanak (eds), *Public Choice and Private Wants: The Political Economy of Agricultural Policy in Africa.*

Wharton, C. 1967: "The Infrastructure for Agricultural Growth." In H. M. Southworth and B. F. Johnston (eds), *Agricultural Development and Economic Growth*, Ithaca, NY: Cornell University Press.

Wilcox, W. W. and Cochrane, W. W. 1951: *Economics of American Agriculture*, New York: Prentice Hall, Inc.

World Bank. 1981: *Accelerated Development of Sub-Saharan Africa: An Agenda for Action.* Washington, DC: World Bank.

World Bank. 1984: *Toward Sustained Development in Sub-Saharan Africa.* Washington, DC: World Bank.

Comments on
"Comparative Advantage and Structural Transformation: A Review of Africa's Economic Development Experience"

GERALD K. HELLEINER

African countries do not figure prominently in the general papers on development presented at the Symposium. There were no Africans on the program; nor, indeed, were there any in attendance. Africa is on the periphery of Raúl Prebisch's periphery. Data limitations have left this continent substantially outside systematic cross-country investigations, such as those of Chenery and friends. Yet if poverty is the reason for our concern with development, surely we must devote more attention to the parts of the world where developmental progress has been most limited.

After the first burst of post-independence activity, sub-Saharan Africa has had little forward motion to analyze and little structural transformation to monitor. With only a few exceptions, African countries were characterized by stagnation in the 1970s and, following devastating shocks from the world economy and the weather, catastrophic decline in the 1980s. In the past few years there has been severe depreciation of both the physical and human capital stock. The World Bank's latest projection of African needs is based on the aspiration of merely returning imports per capita to the already depressed levels of 1980–2 by the end of the decade. Given the prospects for the terms of trade and for net capital flows, even this modest objective, which would permit some increase in capacity utilization by relieving the current "import strangulation," looks beyond reach. The hope of restoring by the end of the eighties the depreciated infrastructure (or less likely, actually achieving significant net capital formation again) is quite remote. What is required for most of sub-Saharan Africa today, far from "development" economics, is increased understanding of the economics (and politics) of decline. There are cumulative processes at work that we do not fully understand. Unfortunately, weak economic performance seems to interact with lowered savings, scarce inputs, inflation, overvaluation, damaged confidence, weaker states, and political disorder. The statistical system has itself been sinking, as increasing proportions of economic activity take place in informal or illegal, in any case unrecorded, markets. The fragility of economic and political systems in low-income countries has perhaps not been sufficiently appreciated before. The endogenization of public policy in models of developing countries, recommended by Ranis and others, is bound to involve unique elements in particularly fragile systems.

The sub-Saharan African countries' experience suggests not only that typology is inescapable in the economics of development, but also that the so-called "initial conditions" are crucially important as a basis for "typing," much more important in this instance than policy choice. The relevant initial conditions in Africa include: low per capita income – and the weak infrastructure and human capital, and the large share of agriculture in overall economic activity that accompany it; typically very small size; a "soft" state; historical influences, such as the high formal sector wage structure bequeathed by colonial rule; and the highly variable resource base. Policy differences among African countries – at least those based on the oversimplified dichotomies which Uma Lele correctly criticizes, such as "open" versus "closed," public versus private, agriculture-oriented versus industry-oriented – have been dwarfed by other influences upon recent performance (for statistical corroboration, see Wheeler, 1984; Helleiner, 1986).

Uma Lele's analysis of the weaknesses that are at the roots of Africa's problems and possible ways out of them focuses upon the micro-foundations of agricultural performance and upon governmental policy. For someone who once wrote an Economic Growth Center book on "Peasant Agriculture, Government and Economic Growth" (in Nigeria), her approach makes excellent sense. Individuals and households in the smallholder agricultural sector are constrained in their access to land and to capital, but it is labor allocation upon which Lele places greatest emphasis. Although there are important issues arising from seasonality of demand and from gender-based division of labor, it is not typically helpful to think in terms of labor surplus in Africa. Farm labor is allocated between food crops, export crops, other farm and rural off-farm activities, and urban migration on the basis of prospective returns. (In Africa, rural-urban migration is often temporary; it is usually still possible for migrants to return to their villages, as indeed many have done in the recent years of urban economic difficulty.) Lele properly devotes particular attention to the importance of risk, as well as return, in farm-level decision-making – risk of changes in prices, yields, and public policies – and to the overarching importance of food security for those who live at the very margin of existence. Also of crucial signific- ance is the limited knowledge that is available concerning the biochemi- cal or seed-fertilizer innovation possibilities in sub-Saharan African conditions. It is worth recalling that the very first Yale Economic Growth Center discussion paper (Green and Hymer, 1966) pertained to the failures of colonial agricultural extension, which they attributed to the fact that the relevant officers did not have all that much that was useful to extend.

As far as government policy is concerned, the key point to be made is that the typical African state has been a very "soft" one. It has been soft both in terms of its sheer managerial capacities – data availability, recognition and implementation lags, expertise, etc. – and, no less important, in terms of its capacity to overcome the influence of specific interests. It has typically been very far from the development-oriented and entrepreneurial state described in Fei's and Ranis's paper published in this volume; rather, it has been bent to serve particular interests and has frequently served them well. When viewed in terms of their contribution to economic development, the agricultural policies of African states can be judged harshly, as Uma Lele and most economists do. If the state is viewed, instead, as a political distributor of economic and other rewards, as Robert Bates (1981) has urged us to do, it has typically performed much "better."

Lele's analysis of smallholder decision-making and governmental performance leads her to advocate an "optimum mix of private incentives and public goods" for improved African agricultural performance. The relevant public goods include agricultural research, infrastructure, and stability. Neither private incentives nor these public goods will alone suffice. Both are necessary. In circumstances of bad weather or severe international economic "shocks," sadly, even the appropriate provision of both may still leave performance weak.

The issues that I consider most important to highlight in the wide-ranging analysis that Uma Lele deploys to make her case are the following:

1   The attention devoted to agricultural research, and particularly to the creation of the basic scientific and technological capacity necessary for the conduct of adaptive research activities, has been quite inadequate in Africa. Lele's assessment in this regard is undoubtedly correct. It is not obvious, however, how she would go about remedying the problem. On the one hand, she says that there has been "too rapid an Africanization of research" in Anglophone Africa; on the other, she says that there has been "excessive reliance on expatriates" in Francophone Africa. How *does* one get the balance right? In any case, the building of the necessary agricultural research base in Africa will certainly take a long time. There are no "quicky" solutions from policy change here.

2   Lele is also correct in her assessment that agriculture has not received a large enough share of resources in the African development effort. Agriculture is, nevertheless, still the prime source of mobilizable savings. (Clearly, the potential for surplus mobilization has fallen with the economic decline of the 1980s.) Higher agricultural prices do not, therefore, always constitute the best use of scarce public resources. There are frequently non-price constraints that can only be addressed

via public expenditure. Lele makes the important observation that the relatively successful agriculture-based African countries have not taxed agriculture significantly less than others; rather, they have used resources better, and in particular, have put more into agricultural infrastructure and other forms of agricultural support. Inappropriate agricultural pricing policy has probably attracted disproportionate attention in recent years. (Perhaps Lele places more emphasis than is warranted on levels of official food prices; market prices frequently bear little relationship to these "announced" ones.) Optimal taxing and pricing is far more complicated than many "market fundamentalists" (a group to which Lele clearly does not belong) make out. It is inappropriate to try to generalize across crops and countries in these matters.

3   Sub-Saharan Africa is now producing well short of its overall potential – it is operating within its production frontier and/or misallocating along it. Lele argues that, given the existing technology, infrastructure, and endowments, most African countries should have been producing more exports relative to food and more agriculture relative to non-agriculture (hence the "comparative advantage" in her title). These misallocations have taken the form of inappropriate deployment of labor, for which governmental policy errors are primarily responsible. Overall, this is probably right.

But there is more that needs to be said: (a) the correction of these misallocations will generate a once-for-all increase in income; this immediate reallocation is of second-order importance, relative to ongoing productivity increases potentially achievable through technical progress; (b) not only is there considerable uncertainty concerning aggregate agricultural supply response (Lele, like others, is forced to rely upon numbers from other parts of the world, and even those are uncertain) but there must also be some concern about the collective impact upon world prices for tropical beverages, oilseeds, fibers, and other agricultural products as a consequence of export expansion in many producing countries; (c) for the past five years, the effect of misallocation upon shortfalls in productive potential, in any case, has been dwarfed by that of foreign exchange scarcity (and subsequent shortages of fuel, inputs, and spare parts) upon capacity utilization.

4   Instability and uncertainty are important elements in farm-level decision-making and welfare. Lele sensibly notes that we do not know exactly what their impact is and urges that we learn more. We do know something, however, about the negative impact of overall economic instability upon economic growth. Instability of import volume, whether in consequence of external shocks or policy oscillation, has been shown to be highly negatively correlated with growth in Africa in the past couple of decades; it is more highly correlated with growth than the investment rate or "openness" (Helleiner, 1986). The stop-go character of importing thus appears to be very costly. Unfortunately, despite larger

international shocks than have been typical in the past, the buffers provided for these countries in the international system have become weaker.

5   In her discussion of the roles of markets and governments, Lele writes: "simply liberalizing markets...may well set back the cause of market development." The encouragement of liberal approaches, she sensibly argues, does not always imply *laissez-faire*. In order to assess the likely impact of privatization, it is important to consider the role of oligopoly and market power, ethnicity and alien influences, and elements of local history. One must hope that an equally sophisticated appreciation of these issues will be found throughout the World Bank as alternatives to existing institutional arrangements are recommended in Africa (and elsewhere).

Some important elements of African experience are inevitably missing in a paper of this length. It may be helpful to offer a short list of those that may be the most important:

1   The future of African exports involves rather more than this paper suggests. The prospect for nonagricultural exports, notably metals and minerals, is important for many African countries and should be factored into any overall assessment of comparative advantage. Unfortunately, that prospect is frequently quite bleak. More broadly, what are the prospects for new and nontraditional exports from Africa? What are the possible African analogues of Taiwan's tinned mushrooms and asparagus?

2   The quality of macroeconomic and financial management can be crucial to overall developmental performance, as well as to agriculture in particular. Overvalued exchange rates, rampant inflation, and an unmanageable external debt have characterized many African countries in the 1980s. Macro-policy has not been "planned" as much as it has emerged through "crisis management," in the same sort of way that Corbo characterized Latin America in the 1930s in this text's previous chapter. While macroeconomic imbalances have not been entirely of the Africans' own making, these problems must, nonetheless, be addressed if sustained growth is to be restored. Sound macroeconomic management includes planning for the prospect of future external shocks.

3   Strategy for the nonagricultural sector must be rethought. If import-substitution industrialization has proven costly, and efforts at major "structural transformation" have been premature, what are the sensible alternatives? Is it really sufficient to return to a primary-producing mode, wait, and hope for the best?

4   Not nearly enough is known about the performance and prospects of small and informal sector enterprise outside of agriculture. As the "modern" economy was buffeted by external blows and domestic mismanagement in recent years, an unrecorded parallel sector – peopled largely by small firms – entered with new vigor into trade, finance, and various directly productive activities. Can and should this small-scale sector be offered more encouragement, and if so, how?

5   As the part of the developing world with the weakest base of educated manpower, Africa must be particularly concerned with the best means of building human capital. Strategies for the formal education system and for other means of learning are likely to be of fundamental importance to longer-run African development.

6   African population growth is now the most rapid of the Third World (Kenya's annual rate of growth is over 4 percent), and fertility still shows little sign of declining. The implications for development and for development policies deserve major attention in any overall review of African prospects.

Africa clearly has a long, long road ahead. If Gus Ranis's "inducement" explanation of policy change is correct, many African governments may be about to shift in directions more conducive to sustained future growth – as some are already doing. But even if so, one must employ a longer time horizon than an impatient world and many impatient development economists prefer. There are no shortcuts through history. The immediate African prospect is bleak.

REFERENCES

Bates, R. 1981: *Markets and States in Tropical Africa: The Political Basis of Agricultural Policies*. Berkeley: University of California Press.

Green, R. H. and Hymer, S. 1966: "The Introduction of Cocoa in the Gold Coast: A Study in the Relations between African Farmers and Colonial Agricultural Experts." Discussion Paper 1, New Haven: Economic Growth Center, Yale University.

Helleiner, G. K. 1966: *Peasant Agriculture, Government and Economic Growth in Nigeria*. For the Economic Growth Center, Yale University. Homewood, Ill.: Richard D. Irwin.

Helleiner, G. K. 1986: "Outward Orientation, Import Instability and African Economic Growth: An Empirical Investigation." In Sanjaya Lall and Frances Stewart (eds), *Theory and Reality in Development*, London: Macmillan, 139–53.

Wheeler, D. 1984: "Sources of Stagnation in Sub-Saharan Africa." *World Development*, 12(1), 1–23.

8

Development Theory and Problems of Socialist Developing Economies

DONG FURENG

Socialist development economics with a well-knit theoretical system is absent in the socialist countries. But this does not mean that there are no development theories in these countries. After the establishment of the socialist system, all the socialist developing countries have been confronted with the question of how to turn their backward economy into a modernized one, or in other words, of how to transform their underdeveloped economy into a developed one. Although they differ from one another in their economic conditions, they are faced with common problems that must be solved in a socialist way, or within the framework of the socialist system; hence the development theories.

In the Soviet Union, there were heated discussions on the development theories in the 1920s as well as in other socialist countries over different periods. In recent years, such discussions have also taken place in China. However, this paper will not deal with these discussions from the historical perspective. Instead, it will offer the author's views on some common problems in the economic development of the socialist developing countries, while resting on the relevant theories with case studies on China.

SOCIALIST PUBLIC OWNERSHIP AND THE DEVELOPMENT OF THE SOCIALIST ECONOMY

According to Marxist theory, ownership of the means of production determines the entire relations of production which, in turn, constitute the foundation of the society and determine the society's superstructure – including the political system and the ideology. Therefore, immediately after victory of the socialist revolution, all the socialist countries began to set up socialist public ownership by: abolishing the private ownership of land and other means of production to establish collective or state ownership in the countryside; abolishing capitalist ownership to establish state ownership (in other words, ownership by the entire people) in cities, and at the same time, transforming individual ownership by the working people into collective ownership. This is what all the socialist countries have done, although they have done it through different processes and approaches.

It is essential for a socialist economy that socialist economic development should presuppose institutional reform, or to be more specific, establishment of socialist public ownership. This theoretical proposition is correct in principle. A case in point is the unprecedented rapid development of agricultural production and the dramatic improvement of the living standard of peasants in China in just a few years from 1953 to 1957, following the abolition of the feudal ownership of land by landlords and the redistribution of land previously owned by landlords or rich peasants among those who had very little or no land, and the establishment of the agricultural producers' cooperatives. In these years the average annual gross output value of agriculture increased by 4.5 percent and the per capita consumption of peasants rose by 3.2 percent.[1] The unprecedented rapid growth of the industrial production and speedy improvement of the living standard of the urban residents in China's First Five-Year plan period (1953–57) offer another proof. In this period, the total annual industrial output value grew by 18 percent[2] and the per capita consumption of nonagricultural residents by 4.8 percent.[3] Compared with those developing countries which have not undergone major social reforms, especially agrarian reform, China's economic development may be of some reference.

However, by saying that the establishment of socialist public ownership is a prerequisite for the development of the socialist economy, the author has limited himself to the extent that this theoretical proposition is correct in principle. One should not regard it as an abstract dogma, as if any form of public ownership can spur the development of the socialist economy. There is no truth in this assumption. In fact, certain forms of public ownership hinder or even impair the growth of the productive forces.

Witness what happened in the Soviet Union, Poland, and some other socialist countries, and even in China after 1957. As is widely known, the Soviet Union suffered an agricultural catastrophe in the course of overall collectivization in agricultural production. Up to 1940, the output of many agricultural products (cotton, beet, meat, etc.) in the Soviet Union failed to reach the pre-October Revolution level in 1913. After the death of Stalin, many resolutions concerning agriculture were adopted, and one minister of agriculture after another was dismissed. However, none of these helped to bring about a notable upturn in its agricultural production. This country of a big grain exporter in the pre-revolution days has become a big grain importer, suffering from a bad shortage of agricultural products.

Beginning from 1958, China, too, experienced a disaster in agricultural production. It was not until 1964 that the total value of agriculture reached the 1957 level. Then, agricultural production grew, but at a rate that was not fast enough: from 1959 to 1978, agricultural production was increased by 52 percent, at an average annual rate of 2.3 percent. It is true that for a time all the socialist economies recorded a fast development rate, but with low economic efficiency and poor economic results. Since the 1960s, the economic development of the Soviet Union and some East European socialist countries has slowed down immensely, particularly in productivity and technology. China was, at one time, faced with a similar situation.

What caused all this? No cause is exclusive, of course. Apart from the choice of development strategy and the economic system which will be dealt with later, it has to do with the form of ownership of the means of production. In fact, some socialist countries are trying to solve this problem. In Poland, collective economic organizations have been dissolved and individual ownership by peasants restored. In Yugoslavia, state ownership has been discarded in favor of ownership by the community under self-management. China is also trying to solve this problem. In the following pages more light will be shed on it, with the emphasis placed on China's experience.

The disaster China experienced in its rural areas beginning from 1958 was, to some extent, similar to what had happened in the course of the overall agricultural collectivization in the Soviet Union. One of the major causes for this disaster can be attributed to the establishment of the system of the people's commune by way of merging the advanced agricultural producers' cooperatives. This merge meant turning the property of the advanced agricultural producers' cooperatives into the common property of the people's communes. Therefore, before joining the people's communes, numbers of cooperatives sold their property, or allocated it among their members, and butchered their livestock, resulting in the destruction of the productive forces. Of course, other causes also contributed to this disaster, such as equalitarian distribution and so on. As a matter of fact, 1957 saw the same thing happen when elementary agricultural producers' cooperatives were merged into advanced ones, except that it was not so serious. This lesson tells us that not every form of socialist public ownership is the basis for the development of a socialist economy; certain forms can hinder and even impair the development of productive forces, because they infringe upon the personal interests of the working people and, consequently, dampen their enthusiasm.

The three-level ownership by the commune, the production brigade and the production team – with the production team (about the size of an elementary agricultural producers' cooperative) as the basic accounting unit, which had been established in China since 1960 – represented a major change to the original idea and form of ownership by the people's commune. This change, however, did not solve the fundamental problem concerning the form of socialist public ownership. In the winter of 1978, the system of contract responsibility with remuneration linked to output began to be put into effect in agricultural production. At first, various forms were tried. Gradually, the household responsibility system became prevalent, with 94.2 percent of the total households in the rural areas adopting it in 1983. Take crop growing as an example. Under this form, each household cultivates a piece of collective land in accordance with certain contracts. The household is entitled to keep all the product surpluses, after delivering the agricultural tax to the state and contributing to the accumulation fund and the public welfare fund of the production team or village. In this way, peasants' income is closely linked to the results of their work, and the decision-making power in production and management is vested in them.

Undoubtedly, this represents a tremendous change in the form of socialist public ownership. On the one hand, land and other means of production and infrastructure, such as water conservation works and roads, are still owned by the collectives and are not to be sold by peasants. On the other hand, individual ownership remains, under which peasants own their investment in soil improvement, means of production (such as farm animals, tools, and vehicles) bought at their own expense, and infrastructure (such as wells) built with their own efforts. Thus, through a "household responsibility system," socialist collective ownership has been combined with individual ownership by peasants, resulting in a combined form of means of production that has stimulated peasants' enthusiasm for production to such a great extent, that agricultural production has increased at an unexpectedly high speed. In the six years from 1979 through 1984, the total value of agricultural output grew by 67.5 percent, averaging an annual growth of 9 percent, far surpassing the 4.5 percent growth rate of the total agricultural output value in the First Five-Year Plan period (1953–7), which also had registered a rapid increase in agricultural production. This shows that only this form of socialist ownership that closely links personal interests of the working people with those of the collectives can lay the foundation for the development of the socialist economy.

The cause for the long stagnation of agricultural production in the Soviet Union should be sought, in the final analysis, in the ownership by the *kolkhozniki*, the members of the Soviet collective farms. This form of socialist ownership cannot be said to be appropriate, because it neglects or even infringes upon the personal interests of peasants and thus dampens their enthusiasm for improving production. In recent years, the system of contracted operation by specialized teams has been employed in the *kolkhoz* in the Soviet Union, but no remarkable results have been achieved. This is because the reform has been confined to the organization of production, and nothing has been done with regard to the ownership by the *kolkhozniki*.

At present, a few Soviet farms are experimenting in a household contract system. However, this does not mean that the household responsibility system, a form of ownership of the means of production prevailing in China's rural areas, is perfect. Under this form, each household is responsible for a very small piece of land, due to the large population and insufficient arable land. Cultivated land per peasant is about one-fifteenth of a hectare in densely populated areas. Working on its own, the household is weak in economic power and short of funds, which obviously is not conducive to the modernization of agriculture. As things stand, the household will remain as the unit in agricultural production for a long time to come. However, the number of households engaged in agriculture will become smaller and the land under their cultivation greater. At the same time, other households will join hands on a voluntary basis in various cooperatives and associations (such as credit cooperatives, supply and marketing cooperatives, transportation cooperatives, and service cooperatives for agricultural production), and enjoy all sorts of services thus provided. By giving play to the initiatives of each household in agricultural production and to the advantages of the collective economy, this form of ownership – which combines operation on a household basis with voluntary cooperation – can overcome possible limitations to production growth of household-based agriculture resulting from large population, insufficient arable land, and lack of funds. And peasants' enthusiasm will be encouraged instead of dampened, as was the case under the former collective ownership. This development trend has begun to emerge in China's countryside today.

Problems concerning the form of socialist public ownership also came up in cities. In China, as well as in the Soviet Union and other socialist countries, ownership by the entire people embodied in the state ownership plays the leading role. This form of ownership has a series of problems, of which the "soft budget constraint" on enterprises (a term used by Hungarian economist Kornai) is a major one. Because of this problem, enterprises are indifferent to profits or losses, with no bankruptcy threatening them. Should losses be incurred, enterprises could still survive, with the state providing subsidies and debt reduction or cancellation – or allowing them to hand in less or no taxes, profits, and interests that would otherwise be delivered. The soft budget constraint results in an indifference of enterprises to improve their operation and management, and it is one of the major causes for poor economic results of state enterprises. A new form of socialist public ownership is needed to change the soft budget constraint into a hard one, whereby state enterprises may be held liable for their profits and losses.

China has embarked on an experiment in which a number of small state-owned enterprises are being transformed into collective ones, or managed by individual employees or employee cooperatives, either on lease or by contract. Some have even been sold to individuals. In 1985, statistics show that 64,671 small commercial enterprises were transformed into collective ones or were managed by individuals on lease, accounting for 75.4 percent of the total small commercial enterprises under state ownership. Also in that year, 20,000 such enterprises were sold to individuals. A very small number of enterprises are being converted into stock companies on an experimental basis, with workers from these or other enterprises or from other organizations as the shareholders. At the same time, a new type of enterprise is developing, with funds pooled in different ways by state enterprises, collective enterprises, or individuals. All these experiments are aimed at linking the interests of enterprises and their workers with the operation and management and making them assume the risks thus involved, so they will not shift the burden onto the state in case of losses.

Provided that socialist public ownership remains predominent, China and some other socialist countries now allow and encourage the development of individually owned enterprises with self-employment, and private enterprises with a limited number of employees, so they may be complementary to socialist public ownership. This is conducive to the development of the economy.

In short, many socialist countries have been confronted with the problem of finding an appropriate form of socialist public ownership and an appropriate ownership structure to promote their economic development. This is an important subject that should be studied in the socialist development economics. Reassessment is being made with regard to formerly popular and dogmatic theories on socialist public ownership, such as the theory on the two-form pattern of public ownership advanced by the Soviet Union and followed as the guide in many socialist countries (that is, the theory that socialist public ownership can take only two forms – ownership by the state or by the entire people, and collective ownership; the former is an advanced form and the latter an elementary form to be transformed into the former, or the two tend to fuse into one). Reassessment is also being made about the theory that socialist public ownership should be all-embracing, and the theory that socialist public ownership and individual ownership by the working people repel each other. The theories and practices concerning socialist public ownership are very important to the development of the socialist economy.

Reforms in the form and structure of ownership of means of production would give rise to two problems: income gaps and unemployment.

First, the problem of widening income gaps. This problem arises from reforms in the form and structure of ownership of means of production. For instance, in the past, workers of the same job but different enterprises received the same pay under China's state-run economy. After some state enterprises were leased or sold to individuals or put under shareholding system, workers of the same job were paid differently. In the rural areas, with the adoption of the household responsibility system, the income of a household depends on its operation and management of the land. Therefore, the income gap among households has become wider. In addition, the income gap among employees under different ownerships has also enlarged, with the rate of income increase for those under individual and private ownerships the greatest, and that of those under collective ownership the second. Proper enlargement of income gaps may be of some use to economic development. However, prevention must be made against gaps that are too large, otherwise they would result in social instability.

Second, the problem of employment. Reforms in the form of ownership of state enterprises are aimed at making those enterprises liable for risks. If their assets could not cover their debts, they should be declared bankrupt (China is formulating the bankruptcy law). Should this happen, unemployment would arise. Changes in production scale and products of enterprises under different forms of ownership, particularly private enterprises with some employees, are also a cause for this problem. They would either increase or decrease employees. Related to the problem of employment is the problem of the labor market. Without this market, it is impossible to make flexible regulations of the supply and demand of labor. Life insurance for the unemployed and labor market are subjects newly put under study in China.

The above-mentioned problems are new ones in the socialist economic development theories. In China, reforms in those two aspects are commonly called transformation of the "eating from the same big pot" system and breaking of the "iron rice bowl." The two problems pose serious challenges to the socialist economic development theories. For in accordance with traditional theories, to realize social equity, income should be roughly equal. Since means of production is publicly owned, the society should provide a guarantee of employment to everybody. Unemployment is impermissible. So is the existence of a labor market. However, experience in all the socialist countries has shown that low efficiency and poor economic results could not be separated from the systems of "eating from the same big pot" and "iron rice bowl." They are major obstacles to the socialist economic development. Now, some socialist countries are undergoing economic restructuring. As it deepens, problems concerning reforms in the form of socialist public ownership and the structure of ownership will become more prominent. Their solution will be the prerequisite for further reforms. This issue will be discussed later in this paper.

CHOICE OF DEVELOPMENT STRATEGY FOR A SOCIALIST ECONOMY

Stalinist development strategy

Following the heated debate on the "problem of industrialization" in the Soviet Union from 1924 to 1928, Stalin worked out a development strategy for industrialization, with the development of heavy industry as the top priority, and he advanced a set of theories accordingly. Advocated as the "road of socialist industrialization," this Soviet strategy was regarded as the unique development strategy, universally applicable in the socialist countries, so much so that it must be adopted by all these countries. Therefore, the other socialist developing countries, China included, either have adopted or for a time followed this strategy. It can be outlined by the following four characteristics:

1   High-speed growth was regarded as the objective in expanding the socialist economy. The question of speed was considered of paramount importance. Stalin asked for "overtaking and outstripping the advanced capitalist countries technically and economically."[4] He emphasized, "the tempo must not be reduced! On the contrary, we must increase it as much as is within our powers and possiblities."[5] This development strategy was similar to the "overtaking and outstripping strategy" once adopted by some developing countries. The party program adopted by the 20th National Congress of the Communist Party of the Soviet Union (CPSU) in 1961 stated, "efforts must be made to augment the industrial output by 2.5 times in the next decade and surpass the level of the industrial development of the United States." In 1958, there was also a call in China to "catch up with and surpass Britain in the output of steel and other major industrial products" in 15 years or even less. All these reflected this development strategy.

2   The development of heavy industry was made the central task in the economic development and enjoyed the top priority. And within heavy industry, the machine-building subsector (as in the Soviet Union) or the iron and steel subsector (as in China) was selected as the center of economic development. Stalin said, "it follows from this that industrialization is to be understood above all as the development of heavy industry in our country, and especially of our own machine-building industry, which is the principal nerve of industry in general."[6] He held that to "commence the industrialization of the country by developing heavy industry" should be the approach for socialist countries.[7] People believed that the development of heavy industry, particularly of the machine-building or iron and steel subsectors, was the driving force for

the development of light industry, agriculture, and other sectors of the economy, leading to overall economic development. This strategy was somewhat similar to the "strategy of the imbalanced development," which was once carried out in some developing countries (although with different priority sectors).

3   Extensive development was adopted as the chief approach to high economic growth. It meant to achieve economic growth mainly by building new enterprises. For example, take China's state industrial enterprises. Of the additions of the total industrial output value from 1953 to 1983, 66.1 percent was contributed by the increase in work force, while 33.9 percent by the improvement in productivity.[8] It is obvious that the industrial growth took the form of extensive development. Stalin took accumulation as the "sole source of reproduction on an extended scale,"[9] because he attached importance to the extensive development of the economy. If a socialist developing country started the high-speed economic development with the building of heavy industry, it would inevitably set great store by extensive development of the economy.

4   Development of the economy was aimed at achieving basic self-sufficiency, thereby reducing dependence on the economy of non-socialist countries and satisfying the financial, material, and technological needs in the economic development with widest possible use of indigenous resources. In the process of industrialization – even when in the last resort, machines, equipment, raw materials and technology had to be imported from non-socialist countries – efforts should be devoted to developing the domestic industries, thereby substituting these imports with domestic products. The degree of self-sufficiency became an important hallmark for the level of economic development. (For example, this degree of machinery and rolled steel was once made such a hallmark in China.)

In the Soviet Union, Ganetsky said, "All those things which our country can produce or has produced should gradually be deleted from our plans for import," and "industry of the Soviet Union should be beefed up in order to rely less and less on foreign countries."[10] Stalin put forward the idea of realizing industrialization by relying on "our devices, without foreign loans, on the basis of the internal resources of our country."[11] This development strategy was implemented in large socialist countries like the Soviet Union and China. Where it was impossible to achieve basic self-sufficiency, such as in some small socialist countries, those countries expected (or were required) to become self-sufficient within the confines of socialist countries. Stalin once put forward the theory of two parallel world markets. Based on this theory, he maintained, "it may be confidently said that, with this pace of industrial development, it will soon come to pass that these countries will not only be in no need of imports from capitalist countries, but will themselves feel the necessity of finding an outside market for their surplus products."[12] This was a self-seclusive development strategy, similar to the "import-substitution" strategy pursued by some developing countries.

China's initial economic achievements

The above-mentioned development strategy came into shape under special historical conditions (here, they will not be discussed in detail). And it has proved of some use. Thanks to this strategy, the Soviet Union succeeded in laying the industrial, particularly the heavy industrial, basis within a short period of time, thus enabling it to resist the German fascist aggression during World War II. The adoption of this development strategy also enabled China to register monumental achievements in its economic development. Four of the main achievements are discussed below.

First, China extricated itself from the long years of stagnation or even retrogression in the pre-liberation days. Its economy developed at a rapid speed that had never been seen before and was beyond the reach of many other developing countries. From 1953 to 1978 (chosen as the end of the period because after that year, China changed its strategy for economic development), China's national income went up 353.2 percent, or 6 percent annually; the gross output value of agriculture grew 129.6 percent, a 3.2 percent annual increase; the total output value of industry increased 1498.6 percent, 11.2 percent annually, of which light industry rose 961 percent, 9.5 percent annually, and heavy industry rose 2891.6 percent, representing a 14 percent annual increase.[13]

Second among China's achievements is that it built an independent and fairly comprehensive system of industry and of national economy, setting up in succession many industrial enterprises that never were seen in old China – such as the automobile and aircraft manufacturing industries, electronics, nuclear and space industries, and petrochemical and chemical fiber industries. Gone forever are the days when old China was only capable of producing limited textiles, other light industrial products and handicrafts, and doing some machine repairing. In the heavy-industry sector, the growth rate was especially high in machine building, chemical, metallurgical, petroleum, synthetics, and electronics industries. The speedy development of industry, particularly of heavy industry, brought about a drastic change in the production structure. In the total industrial and agricultural output value, the share of agriculture dropped from 70 percent in 1949 to 56.9 percent in 1952 and 27.8 percent in 1978, while that of industry rose from 30 percent in 1949 to 43.1 percent in 1952 and 72.2 percent in 1978. In the total output value of industry, the share of light industry decreased from 73.6 percent in 1949 to 64.5 percent in 1952 and 43.1 percent in 1978, while that of heavy industry rose from 26.4 percent in 1949 to 35.5 percent in 1952 and 56.9 percent in 1978.[14] By then China had accomplished the preliminary groundwork for modernization.

Third, China underwent a great change in the geographical distribution of its economy. Many economically backward regions flourished. Before liberation, China's industry concentrated in a few coastal cities, while other areas, especially outlying regions, remained exceptionally underdeveloped. In those days, over 90 percent of the iron and steel works was in the northeast. By contrast, in 1978 a dozen large iron and steel production centers had been set up, and 30 or more medium-sized iron and steel enterprises (each with an annual production capacity of 100,000 tons) and hundreds of small iron and steel enterprises mushroomed across the country. Previously, the textile industry centered in just a few cities such as Shanghai, Qingdao, Tianjin, Wuhan and Wuxi, but by the mid-eighties, all the provinces and autonomous regions had textile mills. A number of industrial centers had emerged, even in the remote provinces and autonomous regions like Inner Mongolia, Xinjiang Uygur Autonomous Region, Qinghai, Gansu, Guizhou, and Yunnan.

The fourth of China's main achievements is a considerable improvement in people's living standards. From 1949 to 1978, China's population increased from 541.67 million to 962.59 million, or by 78.2 percent.[15] Despite the rapid growth of the population, the average consumption level of the Chinese residents registered a rise of 77 percent in 1978 compared to the level in 1952, of which the peasants' consumption level increased by 57.5 percent and that of the non-agricultural residents by 112.9 percent.[16] With arable and cultivated land accounting for only 7 percent of the world's total, the Chinese had a little more than 1.5 mu (1 mu = 0.1647 acre) of cultivated land per head, falling far short of the average world figure 5.5 mu. Limited though it was in arable land, China's grain output increased from 113.18 million tons in 1949 to 304.77 million tons in 1978, a 169.3 percent increase; the output of cotton shot up from 444,000 tons in 1949 to 2,167,000 tons in 1978, a rise of 387.6 percent; the output of oil-bearing crops increased from 2,564,000 tons in 1949 to 5,218,000 tons in 1978, a 103.5 percent increase.[17] The production boom put an end to the miserable life of the pre-liberation days when a wide number of working people lacked food and clothing. By the eighties, people's education and health had improved markedly. Before liberation, the life expectancy averaged 35 years in the rural areas and less than 40 years in the urban areas. In 1981, the figure jumped to 67.9 years.[18]

Adverse effects of development strategy

However, the implementation of the above-mentioned development strategy gave rise to some problems in China, in the Soviet Union and in other countries as well. Their main manifestations may be seen in the following aspects:

First, this strategy exerted an adverse effect on agriculture, which occupies a decisive position in the national economy. In 1952, agriculture accounted for 56.9 percent of the total output value of industry and agriculture.[19] The growth of agriculture has a vital bearing on the economy as a whole. In an effort to build heavy industry at a high speed and give first priority to its expansion, China was confronted with the problem of where to get the huge sum of funds. To build and expand heavy industry requires a great deal of funds, and to do it at full speed necessitates a prodigious amount of funds accumulated within a short period.

It was chiefly through two channels that the state amassed such funds from the agriculture sector:

1 Through agricultural and other taxes levied on the peasants. These taxes accounted for 11 percent of the total agricultural output value in 1952 and 8.55 percent in 1959.[20] Generally, they made up around 10 percent. Being a moderate amount, the taxes did not pose a heavy burden on the peasants.

2 Through the pricing mechanism, namely, the "scissors difference" between prices of industrial and agricultural products. Stalin described this (1955a, p. 53) as "something in the nature of a tribute" that the state gained from the peasants through pricing. He said that the "diversion" of funds from agriculture to industry was "for the purpose of speeding up our industrial development," and that "it is necessary."[21] Through the "scissors difference," the state amassed surplus products from peasants in the form of profits from goods using farm products as raw materials (mainly products of light industry), and from sales to peasants of materials and manufactured goods using industrial products as raw materials. In this way, the state accumulated funds for the development of heavy industry and other undertakings.

The implementation of this strategy turns farm surpluses into accumulated funds for the development of heavy industry through these channels ("scissors difference" being the principal one), which inevitably exerts an adverse effect on the development of agriculture. Since a high-speed development of heavy industry calls for much more in terms of funds, it cannot but disastrously impair agricultural development. What happened in the Soviet Union was a case in point. Mao Zedong pointed out, "the Soviet Union has adopted measures which squeeze the peasants very hard. It takes away too much from the peasants at too low a price through its system of so-called obligatory sales and other measures. This method of capital accumulation has seriously dampened the peasants' enthusiasm for production."[22]

Things were better in China. However, the Chinese committed the same error as the Soviet Union in stressing the need for high-speed development and giving prominence to heavy industry by the adoption of the above-mentioned development strategy. Consequently, China's agricultural development suffered serious damages, as did the economy as a whole.

Another problem that arose from this strategy was that it restrained the growth of the people's consumption, because its objective was to seek high speed, not to meet the people's basic needs. Moreover, under this strategy, the development of heavy industry enjoyed long-term top priority and required huge sums of accumulated funds over a very long period of time. According to statistics, in China investment in light industry generally can be recovered in one year and seven months, while that in heavy industry in five years and seven months. It is true that heavy industry can equip and promote the growth of agriculture and light industry with its own products, namely, the industrial means of production, thus improving the living standard of the people. But it takes a long time to transform the accumulated funds invested in heavy industry into increased consumption by the people. And during this period, the increase of consumption cannot but be restrained. Moreover, an extensive development needs a lot more accumulated funds. Hence, a high rate of accumulation is essential for implementing this development strategy and can be computed as follows:

Accumulation rate = (accumulated funds/national income) × 100%.

When China was overanxious for very high growth rate of heavy industry, the accumulation rate rarely would register high, such as the 43.8 percent reported in 1959. The accumulation rate of the Soviet Union seemed to be lower, accounting for about 25 percent of its national income. However Turetskii, a well-known Soviet economist, estimated that it was about 35 percent, because in the Soviet Union the price of the means of production which comprised the principal part of the accumulation funds was low.[23] Naturally, such a high accumulation rate has a natural inclination to restrain the increase of consumption.

This strategy required a particularly high speed in the development of heavy industry. Therefore, funds, technological facilities, power, raw materials, labor, and technical personnel had to be, first of all, put into heavy industry – leaving agriculture, light industry, and tertiary industry unable to develop correspondingly. As a result, there was a prolonged shortage of consumer goods and services. What is more, in order to develop heavy industry, farm products and light industrial products had to be diverted from the domestic market to the foreign market for the exchange of the means of production needed at home, which only aggravated the shortage of consumer goods. All the countries that adopted this development strategy – such as China, the Soviet Union, or other socialist countries – ran into the problem of relatively high economic growth, with people's consumption lagging behind.

This development strategy also hindered the improvement of the economic results in three ways:

1   In order to attain high-speed growth of the economy charac-terized by an increase of the total output value, enterprises would not balk at any costs in their effort to fulfil and overfulfil the quotas allotted to them. Instead of taking into account the amount of input, they consumed excessive inputs to achieve this end. They never con-cerned themselves with the quality and the applicability of their pro-ducts. This caused prodigious waste.

2   The inordinately high development speed of heavy industry and excessive investments in capital construction, as was required by the strategy, repeatedly caused serious disproportion in economic development. To overcome this disproportion, readjustment had to be made by slowing down the growth rate of heavy industry and suspending some construction projects. Heavy losses were incurred each time such readjustment was made. High speed develop-ment…disproportion…readjustment…high speed development, again… – this almost became a cyclical phenomenon in China's economy.

3   Due to lopsided stress on high-speed growth and extensive development and pursuance of self-sufficiency (to the neglect of comparative economic benefit), technological progress was retarded, and the updating of equipment of the existing enterprises was ignored. Hence, the economic results were poor. For a period of time in China, labor productivity dropped while product cost went up, and national income per 10,000 yuan of accumulation declined: it was 32 yuan in the First Five-Year Plan period, 1 yuan in the Second, 57 yuan between 1963 and 1965 (these were years of readjustment in the wake of a grievous economic setback), 26 yuan in the Third Five-Year Plan period, 16 yuan in the Fourth and 24 yuan in the Fifth (this was a period in the nature of economic readjustment). Many enterprises suffered losses. It is widely known that the econo-mic results in the Soviet Union were poor. Since the 1960s, its capital productivity has registered in negative numbers.

As far as the Soviet Union, China and other socialist countries were concerned, under certain conditions, this development strategy played its role in propelling economic development in the initial stage. However, it could not last long. Once the basic foundation was laid for industrialization, a new development strategy should have been adopted, if the international environment permitted. Otherwise, the defects inherent in the old one would become worse, causing many serious difficulties for the further development of the economy. The opportune moment for China to change its development strategy was the time when the First Five-Year Plan was fulfilled. At that time, basic foundation had been laid for industrialization, various economic sectors were developing more or less in proportion, and the economy had embarked on the path of growth. Although problems occurred, they were not serious and were easy to solve. Moreover, a change took place in the international environment, and China's trade with the West was restored and expanded to some extent. In fact, in the course of drafting the Second Five-Year Plan in 1956, China analyzed its own experience in the execution of the First Five-Year Plan and the errors the Soviet Union made in economic development. As a result, some important ideas and policies for changing the development strategy were advanced – such as reducing the growth rate of heavy industry while accelerating that of agriculture, increasing the proportion of investment in light industry, promoting technological transformation of the national economy, putting a ceiling on the proportion of accumulation in the national income so that this proportion would not be too high, and stressing the need to increase market supplies and improve the people's living standards.

If China had acted in accordance with these ideas and policies systematically, it could have shifted to a new economic development strategy, although at that time the knowledge of problems concerning economic development strategies was not as great as it is today, nor was the international environment so favorable for opening to the outside world. Unfortunately, no sooner had this shift started than it stopped. Beginning in 1958, rather than being changed into a new one, the old development strategy was carried out with its defects further developed. For example, a target was set for doubling the iron and steel output within the year of 1958; a large number of small-sized enterprises that were backward in technology were built; every province, even every people's commune, was required to achieve self-sufficiency; and so on and so forth.

China's new economic strategy

It was not until 1979, when its economy fell into a predicament, that China inaugurated a shift in strategy. The ten principles for economic development advanced by Premier Zhao Ziyang in December 1981 at the Fourth Session of the Fifth National People's Congress represented an unmistakable indication of the shift toward a new economic development strategy in China. This new strategy has the following four characteristics.

It is a strategy with the objective to meet the people's needs; first of all, their basic everyday needs. As is defined in the ten principles: "to give top priority to the people's interests and, first and foremost, to satisfy their basic everyday needs in handling the relationship between productive construction and the people's living conditions – henceforth this is the principle to which we must firmly adhere." The shift from striving for growth rate to satisfying people's needs represents a fundamental change of China's economic development strategy. When growth rate is made the objective, it has to be put above everything else, to be attained at the expense of the people's living standards (for a period of time at least) and to the neglect of economic results, quality of products, and objective demands. When satisfaction of the people's needs is made the objective, it has to be made as the starting point of everything, to be attained on the basis of increased production. Without rapid growth of production, quick improvement of the people's living standards will be out of the question. However, it differs in principle from the first objective, because China's experience shows that an increase in production does not necessarily result in improvement of the people's living standards, and a rapid increase in production is even less certain to lead to the rapid improvement of the people's living standards.

To satisfy the people's needs, it is imperative to set the growth rate with the view of improving the people's living standards gradually, that is, keeping the steps consistent with the growth of the economy. Concerning the growth rate, it is not "the higher the better" in unconditional terms. Rather, the optimum rate is the one that can improve the people's life at the quickest speed possible, not just in the immediate future, but for a long time to come.

To satisfy the people's needs, it is necessary to base economic development on an appropriate business structure, the establishment and development of which will help meet the people's growing needs while the economy grows.

To satisfy the people's needs, it is imperative to make improvement of economic results the precondition and the means for economic development. Only when a rapid growth rate is attained on the basis of increased economic results can the people's living standards be quickly improved.

It is a strategy that facilitates balanced and coordinated development of both the key and other sectors of the economy. The ten principles make it imperative to "accelerate the development of agriculture," "give prominence to the development of consumer goods industries and further reorientate heavy industry," and "radically change the long-standing tendency of undue emphasis on the development of heavy industry and provision of excessive service to new construction projects by some heavy industries." The shift from fixing the development of heavy industry, particularly of the iron and steel industry, as the key in development strategy to balanced and coordinated development of both the key and other sectors represents another fundamental change of China's development strategy. Its implementation presupposes a balanced and coordinated economic development.

There are key sectors. However, they are variable rather than constant, and they are selected with the view of achieving a balanced and coordinated economic development. These key sectors can be the weak links (or bottlenecks) in the national economy, or the crux of fulfilling certain specified tasks of the national economy. They can also be some infant sectors of vital importance. The development of these key sectors must be combined with that of the others. Their importance must not be overstressed, and they certainly must not be developed at the expense of others. However, this strategy should not be taken as one whereby all sectors develop at the same pace. At the present stage of China's development, agriculture, energy, communications, transport, science, and education are the key sectors.

It is a strategy that focuses on improving the economic results and gradually switches over to intensive development. According to the ten principles, "from now on we must tackle all economic problems with better economic results as the fundamental objective." The shift from emphasizing extensive development to emphasizing intensive development is also a fundamental change of China's economic development strategy. Both extensive and intensive development are needed for economic development, and it is difficult to draw a clear-cut demarcation line between them. Therefore, the shift does not mean to reject extensive development. It is always there as a necessary alternative, only that in the future it will play a secondary role in economic development. The adoption of the development strategy that relies mainly on intensive development is required if the people's needs are to be satisfied. For only this strategy can bring about a much better life to the people on the basis of better economic results, while maintaining a relatively high economic growth rate.

It is an economic development strategy of opening to the outside world based on self-reliance. In accordance with the ten principles we should "persist in an open-door policy and enhance our capacity for self-reliance," "we should abandon once and for all autarky, a characteristic of the natural economy," "we should use resources, first the domestic then the international; we should open up markets, first at home then abroad; and we should equip ourselves with the techniques of regulating the domestic economy and of developing external economic relations and foreign trade."

The shift from autarky and a closed-door policy to the policy of opening to the outside world on the basis of self-reliance is also a fundamental change of China's economic development strategy. Opening to the outside world with emphasis on self-reliance will enhance our capability for self-reliance. This strategy differs from both the outward-oriented strategy of some countries and the inward-oriented strategy with self-sufficiency as its objective. It may well be described as an open-door development strategy based on inward-oriented development.

It is not easy to change an economic development strategy. As we all know, the Soviet Union has been emphasizing the need to accelerate the development of its agriculture and light industry ever since the 1950s and the need to shift from extensive development to intensive development ever since the 1960s, but it has achieved very little so far. Although China has been making big strides in changing its development strategy, there is still a long way to go to accomplish the change. Moreover, twists and turns have been made, mainly due to the following reasons.

First, a special business structure had taken shape as a result of long years of implementing the old strategy. For example, heavy industry assumed a large proportion of the economy, and its structure was established mainly for its own expansion. Hence, in order to execute a new strategy, such a structure must be changed, which is no easy task. Before the change is effected, the economy tends to return to the old track.

Second, people are used to the old economic strategy, so when problems or difficulties crop up in implementing the new, they often want to go back to the old strategy. For instance, in 1981 when the production of heavy industry dropped, owing to structural readjustment, calls soared for giving priority to the development of heavy industry.

THE SOCIALIST ECONOMIC SYSTEM AND ECONOMIC DEVELOPMENT

Development of the socialist economy is closely related to the choice of its system. For many years, the highly centralized economic system of the Soviet Union was regarded as the unique, unalterable one.

This economic system, adopted by all other socialist countries, had the following characteristics: (1) the decision-making power was vested in the central authorities, who decided on the distribution of resources through economic planning; (2) the state regulated and exercised direct control over the major part of national economic activities through mandatory planning, leaving the market mechanism an insignificant role to play; (3) economic management was, for the most part, under the charge of administrative systems at the central or local levels – being subordinate to the state administrative departments, state enterprises were devoid of the power to conduct economic activities independently; and (4) administrative measures were the major instruments to promote economic activities, and economic incentives were seldom used.

The introduction of this highly centralized economic system was required by the traditional economic development strategy mentioned above and provided the guarantee for the implementation of that strategy. For it could concentrate the limited resources on the development of heavy industry, ensure the construction of major projects and bring about a speedy growth of the economy. It was suited to development that was mainly extensive and had the inclination to practice closed-doorism and self-seclusion. The major serious defects of this system are as follows:

> Enterprises were deprived of the power to make independent decisions on matters concerning production and management and were not liable for profits and losses, resulting in poor management and economic results.
>
> The economy was not operated smoothly, giving rise to low efficiency and delinkage of production and demand.
>
> Economic sectors were isolated from one another, and economic relations among enterprises were loose, a result of managing the economy by central departments or regional administrative organizations.
>
> Productivity was kept low by egalitarian distribution of income, because diligent workers received no rewards while lazy ones no punishments.

The defects of this economic system became more conspicuous when the economy grew tremendously with the foundation for industrialization built on the newly adopted economic strategy that stressed intensive development, the open-door policy, and satisfaction of the people's needs. This explains why economic reform has become an urgent task for many socialist countries, and why it is needed to execute the new strategy.

China's economic reform started in the rural areas. The introduction of various forms of the contract responsibility system, with remuneration linked to output – mainly the household responsibility system – has greatly stimulated the enthusiasm of peasants for production and brought about a vigorous development of agricultural production and other economic undertakings in the countryside. Promoted by the rural economic reform, experiments have been made to transform the system of urban industry and commerce. Up to now, the major reforms include the following:

1   The coverage of mandatory plans is being reduced step by step and that of guidance plans enlarged. Meanwhile, the entire production and exchange of certain products are now subjected to market regulations.

2   State enterprises have been granted certain decision-making powers. So long as they fulfil state plans and their contracts with the state for the provision of products, enterprises have the right to raise the production of the products that are needed by the country's construction projects or by the market and are entitled to ask for readjustment of plans. Except for items the state does not allow them to sell, enterprises have the right to sell extra-state-plan products, retained products, products that purchase departments do not want to buy, or overhangs.

3   Operation and management of enterprises are linked with their own economic benefits and have become the determinant in profits retention. Gradually, enterprises will be made liable for profits and losses.

4   Reform in the wage system is going on with an experiment to link workers' wages to performance of their enterprise. A progressive excess tax has been levied on above-norm amount of total payroll and bonuses.

5   The systems of direct control of enterprises or corporations by competent administrative departments or local authorities are undergoing gradual changes so that administrative functions may be separated from management of enterprises, thus enabling enterprises to gain a relatively independent position.

6   In commerce, the wholesale process is being simplified. Means of production are entering the market as commodities.

7   Reforms have also been introduced in various regulation systems such as banking and financial systems, and construction and price control systems. For example, beginning in 1985, all investment funds needed by state enterprises are no longer allocated gratis by the state. Instead, they will get loans from the bank and repay the principal and interest as scheduled.

8   A policy has been adopted for opening to the outside world. Four special economic zones have been established and 14 port cities along the coast have been opened to foreign countries.

As a result of these reforms, the market will have a significant role to play as a regulator of the national economy, and enterprises will find it easier to gear production to the changing demand of the market and of the people, which in turn, will promote technological progress and improve economic results.

PRELIMINARY ACHIEVEMENTS AND EXISTING PROBLEMS OF STRATEGIC SHIFT AND REFORM

Since 1979, China's economy has undergone noticeable changes and scored remarkable successes thanks to the shift in the economic development strategy and the initial reform of the economic system (including the transformation in the form and structure of ownership of means of production). The economy has developed with distinctive features that were not seen in the past. They can be outlined as follows:

For example, we see that the economy, especially its agriculture and light industry sectors, is developing at an accelerated pace. The average annual increase of the total agricultural output value during the Sixth Five-Year Plan period (1981–5) was 8.1 percent, while that of industry 11 percent.[24]

And we also note that various sectors of the national economy are developing in better proportion. Serious disproportion in economic development has been eliminated substantially. As for the relation between industry and agriculture, the share of agriculture rose from 27.8 percent in 1978 to 34.8 percent in 1984, while that of industry dropped from 72.2 percent to 65.2 percent.[25] Of the total output value of industry, the proportion of heavy industry fell from 56.9 percent in 1978 to 52.6 percent in 1984, while that of light industry went up from 43.1 percent to 47.4 percent.[26] Much attention has been paid to the development of relatively weak sectors of the national economy, such as energy, communications, and transport, which have obtained more investment from the state.

Another distinctive feature of the economy is that people's living standards have improved much faster than before, and there is a larger supply of consumer goods. The average net income per capita of peasant households was 134 yuan in 1978 and 310 yuan in 1983. In 1981–4, the annual real increase was 3.7 percent, adjusted for price factors. And by contrast, in 1958–78 the figure was 2.9 percent. The annual increase in the income per capita of urban worker families was 4.9 percent, adjusted for price factors.

Economic results have also registered some improvement. For example, in terms of comparable prices, the share each laborer contributed to the national income increased from 894 yuan in 1980 to 1,119 yuan in 1984, representing an annual increase of 5.8 percent.[27]

With the adoption of the policy of opening to the outside world, China has made rapid progress in establishing economic relations with foreign countries. Its exports and imports have expanded by leaps and bounds.

China's economic reform and changes in economic development strategy are just under way. Since the reform can only be achieved gradually over a fairly long period, there will be the coexistence of the new and old systems, operating side by side. For example, on planning, there will be the coexistence of mandatory planning and market regulation; on pricing, the coexistence of the fixed price set by the state and that determined by the market (even for the same category of products, two or even several kinds of price exist); on product flow, the coexistence of unified allocation and appropriation by the state and sales in the market; on investment, the coexistence of investments covered by the state budget (at present, adopting the form of bank loans) and other loans by the bank; on employment of workers, the coexistence of unified allocation by the state and selection of jobs by workers themselves; on enterprise activities, the coexistence of direct control by the state administrative organs and independent decision-making power of enterprises, etc. Such coexistence of the new and old economic systems has major effects upon the economic environment and the behaviors of different economic actors (namely, government, enterprise and individual). It also affects China's economic development strategy.

First, through economic reforms, the role of the market as a regulator of the economy is enhanced. Therefore, it affects the behaviors of different economic actors. Items of means of production under unified allocation of the state have been reduced from 256 to 29. According to a survey made by China's Institute of Economic Restructuring, both the variety and the quantity of materials under unified supply of state planning decreased in 1984 to 73.6 percent of the total amount of the raw materials used by enterprises. An increasing amount of means of production are obtained through the market. According to some statistics, the iron and steel products obtained through market exchanges accounted for 44.6 percent, coal 52.7 percent, wool products 64.8 percent, and cement 81 percent. According to the above-mentioned survey, in 1984 products covered by unified sales of the state decreased to 57.42 percent of the total sales volume, while those sold by enterprises accounted for 32.81 percent.

The prices of more and more products, or of more and more parts of a product, are now determined by the market. The market begins to come into play even in the allocation of capital funds and the labor force. According to the same survey mentioned above, in working out their production plans, 77 percent of enterprises in 1984 took into consideration the market demand; 90 percent had to purchase raw materials from the market; 97 percent had to sell their products or a portion of their products on the market. However, the production and allocation of certain key products are still determined by mandatory planning (in 1985, those covered by the central mandatory planning accounted for 20 percent of the total industrial output value, excluding those under additional mandatory plans of local authorities). The major parts of some key products are priced by the state. The capital market has not yet developed. Labor forces are still mainly allocated by administrative organs, and commodity flows are restricted by geographical administrative division, etc. All these cannot but weaken the regulatory power of the market over economic activities.

Although in recent years, the decision-making power of enterprises has been enlarged with reduced direct administrative interference of their operation and management, functions of government administrative organs and those of enterprises really have not been separated, with enterprises still subordinated to the administrative organs. For these reasons, enterprises have to comply with administrative commands at a higher level while subjecting themselves to market regulations. And activities of large state enterprises are, to a large extent, subjected to administrative decisions.

Following the expansion of the decision-making power of enterprises, enterprises were allowed to retain a portion of profits in their hands and the interests of the enterprise began to be linked with those of the staff and workers. According to the sampling survey of China's Institute of Economic Restructuring, in 1984 the retained profits of enterprises accounted for about 21.59 percent of the total amount of the profits realized, and the bonuses accounted for 30.7 percent of the total retained profits of enterprises. Many enterprises begin to pay attention to improvement of economic results and increase in profit. Nevertheless, enterprises still rely upon the state financially, exempted from the liability for poor performance or losses. The budget constraint on enterprises remains soft. This soft budget constraint has great effects upon enterprise behavior. Since they are not hard pressed by market competition, enterprises lack sufficient motive force for quality improvement, cost reduction, technological innovation and productivity increase. In addition, they are insensitive to market signals or even make wrong reactions.

In the reform, the power of local governments is expanded. Thanks to financial reforms, local governments can now keep a portion of taxes from and profits of their enterprises as local financial revenue. Thus, local governments have the incentive to develop the local economy. However, this also gives rise to some problems. For example, some regions have re-enforced regional economic blockades, not willing to allow products of other regions to enter into their own market, nor let raw materials of their own regions be processed by enterprises of other regions. They would rather have their raw materials processed by local enterprises, even with poor quality and at high cost. Regions are competing for the development of enterprises which are profitable, especially the processing industries.

After the introduction of the market mechanism and the expansion of the decision-making power of enterprises, administrative organs at different levels started to adopt indirect economic means of regulation in economic management. But direct administrative means are still the mainstay. In particular, when relatively serious difficulties emerge in the economy, indirect economic means would be replaced by direct regulation and control of administrative organs. At present, appropriate approaches are yet to be found by which enterprises may shake off their subordinate relations with administrative organs and conduct independent operations and management. Under such circumstances, means and ways adopted by administrative organs under the old system in enterprise management are still playing an important role.

Changes and problems in economic environment and the behavior of economic actors during the period of coexistence of the new and old systems have had an impact on the development of China's economy in four major areas:

1 Although enterprises and government organs pay much more attention than before to the improvement of economic results, the speed at which the improvement is being made is not fast enough. Many departments, regions and enterprises sometimes still concentrate on the economic growth rate alone, regardless of economic results. In the past few years, the problem of an excessively high growth rate has cropped up time and again in China. In particular, from the first half of 1984 to the same period of 1985, the growth rate reached an inconceivable degree, with the total output value of industry and agriculture from January to September 1985 registering an increase of 21.1 percent over the corresponding period in 1984.

In order to reach high growth rates various regions and departments often throw themselves on building new enterprises, and enterprises often expand their scales, neglecting technological transformation and labor productivity increase. In recent years, increases in investments were several times out of control, resulting in decreased investment results.

2 Economic relations are more harmonious because agriculture, light industry and energy have developed rapidly through several years of reform. However, starting from the fall of 1984, when economic growth was accelerated at an excessively high speed and investments increased enormously, a raw material shortage again came up, the energy shortage was aggravated, and the situation in transportation was even worse.

3 In recent years improvement of people's livelihood has enjoyed attention. People have seen their income rise rather fast. Under the

impact of the market, both government organs and enterprises have begun to attach importance to changes in people's demand. However, because the problem of soft budget constraint is still there, the problem of excessive increase in wages and bonuses has arisen. The total amount of wages in 1984 registered an increase of 21.3 percent over 1983, leading to sharp price hike. In the meantime shortages still exist, as the role of the market is not strong enough. Enterprises have not paid enough attention to the improvement of the quality of and the increase in the varieties of consumer goods. They have little interest to produce consumer goods of meager profits.

4   The implementation of the opening-to-the-outside-world policy has given a strong impetus to the expansion of China's international relations. However, since its domestic economic restructuring is just at the initial stage and the market is yet to be developed, China's economy is not adapted to changes and competitions in the world market, and the country has run into some difficulties in opening to the outside world. Therefore, protection of the domestic economy cannot but be enhanced and strict control of foreign trade practiced.

These situations demonstrate that when the old economic system is still playing its role and the establishment of the new one is not completed, China has encountered some difficulties in pursuing the new development strategy. In recent years, the old economic development strategy still has its effect on China's economic development. The new economic development strategy, although already brought into place, will be realized only when the new economic system becomes dominant.

The development of China's economy in recent years shows that it is essential to transform the form and structure of the ownership of means of production. And changes in the old development strategy as well as in the traditional economic system of the socialist economy are needed. In fact, these reforms have played an important role in boosting the economy. As far as socialist developing countries are concerned, the establishment of appropriate forms and structures of means of production, the choice of proper economic development strategy, and the building up of suitable economic system are indivisible. At present, even those socialist countries with developed economies have to solve these three related problems with appropriate measures. Different in economic development and the magnitude of the three problems, both socialist developed countries and developing countries (such as China) have something in common. The experience of China and other socialist countries has enabled us to acquire some new knowledge about the socialist economic development theories. Many of the orthodox theories are now under examination. Some have been discarded, with new theories advanced.

NOTES

[1] See *Almanac of China's Statistics* (Chin. ed.), 1984: Beijing: China's Statistics Publishing House, p. 26.

[2] Ibid.

[3] Ibid., p. 454.

[4] J. V. Stalin, 1954: "Industrialization of the Country and the Right Deviation in the C.P.S.U.(B.)." *Works* (Eng. ed.), Moscow: Foreign Languages Publishing House, vol. 11, p. 259.

[5] J. V. Stalin, 1955: "The Tasks of Business Executives," *Works* (Eng. ed.), Moscow: FLPH, vol. 13, p. 40.

[6] J. V. Stalin, 1954: "The Economic Situation of the Soviet Union and the Policy of the Party." *Works* (Eng. ed.), Moscow: FLPH, vol. 8, p. 128.

[7] J. V. Stalin, 1946: *Speech Delivered at an Election Meeting in the Stalin Election District, Moscow* (Eng. ed.), Moscow: FLPH, p. 16.

[8] Based on data obtained from *Almanac of China's Statistics* (Chin. ed.), 1984: China's Statistics Publishing House, pp. 128, 214 and 297.

[9] J. V. Stalin, 1972: *Economic Problems of Socialism in the USSR* (Eng. ed.), Beijing, Foreign Languages Press, p. 82.

[10] Ganetsky, 1927: "Decade of Soviet Construction," Moscow, p. 111.

[11] J. V. Stalin, 1954: "The Economic Situation of the Soviet Union and the Policy of the Party." *Works* (Eng. ed.), Moscow: FLPH, vol. 8, p. 130.

[12] J. V. Stalin, 1972: *The Economic Problems of Socialism in the USSR* (Eng. ed.), Beijing: Foreign Languages Press, p. 31.

[13] See *Almanac of China's Statistics* (Chin. ed.) 1984: China's Statistics Publishing House, p. 24.

[14] Ibid.

[15] Ibid., p. 81.

[16] Ibid., p. 484.

[17] Ibid., p. 156.

[18] Ibid., p. 95.

[19] Ibid., p. 27.

[20] Li Xiannian, 1959: "Ten Years of Great Financial Achievement of the People's Republic of China." *Selections for the Celebration of the Tenth Anniversary of the People's Republic of China* (Chin. ed.). Beijing, People's Publishing House, p. 362.

[21] J. V. Stalin, 1955: The Right Deviation in the C.P.S.U.(B). *Works* (Eng. ed.), Moscow: FLPH, vol. 12, p. 53.

[22] Mao Zedong, 1977: "On the Ten Major Relations." *Selected Works of Mao Zedong* (Eng. ed.). Beijing: Foreign Languages Press, vol. 5, p. 274.

[23] Sh. Y. Turetskii told me this in 1957.

[24] *People's Daily*, April 4, 1986.

[25] *Almanac of China's Statistics* (Chin. ed.), 1985: China's Statistics Publishing House, p. 18.

[26] Ibid.

[27] *Guangming Daily*, Sept. 14, 1985.

Comments on
"Development Theory and Problems of Socialist Developing Economies"

NICHOLAS R. LARDY

Dong Fureng's paper provides a cogent critique of the Stalinist model of socialist economic development as it was applied in China for almost three decades. He correctly criticizes the model's imbalanced growth strategy with its priority for heavy industrial development and its devastating effects on the growth of farm output, productivity, and income. Second, and closely related, Dong highlights the long-term adverse effect of this strategy on the growth of consumption. That is best captured by pointing out that China's per capita national income, measured in constant prices, almost tripled between 1952 and 1978, while per capita output of the farm sector grew only three-tenths of one percent annually.[1] Third, and in some ways most revealing, total factor productivity growth, in both industry and in agriculture, was significantly negative up through the end of the Maoist period in the late 1970s.[2] In Dong Fureng's view the Stalinist development strategy hindered the improvement of the economic results. Finally, Dong Criticizes the strategy of self-reliance and import substitution that underlays the traditional socialist development model.

Dong is too modest to note the attempt that several Chinese economists made, decades ago, to modify substantially the Soviet model of economic development as it was applied to China. In the mid-1950s, they argued for a radical change in the state's pricing of industrial goods, to reflect the cost of capital used in their production – a revolutionary suggestion in an era when the Soviet Union had not yet accepted the concept of the scarcity of capital goods. Had these proposals been adopted, it might have made the real resource cost of industrialization based primarily on heavy industry more apparent.

Dong and other Chinese economists later argued more explicitly in formal models that the imbalanced growth path of the First Plan (1953–57), with its reliance on extracting resources from the agricultural sector to finance capital intensive development in industry, was inappropriate to an economic setting where the initial levels of per capita farm output were relatively low and in which shortages of consumer goods could serve as the major constraint to sustained rapid development.[3]

These early efforts by China's economists to shift China's development strategy were ignored by China's leadership and the ensuing Great

Leap Forward led to a man-made catastrophe perhaps unprecedented in Chinese history – the death through famine and famine-related diseases of almost 30 million Chinese.[4] In response to that crisis, and perhaps the criticism of imbalanced growth made by Dong and others, there was a partial modification of China's development strategy in the first half of the 1960s. But the Cultural Revolution, with its emphasis on ideological purity, quickly ended that modest attempt to substitute economic for political criteria for resource allocation decisions.

Thus in Dong Fureng's assessment, the fundamental turning point in China's development strategy did not come until 1978. The main components of that shift are well known, since they grow directly out of the critique of the Soviet model. First, balanced growth – with parallel development of agriculture and industry, and of light industry and heavy industry – was to replace the imbalanced strategy of the Maoist era. Second, and closely related, the main objective of growth was no longer simply high-speed development, but improvements in levels of personal income and consumption. Third, the goal was to shift toward what is commonly called a strategy of intensive development, that is, one in which growth is generated, at least in part, through improvements in productivity rather than primarily or even exclusively through the mobilization of more inputs. Finally, the open-door policy was to replace the autarkic policies of the past.

Although Dong describes China's current development strategy as profoundly different from that of the Maoist era and describes the results of China's economic reforms in generally positive terms, I would like to suggest that the elements of continuity of policy are substantial, and that in some respects, the economic results achieved to date may indicate that the reforms, at least in industry and perhaps in foreign trade, are quite superficial.

What are the elements of continuity that make the shift of strategy more modest than Dong has suggested? At least two come immediately to mind. First, the rate of investment in China remains extraordinarily high, given China's modest level of per capita national income. Despite proposals to reduce the rate of accumulation (the ratio of gross investment to net material product) to about 25 percent, the rate in the years 1983 and 1984 averaged over 30 percent, fully equal to the high rate maintained under the extensive growth, resource mobilization strategy of the past.

Second, state investment resources continue to be allocated overwhelmingly to industry and, within industry, the state allocates to the producer goods sector a share of investment that is fully as high as in the periods of imbalanced growth of the past. Nowhere is this more dramatically evident than in the allocation of funds for investment in agriculture. Although the Central Committee of the Chinese Communist Party in 1978 pledged to increase the share of investment allocated to agriculture, the reverse has occurred. The share of state investment flowing to agriculture fell continuously from 1979 to 1984 to reach 5 percent, the lowest share ever recorded in the communist era and far less than in any other socialist country.[5]

While Dong's paper implies that private household investment in soil improvement, transport, machinery, and so forth is now providing the basis for sustained growth of agriculture, that hypothesis is not borne out by empirical evidence. Farm households in recent years have been three times more likely to invest in expanding or improving their privately owned housing than to invest in farming. Similarly they are more likely to invest in financial assets than in farming. And, of course, a large share of incremental farm income is being allocated to finance increased consumption expenditures.[6] In absolute terms, per capita private investment in farming in 1983 was less than it was prior to the time collectives were formed in the winter of 1955–56, an astounding development if one considers how high real per capita farm income was in 1983 compared with almost three decades earlier.[7] In short, even the liberalized long-term land leases now in effect in most of the countryside and the promise of compensation for leasehold improvements in the event a lease is transferred prior to its expiration, do not appear to have encouraged sufficiently large amounts of private investment on what is still publicly owned land.

In summary, state investment in agriculture has fallen, collective investment in farming has shrunk by more than half as decollectivization accelerated, and private investment in agriculture to date has been surprisingly modest. As a result, the farm investment from all sources relative to value added in agriculture in 1983 was only about 7 percent.[8] Similarly there has been surprisingly modest investment in improving the rural infrastructure. Between 1979 and 1983 the highway network, for example, grew by a total of about 4 percent, and the rural road network still completely bypasses one-third of all Chinese villages. Rural electrification, too, has made little progress, and as many as one-half of all rural households have no electricity. Unless the state increases its allocation of resources for agricultural investment, including that for rural infrastructure, and peasant confidence in the long term viability of the current land arrangements increases, it is difficult to see how the underlying rate of growth of agriculture will be more than about two or two and one-half percent – roughly the pace of the pre-reform, imbalanced growth period.

What of the results of the new strategy that Dong outlines? The central point to be noted is the vastly differing results in agriculture, where reforms have been quite profound, and in industry and foreign trade, where reforms have to date been less far-reaching. In agriculture the rate of growth of output was 7.0 percent annually in real terms between 1978 and 1984, fully three times the long-term historic rate achieved between 1952 and 1978. More strikingly, the slow decline in total factor productivity evident between 1957 and 1978 was reversed, and productivity growth accounted for about one-half of the growth of farm output between 1978 and 1984.[9]

Measurement of changes in industrial productivity in a period as short as five years is hazardous, particularly when there is simultaneous restructuring of the composition of output. One would prefer to examine disaggregated productivity trends in branches of industry, rather than aggregate trends that may conceal more than they reveal. But such disaggregated studies are not yet available. Total factor productivity in state-owned industry, which accounted for about 80 percent of industrial output volume in 1978, appears to have declined at an accelerating pace since 1978.[10]

Several features of China's industrial sector are at least consistent with a trend of declining factor productivity. First, the price structure and the price-setting mechanism in industry are largely unreformed. Prices of many products are unrelated to production costs and thus cannot provide the basis for rational decentralized decision-making. Price reform has been on the agenda on and off since 1955, but the results to date have been extremely modest.[11]

Second, industry is characterized by lack of competition. Almost ten years after reform discussion began, there is still no bankruptcy law. And as recently as three years ago, more than a fourth of all state enterprises operated at a loss, even though they paid nothing for their fixed capital. Losses are subsidized by the state treasury, undermining incentives to reduce costs or operate more efficiently. The lack of competition is also reflected in a high degree of protectionism of local markets within China. There is a surprisingly small degree of local specialization in industrial production with many small-scale producers, all operating at far less than optimum scale, serving local markets. Although the domestic market is in principle large enough to support a substantial degree of specialization, this advantage has not been exploited.

Third, the bulk of fixed investment continues to be financed by interest-free budgetary grants that are not repaid. In short, to the manufacturing firm, capital remains largely a free good – in contrast with agriculture, where capital investment input is financed by interest-bearing bank loans that must be repaid. Moreover, enterprises actually have an incentive to maximize the assets under their control, since the current regulations allow them to retain a large share of the depreciation funds that are charged off as a cost. Under those conditions, it should not be surprising that we observe excess demand for machinery and equipment, the adoption of inappropriately capital-intensive production processes, and stagnant or declining total factor productivity.

Results of reform of China's foreign trade system have also been disappointing. The value of the domestic currency has been substantially devalued since 1981 to provide increased incentive for exports.

Steps were also taken to diminish the role of the foreign trade corporations and allow Chinese firms to buy and sell directly on the international market. These and other steps have not been entirely successful. In 1982–5, imports more than doubled while exports rose less than a quarter. In 1985, the trade deficit reached 14.9 billion U.S. dollars, an astounding 54 percent of export earnings. The short-term response has been to reinstate severe controls on imports, to rescind the authority of enterprises to buy and sell directly on the international market, and to re-emphasize import substitution.[12]

In summary, it would be premature to suggest that China's experience since 1978 provides a comprehensive alternative model of socialist economic development. While the reforms have led to dramatic changes in agriculture, many conflicting factors have slowed progress elsewhere, particularly in manufacturing. The result, as Dong's paper makes clear, is the uneasy coexistence of reform and unreformed features within the industrial system. That in turn appears to account for the lackluster productivity performance in manufacturing.

NOTES

[1] Nicholas R. Lardy, 1983: *Agriculture in China's Modern Economic Development*. Cambridge: Cambridge University Press, pp. 2–3.

[2] The most comprehensive studies of total factor productivity in Chinese agriculture are those of Anthony Tang – 1980a: "Food and Agriculture in China: Trends and Projections 1952–77 and 2000," in Anthony Tang and Bruce Stone, *Food Production in the People's Republic of China*, Washington, DC: International Food Policy Research Institute; and 1980b: "Trend, Policy Cycle, and Weather Disturbance in Chinese Agriculture, 1952–78," *American Journal of Agricultural Economics*, May, pp. 339–48. Tang estimates a 15 percent decline in total factor productivity in agriculture between 1952 and 1978. The World Bank estimates industrial productivity declined at an average annual rate of 0.4 percent between 1957 and 1978. *China: Long Term Issues and Options*, Washington, DC: International Bank for Reconstruction and Development, 1985, p. 111.

[3] See the discussion of Dong's analysis in Cyril Chihren Lin, 1985: "The Reinstatement of Economics in China Today," *The China Quarterly*, no. 85 (March), pp. 1–48.

[4] Ansley Coale, 1984: *Rapid Population Change in China 1952–82*, Washington, DC: National Academy of Sciences Press, pp. 66–70.

[5] The share of state investment resources allocated to agriculture was 7.1 percent in 1953–7 (First Five-Year Plan), 9.8 percent in 1971–5, 10.6 percent in 1978 and 11.1 percent in 1979. Since then the share has fallen from 9.3 percent in 1980 to 5.0 percent in 1984, the most recent year for which data are available. State Statistical Bureau, 1985: *Chinese Statistical Yearbook, 1984* (in Chinese), Peking: Statistical Publishing House, pp. 306–7 and Nicholas R. Lardy, 1986: "Dilemmas in the Pattern of Resource Allocation," unpublished manuscript.

[6] In 1983, investment in private housing in the countryside was 23.9 billion yuan, personal savings deposits in rural credit cooperatives rose by 9.2 billion yuan, and rural personal consumption expenditure (excluding housing) increased about 18 billion yuan. By comparison private household investment in farming, including purchase and the construction of fixed assets, in 1983 (the only year for which I have located these data) was only 6.79 billion yuan.

[7] Private farming investment in the First Plan was 17 billion yuan, about three and a half billion yuan annually. Shigeru Ishikawa, 1965: *National Income and Capital Formation in Communist China: An Examination of Official Statistics*, Tokyo: Institute of Asian Economic Affairs, p. 175.

[8] For 1983, total investment in agriculture (excluding rural small-scale industry) is estimated as the sum of state investment (3.545 billion yuan), collective investment (4.390 billion yuan), and private investment (6.790 billion yuan) – or a total of 14.725 billion yuan. Value added in agriculture was 210 billion yuan, but about 10 billion yuan was industrial output of brigade and team enterprises. Farming investment of 14.725 billion yuan is 7 percent of estimated net farm output value.

[9] D. Gale Johnson, 1985: "The Agriculture of the USSR and China: A Contrast in Reform," unpublished manuscript, Sept.

[10] The World Bank estimates that total factor productivity in state-owned industry declined at an average annual rate of 1.9 to 2.0 percent between 1978 and 1982. World Bank, *China: Long Term Issues and Options*, p. 111.

[11] Nicholas R. Lardy, 1986: "Dilemmas in the Pattern of Resource Allocation," unpublished manuscript, April.

[12] Zhao Ziyang, China's ranking Vice-Premier, in his report in March 1986 on China's Seventh Five-Year Plan stated that "China should make every effort to produce at home whatever we can… to expand production of import substitutes and increase the proportion of goods produced at home." From 1986: "Report on the Seventh Five-Year Plan," *Beijing Review*, no. 16, p. 10.

9

Mobilization of the Rural Economy and the Asian Experience

K. N. RAJ

The problems posed by extensive rural poverty in low-income countries have been among the central concerns of development economics from the outset. Ideas on what might be done about it have, however, differed very widely, reflecting differences in political and social philosophies and in the understanding of development processes. Views on the subject also have changed in the light of experience over a period of time. Nowhere, perhaps, have the consequent divergences and shifts in approach to the mobilization of the rural economy found clearer expression than in Asia. Therefore, it is not unreasonable to ask what inferences can be drawn from the wide variety of Asian experience in this critical sector.

To answer this question we shall revert to three models of rural mobilization that have been projected in the earlier theoretical literature on the subject: one based on the mobilization of idle labor in peasant households for capital formation in the rural economy (Nurkse, 1951); another focused mainly on resource transfer from agriculture to industry through the market mechanism (Lewis, 1954; Fei and Ranis, 1964);. and a third highlighting the potential for rapid growth in agriculture opened up by technological advances and the consequent possibility of agriculture itself assuming the role of the leading sector (Schultz, 1963; Mellor, 1976). The scope of limitations of each of these can be examined more closely in the light of the experience in Asian countries that have adopted strategies closely conforming to them.

DIRECT MOBILIZATION OF IDLE LABOR

The idea that idle labor in peasant households represented a latent resource and a potential saving that could be directly deployed for capital formation was among the earliest to be put forward. However, if such labor was to be remunerated at the ruling wage rate (as would be normally required in market economies) and the potential saving still realized, some way had to be found for securing such saving from within these households. The suggestion that this could be done through direct taxation of land (as in Japan, earlier) did not receive wide acceptance, particularly in countries like India, where such taxation had come to be associated with earlier colonial regimes and therefore considered as something to be got rid of. (Even methods of direct taxation of land based on the principle of progression, and therefore confined to the upper strata of farm households, have proved to be unacceptable in India on account of political resistance from these strata). An alternative, however, was to evolve an organizational framework in the rural economy which made it possible to deploy idle labor for capital formation (or other purposes) without additional remuneration. This is precisely what China was able to do through the system based on work teams and brigades within communes.

The information available on mobilization of labor in peasant households and the uses to which it was put within communes is still very limited. Enough is known, however, to warrant the following tentative observations (Ishikawa, 1982):

(a) Even when infra-structural projects were undertaken by the State, their labour-intensive components were separated into several parts, each of which was assigned to a local people's commune to undertake by using its own labour force. The remuneration for this labour came mainly from local production teams by counting work at these construction sites as part of the working days in the teams before determining the relative share of each member in the proceeds from harvest each year. This method of allocation of work and of reward was enforced more thoroughly in the case of commune and brigade projects, since the benefits accrued demonstratively to the members themselves.

(b) While the proportion of total man-days of commune members spent on capital construction projects appears to have risen to unacceptable levels in certain periods (such as during the Great Leap Forward and the Cultural Revolution), views expressed on this issue by Chinese economists indicate that the use of labour for infrastructural investment to the extent of 20 to 30 per cent of the total working days was considered appropriate in the middle of the 1960s (i.e. in the intervening period). A more recent suggestion, from a critic of excessive use of labour for capital construction, points to 30 per cent of labour time as an appropriate national average in the slack agricultural season (i.e. in the winter–spring period) and about 5 per cent of the rural labour force employed in permanent construction groups.

(c) In addition to the labour employed in capital construction projects, about 10 per cent of the rural labour force has been employed in commune and brigade enterprise whose role has been essentially "to enable the economy to proceed with industrialization without being subject to the constraint of an inflexible surplus of foodgrain."

(d) The system also made possible substantial increases in (i) the intensity of labour input in crop cultivation, such as through more working days put in per crop per hectare of paddy land (following particularly the introduction of high yielding varieties and associated changes in technology and farming practices) and greater cropping intensity; as well as (ii) crop yields (as in the case of paddy in which the national average was raised from about $2\frac{3}{4}$ tons per hectare towards the middle of the 1950s to around 4 tons recently, and in some regions to nearly $6\frac{1}{2}$ tons).

What was it then that made the system unviable and led to its substantial dismantling in recent years? Since all the relevant facts are not known one has to depend largely on informed guesses. A major reason was, no doubt, the element of coercion of labor that was always implicit in the system and came to the surface from time to time in varying and sometimes intolerable degrees. Though the organization rules within production teams embodied, perhaps, some of the customary practices associated earlier with decision-making in clans in Chinese village communities (and were in that sense not altogether alien to them), the choices open even to production teams were limited by the extent to which decisions concerning their product-mix and the allocation of labor for work other than for their own subsistence production and investment were in fact not within their control (Ishikawa, 1975 and 1982). Moreover, while appeal to broader social interests could be in principle a major mobilizing force, and was possibly so in China to a considerable extent (particularly in the initial stages when the inequities of the earlier system were still vivid in the minds of the rural community), it was easy for coercion and command to gain dominance at the operational level within a political framework which did not offer adequate opportunity for correction of such tendencies. These alone would have furnished ample grounds for replacing such a system with one that offered greater scope for effective choice to members of the community.

In addition, there evidently were also economic reasons pushing in the same direction. While extensive investment in rural infrastructures and the use of modern inputs such as fertilizers, pesticides, pump-sets, power-tillers and tractors, taken together, made possible more intensive input of labor, it also increased the cost of the material inputs required per hectare of cropped land. "Under such conditions, unless the speed of the increase in per hectare output is greater than that of the increase in cost of inputs per hectare, the profit margin per ton of product will decrease, given the fixed levels of product prices as well as wages (per unit labor remuneration) and it will even become negative. The oft reported fact that in the 1970s the increase in food grain production did not bring about an increase in the income of production teams and their members, and even resulted in their poverty, was related to this situation (Ishikawa, 1982). A stage was, therefore, possibly reached where what mattered most were incentives for productive input of labor and efficient use of other inputs. Peasant farming in separate plots leased out for the purpose from collectively owned land could become then a rational solution from even the broader social point of view, particularly when most of the basic investments required for mobilization of the rural economy had been completed and the rest could be left to be undertaken through the more normal processes of saving and investment.

It needs to be noted that moblizing idle labor had also helped to redress serious regional imbalances within agriculture that had important implications for ensuring grain supplies required for different parts of the country. While nearly two-fifths of China's population lived in the northern regions, and the best half of the cultivated land (in terms of soil quality and terrain) was also located there, most of the available irrigation (as also areas endowed with heavy rainfall and surface flow of water) was earlier in the southern regions (Weins, 1978). Over four-fifths of the increase in grain output during the First Five-Year Plan had, therefore, taken place in the latter, based largely on the restoration and fuller utilization of the traditional infrastructure. Thereafter, extension of water resources to the poorly irrigated regions of the north was adopted as the linchpin of the agricultural strategy, despite the extensive investments it required for effective management of the relatively meager supplies of water in these regions. This had the effect of nearly doubling the annual grain output there in the course of the following two decades, while the increase was only a little over one-half in the southern regions in the same period (Raj, 1983). Such a major shift in the regional distribution of the infrastructure for water management, and thereby in the available grain supply, is not likely to have been feasible but for the scale on which labor could be mobilized for this purpose.

Viewed in this light, the move in China in recent years towards a form of peasant farming in agriculture and a less constrained rural labor market could be interpreted in economic terms as a response to the more favorable conditions created by the earlier strategy, rather than as merely a consequence of its failure. At any rate, this is a hypothesis that needs to be examined more closely before any verdict is passed on the "command approach" associated with the Chinese experiment in direct mobilization of rural labor, particularly since elements of coercion have not been altogether avoided – even in some of the variants of the traditional "market appproach" that have at times received relatively uncritical support.

MOBILIZATION THROUGH MARKET PROCESSES

The idea that unlimited supply of labor from peasant households could help to raise saving and capital formation through market processes, however, initially was not linked at all with mobilization of the rural economy in any clearly articulated form. The availability of such labor was cited only to explain how the relative share of wages and profits in the capitalist sector (whether in agriculture or industry, in the rural economy or in the urban) might be affected by the productivity of labor in the subsistence sector, and how that, in turn, could affect the rate of saving and investment in the economy as a whole. It was pointed out in this context how, precisely for this reason, capitalists (such as plantation owners in Africa) would have a direct interest in holding down the productivity of subsistence workers and might use their political power to suppress technological progress in peasant agriculture (Lewis, 1954).

Any model for resource transfer from agriculture based on this idea could, therefore emerge only when linked to some method for achieving such transfer without holding down the productivity of workers or suppressing technological change in the subsistence sector. An important link suggested by earlier Japanese experience was direct taxation of land, which was believed to have made possible transfer of not only labor but the saving from agriculture. It has, therefore, figured very largely in the literature on the subject (Fei and Ranis, 1963; Johnston, 1966).

How far the land tax in Japan had actually helped in transfering a net surplus in real terms from agriculture for investment in other sectors, and how far it only made farm households more dependent on employment in non-farm enterprises to be able to pay the tax out of the factor incomes so received, is still not very clear. When the revenue from the tax is counted in as a form of forced saving, there appears to have been a large surplus of saving secured from agriculture in financial terms, but it was not matched by a surplus of comparable magnitude in its commodity trade with the rest of the economy. Evidently there were substantial reverse flows to agriculture in the form of factor payments and other transfers on current account. Moreover, a substantial part of the land tax financed current government expenditure, not capital expenditure (Teranishi, 1976; Mody, Mundle and Raj, 1985).

In fact, agriculture in Japan seems to have developed a moderate surplus in commodity trade only in the first two decades of the twentieth century. By then the revenue from land tax was only about 5 percent of the value of gross agricultural produce (following increases in output ւnd a substantial rise in prices), and its real burden had diminished ւurther because of improvement in the terms of trade for agriculture Hirashima, 1980).

The ability of agriculture to demonstrate larger surpluses in its commodity trade with other sectors appears to have depended on a different set of factors, particularly on increase in the productivity of labor within the sector. Such increase in productivity became significant in ʃapan from around the turn of the century, when increases in the labor ɔrce began to get absorbed wholly outside agriculture, and output within the sector continued to grow faster than population. With the ɔaddy supplying the bulk of this output, it was then possible to raise ɔerceptibly the proportion marketed (from about 47 percent of the total n the period 1888–92 to nearly 62 percent by 1909–12). At the same ime, there was no corresponding increase in its imports (expressed as a ɔroportion of output). This was partly because most of the inputs used ɪt that time were of a traditional nature that could be supplied from within. But by then, there also appears to have been a higher rate of ʋoluntary saving, due to increases in income accruing to landowners ʃrom growth in productivity of land, high rents, and decline in the real ɔurden of land tax. A sizeable fraction of saving evidently was invested ɪn small industrial and commercial enterprises within rural areas, which ɑlso absorbed a large part of the growth in the labor force.

This means that, while the land tax was a useful instrument for transfer of purchasing power to the government, the real resources corresponding to it could come only from the entire rural economy, involving both agriculture and industry – initially through heavy reliance on various transfers *into* agriculture, and later through increases in the productivity of labor *within* the sector itself. Since the burden of the land tax got reduced, it could give way to other means of resource transfer, such as through outflow of private savings, although it is not clear whether there was still a large net outflow from agriculture. (The process of mobilization of the rural economy in Japan interpreted in this broader sense, however, requires to be studied more closely with reference to the links between agriculture and rural industry through input-output relations, transfers of factor income, and flows of expenditure and saving in different periods).

A much more striking case of mobilization of resources from agriculture relying primarily on the market mechanism is provided really by Taiwan, where taxation played a relatively minor role, and much higher proportions of agricultural output were still secured as surpluses through the intermediation of landlords and indirectly through terms of trade before World War II (Lee, 1971). This was achieved, of course, within a colonial framework at a time when coercion through use of even the police force was not unknown in the rural economy, and up to one-third of the total rice output could be appropriated as rent by landlords. Moreover, a large part of the surpluses so secured was siphoned away to Japan for its industrialization, and relatively little fo the development of industry in Taiwan. Nevertheless, what is significan analytically is that mobilization of resources from agriculture, ever under these conditions, was perhaps feasible only because output wa: growing at a much faster rate than population, and the productivity o labor was, therefore, rising at a rate that permitted a moderate increase in per capita consumption within the agricultural sector, despite the high rents payable to landlords and the adverse terms of trade.

The rate of growth of agricultural output in Taiwan was, in fact, sc much higher than the rate of growth of population, that productivity pe worker in agriculture more than doubled itself between 1913 and 1937 and was already, in real terms, more than three-quarters as high as ir Japan (where such doubling had taken nearly four decades to achieve due to a lower rate of growth of output). This made the mobilization ol the rural economy much simpler after World War II, when land reform left producers with higher disposable incomes and the availability of higher-yielding varieties of rice made it possible to raise them further. Moreover, despite more rapid population growth, increase in non-agricultural employment opportunities opened up by growth of the domestic market and exports of labor-intensive manufactures enabled transfer of labor from agriculture (thereby raising productivity of laboi still faster within this sector).

Rates of agricultural growth high enough to realize increase in labor productivity were, however, crucially dependent on basic infrastructure investment earlier, particularly in irrigation (Kikuchi and Hayami, 1985). In Japan a substantial part of it had been completed in elementary form during the Tokugawa period, largely through mobilization of local labor in feudal clans, and almost all the area under rice was already irrigated by 1880; the additional investments required thereafter, such as for conversion of wet to dry land, were therefore relatively small. Indeed public investment in irrigation (including even some riparian public works) was negligible in Japan after the Meiji Restoration, although the rate of private investment (part of which was subsidized by government) was around 10 percent of the income from the agricultural sector. In Taiwan, the proportion of land under irrigation was lower at the turn of the century and more investment was needed to cover the entire area; but even here public investment was evidently quite small, and even the total annual investment in agriculture was no more than about 5 percent of the aggregate investment in the economy, except in the 1920s, when it was about 15 percent (Lee, 1971). The relatively modest infrastructural investments required in agriculture for promoting "internal land augmentation" in Japan and Taiwan contributed very materially to the rapid mobilization of the rural economy and to the resource transfer from agriculture thereby made possible.

Such requirements for infrastructural investment in agriculture differ very widely, however, depending on the nature of the terrain and soil, quantum and distribution of rainfall, nature and spread of the available river systems, temperature conditions, etc. Thus, it has been observed that the requirements of supplemental irrigation to sustain crop growth are smaller in much of East Asia than in India, even during the relatively dry periods, due to more even seasonal distribution of rainfall and lower temperatures; and that, with more even seasonal distribution of river flows, it becomes possible also to supplement the supply of water from natural rainfall through relatively simple diversion-type works, small ponds, and lift irrigation instead of having to rely on massive storage-based systems as in South Asia (Vaidyanathan and Jose, 1978). Attention had been drawn still earlier to the special requirements of rice cultivation in areas susceptible to flood conditions, as in the principal alluvial plains close the major rivers (Ishikawa, 1967). The magnitude of the basic infrastructural investment needed for accelerating agricultural growth are, therefore, likely to be very much higher in most countries of South Asia than would appear from the experience of Japan, Taiwan, and even South Korea. This could require substantial resource transfers into the agricultural sector for a while, unless some methods of mobilization of rural labor are devised for this purpose, as in China.

DIFFERENCES IN THE FUNCTIONING OF FACTOR MARKETS

It is essential also to take note of some important differences observable in the functioning of factor markets in South Asia which have tended to make the intensity of labor input in agriculture very much less than in East Asia and raise serious questions about the adequacy and reliability of market processes for the allocation of scarce resources in agriculture. The factors that have influenced the operation of the land-lease market are of particular significance in this context.

In Japan, Taiwan, and most parts of mainland China, the land-lease markets seem to have functioned for a long time in a manner that inequalities in the size distribution of operational holdings were relatively small and few rural households, dependent on agriculture for their livelihood, were left totally landless. Under these conditions, it was in the interest of tenants to raise the productivity of land through more intensive input of labor, even if it helped landlords to increase rent; it was also in the interest of landlords to help them do so through advances of working capital on a selective basis and, where they were far-sighted, through various other initiatives for improving the infra-structure and related farm practices. In South Asia, however, high proportions of rural households have received no land at all or only very small parcels of it through the leasing process and have been, therefore, wholly or largely dependent on wage labor. Most of the land leased out by owners even appears to have gone to relatively privileged categories of households (with often some land of their own), which could thereby operate larger holdings employing such labor. (Although leasing of land to tenants with small holdings has been more widespread in the traditional rice-growing regions of India, combined also with systems of crop-sharing, relatively large holdings dependent primarily on wage labor have persisted in even such regions on an extensive scale). Neither the landlord-tenant nor the employer-employee relationships in such situations have been favorable to intensive use of labor on the available land.

Why the land-lease market has functioned so differently in South Asia from East Asia is not clear. It is perhaps explained in part by the more extensive use of livestock for agricultural operations in South Asia and the decreasing cost in larger operational holdings arising from the indivisibilities on this account. The more extensive use of livestock in India, compared to China, has itself been attributed to differences in soil, climate, terrain, and river systems that made substitution of animal with human power much more difficult, and at the same time possibly encouraged extension of cultivated area in preference to intensive cultivation at an earlier stage of history (Vaidyanathan and Jose, 1978; Booth and Sundrum, 1984). However, while this hypothesis in terms of geophysical conditions offers useful insights into the factors that could have determined the input structure in countries of South Asia over a period of time, it offers no explanation for operational holdings of much larger size than those which can be accounted for by such indivisibility.

An important part of the explanation lies perhaps in sociological factors, particularly the privileges and discriminations associated with the caste system and with hierarchies in rural society created by various systems of collection of land revenue in the past. That such conditioning by earlier social history could materially affect land relations is evident from the pattern as it had evolved in England, where landlords leased out land mainly to "gentleman farmers" who were wholly dependent on wage labor, unlike in Japan where landlords had evidently a strong preference for less well-to-do tenants relying wholly on family labor.

At the same time, we know that tenants relying mainly on family labor came to be preferred in Japan to various forms of labor attached to landowning families, only when shortage of labor began to increase wage rates in the eighteenth century (Smith, 1959). This could not happen in India where "menial castes," estimated at between one-fifth and one-fourth of the rural population from even medieval times, offered a large reserve army of wage labor that could be tied to land in numerous ways (Habib, 1982). The labor requirements of the output-mix could have been also an important consideration, since rice cultivation involving intensive input of labor was dominant in Japan – unlike sheep farming, which required more land than labor and offered much higher returns than crop cultivation in England at an earlier stage.

All this suggests that, while agrarian relations in South Asia could have been shaped by economic factors as much as by social and political factors in the past, the present size distribution of operational holding is likely to reflect also the preferences and biases of landowners within the social structures that evolved over a period of time; therefore, any economic explanations offered for it would have to be based on assumptions of behavior on their part appropriate to such social structures. One such hypothesis, explaining why the ownership distribution of assets may not get transformed through the market but "remain connected with the final distribution in operational use," runs in terms of the preference of landowners under conditions of uncertainty to: (1) hold relatively secure and marketable forms of wealth, and (2) ensure that the probability of loss in such assets does not exceed certain specified limits (Sen, 1981).

Whether any particular explanation such as this is found adequate or not, the existence and extent of such "connectedness" between the ownership distribution of productive assets and their final distribution in operational use within the agrarian economy in South Asia need to be clearly recognized. For, apart from the relatively limited change brought about by leasing of land, the pattern of distribution of credit also appears to correspond fairly closely to the pattern of distribution of operational holdings. (In fact, when classified according to size of operation holdings, the coefficient of concentration of debt has been found to have been generally higher than the coefficient of concentration of land in India early in the 1950s; it does not seem to have changed a great deal since then.)

A major source of advantage in the credit market for those with relatively large operational holdings has been that a higher proportion of their produce could be freely marketed, even in the case of foodgrains; the security offered on this account, along with the collateral provided by their holdings of land, made it possible to borrow at lower rates of interest and without being subjected to credit rationing. On the other hand, when peasants with relatively small holdings and less marketable surpluses sought credit, the only collateral they were in a position to offer was their own labor in addition to the produce of the land; the lenders could then tie advances of credit to such labor and produce and secure them on terms much more favorable than would otherwise have been possible.

RELATION BETWEEN HOLDING SIZE, LABOR INTENSITY, AND PRODUCTIVITY

Given the earlier technology in agriculture, the smaller holdings could, however, not only make more intensive use of labor on the land available to them but also show higher productivity per unit of operated land than the larger ones. Although this inverse size–productivity relationship has been attributed to smaller holdings having a higher proportion of irrigated area, greater cropping intensity, and cropping patterns of higher value, their ability to exploit these sources of productivity was itself a reflection of the greater availability of labor relative to the land operated by them (Bharadwaj, 1974; Dharm Narain and Shyamal Roy, 1980). There has been also evidence of more investment per hectare in small holdings, based in part on borrowing, but largely on direct use of labor for various forms of construction. While even such holdings have been found to supplement family with hired labor, particularly in periods of peak activity, there is little doubt that it was the availability of cheaper family labor that made it possible for them to achieve levels of productivity comparable to and often higher than in the larger holdings.

More recent evidence indicates that, although the smaller holdings continue to have the advantages of the cheaper family labor available to them, modern technology in agriculture (associated with high-yielding varieties, larger inputs of chemical fertilizers and pesticides, and more controlled supplies of water) has made it possible to raise yields on the larger holdings to a degree that the inverse size–productivity relationship widely observed earlier no longer holds in the regions where it has been adopted. However, it has done so without changing significantly the inverse relationship observed all along between size of holding and intensity of labor input.

The explanation for this seems to lie not only in the greater access that operators of larger holdings have to financial resources for securing the necessary inputs, but in the problems of supervision and control of hired labor. This has evidently induced them to undertake mechanization without increasing significantly the use of hired labor, even though such investment could have had land-augmenting effects and made it possible to use labor for promoting cropping patterns of higher value and even multiple cropping on a more extensive scale. There is evidence that, while the inverse relationship between size of holding and intensity of labor input was getting limited to the lower-size groups (in at least certain regions) in the middle of the 1950s, it had spread to the entire spectrum by the middle of the 1970s, with the largest farms tending to increase labor use much less than smaller ones (Chattopadhay and Rudra, 1976; Sen, 1981).

On the other hand, it seems now much more questionable whether the ability of landlords to use the control exercised through land-lease and credit markets for securing labor and the produce of land on terms more favorable to them would necessarily prevent increases in the productivity of land in small tenant holdings. This possibility has been strongly stressed with reference to regions in which, for reasons connected with the earlier evolution of land tenures, the involvement of landlords in agriculture has been combined with deeper interests on their part in moneylending and trade (Bhaduri, 1984). The empirical evidence available for these regions suggests, however, that interlocking of markets does not impose constraints of such severity – even under conditions of "semi-feudalism" – and that, when opportunities for raising significantly the productivity of land (as through adoption of high-yielding varieties) become available, growth in output has been taking place Rudra, 1978; Sen, 1981).

These inferences, although still based on empirical studies of relatively limited range, have important theoretical and practical implications for the process of agrarian transformation (and thereby for mobilization of the rural economy) in countries of South Asia. For instance, it is obvious that in situations in which the values of the marginal product of labor would tend to differ widely, as between operational holdings of different size, allocational efficiency in agriculture cannot be established by demonstrating that the value corresponding to a particular factor proportion is not far out of line with the prevailing wage rate (Saini, 1979; Rudra and Amartya Sen, 1980). Even if these differences can be explained in terms of factors such as risk aversion, costs of supervision of labor, and what is being maximized or minimized in holdings belonging to different size groups (Basu, 1984), they reflect basically systemic constraints that are not overcome through market processes and therefore, in effect, limit the choices within each group.

Moreover, when the "connectedness" reflected in the working of land-lease and credit markets leaves the burden of adjustment largely to the labor market (on which those who are most resource-deficient within the system are dependent), it is incorrect to attribute poverty in agrarian economies wholly to the low quality of material and human capital (even though they may account to a large extent for the relatively low levels of labor productivity in such economies). That the poor make efficient use of the resources available to them should not obscure, at least on the theoretical plane, the scope for raising their productivity and income through institutional changes that would improve efficiency of resource use within the system as a whole.

On the practical plane there are, of course, problems in bringing about such changes. Attempts at radical land reform have been seldom found politically feasible, except when carried through after major upheavals accompanied by substantial changes in power relationships within society (as in China, Japan, South Korea, and Taiwan after World War II). Problems of an administrative nature also have frequently frustrated efforts to improve the availability of credit to peasants with small holdings. Such progress as has been made in these spheres has been, therefore, generally partial and uneven in varying degrees, even within the same country (as in India).

Though agrarian economies have been still found to respond t
opportunities for substantial increases in productivity (as through th
adoption of high-yielding varieties), the extent of the response and th
cost in terms of scarce resources seems to differ a great deal. On presen
evidence, this seems due to differences not only in the geophysica
environments and in the availability of the required infrastructura
facilities, but in the characteristics of the factor markets and thei
impact on production relations over a period of time (which get re
flected in the size-distribution of operational holdings and in the rela
tionship between size of holding, intensity of labor input, and lan
productivity in different size groups).

Where land reform has been effective enough to eliminate very larg
holdings, and more extensive leasing than elsewhere has made it pos
sible for holdings with a certain size range to adjust the area operatec
according to the availability of family labor and draught animals, tech
nological improvements have made it possible to increase yields, even
when the land leased has been on the basis of sharecropping. The ability
of the smaller holdings to achieve levels of productivity comparable tc
those in the large ones is however still in doubt. Moreover, even in the
relatively favorable conditions created by such extensive leasing of land
carefully analyzed evidence offers no clear or conclusive evidence or
the degree of efficiency of resource use. (Bliss and Stern, 1982; Graaff
1984).

Where land leasing has been itself relatively limited, tractorization is
adopted in the larger operational holdings with a stronger bias towards
its labor-saving than its land-augmenting possibilities. The growth in
output that could be secured by more intensive inputs of hired labor is
forgone, the cost of output growth in terms of scarce resources is
inevitably much higher than is required by the inherent properties of the
technology itself. The smaller holdings, on the other hand, have difficulties on account of certain indivisibilities (such as in the draught
animals maintained and in owned irrigation equipment) adversely
affecting their cost structure, as well as for lack of adequate credit to
secure the complementary inputs needed for raising the productivity of
both land and labor. The realized rates of growth, therefore, tend to be
lower than could be otherwise realized, real costs of growth higher, and
the resulting distribution of income from agriculture somewhat more
skewed than under traditional technology (in which the larger holdings
have in such conditions less differential advantage over the smaller).

TECHNOLOGY-BASED GROWTH IN "RURAL-LED" DEVELOPMENT

This poses several problems for a strategy of "rural-led" development
based on the possibilities opened up in agriculture by modern techno-

logy. For it casts agriculture not merely as a source of supply of resources (whether of food, raw materials, labor, or saving), but as a sector that could generate rapidly growing demand for agricultural and non-agricultural products and thereby promote a process of balanced growth. The ability to achieve a high rate of growth of agricultural output is only one of the conditions to be satisfied; it has also to generate a pattern of demand that is conducive to such growth. This depends above all on its potential linkage effects in the rural economy, through expenditure on consumer goods that can be supplied from within, and through the investment outlays so induced.

Assuming that the required rates of growth in agriculture can be achieved without any change in the pattern of distribution of land and the related agrarian relationships, the problems that could arise from the demand side are clear from a quantitative model formulated for India on this basis (Mellor, 1976). Since yield-increasing technological innovations have been mainly in food grain, and the bulk of the increase in income accrues to holders of larger sizes of land, there is a potential imbalance between the incremental increases in supply and demand for food grain itself. For less than a fifth of the increase in the total consumption of the producers of food grain in this range goes directly into it, and the rest of the increase in output has to be absorbed by others.

Fortunately nearly one-third of the increase in consumption expenditure of such producers is on agricultural products other than food grain (such as livestock products, vegetables and fruits, vegetable oil, and unrefined sugar). The additional income so generated in the next round can, therefore, create more demand for food grain within the rural economy, since these are generally more labor-intensive products, and the income from increased output would accrue to a much greater extent to the lower-income groups with higher elasticities of demand for grain. Nevertheless, with all this, much less than one-half of the growth in food-grain output may still get absorbed in the rural economy.

This could be an advantage when the rate of growth of food-grain output is relatively low, and the urban population is dependent on a high proportion of marketed surpluses. In principle, a decline in the relative price of food grain brought about by a higher rate of growth of output could also help the rural poor (Mellor and Desai, 1985), apart from other spin-offs in the economy as a whole. However, when the cost of output growth in terms of scarce resources is high (on account of failure to apply labor intensively enough for realizing their full potential, or due to a rise in the price of essential inputs, such as chemical fertilizers), such decline could not only evoke strong political opposition, but even affect adversely the stimulus required for increasing the output of food grain.

The linkage effects within the rural economy could be, of course, much stronger (generating in the process more demand for food grain) if a significant proportion of the increase in income from growth in food-grain output gets spent on the products of rural industry. This is, however, highly uncertain when the bulk of such increase in income accrues to the upper strata of landowning households, even though a higher proportion of their incremental consumption expenditure tends to be on non-agricultural commodities and services.

In fact, the share of rural industry in several products, such as textiles, has been declining in India for lack of competitiveness in terms of price and quality, and this has not been arrested by fiscal and other measures adopted for the purpose. Not only have more new products emerged, catering to demand hitherto met by traditional industry, but consumer durables account for a relatively high and growing proportion of the expenditure of rural households in the upper-income groups. Without substantial restructuring of rural industry, which itself may not be possible without considerable investment in infrastructural facilities in appropriately located market towns (or as has been attempted in China within the framework of communes), the prospects of its providing significant linkage effects for the development of the rural economy seem more remote now than was the case earlier in Japan.

Under these conditions a higher proportion of the savings accruing from agricultural growth is also likely to be invested outside the rural economy. There has been evidence of such capital outflow in India through direct investment of rural saving in urban enterprises as well as through financial channels. Although private investment within farms has generally increased in response to extension of irrigation through public investment, it has failed to grow when such extension of irrigation itself slowed down (as in Punjab, Gujarat, and Karnataka, where rapid expansion had taken place earlier). Thereafter, the growth in private saving among farmers with relatively large holdings in these regions has gone much more into financial assets (particularly bank deposits) and thus led to net outflow of resources on private account through the agency of financial intermediaries (Mody, 1983).

It also needs to be recalled that rapid agricultural growth could promote a distinct pattern of rural-led development only where more equitable distribution of assets within the agrarian economy, achieved through land reform, was combined with much fuller exploitation of the potential provided by modern technology for land augmentation and intensive use of labor and the resultant broad-based generation of income and demand within rural society (as in China, Taiwan, and South Korea after World War II). It seems an unrealistic expectation that a similar pattern of development can be replicated where much more unequally distributed land has provided the base for the same technology to be used for increasing significantly the share of the upper and middle peasantry in the incremental incomes from agriculture, and as much as one half of the rural population (dependent primarily on labor for its livelihood) remains impoverished by inadequate employment opportunity and diminishing returns to labor, arising from rapid population growth.

Since the scope for more intensive use of labor in agriculture appears to be limited by the technical alternatives now available for increasing output within the given institutional constraints (Ishikawa, 1981; Booth and Sundrum, 1984), the most that can be hoped for is some other variant which offers more employment in the rural economy. Evidently, in many parts of Southeast Asia (such as in the Philippines), a large portion of the increased agricultural income from better irrigation and technology has been getting transferred to laborers through strong patron-client relationships within the agrarian community (Hayami, 1981). In South Asia such relationships are much weaker and the proportion of the rural population dependent on wage employment significantly higher. Massive public works programs supported by the high proportion of food-grain output marketed from the larger holdings, offer a major alternative under these conditions for creating more employment, and in the process, building up the infrastructures required for the development of the rural economy.

While the potentialities of this alternative have been recognized for a long time (in fact, ever since the idea of mobilizing idle rural labor directly for capital formation was first mooted in the 1950s), and considerable experience gained (such as through schemes of guaranteed employment at minimum wages in rural areas operated in some parts of India), there are two important constraints on the scale of the additional employment that can be so created. One of them, set by the limits to mobilization of savings for such investment through public agencies, could become less severe with higher rates of agricultural growth; the availability of much larger marketed surpluses of food grain could itself increase somewhat the scope for deficit spending in support of labor-intensive investment programs without serious inflationary effects. The financing problem would, however, still remain, since the required increase in such investment would be substantial, and there are other competing demands on the resources available to the public sector (such as for investment in transport, communications, energy, and other basic intermediates, like chemical fertilizers).

The other constraint, by far the more difficult, is imposed by problems of organization. Although partly of an administrative and technical nature, they have important social and political dimensions as well, since they are closely linked with the power structure in rural areas and the interests that tend to dominate the deployment of resources available at this level. How far they can be overcome by processes generated through political and administrative decentralization, and interaction with popular movements, is therefore, perhaps the most critical question now for the mobilization of the rural economy in countries of South Asia.

Where social and political movements have helped to correct the biases in the rural power structure, through moderate land reform and organization of rural labor for collective bargaining on a limited scale, the redistributive effects have been significant enough to make some impact on rural poverty (as has been observed in Kerala). When supported by measures for formal and non-formal education for the entire population (including women), and for extension of health facilities to rural areas, it has also been possible to quicken the process of demographic transition, despite relatively low levels of per capita income (Panikar et al., 1975). There has been no evidence of growth in agricultural productivity as a result of such social transformation (Raj and Tharakan, 1983), and this has made it much more difficult to maintain the momentum of change (with consequences that could prove serious). But the failure on this account has been largely due to inadequate understanding – on the political plane – of the imperative need for productive investment and technological change to support processes of social change. If the lesson is learned and acted upon, the progress made through institutional changes and social policies could still provide a firm foundation for more rapid development of the rural economy in the future.

REFERENCES

Basu, Kaushik 1984: *The Less Developed Economy: A Critique of Contemporary Theory.* New York and London: Oxford University Press.
Bhaduri, Amit 1984: *The Economic Structure of Backward Agriculture.* New York: Macmillan.
Bharadwaj, Krishna: *Production Conditions in Indian Agriculture: A Study Based on Farm Management.* Cambridge: University of Cambridge, Dept. of Applied Economics, Occasional Paper 33.
Bliss, C. J. and Stern, N. H. 1982: *Palanpur: The Economy of an Indian Village.* Oxford: Clarendon Press.
Booth, Anne and Sundrum, R.M. 1984: *Labour Absorption in Agriculture.* London and New York: Oxford University Press.
Chattopadhay M. and Rudra, Ashok 1976: "Size-Productivity Revisited." *Economic and Political Weekly* (Review of Agriculture), 11(39), Sept. 25.
Chattopadhay, M. and Rudra, Ashok 1977: "Size-Productivity Revisited: Addendum." *Economic and Political Weekly* (Review of Agriculture), 12(11), March 12.
Fei, C. H. and Ranis, Gustav 1964: *Development of the Labour Surplus Economy: Theory and Policy.* Homewood, Ill: Richard D. Irwin.
Graaff, Jan 1984: "Economic Theory and the Economy of Palanpur." *Oxford Economic Papers* (New Series), 36(3), Nov.
Habib, Irfan 1982: "Agrarian Relations and Land Revenue." In Tapan Raychaudhuri and Irfan Habib, *The Cambridge Economic History of India, vol. I, c. 1200 – c. 1750.* Cambridge: Cambridge University Press.

Hayami, Yujuro 1981: "Agrarian Problems of India: An East and Southeast Asian View." In Yujiro Hayami and Masao Kikutchi, *Asian Village Economy at the Crossroads: An Econometric Approach to Institutional Change*, Tokyo: University of Tokyo Press.

Hirashima, Shigemochi 1980: "Institutional and Macro Aspects of Labour Absorption in Japanese Agriculture." In *Labour Absorption in Agriculture: The East Asian Experience*, ARTEP/ILO.

Ishikawa, Shigeru 1967: *Economic Development in Asian Perspective*. Kinokuniya. 1975: "Peasant Families and the Agrarian Community in Economic Development." In Lloyd G. Reynolds, *Agriculture in Development Theory, New Haven: Yale University Press. 1975. 1981: Essays on Technology, Employment and Institutions in Economic Development*, Tokyo: Kinokuniya. 1982: "Labour Absorption in China's Agriculture." In Shigeru Ishikawa, Saburo Yamada and S. Hirashima, *Labour Absorption and Growth in Agriculture: China and Japan*, ARTEP/ILO.

Johnston, Bruce, F. 1966: "Agriculture and Economic Development: The Relevance of the Japanese Experience." *Food Research Institute Studies*, 6(3).

Kikuchi, Masao and Hayami, Yujiro 1985: "Agricultural Growth against a Land Resource Constraint: Japan, Taiwan, Korea and the Philippines." In Kazushi Ohkawa and Gustav Ranis (eds), *Japan and the Developing Countries*, Oxford: Basil Blackwell.

Lee, Teng-hui 1971: *Intersectoral Capital Flows in the Economic Development of Taiwan, 1895–1900*. Ithaca, New York: Cornell University.

Lewis, Arthur 1954: "Economic Development with Unlimited Supplies of Labour." *The Manchester School*, May.

Mellor, John 1976: *The New Economics of Growth: A Strategy for India and the Developing World*. Ithaca, New York: Cornell University Press.

Mellor, John W. and Desai, Gunvant M. 1985: *Agricultural Change and Rural Poverty: Variations on a Theme by Dharm Narain*. Baltimore, Maryland: The John Hopkins University Press.

Mody, Ashoka 1983: "Rural Resource Generation and Mobilisation." *Economic and Political Weekly* (Annual Number), 18(19–21), May.

Mody, Ashoka; Mundle, Sudipto; and Raj, K. N. 1985: "Resource Flows from Agriculture: Japan and India." Kazushi Ohkawa abnd Gustav Ranis (eds), op. cit.

Narain, Dharm and Roy, Shyamal 1980: *Impact of Irrigation and Labour Availability on Multiple Cropping*. Research Report, International Food Policy Research Institute, Washington DC, Nov.

Nurkse, Ragnar 1953: *Problems of Capital Formation in Underdeveloped Areas*. London and New York: Oxford University Press.

Panikar, P. G. K. et al., 1975: *Poverty, Unemployment and Development Policy: A Case Study of Selected Issues with Reference to Kerala*. New York: United Nations.

Raj, K. N. 1983: "Agricultural Growth in India and China: Role of Price and Non-Price Factors." *Economic and Political Weekly*, 18(3), Jan. 15.

Raj, K. N. and Tharakan, Michael 1983: "Agrarian Reform in Kerala and its Impact on the Rural Economy – A Preliminary Assessment." In Ajit Kumar Ghose (ed.), *Agrarian Reform in Contemporary Developing Countries*, New York: Croom Helm & St Martin's Press.

Rudra, Ashok 1978: "Organisation of Agriculture for Rural Development: the Indian Case." *Cambridge Journal of Economics*, (3), Dec.

Rudra, Ashok and Sen, Amartya 1980: "Farm Size and Labour Use: Analysis and Policy." *Economic and Political Weekly* (Annual Number), 15(5–7), Feb.

Saini, G. R. 1979: *Farm Size, Resource-Use, Efficiency and Income Distribution in India.*

Sen, Abhijit 1981: "Market Failure and Control of Labour Power: Towards an Explanation of 'Structure' and Change in Indian Agriculture." *Cambridge Journal of Economics*, 3 and 4, Sept. and Dec.

Schultz, Theodore, W. 1964: *Transforming Traditional Agriculture.* New Haven: Yale University Press.

Smith, Thomas C. 1959: *The Agrarian Origins of Modern Japan.* Stanford, California: Stanford University Press.

Teranishi, Juro 1976: "The Pattern and Role of Flow of Funds between Agriculture and Non-Agriculture in Japanese Economic Development." In Kuzushi Ohkawa and Yujiro Hayami (eds), *Papers and Proceedings of the Conference on Japan's Historical Development Experience and the Contemporary Developing Countries*, International Development Center of Japan.

Vaidyanathan, A. and Jose, A. V. 1978: "Absorption of Human Labour in Agriculture: A Comparative Study of Some Asian Countries." In P. K. Bardhan et al., *Labour Absorption in Indian Agriculture: Some Explanatory Investigations*, ARTEP/ILO.

Weins, Thomas B. 1978: "The Evolution of Policy and Capabilities in China's Agricultural Technology." In *Chinese Economy Post-Mao*, Washington DC: Joint Economic Committee of U.S. Congress, Nov.

Comments on
"Mobilization of the Rural Economy and the Asian Experience"

HENRY J. BRUTON

In his paper, K. N. Raj studies a variety of aspects of the mobilization of the rural economy. Mobilization implies that there are resources available, or potentially available, that are not currently being used, or not used in a socially acceptable fashion or for a socially acceptable objective. To mobilize such resources means, then, to find a way to take advantage of their existence and to enable them to become more socially productive. The first question, of course, is whether there are such resources or such potential and then, if there are, the next question is why are they not now fully mobilized in the appropriate manner and for the appropriate purpose.

Raj has little to say about whether there are such resources, but clearly believes that there are, at least in Asia, especially South Asia. His explanation of why there is a mobilization problem is mainly in institutional terms – land tenure systems; availability of credit; infrastructure, including especially irrigation; technology; availability of high-yielding seeds, fertilizer, and pesticides; and skills, especially those associated with water management and the capacity of labor to adapt to new demands placed on it by new technologies. He pays little attention to factor prices, and I believe, does not mention either the exchange rate or exports. I found it quite refreshing.

The great merit of this kind of an approach is that it forces the investigator to look closely at the specific situation – the environment, its social, political, and cultural aspects as well as the economic ones. Raj's analyses show that the effectiveness of any policy depends very much on the environment in which it is applied. His main theoretical constructs are those of Ragnar Nurkse, Arthur Lewis, John Fei and Gustav Ranis, and John Mellor. He uses these models sparingly and largely as sources of questions and of insights, rather than as rigid models to be estimated or applied in a once-and-for-all manner. To proceed in this way means that the analyst must be able to examine a particular economy and ascertain why it is the way it is, and from this examination prescribe policies that will be effective at this precise time. Whatever generalizations are possible, then, emerge from these examinations. They are, I believe likely to be few.

I will devote the rest of my comments to identifying some of the points in Raj's paper that illustrate what I have been trying to say, and then raise a couple of questions.

Early in his paper Raj refers to the Nurkse argument that idle labor in peasant households represents a potential for saving that could be used directly for capital formation. To mobilize this potential, the idle labor is employed and must be paid market wages, but to prevent inflation or increased consumption, taxation of the households would be necessary. Direct taxation of this sort was not possible in India, Raj argues, because taxation was associated with the colonial regime, and therefore, was something to be got rid of – not used on a wider scale. Note that this argument is quite different from the more usual one to the effect that sophisticated taxation arrangements are virtually impossible to implement because of lack of a well-trained, well-equipped taxing bureaucracy. To overcome the latter hurdle, training and experience are necessary. To overcome the former, probably only the passage of time is adequate for the job.

He goes on to say that China was able (and willing) to mobilize idle labor for capital formation without paying the labor for this extra work. This seems to have worked reasonably well early on, but has not continued to work in recent years, and indeed the Chinese have moved to greater use of market incentives. He argues that this shift to a less constrained rural labor market is not due to the failure of the previous stage. Indeed it is the exact opposite. The somewhat more coercive command arrangement was necessary and successful earlier in creating the infrastructure (especially the great irrigation works) that corrected marked regional imbalances. Once these objectives were accomplished, it was then possible to rely more fully on market incentives and routine saving and investment processes to produce the continuously rising outputs. One might have wanted Raj to explain a bit more why the command system was necessary at the earlier time to accomplish certain objectives, but the main notion is important: the institutional setting and the objectives at the earlier time did not, in his view, allow the market to work, while after certain modifications in that setting were accomplished, the market became the appropriate instrument. Raj is appropriately cautious, but makes his argument firmly.

He refers to the fact that the successful mobilization of agricultural resources in Taiwan relied mainly on market forces. He argues, however, that this worked because productivity in agriculture was growing very much faster than population. This rapid growth of productivity allowed per capita consumption to rise within the agricultural community, and allowed real incomes in general in the rural sector to increase, despite the transfer of resources out of agriculture. A major source of the increased productivity was the infrastructural investment in Taiwan – as was also the case in Japan and South Korea as well – that had taken place earlier. More importantly, he cites reasons why the costs of infrastructural investment in South Asia are likely to be very much higher than would appear to have been the case in Taiwan and Japan. This, the argument implies, suggests that the market mechanism may be less effective in South Asia than it proved to be in Taiwan.

A final example refers to the land markets in the various countries. Raj tells us that land-lease markets have functioned in Japan and Taiwan for a long time in a way that resulted in a distribution of land such that few rural households that were dependent on agriculture were left totally landless. Under these ownership conditions, it was in the interest of both the tenant and the landlord to find ways to increase land yields. This they did mainly by use of very labor-intensive techniques. In South Asia, however, a large proportion of rural households have received no land at all through the leasing process, and are therefore wholly or largely dependent on wage income. Neither the landlord-tenant nor employer-employee relationship have in these circumstances encouraged the intensive use of labor to get land yields up. So yields remain low, and land reform is made difficult. Raj explains the difference in the way the land-lease market has worked in East Asia from the way it has worked in South Asia in a number of ways, but the argument most congenial to his general position is that in terms of the caste system and the more hierarchical social arrangements in the latter areas. The main point that Raj wants to emphasize is what he calls the connectedness between the ownership distribution of productive assets and their final distribution in operational use in the agrarian society of South Asia. A rural-led development effort of the Mellor kind requires the more equitable distribution of assets that land reform and a fuller exploitation of the potential of modern technology allow. Yet land reform is impeded in South Asia by powerful institutional considerations, so one must search for ways to accomplish increased yields and a more equitable distribution within this existing institutional environment.

One may question a specific argument or empirical conclusion of Raj, but the general point of the paper is surely of fundamental importance, and is one, I believe, most economists accept but often forget. We often urge countries to pursue policies that they simply cannot pursue, and we often have considerable difficulty in convincing ourselves that institutional, political, cultural, or traditional constraints really are there, and, if there, really matter. When a country tries to do the kind of thing that it is not able to do, or not ready to do, the tensions and latent hostility inherent in almost any development effort are exacerbated.

These last considerations suggest two general questions. The first refers to the kind of evidence, empirical or otherwise, that is needed to support the kind of argument that Raj makes. How can one test the argument that taxes could not be effectively applied in India because taxes were associated with the British colonial rule? Similarly, how can we design a test that will show whether the market mechanism will or will not be effective in a particular environment? Although infrastructure is often cited as the basic bottleneck, we also know that infrastructure is often underutilized or not used at all once it is in place. So we need tests to help us see as clearly as possible whether an institution is a bottleneck to be broken or is one that is part of the environment, and development must therefore take place around it.

The second question refers to the relationship between an argument that rests primarily on institutional factors and other arguments, especially those of a more general kind. Institutions of the kind to which Raj calls our attention are very country-specific. They are part of the fundamental features of the social order, the political and cultural traditions, and indeed the geography of a country. On the other hand, we see clearly from the work of Hollis Chenery (and others) growth patterns that appear to be common to a wide number of countries. Evidence has also been accumulated that has convinced many observers (e.g. Balassa and Krueger) that an outward-looking, export-oriented development strategy is an effective development strategy for all developing countries at all times. If institutions and environmental factors are as important as Raj's analysis suggests, and the data support the more general theories as well, then we need to try to marry the general and the specific in a more convincing form than we have done to date.

10

Patterns and Processes of Intersectoral Resource Flows: Comparison of Cases in Asia

SHIGERU ISHIKAWA

INTRODUCTION

In the contemporary developing countries, in particular those in the early development stages, what should be the net direction and magnitude of intersectoral resource flows (ISRF) from the standpoint of agriculture if it is to be beneficial to successful economic development? About two decades ago, I explored the answer to this question on the basis of the case studies of the experiences in a few Asian countries, and suggested the advisability of government policy intervention to bring about a significant resource inflow into agriculture (Ishikawa, 1963, 1967a, 1967b). At that time, a commonplace view prevailed to the effect that the early stage of industrialization of an economy should necessarily be financed largely from a net source outflow from agriculture, and this view was alleged to be founded upon the experiences of Soviet Russia and Japan in their early industrialization stages. However, relating specifically to the Asian context – in which flood control, irrigation, and other basic investments in land and water constituted the prerequisite to productivity increase in its rice-based agriculture, and in which these basic investments were in acute shortage – I wondered strongly whether the attempts of early industrialization should not be caught in difficulties of the type similar to the Ricardian Growth Trap,

I would like to thank Professors H. Myint, Gustav Ranis, Dong Fureng, S. Mundle, N. Lardy and Drs U. Lele and B. Stone for their helpful comments on an earlier version of this paper. In particular, Professor Myint's comments as official discussant of my paper at the symposium reminded me of some weaknesses of my presentation on the framework for analysis and the findings which were very useful in revising the paper. The grant from Nippon Shoken Zaidan, which partly financed this study, is acknowledged with appreciation.

unless the non-agricultural sector was prepared to provide an outflow of resources to the agricultural sector in significant excess of their inflow.

The case studies thus conducted by myself were somewhat preliminary and incomplete, due to the insufficiency of data. They mostly aimed at suggesting the significance of the issue. Later on, however, a fair number of scholars were engaged in the detailed statistical studies of ISRF covering four countries in Asia. As a result, our empirical knowledge relating to this issue has become far richer than before. In such studies, particular mention should be made of Sudipto Mundle (1981) for India with the reference years of 1951/2-70/1, T. H. Lee (1971) for Taiwan with the reference years of 1911-60, and Kazushi Ohkawa et al. (1978) and Juro Teranishi (1982) for Japan with the reference years of 1888-1937 and 1899-1964, respectively.[1] China's study, covering 1952-78, is from my own estimates – revised from my previous ones for this paper (Ishikawa, 1967a and 1967b).[2]

It should be emphasized that these studies have specific analytical aims which go beyond the statistical investigation of ISRF. For example, Mundle aims at investigating the causal relationship between net ISRF and the speed of development, and Teranishi focuses attention on the process of financial development in the Japanese economy since the early Meiji era as the basic factor underlying the changes in ISRF. In this paper, however, I am more concerned about the fact that the statistical findings of these studies, although still with room for statistical improvement, broadly indicate a diversity of the direction and magnitude of net ISRF among the four areas, seemingly suggesting a similar diversity among other developing countries. Keeping this new development of the issue in mind, I plan in this paper to endeavor to answer the following three questions relating to the interpretation of this diversity.

The first question is: What implications do the statistical findings of the diversified pictures of the direction and magnitude of net ISRF have vis-à-vis my earlier policy suggestion mentioned in the above? Was it erroneous? To this question my answer would be that the policy suggestion probably is most relevant in the cases of India and China, but that it may not be so for Taiwan and Japan, as in these areas there was no serious government policy intervention to realize agriculture's net resource inflow, and development of agriculture and the economy as a whole was on the whole successful.

The second question is raised essentially to examine these findings in a more fundamental dimension, namely whether with the progress of the economic development stages, there were likely to be changes in the determinants of ISRF. As for the factors differentiating the stages of economic development, I would put particular emphasis on per capita GNP and the degree of development of the market economy, in particular of "financial development". Thus, my answer would be: (1) where these development factors were in low levels, ISRF tended to be impeded thereby; hence the *raison d'être* of policy intervention of a more direct form, and (2) with the progress of these development stages, these sectors and aspects of the economy in which ISRF was carried on spontaneously and optimally relied upon the market mechanism tended to expand, with the result that the significance of the ISRF problem which assumed the requirement of more direct policy intervention diminished proportionately. The cases of India and China would correspond to (1), whereas those of Taiwan and Japan would be explainable at least partly by (2).

The third question is whether and how these findings about the four areas are relevant in other areas in Asia. Only a brief remark is made about this in the last section.

In the following section, I plan to summarize the statistical findings on the ISRF of the four areas, together with a common statistical framework in which they are presented and compared. In the next section, what may be called an "analytical economic history" approach is briefly introduced as a method to study the three questions above, centering on the second one. In the following four sections, the actual studies are made with respect to the empirical data for the four areas according to that approach. The reference periods under study are confined to those of the above-mentioned ISRF studies for individual countries. Preliminary conclusions are shown in the final section.

STATISTICAL STUDIES OF THE FOUR AREAS – A SUMMARY

Statistical framework for measuring ISRF

1   The concept of agriculture as a unit of resource interflow should typically be a farm (household) sector in the context of "peasant agriculture" which is prevalent in Asian agriculture. This sector consists of the farm households which produce partly for self-consumption and partly for the market, and which integrate the functions of the farms as production enterprises and of the households as consumption units.

2   A non-farm sector as counterpart of the resource interflow, in fact, consists of a number of different sectors with diversified functions and characteristics. Most importantly, it comprises the emerging industry subsector as well as the government subsector, which not only takes care of the industrial subsector but also of the farm sector. It also comprises both the employers (enterprises and governments) and the employees (the households) subsectors. Since, however, our interest is in the role of the farm sector in economic development, the non-farm sector is taken to be an integral sector at least for observing the direction and scale of net resource interflow.

3   Net ISRF is a concept defined either as the sum of net income and capital flows between the two sectors, or net physical flow (the balance of trade in commodities and services) between them. It is measured in two dimensions:

  (a) In real terms, net ISRF consists of a "visible" and an "invisible" component. The "invisible" component is the part of net ISRF which is brought about by the changes in the commodity terms of trade between the two sectors. In the traditional economic analysis, the ISRF is grasped solely by this component, on the implicit assumption that the intersectoral trade always strikes a balance. The "visible" component emerges when the intersectoral trade does not strike a balance. The separation of the net resource flow into these components is formally indicated as follows:

   Net ISRF in real prices $= E/P_e - M/P_m$

   where E stands for exports, M for imports, P_e for the price indices of exports and P_m for those of imports.

   The "invisible" component $= M/P_m(P_m/P_e - 1)$

   in the export-excess case, and $E/P_e(P_e/P_m - 1)$ in the import-excess case.

   The "visible" component $= 1/P_e(E - M)$ or $1/P_m(M - E)$.

  (b) In current price terms, the visible net resource flow is indicated as consisting of three components, as follows:

   $E - M = (i)$ Net factor income earned "off-farm" $(V_1) + (ii)$ Net inflow of transfer income $(V_2) + (iii)$ Net inflow of capital (including changes in cash holdings) (K).

These concepts and measurements are clearly set out from the beginning of the discussion in Ishikawa (1967a) and are generally agreed upon.

It should be noted in connection with item 3(b) that in the course of the discussion, two other ways of conceiving and measuring ISRF were presented. One is to consider the net capital flow (K in the above) as the relevant net resource flow. The other is to consider the sum of the net capital flow and the net income transfer ($K + V_2$) as relevant, considering that the agricultural tax is important and can be taken as a kind of forced saving to be transferred to the non-farm sector. These measures are useful, not as alternative, but as complementary measures to $E - M$. Essentially, $E - M$ is the ultimate measure of overall net movement in real purchasing power between the sectors, K assumes the position of supreme importance only when the total amount of investible resources from the entire economy's point of view is at issue.

Comparative experiences

Overall results of the existing ISRF studies for the four areas are compared for some benchmark years in tables 10.1 and 10.2, and for each of them, changes over time of a few relevant variables are summarized in figures 10.1 through 10.5. From those, the following observations may be made.

1   $E - M$ in current price terms indicates a sharp contrast between China, on the one hand, and India (with the exception of the early 1950s) and Taiwan, on the other. Namely, China's situation was a continuous and ever-increasing net resource inflow into the farm sector, while the situations in India and Taiwan were almost the reverse. The amount of net resource outflow as a ratio of farm income was very large in Taiwan. Observation of the situation in Japan is complicated, as the two estimates indicate entirely opposite results, with the exception of 1923–32. Comparing figure 10.4 with figure 10.5, however, it is apparent that this difference comes mostly from the difference of the estimates of the amount of K, as will be again taken up shortly.

2   As for the items financing $E - M$, the role played by V_1 was by far the most important. In China and Japan, this means that the amount of the farm income earned off-farm was very large and increasing. In the case of Japan, this was so even after the land rental payments to the non-cultivating landlords are netted out. As for Taiwan, the land rental payments were large and increasing in amount and the off-farm income of the farm almost insignificant in the prewar colonial period. The situation reversed after the war. India's situation is not very clear. But the V_1 situation appears to have resembled prewar Taiwan. Tax payment of the farms in the V_2 account was significantly large only in Japan and postcolonial Taiwan.

3   With regard to the K account, significantly large amounts of private flows in both directions are discerned for prewar Japan, and the balance was net outflow from the farm sector. But the amount of this net outflow differs considerably between the two estimates. (It is only to be noted here that as far as K is concerned, only Teranishi's estimates are original and detailed. And in his estimates, the size of net outflow was invariably not very large.) Government investment in the farm sector was supplementing the private saving inflow only to a small extent. In other areas, the amount of private saving flow was small in both directions, and the size of the government investment in the farm sector was competing with the private saving inflow. The direction of K was diverse.

4   The commodity terms of trade between the two sectors measured at the farmyard changed in general in favor of the farm sector, when the base year is selected at a proper earlier year. Exceptions were the

TABLE 10.1 Contrasting structures of intersectoral resource flows of the farm sector. China, India, colonial and post-colonial Taiwan and Japan

	China 1980 (billion current yuan)	India 1968–69 (billion current rupee)	Colonial Taiwan 1931–35 (million current yen)	Post-colonial Taiwan 1956–60 (million current NT$)	Japan 1918–22 (million current yen) I[e]	Japan 1918–22 (million current yen) II[f]
			(annual average; current prices)			
I. Net recourse outflow ($E-M$)	−22.93 (−15)	7.54 (5)	63 (29)	948 (10)	195 (5)	−636 (−18)
						~ −647
a. Outflow of commodities and services (E)	107.96 (71)	78.77 (54)	208 (95)	9,665 (101)	2,626 (62) ⎫	~ −647
b. Inflow of commodities and services (M)	−130.89 (−86)	71.23 (−49)	−146 (−66)	−8,716 (−91)	2,431 (−58) ⎬	
II. Financing of net resource outflow						
1. Net outflow of factor income "abroad" (v_1)	−23.72 (−16)	(14.75)[b] (10)	47 (21)	−813 (−8)	−318 (−9)	−1,139 (−32)
Of it,						
a. Outflow of land rent accrued to non-cultivating landlords (R)	—		56 (25)	739 (8) ⎫	−318 (−9)	133 (4)
b. Inflow of labor income accrued to the farm family members working off the farm and brought in it (W)	−23.72 (−16)		−9 (−4)	−1,552 (−16) ⎬		−1,272 (−36)

2. Net outflow of current income transfer (v_2)	$-1.54\,(-1)$	$(3.95)^a\,(3)$	$17\,(8)$	$1,453\,(15)$	$288\,(8)$	$290\,(8)$
Of it,						
a. Tax and dues paid by the farm sector (X)	$3.91\,(3)$	$(3.95)\,(3)$	$17\,(8)$	$1,453\,(15)$	$288\,(8)$	$\Big\}\ 290\,(8)$
b. Govt subsidies, incl. current expenditures (U)	$-5.45\,(-4)$	$—^c$	$0.3^d\,(0.1)$	$7^d\,(0.01)$	$—$	
3. Net outflow of capital ($K = S_1 + S_2 - I_1 - I_2$)	$2.33\,(2)$	$(-11.16)^a\,(-8)$	$-1\,(0.5)$	$309\,(3)$	$225\,(6)$	$202\,(6)\ \sim 213$
a. Saving outflow through financial intermediaries (S_1)	$6.00\,(4)$	$(0.33)\,(0.2)$	$3\,(1)$	$\Big\}\ 425\,(4)$	$651^g\,(18)$	$388\,(11)\ \sim 399$
b. Increase in cash in circulation in the farm sector (S_2)	$5.24\,(3)$	$(0.20)\,(0.1)$	$—$		$—$	
c. Investment inflow through financial intermediaries (I_1)	$-3.65\,(-2)$	$(-6.99)\,(-5)$	$-3\,(-1)$	$-44\,(-5)$	$-404^g\,(-11)$	$-186\,(-5)$
d. Government investment in the farm sector (I_2)	$-5.26\,(-3)$	$(-4.70)^c\,(-3)$	$1\,(0.5)$	$-65\,(-0.7)$	$-22\,(-1)$	$—$
4. Errors and omissions	0.77			2		
5. Agricultural income	$152.50\,(100)$	$145.02\,(100)$	$220\,(100)$	$9,610\,(100)$	$3,571\,(100)$	

ᵃ These figures, including their components, are considered by the authors, Mody, Mundle, and Raj (1985), as partial estimates, although their negative signs are no doubt relevant. The figures are hence shown within brackets.

ᵇ The figure is what is derivable from the figures of I, II (2) and II (3).

ᶜ The figure is indicated in the source as "public expenditure in the farm sector". It therefore includes the subsidies of both capital and current accounts.

ᵈ The figures are the sum of public investment and subsidy in the capital account.

ᵉ This refers to the Ohkawa group's estimates. The figures are taken from Mundle and Ohkawa (1979), however.

ᶠ This refers to Teranishi's estimates.

ᵍ These figures apparently include savings and investment which were made directly and without passing through financial intermediaries by the farm sectors.

Sources: China: SSB-DTS (1984), SSB (1984); India: Mundle (1981) and Mody, Mundle, and Raj (1985); Japan: Lee (1971); Taiwan: Ohkawa, Shimizu, and Takamatsu (1978), Mundel and Ohkawa (1979) and Teranishi (1982).

TABLE 10.2   Overall net resource outflow of the farm sector and its "visible" and "invisible" components

	China (billion yuan)		India (billion rupee)		Colonial Taiwan (million yen)	Post-colonial Taiwan (T$ million)	Japan (million yen)	
	1966	1980	1960–61	1968–69	1931–35	1956–60	1908–12	1933–37
Export excess in current price as % of agricultural income ($(E-M)/Y_A$)	−3	−15	10	5	24	10	10	9
Export and import price indices								
The base year	1957	1957	1952–53	1960–61	1911–15	1935–37	1988–92	1988–92
Pe	133.9	194.5	121.3	174.9	133.3	2484	233.0	368.9
Pm	102.6	98.8	120.2	150.4	117.8	2975	169.3	292.6
Pe/Pm	130.5	196.9	100.9	116.3	113.2	83.6	137.6	126.1
Export excess in the base year price ($E/Pe-M/Pm$)	−10.4 *(100)*	−71.7 *(100)*	5.5 *(100)*	−2.9 *(100)*	33 *(100)*	96 *(100)*	−52.6 *(100)*	−152.0 *(100)*
Visible component $1/Pe(E-M)$ or in the import excess case $1/Pm(M-E)$	−1.8 *(17)*	−17.9 *(25)*	5.7 *(104)*	3.7 *(−127)*	47 *(143)*	38 *(40)*	57.9 *(−109)*	6.7 *(−4)*
Invisible component $M/Pm(Pm/Pe-1)$ or $E/Pe(Pe/Pm-1)$	−8.6 *(83)*	−53.8 *(75)*	−0.2 *(−4)*	−6.6 *(227)*	−14 *(−43)*	58 *(60)*	−110.1 *(209)*	−158.7 *(104)*

Sources: Table 1 [SSB-DTP, 1984], [SSB, 1984], [Lee, 1971], [Mundle and Ohkawa, 1979] and [Mundle, 1981], [Ohkawa and Shinohara, 1979, pp. 387–8].

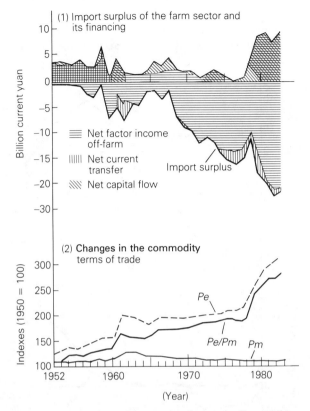

Fig. 10.1   *Overview of intersectoral resource flows: China*
Sources: SSB-DJS (1984) and SSB (1984)

periods in the 1950s and the first half of 1960s in India, of the 1920s in Japan, and of post-colonial Taiwan as compared with the colonial period. As a result, the invisible component of ISRF turned in general to the resource inflow, sometimes of a very large amount, into the farm sector, with the only important exception being post-colonial Taiwan. Also, with regard to China for the whole reference period, India for the 1960s and Japan for the whole reference period, $E - M$ in real terms flows into the farm sector.[3]

THE APPROACH TO COMPARATIVE STUDY – "ANALYTICAL ECONOMIC HISTORY"

Let me now describe the "analytical economic history approach" for our comparative study. While the name itself I borrowed from Professor H. Myint,[4] the following interpretation of the concept is of my own.

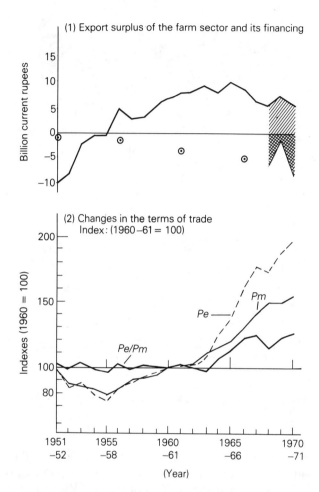

Fig. 10.2   *Overview of intersectoral resource flows: India*

Notes: The statistical scope of Mundle's estimate is, in fact, the agricultural sector. Mody,
Mundle, and Raj (1985) use Ashok Mody's estimates of changes in financial
assets and liabilities of the farm sector for three years from 1968/9 to 1970/1, on
the basis of the estimates of National Council of Applied Economic Research.
The finding was a net borrowing by the farm sector in these three years. These are
shown in this figure with the shaded area of ± ± ± ±. From this we can compute
the combined amount of net current transfer and net factor payment, when the
government investment is assumed away. This combined amount is shown as the
area with shadow ////. Mody also estimated, on the basis of the Reserve Bank of
India's data, the amount of annual public expenditures on the same figure by plot.

Source: Mundle (1981)

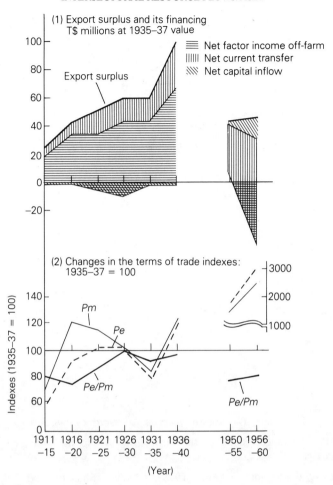

Fig. 10.3   *Overview of intersectoral resource flows: Taiwan*

Source: Lee (1971)

Namely, this is an approach to try to explain a certain specific event of analytical interest as an event of "totality" consisting of combined economic and non-economic factors, the event which emerged under the influence of specific initial conditions. Since the event is taken up as the subject matter of the economics study, the explanation should be done mainly as an analysis via economic theory. However, the "analytical history" approach presumes that of a large number of aspects with which it should deal, existing theories can be applied to only some of them but not to others, and therefore, that when a specific economic development model is formulated for explaining such a "totality" event,

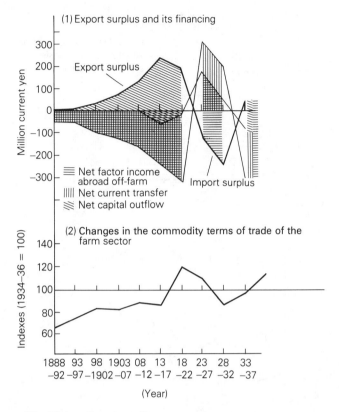

Fig. 10.4   *Overview of intersectoral resource flows: Japan*

Note: The statistical scope of the farm sector is, in fact, identical to the agricultural sector.

Sources: Mundle and Ohkawa (1979); Ohkawa, Shimizu, and Takamatsu (1978)

it inevitably becomes a less formal "historical" theory comprising more or less descriptive components.

Returning to our study, the reason for which the "analytical history" approach is particularly favorable lies in the following two basic assumptions. First, the ISRF is an integral component of the mechanism of saving mobilization and reallocation for the economy as a whole; the impact of the specific pattern of ISRF upon economic development is realized via this overall saving mechanism. Second, this overall saving mechanism is constrained ultimately by the initial conditions and indirectly by the overall economic development mechanism, which in turn, is brought about under direct influence of the above initial conditions.

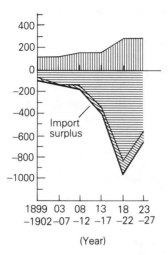

Fig. 10.5   *Alternative estimates of export surplus of the farm sector and its financing*

Source: Teranishi (1982, pp. 240–63)

The first assumption becomes the more important as we expand the scope of our ISRF study to the wider range of the developing countries. So far, we have related the pattern of ISRF too hurridly and too directly to the overall developmental performance. This shortcut may be effective in some cases, for example, when we deal with the countries which are in danger of being caught in the Ricardian-type Growth Trap and hence, a substantial net resource flow into agriculture is in any case a prerequisite for getting out of the trap. But once the countries under study go beyond these, we have to have an analytical approach which is capable of dealing with the process and functions of the ISRF of these countries as well.

As to the second assumption, two points may be made. One, while the initial conditions are always multifaceted, three conditions seem most important for international comparison: resource endowments, stages of economic development, and international environments. Two, the economic development mechanism tends to be summarized analytically as an economic development model, which plays a role of "historical" theory in our approach. Naturally, the economic development model which is relevant to a particular country or a particular group of the countries is conditioned by its initial conditions. There are cases of countries, therefore, in which certain existing development models can be borrowed for application; but in other cases, the development models should be formulated from scratch. Fortunately, some of the existing development models can be borrowed as development models which approximate the development mechanisms conceivable for these four areas.

Thus, our "analytical history" approach stresses causal links among: (1) specific initial conditions, (2) a specific development model, (3) a specific saving mobilization mechanism, (4) a specific pattern of ISRF as part of this mechanism, and (5) a particular development performance. The role of government strategy and policies is significant, but their place in the links is somewhat complicated: They affect the development performance through their influence on (2) and (3), but they are on the other hand conditioned by (1). If we have to be more specific about this relationship, a tentative assumption is that the specific kind of strategy and policy variables that can be adopted are largely determined by the initial conditions, and what government can decide autonomously is almost limited to the choice of specific values to be put to these policy variables.

In the following, the experiences of the four areas are comparatively studied for each of the above causal links in the "analytical history" approach.

INITIAL CONDITIONS

Comparative studies of causal link 1 are made with respect to three aspects of the initial conditions: resource endowments, stages of economic development, and international environments.

Resource endowments

Resource endowments in China, India, and Japan were broadly and commonly characterized as densely populated countries with no untapped arable lands left and with no significant endowments of exportable natural resources. They, however, had a legacy of fairly developed commerce and handicraft, and on that basis they were able to transplant and develop modern industry once they were exposed to the western industrial capitalism.

Initial conditions of Taiwan were somewhat involved. It was developed after the seventeenth century as a sugar-cane and other industrial-crop supply base, mostly for the Chinese mainland. Labor was originally supplied from, and later supplemented by, the mainland immigrants. The export production was expanded with the successive reclamation of new lands, part of which were retained for rice production for the subsistence of peasants producing such exports. This pattern of development, which seems to be approximated by H. Myint's Vent-for-Surplus model (1958), flourished particularly after the opening of two southern ports to the West in the 1860s. However, when

Taiwan was ceded to Japan in 1895, the land frontier almost disappeared, and a further increase in agricultural output had to rely on the increase in yields per hectare of existing cultivated land (Ishikawa, 1971). Colonial Taiwan performed this production task efficiently, and on that basis, specialized as an export economy of crude sugar and rice. This may be interpreted as a continuation of the Vent-for-Surplus-type development by using a "backlog" of transplanted, advanced, agricultural technologies.

The conditions of post-colonial Taiwan were similar to those of the other three countries in the sense that the surplus factor now turned to be labor, and that there already was a modern industrial base to which this surplus labor was capable of being transferred from agriculture.

The stages of economic development

This may be observed both from the level of per capita GNP and of development of the market economy. As for the former, China and India even in the 1980s were among the low-income countries by the World Bank definition, with per capita GNP of the 1980 dollar value both less than US$300. In contrast, per capita GNP of Japan in 1884–90 and Taiwan in 1908–12 were calculated in the 1980 dollar value as US$653 and US$627, respectively.

Similar and even larger differentials seem to have also existed in the agricultural output per head of the agricultural labor force between the four areas. And behind this were the differentials in the state of basic agricultural investments and of the nation's innovating capacity. In the predominantly rice-based Asian agriculture, development of agriculture itself depends on the spread of irrigation and the corresponding progress of breeding and cultivating technologies, and these are measured by the increase in "land productivity" – a proxy of which is the grain output per hectare of cultivated area. From this land productivity viewpoint, the Chinese development outweighed the Indian one, with both the irrigation ratio and the per hectare paddy yield in around 1957 higher by roughly 100 percent in the former than in the latter. But, because of the difference of the man–land ratio in the reverse direction, the difference of the yield per head of agricultural population (a proxy of "labor productivity") was not substantial.

As for Japan, the initial level of irrigation was already high in terms of the irrigation ratio as a result of the investments extensively carried out during the pre-Meiji era, but their qualitative improvements came only after 1900. Additional features were, as for the Meiji era: a large accumulation of technological knowledge in Western Japan, and the existence of the innovative "cultivating landlord" in a large number of localities all over Japan and in the later period; the R&D conducted at the central and prefectural agricultural experiment stations; and the widespread emergence of a new innovator class among the medium-sized farmers. These were the essential sources of the later increases in both land and labor productivities. In Taiwan, the initial land productivity was relatively low, but the later growth rate was remarkably high, due to the substantial irrigation investment and the successful introduction of higher-yielding *japonica* rice varieties and their rapid spread. Average gross agricultural output per farm household in Taiwan thus exceeded even that of Japan after the 1920s. The innovator class in Taiwan was also distinctive, namely the landlords who were non-cultivating, which is different from the rural innovators in Meiji Japan, but were most active in introducing new varieties and new methods (Ishikawa, 1971).

One word on the structural change. Despite the significant initial differentials in per capita GNP and agricultural labor productivity, the initial weight of the rural or agricultural sector in the economy in terms of either population, labor force, or output does not seem to have differed very much among the four countries. A major difference existed in the speed of its change: in India and China it was very slow, and in Japan and Taiwan it was rapid.

Development of the market economy

This concerns development of the economy's organizational arrangements connecting a great number of individual economic units in various kinds of markets: the product markets, the labor markets, the land and land-lease markets, and financial markets. It is to be noted that markets other than financial markets play important roles in directly affecting the realization of those components of ISRF other than K; namely E, M and the debit and credit sides of both V_1 and V_2. But the attention here is focused on development of the financial markets, as its impact is not only upon K, but comprehensive. More specifically, development of the financial markets is capable of bringing about the division of labor of the most developed forms – namely the division of labor between the savers and investors, and that between the saving and holding of primary securities. This is in addition to those kinds of divisions of labor accompanying development in other categories of the market and reflected in the extent of monetarization (Gurley and Shaw, 1967).

Developments of the financial markets in the four areas are compared in table 10.3 on the ratios of M_1 and M_2 to GNP and in table 10.4 on the diffusion of modern financial intermediates, in particular credit cooperatives, in the rural areas. Mainly on the basis of these, the following points may be made. First, seeing from the $M_1/$GNP ratio, an indicator of the degree of monetarization, as well as the $M_2/$GNP ratio, an indicator of the degree of division of labor in the above two essential kinds, the initial financial development in Japan and Taiwan was low,

TABLE 10.3   *Ratios of currency, demand deposits and time and saving deposits to GNP*

		Currency in circulation (GNP)	Demand deposits (GNP)	M_1 (GNP)	Time and saving deposits (GNP)	M_2 (GNP)
China	1957	0.05	—	—	0.03	—
	1979	0.07	0.15	0.22	0.07	0.29
	1983	0.18	0.10	0.28	0.16	0.44
India	1955–56	0.15	—	—	—	—
	1970–71	0.12	0.08	0.20	0.10	0.30
	1980–81	0.12	0.09	0.21	0.28	0.48
Taiwan	1912	0.09	0.06	0.15	0.05	0.20
	1938	0.13	0.11	0.24	0.22	0.46
	1965	0.05	0.09	0.14	0.19	0.33
	1982	0.08	0.21	0.29	0.48	0.76
Japan	1910	0.15	0.23	0.38	0.16	0.54
	1937	0.19	0.11	0.30	0.61	0.91
	1979	0.67	0.25	0.32	0.55	0.87

Sources and Notes: China – Government of PRC, SSB (1983), Government of PRC, SSB-DSTP (1984). Bank deposits by State and collective enterprises and People's Commune and subordinating units are taken to be "demand deposits," and saving deposits by urban and rural resident households as "saving deposits."
India – Government of India, CSO (1979, 1982).
Taiwan – Mizoguchi (1985) for Colonial Taiwan and Taiwan, Executive Yuan (1983).
Japan – Bank of Japan, SO (1966), SO (1979) and Hitotsubashi University IER (1953).

but the speed of their change was quite high. In Japan, the change after the 1890s was distinguished. The former ratio reached already in 1910 a high plateau level in the international standard. The latter ratio began increasing and continued throughout the reference period. Taiwan's change was remarkable after the 1910s. The rapid financial development in Japan is evidenced from the statistical finding that moneylenders' loan rate and the bank deposit rates, as well as the coefficients of variation of prefectural deposit rates, sharply declined between the 1890s and the 1910s. During this period, a well-coordinated modern banking system was established, thus having a significant effect of unifying the segmented financial markets (Teranishi and Patrick, 1978).

In both these indicators, in particular the M_2/GNP ratio, India and China were lagging behind (China's system of non-cash financial settlement in the state enterprises resulted in differences from India in both the cash/GNP and the demand deposit/GNP ratio, but the aggregate M_1/GNP ratio was not significantly different). The M_2/GNP ratio

TABLE 10.4 Financial development as seen from the farm sector

unit: %

	China (%)	India (%)	Taiwan (%)	Japan (%)
Ratio of total borrowing of the farm households which is supplied from modern financial institutions in a farm borrowing survey data (Ratio from agricultural credit cooperatives)		1951–52: 7.3 (3.1); 1961–62: 18.7 (15.5)	1933: 47.4 (19.3); 1940: 73.1 (23.4)	1888: 7.2 (—); 1911: 35.7 (2.5); 1932: 47.3 (16.0)
Ratio of members' deposits in total funds for lending of agricultural credit cooperatives	1966: —; 1979: —; 1982: 90.5	1950–51: 10.9; 1960–61: 5.3; 1970–71: 4.6	1935: 18.9; 1940: 22.2; 1964: 16.3	1903: 19.4; 1917: 64.9; 1937: 76.3
Ratio of lending (and deposits in the higher level financial institutions) to the members' deposits	1966: —; 1979: 22.0; 1982: 31.1 (77.6)	1950–51: 511.2; 1960–61: 719.4; 1970–71: 832.1	1935: —; 1940: —; 1964: 82.2 (64.4)	1903: 451.0; 1917: 87.8; 1937: 25.3 (75.8)
Ratio of members' deposits to agricultural income of the economy	1966: 8.8; 1979: 16.4; 1982: 20.9	1950–51: neg.; 1960–61: 0.2; 1970–71: 0.4		1903: neg.; 1917: 4.6; 1937: 92.8

Sources: China; SSB (1983), UNESCAP (1984), Lu (1980). India; Hayashi (1975), CSO (1984). Taiwan; Tu (1975). Japan; Teranishi (1982), Bank of Japan, SD (1966)

began rising only after the reference period of this study. In India, this occurred as an effect of a series of nationalizations of private commercial banks (the most drastic one took place in 1969) and. the drive for spreading their branch network in all urban and rural areas, an effort to expand the base for saving mobilization. In China, the rise in the ratio was a result of the economic reform after 1980. There is another difference between India and China: in India the financial assets in the forms of insurance funds, annuities, government bonds, and shares have increased a fair degree – 36 percent of entire portfolio of the households in 1979–80 (Hajeda, 1985). In China, they are very small. This difference comes from the difference in the economic and financial system, rather than that of financial development.

Secondly, the differential degree of financial development in the rural districts between Japan and Taiwan, on the one hand, and China and India, on the other, was more distinctive than the above. In Japan financial development in rural districts was rapid, side by side with the establishment around 1900 of the central and preferential networks of semi-official land-mortgage banks, and in particular of the credit cooperatives. The latter provided a strong financial support to the innovating activities of the medium-sized farmers. In Taiwan, a similar type development was exhibited after the 1910s.

One comment on the comparatively better performance of China in rural financial development than in India, as seen in the deposit – agricultural income ratio of credit cooperatives in table 10.4. Again this seems to have come from the systemic difference. Until the 1970s, the amount of saving deposits were normally planned centrally and allocated to the production teams through different levels of the administrative channel. Thus, a high proportion of mobilized savings were centrally absorbed. The default of the borrowers was correspondingly frequent, and the financial basis of the credit cooperative not necessarily sound (Lu, 1980).

Difference in international environment

In India and China, the historical background of political independence brought about a strong national desire for achieving economic independence as quickly as possible. Thus, both aimed at the creation of a "socialist pattern of the society." In the case of China, the political commitment to the Soviet Bloc resulted in isolation from the West in a Cold War context, with the result that the desire for economic independence became greater. Japan in the Meiji era took for granted the market economy as her economic system. But it was not the one of *laissez-faire*. What is called by W. W. Rostow as "reactive nationalism" brought about the leadership and guidance by government.

Taiwan was made a colony of Japan during 1895–1945. But as was different from Korea, another colony of Japan, where the basic policy of

Japan was largely national-defense-oriented, Japan had clear-cut economic objectives *vis-à-vis* Taiwan. In the beginning, Japan intended to turn Taiwan into the crude-sugar supply base. Since the expanding sugar imports were the main cause of trade deficit at that time, import substitution was attempted. Protective tariffs of various forms were the main instruments, as the production costs of Taiwan sugar were much higher than the international prices. In the early 1920s, another aim was superimposed upon the above: raising rice production for export to Japan. This was decided in response to the Rice Riot of 1918 in Japan, an incident which spread all over Japan as spontaneous protest by the low-income population against a sharp rise in rice prices.

With regards to the initial conditions of post-colonial Taiwan, it is most important to note that with the end of the colonial rule, Taiwan became capable of formulating and implementing economic policy to exert influence upon resource mobilization and allocation for its own interests. Moreover, as a result of intensive agricultural development during the colonial days, the technological and infrastructural bases of agriculture in the 1950s became fairly strong. Also, Taiwan at that time had a fairly diversified manufacturing sector centering on the food and chemical industries. This manufacturing development was induced by the inter-industry linkage effect of the export production of sugar and rice.

DEVELOPMENT MODELS

Turning to causal link 2, at first China and India are discussed together. Here, I wish to pay attention to those common aspects of their initial conditions which were characterized, *structurally*, by low agricultural productivity, though endowed with the initial foundation of modern industry and, *in systemic terms,* by introduction of the economic system and strategy which fit to the nation's desire for rapid economic independence and industrialization and also to the state of the underdeveloped market economy. I consider it pertinent to capture the economic mechanism of these two countries by devising an economic model which reflects these characteristics. What are thus devised are: for China's case, the borrowing (in combination) of a Ricardian Growth Trap model and a Fel'dman growth model under centralized planning (Domar, 1957), and in India's case, the same Ricardian Growth Trap Model and a Mahalanobis economic planning model (1953). The Fel'dman and Mahalanobis models are formally identical.

Ricardian Growth Trap model describes, as is well known, the tendency of the agricultural sector, which is under the grip of the law of diminishing returns, impeding the intended growth of the emerging industry sector and sooner or later bringing the economy into a stationary state. The law of diminishing returns could be overcome by technological progress of a sufficient depth and speed, and this would be promoted by proper reallocation of resources between agriculture and industry. In that event, there arises a possibility in which a balanced growth between the two sectors takes place, with labor and wage goods being transferred from agriculture to industry in sufficient quantities. Professor Lewis's well-known dualistic development model (1954) describes this possibility under the context of the densely populated economy, although the necessity of proper technological progress is not made explicit. This means that the Ricardian model is simply a special case of the Lewis model. Referring to the above special case, however, I avoid using the name of the Lewis model, as I stress the fact that both India and China were, until the early 1980s, never removed from the danger of being caught in this trap. In fact China was caught in it twice in 1959–61 and 1970–1, and in order to get out of it, drastic measures were adopted for the cut in the investment and growth rates and also, in the former case, for sending the inflated portion of urban populance to the rural areas (Ishikawa, 1982). In India, a big drought in 1965 and 1966 acted as a trigger to bring the economy into the trap, leading to a later depression of industrial activities.

However, I have three reservations in borrowing the Fel'dman model. First, while the model assumes the operation of the economy under the planner's sovereignty by means of the centralized, physical plans, there is in fact a wide area in the economy in which economic decisions are privately made and the state can only impose certain constraints upon them, such as the compulsory sale quota issued to the production teams of the People's Communes. Borrowing of the Fel'dman model is relevant only because production and distribution of the basic capital and intermediate goods are centrally controlled, and the direction and the speed of the economy's growth thereby are effectively dictated. Secondly, allocation of the goods by physical directives, after all, should be settled financially. Often, it is even replaced by allocation through the directives indicated in money terms. In particular, in those areas where the centralized allocation is not in operation, monetary allocation performs a single commanding function. Hence, even though physical allocation of the investment goods predetermines the basic direction and speed of the economy's growth, there is indeed a danger that a disturbance coming from the monetary side may impede their realization. The basic means to avoid this disturbance is the financial mobilization of savings to the amount that is equivalent to the monetary value of physically planned investment.

Similar points can be made on the application of Mahalanobis's model to India. In particular, there is a difference between the assumed economic system in the planning model and reality, and this difference is much wider than in the Chinese case. The real Indian system is a mixed system that allows the existence of the market mechanism and even of big private businesses. The reason why centralized allocation of the investment goods is still possible is because: (1) the large state-owned enterprises are in operation in the investment-goods sector, and (2) the establishment of private enterprises, their investment, their import and disposition of basic goods are all regulated under the network of licensing systems. The role of the monetary-side activities, particularly the saving mobilization, is far more important for India than for China. The differences in the performance in land reform and in the type of the organization of the agricultural production and management are also important in the same connection.

As for the development mechanism of prewar Japan, a few studies are available which approximate it by Lewis's dualistic development model (Fei and Ranis, 1964; Ohkawa, 1965; Minami, 1973). I agree with such approximation. Only one comment is made. Namely, that thanks to the favorable initial conditions, Japan's agriculture was successful in continuously providing industry with both "unlimited supplies" of labor and the wage goods to feed them since the early Meiji era up to the 1940s. But as noted above, the Rice Riot of 1918 became a trigger for introducing a policy of "Raising Rice Production" in the two colonies. This incident may be considered as symbolizing the emergence of a Ricardian Growth Trap, insofar as it arose because the growth of agricultural output substantially lagged behind the increase in the demand for it, which came from the growth in industrial production.

However, this Ricardian Growth Trap differed in nature from that which emerged in India and Taiwan in the sense that it occurred as a result of misallocation of resources, rather than for the structural reason. It is essential to note that Japan's agriculture then was already capable of achieving continuous technological progress, but that the government did not realize that the same capability could be materialized through increased public investment to make up for the insufficiency of the agricultural infrastructure. It instead resorted to the Raising Rice Production policy in the colonies. In the 1930s, when this policy achieved success and the much increased amount of rice was supplied to the rice market in Japan, the declining tendency of rice prices due to the World Depression was further intensified.

Colonial Taiwan's economic development mechanism is considered, as far as its structural aspect is concerned, to be approximated by the Vent-for-Surplus model of a variant which takes, as observed earlier, a "backlog" of transplanted modern agricultural technologies as a surplus factor. However, there is yet a systemic aspect of the mechanism which related to the fact that the colonial regime in Taiwan played so important a role in accelerating, constraining or even manipulating the operation of this structural model, and this aspect is yet to be stylized and formulated as a particular colonial development model. In this connection, one comment is in order. While the colonial administration of the Japanese government was often considered in the West as beneficial to Taiwan's development (through institutional reforms, infrastructural investment, measures for technological progress in agriculture, etc.), overall it enforced a policy of colonial development that exploited natural resources. Thus, while the earlier stage of colonial development was characterized by metropolitan capital export including government budget transfer, in the later stage, it was rewarded by huge imports of sugar and rice. The direction of resource allocation was essentially geared to the aim of the metropolitan country.

The post-colonial development model has two features. First, structurally, Lewis's dualistic development model seems now "borrowable," although it should be expanded to capture the activities of the important external sector. The change from the Vent-for-Surplus model was made possible by the substantial expansion of the industrial base after the 1930s. But the "turning point" was yet to come during the reference years. Second, systemically, the model of colonial development was replaced by a model of national economy under a strong state leadership and with a substantially large public sector, although under the market economy regime.

SAVING MOBILIZATION AND REALLOCATION

Discussions on causal link 3 are made on the basis of each country.

China

The development model required that a major part of the economy's saving potential be mobilized into the government sector and then reallocated in the form of the investment goods (i.e. of "transformed" savings) among the sectors, such that the economy's saving potential was increased to the largest possible extent. In this reallocation, attention was also necessary to keep the economy out of the Ricardian Growth Trap in both short and long run. The requirement of such a highly centralized saving mechanism seems to have arisen from two factors: (a) a low per capita GNP and a concomitant low saving potential of the economy, and (b) a low level of market development, in particular a low "financial development." The mechanism may be described by separating three phases:

1 Potential savings existing in each of the different sectors of the economy (two major ones being the farm and the nonfarm sectors) are mobilized and centralized to the government subsector as part of the nonfarm sector, using the following two methods simultaneously.

(a) In each sector, the disposable personal income of the working people is kept at a level that is closer to a subsistence level of the classical sense, by use mainly of the policy instruments for determination of a "wage fund" in the nonfarm sector and of the procurement prices of the major agricultural products in the farm sector.

(b) The income and savings of the respective sectors are transferred among themselves partly through manipulation of the intersectoral commodity terms of trade and partly through taxation and subsidization.

The result of using these methods should be that the relative nonlabor's share of the nonfarm sector's income is increased to the maximum possible extent, and the nonlabor's share in the farm sector is kept at a low level. The nonlabor's share of the nonfarm sector income is easily transferred to the central government under the dominant state enterprise system, either by taxation or by compulsory surrender of profits.

2   When the savings and income thus centralized are not sufficient to finance desired government developmental outlays, the government resorts to "deficit financing," defined as the financing of expenditures by the issuance of new notes on the central bank – The People's Bank of China.

3   While the farm sector is forced to serve for efficient saving mobilization in the above two phases, to avoid the difficulty that the Ricardian Growth Trap model describes, the government reallocates an appropriate share of the centralized saving to the farm sector. Main policy instruments are the government budget allocation. Credit rationing is also used.

The overall performance of saving mobilization and of its concentration into the government through phases 1 and 3 seems to have been a considerable success in terms of the government aim. Table 10.5 shows available estimates on national saving for 1978 and 1981. From this (as well as some other crude estimates), it is observed that the national savings ratio in the 1970s was considerably lower than 37 percent for 1978, but is still as high as somewhat exceeding 30 percent, and that the rate of its concentration to the government of 73 percent of total savings in 1978 typified those in the earlier years.

The details of this success can be described straightforwardly only concerning phase 1. The labor's relative share in the industry sector was internationally very low already in the 1950s, but our estimate indicated that it further declined until the late 1970s, when it turned to rise a little bit.[5] The process of manipulating the commodity terms of trade between agriculture and industry (measured at farmyard) was somewhat involved; hence table 10.6 is shown. It indicates that the commodity terms of trade consistently changed in favor of agriculture, but that as the agricultural labor productivity declined sharply at the post Great Leap disaster (1960–1) and the recovery from it required a long time, the index of improvement in income accrued per head of agricultural labor force did not recover the 1957 level until the mid 1970s. This implies that the manipulation of the commodity terms of trade was made under the constraint that per capita real income of the farm sector should not be diminished. In other words, if the agricultural labor productivity had not declined, the government would have manipulated the commodity terms of trade in favor of the nonfarm sector again under the same constraint.[6]

The importance of phase 2 in achieving success is not very clear. While the net balance of the annual receipt and expenditure of the consolidated state budget indicates only a small margin of deficit or even surplus during the years under study, the real deficit and the concomitant increase in the new note issue are said to have frequently arisen through various routes, e.g. when the government stopped disbursing the budgeted expenditure to the state enterprises, and the state enterprises in turn demanded the People's Bank to extend new credits. How large this hidden deficit financing was is not known. Moreover, while the statistical information on currency in circulation has only recently become available, it is not possible to identify how much of its annual increase was due to the deficit financing. It should also be noted that most of the prices in China were under strict control, so a mere knowledge of the amount would not suffice. We have to know how much of the total currency in circulation represented that part which was required for statisfying the public's preference for cash holdings under various kinds of motives, and how much represented the "forced saving" or involuntary accumulation of unrealized purchasing power. Again this is not possible.

However, as far as I know, no critical inflationary situations have been reported that resulted from deficit financing, except for what occurred in the Great Leap disaster (1959–61). On that occasion, deficit financing "in both 'hidden' and 'open' forms", took place – not only due to excessive capital construction, but also due to the requirement of filling the financial losses of a great number of small enterprises by bank credits. The previously mentioned crop failure that triggered a Ricardian Trap coincided with this event. The amount of currency in circulation sharply increased; the retail prices also sharply rose. In 1961, the inflationary situation finally reached a politically and economically intolerable point (Chen, 1981). The deflationary policy was adopted in the same year, with a drastic reduction in government investment. What happened in the years of Cultural Revolution turmoil we are not told.

In phase 3, the ratio of allocation of the capital construction investment to agriculture and forestry in the reference period was around 10 percent – by no means large. By also considering the following three points, the saving reallocation in this phase may be evaluated as fairly successful: (1) China's government investment in land and water infrastructure is mostly made in such a way as to induce local contribution of labor and other low-opportunity-cost resources quite extensively; (2)

TABLE 10.5   Structures of the sources and uses of savings by sector: China and India

I. China

| | IA. 1983 entire society's gross fixed capital investment | | IB. World Bank estimates on gross domestic saving | |
	Sources (%)	Uses (%)	Sources 1978 (%)	Sources 1981 (%)
Government	45.3	} 69.5	73	49
State enterprises	9.5		} 12	} 22
Collective units	} 40.4	11.4		
Households		19.0	15	29
Foreign savings	4.8			
Total	100.0	100.0	100	100
(% of GDP)		(17.1)[a]	(37)	(29)

II. Gross saving (sources) in India – gross capital formation (uses)

	IIA. 1960–61		IIB. 1970–71		IIC. 1978–79	
	Sources (%)	Uses (%)	Sources (%)	Uses (%)	Sources (%)	Uses (%)
Public sector	19	44	16	37	22	44
Private corporate sector	13	19	9	14	7	11
Household sector	56	37	67	50	74	45
Foreign saving	7 (15)		8 (5)		–3 (–6)	
Total	100	100	100	100	100	100
(% of GDP)		(16.1)		(18.4)		(21.8)

[a] Percent of NNP (inflated from NNMP by 16 percent).

Sources: IA. China — SSB (1984, pp. 299 and 302). Note: 1% of NNP (inflated from NNMP by 16%).
   IB.   The World Bank (1985).
   II.   India, Working Group on Savings (1982). Percent figures of sources are derived by taking the amount of gross capital formation as 100. For foreign saving, the figure in brackets is the figure thus derived. The figure outside the brackets is the residual. This discrepancy arises from the fact that we are not able to use the adjusted figures for errors and omissions in estimation. The base figures are all in current price terms and in three-year moving average.

TABLE 10.6 The terms of trade between the agricultural and non-agricultural sector and the indexes of improvement in income accrued to the unit of agricultural labor force with 1957 = 100: China

	Indexes of commodity terms of trade		Indexes of single factoral terms of trade		Indexes of improvement in income accrued to the unit agricultural labor force
	Indexes of procurement prices of agriculture and farm subsidy prices + Indexes of rural manufactured product prices	Indexes of procurement prices of agriculture and farm subsidy prices + Indexes of ex-factory prices of industrial products	Indexes of agricultural labor productivity	Indexes of single factoral terms of trade for agriculture[a]	
	(1)	(2)	(3)	$(1) \times (3)$ (4)	$(3) \times \frac{2}{3} + (4) \times \frac{1}{3}$[b] (5)
1952	85.0	72.5	107.2	91.1	101.8
1957	100.0	100.0	100.0	100.0	100.0
1961	127.4	132.1	72.1	91.9	78.7
1964	118.2	122.8	84.4	99.8	89.5
1966	130.7	139.0	96.6	126.3	106.5
1977	151.5	173.5	106.1	160.7	124.3
1982	207.8	249.2	127.6	265.2	173.5

[a] These indexes indicate the proportionate changes in the value of non-agricultural output acquired per unit of agricultural labor force by commodity exchange. Formally, it is equivalent to (indexes of commodity terms of trade or agriculture) × (indexes of agricultural labor productivity).
[b] The weights of 1/3 and 2/3 refer to those of the agricultural output which are marketed and self-consumed.
Sources: China — SSB (1983).

the current expenditures for operating expenses of agricultural service organizations (such as "Technique Popularization Stations") and for subsidies for various undertakings carried on by the production teams and brigades (such as construction of water conservancy works, agricultural mechanization and other farming improvements) were larger than the capital construction expenditures; and (3) these current and capital expenditures combined to play a decisive role in realizing a continuously increasing amount of import of agricultural producers' goods in the farm sector, which was the main cause of the steady net inflow of the farm sector in China's ISRF.

India

Due to the similarity of the economic development model to that of China, the task required for the overall saving mechanism also was similar. Namely, its purpose ultimately was to achieve the priority growth of the public-sector-led investment goods industry, considering at the same time the requirement to get out of the difficulty of being caught in the Ricardian Growth Trap. On the other hand, the dissimilarity of the economic system dictated that a reasonably large sphere of activities should be retained for the private sector, in particular for its consumer goods sector, and that in achieving the above task the government was allowed to use only conventional instruments of economic policy after admitting the operation of the market forces as a basic resource allocation principle of the economy. More specifically, in individual economic sectors, such direct measures as manipulation of the nonlabor's relative share was not permissible. Conventional measures of fiscal and monetary policies had to be the major reliance. With respect to the intersectoral resource flows, the room for manipulation of the terms of trade was not large, as the socialization of production and distribution was limited.

Therefore, in the study of the saving mechanism of India, the main interest is in identifying the particular instruments of conventional economic policy chosen and their manner of operation in the context of a low per capita GNP and a low development of the market economy.

The overall performance of saving mobilization and concentration through phases 1 and 2 is partly shown in table 10.5. It indicates that the gross saving/GDP ratio achieved a considerable increase from 12 percent in the late 1950s to 22 percent in the late 1970s. It also indicates that the government sector, while originating only around 20 percent of total savings, ultimately commanded (in gross capital formation) as high as around 40 percent of those, although some part of it came from the foreign saving. Overall, the indicated results were remarkable, though not to the extent of China.

The explanation of the good saving results may be in that the fiscal policy efforts to increase tax revenues, in particular corporate and personal income taxes, were considerable. In the field of monetary policy, the effort to promote the rapid spread of financial intermediaries by the successive nationalization of private commercial banks (previously mentioned) and thereby to increase bank deposits was particularly successful. This, together with the increased activities of non-banking financial intermediaries (such as insurance policies, pensions and provident funds, and other government compulsory deposits), resulted in a significant increase in the financial assets holding in the household sector *vis-à-vis* the physical assets holding (Government at India Planning Commission (PC), Working Group on Saving, 1982). Of this increase, the increase in bank deposit was of course most distinguished – the proportion of it in total financial assets of the household increased from 17 percent in 1955–56 to 50 percent in 1979–80 (Hajela, 1985).

With regard to the concentration of the private sector savings to the government sector, the fiscal policy played an important role. In the past Five-Year Plans, an almost equal amount of money to the government savings could be borrowed from the private sector through non-banking financial intermediaries: 24–34 percent of total amount of government capital formation (PC, 1956, 1957, 1961, 1970). This achievement, though, was made possible on the basis of the previous financial development in this nonbanking sphere.

However, regarding the overall performance of saving mobilization and concentration, there is another aspect which relates to the possible impact of deficit financing, an issue in our phase 2. Shortly before, we have noticed a good performance of concentrating the private sector savings to the government savings through "borrowing". But the process of concentration also comprised that of a deficit financing (similarly defined to that in China), and its weight was fairly substantial. In terms of the proportion in the total public sector plan outlay in each Five-Year Plan (FYP), it was 26.4 percent for the 1FYP (1951–1955/6), 20.6 percent for the 2FYP (1956/7–1960/1), and 13.0 percent for the 3FYP (1961/2–1965/6). As suggested in the continuous rise in the saving ratio of the household sector, the resulting new issues of currency were voluntarily absorbed as additional financial assets; the inflationary pressure was then still mild.

However, with the continuous deficit financing, a critical inflation situation was emerging in 1963–64. Money wages and both consumers' and wholesale prices sharply increased. The government deficit further increased. In 1965 and 1966, the earlier mentioned big crop failure occurred, coinciding with this crisis. Inflationary pressure reached some socially intolerable extent, with the result that in 1967 the Fourth Five-Year Plan was officially suspended and a deflationary policy adopted (PC, 1967). The approximately 10 years that followed are called by Dr. V. V. Bhatt (1970) the years of "inflationary recession." The recession was caused by the government investment cut. Inflation, however, continued as the demand for food grains still exceeded the supply. Government had to continue the policy of restraining the increase in public sector investment. This may imply that the concentration of as much private-sector saving as somewhere around 20 percent of GDP, by means including deficit financing, was excessive and beyond the capacity of the private sector to endure.

The long "inflationary recession" was a phenomenon of prolonged Ricardian Growth Trap. As for the cause of it, suggestions are often made on the insufficiency of the fiscal policy effort to tap the potential tax base in the rural sector connected with the high rental income accrued to the landlords and rich farmers.[7] From a somewhat different angle, a policy negligence of agriculture in favor of industry is also suggested. An example is that in the period before the mid-1960s, the commodity terms of trade (as indicated early) were stable, which was mainly due to the large PL480 grain imports. Other government policies *vis-à-vis* procurement and prices of food grains were just ineffective (Mundle, 1981). In the period thereafter, the terms of trade turned in favor of agriculture. A gradual increase in the government procurement of food grains with more favorable prices played a role in it.

The problem of phase 3 on the saving (investment) reallocation among the sectors is closely related to this issue. While the rates of allocation of fixed capital investment to agriculture in the FYPs were much higher than in China, amounting to 20 to 30 percent, the effect of this government investment to induce local contribution of labor and other low-opportunity-cost resources was negligible (Ishikawa, 1965). This was because the government investment was mostly disbursed for large- and medium-scale, water conservancy projects without depending upon local resources. Even when the small-scale local projects were contemplated, local working peasants were not willing to contribute their labor to them. The ratio of total fixed investment to income in agriculture might thus have been smaller than in China. The fact that the proportion of imports of agricultural producer goods to total agricultural imports was much smaller than in China was likely to reflect this phenomenon.

Japan

Japan's development model requires that the saving mobilization mechanism be such as to assure the emerging modern industry sector to proceed with steady capital accumulation and growth, while receiving from the farm sector both "unlimited supplies" of labor and the wage goods to feed it. On the other hand, the initial conditions as to the level of per capita GNP and of development of the market economy, and the fact that the financial markets achieved significant progress around 1900, imply that in Japan, particularly after 1900, this saving mechanism was likely to have worked fairly well through the market forces and by the economic policies based on it or with much less government intervention than in the previous cases. The focus of the study will thus be on investigation of the extent that this likelihood was in fact realized.

As for the framework of study, it is no longer necessary to follow the three-phased one for China and India, as it fits only to the context where substantial government intervention is necessary to make up for the low saving potentials and the weak market mechanism. Here, it is essential to study the saving and investment processes in both the non-agricultural (industry), and the agricultural sectors and the interaction between them, following the sectoral division of the above development model. In studying this interaction, it is important to remember that, as is different from the case where savings and investment of the entire economy or the single sectors are studied independently, the saving flow (K) should be captured in association with the flows of V_1 and V_2, as these three components of the entire resource (or income and saving) transfer are mutually interdependent.

Let me first look at the overall performance of saving mobilization. It was observed as very good. According to the estimates of Ohkawa's group, the saving and investment ratios in the agricultural sector during 1890–1930 were 12–20 percent and 8–12 percent, respectively, and those in the nonagricultural sector 11–24 percent and 15–27 percent, respectively, implying that the agricultural sector was the saving-excess sector and the nonagricultural sector the investment-excess sector (Mundle and Ohkawa, 1979). Teranishi's estimates (1982) divides the economy into four sectors: agriculture, private nonagriculture, government, and foreign. Interesting observations are that private nonagriculture was also a saving-excess sector and government usually the investment-excess sector; the balance of the foreign sector varied.

With regard to the factors behind the relatively high saving ratios in both the agricultural and nonagricultural sectors, many attempts for explanation exist. Suffice it to take note that in the latter sector, capital accumulation was facilitated both by the low supply price of labor from the former sector and by the technology development of the labor-intensive and technological-knowledge-saving character (Ishikawa, 1967a, chap. 4). In the agricultural sector, due to the increases in both land and labor productivity the nearly sufficient increase in the supply of wage goods was made possible. The supply price of labor to the nonfarm sector was yet relatively stable, because labor migration was almost all that of the "underemployed" family labor, and often on a temporary basis.

A more immediate problem is to explain how the overall resource transfer out of agriculture proceeded systemically, the transfer which contributed to the above saving-investment balance in relevant sectors and which was already statistically observed earlier (tables 10.1 and 10.2, and figures 10.4 and 10.5).

V_1 One dominant component of this "net factor income earned off-farm" account was a labor income from the emigrant or commuting family members working off farm. It is apparent that the ever-increasing amount of this component was a function of the stock of "unlimitedly supplied labor" in the nonagricultural sector, or a result of continuous structural changes and market development. An important component which partly counterveiled this labor income was the payment of land rent to the non-cultivating landlords. The question is whether this component served as an institutional apparatus to drain the agricultural sector of the substantial portion of its income, as was the case in colonial Taiwan which will be examined shortly. The answer however is negative. The landlords in Meiji Japan, as mentioned earlier, were largely the cultivating landlords. In the period during and after World War I, when they transformed into non-cultivating or parasitic land-lords, the labor market already was well developed; hence, the institutional land rent lost its force to dictate the landlords' own share. In fact the disintegration of the cultivating-landlord system itself was a result of emergence of the developed labor market. The permanent agricultural laborers who were the mainstay of labor supply in this system were no longer attached to their landlords.

V_2 The main item of this current transfer account, the direct agricultural taxes, occupied more than 90 percent of the government tax revenue in the early Meiji era, and their amount finally came to equal the direct nonagricultural taxes during and after World War II. This was inevitable, as the financial development was on a low level and hence the urban bases of corporate and personal income taxation were under-developed. It constituted the only case in Japan where government intervention in the resource mobilization was made on a large scale, though in the form of fiscal policy.

K As a somewhat microscopic observation of the fact that net saving outflows from agriculture took place mainly via market forces, it is interesting to note the case of *yoyūkin* (surplus funds) of the rural credit cooperatives flowing out from the agricultural sector. In the early period of development of the credit cooperatives, the habit for saving as deposits had not yet been established. Lending was made mostly from share capital. It was only after 1917 that deposits exceeded lending. But as is shown in table 10.4, deposits continued to increase relative to lending, and in 1932 the former became four times larger than the latter. The *yoyūkin* thus arose, which was either directly or through the Credit Cooperative Associations and the Central Agricultural and Forestry Bank, mostly deposited to the private commercial banks or invested in securities. Why did this happen? Because the rates of interest paid by the credit cooperatives had to be as high as those in postal savings and

commercial banks. Thus, the loan interest rates that the credit cooperatives required their borrowers to pay became too high for the peasants
to borrow from them easily. For the purpose of extending low-interest-
rate loans to the poor peasants, the credit cooperatives had to rely after
the 1920s on the disbursement of the low-interest-rate government loan
funds (Ouchi, 1961). This story clearly shows that at that time the
marginal efficiency of capital was generally lower in agriculture than in
industry and that the net saving flow, in fact, took place in the direction
that the difference in it indicated.

E and M   There were only two cases in which the government policy
was used to influence directly the flow of *E* and *M*. They were the
protectionist policy of rice production initiated in 1904 (the nominal
protection rate was estimated as 20–80 percent during 1904–38
(Anderson, 1983) and the Raising Colonial Rice Production Policy
already referred to. The changes in the intersectoral commodity terms
of trade were also basically the results of working of the market forces
with modifications coming from these two policies.

Taiwan

In the light of the development model of colonial Taiwan, inquiry of the
saving mechanism should be two-dimensional: one relates to the organizational dimension, and the other to the systemic dimension, the model
of which, though, is yet to be formulated. In each dimension the inquiry
should cover the saving and investment processes in the farm, nonfarm
(services) and external sectors as well as their interactions. This
approach is similar to one in the study of the saving mechanism in Japan
in the sense that we are assuming a fair level of initial saving potential
and a fairly developed market economy. This means that the colonial
government could mobilize savings without relying on direct, administrative intervention. In the following, however, I will not go into
all these desirable aspects of study as my inquiry is still preliminary. Instead, I will concentrate on two findings relating to the
domestic resource transfer mechanism and the other to the external
resource transfer mechanism.   •

Domestic mechanism   As is seen from table 10.1 and figure 10.3, the
payment of land rent to non-cultivating landlords contributed most to
the continuously large net resource outflow from the farm sector.
Investigation of this fact leads to a finding that a domestic mechanism
was working in which a large amount of net resource outflow from agriculture took place normally.

1   A customary practice of the landlords' claim to taking about a
half of rice yield as land rent was maintained both in the traditional

and *ponlai* rice production (Ishikawa 1971, p. 42). As there was no significant work opportunity outside agriculture (see the small amount of labor income earned off-farm in Taiwan in 1931–5 in table 10.1), this rate of land rent was unlike that maintained in Japan after World War II.

2   The prices of rice were determined exogenously and at a relatively high level. Namely, the prices of *ponlai* rice in Taiwan, the only variety exported to Japan, were determined as a result of interplay of demand in Japan and supply from Taiwan. The result was the tendency of the prices of *ponlai* rice in Taiwan to change in association with the rice prices determined in Japan. A price difference between the two became narrower as time went on. The prices of native *indica* rice also came to follow the same tendency. Moreover, as the rice prices in Japan were protected, the price level of Taiwan rice, in particular *ponlai* rice, was also significantly higher than that in other Southeast Asian countries (Anderson, 1983).

3   As for sugar cane, the purchase prices were manipulated by a monopsonistic system of the "sugar-cane procurement zones," within each of which local farmers were permitted to sell sugar cane only to a specified sugar-producing company. After the advent of the program for Raising Rice Production in 1920, the sugar companies had to decide the sugar-cane purchase prices in association with the rice prices, such that sugar-cane farmers would not shift their production too much to rice, thereby inflicting raw material shortages upon sugar companies. This implies that the prices of sugar cane also became favorable to the landlords.

4   The innovating activities exhibited by the non-cultivating landlords in the spread of *ponlai* rice were largely stimulated by the thus-formed incentive mechanism. Colonial government strongly supported both these innovating landlords and the incentive mechanism.

5   In Taiwan, the proportion of tenants and half-tenants among the farm households was much higher than in Japan: it was approximately 70 percent in the 1920s and 1930s. When their income accrued from rice production was heavily drained off, the imports of the farm sector became necessarily significantly smaller than the exports.

External mechanism   The finding here, as suggested in table 10.7, is that the colonial development process created a mechanism to bring about a continuous export surplus, after a short period of import excess in the early colonial stage. The import excess of the earlier period is explained by the initial capital exports of the sugar companies as well as by the budget transfer of the metropolitan to the colonial government. The huge export surplus of the later period was somewhat involved. It is true that the colonial government achieved financial self-reliance by 1915, and later even became capable of transferring the surplus back to the metropolitan government. But the explanatory power of it was not large. Meanwhile, long-term capital inflow for export production of sugar and related investment continued and was especially large in the boom years in World War I and a short time afterward. In the 1930s, it appears that the marginal returns to investment in sugar industry declined, while the sugar companies attempted diversification of investments. The export surplus was, in the ultimate analysis, found to be largely financed by the short-term capital outflow. According to Yamamoto (1976), short-term capital outflow came partly from the government cash balance held in the Bank of Japan. Another major source was Taiwan Bank's lending activities in Japan, which became larger than that inside Taiwan and flourished already during the period of World War I (Tu, 1975).

Finally, there is another finding relating to table 10.7, which is that the merchandise trade balance exhibits a strikingly close correspondence with the net resource outflow from the farm sector $(E - M)$ of colonial Taiwan in table 10.1. This is shown in table 10.8, together with the fact that these magnitudes were by no means insignificantly small, relative to the magnitudes of total exports and even to GDI. The question is whether there was an internal mechanism working behind this close correspondence between the two. I will not go into this problem, however. In any case, the above two findings indicate that at least one aspect of the colonial saving mechanism in Taiwan could be stylized as a process in which the landlords received a strong incentive from the high institutionalized rate of land rent, introduced agricultural innovation, and brought out the huge amount of *ponlai* rice and sugar cane directly or indirectly for export to Japan. These surplus products were finally exported to Japan through the mechanism of external capital outflow.

Post-colonial Taiwan was much closer to prewar Japan, both in terms of development stage and the economic development model. And yet, the government seems to have exercised much more direct control in saving mobilization and allocation than was considered reasonable under the similar context. This was because of the fact that Taiwan at this stage was in the recovery process from the wartime difficulties, and also due to the causes relating to the postwar military situation. Keeping these in mind, the saving mechanism in operation is observed to have had fairly distinctive features.

1   The large export surplus of colonial Taiwan was reversed to a large import excess. While imports of machinery and industrial raw materials increased, the exports of sugar, rice and other traditional

TABLE 10.7 Balance of payments of colonial Taiwan

[unit: million yen]

	Merchandise balance	Current account balance	General government transfers (net)	Long-term capital balance	Short-term capital balance	Of which net increase of Taiwan bank's credit in Japan
1896–1903	− 2.3	− 49.5	31.7	27.6	− 9.8	− 2.9
1904–8	− 8.4	− 23.3	12.0	19.9	− 8.6	− 4.6
1909–13	26.6	0.6	41.4	30.8	− 72.8	− 5.9
1914–18	167.3	109.3	5.3	62.8	− 177.4	− 225.5
1919–23	212.7	112.0	–	235.4	− 347.4	− 107.0
1924–28	382.9	166.7	–	196.4	− 363.1	218.9
1929–33	354.7	203.2	− 7.9	40.4	− 235.7	25.7
1934–39	666.0	580.7	− 70.9	12.4	− 522.2	24.2
Accumulated total	1,866.2	1,099.7	11.6	625.7	− 1,737.0	− 77.131

Source: Estimates of Yamamoto (1976).

TABLE 10.8 *Correspondence between the net resource outflow from agriculture (A) and the export surplus of external trade (B): Taiwan*

	A	B	$\dfrac{B}{Exports}$	$\dfrac{Exports}{GDI}$
			[unit: million yen at 1985–87 value; annual average]	
1911–15	50	11	0.10	0.36
1916–20	62	41	0.29	0.42
1921–25	60	60	0.34	0.44
1926–30	59	65	0.26	0.44
1931–35	89	91	0.29	0.45
1936–40	90	90	0.24	0.47
1951–55	113	2	− 0.03	0.09
1956–60	96	2	− 0.02	0.11

Source: T. H. Lee (1971).

exports were stagnating. The resulting large deficit, although supported mostly by U.S. aid (which largely ended in 1965), was a symbol of decolonization. It also provided a stimulus for replacing the earlier import-substitution policy by that of vigorous export expansion in the ensuing years.

2   On the basis of this systemic change the government embarked on deliberate industrialization. The initial capital accumulation required for it was economized as the former Japanese manufacturing enterprises were taken over, after the country's defeat in war, and provided the starting base. The large-size enterprises were transferred to state ownership. In 1954, the proportion of total registered capital of the manufacturing companies which were under state ownership was 50 percent. In the 1953 land reform, the former landlords' lands above three hectares were compulsorily purchased by the state for future redistribution. As a principal means for payment, shares of part of the above state enterprises were transferred. Most of the smaller-scale, ex-Japanese enterprises were thus moved into the private sector.

3   During the period under study, roughly one-half of total gross domestic capital formation took place in the state sector. The proportion of the government savings in the government GDCF was only around 10 percent. The difference was mostly financed by U.S. aid and other foreign savings, and the rest from private savings.

4   The main source of this government saving was sought from agriculture. For this purpose, government took the place of the former non-cultivating landlords as the collector of a substantial portion of total rice output. The proportion was approximately 30 percent during 1951–65. The collection was made by various instruments; most importantly, land taxation and a system of rice-fertilizer barter exchange.

ISRF AND DEVELOPMENT PERFORMANCE

Finally, causal links 4 (on ISRF) and 5 (on development performance) are taken up together. It should be cautioned that the ISRF are not simple quantities, but ones which embody the nature and structure of the overall saving mechanism. Particularly, even the net ISRF of the same value has different functions depending upon whether it results from the operation of the market forces, from the exercise of the conventional economic policies, or from a more direct government intervention. It should also be cautioned that development performance is not what can be evaluated with a uniform measure, such as the growth rate of GNP or of its components. It is an overall result of the working of all causal links up to 4. Particularly, it is evaluated with a criterion or criteria that vary depending upon the characteristics of the development models. I wish to emphasize that, as in the discussions thus far, the evaluation of specific ISRF is often made by a simple contrast of its quantitative aspect to the uniform growth aspect of the development performance. In this section, an alternative and proper contrast between the two links will be presented for each of the four areas. Two additional, methodological remarks are in order:

1   The specific quantitative patterns of ISRF are already summarized for individual areas in the section "statistical studies on the four areas." The factors causing them are also already made fairly clear for Japan and Taiwan, as the study of the saving mechanism for the two areas exactly requires that. Regarding China and India, the saving study covered K and V_2 and the changes in the terms of trade. The explanation should be completed by referring to V_1.

2   The specific criteria with which the development performances of the four areas are assessed are now specified. For China and India, one of the criteria is common: the extent that the Ricardian Growth Trap is avoided and even removed. As another criterion: the two countries commonly set high rates of GNP growth and of transformation, but the requirement is much severer in China. For prewar Japan and postwar Taiwan, at least one criterion is to what extent the

Lewisian dualistic development proceeds steadily. As for colonial Taiwan, one of the criteria is the extent that the growth proceeds along the lines of the Vent-for-Surplus model of the variant that the "surplus" factor is an unused backlog of technological knowledge. There is another one: the degree of achievement is evaluated in terms of the colonial development model discussed above.

The contrast thus obtained is described fairly straightforwardly as follows:

China As a result of direct government intervention in the national saving mechanism with the aim of mobilizing and centralizing the economy's saving potential to the government as much as possible, net saving outflow from agriculture was achieved, though not in a large amount. A large inflow of labor income earned off-farm took place, however, basically as spontaneous activities. The net balance was a considerable amount of resource inflow of agriculture. The development performance may be evaluated as good, if we focus on the fact that the Ricardian Trap was avoided, while a high rate of growth of the economy was achieved, except for a few occasions. From the vantage point of the post-1978 economic situation, however, the performance may be more properly evaluated as not good, because we are now informed of the various cases of improper pricing and product-mix policies prevailing in the period after the mid-1960s which brought about a widespread disincentive effect on production. Therefore, what should be emphasized instead may be the fact that China had not been able to escape from the danger of being caught in the Ricardian Trap until recently. The proper contrast between causal links 3 and 4 may thus be that the development performance was unsatisfactory because the government intervention to take out agricultural saving was excessive, or the net resource inflow was insufficient.

India Despite various measures of the fiscal and monetary policies aimed at mobilizing, centralizing, and reallocating the potential national savings into and through the central government, the effect of tapping the incomes of the wealthier class in the rural sector and of reallocating the centralized funds productively to agriculture was not very marked. As a result, K was perhaps inflow and $E - M$ was outflow for agriculture. Only after 1965, when the terms of trade were made in favor of agriculture, $E - M$ in real prices turned to inflow. These are contrasted to the prolonged Ricardian Growth Trap after the mid-1960s, an unsatisfactory development performance.

Colonial Taiwan A large and continuous net resource outflow from agriculture was realized, largely as a result of the working of an institutionalized mechanism of land-rent payment to the non-cultivating landlords under the aegis of the colonial government. This outflow was also synchronized after the 1910s with the continuous export surplus over imports in the external sector, a reflection of a colonial development of the natural resource exploitation type. The development performance is assessed as satisfactory from either of the two models approximated for colonial Taiwan.

Post-colonial Taiwan   Whereas the income level and the market development stage were already not low, the post-colonial transitional situation required a relatively strong government intervention into the ISRF process. Net resource outflow in all levels of the ISRF measurement resulted. Development performance was good in the sense that the Lewis-type dualistic development proceeded steadily. The association between the net resource outflow and good performance is explainable, however, by the fact that the former was basically made possible by a higher development stage as an initial condition.

Japan   The net ISRF, which is equal to $K + V_1$ and is a net outflow from agriculture, was more importantly the result of the working of market forces in the context of a relatively high development stage particularly after 1900. Hence, it can be contrasted properly to a good development performance along the lines of the Lewis model.

TENTATIVE CONCLUSIONS

In this section, I wish to tentatively conclude the above discussion by returning to the three questions raised in the introduction. With regard to the first two questions, part of the answers are already predicted in the introduction. But the full answers are essentially as follows. As to the first question, the answer is that my policy suggestion about the desirability for the government of India and China to have a deliberate policy to realize a net resource inflow of a farm sector is valid for three reasons: (1) a basic development issue of these countries was to avoid and even remove the danger of being caught into the Ricardian Growth Trap; (2) development of the market economy in the two countries was far from the state, such that the ISRF of a sufficient amount and in an optimal pattern would be realized largely by the market forces, and hence the strong government policy intervention was considered desirable to bring about such a state deliberately; and (3) in both countries, performance of agricultural development in most of the reference period was not satisfactory in solving the above issue in (1). One of the basic causes was that in India, the net ISRF was outflow from the farm sector, as government effort to reverse it was insufficient, while in China it was inflow, but excessively so by the strong government intervention with the result of the peasants losing incentives to increase output.

On the other hand, the same policy suggestion is not relevant to post-colonial Taiwan and Japan, where the development stage in which the Ricardian Trap was a real issue was already over. The market economy there also developed to such an extent that the resource flows between the farm and non-farm sectors took place basically by the market forces. This means that regardless of whether the net ISRF was an outflow or inflow, it broadly reflected the optimal resource allocation. Therefore, the direction and magnitude of net ISRF was no longer the issue of economic development. Colonial Taiwan's ISRF was complicated, as the colonial development contributed in shaping it. But the stage of economic development was much closer to Japan and post-colonial Taiwan, and the colonial government simply utilized such a developed economic mechanism to realize the particular ISRF pattern which was favorable to the metropolitan government. Therefore, here also, the net ISRF was basically not an issue of economic development; it was rather an issue of colonial development.

As to the second question about the relationship between the progress of the economic development stage and the changes in the determinants of ISRF, the answer is made in three steps by focusing attention on the extent of "financial development" as the most essential aspect of the development stage.

1   In the stage when the financial market is undeveloped, there is no intercourse between the area or unit where there is a saving capacity but no investment opportunity and the area or unit where there is no saving capacity but with an investment opportunity. The society's production-possibility frontier is significantly inside the maximum potential production frontier when all the investment opportunities under the given saving capacities are not exploited. As the intercourse begins and expands, the welfare of the populace increases. Finally with the full financial development, the maximum potential production frontier is obtained.

2   In the stage of low financial development, such intercourse is possible only within narrowly segmented markets; therefore, the society's interpersonal, interlocal, and intersectoral saving flows are small and irregular in amount, being motivated by weak market forces and often further conditioned by customary rules. With the progress of financial development, the scale of these saving flows becomes the larger, and the extent that these are motivated by market forces the wider. Therefore, the society tends to come closer to the point of maximum efficiency. For the society with low financial development, only when the government intervention – through the conventional economic policy instruments or through more direct means – supplements the weak market forces, is this point of maximum efficiency likely to be approached.

3   As the intercourse between the farm and the nonfarm sectors is the most important intersectoral relation in the context of economic development, the above statement in (2) should be applicable to this aspect most strongly.

The third question was on the relevancy of these findings to other areas in Asia. The study of this question is essentially the task of a new research project, as the estimates of ISRF or its major components have not yet been available for any countries in Asia other than the above. The identification of initial conditions, economic development models or any other causal link of the analytical history approach is also yet to be made systematically. However, if it is permissible to confine attention to the low-income, primary-export economies and to the behaviors of the net ISRF – not in its totality, but only in its marginal portion – some useful observation may be obtained even at this stage.

To elaborate, the meaning of confining attention to the low-income countries is clear from the above observation that in countries at a fairly developed stage, the operation of the market forces is expected to be such that the direction and size of the net ISRF is no longer a serious development problem. Next, the primary export economies are the type of economies which specialize themselves in the production of a few exportable primary products. In the formation stage of most such economies, the countries were sparcely populated but endowed with rich natural resources that were waiting for exploitation; hence, once the world demand began increasing for the primary products that were producible by exploiting these natural resources, the economies started growing. This is exactly the process which is succinctly summarized in the earlier mentioned Vent-for-Surplus theory, and many of the economies of the Asian countries other than the four covered in the above were formed as such economies by the end of the nineteenth century. Therefore, confining attention to the primary export economies implies that a fairly large number of the countries in South and Southeast Asia are in fact covered.

The point I would like to make now is the likelihood in which the answer to the third question depends (although under the above qualifications, particularly in a marginal sense), upon how the government investment resources derived either directly or indirectly from the primary exports were allocated among the alternative uses. Specifically, it appears that those countries in which in the early postwar years the government resources were mainly allocated into agriculture and agriculture-related infrastructure and services were able in later years to transform their economies relatively smoothly toward diversified export production and even toward early industrialization.

During the 1950s, many of these countries were still in a Vent-for-Surplus stage; hence, taxation of primary exports in various forms occupied a significant proportion of total government revenue: one-half in Iran, one-third in Indonesia, one-third to one-fourth in Burma, Malaya and Sarawak, and one-fifth in North Borneo and Thailand (UN-ECAFE, 1961). In addition, the incidence of other major categories of taxation, the import taxes and excise taxes, was considered largest on the peasant producers. On the basis of the actual experience, the main alternative uses of the government investment funds were indicated as (1) basic infrastructure (such as in transport and electricity) and social services (such as in public health and education), (2) manufacturing and mining, (3) development of the non-food, cash crop sector, and (4) development of the food sector. They were to be classified further according to the size of the establishment, the capital–labor ratio, and the ownership pattern. I have a feeling that with the exception of a few countries, most pursued a step-by-step and pragmatic approach to diversification and industrialization. Typically, alternative export crops developed, as the expansion of transport provided to the peasant producers a far better access to the world market; the governments were active in introducing the Green Revolution, sponsoring R&D activities and devising a package deal to diffuse fertilizer application and other improved methods; and industrialization started with the manufacture of power-tillers, pump-sets and other import-substituted farm machines with labor-using and technology-knowledge-saving techniques.

I wish to stress the remarkable difference of this choice pattern from the choice pattern we frequently are informed of, as exhibited by many contemporary primary export economies in some regions such as Africa, where typically a large amount of the government revenue derived (through the Marketing Board) from the export of the primary products was allocated to the non-agricultural sector to initiate a large number of capital and technology-knowledge-intensive projects for establishing large-scale factories and mines, and ambitious infrastructure and social services with a long gestation period. The traditional export crop sector was stagnating in face of the recent downfall of the commodity prices. The domestic food sector was largely neglected. This was particularly the case in the countries that were endowed with oil resources and that suffered after 1973 from the so-called Oil Syndrome. It seems, therefore, that the policy suggestion made for India and China is at least marginally applicable to the primary export economies in Asia as well.

NOTES

[1] Of the two studies on Japan, Ohkawa group's estimates are based on the most competent utilization of the data from monumental national income estimates of Japan by the author of the estimates himself and his associates. They are considered basic for this comparative study. Teranishi's estimates, based on

an unique study on the financial assets and debts of the farm sector, put almost exclusive emphasis on the resource flow on the capital account (K), hence, Teranishi's estimates on this aspect should also be taken into consideration seriously.

[2] Although the comprehensive statistical assessment of ISRF was not carried out, N. Lardy (1983) and B. Stone (1983) are noted as serious studies on various aspects of the ISRF issue when the statistical information was quite insufficient (see note 7).

[3] In the discussion on the long-run trend of the intersectoral commodity terms of trade in prewar Japan, it is sometimes argued that it was relatively constant. The argument is based on the calculation of the terms of trade index by taking as P_M the indices of producer's prices of mining and manufacturing products (Ohkawa et al., 1967) and as P_E the indices of agricultural product prices at the farm gate. However, the relevant terms of trade index for the purpose of our study should be obtained by evaluating both P_E and P_M at the farm gate. In this study we have taken the terms of trade index calculated in Ohkawa, Shimizu, and Takamatsu (1978), table 10.4. According to Mr. Takamatsu, this index is compiled by taking as P_E the indices of agricultural prices at farm and as P_M the combined indices of the current purchased agricultural input prices, the purchased agricultural investment good prices, and the purchased consumer goods prices. Source materials are Umemura et al. (1966) and Ohkawa and Shinohara (1979).

[4] In a private communication.

[5] The estimates were in reference to the state industrial enterprises under the independent accounting system, and based on SSB (1984), World Bank (1981), and some assumptions of mine. The obtained labor's relative share was 39.4% for 1952, 32.1% for 1957, 21.9% for 1968, 21.6% for 1978 and 25.6% for 1982. The details of the estimates will be published soon.

[6] Lardy (1985) and Stone (1983), on the basis of detailed studies on the prices of chemical fertilizers, agricultural machinery, and other modern inputs in the rural markets, doubt the reliability of the officially compiled intersectoral terms of trade indexes. They suspect that the indexes omit incorporating into computation of P_M the prices of these modern inputs. I myself feel that this and related methodological problems should be investigated more before I can make a judgement of my own. Meanwhile, they also presented a view that the relative prices of the food and other farm products to these modern inputs were extremely unfavorable to agriculture and those in themselves imply that a significant resource extraction was made from agriculture. The view on the unfavorableness to agriculture is based on the international comparison of the relative prices and on the monopolistic pricing by state of the modern inputs. It should be remembered however that: (1) since the early 1970s, the supply of modern inputs of various categories from the small-size local enterprises expanded significantly and most of these enterprises were run at financial loss; (2) the official method of pricing the manufactured goods was changed so as to be based on the average cost of all the state enterprises producing the same products, which fit to the above situation of (1); the previous method of basing on the marginal cost was no longer used; hence, the industrial profits accrued in the large and medium enterprises (in the case of chemical fertilizers, producing either ammonium sulphate or urea) should be used for making up for the losses of the small enterprises (ammonium

bicarbonate); and (3) the valuation of E and M by international prices is not relevant for the purpose of the study on ISRF, unless the difference of domestic and import price of imported modern inputs was pooled with the profits of the large-scale enterprises to make up for the losses of the small enterprises. Again, further investigation seems to be necessary for determining these points.

[7] It is interesting to compare the direct tax–net income ratios in both agriculture and nonagriculture in India with those in Japan. In India, the ratios for 1950–70 were in agriculture 1–2% and in nonagriculture 4–6% (Hajela, 1985), whereas in Japan in 1883–1937 the ratios in agriculture gradually decreased from 20% to 7%, and those in nonagriculture increased only slightly from around 2% to 4% (Teranishi, 1981).

REFERENCES

Anderson, Kym 1983: "Growth of Agricultural Protection in East Asia." *Food Policy,* 8 (4), Nov.

The Bank of Japan, Statistics Department 1966: *Meiji-iko Honpo-Shuyo Keizaitokei* (Hundred-year Statistics of the Japanese Economy), Tokyo.

Baosen, Chen 1981: "Theories and Practices on the Fiscal, Monetary and Material Balances." In Ministry of Finance and others (eds), *Zhongguo Caizheng Wen-ti* (Fiscal Problems of China), Tianjiang: Tianjiang Science and Technology Publication Co.

Bhatt, V. V. 1970: "On Inflation and Its Control." In E. A. G. Robinson, and Michael Kidrom (eds), *Economic Development in South Asia,* London: Macmillan.

Chow, Gregory, C. 1985: *The Chinese Economy.* New York: Harper & Row.

Domar, Evsey 1957: *Essays in the Theory of Econmic Growth.* Oxford: Oxford University Press, chap. 9A, Soviet-model of Growth.

Fei, John C. H. and Ranis, Gustav 1964: *Development of the Labor Surplus Economy: Theory and Policy.* Homewood, Illinois: Richard D. Irwin.

Goldsmith, Raymond W. 1969: *Financial Structure and Development.* New Haven: Yale University Press.

Government of India, Central Statistical Organization 1983: *Statistical Abstract of India 1983.* New Delhi.

Government of India, Planning Commission 1956: *Second Five Year Plan.* New Delhi.

Government of India, Planning Commission 1957: *Review of the First Five Year Plan.* New Delhi.

Government of India, Planning Commission 1961: *Third Five Year Plan.* New Delhi.

Government of India, Planning Commission 1967: *The Third Plan: Progress Report 1963–65.* Delhi.

Government of India, Planning Commission 1970: *Fourth Five Year Plan 1969–4.* New Delhi.

Government of India, Workings Group on Savings 1982: "Capital Formation and Saving in India, 1950–51 to 1979–80." Calcutta: Mimeo.

Government of People's Republic of China, State Statistical Bureau 1983. *Zhongguo Tongji Nian Jian 1984* (Chinese Statistical Year Book 1984). Beijing: Chinese Statistical Publication Co.

Government of People's Republic of China, State Statistical Bureau, Department of Statistics on Trade and Prices 1984: *Zhongguo Maoi Wujia Tongji Zuliao* (Materials of Statistics on Trade and Prices in China, 1952–1983). Beijing: Chinese Statistical Publication Co.

Gurley, John G. and Shaw, E. S. 1967: "Financial Structure and Economic Development." *Economic Development in Cultural Change,* 15 (3), April.

Hajela, J. K. 1985: *Monetary and Fiscal Policies in India's Economic Development.* Allahabad: Chugh Publications.

Hayami, Y. and Ruttan, V. W. 1985: *Agricultural Development: An International Perspective.* Baltimore: Johns Hopkins University Press.

Hitotsubashi University, Institute of Economic Research 1953: *Keizai Kaisetsu Tokei* (Annotated Economic Statistics). Tokyo: Iwanami Co.

Ishikawa, Shigeru 1963: "Nihon no Keiken wa Tekiyo Kano Ka (Is Japanese Experience Applicable)." *Keizai Kenkyu* (Economic Research), 14(2), April.

Ishikawa, Shigeru 1965: *National Income and Capital Formation in Mainland China — An Examination of Official Statistics.* Tokyo: The Institute of Asian Economic Affairs.

Ishikawa, Shigeru 1967a: *Economic Development in Asian Perspective.* Tokyo: Kinokuniya Co.

Ishikawa, Shigeru 1967b: "Resource Flow Between Agriculture and Industry — The Chinese Experience." *The Developing Economies,* 5 (1), March.

Ishikawa, Shigeru 1971: "Changes in Taiwan's Agriculture in the Period of Japanese Rule." In Miyohei Shinohara and Shigeru Ishikawa (eds), *Taiwan no Keizaiseicho* (Economic Growth of Taiwan), Tokyo: Institute of Economic Development.

Ishikawa, Shigeru 1981: *Essays on Technology, Employment and Institutions in Economic Development, Comparative Asian Experience.* Tokyo: Kinokuniya Co.

Ishikawa, Shigeru 1982: "Labor Absorption in Asian Agriculture." In Shigeru Ishikawa, S. Yamada and S. Ilirashima, *Labor Absorption and Growth in Agriculture — China and Japan,* Bangkok: ILO-ARTEP.

Kuo, Shirley W.; Ranis, Gustav; and Fei, John C. H. 1981: *The Taiwan Success Story, Rapid Growth with Improved Distribution in the Republic of China 1952–1979.* Boulder, Colorado: Westview Press.

Kuo, Shirley W. 1982: *The Taiwan Economy in Transition.* Boulder, Colorado: Westview Press.

Lardy, Nicholas 1983: *Agriculture in China's Modern Economic Development.* Cambridge: Cambridge University Press.

Lee, Teng-hiu 1971: *Intersectoral Capital Flows in the Economic Development of Taiwan, 1895–1960.* Ithaca, N.V.: Cornell University Press.

Lewis, W. A. 1954: "Economic Development with Unlimited Supplies of Labor." *Manchester School,* May.

Lu Jienxiang 1980: *Xin-Zhongguo Xinyung Hezou Fazhan Jianshi* (Brief History of Development of Credit Cooperatives in New China). Beijing: Agricultural Publicating Co.

Mahalanobis, P. C. 1953: "Some Observations on the Process of Growth of National Income." *Sankhyā,* vol. 12, part 4.

Minami, R. 1973: *The Turning Point in Economic Development: Japan's Experience*. Tokyo: Kinokuniya.

Mizoguchi, Toshiyuki 1985: "'Kyu Nihon-Teikoku' no Keizai-kozo – Kokumin-Keizai Keisan niyoru Bunseki (Economic Structure of 'Former Japan Empire' — Analysis through National Accounting)." Discussion Paper Series No. 129, The Institute of Economic Research, Tokyo: Hitotsubashi University.

Mody, Ashok; Mundle, Sudipto; and Raj, K. N. 1985: "Resource Flows from Agriculture: Japan and India." In Kazushi Ohkawa and Gustav Ranis (eds), *Japan and the Developing Countries: A Comparative Analysis*, Oxford: Basil Blackwell.

Mundle, Sudipto 1981: *Surplus Flows and Growth Imbalances: The Inter-Sectoral Flow of Real Resources in India: 1951–1971*. New Delhi: Allied Publishers Private Ltd.

Mundle, Sudipto and Ohkawa, Kazushi 1979: "Agricultural Surplus Flow in Japan 1888–1937." *The Developing Economies*, 17, Sept.

Musgrave, Richard A. 1969: *Fiscal Systems*. New Haven: Yale University Press.

Myint, H. 1958: "The 'Classical Theory' of International Trade and the Under-Developed Countries." *Economic Journal*, 68, June.

Myint, H. 1972: *Southeast Asia's Economy: Development Policies in the 1970s* (A Study Sponsored by the Asian Development Bank). London: Penguin Books.

Ohkawa, Kazushi 1965: "Agriculture and the Turning Points in Economic Growth." *The Developing Economies*, 3 (4), Dec.

Ohkawa, Kazushi, et al. 1967: *Estimates of Long-Term Economic Statistics of Japan Since 1868: 8 Prices*. Tokyo: Toyo Keizai Shrimposha.

Ohkawa, Kazuishi; Shimizu, Yutaka; and Takamatsu, Nobukiyo 1978: "Agricultural Surplus in an Overall Performance of Savings-Investment." In *Papers and Proceedings of the Conference on Japan's Historical Development Experience and the Contemporary Developing Countries: Issues for Comparative Analysis, February 13–16, 1978,* Tokyo: International Development Center of Japan.

Ohkawa, Kazushi and Shinohara, M. 1979: *Patterns of Japanese Economic Development, Quantitative Appraisal*. New Haven: Yale University Press.

Ouchi, Tsutomu 1961: *Nippon Nogyoron* (On Japan's Agriculture, revised). Tokyo: Iwanami, Co.

Stone, Bruce 1983: "Long-term Intersectoral Resource Flows among Countries Undergoing Technical Transformation of Agriculture: with Special Reference to the People's Republic of China." Paper prepared for the 31st International Congress of Human Science in Asia and North Africa, Sept. 1–3.

Teranishi, Juro and Patrick, Hagh 1978: "The Establishment and Early Development of Banking in Japan: Phases and Politics Prior to World War I." In *Papers and Proceedings of the Conference on Japan's Historical Development Experience and the Contemporary Developing Countries: Issues for Comparative Analysis, February 13–16, 1978,* Tokyo: International Development Center of Japan.

Teranishi, Juro 1982: *Nippon no Keizai-Hatten to Kinyū* (Economic Development of Japan and Finance). Tokyo: Iqanami Co.

Tu, Zhaoyan 1975: *Nihon Teikoku-Shugi Kano Taiwan* (Taiwan under the Imperialist Rule of Japan). Tokyo: University of Tokyo Press.

Umemura, Mataji et al. 1966: *Estimates of Long-Term Economic Statistics of Japan Since 1868: 9 Agriculture and Forestry.* Tokyo: Toyo Keizai Shimposha.

UN-ECAFE 1961: *Economic Survey for Asia and Far East 1961.* Bangkok.

UN-ESCAP 1984: *Agricultural Credit and Banking System in China.* Bangkok.

Wang, Yang-jiao et al. 1984: *Hubei Liutong y Jihua Guanli Sangao Zuliao,* (Reference Materials of Money Circulation and its Planning Management). Beijing: Central Broadcasting and Television University Press.

The World Bank 1985: *China: Long-Term Development Issues and Operations.* Baltimore: Johns Hopkins University Press.

Yamamoto, Yūzo 1976: "Balance of Payments in Taiwan and Korea under the Japanese Rule." In Majaji Umemura, H. Shimbo, S. Nishikawa, and Y. Hayami (eds), *Nippon-Keizai no Hatten — Kindai kara Kindai e* (Development of Japanese Economy — from Modern to Contemporary Times). Tokyo: Nippon-Keizai Shinbunsha.

Comments on
"Patterns and Processes of Intersectoral Resource Flows: Comparison of Cases in Asia"

HLA MYINT

Professor Ishikawa's paper is concerned with a comparative analysis of the patterns of resource flows into or out of the agricultural sector in four Asian countries – Taiwan, China, India, and Japan – during selected periods. It is interesting to start by comparing it with chapter 4 of his book, *Economic Development in Asian Perspective* (1967, Tokyo: Kinokuniya). In that book, he proved the systematic exposition of the conceptual framework for analyzing intersectoral resource flows which is employed in this paper. He also dealt with the same four Asian countries; in the present paper the reference dates are changed to take account of the more recently available statistical studies. But the aim of his two studies is different.

In his 1967 book, Ishikawa was concerned with a critique of the fashionable view of that time that, in order to promote economic development, the underdeveloped countries should extract resources from the agricultural sector to finance domestic industrialization, and that the Japanese experience during the Meiji period provided historical support for such a policy. He pointed out that the historical evidence for a net resource outflow of the agricultural sector during the Meiji period was indecisive and that even if that were true, it was not an appropriate example for the postwar Asian countries to follow. He showed that the level of agricultural productivity in the early Meiji period was already high because of the basic agricultural investments carried out during the preceding Tokugawa period, and that for the other Asian countries which had not yet completed this basic agricultural investment, the government "must be unhesitatingly prepared" to allocate more resources for agricultural investment, particularly in irrigation. He explained in convincing detail why a precise and sophisticated control over water supply would be required to take advantage of the more productive agricultural technology, based on high-yielding seeds and intensive fertilizer application. Thus he advocated a policy of a net injection of resources into the agricultural sector combined with an appropriate choice of technology in "the basic investments and bolder choice of organization in the farm sector" (*op. cit.* especially pp. 181, 319–21 and 347).

In the present paper, Ishikawa is not explicitly concerned with policy questions; his focus is on positive analysis. He believes that "Economic development of a country or a group of countries can be captured, in terms of analytical history, by identifying a particular economic model" which is formulated on the basis of three factors: (1) the stage of economic development, (2) the pattern of resource endowments, and (3) economic strategy and policies pursued. His comparative analysis of intersector resource flows is directed towards the search for a theory of economic development in which the study of the saving ratio may recover its central place.

Table 10.2 of the paper shows a great diversity in the patterns of intersectoral resource flows. Thus we have Taiwan with heavy net outflows of resources from the agricultural sector: 24% of agricultural income during the period 1931–35 and 10% of agricultural income during the period 1956–60. Next we have China with a net inflow of resources into the agricultural sector: 3% of agricultural income in 1966 and 15% in 1980. Thirdly, we have India with a net outflow of resources from the agricultural sector: 10% of agricultural income in 1960–61 and 5% in 1968–69. Finally, we have Japan with a net outflow of resources from the agricultural sector: 10% of agricultural income during 1908–12 and 9% during 1933–37. Table 10.1, however, shows that for the different period of 1918–22, there are two conflicting views about whether there has been a net outflow and a net inflow of resources into the Japanese agricultural sector.

But what are the effects of these different patterns of resource flows on the growth of agricultural output? Does a net outflow of resources from the agricultural sector retard the growth rate of agricultural production and vice versa?

As far as I can make out, there seems to be no simple or obvious relationship between the pattern of resource flow and the rate of growth in agricultural production in the four cases. Thus, Taiwan shows a very rapid rate of growth in agricultural production despite a heavy net outflow of resources from the agricultural sector: 4% a year during the 1923–37 period and 4.4% a year during the 1954–68 period. China shows a rapid rate of agricultural growth together with a heavy net inflow of resources: 3.4% a year during the 1952–80 period. India shows a moderate rate of agricultural growth, 1.9% a year during the 1960–81 period, with a sizeable net outflow of resources from the agricultural sector. Japan's agricultural growth rate was 2% a year during the 1900–20 period.[1]

What then are we to make of this bewildering diversity in the patterns of resource flows and agricultural growth? I would argue that in order to understand the different outcomes, it is necessary to conduct a post-mortem analysis of how productively or otherwise the resources allocated through the intersectoral flows have been used, and that this in turn requires an appraisal of the economic policies which have been applied in the different countries. Ishikawa, of course, appreciates the need to look at the economic policies in addition to the other factors, such as the stage of economic development and factor endowments. But I cannot help feeling that in contrast to his 1967 book, policy considerations have been pushed into the background in his present paper. The reason seems to be partly because he does not like to go over the old ground already extensively covered in his book and partly because he wishes to apply the development models, such as, the "Vent-for-Surplus" model and the "Lewis model" to the different stages of development and the factor endowments in his four countries. My own feeling is that the application of these development models should not be allowed to obscure the policy conditions built into these models.

Both the "Vent-for-Surplus" and the "Lewis" models postulate the pre-existence of underutilized *supplies* of resources in some form or another. They need the introduction of some demand mechanism activated by appropriate policies to put the models into operation. In the Vent-for-Surplus model, the required policy, of course, is the free trade policy of "opening up" a traditional peasant economy to international trade. This connects the potential surplus productive capacity within the country with the world market demand for exports and provides the peasants with the economic incentives to import a wide variety of consumers' goods. Two striking features may be noted: (1) The Vent-for-Surplus type of export expansion is "self-financing" and does not require any substantial savings or inflow of foreign investment. This is so because peasants can clear more land and carry out export production in their "spare time" using their surplus labour while being maintained by their subsistence output.[2] (2) Exports can expand on the basis of unchanged traditional agricultural techniques, simply by bringing in more land under cultivation. This means that while there are general improvements in transport and communications, law and order, and other institutional changes which accompany the extension of the exchange economy, there need not be any special policies to raise agricultural productivity.

Professor Ishikawa is aware of the second aspect of the model when he tries to apply it to Taiwan, not only its earlier colonial period but also to its later period during the 1920s and 1930s when the Japanese colonial administration was introducing new high-yielding varieties of rice. Thus he carefully explains that he is extending the model to include the assimilation of "technical backlogs." But I think that in order to provide a clearer explanation of why Taiwan managed to expand her agricultural production so rapidly despite the heavy net outflow of resources from the agricultural sector during the period, it would still be necessary to consider the role of government policies which raised agricultural productivity sufficiently rapidly to leave some economic incentives for the farmers to expand production, despite the squeeze on their incomes. Ishikawa mentioned the Japanese government policies of subsidizing irrigation projects and introducing improved varieties of rice only in passing presumably because he has already dealt with these policies in his book. I, however, believe that the role of the policies needs to be brought to the forefront of the picture because they laid the foundation of Taiwan's rapid agricultural growth of the post-war period 1950–60 which again enabled her to expand her agricultural production rapidly, despite a heavy net outflow of resources from the agricultural sector.

Similarly, I think that it is necessary to take explicit account of the economic policies required to work the "Lewis model". Thus, in order to apply this model it is not sufficient merely to appeal to the existence of an "unlimited supply of labor". For instance, the reason why the model cannot be applied, say to Bangladesh, but can be applied to Japan and Taiwan is that (apart from the improvements in agricultural productivity) these two latter countries have been successful in pursuing economic policies which have progressively raised labor productivity in the manufacturing sector. Given this, Japan and Taiwan can continue with rapid economic growth despite rising wages and an upward sloping labor supply curve. Without this key condition to activate the model, the mere existence of unlimited supplies of labor can do nothing to promote economic growth in Bangladesh. The examples of the successful countries such as Taiwan, Korea, Hong Kong and Singapore, however, bring out the fact that the economic policies required to raise labor productivity in the manufacturing sector may not be the protectionist policies which Lewis originally suggested but the export expansion policies pushing home the comparative advantage provided by an abundant labor supply.

To sum up: I agree with Professor Ishikawa about the need to have *ex ante* theories of economic development. But statistical studies of the intersectoral resource flows are by their nature *ex post*. Thus in order to go from the *ex post* and to the *ex ante* analysis, it is necessary to introduce a post-mortem appraisal of how far the policies pursued by the governments in the different cases have affected the productivity of the resources allocated through the intersectoral resource flows. This, however, means concentrating on the factors which affect the *productivity* of the resources rather than on the supplies of resources which are captured by the intersectoral flows. Thus, I am not convinced that we should try to restore the study of the saving ratio to the central place in development theory.

NOTES

[1] I have taken the figures for the growth rates in agricultural production from the following sources:

E. Thornbeck 1979: In W. W. Galerson (ed.), *Economic Growth and Structural Change in Taiwan,* Ithaca, N.Y. Cornell University Press, chap. 2.

S. Ishikawa 1983: "China's Economic Growth since 1949 — An Assessment", *The China Quarterly,* June.

The World Development Report 1983: The World Bank.

and Y. Hayami and V. W. Ruttan 1985: *Agricultural Development,* 2nd ed., Baltimore: John Hopkins University Press, p. 167.

[2] In fact, peasant export economies such as Burma, Thailand, and Ghana show export surpluses right from the start of the "opening up" process without having gone through an initial phase of import surplus. Thus the foreign trading companies in the foreign export-import concerns can remit trading profits without any substantial long-term foreign investment but also without reducing the peasants' economic incentives to expand exports. See H. Myint (1956): "The Gains from International Trade and the Backward Countries", *Review of Economic Studies,* 22 (2).

PART III

Crucial Issues, Sectors, and Markets

11

On Investing in Specialized Human Capital to Attain Increasing Returns

THEODORE W. SCHULTZ

Allyn Young began his classic paper, "Increasing Returns and Economic Progress"[1] with these words, "My subject may appear alarmingly formidable, but I did not intend it to be so." My subject may seem no less formidable. To attain and then to gain from increasing returns by allocating resources for this purpose suggests that it is a pursuit beyond the capacity of proper economics.

The idea of increasing returns has not fared well in current growth economics, although it played a considerable role during earlier periods in the thinking of economists. Presently the analytical core of economics belongs to diminishing returns embedded in equilibrium. Surely no economist wants "to go back to a state of innocence before diminishing returns..."[2] But it seems as if we have become locked into diminishing returns in existing states of equilibrium. Thus, we forgo having a growth theory to analyze classes of changes that give rise to increasing returns. Allyn Young's paper should have sprung this lock, and it could have opened economics so that economists could pursue increasing returns. It should have made room for economic growth events that result in increases in output that exceed the increases in inputs, includ-

I am indebted for the criticism and suggestions I received from Zvi Griliches on what I left out on the Residual Issue; from James Heckman for his critical assessment of parts of the evidence I had used; from Robert Lucas noting his results hold even under constant returns; and from Sherwin Rosen, a memo of suggestion which is a gem. George Tolley alerted me to studies of the externalities in cities; and, Jacob Frenkel on international trade studies. T. Paul Schultz called attention to Schumpeter on disequilibria and to my having omitted the limitations of specialization. Richard Barichello provided several helpful suggestions. I am indebted to George Stigler for his comments and for restraint in using his economic razor. John Letiche with good grace helped me in clarifying various issues and alerted me to the extensive growing literature on related issues in international economics (see footnote 36).

ing the gains derived from "Adam Smith's famous theorem that the division of labor depends on the extent of the market."[3] One wonders why economists have not pursued Young's approach. It could be that he turned economists off by asserting, "I suspect, indeed, that the apparatus which economists have built...may stand in the way of a clear view of the more general or elementary aspects of the phenomena of increasing returns...."[4]

It may be elementary but it is often overlooked that increasing return activities do not exist in the axiomatic core of general equilibrium theory, whereas each and every increasing returns event implies that there is a disequilibrium. When such a disequilibrium occurs, there is an opportunity to gain from a reallocation of resources. The human agent who sees such an opportunity and who acts to take advantage of it is an entrepreneur.

Two serious flaws of growth economics are the result of the omission of the properties of the disequilibria that occur during the growth process and the omission of the economic value of the contributions that entrepreneurs make as they deal with these disequilibria. To explain the occurrence of observable economic disequilibria during the growth process is a much neglected part of economics. Schumpeter's approach to economic development is a notable exception.[5] His theory is based on changes in economic conditions that originate from within the economic system. These changes occur as a consequence of what a special set of entrepreneurs do when acting within that system. Schumpeter's entrepreneurs are innovators who create particular economic changes.

I begin with particular pertinent ideas of economists before economic growth models were invented. Some of the early ideas about economic progress have a comprehensiveness that has been lost in the highly specialized parts of today's economics. I then turn to the economic measurements that have all but eliminated the *residual* but in doing so have concealed most of the evidence pertaining to the economics of increasing returns. Lastly, I consider more fully particular aspects of increasing returns with special reference to specialization and human capital.

IDEAS BEFORE GROWTH THEORY

1 Above all there is the magnificent idea pertaining to the division of labor, its origin and its income-producing capacity. The economic importance of the division of labor is presently underrated. It holds the key to specialization, to investment in specialized human capital, and to classes of increasing returns.

2 The early idea about the substance and scope of diminishing returns was far from clear. It was restricted to land, whereas it is applicable to

all factors of production. The rational producer cannot and does not try to avoid diminishing returns; he does not try to grow (Abba Lerner's phrase) "...the world's food in a flower pot."[6] Ricardo's concept based on "the original and indestructable powers of the soil," is a burden in comprehending the increases in the productivity of agricultural land over time.

The early economists observed that agriculture is not only land-specific but that land is location-specific and that nature is niggardly. Their assessment of the then state of knowledge pertaining to agricultural production was, in large measure, correct. They could not have anticipated the development of various substitutes for farm land that have become available since then.

The limits of land productivity, which did in fact seriously limit the economic possibilities of increasing the production of food in England at that period of history, became an essential part of Malthus's theory of population. Thus, it may be said that this particular dated version of temporal "diminishing returns" placed an indelible mark on the history of economic thought.

Lest we forget, distinguished early economists were also bent on land reform. Smith, Ricardo, and Hume viewed agriculture as an unprogressive sector. Hume accused farm people of having a predisposition to indolence. His defamation of them is terse: "A habit of indolence naturally prevails. The greater part of the land lies uncultivated. What is cultivated, yields not its utmost for want of skill and assiduity in the farmers."[7] Smith and Ricardo saw manufacturing and commerce as progressive, whereas agriculture was the sinecure of an unprogressive landed aristocracy. Notwithstanding the notable increases in agricultural production during the period from the first edition of Marshall's *Principles* (1890) to the eighth edition (1920), the preface to the eighth edition indicates that Marshall had not freed himself from Ricardo's static situation assumption and logic with its unique scarcity of land as a factor of production despite changes in economic conditions.[8] There is then a backward jump to a *growth model* with no land in Harrod's *Dynamic Economics.*[9]

The belief that there is a specific *law of diminishing returns* that holds everywhere over time in agriculture is still held by the followers of the Club of Rome. As I have noted elsewhere, that no less an economist than Colin Clark who does not truck with the Club of Rome, no longer ago than 1941, came to the conclusion that the world was in for a dramatic rise in the prices of primary products; namely, by 1960 "...the terms of trade of primary produce will improve by as much as 90 percent from the average of 1925–34."[10] (To speak of such a violent relative increase in these prices as an "improvement" is a neat twist.) His projection went off in the wrong direction. What went wrong? It was not his population variable that did it. The upsurge in population that occurred was larger than he had assumed. So, too, was the rate of increase in industrialization. Clark simply assumed no relaxation o diminishing returns from land, which turned out to be wrong. Could i be that the less agricultural land the better? – to wit Hong Kong and Singapore! Mark Twain would have enjoyed this approach to econo mics.

Neither Clark's Ricardian land, nor Harrod's no-land economi growth model is acceptable. Instead, there are compelling reasons and strong empirical evidence that support the "The Declining Economi Importance of Agricultural Land."[11]

The basic point is that agriculture is not immune to changes i economic conditions that give rise to increasing returns. Consider the Green Revolution in wheat in India: it began in 1966 – production tha year was 11 million tons; by 1984, India's wheat production has increased to 46 million tons. While we await a theory of economi growth to rationalize this extraordinary production event, commor sense suffices to alert one to look for increasing returns in agriculture especially in view of what happened in the Punjab, where the returns to land, fertilizer, equipment, labor, and to the enterpreneurship of farmer all increased.

3   What the early English economists observed were the increases i production by various manufacturing industries in England. They attri buted a part of the additional production to increasing returns. The favorable changes in economic conditions in their day came to be known as the Industrial Revolution. As an economic process it had much in common with what is now referred to as the Green Revolutior in agriculture.

Critics of the early versions of increasing returns argued that the simplistic notion of "improvements" did not suffice to explain such returns. Later, the critics used theory to show the monopoly effects o increasing returns. It became more telling. It implied that increasing returns are incompatible with competition. Therefore, monopoly would prevail. Since monopoly was in fact not pervasive, increasing returns were not pervasive.

Marshall's view of the tendencies to increasing returns with which he concludes Book IV are: (a) Increasing returns from scale effects are either *external* or *internal*; (b) "...the part nature plays in productior shows a tendency to diminishing returns, the part which man plays shows a tendency to increasing returns." Man's part in agriculture con forms to the law of increasing returns (Book VI, chapter X, section 8) and (c) "The *law of increasing return* may be worded thus: an increase o labour and capital leads generally to improved organization, which increases the efficiency of the work of labour and capital." In essence "Increasing Return is a relation between a quantity of effort and sacri fice on the one hand, and a quantity of product on the other."

Marshall's stress on the economic importance of the health, vigor, and the acquired abilities of people foreshadows what we now treat as human capital and so does his assessment of knowledge: "Knowledge is our most powerful engine of production... . The distinction between public and private property in knowledge...is of great and growing importance: in some respects of more importance than that between public and private property in material things."[12]

From Irving Fisher, a great economist, a son of Yale, we have an all-inclusive concept of capital which includes human capital and which in turn includes specialized human capital, an important source of increasing returns.[13]

ENTER ECONOMIC MEASUREMENT

Early economists were not inundated with statistics. They were spared the burden of statistical proof. They relied on history and on personal observations. Now we place our trust in hard data provided they are sanctioned by theory.

A long list of competent studies sponsored by the National Bureau of Economic Research devoted to measurement – brought to a head by Abramovitz[14] drawing on the work of Stigler, Kuznets, Kendrick, Fabricant,[15] Moore, Rees, Long, and still others – reported large gains over time from total factor productivity which became known as The Residual and as The Measure of Our Ignorance. To dispel this state of ignorance some economists were sure that the basic facts were in error. Others relabeled "...these changes as Technical Progress or Advance in Knowledge..." and thus, left the problem of explaining growth in total output unsolved.[16]

It is instructive to recall the search for explanations and the ideas that were advanced for the increases in measured output that exceeded the increases in measured inputs. Among the many solutions for this puzzle of the Residual, one looks in vain for references to increasing returns. No Smith, no Marshall, no Allyn Young. The idea of increasing returns was no longer kosher.

Studies by Denison and those by Jorgenson–Griliches loomed large in this search. In the process they clarified and improved the basic data. Denison's approach is decidedly different from that of Jorgenson–Griliches. They disagreed head-on in a series of polemic publications which dealt with their differences on measurements and on explanations. As economic literature, these papers are major contributions.[17] According to Denison, a substantial part of the postwar growth in national output was due to an increase in productivity; according to Jorgenson–Griliches, almost all of the increase was due to an increase in facto inputs."[18]

In my early efforts to make room in economics for human capital took advantage of Fisher's all-inclusive concept of capital. In principle my approach in making my first estimates of "Capital Formation b Education,"[19] was akin to that of Jorgenson–Griliches. In retrospect i was simplistic of me to have published estimates of stocks of reproduc ible tangible capital, of educational capital in the labor force, includin on-the-job training capital, for 1929 and 1957, in the United States.[20] I took a lot of on-the-job experience on my part to learn that the simplify ing assumption that capital is homogeneous is a disaster for capita theory,[21] and the assumption that the heterogeneity of various forms o measured capital as economic conditions change can be transforme for any given date into a homogeneous stock of capital, is subject t serious doubts.

Capital is two-faced, and what these two faces tell us about economi growth, which is a dynamic process, are, as a rule, inconsistent stories. I must be so, because the cost story is a tale about sunk investments, an the other story pertains to the discounted value of the stream of service that such capital renders, which changes with the shifting sands c growth. But worse still is the capital homogeneity assumption under lying the aggregation of capital in growth models. The dynamics o economic growth is afloat on capital inequalities because of the differ ences in the rates of return when disequilibria prevail, whether the capi tal aggregation is in terms of factor costs or in terms of the discounte value of the lifetime services of its many parts. Nor would a catalog of a existing growth models prove that these inequalities are equalities. Bu why try to square the circle? If we were unable to observe these inequal ities, we would have to invent them – because they are the mainsprin of economic growth, because they are the incentives to invest in growtl Thus, one of the essential parts of economic growth is concealed b such aggregation.[22]

The measurements of Jorgenson–Griliches are an important achieve ment; nevertheless, their estimates do not reckon the differences i marginal productivities and in rates of return as these change over tim Thus the differences in the incentives during each of the dated years t invest in the formation of capital are blunted, if not concealed, in th aggregation process. One must look elsewhere for evidence pertainin to increases in productivity associated with increasing returns events.

3   As I ponder Denison's 1985 update, *Trends in American Economi Growth, 1929–82*,[23] I find his changes in the labor component quit similar to that of Jorgenson–Griliches in terms of reasons that accoun for the magnitude of the changes over time. It is difficult to compare th two approaches on capital. Denison reports no change in land as a input, which is not land as I know it.

Denison's "output per unit of input results" seem plausible in view of his accounting of the factor inputs. Among his 12 explanations for the changes in the measured output per unit of input, there are several that open the analytical door a good bit to get at the origins of the rates of return associated with increasing returns. He states that his scale effects gave rise to opportunities for greater specialization. On this issue I am attracted to Denison's approach, but no supporting evidence is reported.

4   The difficult measurement problems stressed in the preceding section, including estimates of the effects of scale, education, and disequilibria, are identified and dealt with by Griliches in his agricultural productivity studies. Three of his key papers on these issues are cited below.[24,25,26] Most of his results appear in "Research Expenditures, Education, and the Aggregate Agricultural Production Function."[24] Griliches notes that had he "assumed equilibrium and constant returns to scale, it would have begged some of the most important questions we are interested in" (note 25, p. 421). For the purpose at hand, in explaining "cross-sectional differences in output per man, of the two variables, wage rates and education, the latter is the 'stronger' one and 'survives' the introduction of other variables whereas wage rates do not" (note 25, p. 425; see also note 26.) He found substantial economies of scale in agriculture. His results confirm the existences of disequilibria, and the observed behavior reflects the producers' actions to reduce them. In the case of fertilizer, the value of the marginal product exceeded the fertilizer price by a ratio between 3 and 5. Faced with this large disequilibrium, farmers increased their application of fertilizer at a rate of over 7.4 percent per year. This equilibrium gap (VMP/factor price) declined from about 5 in 1949 to 2.7 in 1959 (note 24, p. 968). There was still a substantial disequilibrium at the end of this period.

INCREASING RETURNS, SPECIALIZATION AND HUMAN CAPITAL

1   The idea of increasing returns has become a spoiler at this high table of theory. It conjures up the ideological issues of the value and distribution of *the surplus* and of the *unearned profits* in a capitalist economy. It is also bent on spoiling a part of the usefulness of the axiomatic core of economic equilibrium. But for all that actual, observable, increasing returns appear to improve the economic lot of man.

It is helpful to think of each increasing returns occurrence as an economic event. Most increasing returns are small, micro events, as in the case of a farmer's increase in corn yields made possible by hybrid seed. Such micro events can, as a rule, be identified and measured, and their economic effects are in general ascertainable. But when increasing returns are attributed to large macro events, for example, to the Industrial Revolution, the measurement of the inputs and outputs and their precise effects on productivity is exceedingly difficult to do.

Increasing returns are transitory events. They have a short lifespan that is clearly observable where these events are in the small and occur under open-market competition. When an increasing returns event occurs, there is information that it is worthwhile to reallocate resources. Human agents, acting as entrepreneurs, respond to the expected profits to be had, and their actions account for the transitory nature of these events.

It is hard to think of nature as a substantial source of increasing returns. They are, for all practical and analytical purposes, consequences of the activities of man. They may have their origin either within or outside of the economic system. Those that originate from within would be included in Schumpeter's Theory of Economic Development.

How frequently do increasing returns events occur? Do particular events of this type spawn a series of related events? Does the economy have a built-in capacity to create them? In large measure these questions reach beyond the scope of this essay.

The linkages of increasing returns to specialized human capital via specialization will be considered following a few comments on specialization.

2   We have a myopic view of specialization. We do not reckon the vast extent of the specialization that has occurred over time. For industry, we know about the pin factory. For agriculture, we blithely assume that there is nothing comparable to a pin factory. In international trade, however, specialization has long been a part of trade theory and its applications.

Agriculture is not immune to specialization and to returns from specialized human capital. Today's modern farmer is no Crusoe. The Corn Belt farm family no longer produces eggs, milk, vegetables, and fruit for home consumption. Such food items are purchased. So is the electricity, gas for fuel, telephone service, water not infrequently piped in from off farm sources and paid for. Corn farmers no longer produce their own seed corn. They buy hybrid seed appropriate to their area. Production expenses consist mainly of inputs produced by industry. The production of pigs has become specialized into: (1) producing breeding stock, (2) farrowing and through weaning, (3) producing feeder pigs, and lastly (4) finishing their growth into hogs to suit the market. Yet the myth persists that there is virtually no specialized human capital within agriculture.

It behooves us to keep in mind Marshall's dictum that "Knowledge is the Most Powerful Engine of Production." Is it true? In agriculture it is true – the costs and returns from agricultural research tell us so. Studies of the economic value of agricultural research began to flourish following Zvi Griliches's classic Ph.D. dissertation on hybrid corn, its research costs, and social returns. We now know that the rates of return to expenditures on organized agricultural research in general, since about 1930, have been much higher than the going normal rates of returns on physical capital investments.

What is noteworthy is that agricultural scientists, by virtue of their acquired professional skills, are specialized in human capital. Furthermore, specialization abounds in modern agriculture. Scale effects on returns are well known. The contributions of human capital to increases in farm and farm household productivity are receiving increasing attention. An important factor in the economic success of agricultural research is the specialized human capital of agricultural scientists.

Finis Welch has shown that the value of farmers' education in production is high as agricultural modernization occurs.[27] Welch succeeded in separating the *work* effect from the *allocative* effect of education. The favorable returns to the schooling and higher education of farmers are, in large measure, the result of the allocative effects of education. This acquired allocative ability functions as a specialized form of human capital.

Specialization abounds in our cities and factories, in commerce, manufacturing and in light and heavy industries. But what about the professions? Since economists are not averse to being thought of as one of the knowledge-producing professions, I turn to the production and distribution of knowledge in the United States based on the authority of Fritz Machlup. His 1962 book is a rich vein of information on the vast extent of the specialization that prevails.[28] The last book from Machlup's fertile mind is on the economics of information and human capital within the core of economics.[29] The extent and complexity of the knowledge producing professions bespeak human capital specialization and it accounts in good measure for much of their productivity.

Specialization, however, has its limits. It, too, is subject to diminishing returns. When it is carried too far, there would be losses from the consequences of overspecialization. Not to be concealed is the fact that economists are also vulnerable to overspecialization in what they do. An economist who specializes on what farmers do, fails to comprehend the economics of agriculture as an integral part of the economy. Hayek could say with good grace, "Nobody can be a great economist who is only an economist," and he added, "An economist who is only an economist is likely to be a nuisance if not a positive danger."

3 I now turn to a brief search for economic thinking and for additional evidence to assess the hypothesis which implies that specialized human capital is an important source of increasing return events. We shall not belabor the vast amount of evidence bearing on the performance of entrepreneurs that reveals the rate at which the gains from increasing returns events are realized.

The trade effects of human capital on the composition of the goods that are traded could account for the so-called Leontief paradox, which asserts that contrary to trade theory, capital-rich countries export labor-intensive goods. We now know that the labor services entering into such goods are human-capital-intensive. A capital-rich country exports the services of specialized human capital.

In his *Treatise on the Family*, Becker extends his analysis of the division of labor within the household to that which occurs in international trade. Members of the household specialize their investments and time; "moreover, with constant or increasing returns to scale, *all* members of efficient households must be completely specialized."[30] So, too, the fundamental source of much of the gain from trade is from the advantage of specialized investment and the division of labor. Viner and other trade economists featured and understood the economic reasons why similar countries gained from trade, namely, the gains are a consequence of investments specializing in particular types of human and physical capital and products that utilize such capital intensively.

In a recent paper, Becker returns to his argument that increasing returns from specialized human capital is a strong force creating a division of labor in the allocation of time and investments in human capital between married men and married women.[31]

The economics of two-way trade in similar products between similar countries has been further explored by Daniel Gros.[32] He also argues that increasing returns to scale made possible by specific human capital specialization explains this class of trade. The evidence in support of his argument is as yet sparse.

Rosen came to the issues at hand in his "Substitutions and Division of Labor,"[33] then came his "Specialization and Human Capital," with the following telling argument.

> Incentives for specialization, trade, and the production of comparative advantage through investment are shown to arise from increasing returns to utilization of human capital. Indivisibilities imply fixed-cost elements of investment that are independent of subsequent utilization. Hence, the rate of return is increasing in utilization and is maximized by utilizing specialized skills as intensively as possible. Identically endowed individuals have incentives to specialize their investments in skills and trade with each other for this reason, even if production technology exhibits constant returns to scale. The enormous productivity and complexity of modern economies are in good measure attributable to specialization.[34]

Lucas in his Marshall Lectures, "On The Mechanics of Economic Development,"[35] focuses on the interaction of physical and human capital accumulation and on systems that admit specialized human capital. I shall cite a few clues to his approach. "'Human knowledge' is just human, not Japanese, or Chinese or Korean,…differences in 'technology' across countries…are not…about 'knowledge' in general but about the knowledge of particular people." Knowledge is a form of human capital and human capital is an engine of growth. Lucas assigns a central role to his concept of the *external effects* of human capital. These effects spill over from one person to another, people at each skill level are more productive in high human capital environments, and human capital enhances the productivity of both labor and physical capital. Where Lucas refers to "human capital accumulation as a *social* activity, involving *groups* of people, in a way that has no counterpart in the accumulation of physical capital," it should be restricted to that part of human capital which gives rise to the external effects. In this context, the capacity of human capital as an engine of growth is determined by the returns attributed to the external effects of human capital.

A country's human capital at any given date is an important economic fact in analyzing the production possibilities of the country. The productivity value of this human capital "endowment" depends in large part on its composition in relation to the market opportunities for the services of each part of the composition. What matters in this context is the heterogeneity of human capital. In labor economics, the distinction between general human capital and firm-specific human capital of workers is useful analytically. The concept of specialized human capital encompasses a large number of forms of human capital that pertain to increasing returns events.

Is it possible to anticipate particular forms of specialized human capital that have a high probability of generating increasing return opportunities which would warrant investment in them? It is my contention that it can be done and that it is being done.

In large measure, expenditures on research and development (R&D) qualify. Broadly defined, R&D are major sources of technical advances that originate out of basic and applied research which entail specialized human capital. Thus R&D scientists create new and better techniques for production, the applications of which give rise to increasing return events. Consider organized agricultural research throughout the world. It has become a sizeable subsector of the economy, with annual expenditures equivalent to about 8 billion 1985 U.S. dollars. Then take a close micro look at the acquired scientific ability of a top flight geneticist who devotes his research to increasing the productivity of plants (crops). He is an important cog in the organized agricultural research wheel that has increased greatly the food-producing capacity of agriculture. The prospects are that this important source of gains in agricultural productivity is still far from having been exhausted. Thus, continuing and also increasing investments in this class of specialized human capital is warranted.

Another class of investment in specialized human capital that results in increasing returns over the life span of human beings is exemplified by investment in primary schooling. What is at stake is the acquired ability to have mastered a language sufficiently to *read* efficiently and to *write* with competence. Here, too, marked advances have been achieved in many low-income countries since World War II, measured by the increases in primary schooling. There is a large body of evidence which shows that in countries where agriculture is being modernized, the rate of returns to primary schooling of farmers is high. There continues to be a vast underinvestment in such schools, viewed here as specialized human capital. The high rate of returns to it is a clue that it is a source of increasing returns at this juncture of economic growth.

I have argued that specialized human capital is an important source of increasing returns, and growth theory that excludes the formation of such human capital is far from adequate. Growth theory also excludes the contributions of entrepreneurs to growth. Appreciating the interdependence of these two phenomena is crucial, both for the advance of growth theory and for the explanation of growth experience. On various important issues pertaining to economic progress, early economists had comprehensive insights that growth theory has omitted. Smith's division of labor made possible by specialization constrained by the extent of the market, is a fundamental insight. So are Marshall's tendencies to increasing returns. What is hard to explain is the long silence on the part of economists following Young's classic paper. During the era of the puzzle of the Residual, economic measurement research was unencumbered by Smith, or Marshall, or Young. The search was not for evidence on increasing returns.

There are now indications that specialization, human capital and growth are on the research agenda of a number of economists.[36] Our myopic view of specialization is being corrected by appropriate lenses. Investigations are now at hand and under way that show that specialization, specialized human capital, increasing returns, and growth go hand in hand.

NOTES

[1] Allyn A. Young, 1928: "Increasing Returns and Economic Progress," *The Economic Journal*, Dec., 527–42.

[2] This phrase is from Hicks, 1965: *Capital and Growth*, Oxford: Oxford University Press, p. 134.

[3] Young, op. cit., p. 529.

[4] Young, op. cit., p. 527.

[5] Joseph A. Schumpeter, 1949: *The Theory of Economic Development*, Cambridge, Mass.: Harvard University Press. Also, 1942: *Capitalism, Socialism, and Democracy*, New York: Harper and Brothers, chap. 12.

[6] Abba Lerner, 1941: *The Economics of Control*, New York: Macmillan and Co., p. 161.

[7] David Hume, 1955: *Writing on Economics*, Eugene Rotwein (ed.), Madison: University of Wisconsin Press, p. 10. I am indebted to Nathan Rosenberg on this point.

[8] Alfred Marshall, 1960: *Principles of Economics*, London: Macmillan and Co. In the preface of the eighth edition, dated October 1920, xv–xvi, the following paragraph appears:

There have been stages in social history in which the special features of the income yielded by the ownership of land have dominated human relations: and perhaps they may again assert a pre-eminence. But in the present age, the opening out of new countries, aided by low transport charges on land and sea, has almost suspended the tendency to Diminishing Return, in that sense in which the term was used by Malthus and Ricardo, when the English labourers' wages were often less than the price of half a bushel of good wheat. And yet, if the growth of population should continue for very long even at a quarter of its present rate, the aggregate rental values of land for all its uses (assumed to be as free as now from restraint by public authority) may again exceed the aggregate of incomes derived from all other forms of material property; even though that may then embody twenty times as much labour as now.

[9] R. F. Harrod, 1948: *Towards a Dynamic Economics*, London: Macmillan and Co., p. 20.

[10] Colin Clark, 1953: *The Economics of 1960*, London: Macmillan and Co., p. 52. The "introduction" is dated May 5, 1941.

[11] T. W. Schultz, 1951: "The Declining Economic Importance of Agricultural Land," *Economic Journal*, 61 (Dec.), 725–40.

[12] Marshall, op. cit., book 4, "The Agents of Production," chap. 1, pp. 138 and 139.

[13] Irving Fisher, 1906: *The Nature of Capital and Income*, New York and London: Macmillan and Co.

[14] Moses Abramovitz, 1956: "Resonance and Output Trends in the United States Since 1890," *Occasional paper 52*, New York: National Bureau of Economic Research, 23 pages.

[15] Solomon Fabricant, 1959: "Basic Facts on Productivity Change," *Occasional Paper 63*, New York: National Bureau of Economic Research, 49 pages.

[16] D. W. Jorgenson and Z. Griliches, 1967: "The Explanation of Productivity Change," *The Review of Economic Studies*, July, 249–83.

[17] Five of the principal publications on these issues appear in U.S. Department of Commerce publication Survey of Current Business, 1972: *The Measurement of Productivity*, part 2, 52(5), 1–111. It is also available as Reprint 244 of the Brookings Institution, Washington, DC.

[18] U.S. Department of Commerce, ibid., p. 1.

[19] Theodore W. Schultz, 1960: "Capital Formation by Education," *Journal of Political Economy*, 68 (Dec.) 571–83.

[20] Theodore W. Schultz, 1962: "Reflections on Investment in Man," *Journal of Political Economy* Supplement, 70 (Oct.), 1–8.

[21] John Hicks, 1965: *Capital and Growth*, Oxford: Oxford University Press, p. 35.

[22] Theodore W. Schultz, 1972: "Human Capital: Policy Issues and Research Opportunities," in *Human Resources*, New York: National Bureau of Economic Research, 1–84.

[23] Edward F. Denison, *Trends in American Economic Growth, 1929–82*, Washington, DC: The Brookings Institution, table 8–1, p. 111.

[24] Zvi Griliches, 1964: "Research Expenditures, Education, and the Aggregate Agricultural Production Function," *The American Economic Review*, Dec., 961–74.

[25] Zvi Griliches, 1963: "Specification and Estimation of Agricultural Production Functions," *Journal of Farm Economics*, May.

[26] Zvi Griliches, 1963: "The Sources of Measured Productivity Growth: United States Agriculture, 1940–60," *Journal of Political Economy*, Aug., 331–46.

[27] Finis Welch, "Education in Production," *Journal of Political Economy*, 78, 1970, 35–59.

[28] Fritz Machlup, 1962: *The Production and Distribution of Knowledge in the United States*, Princeton, NJ: Princeton University Press, pp. xix and 416; 1980: *Knowledge and Knowledge Production*, Princeton, NJ: Princeton University Press, pp. xxix and 272; 1982: *The Branches of Learning*, Princeton, NJ: Princeton University Press, pp. xii and 205.

[29] Fritz Machlup, 1984: *The Economics of Information and Human Capital* Princeton, NJ: Princeton University Press, pp. xvi and 644, foreword, and introduction.

[30] Gary S. Becker, 1981: *A Treatise on the Family*, Cambridge, Mass. and London: Harvard University Press, 20–21.

[31] Gary S. Becker, 1985: "Human Capital, Effort, and the Sexual Division of Labor," *Journal of Labor Economics*, 3(1), 533–58.

[32] Daniel Gros, 1984: "Increasing Returns and Human Capital in International Trade," Ph.D. Dissertation, Universtiy of Chicago, 1984.

[33] Sherwin Rosen, 1976: *Economica*, 45(1), 861–8.

[34] Sherwin Rosen, 1983: *Journal of Labor Economics*, 1, 43–9.

[35] Robert E. Lucas, Jr., 1985: "On the Mechanics of Economic Development," *Marshall Lecture*, Cambridge University, May. I am dependent on a draft dated March 1985.

[36] Paul Romer, 1983: "Dynamic Competitive Equilibria With Externalities, Increasing Returns and Unbounded Growth," Ph.D. Dissertation, University of Chicago. For the extensive, growing literature on these issues in international economics, see the references cited in Elhanan Helpman and Paul R. Krugman, 1985: *Market Structure and Foreign Trade: Increasing Returns, Imperfect Competition, and the International Economy*, Mass.: MIT Press; and Avinash Dixit, "Strategic Aspects of Trade Policy, paper delivered at the Fifth World Congress of the Econometric Society, Sept. 1985 (forthcoming).; and, R. W. Jones and P. B. Kenen (eds), 1984: *Handbook of International Economics*, Amsterdam: North-Holland Publishing Co.

Comments on
"On Investing in Specialized Human Capital to Attain Increasing Returns"

MARK ROSENZWEIG

This is a vintage T. W. Schultz paper. It prods us, provocatively, to reorient our thinking, in this case about the processes of economic growth. It is argued that we need to understand better the causes and consequences of periods of increasing returns, i.e., growth in output that exceeds growth in total inputs, if we are to better understand economic development and growth. We must turn away, in part, from our preoccupation with diminishing returns.

One source of increasing returns is, of course, technical change. But another, based on Adam Smith's "theorem" about the division of labor being limited by the extent of the market, is emphasized by Schultz: The basic idea is: (1) There are fixed costs or indivisibilities to investing in specialized knowledge. The returns to such knowledge are thus higher the more such knowledge can be utilized, the larger the market for the services from such knowledge. Growth in exchange opportunities, therefore, expands the scope for specialized human capital investment and allows the exploitation of the increasing returns from indivisibilities. Specialization, market expansion, and increasing returns go hand in hand.

The second major point of the paper is that in situations of increasing returns there are disequilibria, that is, arbitrage opportunities arise. Understanding the behavior of the agents – entrepreneurs – who exploit those opportunities arising from increasing returns is thus a critical part of our understanding of the development process.

The third point is that, (1) given the existence of disequilibria, whatever their sources, and (2) given that human capital is not homogeneous, but differentiated, there are great dangers to aggregating human capital, since the flows of services and rates of return from each type of human capital at any given moment may be quite different. It is not sufficient to say that human capital is an important source of development; the composition of capital matters, too (just as it does for physical capital).

The paper goes on to trace the origins of the idea of increasing returns resulting from human capital specialization in the work of Adam Smith, Alfred Marshall, and Allyn Young as well as in the writing of Schultz's contemporaneous colleagues, Rosen, Becker, and Lucas. The later posits in his recent Marshall Lectures that there are positive externalities associated with human capital investment, the return to an individual's human capital being higher the higher the overall level of human capital in the economy. This is less clearly an example of returns to scale.

The hypothesis linking specialized human capital and increasing returns is an attractive one. First, it provides a building block linking economic growth with qualitative economic development. It does this in two ways. It says that as markets "develop" and expand, as exchange opportunities increase, there will be a tendency for increased human capital specialization. Associated with these two qualitative developments will be growth over and above that due to the standard gains from trade arising from comparative advantage. Moreover, the hypothesis implies that the speed with which the gains are realized will depend on the behavior of entrepreneurs, the agility with which human capital investment resources are rechannelled to specific activities.

An intuitively appealing idea is not necessarily true, of course. What is the evidence for it? How can it be tested? At one level, the idea is not inconsistent with the broad empirical regularities – high-income, high-productivity societies are characterized by reasonably well-integrated markets and by human capital specialization and diversity in all sectors, inclusive of agriculture. Does this mean, however, that economies which invest resources in expanding market opportunities will enter a regime of increasing returns via specialization? This, I think, is the critical question, on which there is little evidence. Indeed, the difficulties of disentangling technical change effects from scale economies in growth accounting exercises are well known.

Evidence is cited that human capital plays an important role in facilitating the exploitation of the gains arising from situations of increasing returns. As cited in the paper, the quantitative studies by Welch and Griliches provide good examples of the returns to human capital in disequilibria. But the sources of disequilibria in these studies based on the U.S. agricultural sector are not necessarily, or likely, the result of the returns from increasing specialization, unless it is thought that all technical change – new ideas – can be attributed to human capital specialization alone.

Let me now attempt to apply the reasoning of the paper to analyze two phenomena in which fixed costs, human capital, specialization and scale economies are linked. First, consider the "green revolution" in India. If that "revolution" is characterized by the initiation of a continuous flow of new technologies, and if there are fixed costs in learning about and adopting the new opportunities, then we would expect that farmers with the largest scale of operations would reap the highest returns to such investments. The new, steady-state dynamic equilibrium would be characterized by farmers with (1) larger operational holdings and (2) higher mean schooling levels compared to the former equilibrium, as farmers with landholdings below some threshold level would find it unprofitable to invest in the new technologies, and would be less productive than larger farmers. The indivisibilities associated with investments in knowledge and the value of knowledge in adapting efficiently to change, two of the central ideas of the paper, thus have implications for the distributional consequences of technical change. Indeed, studies have shown, including work of my own, that Indian farmers with large landholdings and with more schooling were the first to adopt the new high-yielding grain varieties. There was also heavier investment in schooling in areas where the gains from the new technology could be profitably exploited. Of course, these phenomena may have been the result of other factors, inclusive of credit market constraints.

A set of ideas is particularly valuable if it sheds light on a new area of research. I know that T. W. Schultz will agree with me that economics could profitably be applied to the study of language. Language is a form of specialized human capital. However, superficially it would appear that it is an exception to the theory that human capital diversity is associated with or a part of economic growth and development; with the exceptions of countries such as Canada in which governments purposely subsidize the maintenance of language diversity, we generally see a diminution of language diversity with development. Is this a contradiction to the theory? No. Indeed, because we can identify readily different language groups (as opposed to other forms of specialized human capital), we can use language to directly test Smith's proposition about the extent of the market influencing specialized human capital investments, given fixed costs arising from indivisibilities.

Language, besides being a form of specialized human capital, is a medium of exchange. Like currency, it facilitates transactions. The demand for a specific language (the return to investment in it) is thus higher (a) the greater the number of potential transactions requiring it and (b) the higher the gains from such transactions. Thus, we learn Yiddish to better appreciate the writings of Isaac Bashevis Singer; we learn Russian to acquire information about the potentially useful theorems of an obscure Russian mathematician. But we learn the "native" language if we work or live in an area in which most of the population speaks that language. In work I have been engaged in on the foreign-born in the United States in 1900 and 1980 with Guillermina Jasso, we obtained a number of findings consistent with the market scope/scale economies notion: (1) In both 1900 and 1980, a foreign-born person was less likely to learn English the higher the number of persons in his/her local area speaking his/her language, i.e., the proportion of transactions requiring English (market scope) was smaller and thus the returns to investment in English lower; (2) those males who knew less English (treated as an endogneous variable) earned lower wages, but the penalty was smaller the higher the number of persons speaking his language in the local area; and (3) foreign-born males with poor or no English skills were less mobile than other foreign-born males. Their "market" was limited. Investments in a *common* language may therefore decrease the costs of exchange, enlarge the extent of the market, and induce an increase in human capital specialization with a concomitant rise in incomes.

Finally, we often hear complaints about "overspecialization." Everyone knows of scholarly meetings in which the terminology (language?) would not be comprehensible to outsiders. Are there *diminishing returns* to specialization? Have we come full circle? Perhaps not; these difficulties would suggest that there are disequilibrium returns to investing in the specialized human capital devoted to the translation and integration of the ideas that arise from the technically sophisticated specialists into a holistic theory. Perhaps that entrepreneurial role could be played by institutions such as the Yale Economic Growth Center in future years. The field of economic development may then itself enter into a period of increasing returns.

12

The Relationships Between Trade, Employment, and Development

ANNE O. KRUEGER

Of the various subspecialities that comprise the academic field of development economics those of trade and development, on one hand, and of labor markets and development, on the other hand, are probably the two most emotive. Trade issues, ranging all the way from empirical assertions about the terms of trade to policy issues such as the straw man of "import substitution versus export promotion" (when, in fact, the real question is what impact alternative policies have on the efficiency of both), have been extensively and hotly debated. No less contentious were earlier assertions with respect to "disguised unemployment" and the nature of labor markets in developing countries.

In both of these fields, knowledge has evolved remarkably rapidly, and lengthy surveys have been and can be written on each (see Krueger, 1984, and Spraos, 1980, on trade policy issues; and Squire, 1981, and Binswanger and Rosenzweig, 1984, on labor markets). However, until recently, the question of the relationship between trade and employment was at least as much neglected as the two individual fields were researched. In part, this was because an improved understanding both of labor markets and of the implications of alternative trade strategies was required before questions about the relationship could be meaningfully addressed. In part, too, the relative neglect of questions concerning the relationship between trade and employment emanated from the very different focuses of the two subfields, and hence, the reluctance of scholars in each specialty to trespass on the other field.

In this essay, an effort is made to set forth what has been learned about the relationship between trade and employment in the development process and to indicate areas where future research is likely to

I am indebted to Eric Manes and Susan Hume for valuable assistance with the empirical work reported upon in section 3, and to participants in the fall Growth Center symposium for helpful comments.

contribute significantly to knowledge. To do so requires first a brief review of some of the important aspects of the evolution of thought with respect to trade and labor markets separately. Thereafter, attention turns to what (little) is known, or thought to be known, about the relationship between trade and employment. A final section then sets forth areas in which future research is needed.

TRADE AND DEVELOPMENT

As is well known, early thought on development tended to equate "industrialization" with development, and then to focus on the role that international trade might play in industrialization. The key question, clearly, was the type of trade regime that would be most conducive to industrialization.

At least two strands of thought led many development economists to advocate protection. The first was based on the premise that developed countries had such a head start (due, perhaps, to infant-industry reasons) that "industrialization" would not proceed at a satisfactory rate in the absence of protection. The second was based on the belief that developing countries' comparative advantage lay in highly specialized, primary commodity lines, that an open trade regime, therefore, would result in each country's continuing specialization in a few primary commodities, and that the demand for these commodities was both price and income inelastic. That being the case, it seemed self-evident that developing countries could not hope to attain rates of growth above the world average through maintaining their specialization; the income elasticity of demand for importable goods would exceed unity, and hence the relative price of importables could be expected to rise.

"Import substitution" then seemed to be the logical solution: protecting domestic infant industries would encourage them to become "leading growth" sectors and simultaneously their growth would satisfy upward shifts in demand for importables as incomes rose, thereby simultaneously removing pressures that would otherwise arise on the balance of payment.

A first point to note is that, in this view of appropriate trade policies for development, there would be little or no direct linkage between trade and employment.[1] Protection, by its nature, would cut off the domestic economy from the international marketplace, and issues pertaining to employment, therefore, could be addressed in the context of a relatively closed-economy model. Hence, early concerns with trade strategies were of a kind that provided an analytical separation between trade and employment. With hindsight, this is especially surprising in light of the Heckscher–Ohlin model of international trade, which essentially posits a very strong link between employment and comparative advantage (see third section).

The "import-substitution, elasticity-pessimism" view of the role of trade in development was virtually universal in the 1950s. Practice went even further than theory, however. Most developing countries experienced a marked deterioration in their terms of trade at the end of the Korean War commodities boom, and imposed or tightened import restrictions sharply in response. The resulting level of protection to domestic industry was probably far greater than might have been decided upon, had the policy objective remained solely that of fostering domestic industrial development. In many, if not most, developing countries, the extremes to which the trade regime went were far beyond what had originally been intended and imposed significant economic losses upon entire economies. It took some time, however, for the consequences of these policies to play out, and yet further time for them to be recognized.

The first departure from the import-substitution, elasticity-pessimism view of trade policy and its role came with the recognition of two related realities. First, the gains from trade were simply too great to be passed up. Secondly, "foreign exchange shortage" rapidly became a virtually independent constraint to growth in the context of trade and payments regimes employing exchange control, import licensing, and usually prohibitive protection to import-competing industries. Gradually, too, the failure of exports to grow even as much as expected and losses of shares in a rapidly expanding international economy served to highlight the fact that exchange rate overvaluation and protection both discriminated against exports, and that a negative supply response was significantly larger and more quickly forthcoming than had been anticipated.

For present purposes, two other negative consequences of industrialization behind high protective walls may be mentioned. One was the fact that the growth of industry, which was supposed to be a leading growth sector, was not accompanied by significant growth of employment. As noted first by Prebisch (1964), then by Baer and Herve (1966), Morawetz (1974), and others, industrial growth was accompanied by very little employment growth, and the capital intensity of industry rose quickly.

Although it was not recognized at the time, this failure of import substitution to be accompanied by rapid employment growth was part of a negative side of the link between trade and employment, to which attention will return in the third section. The other related negative consequence was the rapid increase in observed incremental capital–output ratios (ICORs) over time. While rising ICORs are to be expected as savings rates rise and capital stock per employee increases, the actual increases were far beyond those that might reasonably have been expected. In part, this was because further import-substitution activities of necessity had to be in more capital-intensive lines, and in part it was because of rising costs of further import substitution as the small size of domestic markets, and other factors, led to ever-higher capital requirements for additional output.

Although the negative consequences of import substitution as actually practiced were becoming increasingly evident, there does not seem in the 1960s to have been a great deal of recognition that slow employment growth, increasing foreign exchange shortage, and other difficulties were at least in significant part a consequence of the import-substitution policies.

However, by that time, some developing countries were altering their trade strategies – and meeting a much greater measure of success than even the advocates of those changes had anticipated. That there was success is not in dispute (see Balassa, 1978; Bhagwati, 1978; and Krueger, 1978), although there is some disagreement as to whether the successful trade strategies were "*laissez-faire*, free trade," or whether instead they were biased toward exports. Nor is there any question that a necessary if not sufficient condition for that success was a different trade strategy. However, the extent of the success was so great that, unless one has an export theory of value, the question immediately turned to the phenomena associated with or accompanying the trade regime that might explain it. The questions still requiring research center largely on the quantitative importance of the various factors that contributed to success.

Here, some of the key hypotheses regarding the reasons for success under the outer-oriented trade strategy are examined, because they affect analysis of the linkage between growth of trade and employment. For most of them, there are suggestive pieces of evidence supporting the hypothesis, some of which are cited, although an exhaustive survey of the evidence to date would require a separate paper exclusively on that subject. Attention returns to some of these hypotheses in the fourth section, where directions for future research are considered.

There are two broad classes of hypotheses, or explanations, of the success of outer-oriented trade regimes.[2] On one hand, there are explanations which focus on the way trade regimes affect macroeconomic variables. Under these explanations, growth proceeds more rapidly because of changes in the macroeconomic environment. Díaz-Alejandro (1976), for example, attributed much of Colombia's faster growth after it altered strategy to the cessation of the "stop-go" cycle, which had earlier centered around sharp shifts in domestic monetary and fiscal policies in response to periodic balance-of-payments crises and foreign exchange shortage. More generally, countries with outer-oriented trade regimes are able to use the international market to counter adverse shifts (such as crop failure) that would otherwise lead to bottlenecks and slower domestic growth.

To the extent that it is the macroeconomic impact of trade strategy that permits more rapid overall growth, the link to employment can be analyzed in a manner similar to that of any other growth-enhancing policy. For analyzing the links between trade and employment, therefore, it is the second, or microeconomic aspects of the link that deserve review. Here, focus is on industry structure (including firm size and size of individual production runs), the degree of competition, and incentives. The effects of different trade strategies on these microeconomic variables is the result both of some negative consequences of highly protective trade regimes and of the positive benefits of a more open trade regime. Later on, in the third section, attention turns to the ways in which incentives can affect export prospects and capital–labor ratios of individual industries.

For present purposes, the question – of whether an outer-oriented trade regime is neutral, as between exportable and import-competing domestic production, or whether there is some bias (although much smaller in magnitude than that toward import-competing production under an import-substitution strategy) toward exportables – can be ignored. The crucial differences, for purposes of analyzing employment, center upon the incentives provided for individual producers, the scope they have for expanding production in individual product lines and for altered market shares, and the ways in which they affect output and growth.

A few stylized facts about import-substitution and outer-oriented regimes will set the stage for discussion. An import-substitution regime is usually characterized by provision of virtually prohibitive protection, most often outright bans on imports, to domestic producers for any product sold on the domestic market; this immediately provides reduced incentives for sale abroad relative to the domestic market. There is typically an overvalued exchange rate, and licensing of all imports and other purchases of foreign exchange is the mechanism through which the balance of payments is constrained. Import licenses, usually only for "essential" intermediate goods and capital goods employed in production, are allocated to producers of commodities for the home market. This directly provides an implicit subsidy to production of these commodities, as the importers receive the implicit premium on the licenses. Both exchange rate overvaluation and the high cost of domestically produced inputs typically serve as disincentives to exporting.

As has been extensively analyzed, the consequences of this sort of trade regime vary somewhat depending on the precise nature of the regime, including the mechanism employed for allocation of licenses, and the offsets, if any, to the disincentives to exporters (such as duty drawbacks or free importation of inputs used in production for re-export).

But in almost all cases; domestic markets are sufficiently small that the protective mechanisms used under import-substitution regimes provide a great deal of monopoly power to producers of commodities competing with importables. They also lead to strong incentives to expand into new import-competing lines (because of the usually automatic protection available and because entry into a new line provides monopoly power for a new activity, whereas expansion into activities competing with other domestic procedures is necessarily more competitive).

These characteristics have a number of consequence. First, because new investment is largely directed to new activities, the capital intensity of new investment in the manufacturing sector rises over time as "easier" import-substitution activities have already been undertaken. The opposite side of the coin for an export-oriented regime, of course, is that firms producing labor-intensive goods can, if successful, expand beyond the size of the domestic market. The capital intensity of production can, therefore, rise much more slowly under an outer-oriented trade regime. This, of course, has immediate implications for employment, as a given savings rate will finance more new jobs at a given real wage. Secondly, because of sheltered positions in the domestic market, the normal market mechanisms that create incentives for lowering costs and that punish inefficient producers and reward efficient producers are much weaker, if they exist at all, under import substitution. Market shares are to a great extent "guaranteed" by the licensing regime whenever intermediate goods are employed in more-or-less fixed proportions to output, both because low-cost producers cannot readily obtain more inputs[3] and because high-cost producers receive the premium on import licenses. Thus, the normal entry and exit mode that provides incentives for efficiency and penalizes those who cannot achieve it is weaker, if it exists at all, under import-substitution regimes. The implications of this set of considerations on labor markets are considered in the third section. Here, it should only be noted that there have been few empirical studies of industrial organization in developing countries that have set about to test the proposition that changes in market shares are less volatile the more restrictive the trade and payments regime. Thus, while it can be stated that the effects are present, further research will be needed to ascertain the quantitative significance of them.

Yet another significant difference between import-substitution and export-oriented regimes lies in the scope that exists for direct controls over domestic markets and in the feedback policy-makers receive as to the consequences of their decisions. This consideration pertains to a wide variety of matters, including the extent to which exchange rate overvaluation can arise and persist, the degree of divergence between international and domestic price relativities, and the impact of tax structures and controls on interest rates and financial institutions on savings and on resource allocation. But of particular relevance for considering the link between labor markets and employment is the scope for labor market interventions. Clearly, when prohibitive protection is provided to a large component of domestic industrial activity, producers can compensate for higher labor costs through exercising their monopoly power better than when they are competing in international markets. To that extent, the scope for intervention in labor markets is linked to the trade regime in important ways. It has often been asserted that countries such as Korea could not have succeeded in their export-oriented development strategy if their labor markets had not been left to function fairly freely in response to market forces. But the opposite is also true: the fact that Korea followed an outer-oriented strategy left policy-makers with less scope for intervention in labor markets, had they considered doing so, than they would have perceived under an alternative trade regime.

One final point deserves mention: for many developing countries, unskilled labor is the abundant factor of production, and comparative advantage within industry (and probably in other economic activities) probably lies in producing and exporting some reasonably labor-intensive goods and services. It is highly misleading to think of comparative advantage in terms of "industries": the number of products within each industry is vast, and the particular subset of commodities that may advantageously and profitably be produced within any one country will depend on the flair of the particular entrepreneur as well as more conventional "trade theoretic" factor supplies. There is nothing in theory to predict that Hong Kong would produce more ladies' short-sleeve cotton blouses, while Korea would produce more ladies' long-sleeve polyester ones. There is, however, something in theory to suggest that Hong Kong, with its free trade regime, would be in a better position to compete in a market in which rapid shifts in production line respond to shifts in fashion than would a country where delays in obtaining import licenses for intermediate goods and raw materials would prevent quick shifts in response (see Morawetz, 1980).

LABOR MARKETS IN DEVELOPING COUNTRIES

Just as international economists initially started out by assuming that goods markets did not function very efficiently, and that protection would be essential if development was to proceed, labor economists in the 1950s and early 1960s assumed that labor markets were not functioning well and that government intervention would be required to correct market failure. Lewis's (1954) classic and insightful contribution was to argue that because there were large rural populations, labor was likely to be in highly elastic supply for nonrural activities for early stages of development. "Highly elastic" was quickly interpreted to mean that this supply could be reallocated at zero price, or at least opportunity cost, and that labor could be regarded as virtually a free good from the viewpoint of resource allocation.

It took considerable research into rural labor markets before the alternative viewpoint prevailed – that there are many aspects of labor

markets in rural areas in developing countries that are not well understood, but that, nonetheless, rural members of the labor force have
positive marginal products (see Binswanger and Rosenzweig, 1984,
chap. 1) and opportunity costs. Whether the observed facts result from
labor scarcity at peak periods with high marginal product (for example,
see Hansen, 1969), and other parts of the year when it is substantially
below the average, from informational frictions (which induce sharecropping, tenancy, and other institutional arrangements, giving rise to
interrelated factor markets – see Bell and Srinivasan, 1985), or from
other causes is not pertinent to the subject at hand here.

More generally, research has demonstrated that labor markets in
developing countries functioned substantially better – in the sense of
workers shifting occupations and locations in response to shifts in
relative rewards – than had earlier been presumed.

Berry and Sabot, for example, reviewed the evidence available as of
1978. Their conclusion is worth quoting at length:

> ...because the efficiency of unconstrained markets is an article of faith
> for some economists, while the pervasiveness of imperfections and their
> dire consequences are premises to which others give uncritical allegiance,
> it is necessary to exercise great caution in interpreting the available
> economic evidence. Nevertheless, certain key features...appear to be
> firmly established.
>
> Our null hypothesis, that labour markets function at a comparatively
> high level of efficiency, is based on well-documented aspects of their
> macro dynamics. As development proceeds, time series and cross-
> country comparisons reveal changes in the occupational, industrial and
> spatial distribution of workers which are consistent with changes in the
> structure of production and economic growth. The success of labour
> markets in mobilizing workers for new growth-generating projects, and in
> other ways altering the distribution of labour services, does not, however,
> exclude the possibility that at any given time labour may be misallocated
> and a significant amount of productive potential be wasted. Furthermore,
> though microeconomic studies of migration and peasant agriculture have
> provided conclusive evidence that workers respond to economic in-
> centives to allocating their time, this is not in itself sufficient to confirm a
> high level of labour market efficiency.
>
> Our conclusion, that in most countries our null hypothesis is accepted,
> rests primarily on the microeconomic evidence of observable causes of
> misallocation...except where it is a genuine search phenomenon (a result
> of inadequate information), it [open unemployment] is in most cases a
> symptom of labour misallocation caused by the decisions of workers,
> more and less educated alike, to forego available low income employ-
> ment opportunities and queue for the few high income positions available
> in a segmented labour market...(Berry and Sabot, pp. 1230–1).

But, as the end of the quote implies, the proposition that labor
markets may function reasonably well in the absence of government

intervention does not imply that governments do not intervene. On the contrary, if one observes the existence of a "few high income positions available in a segmented labor market," it is more likely the result of government intervention than the consequence of inefficient private markets.

Government interventions affecting the conditions of employment and structure of earnings are widespread in developing countries. They include such phenomena as legislation directly governing both conditions of employment (including job security provisions) and fringe benefits (including such diverse items as social insurance, housing and training), the legal framework within which unions are able to bargain, and conditions of employment within the public sector (which can be very large in many developing countries).

Depending on the nature of the regulations and their enforceability (and enforcement), the impact on labor markets can be varied. Employers may be reluctant to hire additional labor, for example, because of their inability to lay off workers once on the payroll, thus tilting their behavior toward selection of more capital-using techniques and production activities than might prevail in the absence of such enforced legislation. Minimum wage legislation may reduce the incentive to hire unskilled workers. And greater enforceability of this sort of regulation in large industrial enterprises than in small-scale activities can and usually does lead to segmented labor markets, with the queue arising as workers vie for jobs in the high-wage, heavily regulated activities (or in public sector jobs).

Other forms of intervention may have quite different effects. In some countries, policies have been put in place to use government-owned parastatals to employ all university graduates who cannot otherwise find satisfactory employment. While the motivation for this sort of policy may have been political, the consequence for rates of return and wage structures are significant: social rates of return may exceed private rates of return for university education by large margins; private firms may wait to observe performance and then "bid away" the more able graduates, leaving others in the public sector (see Krueger, 1972, for an analysis of this phenomenon in Turkey).

Although too little is known about labor markets to be confident about any empirical generalization, a rough guess might be that regulations regarding social insurance and layoff provisions have been the most significant intervention in much of Latin America (see, for example, Corbo on the effects of removing these provisions in Chile); that minimum wages and conditions of employment in public sector enterprises have been effective in driving a sizeable wedge between the "formal" and "informal" sectors in Africa and the Middle East; and that regulations covering employers' obligations to provide housing, education and training, and other social services may have been more significant in South Asia.

These sorts of interventions led to the Harris–Todaro (1970) model of labor market behavior in developing countries: workers earn a supply-and-demand determined wage in the rural areas of developing countries, and know that if they are fortunate enough to find employment in the "formal" sector, they can earn an amount greater than the rural wage by some multiple, m, greater than one. They maximize expected incomes by migrating to urban areas in search of high-compensation jobs, as long as the higher earnings times the probability of finding employment exceeds the rural wage. The probability of finding employment, in turn, can be expressed in several ways (and the possibility of risk aversion can also be used to modify the analysis), of which the simplest is to regard it as equal to the fraction of the labor force who are employed.

There can be a number of outcomes, depending on the precise specification of the model. Open urban unemployment might occur if the basic relationships are as sketched above. An alternative might be that persons in the urban area are employed in an "informal", presumably service or small-scale industry, sector while attempting to obtain high-wage jobs. In that event, there would be less open unemployment, but a significant compensation differential between those working in enterprises subject to the wage and employment regulations and those employed in the informal sector. There would also, of course, be observable differences in the behavior of profit-maximizing employers in the informal and formal sector.

For purposes of understanding the relationship between employment and trade, there are several important conclusions that arise from this. First, if earnings do not more or less appropriately reflect trade-offs and relative scarcity values of different types of labor, the observed distortion is more likely to be a consequence of government intervention than it is of inherent "market failure." Thus, insofar as one wants to analyze the consequence of distortions on the functioning of international trade, one can do so through modeling the various types of labor market interventions sketched out above.

Secondly, while there is every reason to believe that developing countries are relatively well endowed with unskilled labor and, therefore, have a comparative advantage in the production of goods that use unskilled labor relatively intensively, it does not follow that governments must intervene to achieve an efficient trade pattern. Close inspection of models that generate an "unlimited labor supply" suggests that the social opportunity cost (in terms of utility) of labor is likely to be close to the price at which workers are willing to migrate and to offer their services in the labor market.

Thirdly, insofar as there is reason for concern with employment in developing countries, it arises either because the available income-earning opportunities generate very small income streams or because of Harris–Todaro type unemployment. The latter has very different welfare implications from those that would arise if there were no alternative income stream: indeed, a key question is why some should have high-income jobs at the expense of others, and one policy that would reduce unemployment would be to lower wages in the high-wage sector. If concern is with the low incomes that are associated with existing employment opportunities (which is where the social and developmental issue surely lies), then the key policy question is how to shift the demand for labor upward. In the presence of rapid growth of the population and labor force, as is happening in many developing countries, the absence of a sufficiently rapid upward shift may indeed mean even lower earnings for the labor force in the future. It is primarily with regard to this question that the issue of the link between trade and employment is considered in the next section.

It should first be noted, however, that in the presence of Harris–Todaro conditions, it is at least possible that an upward shift in the demand for labor may result in greater unemployment. Suppose, for example, the "stark" version of the model in which rural workers migrate whenever the expected wage, defined as equal to one minus the unemployment rate times the actual urban wage, equals or exceeds the rural wage. For given rural conditions, an upward shift in the demand for urban labor could conceivably induce the migration of enough rural workers so that both urban employment and urban unemployment increased. If such circumstances obtained, urban unemployment would most effectively be reduced by lowering the urban wage; second-best policy might well be to subsidize rural employment; if all else failed, downward shifts in the demand for labor might accomplish some reduction. In what follows, this possibility will be ignored, although the ramifications (via trade flows) of government-induced, wage-setting – above levels that would prevail in the absence of intervention – will be considered.

TRADE AND EMPLOYMENT IN DEVELOPING COUNTRIES

The simple Heckscher–Ohlin model of international trade essentially posits that labor-abundant countries will have a comparative advantage in, and net exports of, labor-intensive goods. This would happen because a well-functioning factor market would ensure that lower wages in labor-abundant countries would render production costs for relatively labor-using commodities lower than in more capital-abundant countries.[4] Thus, it is a model based on the assumption that factor markets function reasonably well.

Conceptually, there are several ways in which trade policies and labor market intervention could singly or through interactions affect the rate at which the demand for unskilled labor shifts upward. First, there is considerable empirical evidence that in the long run, choice of trade policy significantly affects the rate of economic growth. Secondly, if there are systematic differences in choice of technique between import-competing and exportable industries, then alternative trade regimes can affect demand for labor shifting the composition of output. Thirdly, the trade regime may affect the incentives of choice of particular techniques within given economic activities. Finally, regulations in the labor market may affect the quantity of labor demanded through a variety of channels, including especially their impact on the volume and composition of international trade under any particular trade regime.

In this section, these four distinct avenues of impact and interaction are addressed. The first covers the relationship between trade strategies and overall growth rates which are, after all, major determinants of the demand for labor. The second surveys the available evidence corroborating the basic HOS model with respect to developing countries. The third covers the impact of trade regimes on the substitution of capital for labor. Finally, the fourth turns to the predictions that emanate from the HOS model if the link between labor abundance and low wages is broken because of Harris–Todaro or other mechanisms, and the empirical support for such predictions. This last question is the one about which there is least empirical evidence to date, and centers on the extent to which labor market regulation may have choked off potential trade for developing countries.[5]

Alternative trade strategies and growth

There is no need for in-depth analysis to recognize that if there are significant differences in overall rates of economic growth which arise because of differences in trade strategies, that in itself will very likely be the predominant effect of choice of trade strategy on the rate of growth of demand for labor. It would require some very peculiar shifts in the composition of output away from labor-using activities in order for this not to follow. And, in practice, some 50–60 percent of demand growth originates in domestic demand even in highly open, outer-oriented economies.[6]

However, there is little in standard trade theory that predicts any difference in growth rates between a highly restrictive trade regime and an open one, once the static losses associated with a restrictive trade regime have been incurred. One can point to a predicted higher incremental capital–output ratio under an inner-oriented trade regime, and suggest that, for a given investment rate, this would affect the observed growth rate, as noted earlier. Moreover, insofar as the rate of return on investment was higher under an outer-oriented trade regime, savings might rise; theory, however, suggests that for a labor-abundant country, the rate of return on capital might be higher under a restrictive trade regime, and, in any event if capital is internationally mobile, the rate of saving need not equal the rate of investment.

Empirically, however, the available evidence suggests that the impact on growth may be much stronger than consideration of these links alone would indicate. Several cross-country studies (including Balassa, 1978; Krueger, 1978; and Michaely, 1977) have all suggested a strong link: even for sub-Saharan Africa in the 1970s, Balassa found a strong positive effect on growth of less restrictive trade regimes. Direct contrasts of countries' performance with alternative strategies[7] all suggest very strong growth effects of alternative trade strategies, as does direct observation of differences in growth rates.

Comparison of observed incremental capital–output ratios (ICORs) also leads to the same conclusion: Balassa reports incremental capital –output ratios of 1.8 for Singapore, 2.1 in Korea, and 2.4 in Taiwan over the 1960–73 period as a whole; compared to 5.5 in Chile, 9.1 in Uruguay, and 5.7 in India. He also notes that the Brazilian capital-output ratio fell from 3.8 in the 1960–66 period – a period of very high rates of protection to domestic industry – to 2.1 over the 1966–73 period, when the real exchange rate was realigned, protectionist barriers were sharply reduced, and exports grew rapidly.

Thus, there can be little question that there is generally more rapid overall growth when exports are growing more rapidly, and there is ample evidence (see Balassa, 1985, for a review) that exports grow more rapidly when regimes are more outer-oriented. However, if this were the only link between trade strategies and employment, it is not obvious that any separate analysis of trade as it affects employment would be required; the effect of more rapid growth of output on employment would be no different because the origin of more rapid growth was trade, than it would be if it were, e.g., a set of macroeconomic policies more conductive to rational resource allocation.

Factor intensity of exports and imports

The HOS model of trade posits a straightforward linkage between the degree of protection and factor proportions: for countries with a relatively large endowment of unskilled labor, their comparative advantage will lie in exporting labor-intensive goods and importing relatively capital-intensive ones.[8] Indeed, it would be highly likely that some goods would not be produced domestically at all under free trade, if the proportions in which inputs were used were too different from the country's factor endowment. One would expect, under free trade, to observe a reasonably similar factor intensity of all goods produced domestically.

For very labor-abundant countries, protection could induce positive production levels of more capital-intensive goods that would not be produced at free trade. Hence, quite clearly, with protection it would be expected that for labor-abundant countries, capital intensity of protected industries would be greater than that of exportables (and of import-competing industries that would be able to remain competitively in production at free trade). Hence, a decision to move from a more protected trade regime to a more open trade regime would imply a shifting commodity composition of output toward more labor-using activities, and this would shift the demand for labor outward.

Both of these hypotheses – a similarity of input proportions between non-protected import-competing and exportable industries, and a greater labor intensity of exportable than of protected import-competing industries – have been borne out by those empirical studies that have investigated the issue. In the NBER project on Alternative Trade Strategies and Employment, the labor employed per unit of domestic value added (DVA) was greater in exportables than in import-competing industries in all countries but Chile (where intra-Latin American trade dominated); the ratio of labor inputs in exportables to import-competing industries was in excess of 2:1 for Brazil, Indonesia, and Thailand (see Krueger, 1978, p. 96). When labor inputs were disaggregated into the skilled components, the contrasts became even stronger, with exportables using more unskilled labor than protected import-competing industries for all countries for which the data were available (see Krueger, 1983, table 6.1).

Contrasts of the commodity composition of trade before and after Brazil's shift in trade strategy in the late 1960s showed a marked increase in labor intensity (see Carvalho and Haddad, 1981). They estimated the factor inputs per unit of output in exportable and import-competing industries for each year from 1967 to 1974, a period during which Brazil liberalized her trade regime substantially. These estimates were based on the assumption of fixed input–output coefficients for each activity, and thus ignored any substitution that may have taken place during this period. The shifting commodity mix of exports resulting from increased incentives to export is to have led to an increase in workers per unit of output from about 20–22 at the beginning of the period to 28–29 at the end, while the labor inputs per unit of output in import competing industries were unchanged. (Carvalho and Haddad, 1981, p. 53). This would suggest that a 1 percentage point increase in the share of exports in GNP would result in an upward shift in the demand for labor of about one-third of a percentage point. Of course, in well-functioning labor markets, this entire shift would be offset by substitution of capital for labor and higher wages, but that does not diminish its importance. The effect would be to increase the wage rate for unskilled labor.

For Korea, the shift to an outer-oriented strategy also had a pronounced impact on the labor market. The labor intensity of Korea's exports rose markedly over the eight years following the shift to an outer-oriented trade strategy, 1960–68 (see Westphal and Kim, 1977). Nonfarm employment is estimated to have risen from 2.15 million in 1960 to 4.63 million in 1970, during which time real wages rose by 74 percent (see Krueger 1986, Table 9). How much of this increase was attributable to the "mix" effect reported in the Westphal–Kim numbers, and how much was the result of more rapid growth, remains an open question.

There is, thus, a reasonable amount of evidence that the orientation of the trade regime significantly affects the demand for labor; whether the "mix" effect can result in a 25 percent or 100 percent increase in the number of employees firms wish to hire at a given wage remains, however, an open question.

Impact of the trade regime on relative factor prices and substitution between factors

There are a number of mechanisms through which trade policy affects relative factor prices and the choice of technique within activities in developing countries. First and foremost, to the extent that trade strategy shifts the composition of output, it undoubtedly directly affects factor prices. In import-substitution regimes where new investment is directed into skilled-labor and capital-intensive activities, there is the standard trade-theoretic presumption that the relative prices and costs of these scarce factors of production would be driven up. This would imply, if uniform factor payments prevailed for all activities, that the mix of activities was more capital- and skill-intensive than it would be in the absence of protection, but all activities would substitute unskilled labor (whose relative wage would be lower) for scarce capital.[9]

Such a change in factor prices would thus affect the choice of input proportions for all procedures, and would follow directly from the altered composition of output. Little further can be said beyond the previous discussion. There are, however, ways in which the trade regime can affect relative prices confronting producers differentially. Because many capital goods are imported, the most significant effect probably comes about through the impact of the trade regime on the relative price and availability of foreign exchange for the purchase of imported capital equipment.

This effect arises because protectionist trade regimes usually have two opposite impacts. On one hand, because they discourage exports, there is excess demand for imports (at an overvalued exchange rate). Consequently, foreign exchange is allocated among competing claimants. Although governments typically accord "priority" to capital goods imports, not all applications for foreign exchange can be approved. The firms receiving approvals have access to imported capital goods at prices well below the opportunity cost of scarce foreign exchange, while other firms are unable to import legally or, if they can obtain imported capital goods, they do so at "resale" prices. In either case, the end result is that there are two distinct groups of producers, one confronted for most practical purposes with relatively low prices for capital goods and another group confronted with much higher prices.[10]

The profitability of employing cheap goods increases still further if those with licenses can overinvoice their imports and sell the excess foreign exchange on the black market.

In many countries, the differential in capital costs arises between large-scale firms and smaller ones, although in some cases it can arise between public sector enterprises and private firms. For three countries included in the NBER project on Alternative Trade Strategies and Employment – Chile, Pakistan, and Tunisia – the cost of capital was estimated to have been reduced by more than 30 percent by the trade regime,[11] at least for those producers with access to imports at the low prices.

The substitution that occurs in response to these changes in relative costs of employing different factors has by now been well documented. Behrman's estimates, covering 1,723 observations from 27 three-digit industries for 70 countries over the 1967–73 period provided strong support to earlier work, all of which found elasticities of substitution near unity. Behrman's conclusion was that:

> …my estimates provide strong support for an elasticity of substitution between capital and labor across industrial sectors and across countries near the Cobb–Douglas value of 1.0. This result is quite robust under the alternative specifications that I consider with a single caveat about the puzzling role of real per capita GNP… (p. 186).[12]

One other aspect of trade regimes and the impact on factor usage deserves note. Lipsey, Kravis, and Roldan (1982) examined the behavior of multinational firms, and their choice of location, product, and technique across countries. They found a systematic tendency of samples of both Swedish and American multinationals to have more fixed assets per worker in their home countries, and to locate more labor-intensive activities in low-wage countries. However, they found the strongest substitution effect resulted from a shifting of factor proportions in response of relative factor prices. (Lipsey, Kravis and Roldan, pp. 252–3). This raises interesting questions as to the extent to which the trade regime, or domestic wage legislation, induces substitution of labor in one country for that in another. As will be discussed further below, one of the interesting, and difficult-to-research questions, is the extent to which the effects of wage restrictions may be felt through the failure of activities to locate, or develop, in countries with highly restrictive policies.

The impact of labor market distortions on trade

Thus far, attention has focused on the effect of the trade regime on factor markets and employment. Yet, there is another question which may be even more important, on which considerably less empirical research has been done. It focuses upon the impact of labor market regulations and restrictions on the potential for employment under a given trade regime. In its baldest form, the hypothesis would be that labor market interventions can and have choked off export growth, even under trade regimes that are not highly restrictionist.

To a point, theory is fairly clear. Brecher, Helpman, Jones, Magee and others have developed models of trade under the assumption that a factor market distortion prevails.[13] It might be a legislated or union imposed real wage rate throughout the economy at a level higher than was consistent with full employment; it might be such a wage restriction (or its equivalent in terms of job security and fringe benefits) applicable to the "formal" sector.

In the theoretical literature, it has been demonstrated that, in the presence of these sorts of rigidities, almost anything can happen. In particular, the "wrong" good, i.e. the good that would be imported under an efficient allocation of resources, might be exported; the commodity that would be "labor-intensive" when identical factor prices confronted producers in both sectors could be "capital-intensive" if a sufficiently higher wage prevailed than in the rest of the economy; the "right commodity" might be exported but with the "wrong" factor proportions, and there might be open unemployment.

There are also important links between the nominal exchange rate and the real wage. It can be argued that, in some countries, a depreciation of the nominal exchange rate is effective precisely because it lowers the real wage, at least in terms of traded goods. Turning that proposition around, an overvalued exchange rate in a labor-abundant country may make the real wage sufficiently high to reduce or wipe our comparative advantage in labor-intensive industries, and devaluation may in effect be an instrument for lowering the real wage. Even further complexities are introduced if wages are indexed in terms of domestic currency in highly open economies.[14]

From all of this, it is a plausible hypothesis that rapid growth in demand for unskilled labor will occur when the labor market is permitted to function fairly freely in the context of a reasonably open trade regime and a realistic exchange rate. For, if nominal wages were not artificially pegged at an unrealistic level, the prevailing nominal exchange rate would presumably then be reflected in the demand for labor. The converse hypothesis would then also follow: in economies where wages are, through whatever mechanism, held at levels above those that are consistent with their factor endowments, exports would be smaller in absolute value and as a share of GNP than they would be in the context of a well-functioning labor market.

Evidence already cited provides some tentative support for these hypotheses: the Lipsey–Kravis–Roldan analysis suggested that multinationals tend, in part, to choose location based on labor costs; and there does not appear to be any instance of rapid growth in a country with an outer-oriented trade regime and labor market interventions which effectively maintains wages at high levels.

But relative to the possible quantitative importance of this effect surprisingly little research has been done. Some of the reasons why are obvious: an investigator would have carefully to sort out those real wage increases that were endogenous to a growth process (such as, presumably, those in Korea) from those that were imposed upon an economy through regulation; simple examination of legislation and regulations does not suffice to indicate effective intervention, as minimum wage legislation may be set below the prevailing market rate and/or not enforced; in addition, one would have to estimate deviations from "natural" trade levels, which clearly differ for a variety of reasons including natural-resource endowment; and any test would presumably have to be carried out across countries. Furthermore, there appear to be no reliable indicators of real wage levels for unskilled workers on a comparable basis among developing countries.

Nonetheless, the hypothesis that labor market interventions that drive up the real wage may have their largest effect through their impact on export performance is one that is appealing and deserves a great deal more attention than it has so far received. For exporting is a highly visible activity. While it is conceivable that middlemen might export merchandise after purchasing goods produced in the informal sector (not subject to regulations resulting in high labor costs), this does not seem likely. The demands of the international market for uniformity large-scale shipments, and timely delivery (see Morawetz) all imply that the scope for substantial growth of exports based on informal sector production is probably highly limted.

If this is so, regulations raising labor costs to the formal sector would discourage exports even in the presence of a low-wage informal sector Yet this proposition has not been examined empirically in any systematic way, despite its potential importance:

Reasons for the failure to do so are obvious: a meaningful measure of the labor costs distortion and a measure of the "deviation of exports" from what they would have been in the absence of the distortion are both needed. Neither measure is one for which the appropriate analytical construct has an obvious empirical measure.

Yet the potential effects of labor market interventions are significant enough to warrant any effort, no matter how bold, to assess the quantitative significance of the phenomenon. The following discussion reports on the authors' effort to tab at least a preliminary (if heroic) cut at the issue, in the hope that it might stimulate others to devise better tests.

A first problem is how to measure the wage distortion. There are obvious difficulties of across-country measures, yet natural within country measures (such as the ratio of urban and rural per capita incomes or of average wages in industry relative to those in services) that are influenced by a host of variables other than distortions, and in any event, data are not readily available.

An alternative method, and one used here is to hypothesize that the shadow price of unskilled labor of the sort potentially employed in industries producing labor-intensive importables is positively and reasonably closely correlated with a country's per capita income, and that significant deviations of that wage rate relative to per capita income in a formal sector activity are reflections of labor market interventions.

Tourist services, such as luxury hotels and restaurants, are usually visible enough to be in the covered sector, and they typically can attract international capital and management, and are reasonably intensive in the employment of unskilled labor.

Differences in the costs of these services across countries ought, therefore, to reflect primarily differences in labor costs, although other factors (such as site value in large cities) surely enter in.

A good measure of the cost of the tourist services is available in the United Nations per diem allowance in U.S. dollars in capital cities. The advantage of that measure is its availability. There is a presumption that the per diem allowance reflects to some extent the cost of hotel services, restaurants, and taxis, all of which are presumed to be in some measure home goods and to be somewhat labor-intensive. Its major advantage as an indicator is that it is estimated across countries with a similar methodology and that it is changed frequently in response to changing conditions. To be sure, one could always argue that the costs of providing intercontinental hotel services in a very low-income country are likely to be high because of high transport costs or remoteness of the country, and that cannot be ruled out. Nonetheless, one could expect it to reflect to a large extent changes in the realism of the exchange rate, an important component of the real wage for tradeable goods.

Taking the U.N. per diem in dollars relative to estimated per capita income in dollars was therefore used as a proxy for the distortion of the real wage; I shall refer to this variable as the "wage proxy." A higher ratio is presumed to reflect a real wage higher than would be warranted under competitive conditions.

The remaining question is the relevant variable to use for a country's exports relative to their "natural" level. Here again, specification of a full-scale model of the determinants of the share of exports in trade was far beyond the scope of this paper: the variable, used, in fact, was exports per capita. The regression thus estimated was

$$X/P = a + b(UN/y) \qquad (1)$$

where X is dollar value of exports, P population, UN the dollar per diem, and y per capita income. Data were gathered for 33 countries.

Estimates were made for 1968, 1973, 1978, and 1983. The results are reported in table 12.1. Astonishingly, all coefficients are significant at the 95 percent level and have the expected sign.[15]

As can be seen, the coefficient on the wage proxy was surprisingly stable over all four years. The implied elasticity of exports with respect to the wage proxy was close to −0.5 in all estimates. If the proxy accurately reflected real wage movements relative to per capita GNP and if the relationship between the real wage and real income in an efficient development process were truly linear, this elasticity would imply that a 1 percent increase in the real wage (in the formal sector) relative to GNP would result in a reduction of exports of 0.5 percent. Given the tenuous nature of the numbers, it would require too great a stretch of credulity to attempt to complete the specification of how such a reduction would feed through to employment (would resources be shifted to import-competing industries or would the growth of the urban sector be lower and hence more persons remain in rural areas? – what would be the effect of a reduced export growth rate on overall growth?). Nonetheless, the estimates are consistent with the hypothesis that the effects

TABLE 12.1 *Estimated relationship between exports and real wages*

	1968	1973	1978	1983
a	308.25	282.64	319.29	365.97
	(5.69)	(5.85)	(5.99)	(6.13)
b	−1,261.67	−1,106.84	−1,201.13	−1,577.63
	(−2.89)	(−2.60)	(−2.63)	(−3.20)
Implied elasticity at mean	−0.543	−0.498	−0.422	−0.591
R^2	0.20	0.17	0.17	0.24

Countries included are:

Argentina	Indonesia	Philippines
Bolivia	Jamaica	Senegal
Brazil	Japan	Sri Lanka
Chile	Kenya	Thailand
Colombia	Korea	Tunisia
Congo	Mauritius	Turkey
Costa Rica	Mexico	United States
Ecuador	Nigeria	Uruguay
Egypt	Pakistan	Venezuela
Guatemala	Paraguay	Yugoslavia
India	Peru	Zambia

"a" and "b" respectively refer to the intercept and slope of equation 1 on page 375.

of labor market interventions on employment may originate in significant part from their effects on a country's ability to compete in export markets. Given the weaknesses of the data, little weight should be placed on the order of magnitude implied by these estimates. On the other hand, the same qualifications make the fact that the estimates appear to reveal a strong relationship all the more astonishing. The conclusion should not be that there is a strong and well-understood link, but that it is conceivable that labor market interventions may have far greater costs than are revealed in a closed economy framework and that research on this relationship is urgently needed.

AGENDA FOR RESEARCH

The research agenda is large and challenging. Questions range from the effects of trade restrictions on industry structure and competition to the "normal" levels of wages as functions of per capita income levels and other variables. Even such topics as differences in the industrial concentration, the size distribution of firms (and changes over time), and the characteristics of the split (if any) between the formal and informal sectors under open and restrictive trade regimes have hardly been touched.

However, if one were to attempt to identify priorities, an effort to ascertain empirical regularities in relations between urban and rural per capita incomes, between rural per capita incomes and unskilled wages, and other key variables would be very high on the list. This would be a first step, at least, toward estimating the effects of government regulations on wages. They would provide at least some presumptive evidence against which one might attempt to identify countries where these regulations have been effective in altering real wage levels.

There is no way that the underlying question can be definitively answered, but alternative approaches should all prove useful. What is surprising is the degree of our ignorance surrounding wage and labor market issues in a comparative context. Knowledge, even of orders of magnitude, would help narrow the range of uncertainty. What empirical regularities are there between the evolution of real wages and that of per capita income? What meaningful indicators are there, if any, of the extent to which policy interventions affect the real wage? Can ratios of urban to rural incomes, or of average manufacturing wage to per capita income, be meaningfully used? Any data on these issues, across countries, would reduce our ignorance, but they would over time require considerable refinement: to what extent are there differences in experience, education, skill, and other variables between the labor forces in different countries, and especially those entering the urban labor force and seeking essentially unskilled employment in manufacturing? To what extent do social insurance regulations, provisions preventing the discharge of workers, and so on, affect the real cost of labor as perceived by employers? And, above all, to what extent do any of these phenomena affect the real wage relative to that prevailing in a well-functioning labor market?

A second line of research would focus on the effects of effective labor market regulation. In part, this might build on the first, but there are undoubtedly useful pieces of information that might be assembled independently. A major difficulty is that, as is always the case with empirical work on international trade, theory predicts that the effect of intervention may well be to prevent the emergence or growth of particular lines of activity. It is exceptionally difficult to estimate what is not there. Nevertheless, there are enough steps in the linkage between labor market intervention and employment levels that one would expect that research could improve understanding of these links one by one.

If, as trade theory and empirical evidence suggest, the exportation of labor-intensive products is a substitute for the movement of factors of production internationally, trade should be a major mechanism for permitting a rapid expansion of employment, and ultimately, real wages. To the extent that government regulation of the labor market then precludes the full exploitation of the opportunities trade might offer for employment growth, the costs would be significantly higher than a closed-economy model would suggest. And yet, to date, there is little if any research that guides us at all with regard to possible orders of magnitude. Surely, historical experience with shifts in trade regime, the behavior of multinationals, comparative analysis across countries, and/or other techniques can provide a better indication of possible orders of magnitude of these effects than we now have.

The third area for research centers upon the effects of differences in trade orientation on domestic economic variables. As indicated in the second section, there is reason to believe that competitive pressures are more likely to be felt in an outer-oriented trade regime than in a highly protectionist one. To what extent are there differences in industry structure between countries with outer-oriented trade regimes and those with protectionist ones? What differences are there in industry behavior, depending on structure? The question is, of course, of general interest and relates to a variety of areas in addition to the trade-employment linkage. Broader issues cover such phenomena as productivity growth (and the reasons for the sharp differences in growth rates under alternative regimes), differentials and reasons for them. Even with regard to the trade and employment issue, however, questions arise concerning the extent to which protected producers base their decisions to employ unskilled labor, skilled labor, and capital on different factors than do producers expecting to compete in international markets. The degree to which unions can effectively influence the wage might also be expected to differ significantly under alternative trade regimes. Indeed, the environment under the two regimes is so different that one would expect significant differences in behavior in a wide variety of ways. Yet, at the microeconomic level, these questions have barely been touched upon.

An honest summary will convince most of the urgency of the need for further research: given the present state of knowledge, it is equally plausible that labor market restrictions are a major cause of the failure of exports to grow even under inner-oriented regimes, or that they are only negligibly effective in affecting trade patterns, regardless of the nature of the trade regime. Theory suggests that there is some degree of restriction of labor markets sufficient to significantly reduce the potential for trade. However, whether labor markets in developing countries ever are restricted to a degree sufficient to impede trade potential is an open question.

NOTES

[1] To be sure, it was widely recognized that there would be considerable demand for imports in the development process. It was assumed that this demand could be met out of earnings from primary commodity exports (which, to be sure, would grow slowly) and capital inflows. Increases in demand would then largely be satisfied by import substitution.

[2] There are also those who believe that the success was the outcome of a broad set of policy changes, and that the rapid growth of exports, like that of other key variables, was the result of policy changes other than the trade orientation. While it is certainly true that an outer-oriented trade strategy alone was not responsible for the entire increment in the growth rate which resulted, it is hard to see how the shift in trade orientation could not have been a significant, and probably necessary, contributory factor.

[3] To be sure, resale is legal in some regimes, and is a common practice in some cases even where it is not legal. Even then, of course, the seller of the imports will charge the premium-inclusive price. Further, ability to deal with officials in obtaining licenses, etc., is at least as important a determinant of costs as is any other managerial ability with respect to cost minimization. Low-cost operation under protection and an import-licensing regime which confers quasi-monopoly positions probably requires a very different set of skills than managing to compete on the international market when bureaucratic red-tape regarding operations is minimal.

[4] I ignore the possibility of factor price equalization; in the HOS model, at free trade, either countries specialize in producing a range of goods which are "near" to their endowments or there is factor price equalization across countries. Even in that instance, the "net factor export" embodied in the country's trade pattern would be related to the factor endowment.

[5] A question that is not addressed here is the role that human capital plays in labor markets and how the HOS model may be amended to take into account that "third" factor of production. Alternative treatments that have been attempted in the literature include Kenen (1965), in which investible resources are allocated between "raw land" and "raw labor" to increase their

productivity, and three-factor models of trade, such as that of Jones (1971). See also Krueger (1977) for a discussion. Casual empiricism suggests that countries with high per capita incomes typically have more physical and more human capital per person than do countries with lower per capita incomes. For that reason, there is a strong presumption for developing countries that comparative advantage would lie in production of goods with a relatively high share of unskilled labor; for trade among developed countries, the question of relative abundance of physical and human capital might be more important.

[6] See Kim and Roemer (1979) for estimates for Korea. They estimate that, even during the years of rapid export expansion from 1963 to 1973, domestic demand expansion accounted for about 54.7 percent of total output growth, compared to 43.7 percent of exports.

[7] See Banerji and Reidel (1980) contrasting India and Taiwan where shifts toward labor-intensive activities contributed to industrial employment growth of 10 percent annually in Taiwan while shifts toward more capital-intensive activities led to slower employment growth of 3 percent in India despite more rapid productivity growth in Taiwan. See also Fields (1984), Krueger (1986), and Myint (1985).

[8] The factor intensity of different commodities is defined by positing the cost minimizing factor usage that would occur at a particular set of prices of factor inputs, and then ranking commodities from more to less using in terms of the ratios of inputs so derived. It is then assumed that the ranking would be the same for all possible sets of factor input prices. Although there was a time when trade theorists worried about the possibility of "factor-intensity-reversal," subsequent work has indicated that it is not a significant empirical phenomenon. See Leamer (1980) for a discussion of this set of issues.

[9] Using detailed Colombian earnings data, T. Paul Schultz analyzed the impact of protection on earnings of workers and employers in Colombia. He concluded that a large portion of effective protection went to providing quasi-rents to both employers and workers in protected industries, with a 10 percent increase in effective protection raising workers' wages in those industries by about 3 percent, compared to comparable workers in nonprotected industries and employers' wages by an even larger proportion (Schultz, p. 98). Schultz regarded these effects as largely income distributional, implying that much of the effect of protection is to build in quasi-rents which then accounted for a significant portion of observed wage differentials for workers of comparable education and experience. To the extent that the quasi-rent effect of trade regimes is important, that would suggest that the income distribution becomes more unequal under an inward-looking strategy, but that effect would not influence the demand for labor per se.

[10] The differential in relative factor prices confronting different producers is increased still further when one group is subject to various labor market regulations of the type discussed in the second major section, while another group is able to avoid observing them and also ineligible for easy access to import licenses. Credit rationing, and access to credit, may still further increase the differential. Here, focus is only on the impact of the trade regime on relative factor prices.

[11] See Krueger (1983, table 7.1). For Pakistan, Guisinger estimated that the rental cost of capital equipment for those with access to government privileges was about one-fourth what it would have been in a unified market. This

included the implicit subsidy on import licenses, credit rationing, and tax incentives to investors.

[12] See also the study by Corbo and Meller (1981) which was based on detailed Chilean data. They estimated translog production functions but found that the Cobb–Douglas specification was "a satisfactory representation of technology" in a surprisingly high proportion of cases (p. 209).

[13] Because the Heckscher–Ohlin–Samuelson model of trade assumes only two factors of production, it is the wage–rental ratio that affects factor substitution and product mix in the standard trade theoretic model. The ratio changes in the same way, regardless of whether the real wage rate rises (through labor market intervention or for other reasons), or whether the real rental cost of capital falls (as, for example, through the implicit subsidization of capital goods imports discussed previously). In many developing countries, labor market regulations drive up the real wage at the same time as credit rationing at artificially low interest rates, overvaluation of the currency with low nominal tariffs on capital goods imports, and the tax treatment of investment all serve to lower the real cost of employing capital. Since all of these effects work in the same direction, the term "factor market distortion" is often used more or less interchangeably with terms connoting the maintenance of an artificially high real wage; for purposes of analyzing the impact of labor market interventions on trade expansion, however, it is only the labor market regulations that would appear to matter.

[14] For an analysis of one highly open economy with full wage indexation, see Garnaut and Baxter (1984).

[15] Several other variants were estimated using the same basic data, including rates of change of exports and wages, and manufactured exports, rather than total exports. The results were not significant, often of the inappropriate sign, and the coefficients varied widely between the five-year intervals.

REFERENCES

Baer, Werner and Herve, Michel 1966: "Employment and Industrialization in Developing Countries." *Quarterly Journal of Economics*, 80(1), Feb., 88–107.

Balassa, Bela 1978: "Export Incentive and Export Performance in Developing Countries: A Comparative Analysis." *Weltwirtschaftliches Archiv*, 1, 24–61.

Balassa, Bela, 1984: "Outward Orientation." DRD Discussion Paper No. DRD 148, World Bank, July 1985.

Banerji, R. and Riedel, James 1980: "Industrial Employment Expansion under Alternative Trade Strategies: the Case of India and Taiwan: 1950–70." *Journal of Development Economics*, 7, 567–77.

Behrman, J. R. 1982: "Country and Sectoral Variations in Manufacturing Elasticities of Substitution Between Capital and Labor." In A. O. Krueger (ed.), *Trade and Employment in Developing Countries*, vol. 2, Chicago University Press. 195–92.

Bell, Clive and Srinivasan, T. N. 1985: "Agricultural Credit Market in Punjab: Segmentation, Rationing, and Spillover." Development Research Department Working Paper No. 7, World Bank, June.

Berry, A. and Sabot, R. H. 1978: "Labour Market Performance in Developing Countries: A Survey." *World Development*, 6, 1199–242.

Bhagwati, Jagdish 1978: *Foreign Trade Regimes and Economic Development: Anatomy and Consequences of Exchange Control Regimes.* Cambridge, Mass.: Ballinger Press for the National Bureau of Economic Research.

Binswanger, Hans P. and Rosenzweig, Mark R. 1984: *Contractual Arrangements, Employment, and Wages in Rural Labor Markets in Asia.* New Haven: Yale University Press.

Brecher, Richard M. 1974: "Minimum Wage Rates and the pure Theory of International Trade." *Quarterly Journal of Economics*, 8, 96–116.

Carvalho, Jose L. and Haddad, Claudio 1981: "Foreign Trade Strategies and Employment in Brazil." In Anne O. Krueger, H. B. Lary, Terry Monson and Narongchai Akrasanee (eds), *Trade and Employment in Developing Countries*, vol. 1, Chicago: University of Chicago Press.

Corbo, V. and Meller P. 1981: "Alternative Trade Strategies and Employment Implications: Chile." In A. O. Krueger, H. B. Lary, et al., *Trade and Employment in Developing Countries*, vol. 2, Chicago: Chicago University Press, 83–134.

Corbo, Vittorio and Sanchez, Jose Miguel 1985. "Adjustments by Industrial Firms in Chile during 1974–82." In Vittorio Corbo and Jaime de Melo, (eds), "Scrambling for Survival: How Firms Adjusted to the Recent Reforms in Argentina, Chile and Uruguay," Washington, DC: World Bank Staff Working Paper No. 764.

Díaz-Alejandro, Carlos 1976: *Foreign Trade Regimes and Economic Development: Colombia.* New York: Columbia University Press for the National Bureau of Economic Research.

Fields, Gary S. 1984: "Employment, Income Distribution and Economic Growth in Seven Small Open Economies." *Economic Journal*, 94, 74–83.

Garnaut, Ross and Baxter, Paul 1984: *Exchange Rate and Macro-economic Policy in Independent Papua New Guinea.* Canberra: Australian National University.

Guisinger, Stephen 1981: "Trade Policies and Employment: The Case of Pakistan." In Krueger, Lary, et al., op cit.

Hansen, Bent 1969: "Employment and Wages in Rural Egypt." *American Economic Review*, 59.

Harris, John R and Todaro, Michael 1970: "Migration, Unemployment and Development: A Two-Sector Analysis." *American Economic Review*, 60.

Helpman, Elhanan 1977: "Nontraded Goods and Macroeconomic Policy Under a Fixed Exchange Rate." *Quarterly Journal of Economics*, 91, 469–80.

Jones, Ronald W. 1971: "A Three-Factor Model in Theory, Trade, and History," In Jagdish Bhagwati et al., *Trade, Balance of Payments and Growth*, Amsterdam: North-Holland.

Kenen, Peter B. 1965: "Nature, Capital and Trade." *Journal of Political Economy*, 73 (Oct.), 437–60.

Kim, Kwang Suk and Roemer, Michael 1979: *Growth and Structural Transformation, Studies in the Modernization of the Republic of Korea, 1945–75.* Cambridge, Mass.: Harvard University Press.

Krueger, Anne O. 1984: *Comparative Advantage and Development Policy Twenty Years Later.* In Moshe Syrquin, Lance Taylor, and Larry E. Westphal (eds), *Economnic Structure and Performance, Essays in Honor of Hollis B. Chenery*, Orlando, Fla.: Academic Press.

Krueger, Anne O. 1978: *Foreign Trade Regimes and Economic Development: Liberalization Attempts and Consequences.* Cambridge, Mass.: Ballinger Press for the National Bureau of Economic Research.

Krueger, Anne O. 1977: *Growth, Distortions, and Patterns of Trade among Many Countries.* Princeton, NJ: Princeton Studies in International Finance No. 40.

Krueger, Anne O. 1986: "The Importance of Economic Policy in Development: Contrasts between Korea and Turkey." Mimeo.

Krueger, Anne O. 1972: "Rates of Return to Turkish Higher Education." *Journal of Human Resources,* Autumn.

Krueger, Anne O. 1983: *Trade and Employment in Developing Countries: Synthesis and Conclusions.* Chicago: University of Chicago Press.

Krueger, Anne O. 1984: "Trade Policies in Developing Countries." In Ronald W. Jones and Peter B. Kenen (eds), *Handbook of International Economics,* Amsterdam: North-Holland.

Leamer, E. E. 1980: "The Leontief Paradox, Reconsidered." *Journal of Political Economy,* June.

Lewis, W. Arthur, 1954: "Economic Development with Unlimited Supplies of Labour." *Manchester School,* May.

Lipsey, Robert E.; Kravis, Irving B.; and Roldan, Romualdo A. 1982: "Do Multinational Firms Adapt Factor Proportions to Relative Factor Prices?" In Anne O. Krueger (ed.), *Trade and Employment in Developing Countries. Vol. 2. Factor Supply and Substitution.* Chicago: University of Chicago Press for the National Bureau of Economic Research, 215-55.

Magee, Stephen P. 1976: *International Trade and Distortions in Factor Markets.* New York: Marcel Dekker.

Michaely, Michael 1977: "Exports and Growth: An Empirical Investigation." *Journal of Development Economics,* 49-54.

Mirrlees, James 1975: "A Pure Theory of Underdeveloped Economies." In Lloyd Reynolds (ed.), *Agriculture in Development Theory,* New Haven: Yale University Press, 84-106.

Morawetz, David 1974: "Employment Implications of Industrialization in Developing Countries: A Survey." *Economic Journal,* Sept., 491-542.

Morawetz, David 1980: *Why the Emperor's New Clothes are not Made in Colombia.* Washington, DC: World Bank Staff Working Paper No. 368.

Myint, Hla 1985: "The Neoclassical Resurgence in Development Economics: Its Strength and Limitation." Washington, DC: World Bank.

Prebisch, Raúl 1964: *Towards a New Trade Policy for Development.* New York: United Nations.

Schultz, T. Paul 1982: "Effective Protection and the Distribution of Personal Income in Colombia." In Anne O. Krueger (ed.), *Trade and Employment in Developing Countries, vol. 2. Factor Supply and Substitution,* Chicago: University of Chicago Press for the National Bureau of Economic Research, 83-148.

Spraos, J. 1980: "The Statistical Debate on the Net Barrier Terms of Trade between Primary Commodities and Manufacturers." *Economic Journal.*

Squire, Lyn 1981: *Employment Policy in Developing Countries: A Survey of Issues and Evidence.* Oxford: Oxford University Press.

Westphal, L. E. and Kim, Kwang Suk 1977: "Industrial Policy and Development in Korea." Washington, DC: World Bank Staff Working Paper No. 263.

Comments on
"The Relationships Between Trade, Employment, and Development"

MICHAEL BRUNO

Let me first dispose of a small comment of detail, on the regression given in table 12.1. Is the U.N. per diem allowance necessarily correlated with the real wage in the export sector? It is probably more likely to be correlated with the real wage in the informal sector. Anyway, suppose the U.N. variable is correlated with income per capita (y), and log linearly related to it with elasticity $1/s$. In that case the equation on page 375 implies:

$$X/P = a + by^{(1/s-1)}.$$

If $s > 1$ then a negative value for b in the regression can be expected, since it implies an obvious positive correlation between exports per capita and income per capita. Thus, before going further, I would suggest checking first whether the U.N. variable is correlated with real wages for some countries. An alternative suggestion might be to use consumption per capita as a proxy for the real wage. But a negative relation between consumption per capita and exports per capita might be due to foreign aid availability, for which one would have to control separately. Anyway, until a more systematic attempt is made, I would not hasten to draw any conclusion from the regressions of table 12.1.

Let me get to more issues of substance. A key question, also mentioned by Anne Krueger, is the following: Is there any need to separate the effect of trade on employment from any other set of short- and long-run macro-policies that are conducive to better resource allocation? The paper does not give a clear answer to that, and if at all, my conclusion would be negative.

First, the good outward-looking performers (like the "gang of four" and some other countries, including my own country, Israel, in the past) had a good employment record not necessarily because of a preference for exports over import substitution. Most likely they did better because their general macro-policy stance (fewer stop-go policies, etc.) and other conditions (e.g. foreign aid availability) helped them grow more rapidly and thus absorb their labor force.

Second, since more than half of employment, typically, is not in tradeable goods, why stress only the choice of tradeables? A country may absorb labor in construction, housing, and services (including government services), which are labor-intensive and low import-users. Theoretically, at least, one could have a case in which the more profitable exports are in capital- (or human capital-) intensive goods and the optimum is to produce these and solve the unemployment problem by production of non-tradeables.

Next, let me make two points on the real wage issue: (1) A country may have a high and inflexible real wage at a point in time relative to its productivity. With time, it may accumulate capital and bring the marginal product of labor up to the real wage, while using its foreign aid to help absorb labor in non-tradeables. Capital-intensive production in agriculture, for example, may be more conducive to promoting a high rate of technical progress, which in turn may be helpful for development of exports. (2) The problem of real wage is not its high level at a point in time but its flexibility of response to external shocks, as the example of the European countries in the 1970s shows.

Consider a typical European country with advanced trade union legislation, social security, and segmented labor markets; yet its trade is typically highly liberalized by any standards. Its unemployment in the 1970s and 1980s may be partly "classical," partly Keynesian. But none of it has to do with its trade regime or with trade *per se*.

Finally there is a small, yet important, point that has not been mentioned here and yet relates to both employment and trade. Overly quick trade liberalization may cause substantial unemployment (consider Chile in the 1970s), while slow but steady trade liberalization (e.g. Israel) does not. The speed of adjustment certainly matters.

13

Financial Liberalization in Retrospect: Interest Rate Policies in LDCs

RONALD I. McKINNON

When governments tax and otherwise distort their domestic capital market, the economy is said to be financially "repressed."[1] Usury restrictions on interest rates, heavy reserve requirements on bank deposits, and compulsory credit allocations interact with ongoing price inflation to reduce the attractiveness of holding claims on the domestic banking system. In such a repressed financial system, real deposit rates of interest on monetary assets are often negative and are difficult to predict when inflation is high and unstable. Thus, the demand for money – broadly defined to include saving and term deposits as well as checking accounts and currency – falls as a proportion of GNP.

But these monetary assets naturally dominate the financial portfolios of small savers in less developed countries. Thus Edward Shaw and I hypothesized that repressing the monetary system fragments the domestic capital market with highly adverse consequences for the quality of real capital accumulation:

1 The flow of loanable funds through the organized banking system is reduced, forcing potential investors to rely more on self-finance;
2 Interest rates on the truncated flow of bank lending vary arbitrarily from one class of favored or disfavored borrowers to another;
3 The process of self-finance within enterprises and households is itself impaired. If the real yield on deposits — as well as coin and currency — is negative, firms cannot easily accumulate liquid assets in preparation for making discrete investments. Socially costly inflation hedges look more attractive as a means of internal finance.

*Presented to a conference on *The State of Development Economics,* Yale University, April 11–13, 1986. I would like to thank Nathaniel Leff, Jorge de Macedo, and Gustav Ranis for their helpful comments.

4 Significant financial deepening outside of the repressed banking system becomes impossible when firms are dangerously illiquid and/or inflation is high and unstable. Robust open markets in stocks and bonds, or intermediation by trust and insurance companies, require monetary stability.

Remedying financial repression is implicit in its definition. We suggested keeping positive and more uniformly high real rates of interest within comparable categories of bank deposits and loans by eliminating undue reserve requirements, interest ceilings, and mandated credit allocations, on the one hand, while stabilizing the price level through appropriate macroeconomic measures, on the other. Then, savers and investors would better "see" the true scarcity price of capital, and thus reduce the great dispersion in the profitability of investing in different sectors of the economy.

These strictures for liberalizing the financial system seem now like mere truisms to most economists — although not to politicians. Today, both the World Bank and the International Monetary Fund stress the importance of stabilizing the domestic price level and increasing the flow of generally available loanable funds at close to market-clearing interest rates. From the perspective of the 1980s, those countries with substantially positive real interest rates and high real financial growth – such as Japan, Taiwan, and Singapore (as shown in more detail below) – are regarded as leading success stories.

In the 1980s, this new emphasis on the advantages of financial liberalization is quite remarkable. Well into the 1970s, many development economists had still favored the generation of "forced" saving through inflation – or through shifts in the internal distribution of income by such means as turning the internal terms of trade against agriculture in order to transfer an economic "surplus" to the industrial sector. Credit subsidies, at below market rates of interest, were once widely promoted as a means of stimulating socially desirable investments. Unless so manipulated or repressed, the financial sector was not viewed as a leading force in the development process.

Outside the centrally planned economies, however, there is now widespread agreement that flows of saving and investment should be voluntary and significantly decentralized in an open capital market at close to "equilibrium" interest rates.

PITFALLS IN FINANCIAL LIBERALIZATION

Nevertheless, all is not well in the liberal camp. The general case favoring financial liberalization has been called into question by a series of bank panics and collapses in the Southern Cone of Latin America (Díaz-Alejandro, 1985). In the late 1970s and early 1980s, Argentina,

Chile, and Uruguay all made serious efforts to end wild inflations while deregulating and privatizing their commercial banks. Interest rates on both bank deposits and loans were completely freed, with the latter often increasing to unexpectedly high levels in real terms. That these attempted financial liberalizations generally ended in failure – with an undue buildup of foreign indebtedness and government reintervention to prop up failing domestic banks and industrial enterprises – is well documented in a series of revealing studies edited by Vittorio Corbo and Jaime de Melo (1985).

Without retreating to the older view, which elevates repressive financial measures to being potentially desirable instruments of public policy, we now recognize that our knowledge of how best to achieve financial liberalization remains seriously incomplete. The *order* in which the monetary system is stabilized in comparison to the pace of deregulation of banks and other financial institutions must be more carefully considered than had previously been thought.

In this paper, I begin by reviewing the evidence that financial liberalization and significantly positive real rates of interest are, on average, associated with higher economic growth in LDCs. Avoiding financial repression remains very important if the economy's scarce capital is to be allocated efficiently.

However, then I go on to suggest that there are limits to which real rates of interest can be raised in immature bank-based capital markets without incurring undue *adverse risk selection* (Stiglitz and Weiss, 1981) among industrial and agricultural borrowers. Furthermore, when everybody knows that the banks' deposit base is, implicitly or explicitly, insured by the government, macroeconomic instability could well induce considerable *moral hazard* in the banks themselves. Thus macroeconomic instability reduces the socially desirable level of real interest rates in the banking sector, and makes financial liberalization more difficult.

But these propositions, and their implications for public policy, remain to be demonstrated.

A CROSS-COUNTRY ANALYSIS OF REAL INTEREST RATES AND ECONOMIC GROWTH

What lessons have been learned about financial repression in steady states – say over a decade or more? Countries that have sustained higher real rates of interest have generally had robust real financial growth leading to higher real economic growth. Some data on private holdings of "broad" money throw light on these issues. Table 13.1 presents ratios of the broad money supply (M2) to gross national product (GNP).[2] One noticeable characteristic is that even the slower-growing Asian countries (shown in the lower panel) tend to be more financially

TABLE 13.1   *Bank loanable funds in typical semi-industrial LDCs (ratio of M2 to GNP)*

	1960	1965	1970	1975	1980	Mean 1960–80
Argentina	0.245	0.209	0.267	0.168	0.234	0.225
Brazil	0.148	0.156	0.205	0.164	0.175	0.170
Chile	0.123	0.130	0.183	0.099	0.208	0.149
Colombia	0.191	0.204	0.235	—	0.222	0.210
Mean ratio of M2 to GNP for four Latin American countries						0.184
India	0.283	0.262	0.264	0.295	0.382	0.297
Philippines	0.186	0.214	0.235	0.186	0.219	0.208
Sri Lanka	0.284	0.330	0.275	0.255	0.317	0.291
Turkey	0.202	0.223	0.237	0.222	0.136	0.204
Mean ratio of M2 to GNP for four Asian countries						0.247

Source: IMF, *International Financial Statistics* (various issues).

TABLE 13.2   *Bank loanable funds in rapidly growing economies (ratio of M2 to GNP)*

	1955	1960	1965	1970	1975	1980
Germany[a]	0.331	0.294	0.448	0.583	0.727	0.913
Japan	0.554[b]	0.737[b]	0.701[b]	0.863	1.026	1.390
Korea	0.069	0.114	0.102	0.325	0.323	0.337
Taiwan	0.115	0.166	0.331	0.462	0.588	0.750
Singapore	—	—	0.542[b]	0.701	0.668	0.826

[a] As well as deposits and currency, the German series includes bank bonds sold directly to the public.
[b] The bias is downward because deposit information on specialized credit institutions was not collected.
Source: IMF, *International Financial Statistics* (various issues).

developed than typical Latin American countries (shown in the upper panel). However, both groups of slowly or erratically growing economies have fairly low ratios of M2 to GNP, averaging about 0.22.

In contrast, table 13.2 shows financial development in the really rapid-growth economies – West Germany, Japan, South Korea, Taiwan, and Singapore. A high and rising M2/GNP ratio indicates a large real flow of loanable funds. Because capital markets in these economies were dominated by banks, ratios of M2 to GNP encompass the main domestic flow of loanable funds in the system. By 1980 Japan, Taiwan, and Singapore had M2/GNP ratios of 0.75 or more. Only South Korea had a much lower ratio of M2 to GNP (0.34), and had to make up for this shortage of domestic loanable funds by borrowing heavily abroad. The other countries shown in table 13.2 are now net international creditors.

Although a higher rate of financial growth is positively correlated with successful real growth, Patrick's (1966) problem remains unresolved: What is the cause and what is the effect? Is finance a leading sector in economic development, or does it simply follow growth in real output which is generated elsewhere? Perhaps individuals whose incomes grow quickly want financial assets simply as a kind of consumer good (i.e. an incidental outcome of the growth process). To disentangle these issues, table 13.3 presents some data from a recent study on interest rate policies in developing countries (IMF, 1983). Pure data availability and membership of the IMF were the criteria on which countries were selected.

For any one country over time, the real interest rate can vary a great deal, even from positive to negative or vice versa. For the period from 1971 to 1980, the IMF calculated an average real interest rate for each country on a fairly common asset, usually a 30-day deposit. Countries were then classified according to whether their average real interest rate was positive, mildly negative, or highly negative. Because most of these countries have fragmented interest rate structures, a representative interest rate is not easy to select. Nevertheless the IMF managed to devise the three-way classification shown in table 13.3.

Using this same sample of countries from the IMF study, real financial growth (which is not the same as measured personal saving) is shown to be positively correlated with real GDP growth in figure 13.1. The left-hand panel of figure 13.2 shows that those countries that maintain positive real rates of interest have higher growth in real financial assets, as might be expected. Most importantly, the right-hand panel of figure 13.2 shows a significant positive correlation between real rates of interest and real growth in GDP. A similar result was earlier obtained by Maxwell Fry (1978), who regressed real output growth on real interest rates using pooled cross-section and time-series data from a group of Asian LDCs.

With this kind of regression analysis, care must be taken in deciding which variables are exogenous and which endogenous. Positive correlations between° growth in financial assets and growth in GDP do not show which way the causality operates. However, for the purposes of portfolio choice by individual investors, a case can be made for treating the real rate of interest as exogenous. Governments frequently intervene to set ceilings on nominal rates of interest on bank deposits, and at the same time they determine the aggregate rate of price inflation; the real rate of interest, therefore, is very much determined by public policy. Thus the presumption is that nonrepressive financial policies, resulting

TABLE 13.3   *Selected developing countries grouped according to interest-rate policies: growth of real financial assets and real GDP, 1971–80 (compound growth rates, percent per annum)*

	Financial assets[a]	GDP
1. Countries with positive real interest rates		
Malaysia	13.8	8.0
Korea	11.1	8.6
Sri Lanka	10.1	4.7
Nepal	9.6	2.0
Singapore	7.6	9.1
Philippines	5.6	6.2
2. Countries with moderately negative real interest rates		
Pakistan[b]	9.9	5.4
Thailand	8.5	6.9
Morocco	8.2	5.5
Colombia	5.5	5.8
Greece	5.4	4.7
South Africa	4.3	3.7
Kenya	3.6	5.7
Burma	3.5	4.3
Portugal	1.8	4.7
Zambia	−1.1	0.8
3. Countries with severely negative real interest rates		
Peru	3.2	3.4
Turkey	2.2	5.1
Jamaica	−1.9	−0.7
Zaire	−6.8	0.1
Ghana	−7.6	−0.1

[a] Measured as the sum of monetary and quasi-monetary deposits with the banking sector, corrected for changes in the consumer price index.
[b] The period covered is 1974–80.
Source: "Interest Rate Policies in Developing Countries," Occasional Paper, No. 22. International Monetary Fund, October 1983.

in significantly positive real rates of interest, contribute to higher economic growth.

Any positive link between real rates of interest and personal saving, as measured in the GDP accounts, is much less apparent. The results of cross-country statistical studies linking inflation rates to aggregate saving have been quite ambiguous (Leff and Sato, 1980). This ambiguity is puzzling. Shouldn't saving be discouraged as inflation erodes the real values of financial assets?

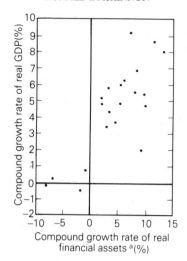

Fig. 13.1   *Selected developing countries: growth of real GDP and real financial assets, 1971–80*

[a]As defined in table 13.3; source: IMF, *International Financial Statistics.*

Source: "Interest Rate Policies in Developing Countries," Occasional Paper No. 22, International Monetary Fund, October 1983

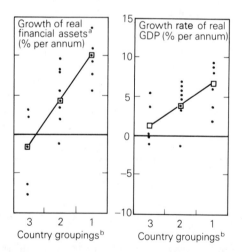

Fig. 13.2   *Selected developing countries grouped according to interest rate policies: growth of real financial assets and real GDP, 1971–80*

[a]As defined in table 13.3.
[b]See table 13.3 for specifications of these groupings.

Source: "Interest Rate Policies in Developing Countries," Occasional Paper No. 22, International Monetary Fund, October 1983

In an inflationary economy, real rates of interest on financial assets are usually negative. Because of the inflation, however, the private sector is forced to abstain from current consumption. Individuals must keep adding to their nominal money balances in order to prevent their real balances from declining. But this inflation "tax" extracted by the government is classified in the GNP accounts as if it were private saving. However, real personal financial assets are not accumulating, and the flow of loanable funds to the private sector may be quite low – even though the flow of private "saving", as measured in the GNP accounts, might be quite high.

Typically, therefore, systematic relationships cannot be derived from cross-sectional data between the flow of personal saving and real rates of interest, or between personal saving and inflation. From cross-country comparisons of "long-run" experiences over a decade or more, however, the positive correlation between real interest rates and real growth seems unambiguous.

Apparently the quality, if not the quantity, of investment improves significantly when interest rates are positive and financial intermediation is robust.

INTEREST RATES AND RAPID ECONOMIC GROWTH IN POSTWAR JAPAN: A REVISIONIST VIEW

Does the postwar Japanese experience support the case for financial liberalization and high interest rates? Starting from very low income per capita after World War II, the Japanese economy grew very rapidly from the early 1950s to the early 1970s. Indeed, Japanese now rather nostalgically refer simply to their "era of rapid economic growth." Moreover, table 13.2 shows robust Japanese real financial growth, with a rapidly increasing ratio of M2 to GNP, during this period.

But, paradoxically, this era was widely considered then – and down to the present time – to be one of financial repression (using our more recent terminology). It was conventional wisdom that Japan was following a "low interest rate" policy in order to provide cheap bank credits, directed by government officials, to support officially sanctioned industrial investments. Interest ceilings in the form of standard loan and deposit rates were observed by all significant banks – and open market sales of corporate bonds and other debt instruments were limited and monitored by government officials. In the documents of the Bank of Japan and the Ministry of Finance, numerous references to administrative guidance could be construed as allocating the flow of most bank loans to officially preferred uses.

However, in his paper "The 'Low Interest Rate Policy' and Economic Growth in Japan," Akiyoshi Horiuchi (1984) provides a convincing alternative view that the Japanese financial system was not significantly repressed after all! For the era of rapid economic growth, Horiuchi shows that officially controlled (real) interest rates in Japan were relatively high by international standards. Moreover he argues that variability in the free interbank call money rate, and in large compensating balances required of business borrowers, meant that the effective loan rates charged Japanese industry fairly accurately reflected the "true" scarcity price of capital in the economy.

Tables 13.4, 13.5, and 13.6 simply reproduce Horiuchi's data comparing Japanese interest rates to those in the United States, Britain, and Germany. One can easily see that nominal interest rates on both the deposit and loan sides were generally higher in Japan from the early 1950s through 1972. And remember that the yen/dollar exchange rate was fixed almost to the very end of this period so that nominal interest rates could be directly compared.

But whether "real" interest rates were higher depends heavily on which index is used to measure Japanese price inflation, i.e., the opportunity cost of holding yen denominated financial assets. If one uses the relatively rapidly increasing consumer price index (CPI) to deflate nominal interest rates, table 13.4 shows that Japanese real interest rates were not so high and, on occasion, were even negative. However, if one uses the slowly growing wholesale price index (WPI) as the relevant deflator, Japanese real interest rates were relatively high: 4 or 5 percent on deposits and 6 or 7 percent on loans.

Elsewhere (McKinnon, 1973, pp. 96–7, and again in McKinnon, 1979, pp. 234–6), I have argued that the WPI – which represents claims on a broad basket of (tradeable) *goods* – is a better deflator than the CPI, which depends heavily on movements in the prices of domestically produced *services,* which cannot be held directly in asset portfolios. In inflationary circumstances, the relevant alternative to holding yen-denominated financial assets is a portfolio of tangible goods (not intangible services), or foreign exchange assets which are a claim on foreign goods.[3] In tables 13.5 and 13.6, Horiuchi recognizes this by using just the WPI to show that, in the 1950s and 1960s, real loan rates in Japan were higher than in the United States and United Kingdom and comparable to those prevailing in Germany – another high growth country.

Horiuchi goes on to show that the Japanese government was far less successful than is commonly believed in influencing the domestic flow of capital. The relatively small flow of government-directed cheap credit was largely allocated to "sunset" or declining industries. Internationally competitive firms had no trouble bidding for funds at close to the market rate of interest. In summary, the Japanese financial system was not significantly repressed in the era of rapid economic growth.

But neither did the Japanese authorities fully "liberalize" their banking system by removing ceilings on deposit rates of interest, or allowing the standard loan rate charged to non-banks to be unrestricted,

TABLE 13.4   *Official discount rates, deposit rates, and monetary market rate (annual average)* (%)

	1953-57	1958-62	1963-67	1968-72	1973-77	1978-82
Japan:						
Discount rate	6.9	7.1	5.9	5.4	7.1	5.6
Call money rate	8.7	9.6	7.4	7.0	8.6	7.1
Deposit rate[a]	5.1	5.3	5.0	5.0	6.0	5.2
WPI rate of change	1.1	−1.0	1.4	1.3	11.4	5.1
CPI rate of change	3.1	3.6	5.6	5.9	13.1	4.6
U.S.:						
Discount rate	2.4	3.1	4.2	5.2	6.5	11.0
TB rate	2.1	2.7	4.0	5.4	6.2	10.7
Deposit rate[d]	2.6	3.2	5.0	5.0	5.5	5.7
WPI rate of change	1.0	0.3	1.1	3.6	10.4	9.1
CPI rate of change	1.2	1.5	2.0	4.6	7.7	9.8
U.K.:						
Discount rate	4.7	4.7	6.4	7.2	11.4	14.5[c]
TB rate	3.5	4.4	5.2	6.6	9.9	12.2
Deposit rate[d]	2.8	2.7	4.4	4.9	8.2	11.2
WPI rate of change	1.7	1.4	2.3	5.8	17.9	11.4
CPI rate of change	2.9	2.2	3.3	6.6	16.3	12.0
Germany:						
Discount rate	3.8	3.4	3.6	4.7	4.6	5.8
Call money rate	3.7	4.0	3.8	5.3	6.3	7.7
Deposit rate[e]	3.5	2.9	3.1	5.4	6.0	6.8
WPI rate of change	−0.5	0.5	0.9	2.6	6.2	5.4
CPI rate of change	0.9	2.0	2.7	3.5	5.7	5.8

[a] The interest rate on six-month deposits.
[b] The interest rate on time deposits less the U.S.−100,000 (maximum). From 1963 to 1967, the maximum rate on deposits of more than one year.
[c] 1978-80. The Bank of England stopped announcing the minimum lending rate, i.e. the discount rate.
[d] The interest rate on deposits account repayable at seven days' notice (maximum).
[e] The interest rate on three-month deposits (maximum).
Source: "The 'Low Interest Rate Policy' and Economic Growth in Postwar Japan" Akiyoshi Horiuchi, *The Developing Economies*, vol. 22, December 1984.

or allowing banks to borrow freely abroad. Nor did the central bank in any way abandon its close monitoring of what the commercial and savings banks were doing in terms of the safety of their asset portfolios. Indeed, because of fiscal surpluses and the absence of a significant market in government bonds, the Bank of Japan was deeply involved in discounting a fairly large proportion of the commercial banks' portfolio of private loans – the famous "overloan" situation – in order to secure

TABLE 13.5   *International comparison of prime rate (annual average)* (%)

	Japan[a]	U.S.[b]	U.K.[c]	Germany[d]
1953–57	7.8 (1.1)	3.7 (1.0)	5.2 (1.7)	8.4 (−0.5)
1958–62	7.4 (−1.0)	4.5 (0.3)	5.2 (1.4)	7.9 (0.5)
1963–67	6.2 (1.4)	5.2 (1.1)	6.9 (2.3)	8.1 (0.9)
1968–72	5.7 (1.3)	6.7 (3.6)	7.7 (5.8)	9.5 (2.6)
1973–77	6.9 (11.4)	8.4 (10.4)	12.4 (17.9)	10.4 (6.2)
1978–82	6.0 (5.1)	15.2 (9.1)	14.6 (11.4)	11.3 (5.4)

Note: The parenthesis presents rates of changes in the WPI.
[a] Discount rate of commercial bills eligible for rediscount by the Bank of Japan (more than Y3 million).
[b] The prime rate.
[c] The interest rate of overdrafts for the prime corporations.
[d] The maximum level of interest rate on overdrafts (until 1966). The interest rate on overdrafts of DM 1 million or less (from 1967).
Source: Bank of Japan, Statistics Department, *Nihon keizai wo chūshin tosuru kokusai hikaku tōkei* [Japan and the world: a comparison by economic and financial statistics], various issues.

TABLE 13.6   *Interest rates on bank loans in Japan (annual average)* (%)

	Loan rates covered by formal control: all banks	Loan rates not covered by formal control: all banks	Rate of change in WPI
1953–57	8.2	9.5	1.1
1958–62	7.6	8.9	−1.0
1963–67	7.1	8.5	1.4
1968–72	6.9	8.2	1.3
1973–77	7.7	8.8	11.4
1978–81	6.6	7.9	6.1

Note: Ceilings have been imposed on interest rates of short-term (less than a year) bank loans by the Temporary Interest Rate Adjustment Law (1947). Within the legal ceilings, the short-term loan rates have been determined by a de facto cartel among the private banks. Though interest rates on other loans have been exempted from the control, they also have been determined by a type of cartel. The Japanese authorities can influence the decision making of these cartels.
Source: "The 'Low Interest Rate Policy' and Economic Growth in Postwar Japan," Akiyoshi Horiuchi, *The Developing Economies*, vol. 22, December 1984.

sufficiently high growth in the monetary base. This greatly facilitated the central bank's monitoring of the quality and safety of loans to the private sector.

From the late 1970s to the present time, the Japanese have greatly liberalized what their commercial banks can do in both foreign and domestic financial markets. The overloan situation has virtually disappeared. But in assessing the quite different Latin American experiences below, what does the earlier Japanese experience suggest for the correct order of financial liberalization?

First, monetary stabilization with a fairly constant domestic price level was the principal mode by which high real interest rates, and high real financial growth, were secured. The Japanese government was not often put into a situation of having to permit (decide on) high nominal interest rates in order to offset high and variable domestic inflation.

Secondly, only after substantial financial deepening in the nonbank parts of the capital market – growth in primary securities trading and increased intermediation by finance and insurance companies, pension funds, and so on – did the authorities substantially loosen up (or begin thinking about loosening up) on what the commercial banks could do.

Thirdly, the domestic banking system was never put in the situation of being the principal financial intermediary for significant amounts of net capital flows from abroad, with its attendant direct or indirect exchange risk. The limited foreign capital coming into Japan was in the form of direct investment – or, more commonly, took the form of company-to-company licensing agreements.

Beginning a decade later in 1960, Taiwan's financial policies roughly paralleled Japan's. Taiwan's dollar exchange rate was quite stable and price inflation was low or nonexistent, except for unanticipated international inflation shocks. Apart from these episodes, real loan rates have been kept between 8 or 9 percent per year, and rates on time deposits were about 6 or 7 percent in real terms (Cheng, 1986). Standard deposit and loan rates suppressed full-scale competition for funds among the Taiwanese banks, which, in any event, were (are) state-owned – unlike their Japanese counterparts.

Only now in the mid-1980s, after substantial financial deepening for more than a decade and a half, is Taiwan seriously considering loosening up on the tight controls over its banking system. Even without this further (and now desirable) liberalization, however, table 13.2 shows how impressively large the flow of loanable funds through Taiwan's banking system has become.

PREMATURE FINANCIAL DECONTROL IN CHILE

Although measured and carefully delimited financial liberalizations have worked well, as in Japan and Taiwan, more sweeping attempts at financial decontrol have sometimes come to grief, as in Turkey, Sri Lanka, and the Southern Cone of Latin America. It is worthwhile tracing out one such experience.

In the late 1970s, all three countries in the Southern Cone had substantially deregulated their banking systems *before* bringing inflation under control and achieving significant financial deepening. Indeed, all three countries suffered from substantial macroeconomic instability at the time that interest ceilings on bank deposits and loans were removed, and banks were allowed to compete freely in the capital market.

Only Chile, however, had sufficient fiscal control to make price stabilization and financial liberalization a fully credible objective of public policy. Thus the Chilean experience from 1976 to 1982 with bank supervision is a somewhat cleaner example of how uncontrolled interest rates might work when inflation is still very high and difficult to predict.

Price inflation started off at over 170 percent per year in 1976, before falling to less than 10 percent in 1981 and then rising again. Table 13.7 summarizes some extensive Chilean financial data provided by Rolf Luders (1985) on the extraordinary pattern of deposit and loan rates – both nominal and real – after most commercial banks had been returned to the private sector by 1976 and official interest ceilings had been removed. Two characteristics stand out.

The first is the very high real interest rate, calculated *ex post* on the basis of experienced inflation rather than on *ex ante* expectations of it. For example, in 1978 the "real" lending rate on peso loans was 42.2 percent on an annualized basis, although lending was typically much less than a year in duration. The net annualized spread between peso deposits and loans was about 10.7 percentage points, after taking out the effects of reserve requirements. To achieve these real yields, the nominal peso loan rate was 85.3 percent, less than one-third of what it had been in the more inflationary year of 1976.

The second striking characteristic of table 13.7 is the large spread between the apparent interest costs of borrowing in pesos compared with borrowing from domestic banks in dollars, which, after the deregulations of the mid-1970s, accounted for almost one-half of total bank loans (Luders, 1985). Adjusted downward for the experienced rate of peso devaluation, this spread was as high as 48.9 percentage points in 1976 and then fell to a still-high 8.6 percentage points in 1980 before increasing to 24.3 percentage points in 1981. It then fell sharply with the "surprise" devaluations of 1982. Indeed, often the "real" cost (adjusted for the domestic rate of price inflation less the rate of exchange devaluation) of borrowing in dollars was negative – even though real borrowing costs in pesos remained very high.

At the time, virtually everyone thought this difference was due to imperfections in financial arbitrage because of the remaining restrictions on foreign capital inflows. Indeed, this belief prompted the authorities to loosen capital restrictions even further in 1980, thus worsening the overborrowing syndrome. Corbo (1985) analyzes the unsustainable real appreciation of the Chilean peso, associated with the

TABLE 13.7   *Chile: Interest rates on 30-day bank deposits and loans*

	1976	1977	1978	1979	1980	1981	1982
			(percent per annum)				
Peso deposits:							
Nominal	197.9	93.7	62.8	45.1	37.4	40.8	47.8
Real[a]	8.6	18.5	24.9	4.4	4.8	28.6	22.4
Peso loans:							
Nominal	350.7	156.4	85.3	62.0	47.0	51.9	63.1
Real[a]	64.3	56.8	42.2	16.6	11.9	38.7	35.1
Gross spread	57.2	33.7	14.5	12.1	7.1	12.3	10.7
Net spread[f]	8.1	17.4	10.7	7.4	5.2	6.3	9.5
Interest differential:[d]							
Peso/dollar deposits	2.9	7.8	0.0	8.7	14.0	19.5	−1.2
Peso/dollar loans	48.9	36.4	8.6	14.1	17.1	24.3	5.6
Dollar deposits:							
Nominal[b]	8.9	8.9	11.1	13.5	15.1	17.8	14.6
Real[e]	−18.1	7.9	4.6	−5.8	12.3	7.6	40.0
Dollar loans:							
Nominal[c]	13.9	13.9	16.1	20.7	19.9	22.2	18.3
Real[e]	−14.3	12.9	9.3	0.1	−8.6	11.6	44.5
Change in consumer prices	174.3	63.5	30.3	38.9	31.2	9.5	20.7

[a] All real peso interest rates are calculated monthly, based on monthly changes in the Chilean Consumer Price Index in pesos, before being annualized.

[b] Nominal dollar deposit rates are costs of borrowing abroad: LIBOR plus average spread charged to Chilean commercial banks.

[c] Nominal dollar loan rates are interest charged domestic customers by Chilean banks.

[d] To calculate interest differential, nominal interest rates in dollars are first adjusted upwards by the (experienced) rate of exchange devaluation.

[e] The "real" interest rate in dollars is:

$$\frac{(1 + \text{nominal rate})(1 + \text{devaluation rate})}{1 + \text{peso inflation rate}} - 1$$

[f] Net spread after effects of compulsory non-interest bearing reserve requirements against peso deposits are taken out.

Source: Rolf Luders *Lessons from Two Financial Liberalization Episodes: Argentina and Chile*, unpublished manuscript, November 1985.

buildup of external debt in 1977–81, which led to a sharp decline in the profitability of the tradeable goods sector.

Sadder but wiser, we now understand that these incredibly high interest rates on peso loans in large part represented the breakdown of proper financial supervision over the Chilean banking system. Neither officials in the commercial banks themselves, nor government regulatory authorities, adequately monitored the credit-worthiness of a broad spectrum of industrial and agricultural borrowers:

> The internal source of difficulty in Chile was a proliferation of bad loans within the banking system. The rolling over of these loans, capitalizing interest along the way, created what I call a "false" demand for credit, which, when added to the demand that would normally be viable, allowed real interest rates to reach unprecedented (and, to many, incredible) levels. (Harberger, 1985, p. 237)

This form of Ponzi game, however, had a peculiarly international flavor in which Chilean financial intermediaries – not only banks – incurred exchange risk as they extended bad loans. James Tybout (1986) and others have shown that the large economic groups, "Grupos," used their control over domestic banks together with their overseas contracts to get dollar credits at relatively low interest rates to re-lend at the extremely high, but which turned out to be false, interest rates denominated in pesos.

Because banks were officially restricted from directly assuming foreign exchange exposure, they simply made dollar loans to the Grupos' industrial companies, which then did most of the ongoing lending in pesos. Thus, by assuming the foreign exchange risk themselves, these Grupos continued to show increases in their non-operating earning in 1980 and 1981, well after their operating earnings had soured because of the exchange overvaluation and continued high interest rates. Some were recording unrealized capital gains, from some very dubious assets, as earnings on their books.

Of course, many Chilean firms need not have known at the time that they were engaged in a Ponzi game. Many probably suffered from excessive optimism regarding future asset values and rates of return – hopes that were ultimately dashed by the real exchange rate over-valuation and downturn in the international economy in 1981–2 that led to massive losses by firms across the export and import-competing sectors. The resulting series of defaults on outstanding bank credits, including those to the large "Grupos", forced bankruptcy on virtually all of Chile's financial intermediaries.

In 1982–3, the Chilean banks were all intervened (renationalized) in order to protect the positions of domestic depositors and foreign creditors – even though the government had not previously committed itself to deposit insurances. In a similar set of bankruptcies in Argentina, official deposit insurance had been more explicit. Nevertheless, the upshot in the two countries was the same. The special position of the banks – as custodians of the nation's money supply – effectively meant that the depositors and the banks could behave *ex ante* as if their deposits would be insured in the event some major financial breakdown occurred.

PRICE-LEVEL STABILIZATION

What are the lessons to be learned from the rather cautious approach to bank deregulation in Japan and Taiwan in comparison to the Southern Cone experiences with complete decontrol? Obviously, sustained stability in the domestic price level is a necessary condition for achieving high real financial growth without undue risk of some major financial panic and collapse. When general macroeconomic and price level instability is pronounced, the use of extremely high nominal rates of interest to offset anticipated inflation, and balance the supply and demand for loanable funds in the capital market, becomes very risky – although perhaps necessary.

However, designing a successful macroeconomic stabilization, where the economy moves from very high to low price inflation, is itself a major problem which I have treated separately (McKinnon, 1973 and 1986). After fiscal control is assured, one can make a case for the government to "forward peg" a few key nominal prices – the exchange rate, wage contracts, standard interest rates on deposit and loans – in order to convince people that the disinflation will be successful. And it is very important that these forward indexed prices be properly aligned with one another to prevent misalignments in relative prices. The Chilean experiment failed, in part, because the real exchange rate became overvalued, leading to a sharp decline in international competitiveness, and real interest rates rose so high they induced unduly risky borrowing and eventually bankruptcies in the industrial and agricultural sectors.

Because this stabilization problem is treated elsewhere (see also Corbo and de Melo, 1985; Edwards, 1985; and Dornbusch, 1985), here I shall focus on the equally important *microeconomic* issues of how best to regulate the risky capital market activities of banks in the face of (possibly) ongoing macroeconomic instability.

THE REGULATORY PROBLEM

In less developed economies with low per capita incomes, open markets for common stocks, bonds, mortgages, or even commercial bills are typically insignificant. Information availability and economies of scale are insufficient for small farmers or merchants to issue their own notes or shares that are publicly traded. Instead, private financial savings in LDCs are largely currency and deposits: claims on central banks, commercial banks, savings banks, postal savings deposits, and so on as measured by M2 in tables 13.1 and 13.2.

This absence of open markets in primary securities – particularly equities – throws more risk on to the bank-based capital market. Combined with greater macroeconomic instability in LDCs, considerable tension is created in achieving a regulatory balance between the two traditional roles of the banking system:

1   The monetary function: providing a stable unit of account, store of value, and means of payment; and
2   Financial intermediation: transferring saving to public and private investors.

Because of the third-party benefits that flow from preventing any impairment of the payments mechanism under (1), banks must be carefully regulated towards safety. And this inherently limits their active risk-taking, but still crucial, role in the capital market under (2).

Governments rely on a wide variety of rules: capital and reserve requirements, restrictions on what can be lent to any one borrower, detailed inspections of the quality of asset portfolios to assure proper loan-loss provisions for each risk category, and so on – to limit the ability of banks to undertake risky investments. Sometimes, for safety reasons, banks are even state-owned, as in the Taiwanese case noted above, and as was true in Korea until recently. Even so, if accounting information from enterprises is poor – and equity or collateral difficult to judge – bank officers and government regulators have trouble distinguishing *ex ante* among borrowers in different risk classes.

Without addressing the complex task of how each of the above regulations might be optimally applied, let us focus simply on optimal interest rate policy for the (commercial) banks. In this one-dimensional analysis based on interest rates, I initially assume that the other safety-first regulations are in effect.

Further narrowing the problem, suppose our hypothetical bank has a given supply of loanable funds from the deposit side (less required reserves) and can divide potential nonbank borrowers into a small number of risk classes, within which each potential borrower is "observationally equivalent," i.e., the subjective probability of default at any given interest rate is the same. The bank's one decision variable is how to set the lending rate of interest, uniform within each risk category, so as to maximize the expected net return per dollar lent.

Following Stiglitz and Weiss (1981), as the real interest rate charged to any one class of borrowers increases, so does the probability of default on loan contracts. Because of the nature of a fixed interest-rate loan, borrowers get to keep any extraordinary profits if their project turns out well, but can default and walk away from unusual losses. Thus, as the interest rate increases,

1   A higher proportion of riskier borrowers will come forward to accept the loan offer; whereas safer borrowers who are unlikely to default will drop out of the applicant pool. This is what Stiglitz and Weiss call "adverse risk selection";
2   Any one borrower will tend to change the nature of his own project (insofar as the bank can't perfectly monitor what he is doing) to make it riskier: what Stiglitz and Weiss call the "incentive effect."

Both effects will induce the bank to limit voluntarily the interest rate charged to any one class of borrowers in order to maximize expected profit. In equilibrium, there will be arbitrary credit rationing with a pool of unsatisfied potential borrowers who are observationally equivalent to those who get loans.

Stiglitz and Weiss simply assumed that their bank would behave in a risk neutral fashion in reaching its rationing equilibrium. Even without regulation by some outside agency, banks would voluntarily limit the interest rate charged in order to avoid undue adverse risk selection and a decline in their expected profit net of defaults. But I shall show that this need not be the case if significant macroeconomic instability causes the returns on projects of the nonbank borrowers to be positively correlated.

ADVERSE RISK SELECTION WHEN THE MACROECONOMY IS STABLE

First, however, let us consider the simpler case of when the macro economy – price level, output, real exchange rate, and so on – is stable, as implicitly assumed by Stiglitz and Weiss. Important aspects of their argument are illustrated in figure 13.3, where the real loan rate is plotted on the horizontal axis and the real net yield per dollar lent on the vertical axis. In a stable macroeconomic environment, one can reasonably assume (with Stiglitz and Weiss) that the distribution of returns among the projects of borrowers are statistically independent of one another, i.e., no positive covariance among the profit positions of firms. Furthermore, suppose that the number of loan applicants in each risk class, R, is "large" so that there is a predictable number of defaults and a deterministic profit to the bank per dollar lent.

Figure 13.3 shows three distinct risk classes: R_1, R_2, and R_3 in ascending order of expected return, and variance in that return, on the borrower's project. R_1 is fully collateralized and perfectly safe with no variance in outcome, with the maximum interest rate the borrower can pay being $r_1 = R_1$. There is no adverse risk selection (or incentive

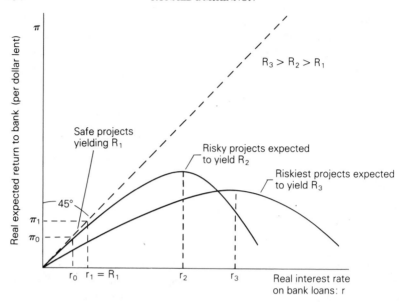

FIG. 13.3 *Bank profit maximization with adverse risk selection and statistically independent default probabilities (three classes of nonbank borrowers)*

effects) so that the profit to the bank increases *pari passu* with *r*, the loan rate, along the solid part of the 45° ray from the origin.

The graph R_2 covers riskier projects with a higher expected yield to the borrower, and lies below and to the right of the 45° ray. Because of incentive effects and adverse risk selection, profits to the bank (per dollar lent) increase more slowly than the loan rate. The maximum profit rate for the bank is to set the loan rate at r_2, after which the influence of adverse risk selection on bank profits more than offsets any further increases in the interest rate.

(Note that the net profits earned by the bank per dollar lent could be wholly paid out to depositors – if the banks were not subject to non-interest-bearing reserve requirements, and "excess" returns to shareholders equity above the loan rate were not significant. Then the net profit on the vertical scale of figure 13.3 could be interpreted as the approximate real deposit rate of interest. As in Stiglitz and Weiss, this geometric model is heuristic and is not itself a complete picture of bank profit maximization, where the returns to bank shareholders are distinguished from the yield to depositors.)

Because the highest returns to the bank (net of defaults) occur when lending is restricted to the R_2 category in figure 13.3, borrowers in R_3 with the most productive projects, but the highest variance in internal returns, are completely rationed out. With adverse risk selection, the bank "with its fixed interest loan contract" sees the net return to itself being too small in category R_3. In effect, the limited bank-based capital market cannot finance some of the economy's potentially more productive investment opportunities, as shown in more detail by Yoon Je Cho (1986). Cho goes on to show that further financial deepening in the form of an equities market would be necessary for risky projects in R_3 to receive adequate financing.

Notice that under the assumption made so far, with the law of large numbers applying within each risk category of statistically independent borrowers, and the bank not being permitted to significantly concentrate its lending on any one borrower, the *bank's optimal strategy is independent of its own risk characteristics*. Because the net yield to the bank is not stochastic, it will choose simply to maximize profits by selecting a (limited) loan rate r_2 applying only to borrowers in category R_2 - with arbitrary rationing (unless the bank runs out of this qualified pool of applicants). Without any official interest rate ceilings, the bank's behaviour will be inherently "conservative" without exhibiting the problems of moral hazard to be discussed below.

Of course, the government can "repress" this financial system by needlessly imposing an even lower interest ceiling - shown by r_0 in figure 13.3. This induces the bank then to shift its loans to the perfectly safe but less productive borrowers in R_1, and completely ration out borrowers in the other two higher-return areas of the economy. Starting from a position of loan-rationing equilibrium, financial repression still hurts if interest rates are forced below that level necessary to prevent undue adverse risk selection.

MACROECONOMIC INSTABILITY AND POSITIVE COVARIANCE IN PROJECT YIELDS

Consider how the behavior of nonbank borrowers, and the banks themselves, might change if macroeconomic instability is introduced into our previous analysis of adverse risk selection based on the assumption of a stable macro economy. The forms that macroeconomic instability might take - changes in the real exchange rate, unexpected inflation or deflations, and so on - are many and varied. Within our narrow analytical framework, however, the introduction of "macroeconomic instability" is taken to mean:

1 *Increased variance* in yields (but without any change in mean) in the real returns of projects being considered by non-bank borrowers; and
2 *New positive covariance* among the expected returns to projects within any one risk class. All (or at least the majority) of projects

will be adversely affected by poor macroeconomic circumstances, and they will collectively have greater profitability in good times.

To further simplify, let us confine the analysis to one preferred class of borrowers: the middle graph in figure 13.4 simply reproduces (from figure 13.3) the R_2 profit function of the banks under the assumption of no macroeconomic instability.

Now assume that there is no problem with moral hazard in the bank itself. The structure of ownership, or the nature of official supervision and control with sufficient required reserves against expected loan losses, is such that the bank behaves as if it were risk-averse. Then the increased macroeconomic instability (requiring increased bank reserves against defaults) is likely to shift the R_2 profit function in figure 13.4 downward to the left to the new graph R'_2. Because of higher variance in individual project returns, *increased adverse risk selection will lower the bank's optimal real loan rate in the presence of macro instability*. Figure 13.4 shows the optimal interest rate associated with R'_2 to be i_1, which is lower than i_2.

However, positive covariance among the projects of the nonbank borrowers also introduces stochastic variance into the bank's own profit

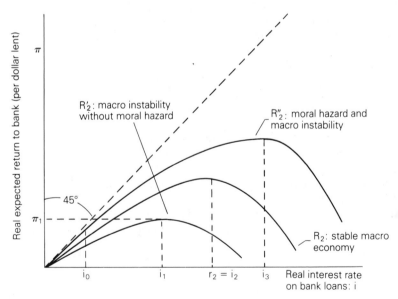

FIG. 13.4 *Moral hazard in maximizing bank profits: macroeconomic instability and positive correlation in default risks (one class of nonbank borrowers)*

net of defaults. The law of large numbers no longer assures the bank of deterministic yield. Although π_1 shows the expected return to the bank, the realized return at the end of the loan period could be considerably more or less because default rates among nonbank borrowers are now positively correlated. Thus even for a risk-averse bank with substantial loan loss provisions, to keep the threat of bankruptcy minimal the regulatory authority might force the bank to select an even lower real interest rate – as shown by i_0 in figure 13.4.

In summary, if banks themselves are properly regulated to be risk-averse, macroeconomic instability will likely force lower real rates of interest and more severe credit rationing on the system.

MACROECONOMIC INSTABILITY INDUCING MORAL HAZARD IN THE BANKS

Suppose now that the commercial banks are privately owned, and that the government's regulatory apparatus for supervising risks assumed by the banks is fairly weak without adequate loan loss provisions. Moreover, the government has implicitly or explicitly committed itself to provide deposit insurance. As the Chilean and Argentinian experiences attest, such deposit insurance creates potentially severe problems of moral hazard within the banking system itself (Kane, 1985).

Any one bank may well undertake very risky lending at unnaturally high real loan rates of interest on the twin presumptions that:

1 favorable outcomes, where the nonbank borrowers succeed in repaying their high interest loans, will lead to large profits to the bank's shareholders; whereas
2 unfavorable outcomes, with highly correlated defaults among the nonbank borrowers, leading to massive losses by the bank in question (and perhaps even the banking system as a whole) will be mainly borne by the monetary authority.

Even though the bank owners might lose their equity or ownership claims under (2), the bulk of the losses will be covered by the deposit insuring agency. Therefore, *ex ante* expected profits from risky lending could well be very high because bank profits are not bounded from above in the case of a favorable outcome. In effect, the bank is the beneficiary of an unfair bet against the government; it gets to keep extraordinary profits without having to pay the full social costs of unusually large losses from risky lending.

Strangely enough, when the macroeconomy is stable, a bank's decision strategy will be unaffected by such moral hazard because the default rates among the "large" number of nonbank borrowers are not positively correlated. The bank will simply maximize (nonstochastic) expected profit – as shown in figure 13.3 and in the middle graph in figure 13.4. (This result depends critically on the maintained assumption that regulation is sufficiently effective to prevent the bank from concentrating its lending in the hands of a few large borrowers.)

However, in the presence of macroeconomic instability, which inevitably creates positive covariance in the default rates of the bank's borrowers, moral hazard on the part of the bank itself becomes a very serious problem. With its own future profit now a random variable, our loosely regulated bank with inadequate loan-loss provisions has undue incentive to make high interest (and therefore risky) loans knowing *ex ante* that a favorable macroeconomic outcome will lead to very high profits – and that it can walk away from heavy losses.

This interaction between bank moral hazard and macroeconomic instability is shown by the upper graph, R_2'', in figure 13.4. The vertical scale now represents the expected revenue per dollar lent *net* of anticipated bank losses to be covered (*ex post facto*) by the deposit insuring agency in the event of unfavorable outcomes. The bank now behaves as *if* it wants to incur risk: its expected profits are uniformly higher than those of a risk-averse (properly regulated) bank because deposit insurance covers any unusual losses. *Thus, in the presence of macroeconomic instability, a bank subject to moral hazard could well set its loan rate at a higher and riskier level*, say i_3, in figure 13.4. In order to cut their own expected losses from providing deposit insurance, however, the authorities could well try to overcome the bank's moral hazard by forcing it to charge a much lower, and safer, loan rate at, say, i_0.

Failure to recognize the need for such official action to limit bank lending rates was, in part, responsible for the financial collapses in the Southern Cone. Of course, proper bank supervision entails much more than simply setting interest ceilings, which is itself a "second-best" response. Preventing concentration of loans to one borrower, limiting foreign exchange risk, requiring adequate reserves against default, and so on are the first line of defense against financial breakdown.

CONCLUSION

The existence of moral hazard in banks, such as that induced by the presence of deposit insurance, implies that the government should probably impose a ceiling on the standard loan (and deposit) rate of interest as well as mandating a number of safety-first requirements, such as larger loan-loss provisions. In the absence of such moral hazard, the banks could be counted on to limit their own interest charges, and behave conservatively by rationing loans. In either case, however, greater macro instability in the economy's price level, real exchange rate, terms of trade, and so on reduces the real interest rate on bank loans which is socially optimal. That said, the empirical evidence underscores the importance of avoiding the opposite, but all too common, syndrome of financial repression: where real interest rates are reduced much below an appropriate loan rationing equilibrium, and are frequently highly negative in real terms. To achieve high real financial growth, successful developing economies have combined domestic price stability with substantial – even if regulated – nominal rates of interest on both deposits and loans.

This analysis, based on the financial effects of alternative steady-state macroeconomic equilibria, does not itself go into the difficult question of how best to achieve price-level stability. The difficult transition problems of moving from high to low inflation are analyzed elsewhere (McKinnon, forthcoming). For sustained and broadly based development, however, there is little doubt that price-level stability and financial deepening are invaluable.

NOTES

[1] Terminology introduced by Edward Shaw [1973] and McKinnon [1973]. Further discussion of optimal financial management in a repressed economy is found in McKinnon and Mathieson [1981]. A more general review of the literature on financial repression and liberalization can be found in Fry [1982].

[2] These ratios are taken from IMF (International Monetary Fund) *International Financial Statistics* (various issues). The IMF defines M2 as money (line 34) plus quasi-money (line 35) plus deposits outside commercial banks (line 45). M2 is a stock tabulated as of June 30 for each calendar year, whereas GNP is the flow of output for that year.

[3] From the well-known Scandinavian model of inflation, we can expect the CPI to increase rapidly when productivity growth is high in tradeables industries but the cost of nontradeable services increases – as was true in Japan. But then I claim that the CPI becomes an invalid deflator for calculating real interest rates.

REFERENCES

Cheng, Hang-Sheng 1986: "Financial Policy and Reform in Taiwan, China." In H. S. Cheng (ed.), *Financial Policy and Reform in Pacific Basin Countries*, Lexington, Massachusetts: Lexington Books.

Cho, Yoon Je 1986: "Inefficiencies from Financial Liberalization in the Absence of Well Functioning Equities Markets." *Journal of Money, Credit and Banking*, 18 (2), May.

Corbo, Vittorio 1985: "Reforms with Macroeconomic Adjustment in Chile during 1974–84." *World Development,* Aug.

Corbo, Vittorio and de Melo, Jaime (eds) 1985: *Liberalization with Stabilization in the Southern Cone of Latin America.* Special issue of *World Development,* Aug.

Díaz-Alejandro, Carlos 1985: "Good-Bye Financial Repression, Hello Financial Crash." *Journal of Development Economics,* 19 (112), Sept.-Oct.

Dornbusch, Rudiger 1985: "Inflation, Exchange Rates and Stabilization." Working Paper 1739, National Bureau of Economic Research, Oct.

Edwards, Sebastian 1985: "Stabilization with Liberalization: An Evaluation of Ten Years of Chile's Free Market Policies, 1973–83." *Economic Development and Cultural Change,* Jan.

Fry, Maxwell J. 1978: "Money and Capital of Financial Deepening in Economic Development." *Journal of Money, Credit and Banking,* 10 (4), Nov.

Fry, Maxwell J. 1982: "Models of Financially Repressed Developing Economies." *World Development,* 10, Sept.

Harberger, Arnold C. 1985: "Lessons for Debtor Country Managers and Policy Makers." In G. W. Smith and John Cuddington (eds), *International Debt and the Developing Countries,* Washington D.C.: The World Bank.

Horiuchi, Akiyoshi 1984: "The 'Low Interest Rate Policy' and Economic Growth in Postwar Japan." *The Developing Economies,* 22 (4), Dec.

International Monetary Fund 1983: *Interest Rate Policies in Developing Economies,* Occasional Paper, no. 22, Oct.

Kane, Edward, J. 1985: *The Gathering Crisis in Federal Deposit Insurance.* Cambridge, Mass: MIT Press.

Leff, Nathaniel and Sato, Kazuo 1980: "Macroeconomic Adjustment in Developing Countries: Instability, Short-Run Growth, and External Dependency." *Review of Economics and Statistics,* May.

Luders, Rolf 1985: *Lessons from Two Financial Liberalization Episodes: Argentina and Chile:* Unpublished manuscript, Nov.

McKinnon, Ronald I. 1973: *Money and Capital in Economic Development.* Washington, D.C.: Brookings Institution.

McKinnon, Ronald I. 1979: *Money in International Exchange: The Convertible Currency System.* New York: Oxford University Press.

McKinnon, Ronald I. 1986: "Monetary Stabilization in LDCs and the International Capital Market." In Lawrence Krause and Kihwan Kim (eds), *The Liberalization Process in Economic Development: Essays in Honor of Kim, Jae-Ik.*

McKinnon, Ronald I. and Mathieson, Donald 1981: "How to Manage a Repressed Economy." Princeton *Essays in International Finance* No. 145, Dec.

Patrick, Hugh 1966: "Financial Development and Economic Growth in Underdeveloped Countries." *Economic Development and Cultural Change,* 14 (2), Jan.

Shaw, Edward, S. 1973: *Financial Deepening in Economic Development.* New York: Oxford University Press.

Stiglitz, Joseph and Weiss, Andrew 1981: "Credit Rationing in Markets with Imperfect Information." *American Economic Review,* 71, June.

Tybout, James 1986: "A Firm Level Chronicle of Financial Crises in the Southern Cone." *Journal of Development Economics.*

Comments on
"Financial Liberalization in Retrospect: Interest Rate Policies in LDCs"

JORGE DE MACEDO

This paper is best interpreted as a list of new topics for the revised edition of McKinnon's influential book *Money and Capital in Economic Development,* published in 1973. The basic message of the old version is that financial repression is bad. The basic message of the new version is that the cure can be worse than the disease. Having succeeded in bringing monetary economics to the Third World, McKinnon can relax his militant posture and recognize the dangers of all-out financial liberalization. He goes as far as arguing that "the government should probably impose a ceiling on the standard loan (and deposit) rate of interest."

The list of new topics is too rich to be reflected in this comment, so I will only pick on one – the extension of the Stiglitz and Weiss (1981) model of equilibrium credit rationing to an unstable macroeconomic environment (first section). To underline the usefulness of McKinnon's assessment of the Chilean experience, I then provide an account of the current Portuguese experience in the same spirit (second section).

Equilibrium credit rationing and macroeconomic instability

If information is perfect and all contracts are enforceable, there is no room for banks. A similar result obtains when the borrower's life is the collateral, as in some underground loan markets. In general, however, lenders don't know the default possibility of a potential borrower, so banks emerge from the incentive to specialize in gathering information about the quality of the projects to be financed. The basic intuition of the Stiglitz–Weiss (1981) model is that as the interest rate charged by lenders rises, the mix of borrowers changes adversely so that it will pay for banks to red-line potential borrowers. In that case the Walrasian equilibrium, where demand equals supply, may not be the competitive equilibrium, which is characterized by excess demand for loanable funds. The result, originally presented for a fixed collateral, generalizes to the case where banks set a combination of interest rate and collateral. As long as the mean return to the bank is not a monotonic function of the interest rate charged to borrowers, there will be equilibrium credit rationing.

This failure of the law of supply and demand is of course not confined to financial markets and has been extensively studied in connection with insurance and labor markets as well. Stiglitz and Weiss (1981) has also been used to rationalize the Chilean experience of banking deregulation in Díaz-Alejandro (1986), and the major critic of financial repression himself had been pointing to potential pitfalls in financial liberalization for some years. Nevertheless, this is the first time that he systematically applied the Stiglitz–Weiss (1981) view in a financial development context.

The application is not without dangers, because of the likely coexistence in such a context of equilibrium and disequilibrium credit rationing, pointed out by Mylonas (1986). Moreover, even if the loan market were perfect, fluctuations in liquid asset balances can lead to persistent fluctuations in economic activity because of the firms' restricted ability to raise equity in external capital markets, as shown by Greenwald and Stiglitz (1986). Similarly, Bernanke and Gertler (1986) show that if there is a sharp, unanticipated fall in the personal stake of managers (available to insulate suppliers of external finance from bad project outcomes) relative to the firms' debt obligations, investment will fall, and vice versa, generating business cycles. Emphasizing the external capital market in the group-dominated Chilean scene may be more convincing than to graft macroeconomic instability in the microeconomic setup, as McKinnon does in this paper.

In sum, the application of Stiglitz–Weiss (1981) does not substitute for an explicit analysis of the role of financial intermediaries in aggregate economic activity, in the best tradition of the "Yale School." That being said, I follow the new McKinnon in rationalizing the behavior of nationalized banks in Portugal.

Delayed financial decontrol in Portugal

Díaz-Alejandro (1970) characterized the interwar Argentine capital market as follows: "Industrialists lucky enough to have access to banking credit granted at negative real rates of interest of course benefitted from the price rise, but industrialists as a whole suffered as a result of the damage done to financial markets by inflation." The statement is applicable to post-revolutionary Portugal if "lucky industrialists" are equated to "state-owned enterprises." Indeed, Maxwell Fry and Edward Shaw identified the problem in a memorandum to the Bank of Portugal in early 1976. Soon thereafter, Fry (1977) presented a paper suggesting measures toward financial liberalization. The discussant (who turns out to be the current prime minister of Portugal) listed several caveats, sounding very much like the ones included in McKinnon's assessment of the Chilean experience. Fry (1980) elaborated on the issue again in late 1979. Since the discussant was then visiting the Growth Center, it may be appropriate to quote his assessment: "…recent examples of financial liberalization in Latin America are not associated with a substantial decline in inflation, in part because the success in increasing central bank reserves may feed monetary growth whilst, by discouraging exports, it may have perverse effects on domestic savings via the current account. That the current account deficit improved dramatically in Portugal, relative to the cases, say, of Argentina or Chile, certainly does not imply that all-out financial liberalization would have reduced inflation and increased domestic saving" (Macedo, 1980).

The point is that the abnormally high level of gold and foreign exchange reserves left by the previous regime changed its nature after the nationalization of all Portuguese commercial banks in 1975. Bank managers, nurtured in the within-groups financial intermediation of the sixties, naturally saw those reserves as a collateral against which the nationalized enterprises were borrowing. They became more willing to lend to risky borrowers, and negative real interest rates, as well as the absence of a stock market, made sure that there would be many of those. Private borrowers were subject to recurrent credit squeezes, due to a stop-and-go macroeconomic policy with the peculiar perversity of being "out of synch" with the main trading partners: when Europe was booming in 1977–9 or 1983–5, Portugal was in recession; and when Europe was in recession in 1980–2, Portugal was booming.

The rise in interest rates which followed the change in U.S. monetary policy in the early 1980s saw the Portuguese banking system with a drastically reduced collateral. The delayed increase in domestic interest rates served, however, to perpetuate the bias towards risky borrowers. It had, furthermore, a disastrous effect on the profitability of banks, and was reflected in the spreading of arrears or bad debts. From being about twice as large as the equity of commercial banks in 1982, non-performing loans were three times as large in July 1985 (the latest official data available), reaching about 18 percent of the commercial loan portfolio.

At the same time, 10 years after the Great Nationalization, the government finally decided to authorize new entrants, both domestic and foreign, into the banking business. While most of the new entrants were not direct competitors of the nationalized banks and while some of the nationalized banks had managed to avoid excessive exposure to bad debts, granting authorization to a dozen new banks made the contrast between "clean" and "stained" banks all too evident. Furthermore, many depositors were lured by attractive interest rates on checking accounts offered by the new banks, so that the potential for risky loans, perhaps to the private sector, was exacerbated.

The new environment certainly called for increased supervision by the monetary authorities, so as to avoid banking crises. Instead of attacking the debt overhang of nationalized banks, however, the government decided to regulate the new banks further by a ceiling on deposit rates and a (retroactive) increase in equity requirements. Also, the proposed implementation in Portugal of a schema of deposit insurance could exacerbate the bias towards bad loans, even on the part of heavily exposed banks. There is already too much insurance, even if it is of the wrong kind. A healthy pattern of evolution requires that the contagion hypothesis will not materialize, so that some "clean" nationalized banks will continue in operation. This cannot be achieved through excess regulation, however, because the neighbouring Spanish financial market is already much less regulated than the Portuguese.

Despite a great number of recent policy measures towards the development of other financial intermediaries and the bullish Lisbon stock market, the Portuguese financial system continues to be dominated by commercial banks and these banks are not as well suited for the financing of medium- and long-term investment as they are for short-term operations. Drawing the lesson from bank deregulation, McKinnon (1985) states "a case can be made for restoring the essential distinction between monetary institutions – where the safety-first rule is paramount – and the 'risk taking' capital market," but the statement is to be understood against the tendency of regulators to "repress deposit rates of interest in both countries (United States and Japan) with undue vigor." Readers of Blinder and Stiglitz (1983) or of Bernanke and Gertler (forthcoming) might add that if commercial banks are too tightly regulated, other financial institutions will create money. Readers of Guttentag and Herring (1986) could sum up McKinnon's creeping agnosticism about financial repression in two propositions: (1) free banking leads to disaster, and (2) bankers have disaster myopia. With Shakespeare to the rescue, one sentence might do: My Kingdom for an hypertropic government.

REFERENCES

Bernanke, B. and Gertler, M. 1986: "Financial Efficiency, Collateral and Business Fluctuations." Draft, Princeton University, June.

Bernanke, B. and Gertler, M. Forthcoming: Banking and Macroeconomic Equilibrium, in Q. Barnett and K. Simpleton (eds), New Approaches to Monetary Economics, Cambridge University Press.

Blinder, A. and Stiglitz, J. 1983: "Money, Credit Constraints and Economic Activity." American Economic Review, May.

Díaz-Alejandro 1970: Essays on the History of the Argentine Republic, New Haven: Yale University Press.

Díaz-Alejandro 1986: "Goodbye Financial Repression, Hello Financial Crash." Journal of Development Economics.

Fry, M. 1977: "Financial Liberalism in Portugal." I International Conference on the Portuguese Economy, Lisbon's Gulbenkian Foundation.

Fry, M. 1980: "Money, Interest and Growth in Portugal." II International Conference on the Portuguese Economy, Lisbon Gulbenkian Foundation.

Greenwald, B. and Stiglitz, J. 1986: Information, Finance Constraints and Business Fluctuations. Draft, NBER, June.

Guttentag, H. and Herring, R. 1986: Disaster Myopia in International Banking. Princeton Essay in International Finance.

Macedo, J. 1980: Comment on Fry (1980) op. cit.

McKinnon, R. 1973: *Money and Capital in Economic Development*, Washington: Brookings Institution.

McKinnon, R. 1985: *Pacific Growth and Financial Interdependence: an Overview of Bank Regulation and Monetary Control*. Reprint No. 226, Center for Research on Economic Growth, Stanford University.

Mylonas, P. 1986: Essays on Credit Rationing. Ph.D. dissertation in progress, Princeton University.

Stiglitz, J. and Weiss, A. 1981: "Credit Rationing in Markets with Imperfect Information." *American Economic Review,* June.

14

Economic Demography and Development: New Directions in an Old Field

T. PAUL SCHULTZ

INTRODUCTION

Three decades ago economists lent their weight to the plausible conclusion that rapid population growth is an important deterrent to economic development in contemporary low-income countries (Notestein, 1945; Coale and Hoover, 1958; National Academy of Sciences, 1971). In the last ten years, the evidence for this conclusion has been reevaluated. A recent working group of the National Academy of Sciences (1986) came to the judgment that, "On balance, we reach the qualitative conclusion that slower population growth would be beneficial to economic development for most developing countries. A rigorous quantitative assessment of these benefits is difficult and context dependent" (p. 90). Nonetheless, public subsidies to voluntary family planning were viewed by this working group as often justified, but not on the economic grounds of relieving society of the evident burdens of social externalities attributed to population growth. These program subsidies were rationalized because they enable "couples to have the number of children they desire" (p. 93), that is, family planning was justified within the public sector on the same basis as public health and farm extension activities, because family planning diffused efficiently and equitably new and poorly understood productive knowledge and thereby helped private households achieve their own objectives. This paper takes stock of recent literature on the economic determinants of household demographic and economic behavior, that has, I shall argue, contri-

This is a revision of a paper presented at the Economic Growth Center's 25th Anniversary Symposium on the State of Development Economics: Progress and Perspectives, April 11–13, 1986. I acknowledge with appreciation the comments of J. Behrman, C. Griffin, and T. W. Schultz and conference participants on an earlier draft of this paper.

buted to this significant reappraisal of the linkages between modern economic growth and population growth.[1]

Reversals of this kind by economists are not uncommon, particularly when issues of public policy are involved. But such reversals can contain lessons. They may signal a fundamental advance in knowledge, or at least an alternative interpretation of accepted facts. They may represent the accumulation of new facts, due to the systematic cataloging of data to reveal empirical regularities where none were previously perceived. In this case, the reversal does not seem to be due to a fundamentally new economic insight, but rather to the proliferation of empirical studies increasingly guided by a common framework that suggests fertility, family labor supply, market-coordinated specialization of production, and investment in humans are closely interrelated activities that have common economic origins. Differences in these forms of demographic and economic behavior of households diffuse through societies with the onset of modern economic growth and can be partially explained by economic variables such as prices, wages, assets, and public sector services and programs that extend information to households. These differences in behavior are evident across countries at one moment in time, and within countries over time, paralleling their demographic transitions from high to low rates of population growth. One interpretation of the evidence is, therefore, that fertility and family specialization between market and nonmarket production activities are reflections of purposive behavior, and can be fruitfully modeled as outcomes of optimizing household production and consumption decision-making, subject however to imperfect information and buffeted by many unexpected events that help to account for noticeable disequilibria.

Consequences of individual fertility decisions that bear on persons outside of the family have proved difficult to quantify, as in many cases where social external diseconomies are thought to be important. Problems of inefficient resource allocation that are often attributed to population growth are increasingly analyzed as originating from market failures, misguided policy interventions, and restricted property rights such as arise with common property resources (National Academy of Sciences, 1986). What remains unclear is precisely when Malthusian (1798) diminishing returns to labor constitute a serious social externality of population growth, and when, conversely, increasing returns to population density, as conjectured by Boserup (1965), are a dominant feature of economic development. With mounting evidence that fertility represents private optimizing behavior of couples, even in premodern societies, the task of assembling convincing empirical evidence on the magnitude of these Malthusian or Boserupian aggregate· effects of population growth becomes substantially more complicated, as discussed below.

Recognition of the ambiguity of the existing evidence of macro-economic consequences of population growth on development may also represent a broader intellectual trend in economics. Macroeconomic systems that lack clearly identified causal relationships have lost their credibility, and microeconomic models of optimizing agents such as individuals, families, farmers, or firms have gained ascendance. This analytical shift in economics may have given impetus to modeling the microeconomic foundations of behavior in the household sector. The next step is to apply these microeconomic models to understand aggregate developments in a general equilibrium framework. But progress in this direction has been slow.

One research strategy is to describe the general equilibrium problem facing individuals, firms, etc., and then specify from a literature review the likely functional form and possible empirical parameters to the component relationships. Simulation of the computable general equilibrium (CGE) framework that is thereby specified can then be used to show how counterfactual changes in conditioning variables might affect the evolution of the aggregate system. Although particular phenomenon have been thoughtfully studied by means of CGE models of this form, such as urbanization in low-income countries (Kelley and Williamson, 1984), these techniques have not been applied with much success to modern household demand models and economic development (Rodgers et al., 1978). Economists have also estimated production functions, factor demand equations, and consumer expenditure systems to measure in a general equilibrium model the empirical importance of Malthusian and Boserupian macroeconomic effects of exogenous population growth on wages and welfare (Evenson, 1984). This innovative empirical strategy for assessing the consequences of population growth has not yet directly sought to incorporate fertility endogenously. That is clearly the next, but far from trivial, task facing economic demographers studying development.

This paper proceeds as follows. The first section reviews the empirical evidence for the most influential general equilibrium model of demographic development, originally proposed by Malthus. The next section states the current microeconomic framework for analyzing household demographic behavior, and the third section illustrates the empirical implementation of this model. The concluding section reconsiders the capacity of empirical studies of household behavior to clarify the consequences of alternative development programs and policies.

MALTHUS'S MODEL AND THE EVIDENCE

For the last 25 years, there has been almost a consensus among social scientists on the nature of the relationships between population growth and economic development. This shared view owes much to the ideas that Malthus (1798) articulated nearly 200 years ago. In many quarters his conceptual framework continues to guide thinking about demographic change during the development process and sets the stage for related policy discussions. A review of the empirical evidence for this historically influential viewpoint is a useful introduction to modern microeconomic analysis of household demographic behavior. It may also clarify why our knowledge of some critical relationships remains so ambiguous.

The model

Three economic relationships constitute the core of Malthus's equilibrium model of economic and demographic development. On the one hand, when real wages fall below some subsistence level, mortality increases. On the other hand, when real wages increase, marriage is encouraged at an earlier age, with a predictable positive effect on lifetime cumulative fertility and thus on population growth. Consequently, there is a dual microeconomic direct dependence of population growth on the wage rate, operating through an economic-biological mortality function and an economic-institutional, marriage-fertility function. Malthus assigns greater weight to the former "positive check" than to the latter "preventive check" as a long-run mechanism governing population growth. The third relationship Malthus relied on was a classical macroeconomic production function in which population growth led to an increase in the labor force and a decrease in the marginal product of labor and hence of real wages. This three-equation system is homeostatic: when shocked from equilibrium, it has a tendency to converge over time to a "natural" or subsistence wage at which there is no population growth, or alternatively, at which population grows, but at an exogenously fixed long-run rate of factor neutral productivity growth.

Mortality: evidence

What is the empirical basis for these three relationships underlying the Malthusian framework? Death rates in preindustrial Europe appear to increase in years when real wages are very depressed (Lee, 1981; Eckstein et al., 1984). It is less certain, however, whether the response of death rates to short-run fluctuations in real wages cumulates or represents primarily a time displacement of deaths that leaves the level of mortality unaffected when averaged over five to ten years.[2] Periods of increased mortality are also often periods of food shortage and hence inflation in food prices that is not reflected in nominal wages (Sen,

1981). Interregional and rural–urban migration during these crisis periods add further uncertainty as to the independent effect of real wage variation on mortality, for the movement of people in search of employment and food observed during crises may be a major factor associated with epidemic and endemic disease and may explain the special age and sex patterns observed in crisis mortality (Galloway, 1985; Watkins and Menken, 1985).

If historical time-series data lend only weak support to Malthus's conjecture that mortality responds to variation in real wages, modern time-series data provide little additional evidence that this connection is quantitatively large in contemporary settings. For one reason, the evidence is generally flawed, because those societies with sufficiently low wage levels to exhibit potentially the Malthusian sensitivity of mortality to wages tend to have the least adequate registration of deaths. Moreover, periods of low real wages continue to be associated with other events – natural disasters, wars, vast movements of population – that leave in their own wake additional consequences as well as below-normal levels of mortality registration.

There are also long phases of industrialization and economic development during which increased wages can be associated with increased mortality. Urbanization, until at least the twentieth century, was often purchased at a social cost in terms of degradation of the health environment. Williamson (1982) argues that the higher wages paid urban English workers compensated them for their loss of longevity in the eighteenth and nineteenth centuries. Increases in wages in the twentieth century in developed countries have supported consumption patterns, such as smoking, alcohol and drug abuse, that have weakened and sometimes even reversed the traditional positive cross-sectional correlation between income and longevity (Fuchs, 1984). In low-income countries, however, mortality remains inversely related to income and occupational status (United Nations, 1980), though education is a far better predictor of lower mortality than is wealth, suggesting that knowledge of hygiene and health practices may today be as important to health as the economic resources to pay for food and health services. The strongest cross-sectional correlate of mortality is the consistent linkage between child mortality and the mother's education, where an additional year's education of the mother is associated with a 5 to 9 percent reduction in child mortality (T. P. Schultz, 1980; Cochrane et al., 1982; Rosenzweig and Schultz, 1982; Farah and Preston, 1982; United Nations, 1985). The lack of convincing contemporary or historical evidence on the empirical magnitude of the relationship from real wages to long-run mortality levels suggests that this plausible link is weak at today's wage levels or attenuated by current public sector capacities and commitment to alleviate extreme poverty and moderate fluctuations in food prices.

Fertility: evidence

Birthrates in Europe before the Industrial Revolution appear to respond positively to wage rates, with a one- to two-year lag rationalized by the requirements of conception and gestation (e.g. Lee, 1977; Eckstein et al., 1984). Good weather and harvests lead predictably to increases in real wages, to increases in marriage, and, in due course, to an increase in fertility (Heckscher, 1954). These preindustrial behavioral patterns that Malthus captured in his agrarian theory are also evident in industrial societies. Covariation between the business cycle, marriage rates, and birthrates is documented in the (later) nineteenth and twentieth centuries for several industrializing countries. The business-cycle relationship is statistically more significant if birthrates are again lagged one to two years (Thomas, 1927; Silver, 1965, 1966). Malthus again may have correctly perceived the short-run responsiveness of births to wage rates, but the cumulative effects of fertility induced by persisting wage changes are less clearly established in existing analyses of time series from England, Sweden, or France (Lee, 1981; Bengtsson, 1984; Eckstein et al., 1984; Richards, 1984).

The major shortcoming of Malthus's framework is not in its failure to provide an adequate explanation for fluctuations in birth and death rates in preindustrial European societies. Its failure is rather to provide no inkling of a secular decline in fertility that occurred shortly after Malthus's death, more or less simultaneously in most industrially advanced countries of Europe (Coale, 1983). To explain this decline in fertility in the face of rising real wages, it is necessary to identify binding constraints on fertility that Malthus overlooked. To find these constraints has led to the assumption of individual optimizing behavior inclusive of fertility, and then the proposition that one or another change in the environment has motivated individuals to want fewer births. Fertility may respond to an increase in the relative cost of children, or to an increase in the return to investments in the schooling of children, or to a decrease in the frequency of child mortality. These and other hypotheses are discussed elsewhere (e.g. T. Paul Schultz, 1976, 1985b).

Revising Malthus on microeconomics

This brief review of the empirical evidence provides several clues as to how the Malthusian framework should be revised. First, in preindustrial periods of the now industrialized countries, the relative emphasis Malthus ascribed to the wage responsiveness of death rates should probably be weakened. Large variations in mortality did occur, but for reasons other than short-run variations in wage rates. Death rates responded only moderately in the short run to wage rates, while birthrates may have varied more substantially with economic conditions. Variation in age-at-marriage was one means by which this occurred. But birthrates within marriage also exhibited positive responsiveness to short-run wage and price variation.[3] As with mortality, the uncertainty as to the magnitude of these relationships increases as we seek evidence on the longer-run wage effects on *cumulative* mortality and fertility (Fogel, 1986). These patterns in historical time series suggest that some measure of voluntary control of fertility within marriage may have existed to avoid births in particularly bad times, even before the onset of the pattern of stopping births according to accumulated family size. This latter form of parity-specific application of birth control became, of course, the dominant means of fertility control during and after the demographic transition (Henry, 1961).

Thus, even in preindustrial periods, the "preventive check" on population growth via fertility occupied a central place, while the role of mortality as a "positive check" on population growth operated relatively independently of wage rates (Lee, 1973). This is more than a minor shift in emphasis between the two reinforcing microeconomic relationships in Malthus's framework; it implies that fertility is not exogenous from the individual's standpoint but is an endogenous variable with an economic life of its own. Making individuals partially responsible for their numbers complicates, as we will see, the interpretation of long swings in population size, which might otherwise provide a clear basis for measuring the third critical Malthusian relationship – that between population size and the marginal product paid to labor in the aggregate economy.

Diminishing returns: evidence

Demographic and economic evidence is broadly consistent with diminishing returns to labor for England from about 1250 to 1700, as illustrated in a variety of general and partial equilibrium models by Lee (1973, 1980). During this period, inputs that complemented labor grew sufficiently fast to absorb at a more or less constant wage a gradual growth of population of about 0.4 percent per year (Lee, 1980). After 1650, as the Industrial Revolution took hold of England, the capacity of the economy to absorb labor may have increased, population growth accelerated, and wages nonetheless continued to increase until the end of the nineteenth century, when birthrates finally declined. In other European countries, reliable long-time series on population size, wages, and prices from preindustrial periods have not been as thoroughly reconstructed and studied. By the nineteenth century, for which data are available for countries such as Sweden, increases in population are not obviously associated with declines in real wages in agriculture (T. Paul Schultz, 1985b). One interpretation of this evidence is that improvements in production technique and nonlabor factors of production were starting to grow more rapidly than did population, despite the acceleration in the growth of population to about one percent per year in the eighteenth and nineteenth centuries.

By the 1950s and 1960s, the gap between crude birthrates and crude death rates in the low-income countries had widened, and population growth in these countries increased to 2 to 4 percent per year. These rates of population growth were several times larger than those ever recorded in Europe during its transition in the nineteenth century. It is remarkable, in retrospect, that the accumulation of nonlabor resources, human capital, and productive knowledge somehow caught up to this very rapid rate of population growth, for real wages in virtually all regions of the world increased, except recently in sub-Saharan Africa and Bangladesh. Diminishing returns to labor induced by rapid population growth must have been fully offset by capital formation and growth in productive knowledge. Although the forecast of a Malthusian trap which would drive wages back to a subsistence level does not fit the historical facts, neither does the available data contradict a tendency for rapid population growth, other things equal, to reduce real wages. The other things which have not remained equal since 1750 in Europe and since 1950 in the low-income world may be viewed two ways. They may be interpreted as economies of increasing output scale effects in nations and world markets, and as economies of population density in providing transportation, communication, and irrigation infrastructures (Boserup, 1965, 1981; Simon, 1977), or they may be seen as due to investment activities that occurred relatively independently of population growth, such as expenditures on mass education, scientific research, and application of new knowledge to productive technology (T. W. Schultz, 1961; Denison, 1962; Kuznets, 1967).

If the former viewpoint of Boserup (1965) is adopted, then the economies of population density may today outweigh the diminishing returns to labor, and Malthus's long-run conclusion must be stood on its head; population growth may trigger economic development as conventionally measured in terms of an increase in per capita income. Alternatively, population pressures on the fixed stock of land may have been offset by the accumulating returns from independent investments in clearing marginal land, draining and improving the fertility of existing land, investing in reproducible physical capital, adding to the average skill level of workers, and producing more knowledge for workers to use. In this latter case, population growth may remain a Malthusian drag on economic growth per head, but apparently not an insurmountable barrier to modern economic growth in the recent, and possibly exceptional, historical period.

Distinguishing between these two different interpretations of our era is complicated further if fertility is an endogenous choice of families. In particular, if fertility responds appreciably to changes in opportunities and adapts to the constraints faced by the individual, this microeconomic adjustment of fertility must be treated simultaneously in a modified macroeconomic Malthusian model of population growth and economic development. To estimate the role of Malthus's diminishing returns to labor or the effect of Boserup's economies of population density, a methodology is required that will hold constant the individual's optimizing behavior that is likely to affect fertility and thereby influence population growth. Assume, for example, that individuals "demand" fewer children when wages rise. Aggregate time series may then reveal that in periods of slow population growth wages increase relatively rapidly, as they did in England from 1250 to 1650 (Lee, 1980). Is this evidence to be viewed as consistent with Malthus's macroeconomic diminishing returns to labor, or is it confirmation of the microeconomic hypothesis that desired fertility is a negative function of wages? To disentangle the critical micro and macro mechanisms on which the Malthusian model rests requires the specification of a more complete microeconomic model of the determinants of fertility (and perhaps mortality) whose parameters can be identified separately from the aggregate consequences of diminishing returns to population growth and increasing returns to population density. The next section reviews more comprehensive microeconomic models of household production and demand that are used today to account empirically for variation in demographic behavior in developing countries.

MICRO FOUNDATIONS FOR HOUSEHOLD DEMOGRAPHIC BEHAVIOR

Economic and demographic behavior of families and households are increasingly studied by economists. Their models of allocational choice are diverse, emphasizing particular conceptual or econometric problems, often at the cost of neglecting other issues. Yet there are common features of these investigations. *First*, the traditional money income budget constraint is replaced by a time budget constraint, endogenizing the allocation of time between market labor supply and non-market activity, especially for women. *Second*, demographic and economic behavior is assumed to depend on a disaggregated reckoning of the household's stocks of human and physical capital. Labor supply is particularly heterogeneous in its productive attributes and alternative uses, and must be valued distinctly for each family member by its marginal opportunity cost. Physical and human capital are costly to transform from one function to another, but, nonetheless, these barriers to adjustment of the asset portfolio of the household are gradually overcome, and adjustments toward equalizing returns across assets occur with time as new productive opportunities are realized. Separate labor supply

:quations for husband, wife, and children are a minimum accommoda-
ion to the existence of the multiperson family where the nuclear family
:oordinates individual interests. Yet the family takes on a variety of
:xtensive forms, and many models may be needed to represent this flex-
ble institution across the world, possibly because different transactions
:osts can modify efficient long-term relationships that are designed to
:oordinate consumption, production, and reproduction in society
Goody, 1976; Ben-Porath, 1980; Pollak, 1985).

Third, the long-term nature of life-cycle commitments in labor
narket training, migration, marriage, children, and savings for retire-
nent focuses economic analysis primarily on permanent and potentially
:oreseen life-cycle conditions, in contrast to transitory and unexpected
developments. Since many of the same long-term opportunities, traits,
expectations, and preferences are attributed a role in determining these
interrelated life-cycle decisions and interdependent resource allocations, it is realistic to view these life-cycle outcomes as occurring simultaneously. In other words, the unexplained deviations in specific
outcomes will tend to be correlated across outcomes within households.
These outcomes are most simply represented as static single-period life-
cycle choice processes, and then complications added as they seem to
clarify particular phenomena. Occasionally observations on entirely
unforeseen events are exploited to understand dynamic adjustment
behavior, but even in these special situations it is not generally possible
to delineate how a sequence of decisions and outcomes feed back on
themselves. An eventual goal of research in this field of economics, as in
many others, is to integrate both evidence on long-run tendencies for
households to optimize their behavior and information on short-run
responses to changing constraints and unexpected realizations. In
the current household context, these unexpected stochastic shocks may
arise from either the salient biological processes, such as those culminating in births and deaths, or the unforeseen and hence exogenous
changes in other more traditional economic constraints, such as prices,
wages, and weather.

Estimation of household demand systems were first based on the
assumption that a block recursive stochastic structure represented
adequately time-ordered behavior of the individual and household
(Wold, 1964). Path analysis was analogously justified in the sociological
study of the unfolding of life-cycle ordered events (Duncan, 1966). But
this simplifying assumption – that errors are independent across
demand equations – is not generally justified in the study of long-run
household life-cycle behavior. For example, how tenable is the assumption that the number of children a woman has is an exogenous determinant of her labor supply behavior, even though the fertility decision
occurred in the past and the labor supply decision continues to accommodate current developments. Preferences of consumers and biological

traits relevant to household production possibilities, such as fertility, are persistent and imperfectly measured. They are, therefore, impounded in statistical errors to equations accounting for many forms of demographic and economic behavior over the life cycle. Identification of recursive structures are thus far from trivial in the household demand framework. Even when plausibly approached as a simultaneous equation system or a multistate duration model, it is very often impossible to identify the structural parameters that in principle may relate one endogenous outcome of the household sector to another endogenous outcome, such as the presumed effect of fertility on a mother's market labor supply.

Fourth, as studies increasingly adopt a common specification of endogenous choice variables determined in the household sector, parallel reduced-form equations are estimated to explain each of these household economic and demographic outcomes in terms of the same list of household endowments, skills, knowledge, and local input and output prices, wages, public sector services, and environmental factors such as climate. Thus, an empirical body of knowledge is accumulating on which to generalize about the size of specific reduced-form parameters. Estimates of the parameters describing household production technology may also exhibit sufficient stability in such areas as reproduction, nutrition or health to encourage replication efforts (Rozenzweig and Schultz, 1986). Progress in the systematic accumulation of knowledge on the regularities of these response and technology parameters over time and across societies can be expected in the future, now that a common analytical framework is being more widely adopted.

The general household demand model clarifies various types of relationships and classifications of variables, but in its unrestricted form it offers few predictions that can be tested empirically. Nonetheless, as with many conceptual frameworks, this form of analytical outline helps to focus subsequent discussion, and illustrate how empirical research has progressed by simplifying and restricting the characteristics of the consumer's utility function (i.e. preferences) or the household production relations (i.e. technology), and where empirical regularities can be relied upon, despite the inability of theory alone to prescribe those regularities.

The general household demand framework

Parents are assumed to maximize their lifetime utility, which depends on seven commodities: their number of children, C, the average education and health of their children, E, and H, the leisure activities of the husband, wife and average child, L_h, L_w, and L_c, respectively, and another composite household commodity, S:

$$U = U(C, E, H, L_h, L_w, L_c, S). \qquad (1)$$

Each of these arguments of the utility function may be thought of as produced in the home with market goods and the non-market time, potentially that of husband, wife, and children:

$$Z_i = \alpha_i(X_i, t_{hi}, t_{wi}, Ct_{ci}, \mu_i), \qquad (2)$$

where $i = C, E, H, L_h, L_w, L_c$ and S, and μ_i represents a couple-specific trait that influences production possibilities and is partially known to the couple, though it is not controlled by them. An example might be exogenous genetic or environmental factors that affect the family's production of child health, or fecundity that affects the capacity of a couple to bear children (Rosenzweig and Schultz, 1983b, 1985a).

The allocation of each individual's time across household production activities is assumed to be mutually exclusive in Becker's (1965) original model, namely, no jointness in production is permitted. This can later be relaxed with little added complexity (Rosenzweig and Schultz, 1983b). Together with time supplied to the market labor force, t_{jm}, the alternative uses of time sum to an exogenously given time budget constraint:

$$\Omega_j = t_{jm} + \sum_i t_{ji,} \qquad (3)$$

where $j = h, w, c$ and $i = C, E, H, L_h, L_w, L_c, S$. Market income is equal to the lifetime or permanent wage rate, w_j, received by each member of the family, times their market labor supply, plus income from non-human capital endowments of husband and wife, V_h and V_w. For simplicity, children are assumed to acquire property only as adults.

$$Y = t_{hm}W_h + t_{wm}W_w + Ct_{cm}W_c + V_h + V_w. \qquad (4)$$

If the household production functions (2) exhibit constant returns to scale, all family members work some time in the market, i.e. $t_{jm} > 0$, full income can be viewed as an exogenous budget constraint, and the shadow prices of the household commodities (i.e. the opportunity value of the market goods and household member's time inputs used to produce a unit of the commodity) are then fixed by the market and do not depend on the bundle of commodities consumed by the household. Otherwise, these shadow prices will depend on parent preferences and returns to scale, and cease to be exogenous (Pollak and Wachter, 1975).[4] If family members withdraw entirely from the market labor force, an interior solution does not occur, and the model takes on added complexity (Heckman, 1987). Because market income in this framework is cleary endogenous, reflecting the family market labor supply decisions, full income is designed to replace market income by a new exogenous resource constraint. But even in this case, the number of children or the composition of the family is endogenous, for it reflects past demographic behavior. The concept of full income, F, thus contains ambiguities for empirical analyses of life-cycle behavior (Gronau, 1984, 1985), but is nonetheless heuristically valuable:

$$F = \Omega_h W_h + \Omega_w W_w + C\Omega_c W_c + V_h + V_w \tag{5}$$

Becker's (1965) household production framework suggests that household behavior can be interpreted as jointly allocating time between market and nonmarket production and combining market goods and nonmarket time to produce commodities that are the final source of utility to the members of the household. It also assumes that the family can be approximated as a unified optimizing consumer, an assumption that has since become standard in neoclassical studies of family labor supply (Ashenfelter and Heckman, 1974; Smith, 1980).[5] This reliance on a well-behaved nuclear family utility function appears to many social scientists to be a limitation of the conceptual framework. In practise, however, economic demographers can always reframe the decision problem in terms of the constraints facing an independent individual, as is standard practice in the study of the factors conditioning the establishment and dissolution of cohabiting relationships or legally/religiously contracted marriages (Becker, 1981; Boulier and Rosenzweig, 1984; Montgomery, 1986). Nash-bargaining models of demand behavior of spouses within marriage draw attention to the distinctive effect of each spouse's own wealth, V_h and V_w, as they influence a spouse's "threat-point." Implementing these individualistic approaches to family behavior underscores the desirability, whenever possible, to know customs associated with family property rights and the origin of family assets, such as inheritances, gifts, or dowry, in order to be able to impute more accurately the ownership of these assets to specific family members. If empirically V_h and V_w influence family demands in the same way, then there is no empirical case for the distinction, and the family utility-maximizing model that generally combines V_w and V_h is the more parsimonious representation of household demand behavior (McElroy and Horney, 1978, 1987).

Reduced-form demand equations for the household production commodities are implied by maximizing (1) subject to (2) and (3) and can be generally written as follows:

$$Z_i = Z_i(P, W_h, W_w, W_c, V_h, V_w, M, e_i), \tag{6}$$

where P is a vector of prices of market goods and public services available to the household, M is the vector of exogenous household-specific traits, μ's, that affect household's production of Z's, and e_i are random disturbances that embody the effects of the couple's preferences and serially uncorrelated errors in measurement, specification and technology.

The reduced-form derived demand functions for market goods and time allocations of household members may be written analogously:

$$X_i = X_i(P, W_h, W_w, W_c, V_h, V_w, M, f_i) \tag{7}$$

$$t_{ij} = t_{ij}(P, W_h, W_w, W_c, V_h, V_w, M, g_{ij}) \tag{8}$$

where f_i and g_{ij} are also serially uncorrelated disturbances.

Since it is assumed that market prices, local public programs, life-cycle market wages, and family nonearned income are exogenous, the reduced-form equations (6), (7), and (8) can usually be estimated consistently by standard single-equation methods. The inability of the researcher to observe typically the productive traits of the couple, M, need not bias the remaining estimates. This depends, of course, on the assumption that the unobserved productive traits of the couple, such as fecundity, are distributed independently of economic endowments, prices, and programs, or that the elements of M are uncorrelated with the P, W's and V's. The reduced-form demand equations embody the more fundamental technological parameters from the household production functions (2) and the behavioral demand parameters from the utility function (1).

EMPIRICAL APPLICATIONS OF THE HOUSEHOLD DEMAND FRAMEWORK

To proceed further in the analysis of such a general household demand model restrictions and simplifications must be adopted. The objective is to direct attention to the more important constraints on choice in a particular setting and to derive predictions that can be tested empirically. One study of district level data from rural India illustrates how this general framework may be restricted in a variety of directions. Rosenzweig and Evenson (1977) focus on three outcomes that can be measured from the 1961 Indian census; surviving fertility (children age 5 to 9 per woman of childbearing age), child school-enrollment rates, and child labor-force-participation rates. These outcomes are explained in terms of district level agricultural wage rates for men, women and children as well as land holdings and other aspects of the district economy, society, and climate.

To assess the likely substitutability or complementarity of household behavioral outcomes, previous empirical studies can provide considerable guidance. For example, the number of children is widely assumed to be a substitute for child schooling and child leisure, while schooling and child leisure are themselves often viewed as complements. Women are generally assumed to contribute time to the "production" of children and the other home commodity (S), whereas children allocate their own time among schooling, labor force work, and leisure. Since only uncompensated price and wage effects are ultimately observed, it is assumed by Rosenzweig and Evenson that compensated substitution effects dominate income effects in the relevant Slutsky equations, leaving the sign of the compensated and uncompensated effects the same. Adult leisure is neglected, whereas child health is viewed as captured in the surviving measure of fertility they analyze, viz. child–woman ratios. These restrictions assure that the own-wage effects are reinforced by cross-wage effects, and that income effects do not outweigh the predictable compensated wage effects. Exogenously higher women's wages should then be associated theoretically with lower levels of fertility, higher child-schooling levels, and lower child labor-force-participation rates. Conversely, exogenously higher child wages should be associated with higher levels of fertility, lower schooling, and higher child labor force participation. Further more controversial restrictions are needed to establish the signs of the effects of the size of land holdings on family size (positive), school enrollments (negative), and employment of children in the labor force (positive). An interesting feature of the child and schooling decisions is that they can be analyzed in most data separately for boys and girls, thereby shedding light on substitution possibilities among these types of family labor and intrahousehold resource allocations (see also Rosenzweig and Schultz, 1982a).

Confirmation of reduced-form partial associations is complicated if data refer only to regional level averages, where the aggregate supply of child and female labor is likely to respond to, and dampen (or reverse), observed variation in wages induced by demand factors. In other words, aggregate labor supply responses can be treated as exogenous when analysis occurs at the household or individual level, and life-cycle market wages are thus exogenous. But at the aggregate regional level, wages also become endogenous. Consequently, Rosenzweig and Evenson (1977) treated their child wage series as endogenous, and based their estimates of the child wage effects on instrumental variables that were logically exogenous and yet may have influenced the derived demands for child labor, such as rainfall, irrigation, and nonfarm employment opportunities. But they persist in treating their female wage series as exogenous.[6] Many of the behavioral patterns implied by their restricted model are empirically confirmed in their district level analysis of wage and farm asset variables that affect fertility, schooling and child labor force participation (by sex). Their restricted household demand model does not imply the sign of the relationship between the husband's wage and the household's demand for numbers of children and their schooling. Regional male wages are empirically found to be positively associated in rural India with surviving fertility and negatively associated with child schooling levels. Most of these patterns are obtained in other studies of fertility in low-income agricultural populations (Schultz, 1976; Mueller, 1984). Wage rates of individual family members play an important role as the opportunity cost of time in explaining many forms of household economic and demographic behavior. Life-cycle wages, as an exogenous constraint on lifetime choices, are difficult to measure, however, because current wages become endogenous over the life cycle as they reflect prior investments in specialized skills, and because current wages are not available for all persons if they currently work only in the home or work as a self-employed or family worker without knowing precisely the marginal product of their labor. Both problems appear to be more serious for inferring the wage of women rather than the wage of men. Having and caring for children competes for the mother's time that could otherwise be invested in gaining skills and experience that are distinctly productive in market work. A standard procedure to approximate the exogenous or initial life-cycle wage profile is to use instrumental variables to impute a value for the wage to each individual, and this wage is thereby uncorrelated with the individual's previous time allocation, career, and fertility decisions, etc. The specification of these instrumental wage equations relies heavily on the human capital earnings function pioneered by Mincer (1974), except that the dependent variable is the logarithm of the wage rate and measures of labor supply, such as weeks worked, are strictly excluded from the instruments because they are endogenous. This instrumental variable human capital wage function is fit for men and women (and potentially for boys and girls) separately, and the imputed value is assigned as the life-cycle wage for each person in the sample, holding post-schooling experience artificially constant at, say, ten years to approximate the overtaking point (Mincer, 1974, p. 93).

However, the instrumental wage equation may nonetheless be biased by the limitation of the estimation to a sample of wage earners and not all those for whom wages must be imputed. This potential sample selection bias can be appraised and corrected by methods described by Heckman (1979) and illustrated with clarity for men (Anderson, 1982) and women (Griffin, 1986) in the context of understanding household demand systems in low-income countries. There are many econometric issues that arise with such wage imputation schemes. Multiple sources of sample selection may be present, such as nonreporting among wage earners (see Behrman and Wolfe, forthcoming), and if the researcher understands what causes the different types of selection, each selection rule can be identified by distinct variables and estimated and corrected. But reliance on functional form alone (i.e. the distribution of the error terms) to achieve identification in such selection problems may not be sufficient to improve empirical results. Economic or institutional knowledge of the selection mechanisms is helpful in dealing with this ever-present econometric problem in survey research.

Interdependencies among endogenous variables

A series of earlier studies at the Rand Corporation of interregiona variation in household demographic and economic behavior analyze jointly household outcomes such as age at marriage, proportion legall and consensually married, cumulative fertility, child–woman ratios female and child labor-force-participation rates, internal migration, th sex ratio of the adult population, and, finally family market incom (DaVanzo, 1971; Maurer et al., 1973; Nerlove and Schultz, 1970; T. I Schultz, 1971, 1972, 1981). These studies provided the first econo metric evidence in low-income countries that increased women' education and wage rates helped to account for women's increase participation in the modern labor force, decreased or delayed marriage and reduced fertility. Census and survey data from Puerto Rico, Taiwan Egypt, Philippines, Chile, and Thailand were analyzed. These investiga tions also sought to go beyond reduced-form estimates, and to measur how various endogenous variables (Z's and t's) affect each other. / priori identification restrictions were exploited across structural be havioral relationships. It has become increasingly clear that the timin of marriage, fertility, and family labor supply behavior are jointly deter mined, but it remains difficult to justify the exclusion restriction needed to identify statistically how one of these outcomes may affect th others. Hence, the growing reticence of economists to assess the conse quences of population growth or the benefits of a fertility decline.

Only under special conditions is it possible to estimate the conse quences of a change in the level of one household demand commodity or choice on another, such as the effect of a decline in fertility on the average level of child schooling. Any of the reduced-form determinants of one outcome in equation (6) may be an important determinant ir other reduced-form equations. The exception to this rule is when one of the commodities is not chosen by the household but is randomly al located, as if by a stochastic rationing mechanism. The clearest example is the occurrence of twins, which can then be related to other adjust ments in the household's pattern of consumption and behavior.[7] In rural India, Rosenzweig and Wolpin (1980a) show evidence that twins are associated with a decrease in the schooling levels of other children in the family. This demand response to an exogenous fertility supply shock (i.e. twins) can be interpreted as the following:

$$\partial E / \partial \bar{C} = (\partial E / \partial \pi_c)_{\bar{u}} / (\partial C / \partial \pi_c)_{\bar{u}} \qquad (9)$$

where the effect of an exogenous change in C and E is equal to the compensated cross (shadow) price effect of π_c on E, divided by the compensated own-price effect on C (see Rosenzweig and Wolpin, 1980a). Since the compensated own-price effect is negative, the negative sign observed in India for $\partial E / \partial \bar{C}$ from twins implies that children and child schooling are substitutes, i.e. $(\partial E/\partial \pi_c)_{\tilde{u}} > 0$. Without further restrictions on the cofactors of the general demand model, it is not possible to discriminate between the interaction of child quality (schooling) and quantity in the full income constraint, as proposed by Becker and Lewis (1974), and the conventional interpretation that child quality and quantity are viewed by parents in their utility function (1) as substitutes.

A parallel analysis of the effect of twins on mother's market labor supply behavior in the United States is also reported by Rosenzweig and Wolpin (1980b). Again the occurrence of this natural experiment, twins, identifies the consequences of an exogenous supply shock of fertility as it affects other household demand (i.e. labor supply) behavior. It should be noted, however, that these "twin"-based estimates of fertility effects do not provide an appropriate measure of how other demands would adjust to *general* changes in fertility, because general changes in fertility embody the demands of couples adjusting to changes in prices, wages, and technology that will be correlated with their other demands. The occurrence of twins is presumably independent of parent preferences or these changing constraints that affect household demands.

One major demographic trend is often interpreted as primarily due to exogenous and unforeseen technological developments. It is the sharp decline in mortality in low-income countries in the period after World War II that had a disproportionate effect on reducing infant and child mortality. Many observers have attributed the change in level of mortality to the spread of new public health technologies that progressed independently of economic development (Stolnitz, 1975). To the extent that this decline in child mortality was unrelated to parent resources, prices, or preferences, the resulting increase in surviving children that parents experienced could be interpreted as an unanticipated shift in the biological "supply" of children (T. Paul Schultz, 1981). The behavioral adjustment of parents to this development may then be analogous to that measured in the twin statistical studies.

It is more realistic to recognize that much of a decline in child mortality over time and variation in child mortality in the cross section is explained by the economic variables that belong in the reduced-form equations of the family demand model. When the partial effects of parent education, wages, and family planning programs on fertility are held constant by statistical means, child mortality is still generally observed to be related to fertility. But such a partial association could still reflect unobserved variables that affect both fertility and child mortality, or the reverse effect of fertility on child mortality. To estimate only the response of parent fertility to exogenous child mortality, an identifying restriction must be imposed. The critical issue is what exogenous factor affects child mortality but does not have a direct influence on parent reproductive goals? The choice of such identification restrictions may in some circumstances be dictated by a well-founded theory or knowledge of the technology of the relevant processes, but more often the identifying restriction statistically imposed is relatively arbitrary. Consequently, the estimates thus obtained are likely to be misleading.[8]

In an analysis of fertility based on the 1973 Colombian Census public use sample, Rosenzweig and Schultz (1982) exploit municipal variation in climate, transportation infrastructure, and malaria control programs to account for exogenous regional differences in only child mortality. Based on these identifying restrictions, they estimate that the fertility response of parents offsets about one-third of the climate- and malaria-related variation in child mortality among urban women.[9] Olson (1980), employing a different statistical methodology, found replacement responses to exogenous child mortality in Colombia in 1973 of the order of 0.2, but this is a lower bound to the total parental response to mortality, because he could not distinguish what portion of the residual correlation might be attributable to an insurance effect of parent "hoarding" or having more births than wanted (in a mortality-free environment) in anticipation of regional levels of child mortality. In a subsequent study, he estimated the hoarding effect of about 0.14, implying a total response of Colombian fertility to child mortality of the order of 0.35 (Olson, 1987).

Estimating household production functions

Another methodological approach for measuring the responsiveness of household demands to exogenous variation in demographic variables involves explicitly estimating more of the structure of the general model to isolate variation in these demographic outcomes that cannot be attributed to behavior, and, therefore, can be viewed as exogenous. First, the reduced-form demand equations, (7) and (8), are estimated for the inputs to the household production function. Individual predictions of input demands based on these estimated equations then permit the estimation of the household production functions (2) parameters by instrumental variable techniques. These estimates are consistent, because the instruments – prices, programs, wages, and family wealth – can be assumed independent of the production trait, μ. Based on the estimates of the technical production parameters to (2), expected outcomes, Z_i^e, are calculated, given the couple's actual input behavior. The deviation of the actual behavioral outcome from that which is expected, $Z_i - Z_i^e$, is then a measure, albeit with error, of the couple-specific trait, μ_i. Data on individual outcomes over time should facilitate more precise estimation of the time-persistent component of this forecast error, which μ_i is intended to represent. This measure of the exogenous variation in, say, child health measured for example by infant mortality, can then be employed to explain subsequent fertility Rosenzweig and Schultz, 1983a). This roundabout procedure provides another way to estimate the reproductive replacement response of parents to exogenous variation in child mortality, i.e. an exogenous biological shock to child health.

Estimation of a household production function (2) for a couple's conception probability leads to analogous instrumental variable estimates of a reproduction function (Rosenzweig and Schultz, 1985a). Technically unexplained deviations in a couple's reproductive performance over time can be interpreted as a measure of exogenous fecundity or variation in the supply of births, again measured with error. This exogenous variation in "fertility supply" can then be employed to explain subsequent modifications in the couple's contraceptive behavior, the wife's market labor supply, and even her market wage rate (Rosenzweig and Schultz, 1985a, 1985b).

The primary conclusion drawn from these estimations of household production models is that a priori structure must be imposed on the household demand model to get behind the reduced-form equations (6), (7), and (8). To estimate the underlying household production-demand structure requires a method to remove the bias caused by heterogeneity in the couple-specific traits, μ_i. Estimates of bias due to omitted variables is a problem at all stages of household demand and production studies. The unavoidable omission of inputs is probably more serious in the estimation of complex *cumulative* household production processes, such as those underlying child health, nutrition, or education than it is in the estimation of shorter and relatively simpler processes underlying the determination of conception and birth or even birth-weight. Because contraceptive behavior is the predominant and readily observed endogenous factor determining conception rates in modern societies, the estimation of reproduction functions is a promising approach to integrate biological and behavioral factors in the study of fertility, a frequently noted goal of demographers (Easterlin, Pollak, and Wachter, 1980).[10]

There are many ways to expand further the household demand framework and add commodities or activities. Savings by the family in the form of physical capital formation for retirement is similar to the formation of human capital in children, in that it extends over many years. Indeed, the Modigliani–Brumberg (1954) life-cycle savings hypothesis is well designed for study in the household demand framework. Savings over the life cycle may foster a variety of human capital investment, insurance arrangements, and even transfers between generations. Economists have long speculated that families may invest in the migration of their members both to augment their income and to diversify their portfolio of human and physical capital, insuring themselves from the vagaries of agriculture or urban business cycles. Little empirical analysis at the household level has yet been undertaken to test the implications of these theories.

Much of the early discussion of the probable consequences of rapid population growth assumed that increases in the size of surviving families would depress private household savings and public productive savings and investments, as conventionally measured (Coale and Hoover, 1958). Empirical evidence is very limited on the direct associa- tion between the composition and level of savings and the size of surviv- ing family (World Bank, 1984). Here again to evaluate the conse- quences of fertility, one must identify the cause of the variation in fertility. Would local child health, family planning, and schooling invest- ments that reduced fertility also raise (or lower) physical savings rates? Are children complements for bequest savings or substitutes for physical savings that provide for retirement at the end of the life cycle? What would be the consequence for household savings, if the increase in surviving fertility were due to exogenous eradication of endemic and epidemic childhood diseases that left more children living? These are hard questions to answer that will require unusually detailed economic and demographic information at the extended household level. But given the centrality of the savings relationship in hypothesized models of demographic and economic development, I would anticipate more research in the future within the household demand framework will analyze the composition and level of savings.

Another way to approach these changes in investments in children, fertility, and savings is to construct a general equilibrium system in which prices are determined endogenously within the model. A general equilibrium approach to the macroeconomic problems of growth, investment and consumption over time has been formulated around a microeconomic theory of exchange between overlapping generations. Although the general framework dates from Samuelson (1958), the redirection of this model from monetary phenomena to the analysis of the demographic-economic transition is recent. This general equili- brium growth framework provides a suitable, if simplified, setting in which to also treat the fertility decision as endogenous. Eckstein and Wolpin (1982) show that as capital accumulates and wage rates increase, there is a substitution away from children and toward the consumption of goods, if the costs of children are linked to the wage rate or the value of time. Also, as income per capita grows, the demand for children increases. The path of fertility generated by this stylized model depends on the relative magnitude of the goods-cost and time- costs of rearing children, and it might plausibly first increase and then decrease as the labor share of output increases with the onset of modern economic growth. Thus, Malthus's model of aggregate growth is pro- vided with a growth path that leads, due to the time-cost of children, to a zero population growth rate while permitting the level of per capita income to secularly increase.

Even though economic theory cannot tell us much about the trade-off in parent preferences between these central dimensions of the family formation process, empirical analysis of various public policies, wage developments, and price changes that are relatively important to the family unit should inform us of certain trade-offs in demand behavior, at least in those cases where income effects are small and can therefore be neglected.[11] Cross-price effects would be more influential when the forms of family behavior are closely related. For example, subsidized birth control programs are observed to reduce fertility because they raise the effective cost of children, and they *also* may increase the schooling (or quality) of children. More accessible or lower-priced schools increase school enrollments (quality) and may also be associated with reduced fertility. Reinforcing cross-program effects of this type have been confirmed in several countries and are reviewed in the next section. Measures of the effectiveness of any one of these programs based only on its direct objective would, in this case, overlook synergistic side effects that may be appropriately attributed to these reinforcing family-oriented welfare programs.

Policy analysis

The consequences of programs and policies on household behavior can be evaluated by estimating reduced-form type relationships, if program activities are allocated across regions in a manner that is independent of individual preferences or unobserved environmental factors (T. Paul Schultz, 1971). Program services may substitute for or complement other consumption and investment activities which are distinct from those targeted by the program. Thus, cross-program effects may be important to the extent that a variety of household commodities are highly complementary or close substitutes for one another. As noted above, the household demand literature has confirmed that child health services, schooling services, and family planning services often exert reinforcing cross-price effects on child health, child educational attainment, and decreased fertility. For example, Rosenzweig and Schultz (1982b) report the local availability of clinics and hospital beds and family planning expenditures per capita are partially associated with both lower child mortality and lower fertility across women in urban areas of Colombia in 1973. The reinforcing effects are generally statistically significant among women from age 15 to 49. Rosenzweig and Wolpin (1982) assess in rural India cross-program effects on fertility, child mortality and schooling, and find reinforcing program effects from family planning clinics, dispensaries, hospitals, and secondary schools.

Rosenzweig and Wolpin (1984) also estimate the direct and cross-program effects of family planning and health clinics on anthropometric indicators of child health and nutritional status in the Philippines. In this study, however, the authors have access to cross-sectional information from repeated rounds of the Laguna Survey. Alternative estimates of the effects of programs on these stock-like measures of child health (viz age-standardized height and weight) are based on three statistical specifications of the same reduced-form equation. When community fixed-effects and child fixed-effects are introduced, bias due to omitted time-invariant community and individual variables is thereby eliminated. But the fixed-effect estimates are also very unstable and imprecise, probably because the fixed-effect specification relies heavily on small changes over time in the anthropometric measures of accumulated nutrition and health, and errors in measuring these variables can be substantial relative to the pertinent "signal". Although the promise of longitudinal data to illuminate the behavioral effects of changes in economic constraints and program interventions is indeed great, means must be found to exploit the panel features of such powerful data without sacrificing the valid information contained in the cross section. The challenge of using time series of cross sections is reflected in earlier household demographic studies based on regional data (Nerlove and Schultz, 1970). The problems and promise of panel data remain at the top of the agenda of research in economic demography (Ashenfelter, Deaton and Solon, 1986).

PERSPECTIVES ON POPULATION POLICY

The purpose of this paper is to assess how microeconomic research on household behavior has in the last 26 years changed our understanding of demographic and economic factors associated with the development process. On the one hand, we are not much closer to knowing under what conditions the "grand dynamics" of Malthus's model of aggregate economic and demographic change are applicable to low-income countries, and when these countries, therefore, sacrifice growth in per capita income by not expending public resources to slow their rate of population growth. Because fertility is increasingly viewed as a household decision variable that responds to changing private opportunities and endowments, a policy to slow population growth beyond what private decisions would otherwise accomplish deprives some individuals of an important benefit – their own children. There is scant evidence of the aggregate gains from slowing of population growth that could be used to compensate individuals whose demands for children would thereby be rationed.

On the other hand, the new economic demography has established a coherent agenda for research that is sufficiently guided by economic theory and econometric tools that the collection in low-income countries of household and community data and its analysis has accelerated. Among the apparent determinants of fertility and mortality are family planning and child health programs, local schools, and infrastructural investments that increase the population's access to these services. There is reason to believe that public extension programs in family planning, child and maternal health, and the schooling of girls can affect substantially fertility and child mortality levels in many parts of the world. There is a strong rationale for more public extension activity in these areas, including at least initially heavy subsidies for contraceptive and health supplies and services, targeted to those populations with the least capacity, both economic and educational, to seek out and use the new technologies available in these fields. As with public sector support for agricultural extension programs to hasten the spread of new productive technologies among the many small farmers of the world, new birth control and public health technologies need to be disseminated widely in a variety of forms and combined with education, not propaganda, if the social barriers erected by past educational policies are not to distort the diffusion of these techniques among all classes of society.

A serious misapprehension of the empirical record of the demographic transition and concurrent developments is that fertility and population growth rates mechanically decline as per capita income increases (Chenery and Syrquin, 1975, p. 47). A principal insight of the economic model of household production and consumption is that where children require substantial time of parents, and particularly of females, it is to be expected that the opportunity cost of children will increase and fertility will decrease as the market wage opportunities available to women improve. Increases in men's wages will not have a comparable effect depressing fertility, and may in fact add to the private demands for children in a traditional agricultural society. In these settings income and substitution effects may even pull together to increase birthrates. Correspondingly, increasing the value and productivity of land and nonhuman capital can add to fertility demands, unless concurrent technological changes and labor mobility increase the returns to parents of investing in their children's schooling and migration. It is not reasonable to assume that economic development must promote a decline in fertility; this widely held view ignores the theoretical logic of the household demand framework and the growing body of supporting empirical evidence that it is not merely the level of per capita income that affects fertility, but the structure of increases in personal income that occurs with development that determines desired fertility. Achieving more equal education investments in girls and boys is one obvious route to facilitate a more rapid decline in fertility, because it is associated with lower child mortality and decreased demands for fertility. Investments that augment private returns on human capital are also likely to raise incomes and lower birthrates. Investments in land development and irrigation projects are less likely to be associated with the same fertility reducing consequences, though these investments may be fully warranted in terms of their social rates of return. The point that has escaped the attention of some policy-makers is that the broader structure of development investments can affect the rate of decline of fertility for a given increase in per capita income. Libya and Hong Kong, for example, might illustrate this distinction, if data were available.

Finally, the new economic demography has clarified the innate problems of measuring the effects of one family choice or behavioral outcome on another. For example, when the inverse association between family size and average child education is discussed in population surveys (World Bank, 1984; National Academy of Sciences, 1986), insufficient emphasis is given to the fact that this salient pattern is not a causal relationship on which policy can operate. It is rather an association between jointly determined family decisions that may reflect bidirectional causation, unobserved variables, and probably heterogeneity in preferences of the population. Unable to use economic theory to justify identifying restrictions that are required to estimate these structural relationships among family choice variables, and rarely able to trace out responses to random shocks from natural experiments, such as is possible with twins, many household researchers have refocused their analysis on unrestricted reduced-form equations from the household production demand system. In other words, they no longer try to disentangle how endogenous family choice outcomes interact, such as fertility and child education. The reduced-form equations for household demographic and economic behavior can still provide a consistent basis for evaluating many programs and policy interventions. Indeed, reduced-form estimates can also assess how the distribution of benefits from these programs differs by exogenous population groups, such as by education or by race (T. Paul Schultz, 1984).

In sum, microeconomic demand studies of household behavior provide a framework that has not yet provided general measures of the aggregate or individual consequences of population growth, but this framework has provided a rationale for voluntary family planning as a technology extension activity that is justifiably undertaken by the public sector. The framework also provides a sophisticated statistical basis for evaluating the effectiveness of family planning and other family welfare programs.

CONCLUSIONS

Several developments have recently led economists to qualify their views that the benefits of slowing population growth clearly outweigh the costs. Fertility is no longer seen as a natural force that is out of control in the world. Though it is a biologically constrained outcome, fertility is also widely regulated by traditional and increasingly modern means of birth control to advance the private interests of individuals and families. Reproductive goals of couples in low-income societies are less rigid than feared by the demographers and economists who first fathomed the magnitude of the contemporary acceleration in population growth (Notestein, 1945). Marriage patterns and marital birthrates can both change rapidly and voluntarily, with the implication that private demands for modern, more effective means of birth control can also expand rapidly. These changes in fertility goals need not occur so as to offset precisely the decrease in mortality. Homeostatic tendencies of fertility to adjust to child mortality appear to be present, but they are difficult to quantify precisely because both outcomes are endogenous within the family production-consumption system. The family demand model implies that certain price, life-cycle wage, and program variables are likely to play a pivotal role in modifying levels of reproductive demands, because these variables change the opportunity cost of time and goods needed to rear children, or affect the productive benefits of child labor versus more educated adult labor, or influence the cost and inconvenience of available technologies of birth control. But the economic model cannot generally prescribe how parents ultimately view children, nor which production and consumption activities compete with children for parent time and other resources. Empirical studies of household demographic and economic behavior confirm that these exogenous conditioning variables not only appear to influence fertility as anticipated, but they also appear to affect parent investments in their children's schooling and health and many other coordinated allocational choices in the household sector. From these empirical regularities, it should be possible to discern whether particular commodities and activities subsidized through public sector programs tend to complement large families or substitute for additional children. If a society determines that it wishes to encourage or discourage fertility, this information may be considered in the formulation of public policy.

At the macroeconomic level much less research has quantified the aggregate consequences of variation in population growth. The expectations of Malthus that rapid population growth would depress real wages and increase income inequalities are not confirmed by a casual inspection of the recent historical record (Kuznets, 1967). Nor have quantitative estimates of Boserup's economies of population density been confirmed by widely accepted methods. This leaves policy-makers unarmed with empirical economic evidence to support their general endorsements of population control policies as a means to accelerate economic development.

Most of the evidence cited in the past to demonstrate the negative consequences of rapid population growth is, with hindsight, simple statistical associations between unfavorable family welfare outcomes and fertility, both of which tend to be endogenous variables determined jointly within the household demand model. For instance, large families have more malnutrition, more mortality, less schooled children, etc. (National Academy of Sciences, 1971). The covariation of such endogenous household variables does not provide a satisfactory basis for inferring causal influence in either direction. The empirical analysis that would clarify the benefits of slowing population growth must be derived within the broader perspective of the family household demand framework outlined above.

Having set aside the global question of the consequences of population growth as not yet answered, development economists can still proceed to seek answers to more appropriately framed questions, such as the effectiveness of public programs and market developments to change the health, education, and fertility of people. Empirical estimates can be calculated representing how local public investments in the number and quality of schools, public health programs, family planning programs, agricultural research and extension programs influence a host of household behavioral outcomes, including, but not limited to, fertility and mortality. It is the synergistic potential of some of these family-oriented human capital investment and development programs that needs to be quantitatively assessed further. The methods as illustrated above are available for this type of research, although they have certain limitations.[12]

An increasing number of low-income countries are investing in the collection of a broad range of economic and demographic survey data collected from households and matched to local information on average prices, wages, and public programs. These data can be directed to answering important policy questions of program effectiveness and the personal distribution of benefits from these public sector activities. Only as these facts are assembled from a sufficient range of environments throughout the world will it be appropriate to venture generalizations. I suspect, however, that the empirical regularities that these investigations will uncover will be no less remarkable than those Engel (1895) found in his early studies of the expenditure shares of workers that established the subsequent direction for research on consumer demands.

NOTES

[1] I shall survey more closely the work I know better. This may give special prominence to the research of economists associated with the Yale Economic Growth Center. Such an imbalance may perhaps be overlooked for a conference marking the Center's 25th anniversary. Regardless, there is a continuity and consistency to the research agenda pursued in economic demography at the Center that provides the focus for this survey.

[2] Changes in real wages are due to two underlying series: nominal wage rates and on prices of basic foodgrains. Most of the time series variation is in food

prices, and therefore in settings where both are available, analysis of the price series alone or real wages yields similar estimates of their effect on vital rates. Here I refer to studies that focus on either food prices or real wages. English mortality appears to have been more responsive to food prices in 1544–1640 than it was in subsequent years, viz. 1641–1745 and 1746–1834 (Lee, 1981). This may have reflected the tendency for English wages to increase over time above subsistence or for other institutions to partially shelter the poor from the life threatening force of food shortages (Fogel, 1986). Smaller response rates are estimated by Richards (1984) for France, 1740–1909, using approximately the same distributed lag methodology as followed by Lee. Bengtsson (1984) found a closer relationship between harvest-price cycles and mortality in southern Sweden in the early nineteenth century than he did in the eighteenth century. The reason offered for the increased sensitivity is the diminished importance of epidemic disease in the nineteenth century. A study by Eckstein et al. (1984) of Swedish national data from 1750 to 1860, based on auto vector regression, found strong evidence of wage induced fluctuations in mortality, particularly among persons over the age of one.

[3] Carlsson (1970) illustrated this point with aggregate time series during the nineteenth century. Ohlin's (1955) thesis found similar evidence much earlier in Sweden and Finland. Lee (1981) shows in England from 1548–1834 that less than half of the incremental births associated with swings in marriage rates must be due to changes in marital fertility rates among women already married. In fact, in southern Sweden at the end of the eighteenth century, marriages are not strongly related to harvest cycles. Marital fertility and the harvest cycle are, however, highly correlated in nineteenth-century Sweden Bengtsson, 1984).

[4] Criticism of the household production approach often notes the fact that in a less specialized home production environment, time is frequently employed to advance several activities at one time, such as the mother's capacity to care for her children while doing some housework, or tending some own account business pursuits. Variable returns to scale are also noted in the household. The properties of household technology that Becker postulated are required to preserve the "adding up" character of full income and the exogeneity of shadow prices. But neither shadow prices or full income are generally observed or analytically needed except to compare welfare in the latter case, which we know is ambiguous anyway with variation in family composition (Gronau, 1985; Deaton and Muellbauer, 1985). Another feature ignored is the public-good aspect of some commodities. Children may be enjoyed by both parents without reducing either's pleasure. How these restrictions on technology actually distort analysis has not been demonstrated, although instances can certainly be found (T. Paul Schultz, 1981; Gronau, 1984).

[5] Aside from casual empiricism, which suggests individuals do not always submerge their individual interests in a consistent manner within a family, there are opportunities to test empirically whether the restrictions implied by demand theory applied to the family are consistent with observed behavior. For example, the income compensated husband's market labor supply response to his wife's wage should be symmetric (equal) to the compensated wife's labor supply response to her husband's wage. Similarly, it is sometimes suggested that the wife values more highly than does her husband certain

allocations of family resources, such as investments in child quality (H, E and perhaps L_c). In this case, increments to her wealth (e.g. dowry) or V_w should increase the demand for these qualitative attributes of children more than would equal increments to the husband's wealth, V_h. Indeed, the standard household model for this reason generally only includes an aggregate nonearned-income variable. Testing for significant differences in the husband and wife wealth effects is one check on the family demand model. This restriction of the family demand theory could not be empirically rejected with U.S. data by McElroy and Horney (1978) who developed a bargaining model of the family designed to explain consumption behavior of U.S. couples. They nest within this bargaining model the neoclassical family demand model. Even if one were to reject the family or household integrated demand model, individual consumption and time allocation behavior would nonetheless depend on the same reduced-form arguments, equations (7) and (8); see Rosenzweig and Schultz, 1984.)

[6] A cross-regional analysis of Sweden from 1850 to 1910 identifies aggregate demand induced changes in adult female and male agricultural wages that help to explain the decline in fertility. The exogenous instruments for the wage series are regional relative output prices and nonfarm employment opportunities. Female wage opportunities are associated with one-fourth of the decline in fertility, and another one-fourth is associated with the decline in child mortality. Increases in male wages shift the age pattern of fertility toward an earlier age, but do not noticeably affect the level of fertility across all ages combined (Schultz, 1985).

[7] The distribution of births by sex is another biologically exogenous outcome that may in turn influence subsequent fertility and other household demand choices to the extent that parents do not regard boys and girls as perfect substitutes.

[8] An even more distressing practice is for the same researcher in companion studies, often on the same data, to change core working assumptions, such as to shift without explanation from treating one household variable as endogenous in one study to being an exogenous instrument in another study. Such practices make the sum of research add up to less than the parts.

[9] The net reproduction rate (NRR) is the average number of female offspring per woman who themselves reach the mean age of childbearing, T. In the long run, such a stable population increases at the annual rate of r:

$$r = \log(\text{NRR})/T.$$

The empirical question is how does the number of births respond to a change in the death rate for children (to say, age 25). If the adjustment were fully offsetting, then $dC/dD = 1$, and NRR would not vary with the decline in child deaths, D. Estimates of this derivative from intercountry comparisons for women of various ages yields estimates of about unity, but this ignores covariates that influence both fertility and child mortality, such as mother's education, so it is undoubtedly upward biased (T. Paul Schultz, 1981). Within countries, controlling for household economic characteristics, family estimates of response patterns range from 0.5 to 1.0. But as the text discusses, there is still likely to be an upward bias in these estimates from unobservables that will tend to have parallel effects on birthrates and death rates in the cross section. Thus, the need to specify a convincing exclusionary restriction to identify the effect of child mortality on fertility. These more restrictive exercises yield response rates on the order of 1/4 to 1/3.

[10] Easterlin and Crimmins (1985) also propose a statistical methodology for disentangling biological and behavioral factors determining fertility, but their procedures can be quite misleading as elaborated elsewhere (see T. Paul Schultz, 1986).

[11] For example, if a family planning clinic lowers fertility and child mortality and raises school enrollment rates in a locality, then a school should increase school enrollment rates and symmetrically lower fertility and child mortality, while child health clinics would lower child mortality and fertility while raising school enrollment rates. Income effects in these cases would raise schooling and lower mortality, but might work to increase fertility, weakening some of the above anticipated program effects on fertility.

[12] A limitation of the framework outlined in this paper is that it is static and treats the life cycle as a single period. It is desirable to characterize the choice problem as one of dynamic optimization in an uncertain environment. Births and deaths are uncertain events and their timing may be important in understanding some forms of household behavior. To model these features within the household life-cycle fertility framework, in a general but estimable form, is attractive. It tends to impose, however, other limitations such as restricting the number of variables that can be treated as endogenous. The computational burden of the estimation methods also effectively restricts the number of conditioning variables that can be considered and the size of sample consulted. Nonetheless, with the decreasing cost of computation this area of research is active and innovative (Wolpin, 1984). Studies have analyzed fertility and child mortality in Malaysia (Olson and Wolpin, 1983; Wolpin, 1984) and Costa Rica (Newman 1987), and fertility and female labor supply in the United States (Vijverberg, 1984).

REFERENCES

Anderson, K. H. 1984: "The Sensitivity of Wage Elasticities to Selection Bias and the Assumption of Normality." *Journal of Human Resources*, 17(4), 594–605.

Anker, R. and Knowles, J. C. 1980: "An Empirical Analysis of Mortality Differentials in Kenya at the Macro and Micro Levels." *Economic Development and Cultural Change*, 29(1), 165–86.

Ashenfelter, O., Deaton, A., and Solon, G. 1986: "Collecting Panel Data in Developing Countries: Does It make Sense?" Living Standards Measurement Study Working Paper No. 23, Washington, DC: The World Bank.

Ashenfelter, O. and Heckman, J. J. 1974: "The Estimation of Income and Substitution Effects in a Model of Family Labor Supply." *Econometrica*, 42(1), 73–85.

Becker, G. S. 1965: "A Theory of the Allocation of Time." *Economic Journal*, 74, 299 and 493–517.

Becker, G. S. 1981: *A Treatise on the Family.* Cambridge, Mass.: Harvard University Press.

Becker, G. S. and Lewis, G. 1984: "Interaction between Quantity and Quality of Children." In T. W. Schultz (ed.), *Economics of the Family*, Chicago: University of Chicago Press.

Behrman, J. R. and Wolfe, B. L. Forthcoming: "Earnings and Labor Force Participation Determinants in a Developing Country." In *Labor Market Discrimination in Developing Economies*, Washington, DC: The World Bank.

Bengtsson, T. 1984: "Harvest Fluctuations and Demographic Response: Southern Sweden 1851–1859." In *Pre-Industrial Population Change*, T. Bengtsson, et al. (eds), Stockholm, Sweden: Almquist and Wicksell International.

Ben-Porath, Y. 1980: "The F Connection." *Population and Development Review*, 6(1), 1–30.

Boserup, E. 1965: *The Conditions of Agricultural Growth: The Economics of Agrarian Change under Population Pressure*. Chicago: Aldine Publishing Co.

Boserup, E. 1981: *Population and Technological Change*. Chicago: University of Chicago Press.

Boulier, B. L. and Rosenzweig, M. R. 1984: "Schooling, Search, and Spouse Selection." *Journal of Political Economy*, 92(4), 712–32.

Carlsson, G. 1970: "Nineteenth Century Fertility Oscillations." *Population Studies*, 24, 413–22.

Chenery, H. D. and Syrquin, M. 1975: *Patterns of Development, 1950–1970*. London: Oxford University Press.

Coale, A. J. and Hoover, E. 1958: *Population Growth and Economic Development in Low Income Countries*. Princeton, New Jersey: Princeton University Press.

Coale, A. J. 1983: "Recent Trends in Fertility in Less Developed Countries." *Science*, 221(4613), 828–32.

Cochrane, S. H. 1980: *The Effects of Education on Health*. World Bank Staff Working Paper No. 405, Washington, DC.

Cochrane, S. H., Leslie, J., O'Hara, D. J. 1982: "Parental Education and Child Health." *Health Policy and Education*, 2 (Feb.).

DaVanzo, J. 1971: *The Determinants of Family Formation in Chile, 1960*. R-830, Santa Monica, CA: The Rand Corp. (Dec.).

Deaton, A. and Muellbauer, J. 1985: "On Measuring Child Costs: With Applications to Poor Countries." Forthcoming in *Journal of Political Economy*.

Denison, E. 1962: *The Sources of Economic Growth in the United States*. New York: Committee for Economic Development.

Deolalikar, A. B. 1984: "Are There Pecuniary Returns to Health in Agricultural Work?" Mimeo, University of Pennsylvania.

Duncan, O. D. 1966: "Path Analysis: Sociological Examples." *American Journal of Sociology*, 72(1), 1–16.

Easterlin, R. A. and Crimmins, E. M. 1985: *The Fertility Revolution: A Supply–Demand Analysis*. Chicago: University of Chicago Press.

Easterlin, R. A., Pollak, R. A., and Wachter, M. L. 1980: "Toward a More General Economic Model of Fertility Determination: Endogenous Preferences and Natural Fertility." In *Population and Economic Change in Developing Countries*, Chicago: University of Chicago Press.

Eckstein, Z. and Wolpin, K. I. 1982: "Endogenous Fertility in an Overlapping Generations Growth Model." Yale Economic Growth Center Discussion Paper No. 416, July.

Eckstein, Z., Schultz, T. P. and Wolpin, K. 1984: "Short Run Fluctuations in Fertility and Mortality in PreIndustrial Sweden." *European Economic Review*, 26, 295-317.

Engel, E. 1895: "*Die Lebenskosten Belgischer Arbeiter-Familien Frueher und Jetzt.*" International Statistical Institute Bulletin, 9, 1-74.

Evenson, R. E. 1984: "Population Growth, Infrastructural Development, Technology and Welfare in Rural North India." IUSSP Seminar on Population and Rural Development, New Delhi, India.

Farah, A. A. and Preston, S. H. 1982: "Child Mortality Differentials in Sudan." *Population and Development Review*, 8(2), 365-83.

Fogel, R. W. 1986: "Nutrition and the Decline in Mortality Since 1700: Some Additional Preliminary Findings." NBER Working Paper No. 1802, Cambridge, Mass.

Fuchs, V. 1984: "Some Economic Aspects of Mortality in Developed Countries." In M. Perlman (ed.), *The Economics of Health and Medical Care*, London: Macmillan.

Galloway, P. R. 1985: "Annual Variation in Deaths by Age, Deaths by Cause, Prices, and Weather in London, 1670 to 1830." *Population Studies*, 39(3), 487-505.

Goldin, C. 1983: "The Changing Economic Role of Women." *Journal of Interdisciplinary History*, 13(4), 707-33.

Goody, J. 1976: *Production and Reproduction*. Cambridge: Cambridge University Press.

Griffin, C. 1986: "Methods for Estimating Value of Time in Low Income Countries with an Application to the Philippines." Mimeo, Yale University, New Haven, Conn.

Gronau, R. 1984: "Home Production – A Survey." NORC Discussion Paper 85-2, Chicago.

Gronau, R. 1985: "The Allocation of Goods within the Household and Estimation of Adult Equivalence Scales." Mimeo, Hebrew University of Jerusalem.

Heckman, J. J. 1979: "Sample Selection Bias as a Specification Error." *Econometrica*, 47(2), 153-61.

Heckman, J. J. 1987: "Time Constraints and Household Demand Functions." Forthcoming in *Research in Population Economics*, T. P. Schultz (ed.), vol. 6, Greenwich, Conn.: JAI Press.

Heckscher, E. R. 1954: *An Economic History of Sweden*. G. Ohlin, (trans.), Cambridge, Mass.: Harvard University Press.

Henry, L. 1961: "Some Data on Natural Fertility," *Eugenics Quarterly*, 8, 81-91.

Hill, M. A. 1983: "Female Labor Force Participation in Developing and Developed Countries – Consideration of the Informal Sector." *Review of Economics and Statistics*, 65(3), 459-68.

Kelley, A. C. and Williamson, J. 1984: *What Drives Third World City Growth*. Princeton, NJ: Princeton University Press.

Kuznets, S. 1967: "Population and Economic Growth." *Proceedings of the American Philosophic Society*, 11, 170-93.

Lee, R. D. 1973: "Population in Preindustrial England: An Econometric Analysis." *Quarterly Journal of Economics*, 84(4), 581-607.

Lee, R. D. 1980: "A Historical Perspective on Economic Aspects of the Population Explosion." In R. A. Easterlin (ed.), *Population and Economic Change in Developing Countries,* Chicago: University of Chicago Press.

Lee, R. D. 1981: "Short Run Fluctuations in Vital Rates, Prices and Weather." In E. A. Wrigley and R. Schofield (eds), *Population Trends in Early Modern England,* Cambridge, Mass.: Harvard University Press.

Levy, V. 1985: "Cropping Pattern, Mechanization, Child Labor and Fertility Behaviour in Rural Egypt." *Economic Development and Cultural Change,* 33(4), 777–91.

Malthus, T. R. 1798: *An Essay on the Principle of Population.* Reprinted, Baltimore: Penguin (1979).

Maurer, K., Ratajczak, R. and Schultz, T. P. 1973: *Marriage, Fertility and Labor Force Participation of Thai Women.* R-829, Santa Monica CA: The Rand Corp., April.

McElroy, M. B. and Horney, J. 1978: "A Nash Bargained Linear Expenditure System: The Demand for Leisure and Goods." Duke University mimeo. Partially published in *International Economic Review,* 22, 333–50 (June 1981), and expanded in (1987), *Research in Population Economics,* T. P. Schultz (ed.), vol. 6, Greenwich, Conn.: JAI Press.

Mincer, J. 1974: *Schooling, Experience, and Earnings.* New York: Columbia University Press.

Modigliani, F. and Brumberg, R. 1954: "Utility Analysis and the Consumption Function: An Interpretation of Cross Sectional Data." In K. Kunilhara (ed.), *Post-Keynesian Economics,* New Btrunswick, N.J.: Rutgers University Press.

Montgomery, M. 1986: "Female First Marriage in East and Southeast Asia: A Kiefer-Neumann Model." Yale University Economic Growth Center Discussion Paper No. 510, Aug. 1986.

Mueller, E. 1984: "Income Aspirations and Fertility in Rural Areas of Less Developed Countries." In W. A. Schutjer and C. S. Stokes (eds), *Rural Development and Human Fertility,* New York: Macmillan Publishing Co.

National Academy of Sciences 1971: *Rapid Population Growth: Consequences and Policy Implicators.* Baltimore: Johns Hopkins University Press.

National Academy of Sciences 1986: *Population Growth and Economic Development: Policy Questions.* Washington, DC: National Academy Press.

Nerlove, M. and Schultz, T. P. 1970: *Love and life Between the Censuses: A Model of Family Decision Making in Puerto Rico, 1950–1960.* R-6322, Santa Monica CA: The Rand Corp., Sept.

Newman, J. 1987: "A Stochastic Dynamic Model of Fertility." Forthcoming in *Research in Population Economics,* T. P. Schultz (ed.), vol. 6, Greenwich, Conn.: JAI Press.

Notestein, F. 1945: "Population – The Long View." In T. W. Schultz (ed.), *Food for the World,* Chicago: University of Chicago Press.

Ohlin, P. G. 1955: "The Posture and Preventive Check: A Study of the Rate of Growth in Preindustrial Populations." Unpublished dissertation, Cambridge, Mass.: Harvard University.

Olson, R. J. 1980: "Estimating The Effects of Child Mortality on the Number of Births." *Demography,* 17(4), 429–44.

Olson, R. J. 1987: "Cross-Sectional Methods for Estimating the Replacement of Infant Deaths." In T. P. Schultz (ed.), *Research in Population Economics,* vol. 6, Greenwich, Conn.: JAI Press.

Olson, R. J. and Wolpin, K. I. 1983: "The Impact of Exogenous Child Mortality on Fertility." *Econometrica*, 51(3), 731–49.

Pollak, R. 1985: "A Transaction Cost Approach to Families and Households." *Journal of Economic Literature*, 32(2), 581–608.

Pollak, R. A. and Wachter, M. L. 1975: "The Relevance of the Household Production Function for the Allocation of Time." *Journal of Political Economy*, 83(2), 255–77.

Ram, R. and Schultz, T. W. 1979: "Life Span, Health, Saving and Productivity." *Economic Development and Cultural Change*, 27(3), 399–421.

Richards, T. 1984: "Weather, Nutrition and the Economy: The Analysis of Short Run Fluctuations in Births, Deaths and Marriages, France 1740–1909." In T. Bengtsson, G. Fridlizius, and R. Ohlsson (eds), *Pre-Industrial Population Change*, Stockholm, Sweden: Almquist and Wicksell International.

Rodgers, G., Hopkins, M. and Wery, R. 1978: *Population Employment and Inequality: Bachue-Philippines*. Guildford Surrey: Saxon House.

Rosenzweig, M. R. and Evenson, R. E. 1977: "Fertility, Schooling and the Economic Contribution of Children in Rural India." *Econometrica*, 45(5) 1065–79.

Rosenzweig, M. R. and Schultz, T. P. 1982a: "Market Opportunities, Genetic Endowments and Intrafamily Resource Distribution." *American Economic Review*, 74(3), 215–35.

Rosenzweig, M. R. and Schultz, T. P. 1982b: *Determinants of Fertility and Child Mortality in Colombia*. Report AID/DSPE-G-0013 mimeo, New Haven, Conn.: Yale University, May.

Rosenzweig, M. R. and Schultz, T. P. 1983a: "Consumer Demand and Household Production." *American Economic Review*, 73(3), 38–42.

Rosenzweig, M. R. and Schultz, T. P. 1983b: "Estimating a Household Production Function: Heterogeneity, The Demand for Health Inputs, and Their Effects on Birth Weights." *Journal of Political Economy*, 91(5), 723–46.

Rosenzweig, M. R. and Schultz, T. P. 1984: "Market Opportunities... Reply." *American Economic Review*, 74(2), 521–2.

Rosenzweig, M. R. and Schultz, T. P. 1985a: "The Demand and Supply of Births: Fertility and Its Life Cycle Consequences." *American Economic Review*, 75(5), Dec.

Rosenzweig, M. R. and Schultz, T. P. 1985b: "Schooling, Information and Non Market Productivity: Contraceptive Use and its Effectiveness." New Haven, Conn.: Yale University Economic Growth Center Discussion Paper No. 490 (Sept.)

Rosenzweig, M. R. and Schultz, T. P. 1986: "Stability of Household Production Technology: A Replication." Yale Economic Growth Center Discussion Paper No. 511, Sept.

Rosenzweig, M. R. and Wolpin, K. I. 1980a: "Testing The Quantity–Quality Fertility Model: The Use of Twins as a National Experiment." *Econometrica*, 48(1), 227–40.

Rosenzweig, M. R. and Wolpin, K. I. 1980b: "Life Cycle Labor Supply and Fertility." *Journal of Political Economy*, 89(2), 1059–85.

Rosenzweig, M. R. and Wolpin, K. I. 1982: "Governmental Interventions and Household Behavior in a Development Country." *Journal of Development Economics*, 10(2), 209–26.

Rosenzweig, M. R. and Wolpin, K. I. 1984: "Optimal Governmental Interventions and Their Consequences." Mimeo, New Haven, Conn.: Yale University.

Samuelson, P. A. 1958: "An Exact Consumption Loan Model of Interest With or Without the Contrivance of Money." *Journal of Political Economy,* 66(6), 467–82.

Schultz, T. Paul 1971: *Evaluation of Population Policies.* R-643, Santa Monica Calif.: The Rand Corp., June.

Schultz, T. Paul 1972: "Fertility Patterns and Their Determinants in the Arab Middle East." C. A. Cooper and S. S. Alexander (eds), *Economic Development and Population Growth in the Middle East,* New York: American Elsevier, 401–500.

Scultz, T. Paul 1976: "Determinants of Fertility." In A. J. Coale (ed.), *Economic Factors in Population Growth,* London: Macmillan Press Ltd.

Schultz, T. Paul 1980: "Interpretation of Relations Among Mortality, Economics of the Household, and the Health Environment." In *Socioeconomic Determinants and Consequences of Mortality Differentials,* Geneva: WHO.

Schultz, T. Paul 1981: *Economics of Population.* Reading, Mass.: Addison Wesley Publishing Co.

Schultz, T. Paul 1983: "Migrant Behavior and The Effects of Regional Prices." Economic Growth Center Discussion Paper No. 443, Aug.

Schultz, T. Paul 1984: "Studying The Impact of Household Economic and Community Variables on Child Mortality." *Population and Development Review,* 10(Aug.) 215–35.

Schultz, T. Paul 1985a: "School Expenditures and Enrollments, 1960–80: The Effect of Income, Prices and Population." New Haven, Conn.: Economic Growth Center Discussion Paper No. 487, July.

Schultz, T. Paul 1985b: "Changing World Prices, Women's Wages and The Fertility Transition." *Journal of Political Economy,* 93(6), 1126–54.

Schultz, T. Paul 1986: "The Fertility Revolution: A Review Essay." *Population and Development Review,* 12(1), March.

Schultz, T. W. 1961: "Investment in Human Capital." *American Economic Review,* 51(1), March.

Schultz, T. W. 1975: "The Ability to Deal with Disequilibria." *Journal of Economic Literature,* 13(Sept.), 827–46.

Sen, A. K. 1981: *Poverty and Famines: An Essay on Entitlements and Deprivation.* Oxford: Clarendon Press.

Silver, M. 1965: "Births, Marriages and the Business Cycle in the United States." *Journal of Political Economy,* 73 (3), 237–55.

Silver, M. 1966: "Births, Marriages and Income Fluctuations in the United Kingdom and Japan." *Economic Development and Cultural Change,* 14(3), 302–15.

Simon, J. L. 1977: *The Economics of Population Growth.* Princeton, N.J.: Princeton University Press.

Smith, J. (ed.) 1980: *Female Labor Supply.* Princeton, N.J.: Princeton University Press.

Stolnitz, G. J. 1975: "International Mortality Trends." In *Population Debate,* New York: United Nations.

Strauss, J. 1985: "Does Nutrition Raise Farm Productivity." Forthcoming in *Journal of Political Economy.*

Thomas, D. S. 1927: *Social Aspects of the Business Cycle*: New York: Knopf.

United Nations 1980: *Socioeconomic Determinants and Consequences of Mortality Differentials.* Geneva: WHO.

United Nations Department of International Economic and Social Affairs 1985: *Socio-Economic Differentials in Child Mortality in Developing Countries.* ST/ESA/SER.A/97, New York: United Nations.

Vijverberg, V. 1984: "Discrete Choices in a Continuous Time Model: Life Cycle Time Allocation and Fertility Decisions." *Research in Population Economics*, vol. 5, Greenwich, Conn.: JAI Press.

Watkin, S. C. and Menken, J. 1985: "Famines in Historical Perspective," *Population and Development Review*, 11(4), 647–76.

Williamson, J. G. 1982: "Was the Industrial Revolution Worth It? Disamenities and Death in 19th Century British Towns." *Explorations in Economic History*, 19(July), 221–45.

Wold, H. O. A. 1964: *Econometric Model Building: Essays on the Causal Chain Approach.* Amsterdam: North-Holland Publishing Co.

Wolpin, K. I. 1984: "An Estimable Dynamic Stochastic Model of Fertility and Child Mortality." *Journal of Political Economy*, 92(3), 852–74.

World Bank 1984: *World Development Report 1984.* New York: Oxford University Press.

Comments on
"Economic Demography and Development: New Directions in an Old Field"

JERE R. BEHRMAN

Schultz's survey has three parts. In his introduction, he discusses the shift in the last decade from the view "that rapid population growth is an important deterrent to economic development in contemporary low-income societies" to a much more qualified perspective quoted from the National Academy of Sciences: "'slower population growth would be beneficial to economic development for most developing countries...(but) a rigorous quantitative assessment of these benefits is difficult and context dependent'" He then reviews the Malthusian population model and relevant empirical evidence. Finally he considers household microeconomic models of demographic behavior and their implications. This survey captures many important dimensions of recent developments in demography and how they relate to economic development. At the same time it raises some questions, both of commission and omission.

Introduction

Schultz suggests that the shift in perspective about population growth being less obviously a deterrent to economic development "does not seem to be due to a fundamentally new economic insight, but rather to the proliferation of empirical studies guided by a common framework..." It seems to me that this characterization understates the role of the "common framework" due to economic theories of household behavioral and fertility, due particularly to Becker but also to Easterlin, Leibenstein, Willis, and others, which provide the framework for much recent economic-demographic analysis. These models have several important characteristics, most of which Schultz describes to various degrees in the second section: emphasis on price as well as income effects, attention to the quality (or human capital) as well as the quantity of children, recognition of time as an important production input and constraint, and incorporation of household production – including that for births and child mortality – into the analysis. I interpret this development of such models to be appropriately characterized as the introduction of a new economic insight (or, in some ways, partially a redevelopment), without which the "proliferation of empirical studies" to which Schultz refers would not have changed consensus perceptions. Thus, I perceive the change to be more than a "shift in economic fashions."

Malthus's model and the evidence

I generally find Schultz's characterization in this section persuasive and useful, but I have two reservations.

First, the section begins:

> "For the last 25 years, there has been almost a consensus among social scientists on the nature of the relationships between population growth and economic development. This shared view owes much to the ideas that Malthus (1798) articulated nearly 200 years ago" (pages 418–19).

While I agree that the Malthusian view has been very influential, to state that it has been the consensus view in the quarter century starting in 1960 is not consistent with Schultz's claim in the introduction that a significant shift has occurred in the past decade, ignores the ferment caused by what I consider to be non-Malthusian contributions by Becker, Leibenstein, Easterlin, Boserup, Simon, and others, and simply does not seem to be true.

Second, much of the evidence that Schultz reviews pertains to the historical relation between real wages (defined as nominal wages deflated by food prices or some broader consumer price index) and mortality or fertility. I personally am not very familiar with these studies. However, it does seem to me natural to ask how relevant are such historical series of real wages likely to be for this analysis. For workers in nonagricultural labor markets who purchase their food in markets, such real wage measures may reflect the construct of interest. But in preindustrial societies, large numbers of individuals are laborers in food production, often paid in kind. For such individuals, an increase in food prices that caused real wages to drop *ceteris paribus* well might be associated with a real income increase. If so, most of the evidence that Schultz cites may not be very damaging to Malthus's basic relations.

Micro formulations of household demographic behavior and empirical evidence

The heart of Schultz's paper is the presentation of the household model for understanding demographic behavior and of empirical studies that are consistent with it, or at least with special cases of it. I agree that the framework provided by this model is very important in understanding certain demographic phenomena; in fact I suggest above that Schultz in his introduction may understate the importance of the development of this framework for changed perceptions of the interrelations between demographic changes and economic development. I also agree that some of the best relevant recent research has been rationalized by this framework. But I think that a number of qualifications, to some of which Schultz alludes, need to be made about this framework:

1   The framework as generally used is static with a one-period lifetime model.[1] But the demographic-economic problems of interest are in some essential respect dynamic – for example, how does fertility evolve in a rapidly changing developing economy? The static framework has many of the same problems on a micro level as does macroanalysis, of which Schultz is critical. How can one deal with expectational formation in an uncertain world, the nature of adjustment paths, and possible irreversibilities?

2   Even the general framework that Schultz presents (and much more the studies that he reviews) abstracts from a number of characteristics that many consider to be important and which, if included, often would preclude identification of structural parameters or change the interpretation considerably. Three examples are endogenous tastes, endowments that affect household and labor market productivity (not just fertility as in Schultz's formulation), and endogenous wages.

Endogenous tastes are hypothesized by some economists and many noneconomists to be important so that, for example, the preference trade-off between the gains from having children (C in relation 1) and consuming the household composite commodity (S) may depend on parental schooling or exposure to the consumption patterns of others (i.e. the "international demonstration effect"). If tastes are endogenous, identification of the household productivity impact of variables such as schooling is much more difficult than is suggested by Schultz's general household model, and individual welfare effects may be quite ambiguous (Easterlin, Pollak and Wachter).

Endowments of genetic and childhood background origin that affect productivity more broadly than just through fertility have been emphasized recently in both theoretical and empirical studies (Becker, 1981; Becker and Tomes, 1976; Behrman, Pollak and Taubman, 1982; Behrman, Hrubec, Taubman and Wales, 1980; Olneck, 1987; Behrman and Wolfe, 1984). If indeed these endowments are important, they may contaminate substantially empirical estimates of many of the structural parameters of interest through un-omitted variable bias[2] and vitiate the empirical equation of schooling and child quality, since schooling may be allocated partially to compensate for such endowments or independently of such endowments (Behrman, 1986).

That wages may be endogenous in poor populations due to health and nutrition effects is a long-standing conjecture in the development literature (Leibenstein, 1957; Stiglitz, 1976; Bliss and Stern, 1978) which recently has received much stronger systematic empirical support in studies by Behrman and Deolalikar (1987), Deolalikar (1986) and Strauss (1986). If wages are endogenous, then they must be treated as such empirically when they are used to represent the opportunity cost of time in the studies under review in order to avoid simultaneity bias, but generally this possible simultaneity is ignored in such studies.

3   The household model on which Schultz concentrates is a model of behavior for an existing nuclear couple. Yet family structures are much more heterogenous than just simple nuclear families in the developing world, which presumably may alter demographic behavior as Leibenstein (1980), Behrman and Deolalikar (1986), and others have emphasized. Moreover, important elements of demographic behavior may reflect the formation or the dissolution of nuclear couples. The age of marriage may be inversely associated with the number of children, and dissolutions may reduce subsequent births and increase mortality. Yet the general household model that Schultz presents says little or nothing about the age of marriage or cohabitation or what leads to dissolutions.

4   In a way not often acknowledged by the practitioners of the use of the household model, the selection of exogenous instruments in order to obtain consistent estimates is a tricky business for several reasons. Community characteristics frequently are used as instruments in such studies, but – as Schultz recognizes – they may not be exogenous if people migrate in response to them. Even if people do not migrate, moreover, endogenous governmental policies may make community characteristics endogenous if, e.g., public hospitals or health clinics are placed where disease incidence is high due to unobserved environmental factors. More broadly, this genre of studies usually does not consider that exogeneity is only one desirable characteristic of good instruments. Also important is that an instrument be highly associated with the uncontaminated (by simultaneity) part of the variable being instrumented – orthogonal exogenous variables will not do. If the instruments are not exogenous or are nearly orthogonal to the variables being instrumented, their use may lead to less informative estimates than the use of ordinary least squares procedures. Yet the authors of this genre of studies seem to think it sufficient to identify some variable that plausibly may be exogenous (often assuming away problems associated with migration and endogenous policies), and then proceeding with perhaps unwarranted confidence about the superiority of their estimates. Finally, if there is more than one endogenous right-hand variable (i.e. several

inputs in the production relation 2), the Schultz recommendation to estimate the reduced-form demand relations for each of these inputs first and then to use these reduced-form estimates as instrumental variable representations of the endogenous variables in the production function seems to be of limited value in many cases. All of the endogenous variables are dependent on the same set of exogenous variables, so their instrumental variable estimates all are (often linear) combinations of the same variables, thus leading to very high collinearity among the instruments so constructed, unless there are arbitrary exclusion restrictions (as often occurs in this literature) or nonlinearities in functional forms (which, as Schultz notes for the selection issue, often is not a very satisfactory way to achieve identification). The high collinearity may make it difficult or impossible to estimate the separate effects of the instrumented endogenous variables in the relation of interest.

Omissions

Perhaps the most striking omission in Schultz's survey is with regard to most studies undertaken by individuals not in residence in New Haven at least part of the last decade. At a celebration of the 25th anniversary of the Economic Growth Center, as Schultz now states in his first note, it perhaps is appropriate to highlight the contributions of those associated with the Center to our understanding. But the density of relevant studies on demography and economic development in the eyes of most individuals in the field is not nearly so dominated by those with current or recent Growth Center affiliations as Schultz's survey suggests. Even though they are not afficionados of the household model with its strengths *and* weaknesses as practiced in New Haven, the inattention to studies in this survey by those such as Easterlin, Preston, and many others is a glaring weakness.

Another striking omission pertains to the topics covered. Even among traditional demographic topics, major areas such as household formation and migration are notable in this survey for the lack of attention given to them. From a broader perspective, surprisingly little attention is devoted to such topics as the implications of public goods and externalities and subsidized schooling and health services for demographic outcomes in developing countries. Just because the household model by itself does not inform us much about the topics does not mean that they are not important in considering demography and development.

Conclusion

Schultz has provided a useful survey primarily of the strengths of the general household model in illuminating questions about demography and economic development. His survey would be even more valuable with greater attention to the limitations of that approach and to a range of important topics in demography and development that are not investigated easily within that framework. But this caveat should not be interpreted to detract from the valuable contribution that Schultz has made in summarizing recent developments in the use of the household model framework for analysis of economic demography and development, and a number of insights that have been offered by this approach that have changed thinking about this topic in important respects.

NOTES

[1] Schultz mentions that almost as an afterthought in note 12 where he also observes that the increasing number of dynamic studies must limit themselves to many fewer endogenous variables, though the expansion of computation options has lessened this constraint.

[2] Rosenzweig and Schultz (1985) a priori avoid such contamination for their more limited definition of endowments by assuming that the endowments are orthogonal in the equation used to estimate the endowments as residuals. The broader the impact of such endowments, the less likely this assumption is legitimate.

REFERENCES

Becker, Gary S. 1981: *A Treatise on the Family.* Cambridge, Mass.: Harvard University Press.

Becker, Gary S. and Tomes, Nigel 1976: "Child Endowments and the Quantity and Quality of Children." *Journal of Political Economy,* 84(4), S143–S162.

Behrman, Jere R. 1986: "Is Child Schooling a Poor Proxy for Child Quality?" Philadelphia: University of Pennsylvania, mimeo.

Behrman, Jere R. and Deolalikar, Anil B. 1986: "Fertility and Family Structure – A Note." Philadelphia: University of Pennsylvania, mimeo.

Behrman, Jere R. 1987: "Wages and Labor Supply in Rural India: The Role of Health, Nutrition and Seasonality." In David E. Sahn (ed.), *Causes and Implications of Seasonal Household Food Security,* Washington, DC: International Food Policy Research Institute.

Behrman, Jere R.; Hrubec, Zdenek; Taubman, Paul; and Wales, Terence J. 1980: *Socioeconomic Success: A Study of the Effects of Genetic Endowments on Family Environment and Schooling.* Amsterdam: North-Holland Publishing Company.

Behrman, Jere R.; Pollak, Robert A.; Taubman, Paul 1982: "Parental Preferences and Provision for Progeny." *Journal of Political Economy,* 90(1), 52–73.

Behrman, Jere R. and Wolfe, Barbara L. 1984: "The Socioeconomic Impact of Schooling in a Developing Country." *Review of Economics and Statistics,* 66(2), 296–303.

Bliss, C. and Stern, N. 1978: "Productivity, Wages and Nutrition; Parts I and II." *Journal of Development Economics*, 5(4), 331-98.

Deolaliker, Anil B. 1986: "The Private Returns to Health and Nutrition in Agricultural Labor: The Case of Rural India." Philadelphia: University of Pennsylvania, mimeo.

Easterlin, R. A., Pollak, R. A. and Wachter, M. L. 1980: "Towards a More General Model of Fertility Determination." In R. A. Esterline (ed.), *Population and Economic Change in Developing Countries,* Chicago: University of Chicago Press, 81-150.

Leibenstein, H. A. 1957: *Economic Backwardness and Economic Growth.* New York: John Wiley.

Leibenstein, H. A. 1980: "Comment." In R. A. Easterlin (ed.), *Population and Economic Change in Developing Countries,* Chicago: University of Chicago Press for N.B.E.R., 135-40.

Olneck, Michael 1977: "On the Use of Sibling Data to Estimate the Effects of Family Background, Cognitive Skills and Schooling: Results from the Kalamazoo Brothers Study." In Paul Taubman (ed.), *Papers in Kinometrics. Determinants of Socioeconomic Success Within and Between Families.* Amsterdam: North-Holland Publishing Company.

Rosenzweig, Mark and Schultz, T. Paul 1985: "The Demand for and Supply of Births." *American Economic Review,* 75(5), 992-1015.

Stiglitz, Joseph 1976: "The Efficiency Wage Hypothesis. Surplus Labour, and the Distribution of Income in LDC's." *Oxford Economic Papers, New Series,* 28, 185-207.

Strauss, John 1986: "Does Better Nutrition Raise Farm Productivity?" *Journal of Political Economy,* 94(2), 297-320.

15
Income Distribution and Economic Growth

GARY S. FIELDS

THE RISE OF INCOME DISTRIBUTION IN DEVELOPMENT ECONOMICS

Who benefits how much from economic growth and why? This question is fundamental to today's development economics. This chapter reviews some of the major lessons learned and major directions for future research in the study of income distribution and economic development.

First, an important note on terminology. I shall use the term "income distribution" as a statistician would and as many specialists who work in the area do, namely, to refer to the overall pattern of incomes and to various summary statistics concerning that pattern. Thus, such ambiguous expressions as a "worsened distribution of income" will be eschewed in favor of clearer ones such as "greater inequality in the distribution of income" or "increased poverty" or "a leftward shift of the frequency distribution of incomes." The term "income distribution," as used here, refers generically to the question of who receives how much income; otherwise, the terms "relative inequality" and "absolute poverty" will be used to distinguish the different aspects of income distribution.

During the 25 years in which the Economic Growth Center has existed, income distribution has gone from being an isolated concern of a scattered few in the Third World to a central concern of all who study or aid economic development. For instance, a conference of leaders in the field was held in the mid-1960s; the proceedings were subsequently published in Adelman and Thorbecke (1966). As stated in the introduction (p. v): "The papers presented at the conference are therefore representative of the most advanced and fruitful techniques, both

Paper prepared for the Yale University Economic Growth Center's 25th Anniversary Symposium on The State of Development Economics: Progress and Perspectives, Gustav Ranis and T. Paul Schultz, editors. I am grateful to the editors for their helpful comments on an earlier draft.

theoretical and applied, available for analysis of the developmen
process in the emerging nations today." The studies were divided int
two main categories: development theory and strategy, and develop
ment planning and programming. The index includes mention o
"disguised unemployment" and related aspects of labor utilization. Bu
no mention is made of words like "poverty," "inequality," and "distribu
tion." This reflects the state of thinking at the time: developmen
economics as a macro phenomenon. Since that time, both Adelman an
Thorbecke have written widely on distributional issues; see, fo
example, Adelman and Morris (1973), Adelman and Robinson (1978
Thorbecke (1973), and Pyatt and Thorbecke (1976). Another exampl
is the widely used readings book by Meier (1984a) entitled *Leadin
Issues in Economic Development.* The latest edition (the fourth) lead
off with a comprehensive examination of income distribution in th
world and in the development experiences of particular countries an
regions. To illustrate how much Meier's thinking had changed, in th
previous edition (the third, published in 1976), he had written: "A
reflected in this new edition, the 'leading issues' now coalesce in
central theme: policies which are designed to eradicate poverty, reduc
inequality, and deal with problems of employment." (Meier, 1976
p. vii). In his first edition (1964), poverty, inequality, and income distribu
tion were virtually absent from consideration. And the Economi
Growth Center itself had undergone a substantial change, as witnesse
by the regular inclusion of income distribution topics in the Center'
current research program, compared to the absence of such topics ir
the country study program of the Center's early years.

What caused this change of thinking? One reason was that voice
from the developing countries themselves were being heard. Particu
larly influential was the work coming out of India. Income distributior
had figured long ago in Indian planning models (Pant, 1974) and ir
academic studies (e.g., Srinivasan and Bardhan, eds., 1974, and the
references cited therein). Changes over time in poverty and inequality
were estimated from household data and projections of income distri
bution were made for the future. Indians no longer viewed developmen
purely in macro terms. That changed perspective reached other Third
World countries. Western writers also became more and more con
cerned about distributional matters. One widely quoted statement is
that of Dudley Seers (1969), who wrote:

> The questions to ask about a country's development are therefore: What
> has been happening to poverty? What has been happening to unemploy-
> ment? What has been happening to inequality? If all three of these have
> declined from high levels, then beyond doubt this has been a period of
> development for the country concerned. If one or two of these central
> problems have been growing worse, especially if all three have, it would
> be strange to call the result 'development' even if per capita income
> doubled.

Shortly thereafter, Seers headed an ILO mission to Colombia aimed at studying that country's employment problem. The Colombia report ILO, 1970) and those that followed for other countries focused both on he fact of employment (or unemployment) and on the returns to employment (including both wages and self-employment income). This concern reflected the belief that better employment opportunities were he principal means by which the poor could earn higher incomes.

But perhaps a more important reason for the shift of development economists' attention toward distributional concerns was the fact that around 1970, those who wished to take income distribution issues seriously began to have the empirical data for doing so. One type of data was cross-sectional. Research programs at the ILO and the World Bank ed to the compilation of inequality estimates for a large number of countries. These were published in Paukert (1973) and Chenery et al. 1974) respectively, and formed the basis for studies of the correlates of inequality by Chenery and Syrquin (1975), Ahluwalia (1976), and others. Around the same time, a second kind of information was being published country by country – the results of comparable household censuses and surveys. Studies continued to come in documenting and explaining the changes in relative income inequality and/or absolute poverty around the world. And thirdly, micro data sets were becoming available for developing countries. These afforded the possibility of looking into the determinants of incomes and income inequality among individuals and households.

Certain definitional matters needed to be faced. Among them were: What is the more appropriate concept: income or consumption? Suppose income is taken as the appropriate concept. What should be included: just cash income or income-in-kind? Which recipient unit should be looked at: individuals or households? What should be emphasized: the incidence of poverty or the duration of poverty? Many times, researchers' choices on these definitional issues were dictated by purely practical considerations, such as the ready availability of certain data and the impossibility of obtaining other data. Then too, when alternatives could be examined, the resultant conclusion often was that it didn't make much practical difference, as long as one examined *either* individuals *or* households, *either* cash income *or* total income, but didn't freely mix the two, as was done in some of the earlier studies based on the Jain (1975) data.

There quickly appeared a veritable plethora of tabulations and cross-tabulations of incomes, poverty profiles, multivariate earnings functions, and decomposition studies. With the improved empirical base, the research need shifted. The next task was to synthesize the results of the very many studies that had been done and to look for patterns and explanations for them. An example of such an effort is Fields (1980b).

We have learned a great deal from the research that has been done thus far. But some very important questions remain to be answered. The balance of this paper addresses in turn the lessons learned and the priorities for future study.

LESSONS LEARNED

An important general lesson, well known to specialists on income distribution but not to development economists in general, should be stated at the outset: Few natural "economic laws" describe the path of income distribution in the course of economic development. By "law," I mean a statistical pattern that holds in a wide variety of places in a wide variety of circumstances. Examples of such economic laws are the tendency as economic growth takes place for agriculture to represent a smaller fraction of economic activity and for more of the labor force to be employed in wage and salary jobs rather than in self-employment or unpaid family labor. At the forefront of such studies of the laws of economic development was Simon Kuznets who, although a professor at Harvard, wrote many papers bearing the imprint of the Economic Growth Center at Yale. Perhaps one of the greater ironies in the history of thought on economic development is that the economic law which today is most often associated with Kuznets and that has come to bear his name – the idea that income inequality increases in the early stages of economic development and decreases in the later stages, thus tracing out an inverted-U curve – receives remarkably little empirical support, either from the evidence presented in Kuznets's writings or in subsequent data. If we consider two possible conclusions – one that income inequality "must" increase before it decreases, the other that income inequality may increase or decrease depending on the type of country and the policies pursued – the latter conclusion is certainly more consistent with the empirical evidence at hand.

The following sections demonstrate both the variety of ways in which economic growth affects income distribution and the paucity of general patterns. The discussion is organized according to the type of data: first, lessons from cross-sectional studies; then lessons from data on changes in different countries over time; and then lessons from micro data.

Lessons from cross-sectional data

Cross-sectional data occupy a prominent place in the study of income distribution, the reason being that these data were widely available before other kinds. Kuznets (1955) pioneered the comparative study of income distribution in a cross section of countries. Among those who followed were Kravis (1960), Oshima (1962), Kuznets (1963), Adelman and Morris (1973), Paukert (1973), Chenery and Syrquin (1975), Ahluwalia (1974, 1976), Ahluwalia, Carter, and Chenery (1979), Saith (1983), and Anand and Kanbur (1984, 1986).

Virtually all these studies examined only income inequality and did not address absolute incomes. Income inequality was found on average to be greater in the less developed countries than in the developed countries. Inequality was also found to be lower on average in the poorest of the less developed countries than in the relatively more-advanced ones. Thus, the cross-sectional evidence compiled over the last 20 years appears to support Kuznets's speculation about the inverted-U.

Or so it seems. If we understand Kuznets to have speculated about *averages* among groups of countries at different stages of economic development, then indeed the cross-sectional evidence supports the inverted-U. But most people do not understand the inverted-U hypothesis that way. They think more in terms of *laws* than of averages. Robinson (1976, p. 437) stated that the inverted-U hypothesis "has acquired the force of economic law" and Fei, Ranis, and Kuo (1978, p. 17) motivated their study of income distribution in Taiwan this way:

> The key question that is raised again and again is whether or not the beginnings of rapid growth in the developing economy must necessarily be associated with a worsening distribution of income [meaning here increasing relative inequality, not absolute immiserization]...The careful examination of even one successful counter-example to any such "historical necessity"...will hopefully provide us with some policy relevant conclusions concerning the precise conditions under which "things do not have to get worse before they can get better."

In fact, the cross-sectional data reveal no such "historical necessity." Rather, there is a great deal of variation around the inverted-U curve. The most recent data on income shares of the poorest 40 percent of households, compiled by Anand and Kanbur (1986), appears in table 15.1.[1] Looking down the last column, one is hard-pressed to see a pronounced inverted-U (or anything else). The wide variation around the average is confirmed by regression studies. Authors such as Cline (1975), Ahluwalia (1976), Fields (1980b), and Anand and Kanbur (1984, 1986), using various inequality measures and various functional forms, have been able to explain at most half the variation in income inequality by national income level, and usually very much less than that. Thus, most of the variation is explained by factors *other than* level of national income; no inevitable relationship between income and inequality is found.

In retrospect, it would have been surprising if countries' income levels *had* been found to provide a powerful explanation for their income inequality. Many leading development economists (e.g., Fei and Ranis, 1964; Kuznets, 1966; Adelman and Morris, 1973) had been saying for a long time that income inequality is determined as much or more by the *type* of economic development (taking account of such

TABLE 15.1   *A minimally consistent data set*

Country	Year	Per capita GNP is year of survey $US at 1970 prices	Percentage income share of the lowest 40 percent
Malawi	1969	80.0	15.0
Pakistan	1963–64	93.7	17.5
	1966–67	104.7	19.2
	1968–69	112.6	20.3
	1969–70	116.8	20.2
	1970–71	118.6	20.6
Tanzania	1967	103.8	13.5
	1969	110.3	7.8
Sri Lanka	1953	83.5	14.6
	1963	91.2	13.7
	1969–70	108.6	17.9
	1969–70	108.6	17.8
	1973	111.3	19.3
India	1953–57	94.2	20.2
	1960	102.9	13.6
	1964–65	111.3	17.2
	1967–68	120.1	13.1
Thailand	1962	142.8	13.2
Philippines	1956	191.8	12.9
	1961	207.2	12.7
	1961	207.2	11.9
	1961	207.2	12.0
	1965	224.4	11.6
	1965	224.4	11.7
	1965	224.4	11.5
	1971	261.8	11.9
Egypt	1964–65	232.8	14.1
Korea	1966	190.5	23.2
	1966	190.5	18.4
	1968	226.5	21.4
	1969	246.5	21.4
	1970	269.2	17.7
	1970	269.2	17.5
	1971	289.9	18.7
	1971	289.9	23.7
Honduras	1967–68	301.0	7.3
	1967–68	301.0	6.4
Zambia	1959	308.2	13.0

TABLE 15.1—*Continued*

Country	Year	Per capita GNP in year of survey $US at 1970 prices	Percentage income share of the lowest 40 percent
Turkey	1968	322.2	9.4
Taiwan	1953	178.6	8.6
	1959–60	216.4	14.9
	1961	234.2	13.5
	1964	283.9	20.3
	1972	457.7	22.3
Malaysia	1957–58	274.1	17.7
	1957–58	274.1	15.7
	1960	286.3	9.6
	1967–68	372.3	10.4
	1970	401.4	11.8
	1970	401.4	11.2
Brazil	1970	456.5	9.2
	1970	456.5	7.7
Jamaica	1958	515.6	8.2
Lebanon	1955–60	588.3	12.3
Costa Rica	1961	450.4	13.0
	1971	617.1	14.6
Mexico	1963	564.7	10.4
	1963	564.7	10.9
	1963	564.7	9.9
	1967–68	662.6	11.2
	1968	673.8	9.8
	1969	696.9	10.2
Uruguay	1967	720.8	14.2
Spain	1964–65	852.1	16.5
Chile	1968	903.5	13.0
Argentina	1961	1,004.6	16.6
Puerto Rico	1963	1,217.4	13.7
Japan	1962	988.2	15.3
	1962	988.2	16.9
	1963	1,083.1	20.4
	1965	1,301.0	16.8
	1968	1,712.8	16.0
	1971	2,255.0	14.8
	1971	2,255.0	22.3

TABLE 15.1—*Continued*

Country	Year	Per capita GNP in year of survey $US at 1970 prices	Percentage income share of the lowest 40 percent
France	1956	1,886.5	11.8
	1962	2,303.1	10.0
United Kingdom	1960	2,028.5	18.1
	1968	2,414.3	18.5
New Zealand	1966	2,278.2	20.9
Australia	1967–68	2,632.4	20.0
West Germany	1968	2,995.3	16.8
	1969	3,100.1	18.9
	1970	3,208.6	16.4
Canada	1961	3,046.6	19.7
	1965	3.509.6	19.0
United States	1960	3,827.1	15.9
	1966	4,623.3	15.4
	1970	5,244.1	15.3
	1971	5,411.9	15.5
	1972	5,585.1	14.1
Yugoslavia	1963	488.0	19.0
	1968	602.3	18.4
East Germany	1967	1,808.7	26.8
	1970	2,046.3	26.3

Source: Anand and Kanbur (1986), based on Jain (1975).

Note: These data are "minimally consistent" in that they are comparable in terms of coverage (national), income receiving unit (household), and income concept (household income).

typological factors as the country's size, natural resource base, and policies followed) as by the *level* of development *per se*. Structural and policy factors need to be considered along with income level or rate of growth.

In the next round of research, they were. Some continued with cross-sectional studies. The work of Chiswick (1971), Adelman and Morris (1973), Chenery and Syrquin (1975), Ahluwalia (1976), and others showed that the extent of inequality in different countries was associated with such factors as education, extent of direct government economic activity, population growth rate, urbanization, and importance of the agricultural sector in total production. These and kindred studies showed that income inequality is associated with a great many variables of *choice* and suggested that policies to affect inequality might make a big difference. This provided a strong motivation for looking at the changes that had taken place *within* individual countries and the reasons for them. The time-series evidence, reviewed below, supports the conclusion from cross-sectional studies that development policy is a fundamental determinant of inequality; the level of national income is not enough. Another conclusion arose from cross-sectional studies but was later discarded. This is the idea that the poor get *absolutely poorer* in the early stages of economic development. The early claims to this effect by Adelman and Morris (1973) were first criticized by Cline (1975) on methodological grounds and were later rejected decisively by the empirical results of Ahluwalia (1976), who found that when countries at different income levels were compared, the average absolute incomes of the poorest 20, 40, or 60 percent all increased monotonically. The absolute impoverishment thesis has been laid to rest.

In recent years, interest in these cross-sectional studies has waned. This is because many of the questions addressed with cross-sectional data were really questions about changes over time, best addressed with intertemporal data within countries. We turn to these studies next.

Lessons from intertemporal data

Researchers working on income distribution in the 1960s and early 1970s had only cross-sectional data with which to work. But as the 1970s began, a second kind of information became available; data on changes in income inequality over time within one or a small number of countries. The first such study of note was Weisskoff's (1970) documentation of changes in income inequality in three Latin American economies (Argentina, Mexico, and Puerto Rico), along with possible explanations for the observed patterns. Soon after, the results of the 1960 and 1970 censuses became available for Brazil. It was possible for Fishlow (1972) to show that the macroeconomic success of the so-called "Brazilian economic miracle" (i.e., the transformation of a stagnant economy with hyper-inflation to one with rapid economic growth and virtual price stability) was not accompanied by marked improvements in income inequality, which was very high both before the economic miracle and afterwards. Other country studies soon followed. By the end of the 1970s, enough data had been accumulated to permit empirical conclusions to be reached on income distribution changes over time.

The intertemporal evidence on less developed countries collected in Fields (1980b) is as follows:

Cases of Qualitative Agreement
   Inequality and poverty both declined: Costa Rica, Pakistan, Singapore, Sri Lanka, and Taiwan

Inequality and poverty both increased: Argentina and the Philippines

Cases of Qualitative Disagreement

Inequality increased and poverty decreased: Bangladesh, Brazil, Mexico, and Puerto Rico

Inequality decreased and poverty increased: India

From these data, we may reach the following conclusions:

- Income inequality increased in about as many countries as it decreased.
- Absolute poverty decreased in most countries.
- The relative inequality and absolute poverty approaches to income distribution are found to agree qualitatively in a bare majority of cases.

These data show that it makes a great deal of difference whether one adopts a relative inequality or absolute poverty approach to measurement of income distribution change. In particular, in many countries' experiences, inequality increased while poverty decreased – a fact that sometimes led to heated debates, as in discussions in the late 1970s of Brazilian income distribution. Thus, the qualitative assessment we reach concerning a country's development experience may depend upon which aspect of income distribution we are most concerned about, relative or absolute. This leads to the issue of the welfare economics of distribution and development, a topic addressed further in the next section.

Moving from data to explanation, why did some countries do better than others? Following all the attention paid to income level in the cross-sectional literature, a natural starting point was to ask whether economic growth *per se* has a bearing on income distribution. The answer depends on whether one's attention is directed toward poverty or toward inequality.

When the evidence is examined from the point of view of absolute poverty, a clear-cut conclusion is reached: rapid economic growth tends to reduce poverty. Of the countries for which we have data, poverty was alleviated rapidly in nearly all of the rapidly growing economies of East Asia and Latin America. Only in the Philippines was rapid economic growth *not* accompanied by reduced poverty. On the other hand, an exception of a different kind is also recorded: Sri Lanka did well in alleviating poverty despite very slow economic growth. Both these exceptions can be explained by policy: not-so-benign neglect of the poor in the case of the Philippines; willingness to sacrifice growth in favor of distribution goals in the case of Sri Lanka. Thus, we may conclude:

- Although rapid economic growth generally reduces poverty, growth is neither necessary nor sufficient for poverty alleviation.

Turning now to the evidence on relative inequality, the intertemporal data reveal surprisingly little association between rapid economic growth and inequality change. Some countries (Brazil, the Philippines) grew rapidly while inequality increased. However, inequality decreased both in rapidly growing economies (Taiwan, Costa Rica) and in slow-growing ones (Sri Lanka). Rapid economic growth is neither necessary nor sufficient for inequality to increase (or, for that matter, to decrease). Nor do we find any evident relationship between the change in inequality and the country's *level* of economic development – certainly no evidence whatever that income inequality increases with economic growth among the poorer countries but decreases with economic growth among the richer countries, as would be predicted by adherents of the inverted-U hypothesis. Again, the differences among countries would appear to be explained by the *type* of economic growth strategy pursued rather than by the *rate* of economic growth *per se*. We have therefore found:

- Whether inequality increases or decreases with economic growth depends on the type of growth rather than on the level of GNP or the rate of GNP growth *per se*.

Having learned that income distribution does not need to change in any inevitable way with economic growth, and having learned that development strategy has an important bearing on who benefits from economic growth, development economists now face a new task. We must look *within countries* to understand what they did and why some fared better in distributional terms than others. In my view, the payoff to further statistical or econometric refinements of "patterns of growth" studies is small relative to the returns to more in-depth country studies. In the section "Where do we go from here?" I offer some suggestions on the kinds of things to look for.

Lessons from micro data

In the late 1960s and early 1970s, for the first time, household sample surveys and public use samples from censuses became available for large numbers of developing countries. A rich and varied literature pertaining to various aspects of income distribution has emerged from micro data analysis.

A first question necessarily preceded all others: How reliable are micro data for less developed countries? Some analysts worried that poor people could not provide sensible answers to questions or that the statistical offices in poor countries could not produce usable data tapes. Both these worries were allayed by actual experience. Inability to answer survey questions would yield noisy data, which would result in low explanatory power of economic models fit to such data sets. Yet, when models comparable to those used in developed country contexts were fit to LDC data, the explanatory power was found to be *better*, not worse. As for developing countries' ability to generate workable data sets, while there have been some frustrating problems, there have also been some remarkable successes. Colombia, for instance, produced a 4 percent sample of census returns within one year, containing computer-readable data on more than three-quarters of a million persons. The U.S. Census Bureau should do as well!

Micro data sets have been used to analyze various aspects of income distribution. Concerning absolute incomes, micro data sets yielded profiles of the poor by various characteristics, as in the work of Fishlow (1972) on Brazil, Srinivasan and Bardhan (1974) on India, and Anand (1977) on Malaysia. High incidences of poverty were found among the poorly educated, rural residents, agricultural workers, women, and so on. The poverty profile literature produced few surprises, though – the poor were found to be those we thought they were.

Where micro data sets proved insightful was in the decomposition of inequality. Much of the early work on income distribution and economic development emphasized the functional distribution of income, i.e., the division of income between capital, labor, land, transfers, and other sources. This concern with functional income distribution, and the corresponding neglect of size distribution, flew in the face of two facts. One is that most families derive little income from non labor sources; they rely primarily if not exclusively on the labor income of family members. The other fact is that some workers receive a great deal more for their labor than do others. These truisms led some researchers to investigate the causes of inequality in the size distribution of income. Fei, Ranis, and Kuo (1978) devised a procedure – later elaborated upon by Pyatt, Chen, and Fei (1980) – for decomposing inequality into "factor inequality weights" indicating the proportion of total inequality due to inequality of capital incomes, inequality of labor incomes, and so on. (Their methodology differs from other decomposition procedures such as the Theil decomposition, both in the decomposition itself and in the type of question to which it is addressed see Fields (1980b) for a comparison of the different decomposition methods.) Fei, Ranis, and Kuo's findings for Taiwan, and the findings using their decomposition procedure for Pakistan (Ayub, 1977) and Colombia (Fields, 1979), demonstrated that *labor* income inequality is the most important source of total income inequality, accounting for more than two-thirds of the total. This finding, coming as a surprise to some and confirming what others had thought all along, directed development economists' attention toward labor markets and the determinants of labor incomes. This is an area that merits considerable attention in the research program of development economics in the coming years, and to which I return in the next section.

Another aspect of income distribution where micro data yielded valuable insight was in the examination of inequality within and between groupings, be they geographical, industrial, racial, or gender. Develop ment models with a small number of economic sectors, perhaps as few as two, are used by many of us. In so doing, we abstract from differences within sectors in order to emphasize the qualitative differences between sectors and the linkages among them. While this has proven very useful in certain contexts – for example, in understanding how industrial development in the urban areas will have a bearing on agriculture through rural-urban migration – thinking in terms of the differences *across* sectors runs the risk of obscuring or even ignoring the importance of differences *within* sectors. Studies analyzing micro data using Analysis of Variance, Theil decomposition, or other similar methods have found that income differences *within* sectors are much more important than income differences *between* sectors, with intrasectoral inequality typically accounting for 80–90 percent of the total (Fields, 1980b, table 4.9).

The predominance of intrasectoral inequality has important policy implications. The finding that inequality within rural and urban areas is much greater than inequality between them means that a policy aimed at channeling development resources toward rural areas because they are poorer might benefit disproportionately the well-to-do rural residents while failing to assist poor city-dwellers. This has evidently happened in Kenya, as in much of Africa (Leys, 1975). Similar leakages would have resulted in Colombia, had the government followed its plan to allocate all its development resources to the poorer one-digit industries, ignoring the much greater inequality within one-digit industries than between them (Fields, 1979). And similar leakages are occurring in Malaysia today, as the government moves ahead with programs to aid the Malays while excluding the Chinese, ignoring the findings of Anand (1983) showing that the two racial groups' income distributions overlap greatly.

A final lesson from micro data to be noted is the work on earnings functions. Psacharopoulos (1973, 1981, 1985), Fields (1980a), and others have shown that in developing countries around the world, multivariate earnings functions exhibit substantial explanatory power, and that much more variation in income is accounted for by education than by regional variables, firm characteristics, or family background variables.[2] These findings direct the attention of income distribution analysts toward understanding the effect of education on income. Here, though, controversy arises. As Blaug (1973), among others, has pointed out, those with more education could be found to be earning higher incomes for a variety of reasons: economic, sociological, or psychological. In a study of Kenya and Tanzania, Boissiere, Knight, and Sabot (1985, pp. 1028–9) examined the various possible explanations and reached the following conclusions:

> Our survey data from East Africa have permitted a sharper test than hitherto of the competing explanations – credentialism, ability, screening,

or human capital – of why workers with secondary education earn more. The direct returns to reasoning ability in the labor market are small, those to years of education are moderate, and those to literacy and numeracy – dimensions of human capital – are large…Our analysis provides strong support for the human capital interpretation of the educational structure of wages. Whether these conclusions should be generalized beyond East Africa to the many other countries in which rates of returns (sic) have been estimated is, however, open to question.

Similar studies elsewhere would be informative.

In all these areas, the findings of micro data sets have told us where to turn and, probably equally importantly, where not to turn to understand better the links between income distribution and economic development. No single approach can give all the answers. However, micro data analysis can help, and indeed has helped, us ask the right questions.

WHERE DO WE GO FROM HERE?

Looking ahead, I would call attention to three lines of research, all interrelated, which would help elucidate some important aspects of income distribution and economic growth:

Understanding constraints on choices

We have learned that people in developing countries respond to the constraint sets they face and will alter what they do if their constraint sets change. More farmers will plant a given crop the higher is its relative price. More workers will locate in a particular area the better are that area's job conditions. More parents will seek education for their children the greater is the relative income of those with education compared to those without. More consumers will buy domestically-made goods in preference to foreign-made goods the lower is the cost of domestically-made goods and the better their other characteristics (product quality, reliability, etc.). Thus, the *rates* at which various economic activities take place depend on the economic returns to various courses of action given the available opportunities and constraints. Incomes are determined accordingly.

Having learned that purposeful behavior is as good a description of choices in developing countries as it is in developed countries, the next task is to understand how the constraints are determined. Here, unfortunately, we know much less than we need to.

The essence of economic underdevelopment is the existence of severe constraints on people's behavior. Take, for example, the situation confronting a poor farmer. He may wish to send his sons and daughters to school, knowing that if they were to acquire an education, their incomes (and hence standards of living) would be very much higher.

Yet, because he lives in a poor country, schooling is not free; the farmer must pay school fees which are a substantial part of his income. And being poor, he faces a double bind: he lacks the money to pay the school fees, and he needs the children to work on the farm during planting and harvesting seasons, since he cannot afford hired labor or mechanized inputs. Suppose, though, that he could somehow overcome all of these difficulties and could scrimp and save in order to send his children to school. Even then, there might not be enough spaces in the schools for all who wish to attend. For all these reasons, the constraints on choices are such that the poor farmer may be unable to send his sons and daughters to school. The children of the poor are apt to be poor.

The essence of economic development is the relaxation of such constraints. As countries get richer, they typically provide more schools and make them free. Furthermore, with economic development, capital markets become more widespread, enabling the poor farmer to borrow at more favorable rates of interest for such worthwhile purposes as purchasing a small tractor with which to complement his labor while freeing his children to attend school during peak periods on the farm. The sons and daughters of the poor farmer therefore face better educational opportunities. Economic development may even enable the poor farmer to cease to be a farmer, for example, by being offered more remunerative work in a factory; or if he is unable to get such employment, his sons and daughters might.

At present, we know much more about the choice aspect of constrained choices than we do about the constraints. High on the agenda of development economics is the need to learn how the constraints on individuals' choices are related to the nature and extent of government involvement in the economy, trade orientation, education and human resource policy, and other aspects of development strategy and performance. We have a good idea of the proximate explanations for behavior. These proximate explanations should be linked more closely than they now are to underlying causes, especially those that might be changed by public policy.

Understanding the labor market mechanisms linking growth and income distribution

We have learned from decomposition studies that labor income inequality is the predominant determinant of total income inequality. Most households receive no significant capital income, unless the imputed value of owner-occupied housing is counted as capital income. Hence, among the majority of households, the major factor determining who is high-income and who is low is whether labor earnings are high or low. Accordingly, the attention of income distribution analysts is directed toward the labor market.

Three kinds of labor market studies would contribute to our understanding of the mechanisms linking growth and income distribution. The first is descriptive-analytic. Labor economics offers many paradigms of labor market functioning, including the competitive model, dual labor market models, labor market segmentation approaches, radical theories, and many others; see, for instance, Gordon (1973) for a summary of these different paradigms. We need empirical evidence that would help us choose among these various analytical approaches in various country contexts. How dispersed are wages for apparently identical workers? With what are these wage differentials correlated? Why? Which persons are employed in which industries, locations, or activities? What explains who is hired and who is promoted? Who are the unemployed? By what mechanisms do they become employed? What is the role of the urban informal sector in job-getting? How important is on-the-job search? To what extent is discrimination practiced? Are there significant impediments to the smooth functioning of supply and demand? What are they? Surveys by such authors as Cain (1976), Berry and Sabot (1978), Squire (1981), and Binswanger and Rosenzweig (1984), provide a good starting point, but more behavioral-institutional labor market studies are needed.

The second need is for more comprehensive and realistic models of labor markets in developing countries. Perhaps the most famous such model is that of Harris and Todaro (1970), devised to fit the labor market circumstances prevailing in East Africa in the late 1960s. It helped explain why job aspirants were flocking to the cities, despite urban unemployment, and why attempts at creating jobs for the urban unemployed made things worse, not better. These insights demonstrate the value of blending behavioral-institutional description with theoretical modeling. Of course, all models are limited, and the Harris-Todaro model is no exception. It did not allow for a number of important aspects of labor markets, among them, heterogeneous labor, the existence of an urban informal sector, a dualistic agricultural sector, on-the-job search, and extended family decision-making. Extensions along these lines have been introduced by quite a number of authors; see Todaro (1976, 1985) for references to this line of literature. Nor can a general model fit in all times and all places. Labor markets in such small economies as Singapore and Hong Kong are best modeled without migration of the Harris-Todaro type. Labor markets in economies as diverse as Puerto Rico, Botswana, Sri Lanka, and Egypt, in which emigration is a viable option, must be modeled differently from closed labor markets. In some countries, preferential hiring may be much more important than probabilistic hiring. And so on. Here again, the insistence on typologically relevant analysis, which was repeatedly impressed upon all who passed through the Economic Growth Center, comes to the fore.

The third need is for dynamic analyses of how labor market conditions change with economic growth. Does growth result in more and better jobs? For whom? Do the patterns vary with stage of economic development? With extent of government economic involvement? With trade and industrialization strategy? With education and human resource policy? To what extent does labor share in economic growth? Evidence on such questions may be found in a study of 12 developing countries in the early 1980s undertaken by the National Bureau of Economic Research and in a project encompassing 13 LDCs in the mid-1980s under the auspices of the World Bank; the main findings of these projects are presented in Krueger (1981) and Klinov (1986), respectively. The results of these large-scale empirical studies, and of the many other studies scattered in the literature, should be systematized and added to. But the most important need I see in this area is for theoretical models of labor market *change* in the course of economic growth, along with the consequences of these changes for inequality and poverty.

Ultimately, development economics must elucidate development *processes*. Static analyses providing a snapshot of events and behavior in developing countries are, of course, worthwhile. But our field runs the risk of going too far with static models, thereby neglecting the dynamic aspects on which development economics is based. High priority should be given to empirically based, theoretical models of the labor market mechanisms linking growth and income distribution.

Rethinking welfare and measurement issues

We have learned that the different aspects of income distribution – inequality, poverty, and economic mobility over the life cycle – are very different from one another. Some observers place heavier weight on one, some on another, but most would want to measure them all, insofar as possible.

When poverty and inequality have been measured, they have been found to have changed very differently in the development experiences of many countries. (Economic mobility has been measured less frequently than the others because of the need for longitudinal and/or retrospective data to measure it.) A pattern arising with some frequency is that inequality rises but poverty falls in a number of countries' economic growth experiences.

These conclusions are derived from particular inequality indices (typically, the Gini coefficient and/or the income shares of particular percentile groups) and particular poverty indices (typically, the headcount ratio). But there exist many other indices of poverty and of inequality. The poverty indices do not necessarily agree among themselves, nor the inequality indices among themselves. This raises the question of which are the "best" inequality and poverty indices to use.

Among the poverty indices, the headcount ratio has certain well-known deficiencies: insensitivity to the amount by which the incomes of the poor fall below the poverty line, and neglect of inequality in the distribution of income among the poor. These omissions were first remedied in the work of Sen (1976), who amalgamated the headcount (H), the income gap of the poor (I), and inequality among the poor (as measured by the Gini coefficient among them, G_p) into a single composite poverty measure:

$$S = H[I + (1 - I)G_p].$$

Since then, Sen's approach has been modified in two kinds of ways. One is to retain Sen's basic structure, but to use inequality indices other than the Gini coefficient or functional forms other than that given in the preceding equation; among those who have worked along these lines are Anand (1977), Thon (1979), Kakwani (1980), and Clark, Hemming, and Ulph (1981). The other approach is to use the family of poverty measures devised by Foster, Greer, and Thorbecke (1984):

$$P_\alpha = (1/n) \sum_{i=1}^{q} ((z - y_i)/y_i)^\alpha$$

where P_α is the poverty index with parameter α, n is the total number of households, q is the number of poor, z is the poverty line, and y_i is the income of household i. Useful overviews of these new directions in poverty measurement may be found in Foster (1984) and Atkinson (1985).

Given all these choices, the applied researcher would naturally want to know which index is best to use to assess how poverty changes with economic growth. Where this line of literature stands as of now is that each class of indices has its own merits and *many* appear suitable. If alternative poverty indices were to be applied and found to give different answers, the practical researcher would be in a quandary about what to conclude. But maybe that would be precisely the right conclusion in such a circumstance: to conclude that the data are inconclusive. The welfare economics of poverty change still need some sorting out.

As for the measurement of inequality, we also have many choices. Fields and Fei (1978) axiomatized the Lorenz criterion, which is used in the great majority of inequality studies. Sen (1973) and others showed which of the commonly used, inequality indices are fully consistent with the Lorenz criterion and which are not. Those inequality indices that are Lorenz-consistent go beyond the Lorenz criterion in ranking the inequality of income distributions, even when the Lorenz criterion cannot. The ways in which these indices complete the ordering have been justified on the basis of decomposability, sensitivity to income changes affecting particular income groups, or ease of computation. What has not been done – and what should be – is to justify the choice of an inequality index on the basis of its suitability for measuring the distributional consequences of economic *growth*. I have attempted to do this in recent work (Fields, 1979, 1985) with limited success. The resolution, we have now learned, rests critically on how inequality varies with the *numbers* of persons in different economic sectors, holding the within-sector income distributions the same. This process is called "modern sector enlargement growth" (Fields, 1979) or "inter-sectoral shifts" (Kuznets, 1955; Anand and Kanbur, 1984). Anand and Kanbur have analyzed the effects of such growth on income inequality as measured by six inequality indices, five of which are Lorenz-consistent (Theil's two indices, the squared coefficient of variation, the Atkinson index, and the Gini coefficient with non-overlapping distributions between high- and low-income groups) and one of which is not (the log variance). All six indices produce a particular pattern: if we suppose that the economy is divided into two sectors, one of which has higher income and higher inequality than the other, as the share of population in the low-income sector goes from 0 to 100 percent, each of the six indices either increases monotonically or follows an inverted-U. And in the case of no within-sector inequality, as is considered in the next paragraph, inequality *must* follow an inverted-U pattern.

The unwary reader should avoid an unwarranted conclusion. Some would argue that inequality "should" first increase and then decrease, because that is what six commonly used, inequality measures do as intersectoral shifts of the prescribed type take place. Yet, consider a five-person economy in which the income distribution goes from $(1,1,1,1,1)$ to $(1,1,1,1,5)$ to $(1,1,1,5,5)$ to $(1,1,5,5,5)$ to $(1,5,5,5,5)$ to $(5,5,5,5,5)$. While inequality "should" increase with the move from $(1,1,1,1,1)$ to $(1,1,1,1,5)$ and "should" decrease in the last step from $(1,5,5,5,5)$ to $(5,5,5,5,5)$, it is not at all apparent what inequality "should" do in between. It is important to examine the underlying data carefully to make such a judgment. Just because six frequently used, inequality indices trace out an inverted-U does not mean that an inverted-U is the "right" pattern. What ought to be cannot be justified on the basis of what is. Those who argue this way are guilty of circular reasoning – not a very helpful method.

More fundamental work on the welfare economics of poverty and inequality change in the course of economic growth is badly needed. Atkinson (1970, 1985), Sen (1973, 1984), and Shorrocks (1983) are among those who have shown us that value judgments cannot be avoided if we are to do such work. It is best that development economists confront value judgments head-on.

A FINAL WORD

To borrow a phrase from Gerald Meier, whose change of thinking was described earlier, the study of income distribution and economic growth is "the economics that really matters" (1984). As we study those aspects of economic development that really matter, the interplay between empirical observation and theoretical modeling must never wander too far from center stage. Facts without analysis are barren. So, too, are deductive theories without empirical foundations. Theory and data must be brought together. Let us have the courage to tackle the difficult but important questions and the judgment to know what they are.

NOTES

[1] The data set is labeled "minimally consistent" because the data are standardized for geographic coverage (national), and income recipient unit (household), and income concept (household income).

[2] An earnings function is a regression equation of the form

$$\log Y = a + b_1 ED + b_2 EXP + b_3 EXP^2 + b_4 FAMBKGD + ...,$$

where Y is the individual's income, ED is years of education, EXP is years of experience, FAMBKGD is a measure of family background. Other explanatory variables might also be included.

REFERENCES

Adelman, Irma and Morris, Cynthia Taft 1973: *Economic Growth and Social Equity in Developing Countries.* Stanford, Calif.: Stanford University Press.

Adelman, Irma and Robinson, Sherman 1978: *Income Distribution Policy in Developing Countries: A Case Study of Korea.* New York: Oxford University Press.

Adelman, Irma and Thorbecke, Erik (eds) 1966: *Theory and Design of Economic Development.* Baltimore: Johns Hopkins University Press.

Ahluwalia, Montek 1974: "Income Inequality: Some Dimensions of the Problem." In Hollis Chenery et al., *Redistribution with Growth,* Oxford: Oxford University Press.

Ahluwalia, Montek 1976: "Inequality, Poverty and Development." *Journal of Development Economics,* Dec.

Ahluwalia, Montek; Carter, Nicholas; and Hollis, Chenery 1979: "Growth and Poverty in Developing Countries." In Hollis Chenery (ed.), *Structural Change and Development Policy.* New York: Oxford.

Anand, Sudhir 1977: "Aspects of Poverty in Malaysia." *Review of Income and Wealth,* March.

Anand, Sudhir 1983: *Inequality and poverty in Malaysia.* Oxford: Oxford University Press.

Anand, Sudhir and Kanbur, Ravi 1984: "The Kuznets Process and the Inequality-Development Relationship." Mimeo.

Anand, Sudhir and Kanbur Ravi 1986: "Inequality and Development: A Critique." Paper prepared for the Yale University Economic Growth Center.

Atkinson, A. B. 1970: "On the Measurement of Inequality." *Journal of Economic Theory,* Sept.

Atkinson, A. B.: "On the Measurement of Poverty." Walras-Bowley Lecture presented at the Econometric Society World Congress, Cambridge, 1985.

Ayub, Mahmood 1977: "Income Inequality in a Growth-Theoretic Context: The Case of Pakistan." Unpublished Doctoral Dissertation, Yale University.

Berry, A. and Sabot, R. H. 1978: "Labor Market Performance in Developing Countries: A Survey," *World Development,* Nov.

Binswanger, Hans P. and Rosenzweig, Mark R. 1984: *Contractual Arrangements, Employment, and Wages in Rural Labor Markets in Asia.* New Haven: Yale University Press.

Blaug, Mark 1973: *Education and the Employment Problem in Developing Countries.* Geneva: International Labour Office.

Boissiere, M., Knight, J. B. and Sabot, R. H. 1985: "Earnings, Schooling, Ability, and Cognitive Skills." *American Economic Review,* Dec.

Cain, Glen 1976: "The Challenge of Segmented Labor Market Theories to Orthodox Theory: A Survey." *Journal of Economic Literature;* Dec.

Chenery, H. 1974: *Redistribution with Growth.* London and New York: Oxford University Press.

Chenery, Hollis and Syrquin, Moises 1975: *Patterns of Development, 1950–1970.* New York: Oxford University Press.

Chiswick, Barry 1971: "Earnings Inequality and Economic Development," *Quarterly Journal of Economics,* Feb.

Clark, S. R., Hemming, R. and Ulph, D. 1981: "On Indices for the Measurement of Poverty." *Economic Journal,* June.

Cline, William R. 1975: "Distribution and Development: A Survey of the Literature." *Journal of Development Economics,* Feb.

Fei, John C. H. and Ranis, Gustav 1964. *Development of the Labor Surplus Economy,* Homewood, Ill.: Irwin.

Fei, John C. H.; Ranis, Gustav; and Kuo, Shirley W. Y. 1978: "Growth and the Family Distribution of Income by Factor Components." *Quarterly Journal of Economics,* Feb.

Fields, Gary S. 1978: "Analyzing Colombian Wage Structure." World Bank, Studies in Employment and Rural Development No. 46, May.

Fields, Gary S. 1979: "Income Inequality in Urban Colombia: A Decomposition Analysis." *Review of Income and Wealth,* Sept.

Fields, Gary S. 1979: "A Welfare Economic Approach to Growth and Distribution in the Dual Economy." *Quarterly Journal of Economics,* Aug.

Fields, Gary S. 1980a: "Education and Income Distribution in Less Developed Countries: With the assistance of Jorge Ducci, World Bank, mimeo.

Fields, Gary S. 1980b: *Poverty, Inequality, and Development.* New York: Cambridge University Press.

Fields, Gary S. 1985: "Measuring Inequality Change in an Economy with

Income Growth." Paper presented at the Econometric Society World Congress, Cambridge, 1985, forthcoming in *Journal of Development Economics.*

Fields, Gary S. and Fei, John C. H. 1978: "On Inequality Comparisons." *Econometrica,* Vol. 46(2).

Fishlow, Albert 1972: "Brazilian Size Distribution of Income." *American Economic Review,* May.

Foster, James E. 1984: "On Economic Poverty: A Survey of Aggregate Measures." *Advances in Econometrics,* vol. 3.

Foster, James E. Forthcoming: "Inequality Measurement." In Peyton Young (ed.) *Fair Allocation,* Proceedings of the Symposium in Applied Mathematics, American Mathematical Society.

Foster, James E., Greer, Joel and Thorbecke, Erik 1984: "A Class of Decomposable Poverty Mesures." *Econometrica,* May.

Gordon, David M. 1973: *Theories of Poverty and Underemployment.* Lexington, Mass.: Heath, Lexington Books.

Harris, John and Todaro, Michael 1970: "Migration, Unemployment, and Development; A Two Sector Analysis." *American Economic Review,* March.

ILO (International Labour Office) 1970: *Towards Full Employment: A Programme for Colombia.* Geneva: ILO.

Jain, Shail 1975: *Size Distribution of Income: A Compilation of Data.* Washington D.C.: World Bank.

Kakwani, Nanak 1980: "On a Class of Poverty Measures." *Econometrica,* Mar.

Klinov, Ruth 1986: "Labor Market Performance in LDCs, 1970–1984: A Cross-Sectional Analysis." World Bank, Development Research Department Working Paper.

Kravis, Irving B. 1960: "International Differences in the Distribution of Income." *Review of Economics and Statistics,* Nov.

Krueger, Anne O. 1981: *Trade and Employment in Developing Countries: Volume 1.* Chicago: University of Chicago Press for the National Bureau of Economic Research.

Krueger, Anne O. 1986: "The Relationships between Trade, Employment and Development." Paper prepared for the Yale University Economic Growth Center Symposium, April.

Kuznets, Simon 1955: "Economic Growth and Income Inequality." *American Economic Review,* Mar.

Kuznets, Simon 1963: "Quantitative Aspects of the Economic Growth of Nations: VIII, Distribution of Income by Size." *Economic Development and Cultural Change,* Jan.

Kuznets, Simon 1966: *Modern Economic Growth.* New Haven: Yale University Press.

Leys, Colin 1975: *Underdevelopment in Kenya.* Berkeley: University of California Press.

Meier, Gerald M. 1984a: *Leading Issues in Economic Development* (1st ed., 1964). New York: Oxford University Press.

Meier, Gerald M. 1984b: *Emerging from Poverty: The Economics that Really Matters.* Oxford: Oxford University Press.

Oshima, Harry 1962: "The International Comparison of Size Distribution of Family Incomes with Special Refeence to Asia." *Review of Economics and Statistics,* Nov.

Pant, Pitambar 1974: "Perspectives of Development, India, 1960–61 to 1975–76: Implications of Planning for a Minimum Level of Living." Reprinted in T. N. Srinivasan and P. K. Bardhan (eds), *Poverty and Income Distribution in India*, Calcutta: Statistical Publishing Society.

Paukert, Felix 1973: "Income Distribution at Different Levels of Development: A Survey of Evidence." *International Labour Review*, Aug.

Psacharopoulos, George 1973: *Returns to Education*. San Fancisco: Jossey-Bass.

Psacharopoulos, George 1981: "Returns to Education: An Updated International Comparison." *Comparative Education*, Vol. 17.

Psacharopoulos, George 1985: "Returns to Education: A Further International Update and Implications." *Journal of Human Resources*, Fall.

Pyatt, Graham and Thorbecke, Erik 1976: *Planning Techniques for a Better Future*. Geneva: International Labour Office.

Pyatt, Graham; Chen, Chau-Nan; and Fei, John 1980: "The Distribution of Income by Factor Components." *Quarterly Journal of Economics*, Nov.

Robinson, Sherman 1976: "A Note on the U Hypothesis Relating Income Inequality and Economic Development." *American Economic Review*, June.

Saith, A. 1983: "Development and Distribution: A Critique of the Cross-Country U-Hypothesis." *Journal of Development Economics*, Dec.

Seers, Dudley 1969: "The Meaning of Development." *International Development Review*, Dec.

Sen, Amartya K. 1973: *On Economic Inequality*. Oxford: The Clarendon Press.

Sen, Amartya K. 1976: "Poverty: An Ordinal Approach to Measurement." *Econometrica*, March.

Sen, Amartya K. 1984: *Resources, Values, and Development*. Cambridge, Mass.: Harvard University Press.

Shorrocks, Anthony 1983: "Ranking Income Distribution." *Econometrica*, Feb.

Squire, Lyn 1981: *Employment Policy in Developing Countries*. New York: Oxford University Press.

Srinivasan, T. N. and Bardhan, P. K. (eds) 1974: *Poverty and Income Distribution in India*. Calcutta: Statistical Publishing Society.

Thon, D. 1979: "On Measuring Poverty." *Review of Income and Wealth*, Dec.

Thornbecke, Erik 1973: "The Employment Problem: A Critical Evaluation of Four ILO Comprehensive Country Reports." *International Labour Review*, May.

Todaro, Michael 1976: *International Migration in Developing Countries*. Geneva: International Labour Office.

Todaro, Michael 1985: *Economic Development in the Third World, Third Edition*. New York: Longman.

Weisskoff, Richard 1970: "Income Distribution and Economic Growth in Puerto Rico, Argentina and Mexico." *Review of Income and Wealth*, Dec.

Comments on
"Income Distribution and Economic Growth"

ALBERT FISHLOW

Gary Fields has contributed a useful review of research on the issue of income distribution over the past 15 years, replete with a selective and helpful bibliography. It is difficult to disagree with his judicious summary reading of the record, i.e., that economic growth is neither necessary nor sufficient for poverty alleviation and that variation in inequality depends on the style of growth, more than its rate or level of income. Despite this evident care and balance, there inevitably remain some questions for further comment. Specifically, I wish to discuss the Kuznets law of increasing and diminishing inequality and the conclusions to be drawn from decomposition analysis, as well as touch upon two largely untreated subjects: the relationship of income distribution to the production structure and the design of appropriate policy.

Even before entering into those matters, however, I wish to register a reservation on Fields's implicit suggestion that the empirical base is now really good enough: "By the end of the 1970s, enough data had been accumulated to permit empirical conclusions to be reached on income distribution changes over time (p. 467). The fact remains that we are still limited to tracing changes over time for relatively few countries and quite short intervals that frequently do not conform to major changes in economic strategy. The broader comparative data still suffer from significant defects in coverage and consistency in definition. For how many countries are movements in real wages, or functional shares, and the size distributions reconciled, or compatible with measured national incomes? To what degree is demographic composition dealt with? These are not casual matters to be dismissed so that one can get on with the analysis. Many of the questions that motivated Simon Kuznets to support the establishment of the Growth Center 25 years ago, in other words, remain. Compilations of very disparate evidence are not the answer. Getting the story right is still a high priority in this field, as well as trying to explain it.

The treatment of the Kuznets curve is illustrative. We have come from facile empirical corroboration in some early studies to more sophisticated rejection in the later. That is a considerable advance. But in this instance, there seems to be an excessive zeal to relegate Kuznets's original insight solely to the realm of observable regularity, and thus to dismiss it. The essential Kuznets point, which remains valid, is that the structural change accompanying economic growth, by initially increasing the weight of groups with greater inequality owing to more complexity, would tend to raise overall inequality. This tendency could obviously be offset by changes in relative income levels as larger numbers of qualified persons were trained, say, or by explicit policy interventions.

One might well expect, therefore, that the performance over time of individual countries would vary in accordance with their development strategies, and that cross-section results relying exclusively on income levels as an explanatory variable would yield poor results without invalidating the direction of the influence of structural change. Indeed, decomposing the observed changes in inequality over time into components derived from changing group weights and relative earnings can afford useful information on the underlying process. In the case of Brazil, between 1960 and 1970, I found that a larger part of the observed change in inequality was due to reinforcing changes in relative incomes than to changes in the composition of the labor force.

It is but a small extension to incorporate probabilities that individuals will exit over time from low-income groups to higher ones. Some see lowered fertility and an altered age distribution in developing countries, and hence, better access to good jobs as a potentially important factor in ameliorating inequality. More generally, a dynamic view of distribution and growth required close attention to the possibility of social mobility. Such studies require more attention. There is more to the Kuznets contribution to the study of inequality than cross-section regressions.

Fields focuses his attention on two other types of decomposition, one based on sources of income, the other on determinants of individual earnings. With respect to the first, he is far too bold in implying a general finding that "*labor* income inequality is the most important source of total income inequality, accounting for more than two-thirds of the total (p. 470). The observations are limited to three, and for one (Colombia), only urban incomes. Clearly, although property income in these cases is more unequally distributed, it will have a small effect on the total when its weight, as in the Taiwan and Colombia data, is one-quarter or less of income. For many developing countries, the share of property income, including entrepreneurial returns, is much higher and the conclusion therefore invalid. I agree that more attention must be paid to the operation of labor markets, and especially the informal sector, and to integrating such analysis with its consequences for inequality. But it would be a mistake to ignore the still relevant contribution of the unequal allocation of assets that provokes not only greater measured inequality but also its perpetuation through unequal access to modern sector opportunities.

In his summary of micro studies, Fields correctly singles out education among the important determinants of individual inequality in a variety of country studies, and duly notes the difference between an absolute human capital and a relative credentialing or signaling hypothesis. He pays too little attention, however, to the possibility that the ubiquitous success of earnings functions in a wide variety of data sets partially derives from the widespread availability of information on education. When other relevant attributes can also be introduced, like position in occupation in the Brazilian case, the contribution of education declines, especially in rural areas. More generally, two lines of potential research deserve notice. One relates to the stability of the contribution of education over time, rather than the statistical significance of the variable in cross-section analysis. The less stable the contribution of education is over time, the less compelling the human capital interpretation of absolute increase in productive capacity. The other is the variance in the distribution of educational attainment itself: is it possible to narrow that inequality significantly over time, or do various societies find new ways of introducing differentiation that widen it again?

In his discussion of income distribution, Fields surprisingly leaves to the side some of the recent efforts to examine production and income generation jointly. Surprisingly, because he exactly emphasizes the importance of development strategy to inequality and poverty outcomes. Yet one can examine such strategy only in the context of a production framework. The construction of social accounting matrices and their utilization in computable general equilibrium models has become more widespread. There are evident difficulties in such modeling, not least the assumptions of stability in the allocation of different forms of income to different population subgroupings. It is difficult to get around the problem of a still-limited degree of explanation of the size distribution. Still, the exercises have a considerable bearing upon policy. A direct focus upon the size distribution in isolation inevitably draws attention to human capital as the central variable – ignoring reallocation of physical assets, as well as the consequences of changes in the productive structure. Since an essential characteristic of poverty in poor countries is the low level of productivity of persons earning low incomes, effective policies necessarily must incorporate information from the production side, rather than more generalized education, or income transfers, alone.

Fields's attention to these policy issues is minimal. They enter principally through the back door of the welfare implications of different measurements of poverty. That is unfortunate. While the measurement problem is certainly of interest, and progress has been made, there is also research on policy instruments – much from the World Bank – to report on and to encourage. Much of the renewed interest in income inequality in developing countries is derived from the hope of improving the distribution of the benefits of economic growth. There has been experimentation with different policy responses to inequality in a number of countries over the last 15 years.

That is not to say that the interventions have been uniformly success-ful. Indeed, the focus upon poverty alleviation, rather than reduction of overall inequality, has not worked out as well as had been hoped. The apparent greater political consensus around such an objective is partially illusory. Commitment to satisfaction of basic needs through nonmarket means conflicts with commitment to price signals and a market style, not to mention its explicit rejection of free household allo-cation of expenditures. These are ideas whose radical implications are readily apparent and not always welcome.

The basic needs approach also has had to confront problems of effi-cient delivery: subsidies always spill over from the target group. Although we may know where the incidence of poverty is concentrated, there is nonetheless an overlap, sometimes considerable, with the non-poor. That complicates the design of eligibility criteria and can readily escalate administrative costs.

But, perhaps above all, serious poverty programs have had to confront an unpropitious context in most developing countries in recent years. When income per capita is declining, and investment rates are low, transfers and productivity enhancing interventions oriented to the poor lose out in competition with other applications of scarce resources. Resumption of immediate growth has become the dominant priority. Stabilization, and the balance of payments, have taken center stage. Even where distribution objectives involve no trade-off with pro-duction in the longer term, they very well may in the short term.

Yet we neglect the issue of inequality at our peril. Resumed growth, especially under the more open political systems that have emerged in many developing countries, will bring demands for improved standards of living for many who have suffered deprivation under austerity. If we are to avoid a fruitless cycle of nominal wage gains eroded by inflation, wasteful increases in public expenditure, and inefficient growth, then development economists – not least those in the Growth Center – will have to apply their accumulated knowledge and extend their research to more effective policy design.

16

Technology, Productivity Growth, and Economic Development

ROBERT EVENSON

Productivity growth has been a very important policy objective of development planners and strategists in the modern (i.e. post-World War II) period. Interest in productivity growth emerged shortly after Abramowitz and others developed empirical measures of productivity change and showed that growth in "output per unit of input" accounted for a large part of output growth. The achievement of increases in output per unit of input has been an essential part of development planning and policy-making.

The economic development literature encompasses many treatments and critiques of productivity measurement and interpretation. It covers theoretical growth models treating productivity growth as synonymous with technical change and determined outside the economic system. Some theoretical models treat technical change as determined or induced by economic variables. Models of R&D investment by firms and public agencies have been developed, and a large empirical literature measuring productivity change and relating it to determining variables has been produced. Another body of literature has studied the consequences of alternative types of productivity (or technical) change in both a positive and normative context.

The 1950s and 1960s were years of high interest in productivity measurement and accounting. Abramovitz, Kendrick, Schultz, Griliches, Denison, Solow and others contributed to the studies of this period. By the late 1960s, interest in this work declined because of controversy over measurement procedures and the implied behavior of producing firms. (See Jorgenson and Griliches, 1967, and Denison, 1968, for a discussion of measurement issues.)

The 1950s and 1960s were also the years of high interest in economic growth models. With the notable exception of Solow and perhaps a few others, growth modelers were content to treat technical change as exogenous to their models and showed little interest in the empirical productivity measurement and accounting studies. This promised to change in the 1960s with the advent of "induced innovation" models. (For a review of this work, see Binswanger and Ruttan.) These models treated technical change as endogenously determined by economic forces. Unfortunately, with a few exceptions (Binswanger and Ruttan), these models were given little empirical content and were soon perceived to be flawed because they did not offer a realistic specification of the technology production process. By the mid-1970s interest both in induced innovation and in growth modeling had all but stopped.

The empirical studies in the field have a somewhat better record in terms of sustained interest. Studies of agricultural productivity change were initiated by Schultz and Griliches and given strong development emphasis by Schultz's influential book, *Transforming Traditional Agriculture* (1963). These studies were initially influenced by the productivity measurement literature and in recent years by developments in the "duality" methodology for estimation of output supply and factor demand systems. The focus of most studies of this type in recent years has been on the statistical association of productivity change with research, extension, schooling, and other infrastructure investments rather than on productivity measurement *per se*.

Studies of manufacturing productivity have similarly sought to measure productivity change and to associate it with R&D investments and industry characteristics. Some useful analytic work is emerging from the field of industrial organization in recent years. Much of it is directed toward developed country industrial questions, but it is influencing development work. In addition, the patents, R&D and productivity work of Griliches and others at the National Bureau of Economic Research is becoming increasingly relevant to development problems.

International trade theorists have considered the *implications* of technical change or productivity change in much the same way that economic growth modelers have. For the most part, this literature has little to say regarding the mechanisms by which technology is produced. It has a little more to say regarding the transfer of technology (i.e. its value in different locations). Recent work by Dixit applying the concepts of industrial organization theory to technology transfer is yielding some useful and relevant insights for development.

In this essay I propose first to review briefly some of the relevant methodological literature. Then I will review data describing international investment patterns in research directed toward technology production (or discovery), with particular reference to investment in developing countries. The next section reviews empirical studies in developing countries associating research and related investments with productivity change. The final section then reviews empirical studies of research investment decisions by private firms and public agencies.

I cannot do justice in this review to more than a limited part of the vast literature that could be generally classified under this topic. I will not attempt to review the normative literature covering North–South issues or the international trade literature on this topic in depth. In discussing the methodological literature, I will focus on the production or discovery and transfer of improved technology, rather than on the economic outcomes associated with exogenously given technology. My focus in reporting the empirical work will also be on the production and transfer of technology, although I will address recent literature on output factor "biases" associated with research investment. Finally, my own research agenda and interests will be reflected in a more complete treatment of the literature dealing with agriculture than with the manufacturing sector.

METHODOLOGY ISSUES

Definitions

Since there is a fair amount of variation in the terminology used in studies in the field it will be useful to begin with a clarification of terms.

Technology encompasses all known *techniques* for producing goods and services. Firms, households, and individuals choose actual techniques according to the market (price), physical, and biological environments in which they produce.

Technological change describes the discovery of new techniques of production which are useful to at least some producers.

Technical change describes the change in actual use by producers of new techniques.

Technology adoption or diffusion describes the process by which a given new technique (or set of techniques) is diffused among a set of producers.

Technology transfer describes or characterizes the relationship between the profitability of a given new technique (or set of techniques) and the market, physical and biological environments that producers are located in. A new technique may increase the profits of producers located in region A by 10 percent when efficiently adopted. The same technique in region B may increase profits when efficiently adopted by only 2 percent, because the techniques interact with soil and climate factors that differ between A and B. The transfer or "spill-in" of technology from region A to region B is thus low in this example.

Inventions are discovered techniques. Inventions can be classified in many ways: by type of technology (chemical, mechanical, electrical, biological, managerial), by function, product or process, by industry of origin, by industry of use, and by degree – major or minor. Some inventions are given legal protection, most are not.

Invention patents are the major form of legal protection provided by countries to an invention. A typical legal system provides for a grant of *limited monopoly rights* to practice an invention in return for public *disclosure* of the invention. A qualifying inventor is given the *right to exclude* others from practicing the invention for a limited period, usually 15 to 20 years. Three major standards must be met for an invention to qualify for an invention patent:

1 The invention must be *useful*.
2 The invention must be *novel*, i.e., new – not known before.
3 The invention must have an *inventive step*, i.e., it must be "un-obvious to one practicing the art."

Utility models are a weaker form of protection to inventions provided by some countries. The qualifying standards are lower in two respects. First, novelty is often, in practice, determined against national or regional standards rather than global standards. More importantly, the inventive step requirement is given a weaker interpretation. The utility model is thus generally regarded as a "petty patent."

Industrial design patents give protection to new designs that do not have an inventive step.

Paris Convention Rights – The Paris Convention is an international agreement between countries in which signatories agree to recognize the inventions made by a citizen of a member country on a par with inventions made by its own citizens.

Productivity is a relationship between output and one or more inputs into a production process.

Productivity change is a change in this relationship. It is related to technical change and technological change in an inexact way. Technological change may or may not be realized as technical change. This depends on the producing environment and on producer behavior. Technical change produces productivity change if producers are efficient. Productivity change can be realized in many ways, e.g., through increases in producer efficiency and through changes in environments.

Productivity measurement

The productivity measurement and accounting literature, itself largely empirical in nature, can be regarded as the point of origin of much of the later theoretical work and virtually all of the empirical work in this field. Partial productivity measures such as output per unit of labor or land, of course, were in general usage long before the development of the more general "total factor productivity" (TFP) measure. Until the development of the more general output per unit of input or total factor productivity index, however, the relationship between the "residual" growth in output per unit of input and growth in output was not fully recognized. Abramovitz, Kendrick, Denison and other early measurers of TFP demonstrated that residual TFP growth clearly was important, even if one could not identify its source.[1]

The productivity "explanation" literature based on adjustments to factor measures was criticized because there was considerable disagreement over the validity of the adjustments made. The "human capital" literature had established a solid foundation for labor force adjustments. Capital stock adjustments, especially regarding rates of capital use, were more controversial. Adjustments based on characteristics of the production function, such as scale economies, were also seen as a translation of the problem into other dimensions (i.e., what caused the scale economies?). (For a treatment of scale economies, see Griliches, 1963.)

Critics of productivity measurement on grounds of capital service flow measurement and noncompetitiveness between firms also contributed to the decline in interest in productivity explanation, but its biggest problems were the internal disagreements over adjustments.[2] The Griliches–Jorgenson–Denison debate in 1967 illustrated this forcefully.[3] Criticisms based on the implied degree of maximizing behavior by firms were also a factor in the decline of this field in recent years (Nelson and Winter, 1974).

A substantial number of productivity measurement and accounting studies, both for the agricultural sector and for manufacturing and other sectors, have now been undertaken (for a recent review, see Kendrick and Vacarra, 1980). The coverage of OECD countries and other developed countries is more complete than the coverage of developing countries (Kravis, 1976, and Mason, 1973). In general, these studies find that when output growth is slow, the TFP residual is negligible, and that when it is high (as in Taiwan, Korea, Japan, Brazil), the TFP residual represents a substantial share of output growth.

Growth models

The early productivity studies inspired several important fields of theoretical and empirical work. The theory studies were of two general classes. The first class of economic growth models drew relatively little from the productivity studies. This body of literature treats productivity (or technical or technological) changes as exogenously determined and thus concentrates on the consequences of alternative rates of productivity growth. These models did raise interest in factor augmentation and embodiment of technology and indirectly contributed to understanding the process of technology discovery, but did not confront these questions directly.

The second class, the "induced innovation" models on the other hand, showed great promise in their early formulations because they appeared to treat not only the rate of technical change, but also the factor intensity or bias as endogenously determined. Binswanger and Ruttan (1978) provide a good review of both theoretical and empirical issues in the induced innovation literature.

These models provided a specification of the "technology of technology production" defined in units familiar to the economist. The "innovation possibilities frontier" (IPF) described a transformation relationship between R&D inputs and inventive outputs measured in terms of factor augmentation or factor shifts. Economic optimization analysis then showed that factor prices (reflecting factor scarcities) would guide the mix of inventive outputs.

As this line of research was developed further, it became increasingly clear that without better knowledge of the technology transformation function (i.e. the IPF), it was not really possible to impose restrictions on the IPF to yield very strong or interesting predictions. Figure 16.1 illustrates the issues.

The IPF depicted in figure 16.1 is defined as $G(\Delta L, \Delta K, R_1, R_2) = 0$

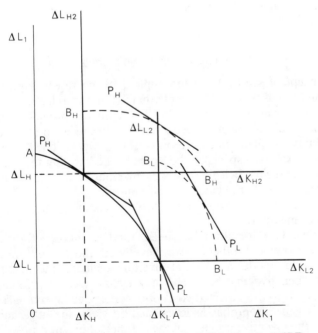

FIG 16.1   *The "innovation possibilities frontier" (IPF)*

For a given level of $R_1 + R_2$ the IPF is AA in figure 16.1. The optimal output mix is $(\Delta L_L, \Delta K_L)$ if the price ratio of L and K is P_L (low-wage economies), and $(\Delta L_H, \Delta K_H)$ if the price ratio is P_H (high-wage economies). This simple version of the theory has predictive power; different mixes of inventive output will emerge under different price regimes. In high-wage economies, the new technology will be relatively labor-saving. The model also has implications for transferability. If no environmental interactions other than price interventions exist (very unlikely), technology produced in high-income countries is worth less in low-income countries then it would be if tailored to the low-income countries.

Now consider a complication of the model by supposing that the R&D actually produced either $(\Delta L_L \Delta K_L)$ or $(\Delta L_H, \Delta K_H)$. What does the next period IPF look like? In particular, does it depend on this period's level of R&D and on this period's prices? It almost certainly does, and it is plausible that the scope for further gains in labor-saving inventions is greater if only ΔL_L gains were produced in this period than if ΔL_H gains were produced. This is reflected in the second-period IPF's $B_L B_L$ and $B_H B_H$. The strong predictions of the first-period model are now modified and weakened. In the long run, factor prices might have little bearing on the ultimate mix of technology produced.

We are thus driven back to the more fundamental issue – what determines the nature of the IPF? The failure of the induced innovation literature to effectively address this issue led to a decline in interest in the model.

Search and invention models

The concept of search has been applied to the research process by Kislev and Evenson, Lee, Dow and others. (For a search model application, see Kislev and Evenson, 1975.) These models provide a rationale for an uncertain discovery process that has been shown to have some applicability to plant breeding and related work. The quantitative genetics literature, especially the animal-breeding literature, actually describes the technological process of inventing in careful detail (Ladd and Gibson, 1978; Englander and Evenson, 1979). One of the important ideas in this literature is that invention is subject to "exhaustion" or diminishing returns.

The invention literature has been another source of theoretical insight. Arrow and others have developed the "single invention" model. In this model a potential inventor evaluates the potential or expected "benefits" that he or she may realize from an invention and compares this to the expected costs of producing an invention. This, of course, is a highly probabilistic calculation given the uncertainty inherent in the inventive process. In the absence of patent protection, the inventor will "appropriate" the benefits only through the actual use of the invention in economic activities and the prevention of imitation through trade secrecy. In this situation, potential inventors who are not employed in production activities where the invention is to be used have little incentive to invent. Potential inventors employed in such activities have some incentives to invent but these may be insufficient to call forth adequate inventive effort. Furthermore, such inventors have strong incentives to maintain trade secrecy.

The patent right grants a *limited* monopoly to the inventor. This legal instrument gives the inventor the right to exclude other parties from using his or her invention for a limited time. This right to exclude is usually limited to a period of 15 to 20 years and applies to the citizens of countries that agree to recognize such rights. This enables an inventor, whether engaged in production or not, to sell or license rights to use his invention. Incentives to invent are thus improved. Most economists see the "distortionary" limited monopoly grant as the price one pays to achieve improved incentives to invent. The legal profession emphasizes the "removal from secrecy" aspect of patent rights (the law requires that the patent document publicly "disclose" the invention) as an important additional benefit.

The economics literature tends to place little weight on the "disclosure" effect emphasized by legal scholars, and somewhat surprisingly, the "removal from secrecy" effect is also not emphasized by economists. This is in part due to the single invention model that has dominated economists' thinking about invention until recently.

A somewhat more realistic model has been put forward more recently, but it does not effectively deal with the disclosure issue. This is the "races" model (Wright, 1984). In this model a number of potential inventors engage in a competitive race to discover an invention. Only the winner obtains the invention (in more sophisticated versions, there are multiple winners). Since each inventor individually does not take into account the effect that his or her presence in the race makes, these models produce a kind of "overfishing" result similar to that obtained in the fishing literature. These models presume that an individual inventor does not know or estimate the number of competitors in the race.

In a recent paper, Dixit (1985) applies models of this type to international invention and obtains the result that only some subset of the competitors in the race will actually stay in the race. Most firms will purchase technology from the winners rather then engage in R&D. This model implicitly considers possible "erosion" in inventive rents but does not consider the disclosure issue very fully.

As noted above, inventors with patent rights receive rents. These rents accrue over a number of years, with the maximum number being the period of the patent grant. The maximum rent accruing will depend on the next best alternative technology. Even if new technologies being developed are inferior to the invention in question, they can cut into the rents to the invention. It is quite rare that rents to an invention still remain at the end of the 15- to 20-year patent period. In most cases, they are eroded within a few years. This would occur even without disclosure effects, but disclosure accelerates the erosion of rents and induces "inventing-around" behavior by competitive firms. As rents are eroded, the gains from invention are transferred from inventors to the consumers of the products and intermediate goods where production is based on the invention in question. As a consequence, rents to inventors, particularly the present value of rents, are generally only a fraction of the ultimate value of the invention.

There are two types of disclosure-induced invention. The first is the inventing-around type, where competing inventors are enabled by disclosure to invent close substitutes to sell and employ in the same market. The second is derivative or adaptive invention. This invention is related to technology transfer. In this case, investors devise minor modifications or adaptations to sell and employ in a different and generally smaller market. This type of invention is highly dependent on disclosure. Inventors tend, therefore, to fall into three broad categories: (1) "*pioneers,*" who initiate technology fields; (2) primary market "*follow-on*" inventors, who compete to produce inventions for the major consumer and factor markets; and (3) "*adaptive*" or derivative inventors, who compete to adapt primary market inventions to secondary markets. The first type of inventor, a special and important type, depends little on within-field disclosure effects. These inventors may respond, however, to disclosure effects from nearby, related technology fields. The second type constitutes the vast majority of inventors and includes most corporate inventors. They respond to disclosure effects by developing substitute inventions which fall just outside the infringement boundaries of other inventions. The third type is almost exclusively dependent on disclosure effects. Most such inventors are in developing countries or in small-scale remnant industries dependent on low-cost labor and partially outdated technology. The value of such inventions depends on the inherent transferability of the invention.

Technology fields tend to have a cycle or cycles. At the beginning of the cycle, pioneer invention occurs, often in an irregular way. Many pioneer inventors are "wildcat" inventors who combine imagination, trial and error skills, and a "venture" or risk preference. In some cases, public sector and university researchers provide pioneer inventions. After commercialization of one, but usually several, of these inventions a period of rapid disclosure-induced invention takes place. Typically this invention tends to be centered on one or more technology "cores," each of which tends to incorporate the assimilated and tested components of individual inventions. In the case where multiple cores exist, disclosure effects across cores can be important. As the invention process proceeds, the market reveals some cores to be inferior. Invention around these inferior cores, as well as the cross-core related invention, then tends to be cut off. Process inventions tend to dominate product inventions in the late stages of the cycle.

Sometime after mainline invention occurs in the primary market, secondary adaptive invention will begin to take place under proper incentives. Multinational firms may engage in some of this invention as they transfer production to low-wage locations. Firms in the secondary markets, however, have an incentive to buy technology from primary markets and to "reverse engineer" this technology, enabling them to engage in adaptive invention for the secondary markets. One could think of this process in terms of "tiers" in which several stages of adaptation take place. The tiers usually are related to levels of development and differences in climate, legal and institutional environments, and factor endowments.

The international market for inventions is then fairly closely linked to comparative advantages in adaptive invention. An ideal patent system from the developing or secondary markets perspective then is one in which low-cost, regularized technology purchase is possible and indigenous adaptive invention is encouraged (Evenson, 1986), that is, it minimizes the cost of technology acquisition by invention and purchase.

Appropriate technology

Induced innovation models influenced at least two further lines of work: one primarily policy-oriented, the second, more empirical.

The policy field in question is the "appropriate" technology literature. It has long been recognized that the *selection* of optimal (or efficient) techniques of production from sets of technologies is determined by relative factor prices (and endowments of soil, climate, traditions, etc.). The induced innovation models showed that there was scope for expanding the technology "appropriate" to a given developing country situation. This implies R&D programs that do not simply continue the multi-period trajectories determined by developed country conditions (see figure 16.1). It implies the development of new tajectories, in some cases building on older technologies. Of course, to the extent that there is a fair amount of "technological determination" in a field, attempts to develop new trajectories may not succeed (Teitel, 1978; Ranis and Saxonhouse, 1977; Pack, 1976; Ranis, 1977).

The production of agricultural technology, in both the public and private sectors, has long been responsive to this principle. Productivity decomposition studies (see below) showed rather clearly that technology trajectories were highly sensitive to soil and climate conditions (Kislev and Evenson, 1975, emphasize this point in their study of productivity changes in agriculture). Accordingly, the international system of research to develop agricultural technology has numerous location-specific technology trajectories, each producing new technology tailored to local soil, climate, and related conditions (Evenson, 1986). Interestingly, as shown later in this paper, this highly adaptive research strategy as regards producing technology adapted to soil and climate conditions has not produced technology highly adapted to factor endowments, i.e., it has not been labor-using/machine-saving.

There is a good deal of normative policy discussion dealing with the merits of subsidizing R&D or conducting public sector R&D to exploit these appropriate technology opportunities. As noted above, private sector invention is generally adaptive, but the actual design and operation of intellectual property systems in developing countries may not encourage such investment. Some of the policy discussion in this field has been influenced by the "small is beautiful" and "self-sufficiency" themes prevalent in some parts of the development literature (Stewart, 1977; Viatsos, 1976).

Technology transfer

The appropriate technology literature does raise the closely related issue of technology transfer. Policy-makers interested in a particular location or region will generally seek access to new technologies of value to producers in the location at minimum cost. If technology provided elsewhere has a high degree of direct transfer (where the degree of direct transfer is measured by the ratio of the profit increase enabled by the technology in a given location to the profit increase enabled in the origin location) appropriate or adaptive R&D may not be justified. If the degree of transfer is low, an adaptive R&D program designed to build on the low direct transfer (and hence achieve indirect transfer) may have a high payoff. If no neighbors are producing inventions with any direct transferability, the location is faced with the problem of developing a free-standing R&D program.

These transfer issues have been addressed in both the empirical productivity decomposition literature and in the investment literature, but very little analytic work has been done on the topic.[4]

Early studies of returns to R&D utilized relatively simple direct project evaluation or benefit-cost methodologies. This often meant comparison of costs, profits or productivity in a "with-without" comparison. In many cases these comparisons were misleading.[5] Later studies utilized "productivity decomposition" methodology, in which productivity indexes were regressed on determining variables, such as R&D expenditure "stocks". This literature required attention to transfer and timing specifications. The third generation of these studies is also of the productivity decomposition type but relies on the costs-profits function or duality-based output supply-function demand systems methodology (see section "Studies of returns to R&D" for further discussion).

Studies of R&D investment in the public and private sector are relatively recent (see final section). Given the extensive emphasis in the international trade literature on the comparative economic growth performance between open and closed economies, it might be expected that trade scholars would have produced a body of comparative studies of investments in R&D and other productivity enhancement investments. The central importance of technology transfer to international trade questions might also be expected to have called forth research on these issues. Unfortunately, this is not the case, and very few studies on these issues have been made.

PATTERNS OF INVESTMENT IN R&D

The purpose of this section is to provide summary data comparing R&D activity in both public and private sectors between different groups of countries. Table 16.1 provides an overview of research intensity measures. The ratio of R&D spending to the value of product in the sector is perhaps the best general comparative indicator of R&D investment. Data for the U.S. and three developing countries of special interest in this paper, Brazil, India and the Philippines, are shown.

The table shows that agricultural research intensities have risen steadily over the past 20 or so years. Industrial research intensities, on the other hand, have fallen in almost all countries since the mid 1960s (see Evenson, 1984). This general trend appears to be reversing itself (as indicated by the U.S. data) in the 1980s. Forestry research is substantial in developed countries but negligible in developing countries (Mergen, Evenson, Judd and Putnam, 1986).

Thus today we have a broad pattern of R&D intensities in developing countries that are roughly one-fifth those of developed countries for industries, and one-third to one-half those for agriculture. Interestingly, the R&D intensities of semi-industrialized economies are not very different from the intensities for developing countries. Licensing data for the Philippines suggest that the payment of license fees to foreigners is roughly two-thirds as much as R&D spending (Mikkelsen, 1984). For India the payment of license and technology fees to foreigners is roughly one-half R&D investments (Deolalikar and Evenson, 1982).

While complete data are not available on technology purchase, it appears that middle-income developing countries are spending as much on technology purchase from abroad as on domestic R&D. The semi-industrialized countries are probably spending considerably more on technology purchase from abroad than on domestic R&D and thus may be as "total spending"-intensive as the industrialized countries.

Table 16.2 provides a descriptive picture of the patterns of invention patents granted in different groups of countries. This table shows that a very small share of the world's invention patents are granted in developing countries. The semi-industrial countries, on the other hand, do grant an appreciable number of invention patents. The planned economies

TABLE 16.1 *Domestic research intensity ratios (R&D/GDP) (100): selected countries, regions, years*

	Industrialized	USA	Semi-industrialized	Middle-income developing	Low-income developing	Planned
Agricultural research (public sector)						
1959	0.68		0.29	0.29	0.15	0.45
1970	1.37		0.54	0.57	0.27	0.75
1980	1.50		0.73	0.81	0.50	0.73
Agricultural extension (public sector)						
1959	0.38		0.29	0.60	0.30	0.29
1970	0.57		0.51	1.01	0.43	0.33
1980	0.62		0.59	0.92	0.44	0.36
Forestry research (public sector)						
1970	0.28		0.10	0.05	0.02	0.17
1984	0.27		0.07	0.06	0.02	0.15
Industrial research (primarily private sector)						
1967	3.25	2.89	0.94	0.31		3.57
1971	2.27	2.48 (1.68)[a]	0.56			2.61
1976	2.06	2.27 (1.68)[a]	0.43			3.37
1979	1.96	2.38 (1.75)[a]	0.43	0.29		3.29
1985	(2.15)	(2.70)(1.89)[a]				
Purchased technology						
1980				0.23		

[a] Non-defense R&D.

Sources: Evenson (1984); Judd, Boyce, and Evenson (1985); Mergen, Evenson, Judd, and Putnam (1986).

TABLE 16.2   *Invention patent summary*

	Industrialized	USA	Semi-industrialized	Developing	Planned
Share of world's invention patents					
1967–71	0.677	0.316	0.043	0.004	0.277
1976–79	0.618	0.233	0.043	0.004	0.336
1983	0.665	0.144	0.063	0.002	0.257
Share of world's industrial design patents					
1975–80	0.918	0.025	0.087	0.010	0.029
Share of world's trademarks					
1975–80	0.556	0.080	0.401	0.036	0.007
Ratio: Patents granted to nationals to total patents					
1967–71	0.53	0.75	0.22	0.11	0.76
1976–79	0.51	0.62	0.25	0.12	0.84
1983	0.43	0.59	0.20	0.06	0.93
Ratio: Patents granted to nationals in other countries to patents granted to nationals in home countries					
1967–71	1.79	1.51	0.21	0.10	0.15
1976–79	1.62	1.69	0.19	0.09	0.11
1981–83	1.71	2.00	0.47	0.90	0.07
Patents granted to nationals per scientist and engineer					
1967	0.238	0.248	0.754	0.053	0.269
1971	0.258	0.214	0.662	0.066	0.218
1976	0.201	0.152	0.422	0.055	0.187
1979	0.200	0.108	0.457	0.052	0.243
Patents granted to nationals per dollar expended on R&D					
1967–71	1.007	1.666	3.807	0.340	1.092
1975–79	1.276	1.463	5.728	0.337	1.297

Source: Evenson (1984).

grant few industrial design patents and very few trademarks. However, as can be noted in the table, these legal instruments are important in the developing and semi-industrialized countries.

The proportion of patents granted that are granted to nationals has been declining in virtually all countries as international trade in inventions has risen, but it continues to be much higher in the developed countries.

The ratio of patents granted abroad to patents originating in the country is an index both of transferability or adaptability, and of "derivativeness" of invention. This measure shows quite clearly that the patents originating in developing countries are more derivative and have lower transferability abroad than those originating in developed countries.

Finally table 16.2 shows that patents granted per scientist and engineer (or R&D dollar) are highest in the semi-industrialized economies and lowest in the developed economies. Patents granted per scientist and engineer have been falling in the developed (and semi-industrialized) countries since 1967. (See Evenson, 1984, for a discussion of these research intensities.)

Table 16.3 provides a summary of data for nine countries operating utility model or petty patent systems. All of these countries are relatively successful in invention, given their levels of development (Brazil introduced its utility model in 1970 and we have only recent data; Italy has not reported recent data). Petty patents are granted primarily to nationals (although West Germany has granted a significant number to foreigners from countries without petty patent systems). They also are granted primarily to individuals, rather than to large corporate firms. Most are granted in mechanical technology, rather than in chemical or biogenetic technology.

The advantage of the petty patent is that it broadens the invention base by providing incentives to encourage individuals and small firms to develop inventions. Some semi-industrialized countries, notably South Korea and now Brazil, are using this legal system effectively. Japan and West Germany have used it effectively in the past.

Table 16.4 provides comparative data by industry of patent origin for the Philippines and for India. Industries are classified as light, chemical and engineering, a classification to be used in further work (see tables 16.5 and 16.11). Table 16.4 provides a general picture of the relationship between industries and the domestic comparative advantage in invention as measured both by the proportion of domestic origin patents and by the ratio of domestic origin utility models to domestic origin invention patents.

As can be seen from the table, there is a positive correlation between the proportion of domestic origin patents in the two countries and between the ratio of utility models to invention patents in the Philippines (data for Brazil show similar patterns). The chemical industries in general (except for paints and photography) have low ratios of domestic origin patents and few utility models. The machinery industry and wood and leather product industries, on the other hand, are industries where high levels of utility models are observed and where domestic patenting is higher.

TABLE 16.3   Utility models (petty patents) granted 1967–80

| | Applications | | | | | | Utility models granted | | | | | |
| | Nationals | | | Foreigners | | | Nationals | | | Foreigners | | |
	1967	1975	1980	1967	1975	1980	1967	1975	1980	1967	1975	1980
W. Germany	42,214	30,114	26,094	11,344	11,938	8,153	20,948	12,099	10,252	2,400	2,181	1,879
Italy	4,418	—	—	778	—	—	3,935	—	—	702	—	—
Japan	109,154	178,992	190,388	1,906	1,668	1,397	20,601	47,449	49,468	721	957	533
Philippines	141	565	762	2	7	24	94	331	465	—	9	3
Poland	1,647	1,896	2,523	22	31	36	411	1,775	1,680	4	25	20
Portugal	139	78	118	25	13	15	77	153	159	9	25	6
Spain	7,601	7,650	5,380	710	1,353	1,162	6,177	4,128	3,845	600	2,041	11,131
Brazil	—	—	1,657	—	—	89	—	—	131	—	—	13
S. Korea	—	7,052	7,936	—	238	622	—	1,032	1,315	—	14	438

Source: Industrial Property Statistical Report, annual issues, World Intellectual Property Organization, Geneva.

TABLE 16.4 Comparative data: patenting in India and the Philippines

| | Domestic origin invention patents 1971–80 | | Proportion domestic origin | | Utility models 1971–80 |
	India	Philippines	India	Philippines	Philippines
Light industries					
Food	119	44	0.35	0.16	1
Beverages	5	8	0.36	0.11	35
Tobacco	6	2	0.12	0.03	10
Textiles	146	47	0.22	0.21	111
Wood and products	25	22	0.40	0.31	50
Paper and printing	71	18	0.29	0.22	81
Leather	21	0	0.36	—	24
Non-metallic minerals	166	6	0.25	0.08	74
Agricultural products	0	36	—	0.55	87
Chemical industries					
Inorganic chemicals	117	9	0.17	0.01	7
Agricultural chemicals	6	6	0.40	0.04	7

Paints	36	27	0.34	0.16	19
Pharmaceuticals	31	19	0.12	0.02	87
Soap – detergent	65	–	0.30	–	–
Explosives	18	48	0.11	0.08	69
Photography	40	–	0.43	–	–
Rubber	18	0	0.08	0	5
Plastics	70	16	0.14	0.05	10
Engineering industries					
Metal products	170	35	0.23	0.16	280
Agricultural machinery	22	11	0.39	0.25	153
Other machinery	143	118	0.28	0.15	395
Electrical equipment	381	62	0.25	0.17	292
Transport	68	24	0.19	0.36	146
Electrical generators	28	35	0.23	0.25	118
Mining	20	15	0.23	0.12	99
Construction	–	6	–	0.03	45
Miscellaneous manufacturing	n.a.	81	n.a.	0.21	618

Sources: Deolalikar and Evenson (1982) and Mikkelson (1984).

TABLE 16.5   *Distribution of patents by origin*

	Light industries[a]		Chemical industries[a]		Engineering industries[a]	
	1954–57	*1975–78*	*1954–57*	*1975–78*	*1954–57*	*1975–78*
Indian	*15.70*	*31.63*	*7.11*	*23.15*	*7.44*	*27.22*
Firms — large[b]	1.48	4.50	0.80	3.80	0.96	2.39
Firms — small[c]	2.00	5.77	1.20	3.63	1.44	4.05
CSIR[d]	2.53	2.42	1.20	5.88	0.72	5.20
University	1.37	4.62	0.46	3.57	0.24	1.89
Individuals	8.32	14.32	3.45	6.57	4.08	13.69
Foreign	*84.30*	*68.37*	*92.89*	*76.55*	*92.96*	*72.78*
Great Britain	25.82	10.97	21.05	8.29	32.61	12.99
France	3.27	3.81	3.59	4.44	5.52	3.55
West Germany	8.54	10.74	6.44	12.67	7.91	9.33
Switzerland	6.11	6.81	5.51	1.67	1.92	1.97
Italy	2.53	2.54	1.59	2.71	1.68	0.58
Japan	3.58	3.12	1.13	3.46	2.16	2.24
U.S.	10.75	13.97	20.58	25.29	19.66	25.10
Other	20.82	16.40	32.20	18.03	21.10	20.10

[a] See table 16.4 for industry classes.
[b] Firms with more than 100 employees.
[c] Firms with 100 or fewer employees.
[d] The Council for Scientific and Industrial Research, supported by the government of India.

Table 16.5 provides further data for the Indian patents showing the origin of patents by broad class. It is of interest to note that patenting by Indian individuals (i.e., not directly employed by registered firms) is quite important, especially in the light and engineering industries. This attests to the fact that inventive capacity is not confined to formal R&D departments in firms. The same fact is shown by the utility model data for the Philippines where most utility models are granted to individuals and employees of small firms. The data also show the importance of public sector invention in India by the Council on Scientific and Industrial Research (CSIR), a publicly funded research organization.

STUDIES OF RETURNS TO R&D

Agricultural studies: first generation

The largest body of literature on returns to R&D is directed toward the agricultural sector. The R&D directed toward agriculture in developing countries is conducted primarily in the public sector. In this section, I review three generations of agricultural studies and three studies of R&D in an agriculturally related industry – the agricultural implements industry.

The first generation of studies used fairly simple measurement techniques of the project evaluation type. The classic study of hybrid corn by Griliches was of this type (1957, 1958). The procedure requires that the new technology or technologies be clearly identified. Then the costs leading to its development can be identified. The benefits are then measured by comparing the cost or profit advantage of the new technology with the older technology. Data on adaptation of the technology are then used to produce an aggregate benefits stream. Standard project analysis methods convert these data into benefit-cost ratios or internal rates of return.

Table 16.6 summarizes several of these first generation studies of agricultural technologies and reports the internal rate of return calculated in them. This methodology is subject to a number of limitations. It requires an identification of a technology or class of technologies and this identification can be quite arbitrary. Many R&D programs produce a "flow" of relatively small incremental inventions. Furthermore, the methodology may lead to a serious bias in that unsuccessful R&D programs are not evaluated.

Agricultural studies: second generation

The second generation of returns to R&D studies sought to overcome this by statistically relating productivity gains to R&D stock variables, thus bypassing the need to identify technology *per se*. Furthermore, the R&D stock implicitly includes both successful and unsuccessful research. This methodology, however, is very demanding regarding specification. It requires a reasonably complete specification of the productivity enhancement relationship, i.e., variables other than the R&D stocks are required (such as producer schooling, extension, infrastructure investments, etc.). It also requires that the transfer and timing dimension be built into the R&D stock specification.

Of course, this specification burden has the merit that a much more complete understanding of the process by which R&D has an impact is enabled by adequate specifications. Nonlinear least squares procedures have been used to estimate the average timing lag between research expenditure and the productivity impact (Kislev and Evenson, 1975; Evenson, 1983).

These estimates indicate that for very-applied agricultural research, the productivity impact reaches a peak roughly nine years after research expenditure in developed countries and somewhat earlier (seven years) in developing countries. Less-applied "pre-invention" or "pre-technology" agricultural science research has a productivity impact reaching a peak roughly 15 years after expenditure. (Evenson, 1984). These

TABLE 16.6 First generation studies of returns to agricultural R&D

Study	Country	Commodity	Time period	Annual internal rate of return (%)
Griliches, 1958	USA	Hybrid corn	1940–55	35–40
Griliches, 1958	USA	Hybrid sorghum	1940–57	20
Peterson, 1967	USA	Poultry	1915–60	21–25
Evenson, 1969	South Africa	Sugarcane	1945–62	40
Barletta, 1970	Mexico	Wheat	1943–63	90
Barletta, 1970	Mexico	Maize	1943–63	35
Ayer, 1970	Brazil	Cotton	1924–67	77+
Schmitz and Seckler, 1970	USA	Tomato harvester, with no compensation to displaced workers	1958–69	37–46
		Tomato harvester, with compensation of displaced workers for 50% of earnings loss		16–28
Ayer and Schuh, 1972	Brazil	Cotton	1924–67	77–110
Hines, 1972	Peru	Maize	1954–67	35–40
				50–55

Hayami and Akino, 1977	Japan	Rice	1915–50	25–27
Hayami and Akino, 1977	Japan	Rice	1930–61	73–75
Hertford, Ardila, Rocha, and Trujillo, 1977	Colombia	Rice	1957–72	60–82
		Soybeans	1960–71	79–96
		Wheat	1953–73	11–12
		Cotton	1953–72	none
Pee, 1977	Malaysia	Rubber	1932–73	24
Peterson and Fitzharris, 1977	USA	Aggregate	1937–42	50
			1947–52	51
			1957–62	49
			1957–72	34
Wennergren and Whitaker, 1977	Bolivia	Sheep	1966–75	44
Pray, 1978	Punjab (British India)	Wheat	1966–75	−48
		Agricultural research and extension	1906–56	34–44
Pray, 1978	Punjab (Pakistan)	Agricultural research and extension	1948–63	23–37
Scobie and Posada, 1978	Bolivia	Rice	1957–64	79–96
Pray, 1980	Bangladesh	Wheat and rice	1961–77	30–35

Source: Evenson (1983). Table references in source.

studies also indicate that for agricultural technology, some depreciation of the impact occurs as biological technology is subject to pest and pathogen attacks.

The spatial or transfer dimension has generally been explored in these specifications. Some attempts to specify transferability between neighboring regions have been made, but have not been very successful. More success has been obtained by using geoclimate classification information. National and international soil/water/temperature-based, geoclimate classifications are available. Kislev and Evenson specified two research stocks using international data, one based on national investment data, the second based on investments in other countries in similar geoclimate regions (Kislev and Evenson, 1975). They found a strong interaction between the two stocks and concluded that most agricultural transfer between developing countries was indirect, i.e., a country did not benefit from a geoclimate neighbor's research program unless it had a domestic research capability.

Table 16.7 summarizes a number of these second generation studies and reports internal rates of return estimates. These internal rates are estimates based on the marginal impact of the research stock variable. Given the timing dimension, this marginal impact can be converted to a marginal internal rate of return. These estimated rates of returns are not strictly comparable to the average returns calculated for first generation studies.

Table 16.8 reports results from a more recent international study (Evenson, 1986) designed to measure the productivity impacts of the International Agricultural Research Centers (IARCs). These IARCs are commodity-oriented and seek to produce technology (mostly crop varietal technology) that will be transferred to a number of developing countries. The specification is one where a productivity index (yield adjusted for acreage change and fertilizer use) for cereal crops (maize, millets, sorghum, rice, wheat) and staples (beans, cassava, groundnuts, potatoes, sweet potatoes) is regressed on a national research stock (NRES) for the commodity, the international research stocks (IARC) for the commodity and a national extension stock (NEXT) and inter-actions.

The upper part of the table reports the coefficients for the stock and interaction variables for regressions pooled for commodities and regions (country and commodity dummy variables are included). The lower part of the table reports the "partial" elasticities for each stock. The data set covers the period 1960–82 for eight developing countries in each region.

The interaction terms show that national research and national extension are not complements in productivity enhancement in developing countries. Similar evidence for U.S. agriculture shows them to be strong complements. In general, except for staples in Latin America, IARC programs do not complement national research programs. They do, however, complement national extension programs in the cereals. This indicates that the IARC system has achieved a fairly high degree of direct transfer of technology.

The productivity elasticities show that national research investments are highly productive, except in Africa for cereal grains (rice and wheat) and Latin America for staples. Implied rates of return are high. They range from 30 to 40 percent for maize in Latin American and maize and staple crops in Africa, to 60 to 70 percent for maize and cereals in Latin America, cereals in Asia, and staple crops in Asia.

National investment in extension programs is also generally productive, except in staples in Latin America and maize in Africa. The elasticities are high enough to justify a spending to value ratio of one-half to 1 percent but not much higher.

IARC investment is productive across the broad. The elasticities for cereal crops are highest in Africa and lowest in Latin America. The reverse is true for staples. The elasticities imply high internal rates of return to IARC investment, in excess of 100 percent everywhere.

As a region, Asia does best with high productivity elasticities for all three forms of investment for all commodities. Latin America has benefited from all investments except in staples. Africa has mixed results. IARC investment has been least productive in staples. National investment has been most productive in staple crops.

Agricultural studies: third generation

The third generation agricultural productivity studies utilize duality-based systems of output supply and factor demand. They represent an advance over the second generation studies in several respects: they allow for multiple outputs or products; and they allow the measurement of separate research impacts on each output supplied and on each variable factor demanded. They are, however, more demanding of data than the simpler production studies.

The essential feature of this methodology is that one estimates a system of output supply and factor demand equations where research, extension, and other fixed factors and environmental variables appear in each equation. The system of equations is derived from a profit maximization model. Symmetry restrictions are usually imposed on cross-price terms in the models. Flexible functional forms (translog, normalized quadratic or generalized Leontief) are used. Estimation requires that farms (or aggregates of farms) be observed under varying prices. Most estimates are based on pooled cross-section, time-series data.

Table 16.9 reports research and extension impacts on output supply and factor demand in three recent studies in India, Brazil and the Philippines. In each country the impacts of research on productivity are high, implying high returns to research (and to extension in India). Of

TABLE 16.7 *Second generation productivity decomposition studies of returns to research*

Study	Country	Commodity	Time period	Annual internal rate of return (%)
Tang, 1963	Japan	Aggregate	1880–1938	35
Griliches, 1964	USA	Aggregate	1949–59	35–40
Latimer, 1964	USA	Aggregate	1949–59	not significant
Peterson, 1967	USA	Poultry	1915–60	21
Evenson, 1968	USA	Aggregate	1949–59	47
Evenson, 1969	South Africa	Sugarcane	1945–58	40
Barletta, 1970	Mexico	Crops	1943–63	45–93
Duncan, 1972	Australia	Pasture improvement	1948–69	58–68
Evenson and Jha, 1973	India	Aggregate	1953–71	40
Cline, 1975 (revised by Knutson and Tweeten, 1979)	USA	Aggregate	1939–48	41–50
		Research and extension	1949–58	39–47
			1959–68	32–39
			1969–72	28–35
Bredahl and Peterson, 1976	USA	Cash grains	1969	36
		Poultry	1969	37
		Dairy	1969	43
		Livestock	1969	47

Study	Location	Commodity/Type	Period	Value
Kahlon, Bal, Saxena, and Jha, 1977	India	Aggregate	1960-61	63
Evenson and Flores, 1978	Asia — national	Rice	1950-65	32-39
			1966-75	73-78
	Asia — international	Rice	1966-75	74-102
Flores, Evenson, and Hayami, 1978	Tropics	Rice	1966-75	46-71
	Philippines	Rice	1966-75	75
Nagy and Furtan, 1978	Canada	Rapeseed	1960-75	95-110
Davis, 1979	USA	Aggregate	1949-59	66-100
			1964-74	37
Evenson, 1979	USA	Aggregate	1868-1926	65
	USA	Technology oriented	1927-50	95
	USA	Science oriented	1927-50	110
	USA	Science oriented	1948-71	45
	Southern USA	Technology oriented	1948-71	130
	Northern USA	Technology oriented	1948-71	93
	Western USA	Technology oriented	1948-71	95
	USA	Farm management research and agricultural extension	1948-71	110

Source: Evenson (1983). Table references in source.

TABLE 16.8 *Regional impact analysis*

Research-extension coefficient	Maize, millets and sorghum			Cereal crops			Staple crops		
	Latin America	Africa	Asia	Latin America	Africa	Asia	Latin America	Africa	Asia
National research stocks	0.0121**	0.0393**	0.0314**	0.0146**	0.854(3)	0.0106**	−0.019**	0.0733**	0.0479**
National extension stocks	0.0331*	−0.609(4)	0.0305**	0.0158**	−0.153(3)	0.0389**	−0.493(2)	0.939(2)**	0.0157*
(1) × (2)	−0.117(2)**	−0.939(3)**	−0.172(2)**	−0.364(3)**	−0.228(3)	−0.597(3)**	0.318(3)**	−0.101(2)*	−0.457(2)**
IARC research stock	0.286(5)	0.809(5)	0.213(6)	0.560(5)**	0.319(5)	0.171(5)	0.237(4)**	0.371(5)	0.514(5)
(1) × (3)	−0.179(6)	0.445(6)	−0.103(5)**	−0.193(6)**	0.157(7)	−0.644(7)**	0.685(6)*	−0.228(5)	0.105(5)
(2) × (3)	0.129(5)**	0.178(6)	0.349(5)**	0.501(7)	0.222(6)**	0.755(6)*	−0.737(6)*	0.653(6)	0.188(5)
Productivity elasticities									
National research	0.0344	0.0505**	0.1168**	0.1435**	−0.0060	0.1135**	−0.0302**	0.0313**	0.1292**
National extension	0.1708*	−0.0129	0.1658**	0.0745**	0.0128	0.1921**	−0.0243**	0.1198**	0.0685
IARC research	0.0317*	0.0355**	0.0416**	0.0298**	0.0543**	0.0428**	0.0412**	0.0187	0.0312*

Numbers in parentheses are $E(-n)$.

* "T" or comparable "F" indicate significance at 5 to 10 percent levels.

** "T" or comparable "F" indicate significance at 5 percent or lower level.

TABLE 16.9 *Estimated comparative impact elasticities of research, HYV and extension programs*

Impact on product supply	North Indian wheat			Brazil	Philippines	
	Research	HYVs	Extension	Research	Research	Extension
Wheat	0.312	0.206	−0.315			
Rice	−0.083	0.124	0.332			
Corn — millets	−0.808	−0.118	0.862			
Industrial crops	0.272	−0.093	0.325	0.054		
Export crops				0.735		
Staple crops				0.011		
Beans				0.011		
Animal products				0.067		
All products	0.166	0.035	0.159	0.250	0.054	−0.048
Demand for						
Labor	0.102	0.105	0.142	0.063	−0.067	−0.126
Animal labor	−0.095	−0.001	0.253	0.020	−	−
Tractors	1.364	−0.042	−1.180	0.106	0.096	0.168
Energy	−	−	−	0.417	−	−
Fertilizer	1.116	0.473	−1.557	0.470	0.635	0.375
All inputs	0.124	0.083	0.020	0.147	−	−
Total variable productivity	0.042	−0.048	0.139	0.10	0.088	0.055

Sources: North India Wheat, Evenson (1985); Philippines, Evenson (1987); Brazil, Evenson (1984).

more interest here, however, are the factor impacts. They provide some insight into the induced innovation question. These results are instructive regarding both factor and product bias. On the product side, the Indian results show that strong crop biases emerge. The HYV Green Revolution impacts are widely recognized to have a factor bias toward wheat and rice. It is not always appreciated that they were biased against corn and millets and other crops. This bias for industrial crops is more than offset by a bias in favor of these crops by the Indian research system. Both the HYVs and the Indian research system are biased against the coarse cereals, corn, millets, sorghum.

On the factor demand side the induced innovation and appropriate technology proponents who argue that domestic origin rather than imported technology (and this is domestic origin) will be labor-using and machinery-saving are not supported by these data. Agricultural technology over the past two to three decades, whether originating in developing or developed countries, has had a persistent bias favoring mechanization over animal-labor use and favoring fertilizer use. It has not had strong labor-using biases. (Extension in India appears to have stimulated labor demand but this is in the Green Revolution region).

Industry studies: agricultural implements – Philippines, India and Brazil

In each of the three reference countries, Brazil, India and the Philippines, a specialized study of the agricultural implements industry was undertaken (Mikkelsen, 1984; Deolalikar and Evenson, 1982; Dahab, 1985). Recall from the descriptive section that agricultural implements represent a field of technology well suited to domestic invention and to petty invention. The Philippines and Brazil have utility model systems, and in both countries small implement manufacturers have utilized these petty patents. India does not have such a system, and the agricultural implements sector in India is effectively without patent protection.

Surveys of firms in the industry in each country were undertaken. Data were collected on:

R&D effort – including "informal" R&D
Inventions made – whether patented or not
Changes in processes actually made – previous five years
Change in products actually made – previous five years
Sales.

In all three countries these surveys showed that almost all firms in the industry engaged in some R&D, although only the largest firms treated it as a formal activity. Almost all firms made some inventions and all changed process and product to some extent. In the Philippines, the 56 firms surveyed were generally small (mean 26.8 employees) but had obtained 5 invention patents and 94 utility models. Only 18 reported formal R&D activity, but 53 reported inventive activity. 52 firms reported changes in product and processes. Statistical analysis showed that patents and changes in products and processes were highly correlated. Analysis also showed that inventive activity did produce changes. The study also showed that technical assistance to some of these firms from the International Rice Research Institute did not stimulate these firms to engage in more inventive activity, but it did increase the number of changes introduced by the firm at a given level of inventive activity.

The Indian study surveyed 45 firms. Statistical analysis showed that R&D activity did stimulate more product and process inventions and more design changes. A second stage analysis showed that these inventions and changes stimulated sales.

The Brazil study also found that a substantial amount of informal R&D effort took place in smaller firms. The larger firms in the industry had ownership and technical agreements with multinational firms. The industry has enjoyed tariff protection for a number of years and was dominated by several large multinational firms until the late 1960s. In the 1970s, small Brazilian firms showed that they could produce and develop new implement designs and produce them for less than the large multinational firms. By 1980 the multinational firms had effectively lost all of the implement markets to aggressive Brazilian firms, except for the most complex machines, tractors and combine harvesters.

The study showed that Brazilian firms did use the utility model and that they did copy and "reverse engineer" new machines developed elsewhere. Inventive effort did produce design changes and increased the competitiveness of smaller firms. This competitiveness of domestic firms appears to be critical to the success of industries given tariff protection.

DETERMINANTS OF R&D

Private firms and individuals and policy-making bodies make decisions regarding investment in R&D as well as investment in alternative sources of productivity growth. Several studies of these decisions have been undertaken in recent years and they are reviewed here with a view toward understanding the perception of decision-makers as to the likely payoff to alternative investments. Public investments in agricultural research and extension are reviewed, as well as private firm investments in R&D.

Two considerations regarding these decisions are relevant. The first is that expenditures on R&D have a lagged and uncertain payoff. The second is that investment in R&D is only one of several competing means to increase the production or supply of a good. The most important alternative for both public sector agencies and private firms to investing in the discovery of technology is to imitate or purchase it. The U.S.-based literature has, until recently, failed to recognize this point. The development literature, on the other hand, has stressed the problems attendant to the purchase and imitation of technology by LDC firms from developed country firms that is inappropriate to LDC environments (Stewart, 1977).

Investment in public sector agricultural research

The inappropriateness or limited transferability of agricultural technology was probably underestimated during the 1950s and part of the 1960s. Many policy-makers stressed investment in extension services in this period on the grounds that "appropriate technology exists, it just isn't being used." The "know-how, show-how" period of foreign technical assistance in agriculture in the 1950s was based on this premise. Most agriculturalists understood very well, however, that virtually all agricultural technology developed in the temperate-zone developed country regions was inappropriate to the sub-tropics and tropics. They pressed for the development of large numbers of experiment station programs with mandates to develop location-specific technology.

By the late 1950s a number of influential international agricultural policy-makers, frustrated with the slow development of national research systems, urged the development of a new set of research institutions, the International Agricultural Research Centers (IARCs). These commodity-oriented centers were expected by some observers to produce a flow of highly appropriate new technology, and the "green revolution" literature attests to substantial success in doing so for wheat and rice. The previous section of this paper reviewed evidence that they have been productive in other commodities as well. However, these impacts were limited in geographic scope.

Given this success, it is of considerable policy interest to ask whether national research system development has been retarded or stimulated by the development of the IARCs. If national policy-makers see the IARCs as sources of highly transferable technology that effectively is a substitute for their own research system products, they may respond by shifting away from doing their own R&D toward simply imitating or copying the technology flowing from the IARCs. On the other hand, the national system may perceive the IARC technology to be imperfectly transferable to their producing environments, and hence, of limited direct value. The IARCs, however, are producing inventions of technology and "pre-invention" scientific findings that are of indirect value to national programs, in that they enhance the invention potential in the national programs. New rice varieties (e.g. IR36) developed at IRRI, for example, have been used in national rice-breeding programs in locations where the IRRI variety is not transferable. This is because many important genetic traits that can be transferred to other more location specific varieties are embodied in the IRRI variety. The response to this opportunity provided by the IARCs should be positive.

The "net response" to IARC investment and to research investment by "geoclimate" neighbors was measured in a recent study by Evenson (1986). Data on research investment by commodity for 24 countries for the recent years were utilized in the analysis. An investment specification was developed which included the following variables as determinants of national program investment:

Economic   production of the commodity, geoclimate diversity of the country, the relative price or costs of research and extension, a measure of the costs of increasing supply via land expansion.

Transfer   cumulated IARC spending in real dollars on the commodity, scientist man-years in geoclimate neighbors.

Political–Economic   imports, exports of the commodity, the urea/ rice price ratio, the proportion of the labor force in agriculture, proportion of population in large cities, deaths from domestic political violence.

The estimates and the rationale for the specification are reported in Evenson (1986). Table 16.10 summarizes the results.

The table shows that as commodity production increases, both research and extension spending rise but at a rate less than proportional to the production increase. The "elasticities" of spending with respect to production evaluated at the mean are in the 0.55 to 0.6 range. This means that at the mean of the sample, a 10 percent increase in production induces a 5.5 or 6 percent increase in spending. This is probably due to fixed costs of undertaking research and extension programs and economies to size of unit. The implied scale parameter is essentially the inverse of this elasticity (i.e. $1/6 = 1.66$). However, it may also reflect an overestimate of scale economies by governments and a tendency on the part of governments to feel that once a substantial research program is in place, it need not be expanded with the importance of the crop.

The table also shows that when the commodity being produced is exported research spending per unit of product is 1.39 times as high for field crops and 1.54 times as high for livestock and horticultural crops as it is for nontraded commodities. (The number for an increase in traded commodity production is the sum of the commodity production numbers and the traded commodity lines). When the commodity is imported, spending per unit of product is 1.29 times as high for field crops and over 4 times as high for livestock and horticultural crops (where imports are generally very low). Countries are apparently placing a high premium on foreign exchange.

TABLE 16.10 *Calculated impacts on national research and extension investment (millions of 1980 dollatrs)*

Policy variable change	Resulting annual research spending, million dollars		
	Field crops	Livestock and horticultural crops	Extension spending
$1 million added to commodity production	0.00164	0.00396	0.00624
$1 million added to commodity exports	0.000634	0.002277	0.00695
$1 million added to commodity imports	0.000472	0.01253	− 0.000937
1 added SY by geoclimate neighboring country	0.0305	0.01901	− 0.1792
10 percent decline in research cost per SY or 10 percent rise in extension cost per EW	− 0.00006	− 0.00053	0.00166
$1 million added to IARC research stock			
(a) first year	0.229	1.084	0.105
(b) after 10 years	2.290	10.840	1.050
$1 million added to general aid for research	1.194	− 0.858	0.047
World Bank aid (for research or extension)	0.285	− 0.063	1.468

The positive response by countries to an added Scientist Year (SY) on the commodity by a geoclimate neighbor is quantitatively significant in field crops and appears to be biased toward all cereals except wheat and toward beans, cassava and groundnuts. The induced spending of $30,000 is large in view of the fact that the cost of the added Scientist Year may be only a little more than that.

The computations for a 10 percent decline in the research costs per Scientist Year has policy relevance. Many countries have options to reduce these costs through improvement of their own capacity to train scientists and through better incentive structures to hold scientists in research positions. In Africa, an expansion in the indigenous scientists component and a reduction in administration costs can easily allow a reduction in costs per scientist.

A decline in the research cost by 10 percent will result in a slight increase in spending on research. This means that the increase in quantity of Scientist Years purchased will rise by a little less than 10 percent for field crop research and by approximately 6 percent for livestock and horticultural crop research. A 10 percent decline in extension costs, on the other hand, will increase the purchase of extension workers by 14.5 to 15.9 percent and will also increase total spending.

The final calculations regarding aid and IARC spending are of most interest. The form of the model measuring IARC impacts was that the stock (i.e. cumulated expenditures in 1980 dollars) of IARC investment had an impact on the annual flow of national research spending. Thus, a $1 million increment to IARC spending in 1978 would raise the value of the stock variable in the analysis in 1978, 1979, etc. If this IARC spending was in field crops, it would stimulate $229,000 added annual national research investment in the first year (1978). (This is calculated as the total of the spending impacts in the 24 countries in the sample. Presumably the scope of influence is wider than for these 24 countries, so this is an underestimate of the effect.) By 1988 a total of $2,290,000 added annual national research investment would have been stimulated by the $1 million expenditure in 1978. With the data at hand, it is not really possible to estimate the deterioration of this effect. It is conservative to suppose that it will last only 10 years (about the average time period for IARC investment in the data set).

This may be compared with the estimates for direct aid. They show that $1 million in general aid increases field crop research by more than $1 million, but at the cost of reduced spending on livestock and horticultural crop research. Thus taking this displacement into account, only $336,000 net incremental research spending takes place for the $1 million aid grant or loan. The same calculation made for World Bank aid shows an even more severe displacement effect. A million dollars in World Bank aid results in only a net increment to spending of $222,000. In rather sharp contrast, it appears the World Bank extension aid has a large stimulus effect on extension spending (Evenson, 1986).

Determinants of R&D in industry

The previous section shows that investment in agricultural R&D, primarily in the public sector in most developing countries, has expanded rapidly. Furthermore, there is little direct transfer of "inappropriate" technology from developed countries (although as noted earlier in this paper, the more appropriate technology produced in agriculture has not met the "ideal" standards of the proponents of appropriate technology). Furthermore, there is considerable evidence of an "indirect transfer" process, especially from the IARCs. This is suggested by the observation that own R&D responds positively to the expansion of R&D by research institutions producing inappropriate technology, pilot inventions, and pre-invention scientific findings.

Does this hold for industry? Many critics of the LDC technology development argue that it does not. They indicate that LDC firms do little adaptive R&D and that policy incentives cause them to imitate or copy inappropriate technology from "upstream". Previously in this paper it was noted that LDC firms do much less R&D than developed country firms and that the R&D is highly adaptive (i.e., LDC patents are seldom taken out in other countries). It was also noted that LDC firms purchase high levels of technology.

In this section, I report results from two recent studies that indicate that significant adaptive indirect technology transfer does occur in LDC industry. This does not mean that investments in R&D by LDC firms are optimal or that the outcome is ideal. (In fact in both India and the Philippines indications are that the mechanisms were working better in the 1960s and early 1970s than in more recent years.)

Indian industry – 1960 to 1970 Deolalikar and Evenson (1982), undertook an analysis of Indian industry data for the 1960 to 1970 period. The study sought to estimate the determinants of both Indian R&D and technology purchase in a jointly determined demand system. This methodology differs from the U.S. based studies where R&D is treated as an investment and unrelated to technology purchase or the inventive activity of other firms.

Data for 50 three- and four-digit industries were utilized. Table 16.11 shows the clustering of industries into three groups, light, chemical and engineering industries. The variable USPATENTS is used as a proxy for international invention (much like the IARC variable in the previous section). Other variables include prices and firm characteristics.

The major findings as regards the determinants of technology impacts and domestic patenting are summarized in elasticity form in table 16.11. The model also included demand functions for production labor, non-production labor and fuel. The Technology Purchase and Domestic Patenting equations were estimated using the SUR model with restrictions across equations. The major findings are:

1 Technology imports are more responsive to prices than are domestic patenting. Rises in production worker wages and fuel prices stimulate technology impacts in the light and engineering industries.

2 Both technology purchase and domestic invention respond positively and strongly to international (U.S.) invention in the light and chemical industries. Responses are lower in the engineering industries. This indicates that Indian firms respond to an increased supply of inventions upstream both by purchasing (and copying) more and by increasing domestic R&D and adaptive invention.

TABLE 16.11 *Elasticities of demand response: technology purchase and domestic patenting*

Elasticities with respect to	Light industries		Chemical industries		Engineering industries	
	Technology impacts	Domestic patenting	Technology impacts	Domestic patenting	Technology impacts	Domestic patenting
Wages, production worker W_P	1.396[b]	−0.003[b]	−0.004[b]	0.001	0.389[b]	−0.001
Wages, non-production workers W_N	−0.443	−0.001[b]	−0.004	0.001	0.115	0.001
Price of fuel PF	2.919[b]	0.002[b]	−0.000	−0.001	0.375[b]	0.001
Growth in U.S. patenting in industry	1.308[b]	1.128[b]	1.107[b]	2.120[b]	0.557[b]	0.196
Foreign share of ownership in industry[a]	0.578	0.159	−0.011	−0.120[b]	0.095	0.027
Public share of industry[a]	−0.258	0.011	0.026	0.216[b]	0.001	0.030
Fixed capital	−0.248	−0.013	−0.157	0.464	−0.357	−0.655[b]
Output	0.114	−0.108[b]	0.025	−0.809[b]	0.391[b]	0.499
Year	0.181[b]	0.101[b]	0.167	0.111[b]	−0.038	−0.114[b]

All elasticities are evaluated at the mean of the industry group, using coefficients reported in tables 4–6 in Deolalikar and Evenson.

[a] These elasticities are partial: they show the percent change in the dependent variable from a one unit change in the independent variable.

[b] The elasticities are statistically significant at the 0.05 level or greater.

Source: Deolalikar and Evenson (1982, tables 8 and 9).

3   Foreign ownership or public ownership has little effect on domestic patenting except in chemical industries where public ownership stimulates domestic invention and foreign ownership reduces it.

Philippine industry Kent Mikkelsen studied the demand for R&D in the Philippines utilizing firm-level data from 375 firms for the 1965–66 and the 1979–80 periods. He developed a model that indicated a threshold size level before R&D investment would be made. He also tested the responsiveness of Philippine firms to inventions obtained abroad in the same industry (i.e. in the U.S.). Industry concentration, international trade experience and multinational ownership were also factors in his study. Mikkelsen concluded:

1   That high concentration deters R&D investment.
2   That import experience enhanced R&D investment in 1966–67 but not in 1979–80.
3   That multinational ownership has little effect on R&D.
4   That U.S. patenting and U.S. R&D stimulated R&D in the Philippines in 1966–67, but that this stimulus effect was much weaker in 1979–80.

While this study was based on limited data, it does raise policy questions as to the transfer mechanism. In both India and the Philippines (and in the Brazilian agricultural implement study), in the 1960s it appears that international invention was stimulating downstream invention largely of an adaptive type. There are some indications that in the 1980s this stimulus mechanism may no longer be functioning. In both the Philippines and India the 1970s were years of relatively poor (certainly disappointing) industrial performance. Neither country sought to encourage aggressive competition among firms during this period, and India clearly weakened its patent system in 1970. Brazil, on the other hand, did encourage domestic competition and invention, and Brazilian industry performed quite well in the 1970s.

CONCLUDING REMARKS

The data and the studies summarized in this paper indicate that institutional development in public sector research programs directed to a limited range of agricultural problems have made great strides in the developing countries. The development of the IARC system has had a major impact. A number of strong national programs have also emerged. The system is still weak for certain crops and for certain regions. Yet progress has been made, and for many poor countries, the only serious effort to improve productivity is taking place in the agricultural sector. Policy-makers have long understood that private incentive structures will not induce research for most agricultural problems. They have also learned that most agricultural technology has very limited transferability.

The system of research institutions developing agricultural technology suited to and targeted to the tropic and sub-tropic regions in developing counries has been highly productive in terms of creating productivity gains. These productivity gains have *not* met the expectations of the appropriate technology proponents. They have not been labor-using and tractor- and fertilizer-saving. They have not become available equally to all farmers in all regions. Some improvement in regional access can be expected in the future, but there is a powerful element of technological determination in the discovery of agricultural technology. Policy-makers have generally understood that this technology is valuable if it reduces costs, even though it is not "utopian."

The picture put forward by the industrial sector is much different. The very poorest countries have no direct policies toward invention and technology purchase. They invest practically nothing in R&D or in the training of engineers and scientists. They do not have effective international research institutions to benefit from. The more advanced developing countries, such as India, have pursued industrial policies with somewhat unclear and confused treatments of invention and technology purchase and imitation. They have patent systems but administer them inefficiently. They belong to the Paris Convention and are frustrated that most of their patent grants are to foreigners. They have generally weakened their system in recent years (India shortened the patent period and proscribed food and pharmaceuticals from protection). The result is that their incentive systems for domestic inventions are weak. These countries do conduct R&D – perhaps one-fifth or so as much as in developed countries.

Several advanced developing and semi-industrialized countries have more aggressive policies to stimulate domestic invention. They do not engage in much more R&D than do developing countries but they obtain many more inventions. They also train and employ more engineers and technicians. The most advanced appear to be following the post-World War II, Japanese pattern of high investment in R&D and employment of scientists and engineers while purchasing technology at a high rate.

The combination of technology purchase and domestic invention, and the complementarity between invention in developed countries and invention in the developing countries, appears to be erratic and inconsistent. While not fully documented, it appears that successful industrial economies have invested heavily in own R&D and in technology purchase, and that a strong complementary relationship between own R&D and R&D upstream is achieved. This combination produces a larger volume of technology flow than an alternative policy of attempting to achieve more appropriateness at the expense of complementarity.

Legal systems are critical to achieving the lowest cost combination of technology purchase and domestic R&D. The Paris Convention system serves the industrial nations well. In some respects it serves some poor country interests, even though they have a relatively low stake in selling technology abroad. Recognition of patent rights of foreign firms may actually lower the real cost of purchasing some (but certainly not all) technology. The utility market system appears to have been effective in stimulating domestic invention in some countries. A very strong utility model could be used to strengthen domestic incentives and weaken foreign rights without risking loss of Paris Convention rights. Other legal instruments are also plausible.

At this stage of our understanding of the role of technology in development, we cannot claim to have delineated all of the issues. It is to be hoped that a new body of studies of invention, of alternative legal systems, of technology transferability and of other dimensions of R&D programs will be forthcoming. Much empirical experience remains to be studied and interpreted.

NOTES

[1] Abramowitz (1956) and Farrell (1957) were among the earliest contributors to this field.

[2] Nelson and Winter (1974) have raised questions about firm behavior and have proposed an evaluationary approach. The weakest behavioral foundation for productivity measurement is probably the simple accounting approach which relies only on the "no profit" condition that the value of outputs equals the value of inputs:

$$\Sigma P_i Y_i = \Sigma R_j X_j \tag{1}$$

Differentiating (1) and expressing it in rate of change form gives:

$$\sum_i S_i \hat{P}_i + \sum_i S_i \hat{Y}_i = \sum C_j \hat{R}_j + \sum C_j \hat{X}_j \text{ or } \hat{P} + \hat{Y} = \hat{R} + \hat{X} \tag{2}$$

where the S_i and C_j are output and factor shares. TFP can then be defined as the residual

$$\hat{T} = \hat{Y} - \hat{X} = \hat{R} - \hat{P}$$

[3] See Jorgenson and Griliches (1967) and Denison (1968) for the debate. Nadiri (1970) provides a succinct review of productivity measurement. Gollop and Jorgenson (1977) report more recent work. Also see Kendrick and Vacarra.

Helleiner (1973), Ranis (1977), Vernon (1966) and others have addressed technology transfer issues.

This was because some of the with-without comparisons were made in experimental settings and were thus not representative of actual production settings.

REFERENCES

Abramovitz, Moses 1956: "Resource and Output Trends in the United States Since 1870." *American Economic Review,* 46(2).

Arrow, Kenneth 1969: "Classification Notes on the Production and Transmission of Technology Knowledge." *American Economic Review,* 59 (May), 29–35.

Berndt, E. R. and Khaled, Mohammed S. 1977: "Energy Prices, Economics of Scale and Biased Productivity Gains in U.S. Manufacturing 1947–71." Discussion Paper 77–23, University of British Columbia, Dept. of Economics, Aug.

Binswanger, H. 1979: "Income Distribution Effects of Technical Change." Economic Growth Center Discussion Paper No. 281, May.

Binswanger, H. 1974: "A Microeconomic Approach to Induced Innovation." *Economic Journal,* 84(Dec.) 940–58.

Binswanger, H. P. and Ruttan, V. W. 1978: *Induced Innovation and Development.* Baltimore: Johns Hopkins University Press.

Dahab, S. 1985: "The Agricultural Machinery and Implement Industry in Brazil: Its Historical Development and Inventive Activity." Ph.D. dissertation, Yale University, Sept.

Deolalikar, A. and Evenson, R. E. 1982: "Technology Production and Technology Purchase in Indian Industry: An Econometric Analysis." Yale University, Economic Growth Center Discussion Paper No. 421, July.

Denison, E. F. 1968: "Some Major Issues in Productivity Analysis: An Examination of Estimates by Jorgenson and Griliches." *Survey of Current Business,* U.S. Government Printing Office, vol. 49, part 2, 1–27.

Disch, Arne 1983: "Agricultural Policies and Real Income Changes: An Application of Duality Theory to Brazilian Agriculture." Ph.D. dissertation, Yale University, Oct.

Dixit, A. 1985: "The Cutting Edge of International Terchnological Competition." Unpublished.

Englander, A. S., and Evenson, R. E. 1979: "Stability, Adaptability and Targeting in Crop Breeding Programs." Paper presented at the Annual Meeting of the American Agricultural Economics Association, Washington State University, July 29–Aug. 1.

Evenson, R. E. 1983: "Economic Benefits from Research," *Twentieth Century Agricultural Science,* Beltsville, Maryland: National Agricultural Library.

Evenson, R. E. 1984: "International Invention: Implications for Technology Market Analysis." In *R&D, Patents, and Productivity,* Z. Griliches (ed.), Chicago: University of Chicago Press.

Evenson, R. E. 1985: "Output Supply and Input Demand Effects of High Yielding Rice and Wheat Varieties in North Indian Agriculture." *Indian Journal of Quantitative Economics,* 1(1), Punjab School of Economics, G.N.D. University, Amritsar, India.

Evenson, R. E. 1986: "The CGIAR Centers: Measures of Impact on Nation: Research, Extension and Productivity." Consultative Group in Internation: Agricultural Research, The World Bank.

Evenson, R. E. 1987: "Productivity in Philippine Agricultural Regions." Fortl coming in *Philippine Journal of Development*.

Evenson, R. E. and Kislev, Y. 1976: "A Stochastic Model of Applied Research *Journal of Political Economy*, 84(2), April.

Farrell, M. J. 1957: "The Measurement of Productivity Efficiency." *Journal c the Royal Statistical Society*, (Series A, general), vol. 120, part 3, 253–81.

Gollop, Frank M. and Jorgenson, D. W. 1977: "U.S. Productivity Growth b Industry 1947–73." Discussion Paper No. 570, Harvard Institute c Economic Research.

Griliches, Zvi 1952: "Hybrid Corn: An Exploration in the Economics o Technological Change." *Econometrica*, 25 (Oct.), 501–22.

Griliches, Zvi 1958: "Research Costs and Social Returns: Hybrid Corn an Related Innovations", *Journal of Political Economy*, 66 (Oct.) 419–31.

Griliches, Zvi 1963: "The Sources of Measured Productivity Growth: U.S Agriculture, 1940–60." *Journal of Political Economy*, 71(4), 331–46.

Helleiner, G. 1973 "Manufactured Exports from Less Developed Countrie and Multinational Firms", *Economic Journal*, March.

Jorgenson, D. W. and Griliches, Zvi 1967: "The Explanation of Productivit Change." *Review of Economic Studies*, 34(3), 249–83 (also in *Survey o Current Business*).

Kendrick, John 1973: *Post-War Productivity Trends in the United State 1948–69*. New York: National Bureau of Economic Research.

Kendrick, John W. and Vaccara, Beatrice N. (eds) 1980: *New Developments i Productivity Measurement and Analysis*. National Bureau of Economi Research, *Studies in Income and Wealth*, vol. 44, Chicago: University o Chicago Press.

Judd, M. A., Boyce, J. K. and Evenson, R. E. 1986: "Investing in Agricultura Supply." *Economic Development and Cultural Change*, 30(1), Oct.

Kislev, Y. and Evenson, R. E. 1974: *Agricultural Research and Productivity* New Haven: Yale University Press.

Kravis, I. B. 1976: "A Survey of International Comparisons of Productivity." *Economic Journal*, 86 (March), 1–44.

Ladd, George W. and Gibson, Craig 1978: "Microeconomics of Technica Change: What's a Better Animal Worth?" *American Journal of Agricultura Economics*, 60, 236–40.

Mason, R. H. 1973: "Some Observations on the Choice of Technology by Multinational Firms in Developing Countries." *Review of Economics anc Statistics*, 55(3), Aug.

Mergen, F., Evenson, R. E., Judd, M. A. and Putnam, J. 1986: "Forestry Research: a Provisional Global Inventory." Center Discussion Paper No. 503, Economic Growth Center, Yale University, May.

Mikkelsen, K. 1984: "Inventive Activity in Philippine Industry." Ph.D. dissertation, Yale University, May.

Nadiri, Ishaq 1970: "Some Approaches to the Theory and Measurement of Total Factor Productivity: A Survey." *Journal of Economic Literature*. 7(4), 1137–77.

Nelson, R. R. 1951: "The Simple Economics of Basic Scientific Research." *Journal of Political Economy,* June, 247–306.

Nelson, R. R. and Winter, Sidney G. 1974: "Neoclassical vs. Evolutionary Theories of Economic Growth: Critique and Prospectus." *Economic Journal,* 84, 886–905.

Quizon, J. and Binswanger, Hans "Technical Change and Factor Income." Mimeo.

Pack, H. 1976: "The Substitution of Labor for Capital in Kenyan Manufacturing." *Economic Journal,* 86 (March), 45–58.

Penrose, E. 1973: "International Patenting and the Less Developed Countries." *Economic Journal,* 83 (Sept.) 768–86.

Ranis, G. 1977: "Industrial Technology Choice and Employment: A Review of Developing Country Evidence." *Intercencia,* 2(1).

Ranis, G. 1979: "Appropriate Tech nology: Obstacles and opportunities." In T. Stanley and S. Rosenblatt (eds), *Technology and Economic Development: A Realistic Perspective,* Boulder, Colorado: Westview Press.

Ranis, G. and Saxonhouse, G. 1977: "Technology Choice, Adaptation and the Quality Dimension in the Japanese Textile Industry." Economic Growth Center, Yale University, Nov.

Rosenberg, N. 1974: "Science, Invention and Economic Growth." *Economic Journal,* March.

Schmookler, J. 1966: *Invention and Economic Growth.* Cambridge, Mass.: Harvard University Press.

Schultz, T. W. 1963: *Transforming Traditional Agriculture.* New Haven: Yale University Press.

Solow, R. M. 1962: "Technical Progress, Capital Formation and Economic Growth." *American Economic Review,* 52 (May), 76–86.

Stewart, Frances 1977: *Technology and Underdevelopment.* London: Macmillan Press Ltd.

Teece, D. J. 1977: "Technology Transfer by Multinational Firms, the Resource Cost of Transferring Technological Knowhow." *Economic Journal,* 87 (June), 242–61.

Teitel, Simon 1978: "On the Concept of Appropriate Technology for Less Industrialized Countries." *Social Change,* 12, 123–43.

Viatsos, C. 1976: "The Revision of the International Patent System: Legal Considerations for a Third World Position." *World Development,* Sept.

Vernon, R. 1966: "International Investment and International Trade in the Product Cycle." *Quarterly Journal of Economics,* 80(2) May, 190–207.

Wright, Brian D. 1984: "The Effects of Price Uncertainty on the Competitive Firm." Economic Growth Center Discussion Paper No. 466, Yale University, May.

Comments on
"Technology, Productivity Growth, and Economic Development"

FRANCES STEWART

The subject of technology and development is of enormous importance both from a substantive point of view and for the light it sheds on th methodology of development economics. Substantively, it is widel agreed that technological change accounts for a very large part o economic growth. In developing countries, especially in agriculture indigenous research and development and subsequent technolog change has been extremely productive in many Asian econo mies – largely instrumental in transforming their agricultural prospects which in turn has been responsible for greatly improving their genera economic achievements and outlook. In addition to the effects or sectoral and aggregate growth, technology change may greatly influenc income distribution, affecting both the earnings opportunities of dif ferent categories of people (e.g. small farmers versus large, labor versus capital, dry regions versus wet), and also the quality and availability o different types of goods (improving sophisticated products consumed by the rich, or basic goods consumed by the poor). Methodologically analysis of technology represents one of the most challenging areas fo social scientists, vividly illuminating many of the debates of this sympo sium. A comprehensive discussion of technology highlights the limita tions of a pure "market" approach; the need to extend the analysis to include a wider set of motivations, institutions, and selection mech anisms; to encompass elements of political economy and of sociology and to appreciate the discontinuities that make being a late-comer require special analysis and policies, and give meaning to ideas of "dependency."

Bob Evenson's paper represents an ambitious attempt to encompass the major issues related to the production and transfer of technology and its role in development: he covers both theory and empirical material, agriculture and industry. Inevitably, the task turns out to be too big for a single paper, so that the result is uneven, with some issues just named and not discussed, some missed out altogether, and others developed in depth. It would almost certainly have been better to de lineate the topic more narrowly in order to produce a tight and consist ently argued paper, but the breadth of the paper provides a stimulating introduction.

The paper provides a useful guide to definitions in an area where definitions are unavoidably somewhat arbitrary, but nonetheless essential for comprehensible discourse. There is a brief overview of the more conventional theoretical literature and a survey of many of the empirical findings on patents, returns to R&D and the determinants of R&D in developing countries.

The empirical sections of the paper are particularly rich and insightful, providing a useful and up-to-date review of findings on agricultural research and extension, and on the determinants of R&D. The paper is much less comprehensive in its treatment of industrial R&D and technology change, with some major studies being omitted (notably all the work of Katz and others in Latin America and of Dahlman and Westphal, Lall, and others in Asia and elsewhere). On agricultural research and development, three findings are especially worth emphasizing: (1) that in general the returns to R&D in agriculture in developing countries appear very high; (2) that the "output" of R&D has not been particularly appropriate, in terms of resource and factor use or crop composition – indeed, many would go further and argue that while it has been productivity raising, it has also definitely been inappropriate in some cases, permitting, or even causing, rising underemployment and poverty to accompany the rising output (e.g., see Pearse and Griffin). In principle, these distributional concerns should be explicitly introduced into the "rate of return" estimates; and (3) that international research has been complementary to – and not a substitute for – domestic efforts. Taking the first and third of these findings together, Evenson forcibly argues that support for R&D is a particularly good use for international funds. However, one should also take into account the question of appropriateness of the new technologies and the contribution of the R&D to the elimination of poverty.

My major comments on Evenson's paper are two-fold. First, a disagreement with his view that the income distribution effects of technology may be ignored. Secondly, I believe that to understand technology choice, transfer, and change, we have to go beyond the empirical relationships to an attempt to arrive at a comprehensive understanding of what lies behind them. Presenting a more comprehensive view of the elements involved also helps identify an agenda for research in this area.

In the introduction to his paper, Evenson states that "The literature is further clouded by treatises arguing distributional matters and class conflict," with the implication that the distributional implications of technology may be ignored. The rest of the paper ignores distributional considerations. Taking a "neutral" view of distributional issues permits Evenson to avoid analysis of important questions about the determinants of distributional effects, and to state that the outcome of technical change following agricultural R&D has often been inappropriate, without analyzing *why* this has been so.

In my view, technical change generally does have distributional con
sequences, often important ones, as well as raising output and pro
ductivity. Clearly, for example, in agriculture, the crop composition o
R&D affects both regional and household income distribution. Th
relative neglect of R&D in Africa has affected intercontinental incom
distribution. Whether industrial R&D produces labor-intensive o
capital-intensive, small-scale or large-scale technologies, will influenc
the distribution of income as between labor and capital, and amon
wage earners, as between wage earners and the self-employed, and th
employed and the un- and underemployed. Moreover, the type of *pro
ducts* produced by R&D – e.g. whether they consist in improve
housing materials of cooking stoves for the low-income, or mor
sophisticated cars or air-conditioners for the high-income – affects th
distribution of welfare. While, obviously, other factors are also im
portant – and the same technology may have different effects o
income distribution according to the circumstances (as for example
hand-threshers, which have improved incomes among the low-incom
farmers in Thailand and worsened the situation of the landless in th
Philippines (Duff, 1986) – the design of technology is an importan
influence on income distribution. This emerges also from an analysis o
the major macro-theories of income distribution, ranging from th
neoclassical to the Marxist.

My second main comment is that Evenson takes too narrowl
empirical a view of the technology issue. In part this stems from hi
review of theory. He provides a useful review and critique of som
approaches – notably of the Innovation Possibility Frontier, whic
proved abortive because its shape, which is critical to the outcome a
Evenson shows, is completely unknown. His findings on theory ar
summarized in the statement that "unfortunately our renewed interest i
growth and efficiency is not aided much by the theorists in our profession." In his own work, and in this paper, Evenson has therefore focuse
on identifying empirical relationships, doing some pioneering work i
this difficult field, where problems of data are notoriously tricky.

As we all know regression techniques can tell us about empirica
associations. They do not tell us *why* these associations occur. Withou
supporting theoretical insights, the results may appear random – no
necessarily to be repeated in new circumstances. Evenson concludes
for example: "National research investments are highly productive
except in Africa for cereal grains…and Latin America for staples" and
he comes to a similar conclusion for national investment in extension
What we need to know is the reason for the failures – failures both with
respect to distribution and appropriate technology in Asia and with
respect to productivity in Africa and Latin America – because it is here
that new policies are urgently needed, if the problems of rural poverty
are to be tackled. The econometrics reviewed by Evenson provide a
useful starting point, suggesting where we need to look. But they are not

sufficient to understand the relationships involved. Now that some basic empirical relationships have been established, there is a need to try and unravel the black boxes represented by the empirical work. For this a more comprehensive approach is needed which brings us back to the methodological issues and how to understand technology choice and change in developing countries.

Many of the elements involved are sketched in Evenson's paper. Here I shall say a bit more about them, not to be comprehensive (which would be impossible), but to shed some light on methodological approaches and on future directions for research.

My starting point is fundamental disagreement with one sentence in Evenson's paper (a sentence which is not in fact really followed up in the remainder of the paper). Evenson states, "In this essay I shall argue that the treatment of technology as a commodity that is designed and produced (invented) and exchanged in a market-like fashion can contribute to a better understanding of technology in development." In my view, to treat technology as an ordinary market commodity leads to fundamental *misunderstanding* of its role. This is for two reasons. First, because whether one is buying technology or developing it, one does not know what one is getting, until one has acquired it. Consequently, it cannot be treated like a normal commodity whose costs and benefits are known before the purchase (or investment) is undertaken. Secondly, because of the public-good characteristics of most technology, once developed, its costs of transmission are relatively low. Because of this, markets have to be artificially created (by patents, oligopoly, secrecy, etc.) if they are to work at all in this area. If markets are created in this way there is no competitive "right" price but a price arbitrarily determined by legal fiat or bargaining. The essential ignorance of buyers about what they are buying means that unequal bargaining power and, in some sense, "unfair" prices are very common. The fact that technology is *not* an ordinary commodity like tables and chairs is of enormous importance to institutions, incentives, and resource use. It explains the prevalence of public R&D; the need to "create" a market if private institutions are to play a significant role; while in some cases, private production and sale of technology may be efficient from the perspective of securing rapid technological change, the resource allocation involved cannot be justified by normal static welfare economics; and where private rents or monopolies are permitted to create incentives to innovate, continuous care is needed so these are not abused. It is this aspect of technology that explains and may justify the prevalent view among many developing countries that they are being exploited in the North–South sale of technology and that they need to create new institutions to offset this. Government intervention – either directly in the form of R&D institutions, or indirectly in the form of patents, utilities, etc. – becomes essential to regulate the technology market. It is worth noting that with the rapid development of the communications industry, which also does not generate tables and chairs-type commodities, the role of "ordinary" commodities and the relevance of that part of economics (viz. the bulk of welfare economics) designed for such commodities is becoming significantly smaller.

Public institutions to undertake R&D are therefore important, especially in industries in developing countries where foreign technology is largely inapplicable and where small units of production dominate. This situation prevails in much of agriculture, and public institutions have been developed. It also applies to much small-scale industry, but here there remains a major institutional lacuna, as Evenson notes. A fundamental aspect of understanding R&D and technology change is understanding the workings of public R&D institutions. This is necessary if we are to make these institutions more effective and more relevant to their major clients (especially small farmers, in the case of agriculture). To understand these institutions better, the following elements need to be incorporated:

1   The motivation of those determining the allocation of resources within them. This would extend to the influences of political economy, viz. the influence of various interest groups domestically and abroad (for example, see Rudra, 1986, who explains the choice of technology in India in the Green Revolution very largely with reference to the power and interests of a symbiosis of local large farmers, tractor and fertilizer manufacturers, and foreign technology suppliers and aid donors); bureaucratic motivations (James, 1986); the objectives and influence of scientists and technologists (see Biggs 1981, 1984).

2   The impact of the environment. This includes factor prices (as in Binswanger and Ruttan's theory of induced innovation, 1978); land distribution (see Biggs and Clay, 1983); the competitive environment and institutional arrangements (see Ranis and Saxonhouse, 1986).

3   The operations and procedures of the institutions. While it is now widely accepted that technology has to be adapted when transferred from a different environment, there has been much less attention to the need for institutional adaptation. Biggs has argued that *transferring* institutions from developed countries, as against *evolving* them in local conditions has been responsible for many failures of R&D institutions to respond to the needs of small farmers.

Incorporating these considerations into the analysis of public R&D institutions explains the tendency noted by Evenson for new technologies to be inappropriate. These aspects, plus essential organizational features, such as the scale and resources of institutions, and the skills and experience of their researchers, are also essential to help explain the failures observed, such as those that abound in sub-Saharan Africa.

A similar typology would be relevant to understanding private sector R&D, although here, market forces have more direct influence on decisions. However, detailed empirical work on private sector technology change (see Dahlman and Westphal, 1982; Maxwell, 1986; Lall, 1986; Katz, 1980; Pack, 1986) has shown a similar complexity of influences, with the outcome depending on interaction between motivations, institutions, human capacity, and the environment.

As a research agenda, further unraveling the "black-box" of R&D institutions both in the public and the private sector should be high on the agenda. This would require a comprehensive view of institutions, motivations, and selection mechanisms. A similar need for a comprehensive approach encompassing these variables applies to many areas of interest in developing countries. What this suggests is not that a pure market approach is necessarily incorrect, but that *it is necessarily incomplete*: in many environments its application, without other complementary action, may lead to no improvement or even a worsening in meeting objectives.

Lack of symmetry in the characteristics of developed and developing countries is a pervasive feature. This leads to discontinuities and inequalities, which in turn may lead to imbalances. In a general way, discontinuities are a major reason for limited applicability of conventional economics. In technology, the fundamental asymmetry arises from the heavy *dependence* of developing countries on technology generated in the developed countries. This remains a most fundamental dimension of technology for most Third World countries, although it seems to have become less fashionable to talk about it. As is well known, R&D continues to be dominated by work in the developed countries, especially in industry, as is powerfully shown by Evenson's figures on research intensity (table 16.1) and patents (table 16.2). The industrialized countries account for 67 percent of the world's invention patents, and 92 percent of industrial design patents. Only 20 percent of patents issued in semi-industrialized countries and 6 percent issued in developing countries are issued to nationals. This continued domination means that the broad directions of change are determined in the developed countries. This leads to marked discontinuities in productivity between traditional techniques and advanced technologies coming from the developed countries. There is an automatic tendency for traditional and small-scale technologies to fall behind modern technologies over time, which means that they will tend to be displaced unless special efforts are made to improve their productivity. This is especially true of product characteristics (research into new products forms a much smaller proportion of total industrial research in developing countries). This discontinuity in technology is one important feature of being a late-comer. It can be viewed as an advantage – since it offers developing countries the opportunity of big leaps in productivity – but it may also present severe problems of factor-use, distribution and employment (see Stewart in Passinetti (ed.), 1986). In the past, the situation has been rather different in agriculture, and the issue of transfer has related more to institutions than to agricultural technology. But this may be changed by the advent of biotechnology, which promises to be enormously productivity-raising, but also highly capital-intensive, technology-intensive, and large-scale (see Buttel et al., 1985). If this is so, it will raise again the conflict between output, employment, and distribution and highlight the issue of technological dependency.

The continued technological dependence also means that the balance of trade in technology is likely to remain very much in favor of the developed countries, and the terms of trade in technology are likely to be a continuing source of dispute (see Krugman, 1979).

While dependence remains a basic fact of technological life, it is now acknowledged that *local technological capability* is essential to make imported technology work efficiently, adapt it to the local environment, etc. What is needed, as Evenson concludes, is the right mixture of imported technology and local efforts. While I fully agree with Evenson's conclusions, there is a need for research to identify the best policy environment to build up local capability and the best institutional mechanisms for achieving an effective symbiosis between imported and local technological development.

The rapid evolution of technology promises to change dynamic comparative advantage. Some industries which had been "labor-intensive" may become relatively capital- or skill-intensive (e.g. parts of the textiles industry). While some of the new technologies requiring skills and attitudes may be more prevalent in the NICs than in the older industrialized countries, they may create renewed advantages for these economies, but diminished opportunities for the least developed countries. The evolution of dynamic comparative advantage, and the product cycle is a high priority area for research.

To summarize, I disagree little with much of the paper, but I feel it is essential to locate the observations in a wider context of:

Motivations of decision-makers;
Technology institutions and their operations;
The wider environment, including markets, prices, asset distribution political economy;
The technology market, nationally and internationally; and
Technological dependence

if we are to understand how our fundamental objectives may best be served.

REFERENCES

Biggs, S. and Clay E. 1983: "Generation and Diffusion of Agricultural Technology: A Review of Theories and Experiences." *World Employment Programme*, 2–22, Working Paper 122, International Labor Organization.

Biggs, S. 1981: "Institutions and Decision Making in Agricultural Research." In F. Stewart and J. James (eds), *The Economics of New Technology in Developing Countries*, London: Frances Pinter.

Biggs, S. 1984: "Awkward but Common Themes in Agricultural Policy." In E. Clay and B. Schaffer (eds), *Room for Manoeuvre: An Exploration of Public Policy in Agriculture and Rural Development*, London: Heinemann.

Binswanger, H. P. and Ruttan, V. W. 1979: *Induced Innovation: Technology Institutions and Development.* Baltimore: John Hopkins.

Buttel, F. H., Kenney, M., and Kloppenburg Jr., J. 1985: "From Green Revolution to Biorevolution: Some Observations on the Changing Technological Bases of Economic Transformation in the Third World." *Economic Development and Cultural Change*, 34(1).

Dahlman, C. and Westphal, L. E. 1982: "Technological Effort in Industrial Development: An Interpretative Survey of Recent Research." In F. Stewart and J. James (eds), *The Economics of New Technology in Developing Countries*, London: Frances Pinter.

Duff, B. 1986: "Changes in Small Farm Paddy Threshing Technology in Thailand and Philippines." In F. Stewart (ed.), *Macro-Policies for Appropriate Technology.* Boulder, Colorado: Westview Press.

Griffin, K. 1974: *The Political Economy of Agrarian Change.* London: Macmillan.

James, J. 1986: "Beaucratic, Engineering and Economic Men: Decision Making for Technology in Tanzania's State and World Enterprises." In S. Lall and F. Stewart (eds), *Theory and Reality in Development*, London: Macmillan.

Katz, J. M. 1980: "Domestic Technology Generation in LDCs: A Review of Research Findings." IDB/ECLA Working Paper 35, Buenos Aires: CEPAL.

Krugman, P. 1979: "A Model of Innovation, Technology Transfer, and the World Distribution of Income." *Journal of Political Economy*, 87.

Lall, S. 1986: *Learning to Industrialize: the Acquisition of Technological Capability in India.* London: Macmillan.

Maxwell, P. 1986: "Technical Change and Appropriate Technology: A Review of some Latin American Studies." In F. Stewart (ed.), *Macro-Policies for Appropriate Technology.* Boulder, Colorado: Westview Press.

Pack, H. 1986: *Productivity, Technology and Industrial Development.* Oxford University Press.

Pearse, A. 1980: *Seeds of Plenty, Seeds of Want: Social and Economic Implications of the Green Revolution.* Oxford University Press.

Ranis, G. and Saxonhouse G. 1985: "Technology Choice and the Quality Dimension in the Japanese Cotton Textile Industry". In K. Ohkawa and G. Ranis (eds), *Japan and the Developing Countries: A Comparative Analysis.* Oxford: Basil Blackwell.

Rudra, A. 1986: "Technology Choice in Agriculture over the Past Three Decades." In F. Stewart (ed.) *Macro-Policies for Appropriate Technology.* Boulder, Colorado: Westview Press.

Stewart, F. 1986: "Technology change in the North: Some Implications for the South." In L. Passinetti (ed.) Proceedings of the 7th World Congress of Economists, London: Macmillan.

17

International Trade and Factor Movements in Development Theory, Policy, and Experience

T. N. SRINIVASAN

The role of international trade and factor movements in the process of economic development of less developed countries has continued to attract the attention of economic theorists, policy-makers, and chroniclers of economic development. While it is too much to expect a consensus view of this role to emerge based on the confrontation of alternative theories with the development experience of many countries since World War II, it is fair to say that first, the divergence of views has narrowed, and second, the proponents of alternative views are able to support them by drawing upon (albeit selectively) an impressive accumulation of analytical and empirical studies.

The 25 years since the birth of the Economic Growth Center at Yale have witnessed a sea-change in the world economic system: the nations of the world have become, to use a hackneyed phrase, more *inter-dependent* – both in the sense that a larger proportion of world output is traded in world markets, and in the sense that world capital markets have become integrated to a considerable extent. And the system has absorbed significant shocks – the collapse of the Bretton Woods system of fixed exchange rates, the two massive oil-price increases in 1973 and 1979, and the related phenomena of recessions in industrialized countries and the unprecedented increase in real interest rates. Whether the recent fall in oil prices and interest rates will sustain the ongoing recovery and help the oil importers, or whether it will end it through its effect on some oil-exporting countries (mainly the heavily indebted ones) and the capital exporters, is too soon to tell. Be that as it may, the experiences of countries that have followed development strategies which differed in their orientation towards foreign trade in adjusting to

I thank Bela Balassa, Willem Buiter, Michael Jones, Kenneth Kletzer, Pradeep Mitra, and Gustav Ranis for their valuable comments on an earlier draft.

an external economic environment that was subjected to shocks provided an unusual opportunity for assessing the strengths and weaknesses
of the strategies pursued.

The period since World War II also witnessed several rounds of
multilateral negotiations and agreements for reducing the tariff and
non-tariff barriers to international trade. A number of innovations in
reducing the political and other risks involved in foreign investment
have also taken place. Also a set of proposals for a New International
Economic Order was put forward by the developing countries in the
second half of the 1970s. The so-called North–South negotiations
between the developed (North) and developing (South) countries on
these proposals have been held off and on since then. While a few of
these proposals were accepted by the North in some diluted form, they
have all been the subject of a number of studies, which by and large
conclude that most of them were unlikely to benefit all developing
countries, if they benefit any at all. For all intents and purposes, these
proposals are dead, but perhaps not quite buried yet.

Besides the shocks and shifts in the global economic system of the
last 25 years, there have also been significant additions to the analytical
tool kit of economists in general and development economists in particular. Some of the analytical problems that were once thought to be
peculiar to development economics have now become part of the mainstream. Equally, advances in economic theory, in particular the attempts
to provide a more satisfactory theory of expectation formations and
(microeconomic) foundations for macroeconomics, the development of
models incorporating features of industrial organization theory in analyzing problems of international trade, and analysis of the implications
of viewing nonmarket institutions and processes as serving the functions
of nonexistent or imperfectly functioning markets in a context of asymmetric information, moral hazard, adverse selection, etc., have all influenced development theorizing. There has been an enormous increase in
the quantity (if not to the same extent in the quality) of economic data
on developing countries. At the same time, a vast array of new econometric tools and the computational capacity to use them have become
available, enabling analysts to use simulation with empirical models as a
technique for understanding the implications of complex policy scenarios and shocks to the system, a task that is not easy to accomplish only
with a priori theorizing even of the most sophisticated kind.

The developments in the world economy, in theorizing about them,
in empirically modeling the functioning of the economic system and
simulating the effects of counterfactual policy variants and other shocks
to the system have been substantial. It is impossible to discuss all of
them in a coherent manner in one paper, even if one were indeed
equipped to do so. A more modest approach is taken here of reviewing
a *few* theoretical advances and empirical studies relating to international
trade and factor movements. More specifically, the first section is

devoted to the continuing debate on outward versus inward orientation in development strategy and the light thrown on it by recent empirical studies. The following section focuses on some theoretical constructs, such as the so-called North–South models, rent- and revenue-seeking models, etc. and relates them to the empirical studies of the former section. The next discussion is concerned with international factor movements in theory and in the world economy. The final section concludes the paper.

THE FOREIGN SECTOR IN DEVELOPMENT STRATEGY

Early perceptions and subsequent experience

It is useful to begin with some facts at the aggregate level. Contrary to the widespread belief in the immediate post-World War II years that the prospects were dim for substantial growth in world trade and per capita income of the poor countries, the realized growth was remarkable, although it is too soon to assess whether the growth path of the pre-first-oil-shock period has been restored since 1984. The available data are in tables 17.1 and 17.2. The realized average growth rate of per capita income over the period 1950–83 at about 3 percent per annum

TABLE 17.1   *Growth of world merchandise trade and production*

	Annual percentage rate of change		
	1963–73	*1973–83*	*1984*
Volume of exports			
All merchandise	9.0	3.0	9.0
Agricultural products	4.0	3.0	7.0
Minerals	7.5	−2.0	3.0
Manufacturing	11.5	4.5	12.0
Volume of production			
All merchandise	6.0	2.0	5.5
Agriculture	2.5	2.0	5.0
Minerals	5.5	0.5	2.0
Manufacturing	7.5	2.5	7.5
Share of developing countries	*1963*	*1973*	*1984*
In world exports	20.5	19.0	24.5
In world imports	21.0	18.0	23.5

Source: GATT, 1985, tables 1 and 2, pp. 4–6.

TABLE 17.2 *Growth of per capita real GNP*

	1955–70	1965–73	1973–80	1981	1982	1983	1984[a]	1985[b]
All developing countries								
Low-income	3.1	4.1	3.2	1.0	−0.7	−0.0	3.3	2.4
Middle-income	1.6	3.0	2.7	3.0	3.2	6.1	7.4	6.1
Major exporters of manufactures	3.9	4.6	3.1	−0.8	−2.0	−1.6	1.8	1.0
Other oil importers	3.2							
Oil exporters	3.4	4.6	3.4	1.5	−2.8	−4.4	0.7	0.0
High-income oil exporters	5.8	4.1	5.9	−0.7	−7.6	−15.7	−3.0	−8.5
Industrial market economies	3.6	3.7	2.1	−1.1	−1.3	1.6	3.9	2.4

[a] Estimated.
[b] Projected (on the basis of GDP).
Source: The World Bank (1982, table 3.1; 1986, table A.2).

exceeds by one-third the growth rate achieved by most of today's industrialized countries over a century ending in 1960. Equally, if not more impressive, is the fact that the volume of world trade as a whole grew faster than world GDP. Even the volume of trade in primary products (agricultural and mineral) seems to have grown faster than the growth in their output. Needless to say, this aggregate picture masks substantial variations among countries, in part explainable by their policies. Nevertheless, the pessimistic perspective on the elasticity of trade with respect to output and income that colored early development theorizing and policy-making has been clearly belied by history.

This pessimism led to the identification of a shortage of foreign exchange as one of the *key* (if not the sole) constraints on economic development. Cairncross (1960) put the dominant view succinctly:

> The majority of the underdeveloped countries are monocultures, dependent for their earnings of foreign exchange on a single commodity (or at most two or three). These earnings are *highly inelastic* except when exports of the principal commodity form a small fraction of the world's consumption. At the same time, nearly all the plant and machinery that they require has to be imported, so that the scale of *industrial development* is limited by the foreign exchange available to pay for it. (my italics).

It is indeed ironic that this view of a single primary commodity export with (income) inelastic foreign demand constraining the imports of capital goods needed (often in fixed proportion to output) for industrial development continues to underpin some of the recent structuralist North–South models (to be discussed in the next section), thus suggesting that some form of theorizing is unlikely to be influenced by inconvenient facts.

Evolution of analytical models: two gaps to applied general equilibrium

The early development models (Chenery and Bruno, 1962; Chenery and Strout, 1966) encapsulated a rigid foreign exchange gap (in addition to a domestic savings gap) that can prove to be a binding constraint on development, given the assumed exogeneity of export earnings. When it was binding, which implied that there was a realizable but unrealized pool of domestic savings, foreign aid became twice blessed – once for relieving the constraint on imports of capital goods, and once again by realizing the potential domestic savings and converting it (together with aid-financed equipment imports) into productive capacity in the form of plant and equipment. In time the two-gap models begat a generation of multisector development planning models. The analytics of these models were summarized in Blitzer et al. (1975). I discussed their treatment of foreign trade in chapter 6 of that volume. Some limited input substitution in production was included in these models in the form of alternative activities that used inputs in different but fixed proportions. Even more limited commodity substitution in demand was allowed in an ad hoc way. The choice among alternative production and consumption activities was the consequence of the optimization of the specified objective functions of these models. Put in another way, their choice was not necessarily the result of the response, given their objectives, of producers, consumers, and traders to the relevant *prices* and *constraints* in fact faced by them. Rather it was as if these agents faced the "shadow prices" associated with the "optimum" solution to the model and their actual decision environment was adequately described in the model. Implicit in this was also the belief, though not necessarily shared by all modelers, that the planner (i.e. the state) had enough fiscal and other instruments in his arsenal to assure that the "shadow prices" were in fact the actual prices faced by consumers and producers. Thus, a purposive planner, imbued with the long-term interests of the society, having at hand an appropriately formulated model of the economy, was supposed to use the model as a tool to analyze the implications, alternative strategies, and policies and arrive at the most suitable (if not the *optimal*) strategy, together with a description of taxes, subsidies, etc., needed to implement the strategy. It must be added, however, that the more perceptive among planners did not share this view of the modeling exercise and instead viewed the models only as computationally convenient but necessarily rough approximations, although far more useful than other methods to check the internal consistency of alternative plan proposals. They rightly believed that the planning models cannot eliminate the role of judgment in making hard *political* and *socioeconomic* choices. Forgetting this important fact can lead to unfortunate consequences. For example, Rosen (1985) provides a fascinating account of the entanglement in Indian politics of a (in many ways) pioneering, planning model put together in the 1960s by Indian and foreign economists working for the Center for International Studies at the Massachusetts Institute of Technology (MIT).

As the many limitations of economy-wide planning models – and in particular, their underplaying the role of prices and markets and exaggerating that of the state in steering the economy along an efficient development path – were becoming increasingly transparent, the capacity to build an empirical analogue of a price-endogenous Walrasian General Equilibrium Model and algorithms to compute its equilibrium became available in the mid-seventies. This new tool of applied general equilibrium analysis was quickly put to use for analyzing domestic fiscal policies in a number of countries (see Shoven and Whalley, 1984, for a survey). Their multicountry variants have been used to analyze foreign trade policies, particularly unilateral and multilateral trade liberalization. Such models have been put together for several developing countries, largely under the sponsorship of the World Bank but also at the International Institute for Applied Systems Analysis in Austria, starting from the pioneering effort of Adelman and Robinson (1978) for Korea.[1] The attractions of such a model are obvious enough: not only the allocative efficiency implications of policies that distort the equilibrium set of market prices can be analyzed, but through their effect on equilibrium returns to primary factors, the income distributional implications can be drawn as well. Provided one is willing to specify the processes of formation of price expectations, accumulation of primary factors and of technical change, a sequence (in time) of equilibria can be computed as well. The elements of such a sequence are not, of course, components of an intertemporal competitive equilibrium but simply of Hicksian *temporary* equilibria. Thus, static as well as dynamic efficiency and equity implications of alternative development strategies could be analyzed, or so it was hoped. Clive Bell and I (Bell and Srinivasan, 1984) have critically examined the strengths and weaknesses of such models for understanding the development processes. It suffices here to say that these models have been far more useful in examining issues of allocation and efficiency than as tools for analyzing *processes*.

The evolution of another useful tool, namely, social benefit-cost analysis, for analyzing choice at the sectoral and project level rather than at the economy-wide level needs to be briefly noted. Although benefit-cost analysis as a tool for making public investment choice is not a new development, its refinement to incorporate a wide spectrum of social objectives (including, in particular, those relating to the distribution of income along socioeconomic groups at a point in time and over time) and the derivation of procedures for the evaluation of *individual projects* from an explicit or implicit *economy-wide model* indeed is. Such derivation can be linked to the evolution of economy-wide models. Simply stated, the problem of project evaluation is to arrive at a set of social or shadow prices to inputs and outputs of a project during its lifetime so that the net present value of the project at these prices indicates its social welfare impact. Analogous to the use of simple models, such as the two-gap model, initially there were attempts to derive shadow pricing formulas for a few key factors such as unskilled labor, capital, and foreign exchange. As the simple one- and two-sector models evolved into their multisector, multiperiod programming variants, the shadow prices for inputs and outputs associated with the optimum solution to the economy-wide programming problem suggested themselves as the relevant ones for use in project evaluation. Unfortunately, apart from the conceptual problem – that each ad hoc constraint introduced to approximate some aspect of reality in a programming model acquired a shadow price that was not easily interpretable and usable in a project evaluation context – it turned out that the shadow price vector was not very robust, even to minor changes in the specification of the model. By viewing a project as a small perturbation of an initial equilibrium, one could in principle derive project evaluation criteria from the applied general equilibrium models as well. The same robustness problem with respect to model specification arises in this case also.

Workable procedures of evaluation have to be robust, theoretically sound, and simple in computation. The two basic project evaluation guidebooks that emerged from a search for workable procedures, namely, the OECD manual authored by Little and Mirrlees (1974) and the UNIDO Guidelines authored by Dasgupta et al. (1972) both fulfill the above criteria. A central result of these authors is that for a small open economy (i.e. an economy that cannot influence the relative prices of internationally traded goods) shadow prices for traded goods are their "border" prices (i.e., f.o.b. prices for exports and c.i.f. prices for imports). The shadow prices for non-traded goods and primary factors can often be derived from traded goods prices. These results are fairly robust (as long as the economy is a price-taker in world markets and distortions are not due to quantitative interventions, such as import quotas etc.) and can be rigorously derived from a general equilibrium model of the economy (Srinivasan, 1982), thus making the procedure theoretically sound. Since border prices for traded goods are easily available and the procedure for deriving other prices usually requires no more than an input-output table, the procedure is easily implemented.

Outward- and inward-oriented development strategies

The early pessimism with respect to foreign demand for exports was in part based on the dismal experience with foreign trade during the interwar period in general and the depression period in particular. This pessimism, apart from its impact on analytical modeling of development discussed above, was a major cause that led many developing countries to adopt an "inward-oriented" strategy of development, in spite of the potential static and dynamic gains of an "outward-oriented" strategy. To avoid the all too frequent misidentification of outward-orientation either with active export promotion or with *laissez-faire*, let me define an outward-oriented strategy as one that has no significant bias, first towards autarkic development, and second, toward either export promotion (more generally, *earning* of foreign exchange) or import substitution (*saving* of foreign exchange). Besides adopting a development strategy that was biased toward import substitution (*beyond* what would occur if dictates of comparative advantages were followed), many countries implemented it mainly through a regime of *quantitative* restrictions on imports and exports of goods and services, domestic and foreign investment, import of technology, etc., although tariffs and price interventions were not altogether absent. By the mid-1960s the failure of this strategy was becoming clear. Although few countries abandoned it altogether, several experimented with liberalizing their foreign trade and payments regimes.

These liberalization episodes – as well as the claims of rapid industrialization, enhanced investment rates, greater employment creation and faster technical progress, etc., made in favor of the inward-oriented strategy – were examined in a number of theoretical and empirical studies in the late seventies (Balassa, 1982; Little et al., 1970; Bhagwati, 1978; Bhagwati and Srinivasan, 1979; Krueger, 1978 and 1983). Very few, if any, of the claims made for inward orientation were supported by the experience of the countries studied. The strong conclusion emerging from these studies is simply that trade liberalization is beneficial and the performance of countries that either switched to, or pursued from early on, a version of the outward-oriented strategy far outstripped that of others. Bhagwati (1986) persuasively argues that the attribution of success of the outward-oriented strategy for eastern countries Singapore, Taiwan, and South Korea to their authoritarian regimes is simply an assertion without any convincing evidence to support it.

An apparently unfavorable assessment of outward orientation emerges from studies of trade liberalization, using the newer tool of applied general equilibrium modeling. Whalley (1984) and Srinivasan and Whalley (1986) report on several of these studies. Since the results of most are similar let me draw on Whalley (1984) for illustration. His model distinguishes seven regions: the United States, European Economic Community (EEC), Japan, other developed countries (ODCs), Organization of Petroleum Exporting Countries (OPEC), newly industrializing countries (NICs), and other less developed countries (LDCs). Six aggregate products are produced in each region, with five of them being internationally traded. He makes four counterfactual simulations or scenarios. In the first, only the North (USA, EEC, Japan and ODC), in the second only the South (OPEC, NIC and LDC), and in the third, all seven regions abolish tariff and non-tariff barriers. In the fourth scenario, the last three regions grow faster in the post-1978 period than the first four, as they did in the pre-1978 period. The welfare impact of liberalization is assessed by Hicksian Equivalent Variation of income. The results are shown in table 17.3.

The global gains to trade liberalization are extremely modest, varying from 0.28 percent of 1977 GNP in scenarios 1 and 2, to 0.36 percent in scenario 3, when the whole world achieves the Nirvana of free trade. The NIC-LDC group lose almost 5 percent of their GDP by unilaterally liberalizing, and about 4 percent when the rest of the world joins them in liberalizing. Further, as in scenario 4, if the LDCs and the South generally continued to grow faster and attempt to catch up with the North, their terms of trade deteriorate. Should we conclude from this that outward orientation makes only a marginal difference to world welfare but definitely harms the LDCs and NICs?

TABLE 17.3a   *Annual welfare impact of trade liberalization scenario*
(1977, $ billion)

Region	GNP (1977)	Scenario		
		1	2	3
EEC	1,629	−3.1	37.2	33.1
USA	1,897	−0.1	12.1	10.1
Japan	737	−0.8	21.0	21.2
ODC	2,024	3.4	4.5	5.6
OPEC	303	1.7	7.0	4.4
NICs	461	9.2	−31.6	−24.3
LDCs	773	11.8	−28.2	−23.0
World	7,824	22.1	22.0	27.8

TABLE 17.3b   *Terms of trade impact of differential growth*

Region	Annual growth rate (percent)	Terms of trade change (percent) relative to base case		
		After 5 years	After 10 years	After 20 years
EEC	3.3	3.4	6.8	13.9
USA	2.8	3.4	6.9	14.0
Japan	4.8	−3.4	−6.7	−13.1
ODC	4.1	−2.8	−5.7	−11.1
OPEC	3.5	0.9	1.8	3.5
NICs	5.2	−4.6	−8.9	−17.2
LDCs	4.5	−3.1	−6.1	−12.1

Source: Whalley (1984, tables 4 and 5).

I have argued elsewhere (Srinivasan, 1986) that such a conclusion would be wrong for several reasons that have to do with both the *competitive* general equilibrium features of the models, particularly their inadequacy in capturing the necessarily forward-looking and dynamic processes of factor accumulation and technical change, and their manipulation of data (as well as the specification of crucial elasticity parameters) to make them an internally consistent *equilibrium* set. For the present purposes, I wish to emphasize two features that are likely to understate the gains from outward orientation in developing countries. The first relates to the fact that the models assume away rent-seeking activities triggered by the policy instruments used in implementing an inward-oriented strategy. Such rent-seeking diverts resources away from producing goods and services demanded by final consumers, a diversion that will by definition disappear with liberalization. The second is the assumption that production takes place under constant returns to scale technologies and competitive market structures. Yet the policies used to sustain inward orientation (particularly those relating to the industrial sector, such as investment licensing, allocation of capital goods imports, etc.) restrict competition not only from imports but also among domestic producers. In fact, they create domestic oligopolies and even monopolies, besides establishing high-cost domestic capacity of non-optimal scale for the production of import substitutes. Again, gains from liberalization arising from the elimination of deadweight losses due to imperfect competition are not captured by the models. I will return to the analytics of rent-seeking and imperfect competition and international trade later in this paper. It is worth drawing attention at this stage to two studies that estimate the gains from liberalizing an economy in which rent-seeking or imperfect competition is prevalent. The first by Grais and Urata (1986) models the rent-seeking associated with import quotas in the Turkish economy. It finds that while the gain to the removal of tariffs only (while keeping the quotas intact) was negligible, the removal of quotas increased real GDP compared to its base or reference value by anywhere between 5 and 10 percent. The second, by Harris (1983) for Canada, models economies of scale and imperfect competition. He finds that Canada's participation in a multilateral reduction of all tariffs yields a welfare gain in excess of 5 percent of GNP.

Outward orientation and adjustment to external shocks

In the literature on the role of international trade and development, it is sometimes argued that outward orientation may expose a developing economy to disturbances that have their origins elsewhere in the trading world. In particular, a small open economy engaging in free trade (and capital movements) will be at the same time exposing itself to uncertain terms of trade (and interest rates). Of course if the small open economy faces a complete set of contingent commodity markets in the Arrow–Debreu sense, the argument in favor of the optimality of free trade is unaffected. But in the real world of incomplete markets, a general answer as to the (expected) welfare impact of trade restrictions cannot be given. However, to the extent that uncertainties can originate in the home economy as well as the rest of the world, opening the economy to foreign trade offers insurance against risks originating at home. For example, the ability to import from the rest of the world reduces the risk associated with crop failures at home, as long as such failures are not correlated with those abroad.

The problem of adjustment to shocks should be conceptually distinguished from the issue of whether or not to trade in a world in which the variables exogenous to the decisions of an economy (e.g. its terms of trade, if it is a small open economy) are uncertain but with a known objective or perceived probability distribution. One definition of an external *shock*, though not a universally accepted one, is that it is an *unanticipated*, temporary or permanent, change in (the joint probability distribution) of one (or more) variables exogenous to the economy. *Adjustment* to a shock then can be defined as changes in the time path of the endogenous variables, in particular, policy instruments, that are occasioned by the shock. Given some indicator of the "cost" of adjustment one could compare alternative policy responses to the shock. In principle, the development strategy pursued by a country will affect its adjustment process: conceivably one strategy as compared to another may *expand* the set of feasible policy responses to a given shock, and as such, will be better from the point of view of the adjustment, regardless of how the cost of adjustment is defined. Even if such a strong ranking of two strategies is not always possible, one can compare them given an indicator of adjustment costs.

One could view, as Neary (1985) does in his lucid analysis, the problem of adjustment as tracing out the consequences of an exogenous shock to an initial (steady state) equilibrium of an economy until a new equilibrium is reached. Loosely speaking, the process by which the economy reaches a new equilibrium once it is out of an initial equilibrium can be specified in alternative ways, depending on the flexibility with which resources move between sectors, the time horizon involved, and the policy instruments used to influence the process. Again as Neary argues, while conceptually such an analysis is appealing, the fact that in the real world the economy is likely to be bombarded by a sequence of shocks – each one coming before the adjustment to all the earlier ones have completely worked themselves out – makes analysis of the efficacy and welfare cost of particular policy interventions or of development strategies in the adjustment process particularly difficult.

A number of studies at the World Bank of Balassa (1982, 1985, 1986a, 1986b) and Mitra (1986a, 1986b) view the OPEC-induced increase in real oil prices of 1973 and 1979, as well as the increase in real interest costs of international borrowing in the early eighties, as shocks. They attempt to quantify these shocks as they affect different countries and compare their adjustment policies in terms of certain indicators. Balassa concludes from such a comparison that developing countries pursuing an outward-oriented development strategy were more successful in their adjustment. While this is in many ways a comforting conclusion, there are some problems with the approach used in arriving at it.

Balassa defines adjustment policies as responses to external (and internal) shocks that have as their objective regaining the pre-shock growth path of the national economy. Such a definition presumes that regaining the pre-shock growth path is not only feasible but also optimal in the sense of minimizing the costs (or maximizing the gains, in the case of favorable shocks) of adjustment. Although Balassa's definition of external shocks as "unanticipated changes in world economic conditions" is not too different from the definition given above, his methodology of quantifying the shocks involves the assumption of static expectations. Thus, any difference in a country's average terms of trade during the shock-adjustment period (1974–78 or 1979–83) compared to the average during the immediate pre-shock period (1971–73 and 1976–78, respectively) is viewed as the magnitude of a terms of trade shock. Similarly the difference between the average interest rates during 1976–78 and the average during 1979–83 is viewed as the *magnitude* of an interest rate shock. The magnitude of the shock to foreign demand for a country's export is identified as any deviation from its pre-shock share in the trend value of world exports. Of course, it is not easy to specify the anticipated or expected path (or more precisely the stochastic process) of the exogenous variables so that departures from it could be deemed a shock. But it seems somewhat extreme to postulate static expectations. Adjustment policies consisted of export promotion (increases in export market shares), increased borrowing (relative to past trends), import substitution (decreases in income elasticity of import demand compared to the period 1963–73) and deflation (reduction in income growth relative to the 1963–73 trend).

Mitra (1986a, 1986b) quantifies shocks (or more precisely the quantitative impact thereof) through an open economy macroeconomic model of each country studied. The model was estimated using annual data for 1963–81 and introducing a dummy variable in the slopes and intercepts of each of the four structural equations of the model to distinguish the shock and adjustment period 1974–81 (dummy taking the value 1) from the pre-shock period of 1963–73 (dummy taking the value zero). The predictions from the model for the period 1974–81 are compared with the predictions for the same period obtained by assuming that the coefficients of the slope and intercept dummies were zero, i.e., assuming that the pre-shock structure prevailed in the post-shock period and that there was no shock to the exogenous variables. The difference in the two predictions for each of the relevant macroeconomic variables is the impact of the shock. It is then decomposed through straightforward accounting into price and quantity changes.

The exogenous variables were: (1) the trend value of the export and trade-weighted average of GDP in the three most important trading partners of a country, (2) the index of the "price" of its exports relative to the price of manufactured exports of OECD countries (i.e. a deflator of nominal export earnings used to obtain its purchasing power), (3) the index of the "price" of its imports relative to the same numeraire, (4) real investment, (5) real net factor income from abroad. Absence of shock is assumed to imply that the first variable continued along its 1961-73 trend in the post-1973 period, the second and third stayed at their 1971-73 values, the share of real investment in real GNP stayed at its 1971-73 value, and real factor income in the post-shock period equaled its actual value. Thus Mitra's counterfactual is a combination of Balassa's static expectations and extrapolation of past trends, with respect to some variables, and perfect foresight, with respect to real factor incomes.

Mitra groups countries into five classes according to their modes of adjustment (italicized countries are semi-industrial and their adjustment to shocks is analyzed in Mitra, 1986b):

Group 1 – *Chile,* Costa Rica, *the Philippines, Singapore, South Korea* and *Taiwan* – adjusted principally through export expansion *and* public resource mobilization (i.e. policies affecting the response of public consumption and revenues to income).

Group 2 – *Argentina, Brazil,* Guatemala, Honduras, India, Kenya, Malawi, Mali, Thailand, *Turkey* and *Uruguay* – relied on either export expansion *or* public resource mobilization.

Group 3 – Jamaica, *Portugal* and *Yugoslavia* – adjusted through import substitution and negative public resource mobilization.

Group 4 – El Salvador, *Mexico,* Morocco, Pakistan and Spain – resorted to financing without domestic adjustment.

Group 5 – Benin, Bolivia, *Colombia.* Indonesia, the Ivory Coast, Malaysia, Niger, Nigeria and Tunisia – were lucky enough to have experienced favorable shocks.

The magnitude of the shocks and the adjustments as per the Balassa and Mitra methodologies are shown in tables 17.4 and 17.5. I very much agree with Balassa's a priori arguments that outward-oriented economies are better placed to adjust to external shock, even though the very fact that they are integrated to a greater extent with the rest of the world than the inward-oriented ones tends to magnify their external shocks. For instance, in the inward-oriented economies, the import control regimes usually would have succeeded in eliminating all imports other than those related to the operation and expansion of productive capacity (mostly industrial and infrastructural capacity), and in establishing high-cost, uneconomically sized plants producing domestic substitutes. It is also likely that their steps towards attenuating some of the deleterious effects of excessive import substitution through export promotion are also likely to involve direct subsidization of non-traditional exports while continuing to penalize their traditional exports. All this means that when any external shock hits the economy, very little of imports can be cut without jeopardizing growth, and further import

TABLE 17.4   External shocks and policy responses to those shocks for groups of developing economies

		Terms of trade effects	Export volume effects	External shock total	Interest rate effect	Together	Additional net external financing	Export promotion	Import substitution	Effects of lower GDP growth
		(as a percentage of GNP)					(as percentage of external shock)			
Outward-oriented NICs	1974–78	6.5	2.9	9.4	—	9.4	−50.1	54.0	71.7	24.4
	1979–83	8.9	6.1	15.0	1.8	16.8	−24.7	29.3	29.1	66.3
Outward-oriented LDCs	1974–78	5.9	1.2	7.0	—	7.0	57.0	29.8	11.5	1.7
	1979–83	7.0	1.4	8.4	1.3	9.7	53.3	27.5	1.6	17.6
Outward-oriented NICs and LDCs	1974–78	6.3	2.4	8.8	—	8.8	−26.5	48.7	58.5	19.4
	1979–83	8.4	4.9	13.3	1.7	15.0	−11.5	29.0	24.5	58.1
Inward-oriented NICs	1974–78	3.6	0.8	4.5	—	4.5	58.5	−13.6	41.2	13.9
	1979–83	2.1	0.4	2.5	2.0	4.6	5.1	22.8	15.4	56.7
Inward-oriented LDCs	1974–78	3.4	1.0	4.4	—	4.4	150.6	−17.6	−36.5	3.5
	1979–83	4.5	0.9	5.4	0.7	6.1	96.7	−9.0	−0.6	12.9
Inward-oriented NICs and LDCs	1974–78	3.6	0.9	4.5	—	4.5	89.0	−14.9	15.4	10.5
	1979–83	2.8	0.6	3.4	1.6	5.0	37.6	11.5	9.8	41.2

Source: Private communication from B. Balassa.

TABLE 17.5 Balance-of-payments effects of external shocks and modes of adjustment: 1974–78 and 1974–81 averages (percentage of local currency GNP)

	Group I		Group II		Group III		Group IV		Group V	
	1974–78	1974–81	1974–78	1974–81	1974–78	1974–81	1974–78	1974–81	1974–78	1974–81
External shocks										
1. International price effects										
a. Export price effect										
(i) Direct effect	−1.97	−2.87	−0.63	−0.45	−3.86	−3.24	−3.16	−2.31	−7.59	−9.26
(ii) Indirect effect	−2.38	−3.05	−0.37	−0.37	−2.87	−2.34	−1.75	−1.06	−2.93	−3.57
Difference (i − ii)	0.41	0.18	−0.27	−0.08	−0.99	−0.89	−1.41	−1.25	−4.66	−5.69
Import price effect										
(i) Direct effect	6.08	8.06	3.16	3.71	4.55	4.98	2.03	1.28	2.03	2.41
(ii) Indirect effect	4.81	5.80	1.44	1.72	3.20	3.47	1.03	0.53	0.90	1.24
Difference (i − ii)	1.27	2.25	1.72	2.00	1.34	1.51	1.00	0.75	1.13	1.17
Sum (1a + 1b)	1.68	2.43	1.45	1.91	0.35	0.61	−0.41	−0.50	−3.53	−4.52
2. Recession-induced effect										
a. Export volume effect	1.97	2.04	0.60	0.69	1.18	1.30	1.22	1.46	0.73	1.27
b. Import saving effect	1.27	1.28	0.30	0.39	0.84	0.91	0.65	0.81	0.08	0.33
Difference (2a − 2b)	0.70	0.76	0.30	0.30	0.34	0.39	0.57	0.66	0.65	0.93
3. Net interest rate effect										
a. Payments effect										
(i) Medium- and long-term	−0.11	0.68	−0.09	0.18	0.05	0.72	0.06	0.45	0.10	0.75
(ii) Short-term	−0.01	0.87	−0.01	0.16	0.00	0.40	−0.03	0.22	−0.01	0.15
Sum (i + ii)	0.10	1.54	−0.10	0.34	0.04	1.12	0.03	0.68	0.09	0.90

b. Receipts effect	0.28	0.00	0.06	0.00	−0.15	−0.10	0.09	−0.01	0.76	0.01
Difference (3a − 3b)	0.63	0.09	0.62	0.04	1.27	−0.14	−0.25	−0.09	0.78	0.10
4. Total shock (1 + 2 + 3)	−2.96	−2.79	0.77	0.20	2.27	0.83	2.47	1.66	3.98	2.48
Modes of adjustment										
1. Trade adjustment										
a. Export expansion										
(i) Direct effect	0.25	−0.02	0.02	0.63	−7.31	−7.60	1.66	0.75	17.05	12.79
(ii) Import-augmenting effect	−0.58	−0.91	−0.13	0.32	−5.23	−5.41	0.55	0.18	11.60	9.09
Difference (i − ii)	0.83	0.89	0.15	0.31	−2.08	−2.19	1.11	0.57	5.45	3.70
b. Import substitution										
(i) Direct effect	−5.04	−3.88	−3.28	−3.32	4.43	4.68	0.85	0.87	−4.20	0.97
(ii) Indirect effect	−0.36	−0.17	−1.28	−1.55	3.13	3.38	0.38	0.36	−2.59	1.45
Difference (i − ii)	−4.68	−3.71	−2.00	−1.77	1.30	1.31	0.48	0.50	−1.61	−0.48
Sum (1a + 1b)	−3.85	−2.82	−1.86	−1.46	−0.78	−0.88	1.59	1.07	3.84	3.22
2. Resource mobilization										
a. Private	1.27	0.98	0.65	0.72	−0.96	−1.53	−0.44	−0.61	0.54	1.08
b. Public										
(i) Public consumption restraint	0.16	0.25	−0.87	0.61	−4.04	−2.93	−0.88	−0.69	0.19	−0.09
(ii) Tax intensification	−1.14	−0.86	−0.24	−0.25	0.39	0.28	−0.12	−0.10	0.49	0.49
Sum (i + ii)	−0.98	−0.61	−1.11	−0.86	−3.64	−2.65	−1.00	−0.79	0.68	0.40
Sum (2a + 2b)	0.29	−1.37	−0.46	−0.14	−4.61	−4.18	−1.44	−1.39	1.22	1.48
3. Investment slowdown	−1.74	−1.31	−0.84	−1.60	2.78	2.48	−0.69	−0.46	−1.91	−1.13
4. Net additional external financing	2.34	0.97	3.39	3.39	4.88	3.41	3.01	2.45	0.83	−1.09
5. Total (1 + 2 + 3 + 4)	−2.96	−2.79	0.77	0.20	2.27	0.83	2.47	1.66	3.98	2.48

Source: Mitra (1986a, table 4.1).

substitution or export promotion (along the same lines as before the shock) can be achieved only at increasing costs. Thus, a priori, inward orientation can increase the *cost* of adjustment substantially.

It is not clear, however, whether the increased cost of inward orientation can be inferred from the a posteriori results of table 17.4. After all is said and done, these portray the effects on two sides of an accounting equation: on the one side, external shocks affect export earnings, import payments, and interest on foreign debt; on the other side, adjustment involves financing (without domestic adjustment), domestic adjustments that relate to export supplies, import demands, and those that relate to components of GDP. The fact that components relating to adjustment differed between countries does not in and of itself indicate whether all modes of adjustment were feasible for all countries, and even more important, whether a particular mode was more or less costly in some well-defined sense than the other.

Balassa was careful to define his indicator of success of adjustment as GDP growth rate, and as such he relates the adjustment path as revealed by the magnitude of different components in table 17.4 to growth performance. Yet, without a well-specified model of the relationship between the set of feasible paths of adjustment and the development strategy adopted by a country, it is hard to assess his argument that in response to the initial shock of 1973, the outward-oriented economies did not increase their external debt but relied on output-increasing policies of export promotion and import substitution after initially deflating their economies. Table 17.4 reveals that the *dominant* response of outward-oriented LDCs in fact was external financing, and import substitution played a minor role. In the case of outward-oriented NICs, deflation was the dominant mode of adjustment in the period 1979–83. Even when the outward-oriented NICs and LDCs are put together, the dominant response in 1979–83 is not *output-raising* policies but the *output-reducing* policies of lower GDP growth.

The analysis of Mitra, based as it is on a macroeconomic structural model, incorporates behavioral responses to the evolution of exogenous variables (with the break in the structure after 1973) as well as to shocks in their evolution. The structural system is driven only by gross national income (corrected both for capital gains and losses on net debt, as well as terms of trade changes). This is admittedly a simple framework for analyzing adjustments. Nevertheless, his conclusions – that in many semi-industrial countries attempts to adjust to exogenous external shocks were compromised by domestic public sector profligacy, and the use of exchange rate policy to counter inflation generated by such profligacy was counterproductive – are of important policy significance, if they are confirmed, as is likely, by a more elaborate analysis including more countries.

SOME RECENT THEORETICAL MODELS OF TRADE AND DEVELOPMENT

Rent-seeking and DUP activities

It was noted in the last section that policy instruments used to implement an inward-oriented strategy of development are likely to trigger rent-seeking activities. Since Anne Krueger's (1974) classic article on the diversion of resources towards rent-seeking, an analytical framework for integrating such activities, which have been characterized by Bhagwati (1980) as Directly Unproductive Profit (DUP)-seeking activities, into traditional models of trade theory has emerged. With this framework, a number of diverse theoretical results and empirical observations – such as immiserizing growth (Bhagwati, 1958), *negative* value added at *world prices* of heavily protected domestic activities in developing countries, *negative shadow* prices for factors in project evaluation, the impact of rent- and revenue-seeking on domestic welfare and on the ranking of alternative policy interventions for achieving noneconomic objectives – can all be seen as arising from basically the same underlying structural feature of a distorted economy. It is this: given an existing distortion (such as an import tariff in a small open economy or some other non-optimal taxes), any addition to factor supplies through accumulation or diversion of factors from their existing use towards a project (or for rent-seeking, revenue seeking and lobbying) can *reduce* welfare, as in the case of immiserizing growth, by *accentuating* the effects of that distortion or *improve* welfare, as in the case of a negative shadow price for a factor, by *attenuating* them. It also turns out that if the diversion of resources to rent-seeking are of the same value in equilibrium as the rents sought, then a policy, such as an import tariff, which is *inferior* in terms of its welfare cost in the absence of revenue-seeking to a production tax in achieving a noneconomic objective of raising the output of a sector (beyond the level achieved in a *laissez-faire* equilibrium), can become superior to it with revenue-seeking present (Bhagwati et al., 1984).

One implication of the presence of rent-seeking was already mentioned: the gains to those policies that eliminate the distortion that triggered the rent-seeking could be substantially greater than the estimates of the cost of the same distortion in the absence of rent-seeking. If we also include the resources devoted to lobbying for the adoption of a distortionary policy in the cost of distortion, it can be substantial. This is easily illustrated by using the traditional approach to the cost of protection. In figure 17.1, AB represents the production possibility (*PP*) curve of a small open economy if all its resources are devoted to

Importable

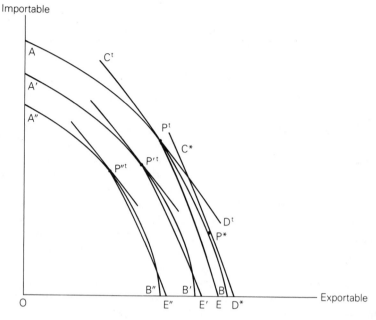

FIG. 17.1   *Cost of protection and DUP activities*

production activities. C^*D^* represents an iso-value line at world prices. The economy will operate at P^* under free trade. If a tariff is imposed by the government without anyone lobbying for its imposition or for the diversion of revenues it generates once imposed, the iso-value line becomes C^tD^t and the economy will produce at P^t; the production cost of protection is measured by the difference ED^* between the value at world prices of P^* as compared to P^t. Now, first introduce lobbying for the tariff, rather than its being imposed autonomously. The resources diverted to the lobbying activity (which remain diverted, because a tariff once imposed may not remain in place unless the lobby continues to plead for it!) shrinks the PP curve to $A'B'$ and the production point shifts to P'^t. If there is a resource-using struggle for the disposition of the revenue generated by the tariff, the PP curve shrinks further to $A''B''$ and the production point moves to P''^t. The total (production) cost of protection then is $E''D^*$, consisting of the sum of cost of revenue-seeking $E''E'$, the cost of lobbying for the tariff $E'E$, and the traditional cost ED^*.

On the other hand, if rent-seeking in fact had the effect of reducing the cost of the distortion that triggered it, as in some of the examples above, the gains from elimination of the distortion may be less. Indeed, some forms of corruption and extra legal transactions in developing countries and some centrally planned economies may even improve the efficiency of an otherwise extremely inefficient bureaucratic allocation system. In such cases, the economic gains towards a less bureaucratic allocation system may be less than what might seem on the surface.

North–South models

The so-called North–South models build on an assumed structural difference between the developed North and developing South. In the Findlay (1980) version, each region is *specialized* in producing its export good. The North produces a single homogeneous manufactured good under a constant returns to scale neoclassical technology with capital and labor as inputs, saves a fixed proportion of its output, and fully employs its exponentially growing labor force in a competitive market for goods and factors. The part of the output that is not saved (and invested) is spent either on domestic manufactures or on imports of primary products from the South. South's technology for the production of exports is again neoclassical, with capital and labor as inputs – except that labor supply to the export sector is infinitely elastic at a fixed product wage. Southern workers consume all their wages and capitalists save part of their profits. Consumption expenditures of workers and capitalists is divided between spending on home-produced primary products and imported manufactures, depending upon relative prices.

A unique steady state equilibrium in which North and South grow at a rate equal to the growth rate of the effective supply of labor in the North is shown to exist. Also convergence to this steady state from arbitrary initial conditions is established. The comparative dynamics (i.e. impact on the steady state equilibrium) of increases in the Northern propensity to save and improvements in its technology are simply that its per capita income increases and its terms of trade improve, while the South loses on both counts. As Findlay himself admits, the assumptions of the model – such as the absence of capital mobility in response to differing profit rates between North and South, production specialization, and above all, the assumption of unlimited labor supply at a fixed real wage in the South – are very restrictive. I would add the exogenously specified savings propensities and population growth rates to his list. But the fundamental problem is that while these rigidities and fixities may make some sense in the short or even medium run, to keep them fixed forever and take the comparative dynamics of the long-run steady states emerging from them as stylized development stories is seriously misleading. Besides, the intertemporal gains or losses along the transitional path toward the new steady state are ignored in focusing exclusively on the steady state. Such gains or losses may reverse the conclusions derived from steady state comparisons.

Another North–South model which builds in even more rigidities than Findlay's is attributed to Kaldor (Vines, 1985). In this model also, the North is specialized in producing an industrial output using capital and labor in fixed proportions to output. Real wages are *exogenous* and *fixed* and any surplus of output over sales to the South and Northern consumption is invested. The South is *specialized* in producing an agricultural good using land, labor and capital. The capital–labor ratio is *fixed*. In the short run and intermediate run, diminishing returns arising from the fixity of land are assumed absent so that the capital–output ratio in agriculture is *constant*. In the long run, substitution (at a diminishing marginal rate) between land and labor is allowed. Southern real wage is also *fixed* (in terms of the agricultural good). Wages and rents are consumed in agricultural goods, while all profits are invested. Thus, the agricultural surplus of the South is exchanged for Northern capital goods. Northern workers also do not save, but split their consumption between the industrial good and agricultural good depending on relative prices.

It is shown that in the short run, with given stocks of capital in the North and South, the two regions do not grow at the same rate – the two growth rates being determined by the equilibrium terms of trade, with more favorable terms of trade for the South leading to its faster growth. In the medium run, the equilibrium capital stocks as well as the terms of trade are jointly determined. The two capital stocks grow at the same equilibrium rate, depending on capital productivity in the two regions and on their share of consumption in output. In the long run, the growth rate of the system is the same as that of the effective stock of agricultural land. Another feature of this model is that adjustments to an exogenous fall in Southern productivity may involve *overshooting*, in the sense that the terms of trade rise above their medium-run equilibrium value and gradually fall towards it. Furthermore, the path towards long-run equilibrium value of the ratio of capital stocks in the two regions and the land to capital ratio in the South may involve cyclical behavior. The overshooting and cylical adjustment are viewed by Vines as formally establishing Kaldor's indictment of the price mechanism as a perverse and slow-acting mechanism that creates unnecessary cycles in world industrial activity! As in Findlay's model, the extreme assumptions of this model appear to be ill-suited to an analysis of the long-run development process.

Vines and Kanbur (1986) use a simpler version of the Vines model, in which Southern output of agriculture is price-inelastic and Northern macro economy is Keynesian, to argue that benefits to the stabilization of agricultural prices through a buffer stock operation can yield substantial benefits to the North, if Northern real wages are sticky. Buffer stock operation avoids a deflationary policy that would otherwise be necessary to contain inflation whenever agricultural prices rise because of harvest failure in the South. By ignoring *private* stock operations, the role of price expectations and speculation, and by exaggerating the inflexiblities in the system (besides real wage inflexibilities) through the assumption of fixed propensities, the model is likely to exaggerate the gains that accrue from *publicly* funded buffer stocks.

Recent models of international trade

Turning now to developments in the theory of international trade, only two will be briefly noted. One is the application of neo-Ricardian, time-phased models and neo-Marxian analysis (under the broad theme of Unequal Exchange) of international trade. Evans (1984) offers a perceptive critique of these models. The second is the intellectual arbitrage between industrial organization theory and international trade theory by Krugman (1979a, 1979b, 1980), Helpman (1981) and others. Stewart (1984) has attempted to derive some implications for the South of this theory.

The time-phased Ricardian models (Steedman, 1979a and 1979b) are viewed by their builders as repairing what they consider as two damaging features of traditional models of trade and growth, namely, their treatment of capital as a homogeneous aggregate and their ignoring the time lags involved in production. By adopting Von Neumann's formulation of production in terms of activities that transform a *vector* of inputs into a *vector* of outputs one period later, they address both the concerns.[2] They focus only on the steady state (the state of balanced growth) of the system. The two conclusions of this body of theory are worth noting: first, for a small open economy the steady state associated with *autarky* (or with restrictions on international trade) may yield *higher* consumption every period than that associated with free trade; second, the commodity pattern of trade can change along the approach to the steady state. Indeed it can be reversed; a commodity that is exported at one point of time is imported at another. It should be pointed out that neither conclusion depends on the Ricardian time-phased structure of the model: a standard two-commodity, two-factor, Heckscher–Ohlin–Samuelson model in its dynamic version, in which one of the commodities is an investment good and in which there are no time lags in production, can be used to derive them. More important, the fact that trade restrictions lead to higher consumption than free trade in a *steady state*, does not imply that restricting trade is *intertemporally* optimal, indeed the contrary is true, for a small open-economy free trade is the intertemporally optimal policy (Bhagwati and Srinivasan, 1980; Samuelson, 1975).

In the literature on Unequal Exchange (Emmanuel, 1972), the North is the center and the South is the periphery. The process of international exchange and investment is assumed to equalize the rate of return to capital in the center and the periphery. The return to labor is not however equalized and indeed, this inequality is alleged to grow. Since the exchange between the center and the periphery is voluntary, whether unequal wages between regions should be viewed as indicating that the commodity exchange itself is "unequal," in some sense is unclear. However, if one is prepared to define suitably the content of "socially necessary labor" in commodities being exchanged (using a model that will enable one to do so unambiguously), one can arrive at a precise definition of "unequal exchange" as exchange of commodities of unequal content of socially necessary labor. Roemer (1984) follows this route. Few would be bold enough to infer policy-relevant conclusions from the existence of unequal exchange in the sense of Roemer.

The intellectual arbitrage between industrial organization theory and international trade theory came about initially as an attempt to explain (better than conventional theory) certain stylized facts of international trade. These were: (1) that even at the most disaggregated level the trade among industrialized countries appears to consist largely of *intra*-industry trade, each country *exporting* as well as *importing* commodities that would be classified as falling within the same industry category; (2) significant economies of scale in production appeared to characterize the technology of some of these industries; and (3) in many countries such industries appeared to be highly concentrated, often with very few firms. By drawing on the model of monopolistic competition in an industry producing a set of differentiated products under increasing returns to scale and setting it in the context of international trade, recent theories "explain" the above stylized facts. An interesting result is that in contrast to traditional theories, gainful exchanges will arise – even between two economies which are identical in every respect. Given economies of scale each country will produce a *different* set of (differentiated) products of the same industry, but *consumers* in each will be able to buy products produced in *both*. This raises consumer welfare in both countries, compared to what could be achieved by each under autarky. A consequence of the oligopolistic equilibrium that characterizes international exchange in some of the models is that it would be in the interest of each country to attempt to capture more of the oligopolistic rents that arise from the divergence between equilibrium prices and marginal costs. This brings in a role for active strategic trade interventions that is not present in traditional theories.

The implications of the above for the developing countries are far from obvious. First, the case for strategic intervention and the *type* of intervention are very sensitive to the specification of the model and the concept of equilibrium used. Second, the arguments for trade interventions that the new theory allows cannot be taken as analytical support for the particular interventions that developing countries have imposed in totally different contexts. Starting from the premise that few developing countries will be able to establish a viable industry producing differentiated products under economies of scale, Stewart (1984) has suggested that the South as a group could, however, do so – if each country specialized in one or at most a *few* products and traded with each other in these products. This argument for the *South–South* trade, however, does not follow from the above theory except in that there is a common assumption that, *ceteris paribus*, the greater the variety of products consumed, the greater is consumer welfare. Since the argument also assumes protection against imports from the North of the products of the same industry, it really involves *diverting* trade with the North and *creating* trade among countries of the South. There is no presumption that this is necessarily welfare-improving for the South.

Even though the trade among the developed industrialized economies with similar tastes, technologies, and factor endowments is in large measure intra-industry, two-way trade (and this is the starting point of newer theories of trade), significant intra-industry trade takes place among developing countries as well. Havrylyshyn and Civan (1983) find in a regression analysis that per capita income and the diversity of manufactured goods exports besides membership in a successful trade grouping (e.g. EEC) explain a significant proportion of the variation in intra-industry trade among countries. The stage of development also matters. While 60–80 percent of all trade in industrialized countries is intra-industry, the percentage is between 40 and 50 in the newly industrialized countries and is only between 10 and 20 in other developing countries. The authors argue that this link with stage of development of intra-industry trade in differentiated products implies that as development proceeds, the penetration of developing countries into the developed country markets will be diffused over a number of products. As such, such penetration may appear less threatening and invoke less of a protectionist response from the developed countries. This is not entirely convincing. After all, the differentiated *products* presumably come from the same set of *industries* and lobbying for protection is likely to be industry-based rather than narrow product-based. There is no reason to believe that such lobbying will be blunted.

A few words about trends in South–South trade are in order in concluding this section. It is sometimes suggested (Stewart, 1976) that the patterns of financial, transport, and marketing arrangements developed during the colonial era have precluded developing countries from changing their colonial trade patterns toward trading among themselves to greater mutual benefit. This argument is not valid for all developing countries, if it is at all valid for any. For example, India was able to change, fairly soon after its independence, the geographical concentration of its exports substantially, from the United Kingdom to other developed countries such as the United States and the USSR, although not as much to other developing countries. Havrylyshyn and Wolf (1983) show that the share of non-fuel trade among developing countries in their total trade did not change between 1963 and 1977. However, this constant share is the sum of a *falling* share of manufactures and a *rising* share of primary products. They did not find any bias against trade among developing countries, other than the effect (if any) of their own trade restrictions. Exports of manufactures from developing countries to other developing countries are found to be more capital-intensive than exports to developed countries, a pattern not inconsistent with multicountry generalizations of the Heckscher–Ohlin theory. However the pattern may also have been influenced by trade restrictions in developing countries (Krueger, 1978). Be that as it may, to repeat it is not clear whether promoting South–South trade through distortionary restrictive trading arrangements will mean that gains from trade creation will outweigh the losses from trade diversion and distortions.

INTERNATIONAL FACTOR MOVEMENTS

The welfare implications of international factor mobility have been analyzed extensively by trade theorists in the last several years. The so-called "brain-drain" from developing countries, foreign investment in such countries, and the use of immigrant labor in declining industries in developed countries as a way of reducing labor costs (in an attempt to remain viable in the face of competition from developing countries) have all been analyzed. Models used in the analysis have been varied, including the traditional Heckscher–Ohlin model, the specific factors model, and models incorporating increasing returns and monopolistic competition. Even lobbying activities have been incorporated in the analysis. First-best and second-best policies towards factor movements have also received attention.

In the standard H–O–S, two-factor-two-commodity model of a small open economy, *under a free trade regime*, if foreign investors of imported capital (or immigrant laborers) are paid its marginal value product in the importing country and these returns are repatriated, as long as the economy remains incompletely specialized before and after the import of capital (labor), such factor imports do not change consumer welfare. If the economy becomes specialized in the capital-(labor-)intensive good after capital (labor) imports from an initial position of incomplete specialization – or specialization in the labor-(capital-)intensive good – then clearly welfare increases. For in such a situation, the additional capital (labor) import at the margin *reduces* its marginal product, thereby reducing the cost to the economy in terms of payments to intramarginal units of foreign capital (labor).

Brecher and Díaz-Alejandro (1977) were the first to show that the above favorable welfare consequences of inflow of foreign factors need not hold if the economy is not following its optimal free trade policy. Indeed, given an existing import tariff, if importables are capital- (labor-) intensive – even if the economy is incompletely specialized before and after foreign capital (labor) inflow – there is a welfare *loss* associated with their capital-intensive manufactures and such protection induces the "tariff-jumping" type of foreign investment, the Brecher–Díaz-Alejandro result points to the *additional* welfare loss (over the above primary loss associated with the protective tariff in the absence of foreign investment) that inward-oriented policies generate. Bhagwati and Srinivasan (1979) have argued that outward-oriented policies on the other hand are likely to attract welfare-improving foreign investment that takes advantage of the relative cheapness of a country's more abundant factor.

A number of subsequent studies have examined the welfare consequences for the home economy of alternate trade policies (first-best and second-best) in the presence of foreign-owned factors of production (Bhagwati and Brecher, 1981; Brecher, 1983; Srinivasan, 1983). Other authors consider the choice between emigration of home labor (investment abroad of home capital) and attracting foreign investment (attracting foreign workers). They extend and generalize a result originally due to Ramaswami (1968, 1970). He considered a model in which a single homogeneous commodity was produced under constant returns to scale in two countries using capital and labor as inputs. Although there is no incentive for commodity trade in this model, incentives for factor movements arise because of different factor endowment ratios in the two countries. He shows that for the capital-poor country that can optimally tax earnings of foreign capital or the income of its nationals working abroad, the optimal policy is to attract and tax foreign capital, rather than let home workers emigrate and tax their earnings. This result or variants of it survive in more general contexts (Bhagwati and Srinivasan, 1983; Calvo and Wellisz, 1983; Jones, Coelho and Easton, 1986; Wong, 1983; Saavedra-Rivano and Wooton, 1983). Except for Saavedra-Rivano and Wooton, who work with a dynamic North–South model of the Findlay (1980) type, the analysis of the above authors is static. On the other hand Buiter (1981) analyzes the pattern of capital formation, balance-of-payments behavior and welfare in a dynamic, two-country, overlapping generation, general equilibrium model in which countries differ only in their pure rates of time preference and there is perfect international capital mobility. With a positive rate of natural growth, the low-time-preference country runs a current account surplus (i.e. exports capital) in the steady state, although not necessarily outside it. The ranking of steady state utility levels under autarky and free trade and capital mobility is ambiguous. Galor (1986), independently of Buiter, uses essentially the same model to analyze the implications of international migration. He finds that there is unilateral migration from the country with high- (low-)time preference to the country with low- (high-)time preference if the autarkic steady state equilibrium in *both* countries is characterized by under (over) investment relative to the Golden Rule. Bilateral migration occurs if the two countries are located on the opposite sides of the Golden Rule. In contrast with the other analyses discussed above, in Galor's model unilateral migration immiserizes the non-migrants in the immigration country while non-migrants in the emigration country are no worse off.

Leontief (1936) suggested that a unilateral transfer of income from one country to another in a two-country, two-commodity, pure-exchange world may immiserize the *recipient* while enriching the donor; Samuelson (1947) showed that such a possibility cannot arise unless the equilibrium is Walrasian-stable. This so-called transfer paradox has recently received independent attention from several authors. By introducing a third country, or by introducing domestic distortions, one can resurrect the transfer paradox even in a stable equilibrium. Equally the possibility arises that both *the donor and the recipient* are enriched by the transfer (Bhagwati, Brecher and Hatta 1983, 1985, and the literature cited therein). This literature obviously has no connection with that on factor mobility. However, some may jump to the conclusion that the transfer paradox has the implication that foreign aid can immiserize developing countries. Such a conclusion will be hasty, in part because the transfer-induced change in equilibrium terms of trade on which the paradox depends is unlikely, since aid is quantitatively very small relative to the value of global trade, and in part because the above analyses ignore policy responses (such as removal of distortion, etc.) that can negate the paradoxical outcome.

One particular institutional arrangement under which international investments and technology transfer have taken place – namely, the multinational corporation – has received theoretical and empirical attention (Helleiner, 1981). For reasons of brevity this literature and that on direct foreign investment (Michalopoulos, 1985) are not discussed here.

In concluding this section, recent experience with international migration must be mentioned. The boom in the oil-rich West Asian countries after the first oil shock induced a substantial emigration of labor from South and East Asia, as well as the Arab world to these countries. At their peak, the remittance to their families at home by these emigrant workers constituted one-half or more of the foreign exchange earnings of many of the countries of origin. With the decline in oil prices and the contraction of investment in the oil-exporting countries, growth in the use of immigrant labor in these countries is unlikely in the near future, and in fact, the net flow will probably turn negative. The investment of remittances by the families of emigrants in housing, small enterprises, and other activities has transformed some parts of South Asia with an unusual concentration of such emigrants. The returning emigrants brought with them (in addition to their savings) skills, knowledge, and an altered outlook acquired during their sojourn abroad (Swamy, 1985; World Bank, 1984).

CONCLUSION

The development of sharper theoretical and econometric tools and the accumulation of a large and growing body of economic data relating to developing countries have enabled a number of analysts to compare outward- and inward-oriented strategies of development. Most of the analysts, though not all, have concluded that countries that followed an outward-oriented strategy not only did better by most indicators of development, but also weathered better the shocks to the world economy. Recent policy changes in the two giants of the developing world, namely, India and China, towards economic liberalization suggest that the lessons of three decades of development have been learned. Some pessimists argue that if the two giants and the rest of the developing countries were to adopt an outward orientation, it would exacerbate the rising tide of protectionism in the industrialized world, besides imposing terms of trade losses on the developing countries. However, given that the manufactured exports of the developing world still form less than 5 percent of the apparent consumption of such commodities in the developed world, as long as the recovery in the industrialized world continues, such fears seem exaggerated. This is not to say, however, that problems cannot arise with regard to particular commodities and/or countries.

NOTES

[1] It is interesting that the earliest empirical *planning model* for any developing country was by Sandee (1960) for India. However, a *price-endogenous model* for India came years after Adelman and Robinson's for Korea, as if the attitudes of policy-makers towards prices and markets in the two countries influenced the modelers!

[2] The issue of heterogeneity of capital attracted some extensive attention in the so-called Cambridge (Massachusetts) versus Cambridge (England) controversies in capital theory. A few of the uninformed have somehow come to the conclusion that neoclassical economic theory stands or falls on the validity of the homogeneity of capital. Malinvaud (1953) in his seminal paper on capital accumulation had, among other things, given a perfectly rigorous meaning for the concept of marginal productivity of capital in a model in which capital *goods* were *heterogeneous*. This paper apparently was not read by many of the neo-Ricardians or Sraffians. Hahn (1982) lucidly exposes the misunderstanding and confusion that surround the neo-Ricardian discussion of the neoclassical economics.

REFERENCES

Adelman, I. and Robinson, S. 1978: *Income Distribution Policy in Developing Countries: A Case Study of Korea.* London: Oxford University Press.

Balassa, B. 1982: *Development Strategies in Semi-industrial Economies.* Baltimore: Johns Hopkins University Press.

Balassa, B. 1985: "Developing Country Debt: Policies and Prospects." Report No. DRD 149, Development Research Center, Washington DC: World Bank.

Balassa, B. 1986a: *Change and Challenge in the World Economy.* London Macmillan, part 2.

Balassa, B. 1986b: "Policy Responses to Exogenous Shocks in Developing Countries." *American Economic Review, Papers and Proceedings*, 75–8.

Bell, C. L. G. and Srinivasan, T. N. 1984: "On the Uses and Abuses of Economywide Models in Development Policy Analysis." In M. Syrquin, L. Taylor and L. Westphal (eds), *Economic Structure and Performance*, New York: Academic Press, chap. 22, 451–76.

Bhagwati, J. N. 1958: "Immiserizing Growth: A Geometrical Note." *The Review of Economic Studies*, 25, 201–5.

Bhagwati, J. N. 1978: *Foreign Trade Regimes and Economic Development. Anatomy and Consequences of Exchange Control Regimes.* Cambridge: Ballinger Press.

Bhagwati, J. N. 1980: "Lobbying and Welfare." *Journal of Public Economics*, 14 (Dec.), 355–63.

Bhagwati, J. N. 1986: "Rethinking Trade Strategy." In J. P. Lewis and V. Kallab (eds), *Development Strategies Reconsidered*, Washington, DC: Overseas Development Council, 91–104.

Bhagwati, J. N. and Brecher, R. 1981: "Foreign Ownership and the Theory of Trade and Welfare." *Journal of Political Economy*, 89, 497–511.

Bhagwati, J. N., Brecher, R. and Hatta, T. 1983: "The Generalized Theory of Transfers and Welfare: Bilateral Transfers in a Multilateral World." *American Economic Review*, 83, 606–18.

Bhagwati, J. N., Brecher, R. and Hatta, T. 1985: "The Generalized Theory of Transfers and Welfare: Exogeneous (Policy-Imposed) and Endogenous (Transfer Induced) Distortions." *Quarterly Journal of Economics*, 13, 353–64.

Bhagwati, J. N., Brecher, R. and Srinivasan, T. N. 1984: "DUP Activities and Economic Theory." in D. Colander (ed.), *Neo-Classical Political Economy.* Cambridge: Ballinger, chap. 1, 17–32.

Bhagwati, J. N. and Srinivasan, T. N. 1979: "Trade Policy and Development." In R. Dornbusch and J. A. Frenkel (eds), *International Economic Policy: Theory and Evidence*, Baltimore: Johns Hopkins Press, 1–35.

Bhagwati, J. N. and Srinivasan, T. N. 1980: "Trade and Welfare in a Steady State." In J. S. Chipman and C. P. Kindleburger (eds), *Flexible Exchange Rates and Balance of Payments.* Amsterdam: North-Holland Publishing, 341–53.

Bhagwati, J. N. and Srinivasan, T. N. 1983: "On the Choice Between Capital and Labour Mobility." *Journal of International Economics*, 14, 209–22.

Blitzer, C. R., Clark, P. B. and Taylor, L. (eds) 1975: *Economy-Wide Models and Development Planning*. London: Oxford University Press.

Brecher, R. A. 1983: "Second Best Policy for International Trade and Investment." *Journal of International Economics*, 14, 313–20.

Brecher, R. A. and Díaz-Alejandro, C. 1977: "Tariffs, Foreign Capital and Immiserizing Growth." *Journal of International Economics*, 7, 317–22.

Buiter, W. H. 1981: "Time Preference and International Lending and Borrowing in an Overlapping-Generations Model." *Journal of Political Economy*, 89(4), 769–97.

Cairncross, A. K. 1960: "International Trade and Economic Development." *Kyklos*, 13 fasc. 4.

Calvo, G. and Wellisz, S. 1983: "International Factor Mobility and National Advantage." *Journal of International Economics*, 14, 103–14.

Chenery, H. B. and Bruno, M. 1962: "Development Alternatives in an Open Economy." *Economic Journal*, 72, 79–103.

Chenery, H. B. and Strout, A. 1966: "Foreign Assistance and Economic Development." *American Economic Review*, 56, 679–733.

Dasgupta, P., Marglin, S., and Sen, A. K. 1972: *Guidelines for Project Evaluation*. New York: United Nations.

Emmanuel, A. 1972: *Unequal Exchange: A Study of the Imperialism of Trade*. New York: Monthly Review Press.

Evans, D. 1984: "A Critical Assessment of Some Neo-Marxian Trade Theories." *The Journal of Development Studies*, 202–26.

Findlay, R. 1980: "The Terms of Trade and Equilibrium Growth in the World Economy." *American Economic Review*, 70, 291–9.

Galor, O. 1985: "Time Preference and International Labour Migration." *Journal of Economic Theory*, 38(1), 1–20.

GATT 1985: *International Trade 1984/85*. Geneva: General Agreement on Tariffs and Trade.

Grais, W., Demelo, J., and Urata, S. 1986: A General Equilibrium Estimation of the Reduction of Tariffs and Quantitative Restrictions in Turkey in 1978." Forthcoming in T. N. Srinivasan and J. Whalley (eds), *General Equilibrium Trade Policy Modeling*, Cambridge, Mass.: MIT Press, 61–88.

Hahn, F. 1982: "The Neo-Ricardians." *Cambridge Journal of Economics*, 6, 353–74.

Harris, R. 1983: *Trade, Industrial Policy, and Canadian Manufacturing*. Toronto: Ontario Economic Council.

Havrylyshyn, O. and Civan, E. 1983: "Intra-Industry Trade and Stage of Development." In P. K. M. Tharakan (ed.), *Intra-Industry Trade: Empirical and Methdological Aspects*. Amsterdam: North-Holland, 111–40.

Havrylyshyn, O. and Wolf, M. 1983: "Recent Trends in Trade Among Developing Countries." *European Economic Review*, 21, 333–62.

Helleiner, G. 1981: *Intra-firm Trade and the Developing Countries*. London: Macmillan.

Helpman, E. 1981: "International Trade in the Presence of Product Differentiation, Economies of Scale and Monopolistic Competition." *Journal of International Economics*, 11, 305–40.

Jones, R. W., Coelho, I., and Easton, S. T. 1986: "The Theory of International Factor Flows: The Basic Model." *Journal of International Economics*, 20, 313–28.

Krueger, A. 1974: "The Political Economy of the Rent Seeking Society." *American Economic Review,* 64, 291–303.

Krueger, A. 1978: *Foreign Trade Regimes and Economic Development: Liberalization Attempts and Consequences.* Cambridge: Ballinger.

Krueger, A. 1983: *Alternative Trade Strategies: Volume 3: Synthesis and Conclusions.* Chicago: Chicago University Press.

Krugman, P. 1979a: "Increasing Returns, Monopolistic Competition and International Trade." *Journal of International Economics,* 9, 469–79.

Krugman, P. 1979b: "A Model of Innovation, Technology Transfer and the World Distribution of Income." *Journal of Political Economy,* 82, 253–366.

Krugman, P. 1980: "Scale Economies, Product Differentiation and the Pattern of Trade." *American Economic Review,* 70, 950–9.

Leontief, W. 1936: "Note on the Pure Theory of Capital Transfers." In *Explorations in Economics: Notes and Essays Contributed in Honor of F. W. Taussig,* New York: McGraw Hill.

Little, I. M. D., Scitovsky, T., and Scott, M. 1970: *Industry and Trade in Some Developing Countries: A Comparative Study,* London and New York: Oxford University Press.

Little, I. M. D. and Mirrlees, J. A. 1974: Project Appraisal and Planning for Developing Countries. London: Heinemann.

Malinvaud, E. 1953: "Capital Accumulation and Efficient Allocation of Resources." *Econometrica,* 21, 233, 268.

Malinvaud, E. 1962: "Efficient Capital Accumulation: A Corrigendum." *Econometrica,* 30, 570–3.

Michalopoulos, C. 1985: "Private Direct Investment, Finance and Development." *Asian Development Review,* 3, 59–71.

Mitra, P. 1986a: "A Description of Adjustment to External Shocks: Country Groups." In D. Lal and M. Wolf (eds), *Stagflation Savings and the State of Perspectives on the Global Economy,* New York: Oxford University Press, 103–114.

Mitra, P. 1986b: "Adjustment to External Shocks in Selected Semi-Industrial Countries, 1974–81." Forthcoming in P. Ferri and G. Ragazzi (eds), *Adjust-in to Shocks: A North–South Perspective.* Amsterdam: North-Holland Publishing.

Neary, P. 1985: "Theory and Policy of Adjustment in an Open Economy." Discussion Paper 61, London: Center for Economic Policy Research.

Ramaswami, V. K. 1968: "International Factor Movements and National Advantage." *Economica,* 35, 309–10.

Ramaswami, V. K. 1970: "International Factor Movements and National Advantage: Reply." *Economica,* 37, 85.

Roemer, J. 1984: "Unequal Exchange, Labour Migration and International Capital Flows: A Theoretical Synthesis." In P. Desai (ed.), *Marxism, Central Planning and The Soviet Economy, Essays in Honor of Alexander Ehrlich,* Cambridge, Mass.: MIT Press, 34–60.

Rosen, G. 1985: *Western Economists and Eastern Societies* Baltimore: Johns Hopkins University Press, 128–38.

Saavedra-Rivano, N. and Wooton, I. 1983: "The Choice Between Labour and Capital Mobility in a Dynamic Model of North–South Trade." *Journal of International Economics,* 14, 251–62.

Samuelson, P. 1947: *Foundation of Economic Analysis.* Cambridge, Mass.: Harvard University Press.

Samuelson, P. 1975: "Trade Pattern Reversals in Time-Phased Systems and International Efficiency." *Journal of International Economics*, 5, 339–64.

Sandee, J. 1960: *A Demonstration Planning Model for India*. Bombay: Asia Publishing House.

Shoven, J. and Whalley, J. 1984: "Applied General Equilibrium Models of Taxation and International Trade: An Introduction and a Survey." *Journal of Economic Literature*, 22, 1007–51.

Srinivasan, T. N. 1982: "General Equilibrium Theory, Project Evaluation and Economic Development." In M. Gersovitz, C. Díaz-Alejandro, G. Ranis and M. Rosenzweig (eds), *The Theory and Experience of Economic Development*, London: Allen and Unwin, 229–51.

Srinivasan, T. N. 1983: "International Factor Movements, Commodity Trade and Commercial Policy in a Specific Factor Model." *Journal of International Economics*, 14, 289–312.

Srinivasan, T. N. 1986: "Development and Strategy: Is the Success of Outward Orientation at an End?" In M. R. Shroff and S. Guhan (eds), *Economic Progress and Welfare: Essays in Honor of I. G. Patel*, Delhi: Oxford University Press.

Srinivasan, T. N. and Whalley, J. 1986: *General Equilibrium Trade Policy Modeling*. Cambridge, Mass.: MIT Press.

Steedman, I. (ed.) 1979a: *Fundamental Issues in Trade Theory*. London: Macmillan.

Steedman, I. 1979b: *Trade Among Growing Economies*. Cambridge: Cambridge University Press.

Stewart, F. 1976: The Direction of International Trade: Gains and Losses for the Third World. In G. K. Helleiner (ed.), *A World Divided: the Less Developed Countries in the International Economy*. Cambridge: Cambridge University Press, 89–110.

Stewart, F. 1984: "Recent Theories of International Trade Some Implications for the South." In H. Kierzkowski (ed.), *Monopolistic Competition and International Trade*, London: Oxford University Press, 84–107.

Swamy, G. 1985: "Population and International Migration." Staff Working Paper No. 689, Washington DC: World Bank.

Vines, D. 1985: "North South Growth Model Along Kaldorian Lines." Discussion Paper No. 26, London: Centre for Economic Policy Research.

Vines, D. and Kanbur, R. 1986: "North South Interaction and Commod Control." *Journal of Development Economics*, 23(2), 371–87.

Whalley, J. 1984: "The North South Debate and the Terms of Trade: An Applied General Equilibrium Approach." *Review of Economics and Statistics*, 66, 224–34.

Wong, K. 1983: "On Choosing Among Trade in Goods and International Capital and Labour Mobility: A Theoretical Analysis." *Journal of International Economics*, 14, 223–50.

World Bank 1982, 1984, 1986: *World Development Report*. New York: Oxford University Press.

Comments on
"International Trade and Factor Movements in Development Theory, Policy, and Experience"

BELA BALASSA

In his excellent paper, T. N. Srinivasan deals with a number of theoretical and policy issues relating to international trade and factor movements. In this note, I will concentrate on two areas: the appropriateness of the assumptions made in models concerning North–South trade, and the issues involved in evaluating policy responses to external shocks.

Complete specialization, elasticity pessimism, and the cost of protection in developing countries

Srinivasan cites a number of models concerned with bilateral North–South relationships. These models have some common features: they assume complete specialization, with the North (the industrial countries or the center) producing manufactured goods, and the South (the developing countries or the periphery) specializing in primary commodities; they also exhibit elasticity pessimism.

One may begin with the ECLA model, originating with Raúl Prebisch, which posited less-than-unitary income and price elasticities in the industrial countries for primary commodities exported by the developing countries. These assumptions led to the conclusion that, under free trade, productivity improvements in the periphery would in part be appropriated by the center through lower prices, entailing the deterioration of the periphery's terms of trade.

In turn, early two-gap models assumed that the exports of the developing countries were exogenously determined by demand on the part of the industrial countries. Later model variants modified this assumption without, however, removing the rigidities characteristic of this family of models.

Complete specialization models again came into vogue during the last decade. Postulating less-than-unitary income elasticities in the North for the exports of the South led Taylor (1981) to the conclusion that productivity increases in the South will reduce its terms of trade and growth rate, and hence, per capita incomes. In the models of Vines (1985), and Vines and Kanbur (1986), the terms of trade of the South deteriorate as productivity increases are not matched by wage increases – except that in the long run, diminishing returns to land may provide an offset.

In Findlay's model (1980), too, productivity growth in the South will engender a fall in its terms of trade and a decline in per capita incomes, measured in terms of manufactured goods, on the assumption of a unitary income elasticity for its exports in the North. It is added, however, that the deterioration of the terms of trade may be compensated by increases in employment if import price elasticities in the North and the South are sufficiently high.

The latter point was formalized by Bacha (1978), who criticized Prebisch as well as Emmanuel (1972)[1] for having disregarded the possibility that productivity growth would lead to welfare improvements in the South through increases in employment. Bacha showed that the South's welfare will decline only if the Johnson (1954) immiserization condition obtains; i.e., the income elasticity of demand in the South for the manufactured exports of the North exceeds the sum of the price elasticities of import demand in the North and in the South, less one. In turn, economic growth in the North will unambiguously benefit the South.

In view of the recent proliferation of models of complete specialization, it may come as a surprise that the pattern of international trade has increasingly become one of incomplete specialization between the North and the South. Apart from tropical beverages, which account for less than 5 percent of the exports of the developing countries, there are competing suppliers and/or substitutes for all developing country exports in the industrial countries.

In the latter instances, the South limiting its primary exports – whether directly through export taxes or indirectly through import protection – has in fact led to declines in export market shares in favor of producers in the North, rather than to a terms of trade improvement in the South. This has occurred in regard to temperate-zone agricultural products, tropical-zone products competing with those produced under a temperate climate, as well as non-fuel minerals and metals (Balassa, 1987).

A similar result has recently been observed in the case of petroleum. OPEC's share in world production declined from 68 percent in 1973 to 40 percent in 1985 as alternative suppliers emerged in response to the high prices maintained by OPEC, with prices subsequently declining by over two-thirds from their peak of $34 per barrel in 1980. In fact, in mid-1986, the real price of petroleum, deflated by the industrial countries' export price index for manufactured goods, was only two-thirds higher than in 1973 prior to the quadrupling of petroleum prices in late 1973.

Considering further that manufactured goods exported by the South, which have come to account for nearly one-third of its total exports, compete with the products of the industrial countries, it will be apparent that trade between the two areas is characterized by incomplete rather than by complete specialization. Correspondingly, rather than the Johnson conditions, it is the Bhagwati conditions that will be relevant.

Bhagwati (1958) showed that for growth to be immiserizing under incomplete specialization, a necessary but not a sufficient condition is that demand for the growing country's exports is price-inelastic or that growth reduces the domestic production of importables. Limiting attention for the time being to the first condition, this is unlikely to occur under incomplete specialization, since import demand is derived from domestic demand and domestic supply, and the price elasticity of import demand may exceed the domestic demand and supply elasticities several times.

The relevant formula is:

$$\eta_m = \eta \, \frac{C}{M} + \varepsilon \frac{P}{M}$$

where η_m, η, and ε are the price elasticities of import demand, domestic demand, and domestic supply, respectively; M denotes imports, C domestic consumption, and P domestic production. If, for example, imports account for 10 percent of domestic consumption and the domestic demand and supply elasticities are both unity, the import demand elasticity will be 19.[2]

In the traditional small-country case, the foreign import demand and the export supply elasticities are infinite. Now, the Prebisch–Emmanuel thesis is turned on its head as immiserizing growth cannot occur under free trade but it may be the result of import protection (Johnson, 1967). This is because resources are reallocated from labor-intensive export industries to capital-intensive, import-competing industries in response to protection as capital accumulates. In the small-country case, the condition for immiserizing growth is that one plus the tariff in the import-competing industry exceeds the ratio of labor's share in the labor-intensive to that of the capital-intensive industry (Martin, 1977).

Given the high protection observed in many developing countries, the fulfillment of this condition is in the realm of possibilities. Conversely, the second Bhagwati condition will not be fulfilled under protection as resources will be reallocated from export- to import-competing industries, rather than vice versa. And even if it were fulfilled under free trade, it would require an unrealistically low foreign import demand elasticity to lead to immiserization.

In intermediate cases when a country can influence the world market prices of at least some of its exports, the efficiency cost of protection has to be set against its beneficial terms of trade effects. In practice, it has been shown that the former greatly outweighs the latter. Thus, partial equilibrium estimates for Brazil, Chile, and Pakistan show that the cost of protection was between 5 and 10 percent of the gross domestic product in the mid-sixties (Balassa and associates, 1971, p. 82). The cost of protection estimated in a general equilibrium framework was even higher, 11 or 16 percent of GNP under an optimal tax for coffee, depending on the assumptions made about labor markets, in Colombia even though its tariffs were lower than those of the aforementioned three countries (de Melo, 1978).

Nor is there evidence that the cost of protection would have been offset by superior productivity improvements over time. In fact, results obtained by Bruton (1967) and Elias (1978) for the post-1940 years showed that total factor productivity generally increased less rapidly (if at all) under protection than during periods of relatively free trade in Latin America. As a result, these countries increasingly showed a tendency to fall behind the industrial countries. Or, as Bruton expressed it, "the misallocation produced by conventional IS [import-substitutional] policies not only reduces total output but it also reduces the growth rates, principally through its effect on productivity growth and the flexibility of the economy" (Bruton, 1970, p. 140).

This conclusion is supported by the experience of the 1960–85 period in Latin America, where the pursuit of inward-oriented policies has contributed to the retardation of the growth process. Latin American countries first fell behind the semi-industrial countries of Western Europe, such as Austria, Italy, and Finland; they were subsequently surpassed by Japan and the countries of Southern Europe; and they were finally overtaken by the four Far Eastern NICs. At the same time, subperiods characterized by relatively outward-oriented policies exhibited higher growth rates, as did countries where protection rates were lower (Balassa, Bueno, Kuczynski, and Simonsen, 1986).

Furthermore, Nishimizu and Robinson (1984) found that export expansion is positively, and import substitution negatively, correlated with changes in total factor productivity in 13 Korean, Turkish, and Yugoslav industries. The negative result obtained for import substitution in Turkey confirms the conclusions earlier obtained by Krueger and Tuncer (1980) for this country.

Also, India, which had a particularly pronounced inward orientation during the postwar period, experienced a decline in total factor productivity between 1959–60 and 1979–80 (Ahluwalia, 1985). The same result has been obtained in a World Bank study for Mexico for the period 1970–82, when the economy became increasingly inward-oriented.

The findings lead to the conclusion that liberalizing trade will increase national income in developing countries. This conclusion conflicts with that of Whalley (1984), obtained in the framework of a general equilibrium model for the world economy. Thus, according to

Whalley, unilateral trade liberalization, and even the multilateral liberalization of trade, would give rise to income losses in the South. These results do not stand up to scrutiny, however.

To begin with, by reason of its static assumptions, Whalley's model does not incorporate differences in the rate of growth of productivity under alternative trade policies. Also, it excludes economies of scale, which have been shown to account for much of the cost of protection, equaling 5 percent of GNP, in Canada (Harris, 1983). And Whalley's estimates are open to criticism on their own grounds, by reason of the assumed low price elasticities of demand, derived from estimates subject to a downward bias because of the use of single least-squares procedures.

The sensitivity of the estimates to the assumed elasticities is shown by the results obtained in the general equilibrium model of Ginsburgh and Waelbroeck (1981). Using conventional elasticity estimates, the results of these authors show a gain from multilateral trade liberalization of 1.5 percent, and a loss from unilateral liberalization of 0.8 percent, of the gross national product of the developing countries. However, gains of 5.6 and 3.7 percent, respectively, are obtained when more realistic elasticities are used (pp. 330, 336).

Evaluating policy responses to external shocks

I come next to Srinivasan's comments on my own work on policy adjustment to external shocks. These comments pertain to the methodology applied, the interpretation of the results, and the implications of the policies applied for the rate of economic growth. They will be taken up in turn.

Srinivasan suggests that my "methodology of the quantifying shocks involves the assumption of static expectations." He adds: "of course, it is not easy to specify the anticipated or expected path (or more precisely the stochastic process) of the exogenous variables so that departures from it could be deemed a shock. But it seems somewhat of an extreme to postulate static expectations."

Past trends in world exports, in the country's economic growth, in the relationship of the country's imports to its gross domestic product, and in its external financing, however, represent the outcome of a dynamic process. The calculations are predicated on the assumption that this dynamic process would have continued in the absence of external shocks.

Departures of the expected path from past trends would have had to be defined country by country. At the same time, the integrity of the method applied may have been compromised if adjustments were made in regard to individual countries, since such adjustments necessarily involve a certain degree of arbitrariness. The difficulties multiply if we consider that the calculations pertain to 43 countries. Thus, it has appeared preferable to follow the same procedure in regard to every country.

Table 17.4 provides my unpublished results of the balance-of-payments effects of external shocks and of policy responses to these shocks in the 1974–78 and 1979–83 periods for outward-oriented and inward-oriented NICs and LDCs. According to Srinivasan, "It is not clear, however, whether the increased cost of inward orientation can be inferred from the a posteriori results of table 17.4. After all is said and done these portray the effects on two sides of an accounting equation" (p. 554).

To begin with the latter point, the results reported in table 17.4 compare actual observations with the "anti-monde" based on the stated assumptions in an accounting framework. They are meant to convey information on the modes of adjustment rather than on their cost. At the same time, Srinivasan's statement – "it is hard to assess his argument that in response to the initial shock of 1973, the outward-oriented economies did not increase their external debt but relied on output-increasing policies of export promotion and import substitution after initially deflating their economies" – conflicts with the facts.

Thus, while the ratio of the external debt to the exports of outward-oriented developing countries increased by less than one-fourth during the period, the ratio for inward-oriented countries more than doubled (Balassa, 1986, table 3). Also, the annual estimates show the shift from deflationary policies to output-increasing policies in outward-oriented countries occurring over time. This shift is also indicated by the growth rates reported in table 17.1 that show an acceleration of economic growth that took place after a deceleration in the years immediately following the external shocks. Thus, while deflationary policies were of importance in outward-oriented countries in the 1979–83 period, on the average this average conceals the changes that occurred during the period.

Additional information is provided in a cross-section study of 43 developing countries where a continuous variable was used to define trade orientation, thereby overcoming the problems involved in the binary classification of outward and inward orientation (Balassa, 1985). In this study, the contribution to economic growth of initial trade orientation and of policy responses to external shocks during the 1973–79 period have been separately estimated.

The extent of trade orientation has been defined as deviations of actual from hypothetical values of per capita exports, the latter having been derived in a regression equation that includes per capita incomes, population, and the ratio of mineral exports to the gross national product as explanatory variables. In turn, alternative policy responses have been represented by relating the balance-of-payments effects of export promotion, import substitution, and additional net external financing to the balance-of-payments effects of external shocks.

TABLE 17.6   *Rates of growth of GDP*

	1963–73	1973–76	1976–79	1973–79	1979–82	1982–85	1979–85
Outward-oriented NICs	7.1	5.0	9.2	7.1	3.4	5.8	4.6
Outward-oriented LDCs	7.2	6.5	7.2	6.8	4.8	5.0	4.9
Outward-oriented NICs and LDCs	7.1	5.4	8.6	7.0	3.8	5.6	4.7
Inward-oriented NICs	6.9	5.9	5.3	5.6	2.2	1.8	2.0
Inward-oriented LDCs	3.7	4.5	3.6	4.1	4.9	3.6	4.3
Inward-oriented NICs and LDCs	5.7	5.4	4.8	5.1	3.0	2.4	2.7

Source: World Bank data base.

The impact of trade orientation on economic growth has been indicated by estimating differences in GNP growth rates between a country in the upper quartile of the distribution in terms of trade orientation, representing the median among outward-oriented countries, and the neutral case where the trade orientation variable takes a zero value. The results show a gain of 0.5 percentage points for the country concerned. In turn, a country in the lower quartile of the distribution, representing the median among inward-oriented countries, is shown to experience a shortfall of 0.5 percentage points in its GNP growth rate. *Ceteris paribus*, there is thus a difference in GNP growth rates of 1.0 percentage points between the median outward-oriented and the median inward-oriented country.

Furthermore, the regression coefficient of the export promotion variable exceeds that of the import substitution and the additional net external financing variables two to two-and-a-half times, indicating that greater reliance on export promotion in response to external shocks permits reaching higher GNP growth rates. Correspondingly, increasing export promotion by 10 percentage points at the expense of import substitution and additional net external financing would add 0.3 percentage points to the rate of economic growth. The gain is 0.7 percentage points if comparison is made between the upper quartile and the median in terms of reliance on export promotion, and a loss of 0.4 percentage points in GNP growth is shown if a country at the lower quartile of the distribution is compared to the median. Comparing the two quartiles, a gain of 1.2 percentage points is obtained.

The results are cumulative, indicating that both initial trade orientation and the choice of adjustment policies in response to external shocks importantly contributed to economic growth during the period under review. In fact, these factors explain a large proportion of inter-country differences in GNP growth rates that averaged 5.0 percent in the 43 developing countries under consideration during the 1973–79 period, with an upper quartile of 6.5 percent and a lower quartile of 3.3 percent.

These results strengthen the findings obtained by using the binary classification scheme and reported in Srinivasan's table 17.4 and in table 17.6 of the present note. They show the crucial importance of policy choice in coping with external shocks for a country's growth performance.

NOTES

[1] Emmanuel's model is identical to that of Prebisch, except for his assumption of the international equalization of the rates of return to capital, which are assumed to differ between the North and the South in the Prebisch model.

[2] While this expression will be appropriate for primary products and intermediate goods that are standardized commodities, it will have to be modified

in the case of differentiated manufactured goods where, *ceteris paribus*, the differences between import and domestic price elasticities will be smaller.

REFERENCES

Ahluwalia, I.J. 1985: *Industrial Growth in India.* Delhi: Oxford University Press.

Bacha, E. 1978: "An Interpretation of Unequal Exchange from Prebisch-Singer to Emmanuel." *Journal of Development Economics*, 5, 319–30.

Balassa, Bela 1985: "Exports, Policy Choices and Economic Growth in Developing Countries After the 1973 Oil Shock." *Journal of Development Economics*, 18, 23–36.

Balassa, Bela 1986: "Developing Country Debt: Policies and Prospects." In Herbert Giersch (ed.), *The International Debt Problem: Lessons for the Future,* Tübingen: J. C. B. Mohr (Paul Siebeck), 103–22.

Balassa, Bela 1987: "Outward Orientation." Forthcoming in H. B. Chenery and T. N. Srinivasan (eds), *Handbook for Development Economics,* Amsterdam: North-Holland.

Balassa, B. and associates 1971: "The Structure of Protection in Developing Countries." Baltimore: Johns Hopkins University Press.

Balassa, Bela; Bueno, Gerardo; Kuczynski, Pedro Pablo and Simonsen, Mario 1986: *Toward Regaining Economic Growth.* Washington, DC: Institute for International Economics.

Bhagwati, J. 1958: "International Trade and Economic Expansion." *American Economic Review*, 48, 941–53.

Bruton, H. J. 1967: "Productivity Growth in Latin America." *American Economic Review*, 57, 1099–107.

Bruton, H. J. 1970: "The Import Substitution Strategy of Economic Development: A Survey." *Pakistan Development Review*, 10, 124–46.

De Melo, J. 1978: "Estimating the Cost of Protection: A General Equilibrium Approach." *Quarterly Journal of Economics*, 62, 209–26.

Elias, V. J. 1978: "Sources of Economic Growth in Latin American Countries." *Review of Economics and Statistics*, 60, 362–70.

Ginsburgh, V. A. and Waelbroeck, J. L. 1984: *Activity Analysis and General Equilibrium Modelling.* Amsterdam: North-Holland.

Johnson, H. G. 1954: "Increasing Productivity, Trends and the Trade Balance." *Economic Journal*, 36.

Johnson, H. G. 1967: "The Possibility of Income Losses from Increased Efficiency Factor Accumulation in the Presence of Tariffs." *Economic Journal*, 17, 151–4.

Krueger, A. O. and Tuncer, B. 1980: "An Empirical Test of the Infant Industry Argument." *American Economic Review*, 5, 1142–52.

Martin, R. 1977: "Immiserizing Growth for a Tariff-Distorted, Small Economy: Further Analysis." *Journal of International Economics*, 7, 223–8.

Nishimizu, M. and Robinson, S. 1984: "Trade Policies and Productivity Change in Semi-Industrialized Countries." *Journal of Development Economics*, 16, 177–206.

Taylor, L. 1981: "South-South Trade and Southern Growth: Bleak Prospects from the Structuralist Point of View." *Journal of International Economics*, 11, 589–602.

18

External Borrowing by LDCs: A Survey of Some Theoretical Issues

KENNETH KLETZER

INTRODUCTION

Inflows of foreign capital have played a role in the growth of developing regions for several centuries. Portfolio lending to developing countries experienced an extended period of expansion during the late nineteenth and early twentieth centuries. Although lending by the OECD countries to the LDCs grew steadily during the 1960s, the rapid growth of syndicated bank loans after 1973 and reschedulings of the 1980s have recently brought widespread attention to the role of risk in international lending.

International credit transactions are subject to the risks created by the sovereign immunity of debtors. In any setting, lenders encounter problems of the enforceability of contracts and of imperfect information about the characteristics and behavior of borrowers. One of the parties to a contract may later find reneging on some of their obligations to be in their best interests. Parties subject to the same legal jurisdictions can rely upon the authority of the state for a degree of enforcement of contracts. Loan contracts can incorporate performance requirements for debtors which rely on the legal institutions of the country for fulfillment in some contingencies. However, loans between governments or the nationals of different countries cannot rely on third party enforcement. Relationships between borrowers and lenders must be self-enforcing. Contractual terms are viable for which fulfillment is in the enlightened self-interest of the debtor. With the absence of an external authority to enforce directly contractual obligations and the protection of debtor assets afforded by sovereignty, the enforcement of contracts necessarily occurs through the credibility of indirect sanctions for default. The interruption of other transactions, such as future credit

I am grateful to Willem Buiter and T. Paul Schultz for their many helpful comments on an earlier draft of this survey. I remain solely responsible for all remaining errors or oversights.

flows and trade agreements, between creditors and recalcitrant debtors provide the primary means of enforcement.

Many writers on LDC debt have concentrated on the question of whether repayment difficulties are the result of a lack of debtor solvency or liquidity. In only a few instances, can an argument even be made that a country's net worth is negative; even if the output counted includes only that readily transferable to foreigners, the present value of the stream of resources available for repayment exceeds the debt of almost all borrowers. If the current problems are ones of liquidity, then an explanation is needed of why lenders fail to provide additional loans to ultimately solvent debtors. The theoretical literature on lending with potential repudiation provides a starting point for modeling this issue. The ability of debtors to default on their external obligations implies that credit transactions are constrained by the proclivity of borrowers to repay, rather than by their ability. The amount of debt that is likely to be voluntarily repaid, under the threat of sanctions, is less than that which could eventually be serviced.

Lender's imperfect information about the actions and characteristics of borrowers can lead to major imperfections in the international credit market. Asymmetries of information lead to a variety of moral hazard and adverse selection issues in all credit transactions (for example, see Stiglitz and Weiss, 1981 and 1983). In domestic markets, covenants to loan contracts specifying borrower and lender behavior in various contingencies, and legal institutions establishing bankruptcy procedures, reduce many of these problems to a degree. In international lending, most loan covenants – for example, those establishing debt priorities – are not enforceable against a debtor. Because the penalties for default are indirect, moral hazard issues can arise through the ability of borrowers to take actions which reduce the costs of sanctions or the probability of penalization.

Short-term contracts may govern long-term, debtor-creditor relationships because they allow frequent renegotiation of the terms of the relationship. When creditors have a limited ability to observe and restrain debtors' actions, many possible covenants to loan contracts specifying debtor behavior in various contingencies are unenforceable. The restricted ability of lenders to observe realizations of debtor income can lead to rescheduling of outstanding short-term debt. In one interpretation, rescheduling can be viewed as an outcome in some contingencies which is anticipated by both sides of the market; loan terms are rationally expected to be state-contingent. Another aspect of rescheduling is the strategic behavior of debtors and creditors, even when initial loans are made under competitive conditions. The success of lenders to incorporate private sector loans extended without government guarantees into rescheduled public debt is evidence of their market power.

This paper is intended to survey those insights that can be obtained from the theoretical literature on credit market imperfections, in general, and on lending with sovereign risk, in particular, for understanding the determinants of portfolio capital flows to the LDCs. Several implications of these basic models and of results from the theory of games for the institutions observed in LDC borrowing are suggested which have not yet been formally modeled.

Four motives for external borrowing can be distinguished. If the value of output is subject to fluctuations, then borrowing to smooth consumption over time is advantageous when consumers are risk-averse. Borrowing to finance capital accumulation can allow investment at a higher rate than otherwise optimal in a country with marginal productivity of capital exceeding the foreign rate of interest. The adjustment of consumption and investment following exogenous events, such as terms of trade shifts, can be eased through foreign borrowing. Debt can also provide a medium of exchange for international transactions, for example, the use of suppliers' credits for commodity trade.

The next section discusses optimizing models of the pattern of borrowing for the first two motives which exclude the possibility of repudiation. The implications of imposing a solvency-type budget constraint are presented. Problems encountered by studying non-optimizing models are also discussed. The simple motives of lenders to extend credit beyond that which can be repaid in full with certainty are discussed.

The following section discusses the enforcement problem in international credit transactions and the possible sanctions for default. The credibility of threatened penalties is also examined. The points emphasized in this section are made in a variety of other sources; this exposition is quite similar to that given by Eaton, Gersovitz, and Stiglitz (1986), where the reader will find elaboration of many of the issues raised.

The role of informational asymmetries for international credit transactions is surveyed in the subsequent section. A simple stochastic model of borrowing with potential default is presented to aid the exposition. The inability of creditors to monitor many of the actions of debtors and observe realizations of debtor-specific exogenous events can be related to a number of important market outcomes. The dominance of syndicated bank loans over bond debt, short original maturities of loans, debt-rescheduling, and reserve-holding behavior of debtors are discussed separately, although they are interrelated phenomena. One consequence of short-maturity structure, credit-rationing, and renegotiation is the possible procyclical pattern of lending in a consumption-smoothing framework. The role of borrowers' reputations in repeated lending games of incomplete information is also discussed; the co-existence of bond debt with syndicated bank loans and its apparent informal priority is given as an example of the potential insights game theory may provide.

The sixth section discusses the flight of private capital from debtor nations. Capital flight can result from public guarantees of private sector foreign debt, because foreign asset income usually escapes the increased taxation of domestic capital earnings implied by bankruptcies. The next two sections briefly discuss the effects of select debtor country policies on indebtedness and the possible implications of deposit insurance and inadequate regulation of intermediaries in creditor countries, respectively. The last section contains a brief review of econometric studies of the determinants of external credit flows and repayment crises.

SOLVENCY AND INTERNATIONAL LENDING

A natural starting point for a description of equilibrium lending to LDCs are models of external borrowing in the absence of potential default. Such models provide insights into the pattern of borrowing under alternative motives and serve as benchmark cases for the analysis of the effects of external disturbances and domestic policy choices on the borrowing behavior of households and firms. A number of papers on foreign borrowing use two-period models.[1] In these models, both the principal and interest on debts incurred in the first period must be repaid by the end of the second period; therefore, solvency requires that second period income equal or exceed indebtedness and the debt-service obligation. In any finite horizon model, the dynamics of borrowing are determined by the exogenously set terminal level of debt. In an infinite horizon framework, debt principals need never be repaid; rather, the present value of debt-service payments must exceed the value of the principal. The steady-state net external asset position of the country is endogenously determined by optimization of some objective function. The solvency budget constraint requires that the present value of the stream of future income is not less than the current indebtedness.

The pattern of borrowing and lending under the consumption smoothing motive can be examined in the absence of default risk in either finite or infinite horizon models. Clarida (1986) studies optimal borrowing in an infinite horizon general equilibrium model with stochastic income under the imposition of the constraint that a debtor is solvent with unit probability. Borrowing is countercylical, and any level of debt which can be serviced given the equilibrium interest rate is reached with positive probability.

Optimal borrowing by an initially capital-poor country for the purpose of accumulation has been modeled for one-sector economies by Bardhan (1967), for the small-country case, and Hamada (1966), in a two-country model. Since the domestic marginal productivity of capital initially exceeds that abroad, an exchange of bonds for capital leads to an increase in wealth and consumption. Current account deficits occur as the capital stock and consumption increase. In the steady state, the current account is balanced and trade surpluses cover interest payments on a permanent level of debt. In two-sector economy models, early period current account deficits can be followed by surpluses for an initially capital-poor country. Engel and Kletzer (1985a) display such stages in the balance of payments in an optimal savings model with a tradeable investment good and a non-tradeable consumable under the usual Heckscher–Ohlin assumptions. Initially, bonds are traded for capital as resources move to the traded-goods-producing sector. Thereafter, current account surpluses occur as resources shift toward the consumption goods producing industry; the capital stock rises or falls as wealth increases, depending upon the relative capital-intensity of the sectors. In the steady-state, the country can be either a net debtor or creditor.[2]

Another literature which emphasizes the ability of debtors to repay exists. Domar (1950) presents a simple way in which debt and debt-service can permanently grow: the growth rate of new lending must exceed the interest rate (Avramovic, 1964, presents a similar analysis). Under this scheme, the initial principal is provided in exchange for nothing. This line of modeling is adopted by Kharas (1984) and Sachs (1984) in the context of borrowing in the presence of constraints on government revenue. When governments incur external debts, repayment is constrained by the ability of the government to raise revenue and transfer it abroad. In the absence of lump-sum taxation, deadweight losses and national income are endogenous to the level of revenue-raising attempted. In the Kharas paper, the debtor's growth rate is exogenous and exceeds the interest rate, so that an equilibrium in international asset markets will fail to exist. The growth rate should be treated as an endogenous variable. Sachs (1984) uses a two-period optimizing model with an exogenously imposed constraint on government revenue in the second period. This leads to a higher marginal cost of revenue in that period and to optimal borrowing up to a point below that which equates the domestic marginal productivity of capital to the interest rate. As Eaton, Gersovitz and Stiglitz (1986) emphasize, switching the period in which the constraint is binding reverses the result. While equilibrium intertemporal optimizing models only serve as a benchmark case, models which adopt arbitrary assumptions can lead to special or untenable conclusions.

Solvency models exogenously impose a constraint on borrowing, rather than deriving such constraints on the supply of loans from creditors' optimizing behavior. In a stochastic income framework, loans can serve risk-sharing purposes, in addition to providing intertemporal trades. If repayment capacity is uncertain, then a lender generally will lend more than can be repaid in all contingencies on schedule. A risk-neutral creditor seeking to maximize expected profit will extend credit beyond that amount which can be serviced with certainty. Jaffee and Modigliani (1969) demonstrate that such a lender would place an upper bound on the amount lent and incur a possibility of *ex post* losses.

The maximum debt for which a borrower remains solvent may itself be endogenous because the resources available for repayment can depend upon repayment obligations. Stiglitz and Weiss (1981) show that the choice of investment can vary with the loan contract taken. If lenders cannot observe directly the project selection of a borrower, then adverse selection results in their model. Increasing the interest rate increases the riskiness of loans and can lead to a decrease in expected profits; therefore, credit-rationing can result. An important implication is that solvency cannot be defined independently of the actions of agents on both sides of the market.

A surprisingly large percentage of the discussion about the indebtedness of the LDCs has focused on the solvency or liquidity of debtor governments. The debts of countries are clearly less than the value of assets owned by governments and nationals in almost all cases. While the government may face limits in its ability to appropriate these assets, this action involves a set of trade-offs and is a choice taken by the government. As Gersovitz (1985) points out, Mexican oil reserves alone (the property of a parastatal) probably are adequate to cover Mexico's external debt. The other popular view is that borrowers have positive net worth but are illiquid. Clearly, the question arises of why lenders are unwilling to supply new credit.

Instead, sovereign governments can elect to default on terms of a contract or repudiate outright external obligations. This ability impedes the international movement of capital. The subsequent sections discuss the implications of sovereign risk for modeling external borrowing by the LDCs.

SOVEREIGN IMMUNITY AND THE VOLUNTARINESS OF REPAYMENT

Any credit transaction is subject to a potential problem of enforcement of the terms of the exchange. Nationals of the same country who enter into a contract can appeal to the external authority of the state in the event of one party's reneging upon an obligation. To varying degrees, the legal frameworks of nations provide protection for parties to a contract in the event of the inability or unwillingness of one of them to abide by the terms of the contract. Contracts written between nationals of one country and nationals or the government of another, however, are subject to a potential problem of sovereign immunity. Generally, creditors have little or no hope of obtaining compensation for nonperformance in the debtor's own political and legal jurisdiction. The sovereignty of nations rules out the existence of a credible third party to enforce terms of contracts involving governments. Therefore, many international credit transactions can involve only contract terms which would be in the best interests *ex post* of the borrower to honor. Many of the institutions surrounding international lending can be understood best in terms of this need for contracts to be self-enforcing. The primary impediment to international capital flows to the LDCs is not seen in the ability of countries to repay, but instead in the voluntariness of fulfilling contract obligations.

The major difference between international and domestic credit contracts is that the latter are legal obligations which are subject to enforcement under the power of the state. Debtors who are unable to repay may file for bankruptcy, obtain protection from creditors and discharge of their obligations. Because repayment of external debt is largely voluntary, the penalties which can be imposed on a recalcitrant debtor country are necessarily indirect. A nation may suffer the consequences of incurring debt-service obligations it cannot service for an arbitrary period of time. Furthermore, while collateral plays a significant role in domestic lending, it plays virtually no role in international credit markets. Collateral remaining in the debtor country cannot be seized, and physical assets outside the country are often of little productive value (the exceptions tend to comprise value far less than outstanding debts of the LDCs).

In any context, a loan is a particular form of contract between parties governing an intertemporal exchange. The contract specifies repayment terms and actions which may be taken by debtors and creditors in a variety of contingencies. The possibility that repayment obligations may not be met as contracted is reflected in the covenants of the loan contract. These covenants are intended to ensure that the borrower engage in certain activities and not engage in others which affect the likelihood of full repayment. Contracts also specify conditions under which the lender can suspend terms of the contract prior to its expiration (in LDC lending, cross-default clauses serve this purpose).

Loan covenants are useful only if the contingencies to which they apply and debtor's actions they stipulate are observable by the lenders. A crucial determinant of the nature of the relationship between lender and borrower is the set of actions and outcomes that are observable by both and upon which covenants can be written. Debt contracts specify an amount to be lent and a schedule of repayments of interest and principal to be made, but these are, to varying degrees, state-contingent terms. The degree to which observability is incomplete affects the extent that debtor-creditor relationships are governed by explicit and by implicit contracts. The lesser the ability of creditors to restrain the actions of debtors during a contract's term, the greater is the incentive to offer short-term agreements in long-term credit relationships. Short-term loans allow for frequent recontracting of the terms of the agreements, therefore, a finer degree of conditioning on borrowers' actions.

The role of repetition of the relationship between borrower and lender should not be ignored. In a two-period framework, a borrower can either provide full repayment of a loan at the second date or default. A default is merely a payment of anything less than the principal plus agreed-upon interest. In a multi-period setting, deviations from a repayment schedule do not necessarily imply that future payments will not maintain the present value of the loan. When credit relationships potentially last a number of periods, contracts may be renegotiated and entered into under full recognition of this possibility. A variety of responses by creditors to violations of the terms of the agreement are possible. As Eaton, Gersovitz and Stiglitz (1986) point out, declaration of a default is only one of these. They define a default as occurring whenever a creditor formally declares that there has been a violation of a condition of the loan. The contract conveys upon the lender the right to declare a borrower in default; creditors may or may not choose to exercise this right. Therefore, default is the result of a sequence of decisions, not an automatic outcome. Insolvency of a debtor is not an adequate condition for the declaration of a default; the lender may lose the ability to obtain partial repayment by doing so. On the other hand, a default may be declared when a borrower has positive net worth. For example, declaration can follow the unwillingness of the debtor to repay other loans or the inability of the creditor to restrict actions of the borrower which increase the riskiness of outstanding debt. Formal declaration of a default in international lending can result in costly actions by regulators for both lenders and borrowers. The imposition of penalties by other governments on countries in default will tend to lower the expected flow of payments to existing creditors, even if anticipated payments fall below the amount lent in present value.

Penalization of default

The willingness of sovereign debtors to abide by the terms of loan contracts depends upon the degree to which default can be penalized and the resolve of lenders to impose penalties. The penalties available to creditors include exclusion from future access to credit, interference with commodity trade, and disruption of access to trade finance. In the nineteenth century, military threats against debtor nations and even the loss of sovereignty (Egypt) appear to have been credible threats. The suspension of favorable trade agreements, for example, revoking and granting to alternate suppliers voluntary quota arrangements, are probably credible contemporary threats along with embargoes on future lending. The nature of penalties is crucial to informative modeling of the international credit market, since the extent of capital flows to the LDCs depends upon the credibility of a borrower's willingness to repay. Kaletsky (1985) provides a comprehensive overview of the legal, political, and institutional issues involved in penalization of default. Eaton and Gersovitz (1981b) review U.S. legislation which provides for potential penalities to be imposed in the event of default on foreign obligations to the U.S. government or intermediaries.

Exclusion from future credit access is an often cited potential penalty (the Eaton and Gersovitz, 1981a, and Kletzer, 1984, models adopt this penalty structure). A denial of future credit access only makes sense in an infinite (or equivalently, uncertain) horizon model, since in a finite horizon setting, the penalty has no force in the last period. Therefore, no loans are made in the next to last, and the penalty has no force in that period as well. A loan market is unsustainable. Similarly, moratoria on future lending are inadequate penalties to maintain loan transactions if a date will be reached after which the debtor only makes positive net payments. In the standard infinite-horizon, optimal capital accumulation models, such a point is attained when the marginal productivity of capital is drawn into equality with the interest rate. As the capital stock grows, the potential cost of the penalty declines toward zero. In this context, exclusion from the credit market is an insufficient penalty to support any credit transactions by backward recursion.

Furthermore, moratoria on credit access provide an adequate penalty to sustain lending only in infinite-horizon models with stochastic debtor income. In this context, future flow of funds is in both directions so that the penalty can impose a cost on the debtor in any time period. If borrowers are risk-averse, then the desire to borrow and the cost of moratoria derives from a motive to smooth consumption. Risk-neutrality on the part of lenders assures that some degree of lending will occur. In a capital-accumulation model with stochastic output, the threatened denial of future credit can sustain lending for the purpose of investment if the borrower is risk-averse, since there is a cost to repudiation in the long run. However, the flow of capital to the country will be constrained by the extent of the penalty, so that, generally, the expected marginal productivity of capital will exceed the interest rate for extended periods.

In the Eaton and Gersovitz and Kletzer models, increases in the cost of losing access to credit shift outward the supply schedule of loans. The penalty for default is higher the lower the rate of discount, greater the borrower's degree of risk aversion, greater the variance in income, lower the interest rate, and more costly are domestically available avenues for consumption smoothing. Increasing the penalty raises the amount lent in these models, which benefits the borrower. However, since output is stochastic, risk-neutral lenders will extend credit to a point where default occurs with positive probability. In these states, debtors are worse off, and the states of default are less probable, reducing the insurance benefits of potential default for the borrowers. Therefore, the expected utility of debtors can either increase or decrease.

An important role of international lending is in the financing of international trade. The cost of conducting barter trade is presumed widely to be quite high. Threatened trade embargoes or suspension of trade preferences can also provide incentives against debt repudiation.

A set of issues can arise in applying penalties if the actions of a borrower affect the burden of sanctions. Commitment to actions which lenders perceive as raising the burden will improve the supply of credit, and conversely. However, such actions must be observable by lenders and not easily reversed.

The potential disruption of trade finance can be partially offset. Debtors have an incentive to accumulate foreign reserves in anticipation of a default, instead of fully meeting their debt-service obligations. At the same time, forestalling a declaration of default by creditors allows the time required for this accumulation. Many people may see the 1986 Peruvian limitation of private market debt-service payments and maintenance of service on official (non-IMF) credits, while foreign reserves rose, in these terms. The efficacy of the penalty may be diminished because a default declaration is not currently in the creditors' interests.

Penalization of a recalcitrant debtor through disruption of its international trade may be quite credible. If a debtor attempts to transact trade through banks on which it has defaulted, then any transactions balances can be attached to cover its debt obligations. Avoidance of the international banking system can significantly increase the cost of trading. Although punishment of a defaulter will often not increase the likelihood of ultimate repayment, a lender can credibly threaten to offset loan obligations against other balances of a non-performing borrower.

Gersovitz (1983) and Alexander (1985) study models in which the penalty for default depends positively upon the importance of trade to the debtor. A commitment to raise investment leads to an increase in the supply of credit if it increases the value of trading opportunities. If investment occurs in import-substituting industries, then it reduces the repayment incentive.

A number of papers (Sachs, 1984; Cooper and Sachs, 1985; Sachs and Cohen, 1985) assume that the penalty for default is a loss of income proportional to GNP. Among the conclusions they derive is the implication that if a credit-constrained debtor can commit funds to investment, instead of to consumption, then the supply of credit will expand. As Gersovitz (1985) makes clear, this conclusion easily fails to hold in models adopting penalties of credit or trade embargoes. Also, a reasonable argument can be given that the higher a debtor's income, the more able it will be to accommodate itself to sanctions.

The credibility of embargoes in future lending

While governments and banks may reasonably be expected to reduce a country's trading opportunities in the event of a default, threatened moratoria on future credit access may not always be credible. Current creditors or other potential lenders may find continued flows of credit to a recalcitrant borrower profitable. In particular, the full suspension of future borrowing possibilities will not increase the probability of even partial repayment of old debt.

In Eaton and Gersovitz (1981a), lenders are competitive so that any loan earns zero profit. They argue, therefore, that the costs of refraining from future lending are also zero. However, this equilibrium can be difficult to support under noncooperative behavior among lenders. If all other creditors refrain from lending in the future to a defaulter, then any particular lender can provide a profitable loan. A cooperative outcome can arise in the infinite horizon case when borrowers' and lenders' identities are subject to recall by the other players in the repeated game. A player who fails to cooperate at one point (e.g. by defaulting) will face noncooperative strategies chosen by the other players for some number of subsequent plays. The literature on repeated noncooperative games can be appealed to for a number of results, notably when discount rates are small, a degree of cooperation can emerge in equilibrium (see Fudenberg and Maskin, 1986).

The entry of new lenders during a moratorium on credit access enforced by old creditors can be restricted in repeated game models with imperfect information. The refusal of current creditors to lend may easily convey information to other potential creditors in this context. Also, the relatively small number of international banks may be capable of cooperating in the exclusion of defaulters. The banks themselves may be able to enforce an embargo through their other transactions with each other. The syndication of bank loans to the LDCs may be seen partly as a response to the need to credibly impose sanctions for default. Additionally, a current lender faces the possibility of recovering previous loans if it makes new loans to a debtor having repayment difficulties. Therefore, new lenders may have less to gain by negotiating loans to a problem debtor than do existing creditors.

Another possibility is that creditors can write covenants in loan contracts which pertain to other creditors' actions. These provisions, particularly seniority clauses, could be enforced in developed country courts to which both lenders are subject. Covenants of this type allow a creditor to obtain an enforceable judgment against another creditor in a common legal jurisdiction rather than attempt to enforce a contract with a sovereign borrower.[3] Cross-default and seniority clauses in IMF and World Bank loan agreements may also lend credibility to sanctions.

Stiglitz and Weiss (1983) discuss the potential incentive effects of debt seniority clauses and show that a refusal of a current creditor to lend leads to refusals of new lenders as well.

Eaton (1985) emphasizes the importance of banks' reputations for punishing defaulters in maintaining the value of their equity. Owners of intermediaries are concerned with preserving their equity investments, and the failure to punish defaulting debtors causes this equity to lose its value. Eaton shows that the value of the equity must exceed the costs of penalizing borrowers. Therefore, if punishment is costly, banks' profits must be positive. This mechanism leads to a credible threat of punishment in an infinitely repeated game and to a lending rate of interest exceeding the deposit rate even if defaults never occur (e.g. in a nonstochastic model).

The difficulty for a lender to credibly commit to a cut-off of credit to debtors is demonstrated by Hellwig (1977). In his model, lenders extend a line of credit to a borrower with income following a simple hazard process. The borrower's income is zero until it jumps to a permanent positive level; the probability of the jump is the same each period. Default occurs if before the jump has occurred, the credit ceiling is reached and no new credit is forthcoming. The lender always has an incentive to increase the credit line if it is exhausted prior to the increase in income. Otherwise, no repayment takes place, while new loans embody the possibility of servicing of old debt as well. The new loans need not be profitable if viewed on their own, and good money is thrown after bad. Debtors have the incentive to increase their consumption in zero-income periods, running down their credit lines rapidly. Therefore, by making an initial loan, a creditor enters a relationship in which additional loans may be profitably written, but the total debt provides negative expected profits. Consequently, the loan market breaks down.

INSTITUTIONAL CHARACTERISTICS OF LDC BORROWING

The necessity for lenders to rely upon the enlightened self-interest of sovereign borrowers for repayment can be related to the characteristics which distinguish international credit markets from domestic ones in the developed countries. Informational imperfections may be responsible for many of the market outcomes and institutions surrounding capital flows to the LDCs. The inability of creditors to observe certain actions taken by debtors and outcomes leads to restrictions on the types of contracts which can be enforced, hence entered into. The domination of syndicated bank lending over bond lending, short maturity lending in long-term debtor–creditor relationships, and rescheduling of debts can be seen as outcomes of the enforceability problem in sovereign lending.

In this section, a basic model of borrowing with potential repudiation is presented in which debtor income is stochastic. The model makes a number of overly simplifying assumptions and is intended to serve only for drawing a few basic implications for modeling and serve as an aid to expositing the role of imperfect information in the loan market.

Basic stochastic model

The simple model adopted is a variant of the Eaton and Gersovitz (1981a) one, following Kletzer (1984). Output is a random variable, which is identically independently distributed across periods. Debtors obtain utility from a discounted stream of felicity (current period utility) of consumption each period and face a moratorium on future lending if they default. Utility is given by,

$$V = E \sum_{t=0}^{\infty} \beta^t U(c_t),$$

where $0 < \beta < 1$ and $E(.)$ is the expectation operator. Output cannot be stored, and, for simplicity, the moratoria last forever.

In the event of debt repayment, a borrower's utility is,

$$V^r(y_t, R_t) = U(y_t + l_t - R_t) + \beta E[\max\{V^r(y_{t+1}, R_{t+1}), V^d(y_{t+1})\}]$$

and, if default is chosen,

$$V^d(y_t) = U(y_t) + (\beta/(1 - \beta))E(U(y)),$$

where R_t is the current debt-service obligation, l_t is the current new loan, and y_t is the output, a random variable.

The borrower defaults whenever $V^d(y_t) > V^r(y_t, R_t)$. The model assumes that default or full repayment are the only options available to a debtor.

If loans mature in one period, then the expected profits to lenders are given by

$$E\pi = l \cdot (P \cdot (1 + r) - (1 + \rho)),$$

where ρ is the opportunity cost of funds and r and l are the interest rate and size of the debt. P is the probability of repayment which depends upon the terms of the current and anticipated future loan contracts. Kletzer (1984) shows that if the range of possible values for output is bounded and felicity is concave, then the probability of default increases with the interest rate and, eventually, with the amount lent. Expected profits fall below zero for any interest rate as the principal passes beyond an upper bound and for any positive principal as the interest rises beyond a finite bound. Therefore, the set of positive loan contracts which provide non-negative expected profits is bounded in both the amount lent and the rate of interest charged. These results are depicted in figure 18.1, where continuity of the cumulative distribution of output and some additional degree of concavity have been assumed. The set of loan contracts in figure 18.1 are those available to a particular debtor.

Lenders may be assumed to be risk-neutral. However, a concept of equilibrium must be explicitly adopted. Competition amongst lenders is a useful starting point for examining market outcomes. In this model, free entry in loan contracts (interest rates and quantity lent) is a natural characterization of perfect competition. If there are no asymmetries of information between lenders, then it is appropriate to examine Nash equilibria in loan contracts. In this model, a Nash equilibrium in loan

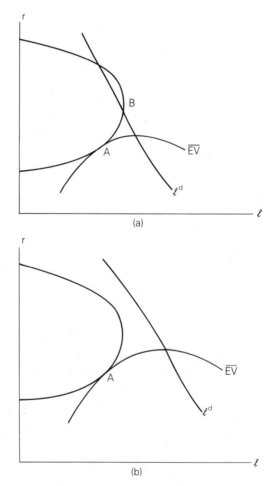

FIG. 18.1   *Nash equilibrium in loan contracts*

contracts is simply the best pair of interest rate and amount lent for the borrower from among those loan contracts which provide non-negative expected profits.

An important point is that the probability of repayment depends upon total debt-service obligations, so that the amount any particular lender will provide in equilibrium depends upon the amount lent by others. A Nash equilibrium is an equilibrium with free entry in loan contracts if each creditor can observe the amount lent by others. In equilibrium, a contract must specify the interest rate and total concurrent amount lent to the borrower from all sources. Such contracts are enforceable only if the total debt service obligations at each date are observable by each creditor.[4] With general maturities of loans, contracts will need to specify the repayment schedule as a function of the stream of total debt-service obligations of the borrower at each date when a repayment is to occur.

A Nash equilibrium in loan contracts is depicted in figure 18.1, taken from Kletzer (1984). The concave curve, $\overline{EV}$, passing through the equilibrium point, A, is an indifference curve for the debtor (constant expected utility given optimal default behavior). The loan demand curve, denoted l^d, gives the amount of credit which would be desired at each given rate of interest. In the presence of possible default, borrowers demand more credit than they would in its absence. For this consumption-smoothing model, the indifference curves and curve l^d all vary with the realization of income, y. A smaller (that is, lower amount and interest rate) debt contract will be chosen with higher realized output.

The first implication that can be drawn from this model is that in an equilibrium with observability of total indebtedness, credit must be rationed. The contract equilibrium can be supported using a non-linear interest schedule, that is, the interest rate as a given function of total concurrent indebtedness. However, the borrower cannot obtain all the credit demanded at the equilibrium rate of interest. This is the same type of credit-rationing demonstrated by Jaffee and Russell (1976).[5]

The main point to be made here is that the terms of the loan contract are simultaneously determined. The interest rate and amount lent are both endogenous; the information of lenders which determines loan supply also determines the interest spread over the opportunity rate of interest. This point has been ignored in empirical studies of LDC credit flows.[6]

Furthermore, the interest spread cannot be interpreted in terms of a risk premium. For example, an increase in the borrower's discount rate reduces the penalty for default and leads to a contraction of the set of loan contracts which provide creditors with non-negative expected profits. The resulting equilibrium loan contract can be shown to entail a reduction in the amount lent (more severely rationed credit, since the demand curve shifts outward with the increase in default probability for constant contracts) and either an increase or decrease in the interest rate charged. The risk of default is reflected in both terms of loan contracts. In the presence of equilibrium rationing, reductions in the amount lent reflect increases in risk; because the probability of default declines with decreases in the interest spread, the change in the spread is ambiguous.

An increase in the opportunity cost of capital to lenders or adverse shifts in the distribution of borrowers' incomes lead to a shrinkage of the set of loan contracts attaining non-negative expected profits. Because the set is bounded for principal amounts exceeding zero, combinations of given opportunity cost and low ranges of possible income can yield no positive profitable contracts. This may be seen as the source of exclusion of the low-income LDCs from the private external loan market.

Syndicated bank lending

One of the prominent institutional features of recent LDC borrowing has been the predominance of bank over bond lending, particularly through syndicated loans. Banks may be more able to enforce and monitor terms of loan contracts than bondholders. For example, the ability of banks to enforce seniority clauses and other covenants (such as cross-default clauses) between each other enhances their abilities to impose penalties upon reluctant debtors and renegotiate loan terms. Bondholders may be unable to agree upon terms of loan renegotiation because of their diverse interests or face significant transactions costs in doing so. While the value of bonds fluctuates on the secondary market varying the return to lenders, debtors may face only two options: continued full debt-service or default. Syndicated bank debt can be renegotiated changing both the value of the lenders' assets and the repayment obligations of borrowers. In the presence of sovereign immunity and indirect enforceability, the ability of syndicates to reschedule loan payments through cooperation between creditors can give an advantage to bank over bond lending.

Another important point is that the credit-rationing equilibrium described above requires that lenders can observe, therefore condition loan terms upon, the total concurrent debt-service obligations of their borrowers. Restricting total lending, when the priority of debt is unclear, requires cooperation between lenders. This may be costly in the case of bondholders and fairly easy to do through syndication. An example of an equilibrium notion suitable to the case of nonobservability of total indebtedness by creditors is a interest-rate-taking free-entry equilibrium in the model of figure 18.1. Such an equilibrium, if one exists, will result in a contract on the borrower's loan demand curve at its lowest intersection with the set of zero expected profit loan contracts (point B in figure 18.1a). Contracts along the demand curve above this point will be dominated, for the borrower, by this contract. In general, such equilibria may fail to exist (in figure 18.1b, l^d does not intersect the set of zero expected profit contracts). If this type of equilibrium exists, then the debtor is always at least as well off in the Nash equilibrium with observed total indebtedness.[7]

Syndicated bank loans may dominate LDC borrowing because of this potential asymmetry of information between lenders and each borrower. The ability of creditors to monitor total concurrent debt-service obligations has social value in this model. Because providing additional loans raises the probability of default on all debt, lenders have an incentive to form a syndicate through which they can correctly observe the total lending by other members. A guarantee that an initial sale of bonds (at the Nash equilibrium level) will not be expanded subsequently is not credible in this model. Investment banks may or may not be able to credibly restrict bond issues they register through the equity value of their reputations. There are incentives to increase indebtedness *ex post* selling new bonds with higher yields.

Debt maturities

The basic model above (as in Eaton and Gersovitz (1981a)) assumes loan principals and interest payments are due after one period. Incentives to borrow using longer maturities are common, for example, gestation lags or investment costs with non-concavities in production may exist. In the simple repay-default framework, the accumulation of additional debt while paying debt-service without retiring principals on old debt generally will be an attractive option to debtors. In the consumption smoothing model without default, there would be no reason for particular debt-maturities to appear. However, the insurance aspects of the option of defaulting provide incentives for borrowers to prefer longer-maturity debt contracts.

An important aspect of sovereign risk is the inability to enforce many bond covenants common to domestic capital markets. Covenants restricting debt dilution and establishing debt priorities are essential to the use of long-term loan contracts. Because increased lending reduces the profitability of current debt in the moral hazard model, long-term loans must anticipate possible subsequent additions to debt. New loans will be made which require concurrent debt-service with long-term loans if they are profitable. Because new lenders may possess more information than was available when an old contract was made in a stochastic framework, additional debt will often be profitable. The increase in debt which occurs with positive events (e.g. information that reveals an increase in the *ex ante* probability of repayment) reduces the *ex ante* profitability of a given long-term loan contract. If additional shorter-term loans are expected to be profitable, then with free entry of lenders, both new creditors and the current providers of long-term debt have the same incentive to make such loans. Therefore, covenants restraining additional future borrowing cannot be credibly enforced in this setting.

Sachs and Cohen (1985) argue that the interest spread on longer-term debt must rise as a consequence and that this can lead borrowers to choose shorter-term lower interest rate contracts. However, debtors may prefer longer-term contracts with higher interest rates and lower probabilities of full repayment, if they are offered, due to the insurance roles of long-term debt. Kletzer (1984) points out that since the set of loan contracts which provide non-negative expected profits is bounded from above in the interest rate, the entire set of loan contracts which will be offered shrinks with increasing maturities if information about ultimate outcomes is revealed over time. This implies that for maturities beyond some length, there may be no contract with a positive principal that creditors will offer. In a stochastic setting, only short- and medium-original term debt may be offered.

While many motives for long-term, debtor-creditor relationships exist, transactions may take place only through a sequence of short-term contracts because lenders are unable to observe and, therefore, restrain subsequent actions by borrowers. The lack of enforceability of debt dilution and seniority clauses are only a single cause; a variety of moral hazard and adverse selection problems may also give rise to short-term debt obligations. For example, Stiglitz and Weiss (1981) demonstrate that borrowers' choices amongst risky projects depends upon the terms of loan contracts and are subject to adverse selection from the creditors' viewpoint. In the presence of asymmetries of information between debtor and creditor, the ability to change the terms of a relationship with greater frequency will be valuable. Contracts cannot rely on covenants which are not credibly enforceable; periodic renegotiation of the terms of the relationship provides incentives for performance on the part of the debtor, which long-term contracts may be incapable of achieving due to imperfect information.

Debt rescheduling

In the simple stochastic Eaton and Gersovitz (1981a) model of lending with potential repudiation, creditors have an incentive to renegotiate contract terms *ex post* when borrowers prefer default to full repayment. Since the original interest rate exceeds the opportunity cost of funds, creditors can still realize positive profits *ex post* for some reductions of repayment obligations, while incurring smaller losses in other instances than they would suffer by declaring a default. Likewise, debtors will prefer to pay something less than originally contracted and avoid the penalties consequent with default. When creditors possess complete information about debtors, debt-equity type contracts should emerge which allow, either explicitly or implicitly, for varying repayment obligations with the realized state of nature. Grossman and Van Huyck (1985) take this approach to interpreting debt-rescheduling. They suggest that since the conventional explicit legal contract only specifies a given rate of interest (which may float), lenders cannot increase the debt-service obligation prior to the contracted repayment date. Therefore, the set repayment schedule is the maximum of payments over states of nature. Lenders expect to receive less in many outcomes, and a default only occurs if the payment is less than the anticipated acceptable one for a given realized outcome. In the presence of sovereign immunity and credible penalties for outright repudiation, the basic model of this section can be used to show that risk-neutral lenders do not fully insure, that is, entirely smooth the consumption streams of, borrowers. Equity-debt contracts specifying state-contingent repayment obligations will be rationed in equilibrium.

If the income realizations of debtors can be observed by creditors, then loan contracts explicitly specifying state-contingent payments would arise. However, the standard debt-contract has been shown to be the optimal form of incentive-compatible contract for lending in two-period models when the state of nature can be observed only at a cost by the creditor (see Townsend, 1978; Gale and Hellwig, 1985). Costly observation of the realized income of debtors in a multi-period model with potential default could generate equilibrium standard debt contracts with renegotiation. The combination of the ability of borrowers to default and indirectness of penalties imply that equilibrium contracts will be of shorter original maturity than developed country corporate debt contracts and entail anticipated potential renegotiation of repayment terms when outcomes can be observed, but only at a cost, by creditors. This is one interpretation of debt-rescheduling.

The presence of creditors' incomplete information about debtors' characteristics can significantly affect the nature of debt renegotiations. For example, lenders may be uncertain about the perceptions of borrowers of the costs of default penalization or the probability of particular sanctions being imposed. Even if lenders cannot observe the realized state of nature, debt-rescheduling could still take place. Debtors can be inhibited from persistently reporting poor outcomes because of the loss of reputation and deterioration of loan terms that result. Similarly, cooperation between lenders can arise, so that only certain types of arrangements result, such as a lack of individual debt renegotiation in favor of simultaneous rescheduling of all outstanding debt.

Debt renegotiations in which debtors seek to obtain new net capital inflows and those in which they desire to lengthen the horizon over which principals are repaid or reduce interest obligations can lead to basically different outcomes. Most recent reschedulings have involved debt-service postponement by countries attempting to reduce their external indebtedness; net payments are made to creditors, which are smaller than required by the original contracts.

In the simple stochastic model of borrowing with potential repudiation, new lenders will assume only debt which assures non-negative expected profits. When a debtor realizes a poor output state, default with consequent penalization can be superior to full repayment and selection of a new zero expected profit debt contract. In this case, old creditors have an incentive to reduce debt-service obligations so that the borrower will choose not to default. If a debtor does not desire new inflows of capital, rescheduling results in a reduction in the present-value of the stream of repayments.

When a debtor seeks a new net inflow of funds, old creditors are more likely to supply them. Existing creditors have the possibility of recovering old debt-service in addition to new repayments when they provide new loans. In a low-income state, a borrower will choose between full default with penalization and accepting a renegotiated debt contract offered by existing creditors. Because new lenders will not assume the old debts on terms which the borrower would accept (full repayment in this event is inferior to default), old lenders can offer a rescheduling of existing debt-service combined with new loans with repayment terms exceeding those available in the competitive market. New lenders may be willing to extend more favorable terms on new inflows if the old debts are rescheduled, but existing creditors can offer the rescheduling and new loans as a single take-it or leave-it package. Even if the original loans were made in a competitive market (that is, with free entry in contracts), debt-renegotiation involves strategic behavior on the part of both lenders and borrowers.

Ozler (1984) presents a simple model of bilateral monopoly between lender and borrower. When the loan is made, second-period income and the penalty cost are both uncertain, but the borrower is known to be solvent. If income and penalty both exceed debt-service, then the debtor repays as contracted. If income falls below the repayment obligation, then the debtor seeks a rescheduling of debt-sevice. The new loan is made on more favorable terms for the lender than the initial loan because of the monopoly power the lender now has. On the other hand, if the penalty falls below the debt-service obligation, then the borrower threatens default and extracts concessionary terms from the lender. Ozler examines the effects of rescheduling announcements on the equity value of banks and finds that reschedulings during the late 1970s increased bank market values while those during the early 1980s reduced them.

Of course, other explanations of rescheduling exist. Banks may agree to postpone debt-service for insolvent or recalcitrant borrowers because managers are wrong about a debtor's proclivity or ability to repay, acting in the best interests of their own careers and moving on, acting in shareholders' best interest by postponing costs regulators will impose, or hoping that official and multilateral agency creditors will take over portions of the debt.

Potential problems for lending can be created by the short-term nature of original loans in the presence of potential default and consequent credit-rationing. If the simple model of borrowing is extended to allow more general stochastic income processes (other than identically independently distributed ones), then low-income states can lead to reductions in the amount of debt lenders wish to hold. For example, when output realizations are positively serially correlated and debt matures in one period, the set of loan contracts providing non-negative expected profits shrinks inward in low-income states. Because original maturities are shortened for reasons of imperfect information, lending becomes procyclic in the consumption-smoothing framework. Net principal retirements are desired by creditors when income is low and additions to debt forthcoming when income is high. Besides providing a reason in addition to borrowing for investment for the observed strongly procyclical pattern of lending to LDCs, this model could provide a basis for depicting panics amongst lenders.

Diamond and Dybvig (1983) present a game model of bank runs. Each depositor is better off withdrawing funds if others do so, but everybody benefits if nobody withdraws their deposits. Essential to the result is the assumption that deposits are refunded in full on a first-come, first-served basis. When lenders wish to hold fewer assets in a country, the net payments required rise (at the same time the value of output falls) which raises the probability of default. As one creditor withdraws, the profitability of others' loans are adversely affected. Without well-defined debt seniorities, this could potentially lead to a crisis.

Sachs (1984) and Krugman (1985) suggest models similar to Diamond and Dybvig (1983), substituting syndicated bank loans for bank deposits and allowing current income to fall short of debt-service obligations. Sachs assumes that each bank faces an upward-sloping marginal cost curve of loans; banking regulations or risk aversion are cited as possible sources. This implies that a single creditor may find it unprofitable to extend the entire loan to avoid default. Because the refusal of one creditor to relend raises the probability of default on other loans of other creditors, an externality exists so that cooperation between lenders can lead to a superior outcome. However, as already noted, a new loan need not be expected to be profitable on its own to be offered by an existing creditor. The bank already holding the largest amount of debt will be the most willing to extend further credit.

Gersovitz (1985) points out that both the Sachs and Krugman models really explain the prorating of payments moratoria and reschedulings across lenders and not rescheduling itself. In the Diamond and Dybvig model, intermediaries are unable to recoup the full value of their investments after one period, but depositors are able to claim the full value of their deposits on a first-come, first-served basis so that a depositor panic can result. A sovereign debtor for which resources available for repayment fall below debt-service obligations has an incentive to unilaterally reschedule payments, proportionally revaluing the assets of creditors. If creditors all face the same increasing marginal cost of funds, then creditors will each minimize their losses by accepting partial proportional payments if a debtor is incapable of servicing the complete debt. A lender panic does not occur for the same type of reason runs on mutual funds do not occur.

Debt and reserve-holding

Eaton and Gersovitz (1980) present an interesting empirical finding: foreign reserves rise as debtor countries are rationed more severely on international credit markets. Reserve-holding by debtors can be justified by the same transactions cost arguments that serve for creditors. However, credit market imperfections and default sanctions can be identified as additional sources of motives for reserve-holding and help explain the pattern of reserve accumulation by borrowers.

The difficulty encountered in explaining reserve-holding by debtors in the absence of transactions costs is that the interest paid on debt should equal or exceed that earned on reserves. We have already argued that short original debt maturities in a model of credit-rationing under potential repudiation with a general stochastic income process can lead to a procyclical pattern of lending (which happens to be socially inefficient). The supply curve of credit shifts inward with low-income realizations, so that the cost of credit increases and eventually becomes infinite. The gap between the marginal borrowing rate of interest and the discount rate during low-income events can compensate for the gap between the interest rate on debt (or, more, generally, the marginal productivity of domestic capital) and the interest earned on reserves. This motive for further consumption-smoothing through saving in the form of reserves derives from the presence of a credit constraint. In general terms, uncertainty about the future marginal rate of substitution of consumption between periods and the future marginal cost of borrowing leads to the holding of precautionary reserves. The imperfection in credit markets creates the insurance role for reserves. The addition of capital accumulation to the model will introduce possible precautionary motives in investment.

The costs of default penalization also provide a precautionary motive for reserve-holding for the same reason in the same framework. The cost of accumulating some reserves *ex ante* may be offset by the reduction in the likelihood of default they facilitate. Available reserves allow continued debt-service with a smaller reduction in current consumption, so that the benefits in low-income events are simultaneously increased consumption and reduction in the probability of facing default and consequent sanctions. In the context of borrowing and lending with imperfect information, reserves provide insurance to allow continued debt-service payments during low-income events, so that the possible reputation costs of debt-rescheduling can be avoided. Losses of reputation can lead to adverse shifts in the supply of loans in any given future event. These costs will also offset the current opportunity cost of holding foreign reserves.

The discussion so far implies that an autonomous increase in the reserves held by debtors during poor events will have a positive impact on the probability of repayment and functioning of the international credit market. However, reserves may rise in anticipation of repudiation, as was noted previously. If default sanctions include interference with access to trade finance, then increasing foreign reserves reduces the cost of penalization – as long as reserves cannot be confiscated by creditors. The probability of default may rise instead of fall because reserves are precautionary savings against default sanctions.[8]

Debtors' reputations and repeated games of incomplete information

A number of references have been made to the possible role of borrowers' reputations in models that emphasize asymmetries of information in the credit market. Recent results in the theory of games with incomplete information are likely to find widespread use in theoretical models of international financial markets. Aizenman (1986) presents a variant of the Eaton and Gersovitz (1981a) certainty model of lending with potential repudiation in which creditors possess incomplete information about the perceptions of debtors of the costs of penalties for default. Lenders form beliefs about borrowers' penalty cost perceptions which are summarized by a probability distribution. Debtors know the exact cost of sanctions. Aizenman uses the model to generate an upward-sloping, then backward-bending, supply curve of loans analogous to that derived from a stochastic model (e.g. figure 18.1).

Some insights might be gained by stating an explicit equilibrium notion for this model. The setup can be represented by an extensive form game with incomplete information. An appropriate equilibrium concept is the sequential equilibrium one proposed by Kreps and Wilson (1982b). Multiple sequential equilibria exist for the model. Restricting attention to those equilibria in which default never occurs yields a potentially useful insight. In such equilibria, loan contracts are offered which provide non-negative expected profits given lenders' prior beliefs about a debtor's perceived default penalty, and equilibrium repayment obligations are less than the actual penalty perceptions of debtors. Even though repudiations never occur in such sequential equilibria, creditors' beliefs are not controverted. However, updating priors may be inappropriate, because extending more favorable loan terms may lead to a default. Therefore, learning by creditors is costly.

Information which adversely alters a debtor's reputation can have persistent effects.

An example of the applicability of games of incomplete information to the interpretation of international credit market institutions is the existence of bond lending to LDCs along with syndicated bank loans. The dominance of bank over bond lending has already been discussed. However, a large number of medium- and high-income LDCs have floated bonds on international markets since 1973, and approximately $27 billion of bond debt is currently outstanding (the bulk is Mexican and Brazilian). Furthermore, during recent debt rescheduling, interest payments on and amortization of bond debt continued. Bondholders have little option to declaring default if payments are suspended; the prospect of repayment is already reflected in the value of bonds on the secondary market. Therefore, lenders will hold bonds only if the borrower is inhibited from defaulting on individual bonds. An equilibrium with positive bond debt under potential default is possible in a reputational game because the ability to issue future bond debt depends upon maintaining the servicing of existing bonds; the cost of a failure to completely fulfill obligations to current bondholders is the loss of any access to the bond market. Moreover, the cost of defaulting on bond obligations, however small, can lead to a loss of reputation in all asset markets in a game of incomplete information, so that the supply of bank loans is contracted or a default is declared by other creditors.

Many of the characteristics of external lending to the LDCs might find explanations in repeated games of incomplete information. However, these games typically possess multiple equilibria, and the qualitative nature of equilibria often is very sensitive to the particular assumptions made about the information possessed by different players. While some insights might be gained into the role of debtors' and creditors' reputations in the market, the approach is unlikely to yield empirically testable models. Models based on the characteristics of perfect equilibria in repeated stochastic games of complete information which incorporate the enforceability problem are difficult to handle but may be much more promising.

PRIVATE CAPITAL FLIGHT AND PUBLIC DEBT

A widely publicized feature of large debtor countries is the significant extent of the acquisition of foreign assets by their citizens. Using different methodologies, Dooley et al. (1983) and Cuddington (1985) estimate that up to one-half, and possibly more, of the increase in the gross indebtedness of Argentina, Mexico, and Venezuela during the period 1974–82 was offset by private outflows of capital. Standard portfolio diversification can explain large two-way flows. If capital flight is a result of such motives, then it is not the outcome of a market failure requiring intervention. However, the imperfect enforceability of international debt contracts provides a basis for concern.

In the presence of sovereign immunity, lenders may have little ability to impose penalties on individual private debtors or assess the value of their assets in the event of bankruptcy. Creditors are likely to have a greater ability to penalize the country as a whole for default, so that capital inflows are in the form of loans to the government or to private borrowers with government guarantees.

The majority of lending to the LDCs has taken the form of public or publicly-guaranteed debt. In the absence of *ex ante* explicit guarantees, governments have been held accountable by lenders for the debts of private borrowers. Díaz-Alejandro (1985) gives an example of the extent of implicit public guarantees of private debt. The Chilean government explicitly did not guarantee foreign loans to several private banks. However, when these banks failed, creditors demanded and received repayment from the government.

Díaz-Alejandro (1984) links capital flight from large Latin American debtors to the subsidization and public guaranteeing of private debt and the ability of nationals to avoid domestic taxation of the income from foreign assets. Eaton (1986) presents a model in which capital flight can be generated by the tax obligations implied by the potential nationalization of private debt. Explicit and implicit government guarantees create an interdependence between private investment decisions through the public sector budget constraint. Actions which raise the probability of one borrower's default increase the anticipated tax obligations of other borrowers. The other borrowers have an incentive to place their assets abroad, thereby increasing the probability of default on their own loans.

Multiple equilibria exist in each version of Eaton's model. In one of these, all creditors restrict loan amounts given debtors' tax obligations, so that investing domestically and fully repaying debts are in each borrower's self-interest. Potential nationalization of private debts provides an incentive to borrowers to invest abroad, raising the expected tax obligations of all borrowers. Therefore, another equilibrium exists in which all debtors invest abroad and the government defaults on foreign debt.

A similar approach is taken in Eaton and Gersovitz (1986), in which public borrowing is shown to lead to possible capital flight because of the implied increases in the taxation of domestic investment income with increased debt. Khan and Haque (1985) model capital flight as a response to an asymmetry in the risk of expropriation facing domestic and foreign investors. Nationals face a higher risk of expropriation by their government, so they invest abroad. Consequently, domestic investment is financed with foreign loans. Using the Eaton and Gersovitz (1986) argument, the government's expropriation decision can be related to public indebtedness. Expropriation and other forms of taxation are a means for raising government revenue to meet external debt-service obligations. Increases in public debt contribute to the private sector's anticipated taxation. If assets located abroad escape taxation and the risk of expropriation, then capital flight can be a consequence of extensive foreign borrowing.

Much discussion of capital flight from Latin American debtors has emphasized the role of overvalued currencies and domestic financial instability. Dornbusch (1985) points out that the threat of devaluation in the presence of currency overvaluation is a primary source of capital flight. Inflationary finance, a form of taxation of domestic capital, can lead to capital flight as an application of the analysis of Eaton (1986).

DEBTOR COUNTRY POLICIES

The consequences of domestic policies for external borrowing are a significant concern for countries facing imperfect international credit access. Debtor countries having repayment difficulties will undertake policies intended to improve their current account balances. Furthermore, the option of defaulting introduces moral hazard issues in the selection of domestic policy; part of the risk of policy choices is borne by creditors. Poor policy-making is cited as a source of repayment difficulties, often because capital flight is a perceived outcome.

The presence of a rising cost of external credit with country-wide indebtedness implies that an optimal policy response is to assure that the domestic rate of interest equals the marginal cost of foreign credit rather than the average cost. Aizenman (1986) shows that this can be achieved through borrowing taxes if domestic credit markets are not subject to imperfections. If moral hazard, adverse selection, or enforceability problems arise in domestic credit transactions, then additional time-varying taxes and subsidies are necessary. Adoption of optimal taxes on foreign borrowing and second-best commodity taxes and subsidies in the presence of domestic market imperfections requires policymakers to possess complete information on the external indebtedness of the country. Recent experience has shown that most large debtor nations have had a very limited accounting of public and publicly-guaranteed foreign borrowing.

The adoption of policies to improve the current account is widespread, as is concern that liberalization of trade can lead to debt problems. Tariffs are widely thought to bring about current account improvements because they raise the relative price of importables. In a general equilibrium context, this is not necessarily the case. The effect of tariffs on the excess of saving over investment depends on their effects on the desired long-run levels of physical capital and wealth in the economy. Engel and Kletzer (1985b) show that permanent tariff increases have an ambiguous effect on the rate at which a country borrows from abroad; the result depends crucially upon the particular formulation of household objectives in an optimizing framework. Calvo (1985) demonstrates that temporary liberalization often leads to increasing indebtedness because consumers' intertemporal consumption plans anticipate the future change in relative prices. The implication is that an intended permanent liberalization can lead to current account deficits if households perceive the possibility of future reversal. As a consequence, a reversal of the plan can become optimal. Calvo proposes that borrowing restraints accompany trade liberalization programs.

A much less rigorously studied issue is debtor-optimal policy choice under potential default. If debtors are able to commit themselves to follow some policies over others, then improved loan terms will be forthcoming. Commitment is essential, since increased lending is accompanied by moral hazard problems when default is possible. The presence of moral hazard and adverse selection in policy choices suggests an important role for multilateral agencies in the coordination of lending to the LDCs. IMF conditionality can be seen as potentially imposing commitment to policies from which a debtor would optimally deviate *ex post*. In the presence of creditor imperfect information, IMF involvement may be essential to the terms of loan contracts. When lenders infer information about debtor characteristics from other lenders' actions, IMF and World Bank lending may play important roles in the formation of borrower reputations.

CREDITOR COUNTRY REGULATION

Since the debt crises of 1982 began, a popular view in the creditor nations has been that the banks lent too much. Although bankers may have made *ex ante* profitable loans which *ex post* they would prefer not to have written, there is the possibility that market imperfections lead to inefficient lending practices. The implications of basic models of lending with enforceability problems is that credit is rationed and capital flows are less than would occur if potential sovereign default were not possible.

Kletzer (1984) discusses the potentially important inefficiency in international lending which results when lenders are unable to observe the magnitude of concurrent lending. Since the lending of each additional amount raises debt-service obligations, the probability of default on all outstanding debt increases. Therefore, in a rationing equilibrium the interest rate depends on the total amount borrowed from all sources and not on the size of the particular loan. In the absence of observability of total concurrent indebtedness, if an equilibrium exists, then more is lent at a higher rate of interest than in an equilibrium with observability.

The debtor is worse off as a result. Because seniority clauses are less extensive and foreign loans are often made to a variety of government agencies, public enterprises, and private sector firms under government guarantee, the problem of observability of total debt may be significant for international lending. The dissemination of information on the external private and official debt of LDCs could be coordinated by the IMF and World Bank in an effort to alleviate this type of international credit market imperfection.

Because lenders have less information about their borrowers than the debtors themselves or different information than do other lenders, another informational externality arises. Information about the credit-worthiness of borrowers can be inferred by the willingness or lack thereof of other creditors to lend. This externality could contribute to panics by lenders, in which each lender's attempt to protect himself by withdrawing increases the likelihood others will also, so that no one is able to recover their assets. The revision of a debtor's reputation induced by other lenders' cutbacks can lead to a further reduction in the willingness to lend, increasing the probability of default.

Public insurance of bank deposits is widespread in the developed countries. This insurance promotes capital market efficiency by reducing the need for depositors to monitor bank activities or demand large risk premia. As a result of deposit insurance, banks have incentives to increase the riskiness of their portfolios. Bank regulation accompanies insurance to restrain moral hazard on the part of management.

The amount of bank capital lent to a single borrower is restricted in the United States; however, countries or individual agencies in countries were not classified as a single borrower. Therefore, banks could increase insurers' exposure to risk while raising expected profits.

Regulators could take two steps to deter moral hazard problems. The first is adopt full disclosure of lending to individual countries. Increased reporting (which has occurred in the United States) can allow more extensive monitoring of banks' portfolios by depositors and share-holders and reduce the problems created by incomplete observation of indebtedness by all lenders. The other step is to require bank capital increases. The rescheduling of loans otherwise in default allows banks to pay dividends on interest income created by new loans. This act can raise the upper bound on an insurance claim arbitrarily high.

Compensation of bank managers can also create moral hazard dif-ficulties. The performance of one bank's management is likely to be judged by that of other banks. A manager who fails to undertake a high-yield, high-risk loan that is repaid will suffer, while if all banks make loans that fall into default, then any particular manager is unlikely to be blamed. This can lead to significant correlation of risk between banks' portfolios. Regulations restricting management actions and increasing disclosure can partially offset the adverse effects of these incentives.

EMPIRICAL IMPLEMENTATION OF THEORIES OF
SOVEREIGN BORROWING

A number of econometric studies of LDC borrowing are available. This section critically reviews the general approach of many of these studies in terms of the theoretical analysis of sovereign lending. A comprehensive review of the empirical literature is not intended.

Existing econometric work investigates sovereign borrowing and lending in two circumstances. Several studies examine voluntary lending and attempt to identify determinants of the level of debt and the terms on which it was contracted. A second group concentrates on when debt problems occur. The factors influencing a resumption of voluntary lending to problem debtors have not been modeled.

Empirical implementation of theories of lending under sovereign risk faces two basic problems. Information on the terms of loans is incomplete; studies must use some level of aggregation over loan contracts. Cumulative debt figures include public foreign debt and private debt covered by varying degrees of government guarantee, explicit or implicit. Another problem is the absence of suitable exogenous variables which vary across debtors. The terms of trade are an important source of external disturbances which may be treated as roughly exogenous for many LDCs; however, few other variables exist. A primary problem with much of the extant empirical literature is the inclusion of variables endogenous to external capital flows as explanatory variables.

Estimation of the determinants of outstanding debt and voluntary credit flows requires allowing for the possibility that desired debt levels exceed a creditor imposed debt ceiling. In the absence of repayment problems, two-regime models must be used. With problem debtors in the sample, three (or more) regimes are necessary to allow for both voluntary and involuntary lending.

Eaton and Gersovitz (1980 and 1981a) estimated a two-regime version of their model using data from forty-five countries for the two years 1970 and 1974. They find that the credit-constrained regime is more prevalent than the unconstrained one. Hajivassiliou (1985) estimates a three-regime model using a panel set of data for seventy-nine countries over the period 1970–82. By accounting for unobserved heterogeneity across debtors, persistent country effects are found over time.

Bank loans to the LDCs typically specify the interest rate as the sum of a reference rate, usually the London Inter-Bank Offer Rate, and a spread. The spread is fixed for the term of the loan, while the reference rate floats. In general, the quantity lent and repayment terms are jointly determined. In a stochastic setting, the interest spread is endogenous to the same set of variables that determine quantity (in the certainty version of the Eaton–Gersovitz model, the spread is zero). However, several studies treat the rate as exogenous. An alternative econometric approach to that taken by all authors would be simultaneous estimation of the spread and amount lent; however, such an exercise may require extensive individual loan data rather than the aggregated loan data available to these authors. Hajivassiliou (1985) cites evidence that interest spreads are not responsive to the same variables which determine credit inflows. More complete information on loan terms is necessary to adequately test for exogeneity. In particular, interest payments do not comprise the full return to lenders, for example, front-end fees are widespread in sovereign lending.

Interest spreads reflect the riskiness of loans but are not strictly risk premia, because the amount lent is rationed and also reflects lenders' perceptions of risk. McDonald (1982) surveys a number of studies which attempt to interpret the spread as a risk premium. In addition to poorly revealing creditor's risk assessments, spreads should reflect other factors, such as differing tax treatment of interest income across borrowers. These studies use a number of explanatory variables the inclusion of which is not derived from a well-stated model of sovereign lending. For example, while the maturity of debt is not exogenous to the other terms of loan contracts, the term structure of debt is often included as an independent variable.

A large number of econometric studies of LDC borrowing concentrate on debtor nations which experienced debt-servicing difficulties. McDonald (1982) provides a review of a number of these papers. McFadden et al. (1985) adopts a multi-regime model which emphasizes borrowers falling first into arrears and then possibly rescheduling. Events are analyzed rather than credit flows. The use of the occurrence of a debt problem as a dependent variable creates a number of difficulties: debt problems are hard to define. Because the formal declaration of a default can be costly to lenders, some debtors experiencing debt-servicing problems may not be identified. Borrowers may not choose to explicitly repudiate so that penalties are delayed and reduced. Rescheduling of some loans may not reduce the present-value of the debt, while in other cases, it will. The adoption of the event of rescheduling as a dependent variable does not allow for a distinction between these instances. Of primary interest in debt-servicing problem cases are the determinants of the future flows of capital. The study by Hajivassiliou (1985) which includes incidences of repayment problems in an analysis of the determinants of the flows of funds is a step in this direction.

Edwards (1984) also analyzes problem debtors. The interest spread is selected for the dependent variable, while the amount lent is used as an independent variable. As in many other papers, Edwards uses explanatory variables which are likely to be jointly determined with the dependent variable, for example, international reserves to GNP ratio, capital inflow to debt-service ratio, and investment to GNP ratio.

CONCLUSION

This paper has attempted to survey ideas developed in the literature on the role of sovereign immunity in international capital markets. A number of implications of the enforcement problems and informational imperfections in international credit markets for the nature of capital flows to the LDCs have been discussed; many of these have not yet been modeled rigorously. The relationship between sovereign immunity and debtor country macroeconomic policy choices and the role of multilateral agency and official lending for coordinating capital flows have received sparse attention in the theoretical literature. Many of the econometric studies of sovereign borrowing have not taken account of the theoretical analysis and fail to recognize the simultaneity of the determination of dependent and explanatory variables. The inadequacy of data on private sector loans and difficulties for defining problem cases hamper the best efforts.

NOTES

[1] For example, see Sachs (1984).

[2] Fischer and Frenkel (1975) display stages in the balance of payments in a non-optimizing model with a fixed saving rate. The results of Engel and Kletzer (1986) are derived in a small-country model with endogenous time preference, but they clearly generalize to other saving formulations and to a two-country framework.

[3] See Eaton, Gersovitz, and Stiglitz (1986).

[4] Arnott and Stiglitz (1982) discuss the importance of observability of total insurance purchases in moral hazard models at length. The comparison between credit market equilibria with and without observability in Kletzer (1984) draws on this paper extensively.

[5] This type of equilibrium credit-rationing contrasts with that derived by Stiglitz and Weiss (1981). Here (and in Jaffee and Russell (1976)), each borrower receives a loan smaller than what they demand at the equilibrium rate of interest. In the Stiglitz–Weiss adverse selection model, some borrowers' projects are fully funded and other potential borrowers receive no funds, even though they demand them at the equilibrium rate of interest.

[6] For example, see McFadden et al. (1985) and Edwards (1984).

[7] See Kletzer (1984) and, also, Gale and Hellwig (1985).

[8] O'Connell (1986) discusses these issues in a game with incomplete information.

REFERENCES

Aizenman, J. 1986: "Country Risk, Asymmetric Information and Domestic Policies." NBER Working Paper Series, No. 1880, April.

Alexander, L. S. 1985: "Trade and Sovereign Lending," Federal Reserve Board of Governors, manuscript.

Arnott, R. and Stiglitz, J. E. 1982: "Equilibrium in Competitive Insurance Markets: The Welfare Economics of Moral Hazard." Queen's University Institute of Economic Research, Discussion Paper No. 465.

Avramovic, D. et al. 1964: *Economic Growth and External Debt*. Baltimore: Johns Hopkins University Press.

Bardhan, P. K. 1967: "Optimum Foreign Borrowing." In K. Shell (ed.), *Essays on the Theory of Optimal Economic Growth*, Cambridge, Mass.: MIT Press, 117–28.

Calvo, G. 1985: "On the Costs of Temporary Liberalization/Stabilization Experiments." Columbia University Department of Economics, mimeo, Sept.

Clarida, R. 1986: "International Lending and Borrowing in a Stochastic Sequence Equilibrium." NBER Working Paper Series, No. 1944, June.

Cooper, R. and Sachs, J. D. 1985: "Borrowing Abroad: The Debtor's Perspective." In Gordon W. Smith and John T. Cuddington (eds), *International Debt and the Developing Countries*, Washington, DC: IBRD, 21–60.

Cuddington, J. 1985: "Capital Flight: Issues, Estimates and Explorations," World Bank, unpublished.

Diamond, D. and Dybvig, P. 1983: "Bank Runs, Deposit Insurance, and Liquidity." *Journal of Political Economy*, 91, 401–9.

Díaz-Alejandro, C. 1984: "Latin American Debt: I Don't Think We are in Kansas Anymore." *Brookings Papers on Economic Activity*, 2, 335–403.

Díaz-Alejandro, C. 1984: "Good-bye Financial Repression, Hello Financial Crash," *Journal of Development Economics*, 19, 1–24.

Domar, E. 1950: "The Effects of Investment on the Balance of Payments." *American Economic Review*, 40, 805–26.

Dooley, M. et al. 1983: "An Analysis of the External Debt Positions of Eight Developing Countries through 1990," Federal Reserve Board of Governors, International Finance Discussion Paper, No. 227.

Dornbusch, R. 1985: "External Debt, Budget Deficits, and Disequilibrium Exchange Rates." In G. Smith and J. Cuddington (eds), *International Debt and the Developing Countries*. Washington, DC: IBRD.

Eaton, J. 1985: "Lending with Costly Enforcement of Repayment and Potential Fraud." University of Virginia, Department of Economics, mimeo.

Eaton, J. 1986: "Public Debt Guarantees and Private Capital Flight," World Bank, Development Research Department, mimeo, Aug.

Eaton, J. and Gersovitz, M. 1980: "LDC Participation in International Financial Markets: Debt and Reserves." *Journal of Development Economics*, 7, 3–21.

Eaton, J. and Gersovitz, M. 1981a: "Debt with Potential Repudiation: Theoretical and Empirical Analysis." *Review of Economic Studies*, 48, 289–309.

Eaton, J. and Gersovitz, M. 1981b: *Poor Country Borrowing and the Repudiation Issue*. Princeton, NJ: Princeton Studies in International Finance, No. 4.

Eaton, J. and Gersovitz, M. 1986: "Country Risk and the Organization of International Capital Transfer," World Bank, Development Research Department, mimeo, Aug.

Eaton, J., Gersovitz, M. and Stiglitz, J. E. 1986: "The Pure Theory of Country Risk." *European Economic Review*, 30, 481–513.

Edwards, S. 1984: "LDC Foreign Borrowing and Default Risk: An Empirical Investigation, 1976–80." *American Economic Review*, 74, 726–34.

Engel, C. and Kletzer, K. 1986a: "International Borrowing to Finance Investment." NBER Working Paper Series, No. 1865, March.

Engel, C. and Kletzer, K. 1986b: "Tariffs, Savings and the Current Account." NBER Working Paper Series, No. 1869, March.

Fischer, S. and Frenkel, J. 1974: "Economic Growth and the Stages in the Balance of Payments." In G. Horwich and P. Samuelson (eds), *Trade, Stability, and Macroeconomics*, New York: Academic Press.

Fudenberg, D. and Maskin, E. 1986: "The Folk Theorem in Repeated Games with Discounting and with Incomplete Information." *Econometrica*, 50, 863–94.

Gale, D. and Hellwig, M. 1985: "Incentive-Compatible Debt Contracts: The One-Period Problem." *Review of Economic Studies*, 52, 647–63.

Gersovitz, M. 1983: "Trade, Capital Mobility and Sovereign Immunity." Research Program in Development Studies, Discussion Paper No. 108, Princeton University, Sept.

Gersovitz, M. 1985: "Banks' International Lending Decisions: What we know and implications for future research." In G. Smith and J. Cuddington (eds), *International Debt and the Developing Countries*, Washington, DC: IBRD, 61–78.

Grossman, H. and Van Huyck, J. B. 1985: "Sovereign Debt as a Contingent Claim: Excusable Default, Repudiation, and Reputation." Brown University, mimeo.

Hajivassiliou, V. 1985: "Analyzing the Determinants of the External Debt Repayments Problems of LDCs: Econometric Modelling using a Panel Set of Data," Yale University, Economic Growth Center Discussion Paper Series, No. 495, Dec.

Hamada, K. 1966: "Economic Growth and Long-Term International Capital Movements." *Yale Economic Essays*, 6, 41–96.

Hellwig, M. 1977: "A Model of Borrowing and Lending with Bankruptcy." *Econometrica*, 45, 1879–1906.

Jaffee, D. and Modigliani, F. 1969: "A Theory and Test of Credit Rationing." *American Economic Review*, 59, 850–72.

Jaffee, D. and Russell, T. 1976: "Imperfect Information, Uncertainty and Credit Rationing." *Quarterly Journal of Economics*, 90, 651–66.

Kaletsky, A. 1985: *The Costs of Default*. New York: Priority Press.

Khan, M. S. and Hague, N. 1985: "Foreign Borrowing and Capital Flight: A Formal Analysis," *IMF Staff Papers*, 32, 606–28.

Kharas, H. 1984: "The Long-Run Creditworthiness of Developing Countries: Theory and Practice." *Quarterly Journal of Economics*, 99, 415–39.

Kletzer, K. 1984: "Asymmetries of Information and LDC Borrowing with Sovereign Risk." *Economic Journal*, 94, 287–307.

Kreps, D. M. and Wilson, R. 1982: "Sequential Equilibria." *Econometrica*, 50, 863–94.

Krugman, P. 1985: "International Debt Problems in an Uncertain World." In G. Smith and J. Cuddington (eds), *International Debt and the Developing Countries*. Washington, DC: IBRD, 79–100.

McDonald, C. D. 1982: "Debt Capacity and Developing Country Borrowing: A Survey of the Literature," *IMF Staff Papers*, 29, 603–46.

McFadden, D. et al. 1985: "Is There Life After Debt? An Econometric Analysis of the Creditworthiness of Developing Countries." In G. Smith and J. Cuddington (eds), *International Debt and the Developing Countries*. Washington, DC: IBRD, 179–209.

O'Connell, S. A. 1986: "Reserves and Debt in LDCs." University of Pennsylvania Department of Economics, mimeo, March.

Ozler, S. 1984: "Rescheduling of Sovereign Government Bank Debt." Stanford University, mimeo.

Sachs, J. 1984: *Theoretical Issues in International Borrowing*. Princeton, NJ: Princeton Studies in International Finance, No. 54.

Sachs, J. and Cohen, D. 1985: "LDC Borrowing with Default Risk." Forthcoming in *Kredit and Kapital*.

Stiglitz, J. E. and Weiss, A. 1981: "Credit Rationing in Markets with Imperfect Information." *American Economic Review*, 71, 393–411.

Stiglitz, J. E. and Weiss, A. 1983: "Incentive Effects of Terminations." *American Economic Review*, 73, 912–27.

Townsend, R. 1978: "Optimal Contracts and Competitive Markets with Costly State Verifications." *Journal of Economic Theory*, 21, 417–25.

Comments on
"External Borrowing by LDCs:
A Survey of Some Theoretical Issues"

WILLEM H. BUITER

This is a fine, thoughtful survey of an important subject area. Rather than attempting a survey of the survey, I shall focus on some loosely connected ideas and questions prompted by Kletzer's very useful paper.

More theory, please

One thing that strikes an outsider to this field is how little theoretical work has been done on the subject of sovereign borrowing. The literature from before the recent debt crisis (1980, if Eastern Europe is one's area of reference; 1982 for Central and South America) by and large ignored the problem of incentive-compatible debt contracts for sovereign borrowers. Hellwig's paper in *Econometrica* (1977) was an important contribution, even though it was not written with sovereign borrowing in mind. Eaton and Gersovitz (1980, 1981a, 1981b) finally provided the field of sovereign borrowing with rigorous theoretical foundations, through a series of papers that represented an unusually happy marriage between innovative theoretical analysis and systematic empirical testing. Since then there has been the elegant paper by Kletzer (1984) on sovereign borrowing and asymmetric information, a paper by Cohen and Sachs (1984), further papers by Eaton (1985) and Gersovitz (1983), applications of the "bank runs" paper by Diamond and Dybvig (1983) to the issues of panics by lenders (Sachs, 1984; Krugman, 1985) and of capital flight (Eaton, 1983), and various applications of the theory of repeated games and of endogenous reputations (Kreps and Wilson, 1982; Fudenberg and Maskin, 1986.

Convincing models of self-enforcing contracts between rational borrowers, existing lenders, and new lenders are few and far between. The tacit assumption in many recent discussions of the debt problem that borrowers' concern with their reputations for dutiful debt service significantly lessens the threat of repudiation and raises safe credit ceilings seems unwarranted. Where the reputation story is grounded in assumptions about lenders' ignorance concerning the true objectives or true nature of the borrower, it seems totally implausible. The uncertainty that matters is strategic uncertainty, not asymmetric information about the borrowers' tastes and/or opportunity sets. Further theoretical work on lender-borrower games would seem to be a high priority if we are to get a real handle on the rescheduling phenomenon. Increased emphasis on lender behavior (including the games played between "old" and "new" lenders) would seem proper to correct the relative neglect of this area hitherto.

The omnipotent planner-borrower

Much of the theoretical literature approaches the borrowing decision through the intertemporal optimizing decisions of a single, omniscient, and omnipotent central planner, constrained only by material balances and by what the rest of the world is willing to lend. This obviously greatly overstates the command over domestic resources that is actually achievable by the borrowing countries' governments, some of which are staggeringly incompetent. Clearly, the borrowing government's domestic control problem is to be solved simultaneously with its external debt strategy. Private agents as producers, consumers, borrowers, and foreign investors (legal or illegal) should not be subsumed under an all-encompassing government. In those few cases when the private and public sectors are modeled separately, the revenue-raising ability of the government is either overstated or constrained in an ad hoc manner.

The cost of repudiation

Costs to the borrower of repudiation are generally broken down into two categories: cost of exclusion from the international capital market, and a "direct" cost. There is some disagreement about the comprehensiveness and the duration of the capital market exclusion penalty. The theoretical literature assumes one extreme – complete exclusion forever. Historically, most of the countries that defaulted in the 1930s were back borrowing abroad in the 1960s and a significant number of them are involved in the current debt crises. Note, however, that sufficiently high discount rates will greatly diminish the difference between exclusion for 20 years and exclusion forever. Furthermore, it might be argued that the defaulters of the thirties "benefited" from the global cataclysm of World War II, which may have swept such comparatively trivial issues as punishing bad debtors from the minds of those who were supposed to impose and enforce sanctions.

The "direct costs" are a bit of a grab-bag. They include any trade sanctions that may be imposed, the attachment of assets by creditors, whenever such assets are located in a jurisdiction that is friendly to the creditor, the costs of cash-in-advance trading, etc. Such costs increase with the "external vulnerability" of a country. This external vulnerability is not (except possibly in special cases) measured by the *size* of the economy or the size of the domestic capital stock, a specification that has become quite popular (for example, see Cohen and Sachs, 1986).

This permits a country literally to "invest" in credit-worthiness. By accumulating capital, the direct default penalty is increased and, *ceteris paribus*, lenders are willing to raise the credit ceiling. That this kind of analysis can lead to very grave lending errors (from the viewpoint of the lender) becomes obvious, if we assume that the investment is in import-substituting activities rather than in export-oriented activities. By pursuing and investing in self-sufficiency, a country may reduce its vulnerability to direct external penalties, and thus, *ceteris paribus*, lower its credit ceiling.

The literature is never very precise about whether the penalty is to be thought of in per capita terms or in aggregate terms. (This probably reflects the virtually universal "single representative agent-cum omnipotent planner" modeling approach in the theoretical debt literature already referred to.) The relationship between penalty and size will have to be clarified before empirical work is undertaken.

Eastern European debt

The literature abound with studies of the Latin American debt crisis. There is some work on African and Asian debt. Serious study of the Eastern European debt crisis is almost entirely absent, however. Eastern Europe would seem to offer a very interesting area of study. The recent debt crisis struck there first (in 1980, when Poland could no longer meet its obligations, well before Mexico went into arrears). The debtor countries are heterogeneous in terms of per capita income,

TABLE 18.1   *Bid-ask spreads for bank debt of Poland, Yugoslavia and Romania*

Month/year	Poland	Yugoslavia	Romania
		(cents per dollar of debt)	
July 1985	55–60	74–77	85–89
January 1986	50–53	78–81	91–94
February 1986	49–53	78–81	91–93
March 1986	48–53	78–81	89–92
April 1986	48–53	78–81	90–93
May 1986	48–53	78–81	90–92
June 1986	43–46	77–79	89–92
July 1986	42–45	75–78	86–89
August 1986	42–45	75–78	86–90
September 1986	43–45	75–78	86–89
October 1986	42–44	77–80	86–89
November 1986	41–44	77–81	86–89

Source: Shearson Lehman Asset Trading Inc.

economic and industrial structure, and as regards methods of planning and economic and political control (Poland, Hungary, Yugoslavia, Romania, Bulgaria, East Germany, etc.). The discounts at which their debts trade in the informal interbank market are comparable to those applied to some of the Latin American debtors. Table 18.1 shows these discounts from July 1985 to November 1986 for Poland, Yugoslavia, and Romania.

Obvious differences with the Latin American debtors include a much smaller role for the IMF and the World Bank. It would seem that a considerable amount of information is waiting to be mined in these countries.

REFERENCES

Cohen, D. and Sachs, J. 1984: "LDC Borrowing with Default Risk." Forthcoming in *Kredit and Kapital*.

Cohen, D. and Sachs, J. 1986: "Growth, External Debt and Risk of Debt Repudiation." *European Economic Review*, 30(3), 529–60.

Diamond, D. and Dybvig, P. 1983: "Bank Runs, Deposit Insurance, and Liquidity." *Journal of Political Economy*, 91, 401–9.

Eaton, J. and Gersovitz, M. 1980: "LDC Participation in International Financial Markets: Debt and Reserves." *Journal of Development Economics*, 7, 3–21.

Eaton, J. and Gersovitz, M. 1981a: "Debt with Potential Repudiation: Theoretical and Empirical Analysis." *Review of Economic Studies*, 48, 289–309.

Eaton, J. and Gersovitz, M. 1981b: *Poor Country Borrowing and the Repudiation Issue*. Princeton, NJ: Princeton Studies in International Finance, No. 4.

Eaton, J. 1985: "Lending with Costly Enforcement of Repayment and Potential Fraud." University of Virginia, Department of Economics, mimeo.

J. Eaton 1986: "Public Debt Guarantees and Private Capital Flight." World Bank, Development Research Department Discussion Paper No. 183, Sept.

Fudenberg, D. and Maskin, E. 1986: "The Folk Theorem in Repeated Games with Discounting and with Incomplete Information." *Econometrica*, 50, 863–94.

Gersovitz, M. 1983: "Trade, Capital Mobility and Sovereign Immunity." Research Program in Development Studies, Discussion Paper No. 108, Princeton University, Sept.

Hellwig, M. 1977: "A Model of Borrowing and Lending with Bankruptcy." *Econometrica*, 45, 1879–906.

Kletzer, K. 1984: "Asymmetries of Information and LDC Borrowing with Sovereign Risk." *Economic Journal*, 94, 287–307.

Kreps, D. M. and Wilson, R. 1982: "Sequential Equilibria." *Econometrica*, 50, 863–94.

Krugman, P. 1985: "International Debt Problems in an Uncertain World." In G. Smith and J. Cuddington (eds), *International Debt and the Developing Countries*, Washington, DC: IBRD, 79–100.

Sachs 1984: "Theoretical Issues in International Borrowing." Princeton Studies in International Finance, No. 54.

Author Index

Subject Index